AIR FORCE SPOKEN HERE

James Parton
"Air Force Spoken Here"
General Ira Eaker and the Command of the Air

In cooperation with the
Air Force Historical Foundation

ADLER&ADLER

Published in the United States in 1986 by
Adler & Adler, Publishers, Inc.
4550 Montgomery Avenue
Bethesda, Maryland 20814

Library of Congress Cataloging-in-Publication Data

"In Cooperation with the Air Force Historical Foundation."
Includes index.
1. Eaker, Ira, 1896– . 2. Generals-United
States—Biography. 3. United States. Air Force—
Biography. I. Air Force Historical Foundation.
II. Title.
UG626.E24P37   1986   358.4′0092′4   [B]   85-28633
ISBN 0-917561-15-5

First Edition
Printed in the United States of America

For J.P. III, Dana, and Sara

Contents

Illustrations ix
Preface xi

PART ONE
The Command of the Air
3

PART TWO
Pioneer Aviator
15

PART THREE
Night vs. Day Bombing
105

PART FOUR
The Combined Bomber Offensive
259

PART FIVE
Cassino, Ploesti, and Rift with Russia
349

PART SIX
Mr. U.S. Air Force
451

Sources 495
Notes 499
Glossary 527
Bibliography 531
Acknowledgments 535
Index 539

Illustrations

i "Nameplate" from Eaker's desk, 1960–80

2 C-in-C, Mediterranean Allied Air Forces, 1944

8 Deane, Nikitin and Novikov

10 Perminov greets Eaker at Poltava

11 Eaker and Harriman, Moscow, June 5, 1944

14 Captain Eaker, Philippines, 1921

19 The Eaker family about 1900

28 Private Eaker, 1917

29 The first five to enlist from Eaker's class

37 Captain Eaker and his DH, Philippines, 1920

40 Visiting China—Lieutenant Longfellow and Captain Eaker

42 Major Spaatz, Captain Eaker and Eaker's first wife, Leah

49 General Patrick, Chief of the Air Service

53 Major Dargue and Captain Eaker study Pan Am flight map

57 Captain Eaker and Lieutenant Fairchild arriving in Rio de Janeiro

59 President Coolidge awarding Eaker the DFC

63 Captain Eaker and General Fechet

72 The *Question Mark* refueling in air

73 The *Question Mark*'s "flying blackboard"

74 The *Question Mark* crew, just landed

81 Eaker on crutches after forced parachute jump

82 Eaker about to start transcontinental flight

83 Eaker on wing of his cracked-up plane

84 Ruth Apperson Eaker soon after her marriage, 1931

100 First "blind" flight across the U.S.

104 Arnold, Harris and Eaker, England, 1943

111 B-17s intercepting the *Rex*, 1938

114 Eaker, Westover, Hughes and Arnold, 1938

137 Jackie Harris with Arnold and Eaker, 1943

150 The five famous names over the doors at PINETREE

152 Wycombe Abbey

162 Eaker and his puppy

165 Eaker, Eisenhower and Ambassador Bullitt

176 Eaker and newsmen after first B-17 mission

180 Ruth Eaker, 1942

186 Eaker being briefed in PINETREE war room

187 Eaker and group in PINETREE operations room

196 Spaatz, Eaker and Longfellow meet King George VI

199 Eaker decorating Frank Armstrong

206 Hansell and LeMay, May 1943

Illustrations

219 Eaker and Arnold, 1943

225 Eaker and Portal, 1943

236 LeMay briefing his commanders before Normandy

255 Wreckage of the B-24 in which Andrews crashed, 1943

258 Churchill, Andrews, Harris, Eaker and others, 1943

267 Inquest after the B-26 disaster, May 1943

269 Eaker and Lovett, 1943

275 Head table at a PINETREE "Bomber Night," 1943

286 Churchill and Eaker talking with Lieutenant McFann, 1943

296 Devers and Eaker sending the *Memphis Belle* home

301 LeMay's B-17s over Regensburg

310 An Eighth Air Force combat wing en route to Germany, 1943

314 Marienburg

317 Schweinfurt II

321 Eaker awards Air Medal to Fechet, 1943

337 Eaker looking grim

348 Cassino as seen from a bomber above it

352 Slessor and Eaker, Caserta, 1945

358 Truscott and Eaker at Anzio

362–63 The Cassino Abbey before, during and after the bombing

368–69 The marathon poker match in the palace

374 The first bombs hitting the town of Cassino

375 Cassino after the bombing

387 Eaker and Twining at Bucharest

388 The Royal Palace of Caserta

397 Spaatz, Twining and Eaker at Bari, 1944

402 Eaker playing volleyball against the Russians, Poltava

417 The air commanders meet in central France

423 Kraigher about to take off on a supply drop mission

428 Eaker and Tito, Belgrade, 1945

437 Eaker and Chennault, Kunming, China, 1945

444 President Truman, Spaatz and Eaker at the White House, 1946

447 Eaker receiving the DSM from Eisenhower with Spaatz alongside

449 Pentagon display—air winners of the Congressional Gold Medal

462 The Eakers with Wernher von Braun

465 Reunion at Whitney's plantation

479 U.S. Strategic Institute planning session

486 Doolittle and Eaker with General Jones

488 Eaker and Spaatz talk with Neil Armstrong

492 Fourth star presentation to Eaker, April 26, 1985

Preface

I T WAS my good fortune to land on General Eaker's staff in England very early in World War II—May 1942. Initially in intelligence, I became his aide and confidant throughout the war and then his friend and associate in many matters during the subsequent years. The closeness of our relationship as well as his gift for cloaking human sentiment with sardonic humor are evident in his reply when I asked him in 1950 if he would be best man at my wedding: "Jimmy, since you were my aide for almost four years it seems only fair that I should be yours for a few hours."

Thirty-three years later Lt. Gen. John B. McPherson, then president of the Air Force Historical Foundation, of which I am a trustee, surprised me with the suggestion that I write Eaker's biography. Since I had given up the hard and solitary drill of writing years back for the much easier and more gregarious duties of a publisher, I was dubious at first. But I agreed because I concluded that Eaker richly deserves a biography both to commemorate his career as a remarkable commander and as America's most articulate spokesman for the responsible use of air power.

In a letter we executed jointly he promised "full cooperation" and I undertook to show the manuscript to the Office of Air Force History "to check for accuracy and to point out any interpretations which might seem open to question. But," I added, "in the interest of complete scholarly objectivity, final decision on judgments and interpretations shall rest with the author."

The Office of Air Force History *did* find several factual mistakes and made some significant and useful suggestions regarding interpretations, most, but not all, of which I adopted. Neither Eaker nor his wife held back from answering even the most sensitive questions.

xi

Their cooperation could not have been more complete or more fruitful and I am immensely grateful to them both.

Nor did they ever ask to see the manuscript or try to influence my conclusions on any basis other than accuracy. As a skilled journalist himself, Eaker knew that I should and would do my best to adhere to Cromwell's famous admonition to Sir Peter Lely, his portrait artist, "not to flatter me at all; but remark all those roughnesses, pimples, warts and everything as you see me: otherwise I will never pay one farthing for it."

"Air Force Spoken Here"

Ira C. Eaker, commander-in-chief, Mediterranean Allied Air Forces, 1944.

ONE

The Command of the Air

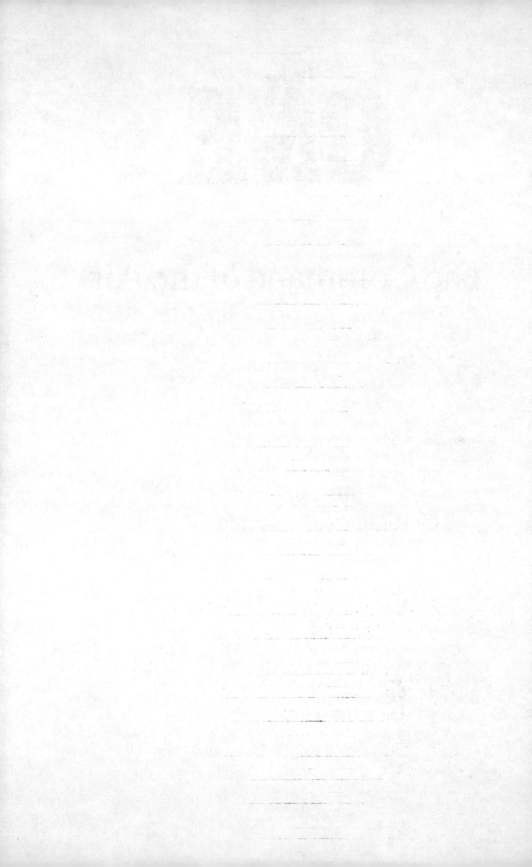

1

"Air power may either end war or end civilization."

—WINSTON S. CHURCHILL, HOUSE OF COMMONS,
MARCH 14, 1933

WHEN AMERICAN and British troops stormed the beaches of Normandy on June 6, 1944, Lt. Gen. Ira C. Eaker of the U.S. Army Air Forces was in Moscow. This was ironic, for Eaker was the man chiefly responsible for creating the air force, "the Mighty Eighth," which made the landings possible. He would have preferred to be piloting a fighter over the beaches that day as his successor in command of the Eighth, Lt. Gen. James H. "Jimmy" Doolittle, was in fact doing.

But Eaker had been promoted six months before, despite his anguished objections, to a bigger, though less decisive, post—commander in chief, Mediterranean Allied Air Forces, in charge of four air forces, the American Twelfth and Fifteenth and the British Desert and Balkan. He found this new task much more challenging and adventurous than he expected. It was an assignment that drew on all his skills as combat commander, executive and diplomat, as his trip to Moscow exemplified. He had brought 129 B–17 Flying Fortresses and 150 escorting P–51 Mustangs of the Fifteenth Air Force on the first "shuttle-bombing" mission. They had taken off June 2 from Foggia, Italy, bombed a railway yard in Hungary and then, to the surprise of the Germans, instead of turning for home, flew on east to three new American air bases secretly established in the Poltava area of the Ukraine. This spectacular and successful attack (target heavily damaged, only one B–17 lost) had enormous immediate and long-term importance. For the immediate, it opened a third air front for the strategic bombardment of German war industries; for the longer future, it was America's most dramatic effort to establish a complete, trusting relationship with Russia.

Eaker's heart that week, however, was far away in Normandy. When he learned that the beachhead had been secured, he sent a signal through American embassy channels to Lt. Gen. Walter Bedell Smith, chief of staff for Gen. Dwight D. Eisenhower, asking what opposition had come from the German air force.

Smith's reply was laconic: "The Luftwaffe didn't show."

The air statistics from Normandy were specific: during the first twenty-four hours of the battle the American and British air forces jointly mounted 14,674 sorties, the German air force but 319.[1] Here was the clearest possible evidence of Allied command of the air. And it had always been recognized, as well as repeatedly asserted, by the Allied leaders that, without air superiority, no invasion across the English Channel could succeed.

Winston Churchill wrote, "For our air superiority . . . full tribute must be paid to the United States Eighth Air Force."[2]

"That," said Eaker years later, "was my greatest satisfaction of the war."[3]

In Russia the news had an electrifying effect. Ambassador W. Averell Harriman wrote, "Moscow was awash in boozy good feeling. Edward Page, second secretary of the American embassy, who was dining out that evening in a newly opened restaurant, found himself being toasted and embraced all night long by Russians he had never met."[4] The author of this book, one of three staff officers who flew with Eaker to Russia, was walking around Red Square in U.S. Army uniform when a short, young, pimply-faced Soviet soldier in rumpled fatigues and jack-boots fell into step alongside. He chattered in Russian, which I, of course, could not understand. But presently I heard him ask, "Poleski? Francski? Jugoslavski?" and realized he was asking what nationality I was. I replied with the only Russian phrase we had been taught, for use in case we got shot down on the way in, "Ya Amerikanyets," meaning "I am an American." The Russian soldier stopped dead in his tracks, broke into a broad grin that revealed two missing front teeth, thrust out his hand for mine and said, "Rooseveltski!"

The night before D–Day Eaker and I and a few others were sharing a nightcap with Ambassador Harriman and his daughter

Kathleen in his private sitting room upstairs at Spasso House, as the American embassy was called, when Second Secretary Page came in with a signal from England. Harriman opened it, smiled, stood up and said, "Our troops are landing in Normandy in a few hours. I must go tell Uncle Joe."

Stalin had been demanding the invasion for over two years, becoming increasingly caustic about the repeated delays. A cross-channel attack had been planned for 1942, then canceled. Again in 1943 it was put off, this time in favor of the invasion of Sicily and then Italy itself, at which Stalin sneered. In 1944 it was first set for May, then for June 2. When the attack at last came on June 6, the outcome was uncertain for several days. By June 10, however, when Harriman took further details to the Kremlin, "This was a different Stalin," he reported, "unstinting in his praise. . . . Oblivious to the bitter recriminations of the past . . . Stalin at last acknowledged the tremendous achievement of Allied arms in successfully crossing the Channel. He said . . . 'The history of war has never witnessed such a grandiose operation.' "[5]

Early June 1944 marked, in short, a new high in American relations with Russia at the top level of diplomacy and authority. Similarly, the successful execution of the first shuttle mission "marked the high tide of our military relations," as Maj. Gen. John R. Deane, chief of the U.S. military mission in Moscow, put it.[6] It appeared that true harmony between the two great powers was really being achieved. Eaker briefly thought so. He had two amiable business meetings with Foreign Minister Vyacheslav M. Molotov and with Lt. Gen. N. V. Slavin of the Russian general staff—the designated "contact" with the U.S. military mission. Slavin introduced him to the two top Soviet airmen, Marshal A. A. Novikov and Col. Gen. A. V. Nikitin. Airmen, whatever their tongues, speak the same language and the soft-voiced Texan hit it off immediately with both of them as he did with Maj. Gen. A. R. Perminov, the Russian base commander back at Poltava.

Novikov, "the General Arnold of the Red Air Force," as Deane described him, "was short, clean cut, with closely cropped brown curly hair and blue eyes." Nikitin was "tall, thin and stooped . . . quiet, courteous and reserved, and had a good sense of humor. It was he who was put in charge of the Russian end of our combined operations, and had he been free of interference our success would have been ten-fold."[7] Eaker talked with them and others of the Russian

Deane   Nikitin   Novikov

air force staff from 1:30 to 4:00 A.M. at the Kremlin—hours that apparently were regarded as normal by the Soviet hierarchy. He recalled: "They asked me a number of questions about our operations. . . . When it came my time to ask questions I said, 'We have found it better to destroy the German tanks and fighters at the factory rather than meet them on the battlefield, so I've been wondering why you have not had more of a strategic operational effort.' Novikov said, 'That's a good question. We have observed your very successful effort of knocking down a lot of factories and we know about it and applaud it, as it is helping us too. . . . When the Germans invaded our motherland, we took full stock of our resources and we thought we just might stop them if we put every resource we had to stopping those vast land armies with air support. So we devoted all our air effort to air support. Now we've got them on the run. We're beginning to think about some strategic aircraft operations." Novikov added that he had just seen a Kremlin memorandum to Harriman asking for four hundred heavy bombers from the U.S.[8]

In addition to that sort of flier-talk comparison of ideas and tactics, the two commanders made some significant immediate operational decisions. A notable example had to do with target selection for the American shuttle missions. On the way to Poltava, Eaker's B-17s had bombed a trivial target, the rail yards in Debrecen, Hungary, because the Soviet leadership for undisclosed reasons had refused approval of more vital targets such as German aircraft facto-

8

ries or synthetic oil works. Eaker wanted approval to hit some German airfields on the way back to Italy, and Novikov gave it to him.[9]

The next day, by way of reciprocity and to demonstrate that the United States was holding nothing back from the Soviets, Eaker took several Russian air officers designated by Novikov up over Moscow in his B-17 and showed them how its H2X radar worked. It was a day of thick overcast with nothing visible to the naked eye from ten thousand feet above the city. But through the radar they could easily see the river snaking past the Kremlin and make out other prominent buildings. The Russians knew something of this sort existed but they had never seen it in action and were volubly impressed.[10]

The following day, June 5, Eaker lunched with Foreign Minister Molotov and was Harriman's guest of honor at a large, formal reception at Spasso House where the most prominent Soviet guest was Andrei Vishinsky, the notorious prosecutor of the 1937 purge trials that sent several hundred of the top Soviet army officer corps to be executed. Two other guests were Novikov and Nikitin. Eaker decorated both of them with the Legion of Merit. A year later Novikov was relieved as Soviet air chief and sent to Siberia, from which he was rehabilitated after Stalin's death. Eaker concluded, "Stalin evidently presumed he was too friendly with the Americans."[11]

There was also a sinister overtone in Eaker's quickly established friendship with General Perminov. "When I returned to Poltava from Moscow," Eaker's memoir continues, "General Perminov asked me to have dinner with him. When I arrived at the battered, partially destroyed officers club I was ushered in to see General Perminov by a tall, robust Russian girl in a captain's uniform who stood just inside the door. . . ." Eaker particularly wanted to ask about arranging air corridors or courses to and from German targets, but each time he broached that or any other military topic Perminov ducked reply. "As midnight approached the tall captain at the door left the room. Perminov responded to her exit at once, saying, 'She is my aide but I didn't pick her. She was picked by the KGB, and she has gone to report to Moscow about you and me. Now we can get on with the war. Let me see those maps.' And he promptly drew the corridors."[12]

Poltava itself represented still a third aspect of the new American-Russian teamwork. Twelve hundred Americans were stationed there to service the incoming and outgoing shuttle missions of over one thousand men each time from Italy and England, while

Eaker is greeted at Poltava by Perminov, the Russian base commander. Despite the latter's skeptical stare, the two became trusting comrades.

housekeeping, base management and protection were provided by the Russians. In a letter to Eaker three months before the first shuttle mission Harriman commented on the unique precedent this set: "We have to realize that the establishment within the country of armed forces of a foreign nation under their own command has never before been permitted to my knowledge in the history of Russia, and there are many inhibitions to break down."[13] The U.S. bases at Poltava were, in effect, America in microcosm plunked down into a swarm of Russians. How would G.I. Joe and Ivan Ivanovitch get along together? In June 1944 they seemed to be getting along just fine.

And there was yet a fourth major aspect of the new teamwork —the bases at Poltava were intended to be the first step toward establishing similar bases for the U.S. in the Vladivostok area so American bombers could get at Japan. Stalin had approved this plan "in principle," but it was top secret for more than the usual security reasons: Russia and Japan were not at war with each other and Stalin made it clear that he had no intention of fighting on a second front until Germany was beaten. Harriman and Eaker of course knew of these long-term objectives. They had been friends and allies since 1942 when Eaker was organizing the VIII Bomber Command in

Eaker and Harriman in Moscow the night before D-Day in Normandy.

England and Harriman was lend-lease ambassador from the United States to Great Britain.[14]

From Poltava Eaker dispatched some of his B-17s to bomb a German airfield in Rumania with good results and no losses and return to Poltava. And on June 11 he accompanied the whole force back to Italy, bombing another German airfield in Rumania with accuracy and minor losses (one B-17 and two P-51s).[15] That same week, halfway around the globe, a huge American task force began the invasion of the Mariana Islands in the Pacific. Their conquest gave the U.S. bases for the B-29 bombardment of Japan and eliminated the need for airfields near Vladivostok. This was doubly fortunate, for it soon became clear that Stalin had only pretended to be sincere about giving the Americans any such foothold near the Pacific.

The shuttle missions, eighteen of which were accomplished, dramatized how deep were the philosophic and practical differences between Russia and the United States. Eaker returned from the first one sorely aware of the ruthless and unscrupulous methods of the hierarchy while also having observed how well twelve hundred Americans in the heart of Russia could get along with the ordinary people and how he could achieve effective coordination with his military opposite numbers if only there were no interference from the Kremlin.

The American-Russian relationship deteriorated steadily in the final year of the war, and Eaker was uniquely positioned to observe the deterioration. That was because his Mediterranean Allied Air Forces were the closest to the Russian front as Soviet armies advanced through the Balkans and into Hungary, Czechoslovakia and Poland. There were many ways besides shuttles that MAAF could have helped the Russian advance, and Eaker made many wholehearted offers. But they were increasingly rebuffed. It became clear as the Soviets felt their triumph coming that they wanted no direct military help and no sharing of credit for their conquests. Nor, Eaker and others observed, could they be trusted to do what they said they would do. MAAF's courageous and costly attempts to drop supplies to the beleaguered Polish liberation army in Warsaw while the Russian army sat on its hands a few miles away was the worst of many ugly episodes. Eaker became entirely disillusioned with the Soviets but not the Russian people—a cynicism he found no reason to change in the subsequent forty years.

After the war, as the wartime alliance fell totally apart and into outright confrontation, Eaker became a sort of modern Paul Revere. For a few years he savored the cushy comforts of U.S. corporate life, building Hughes Aircraft from $2 million annual sales in 1947 to $200 million in 1957. Then, instead of retiring, he threw himself full-time into writing, lecturing and lobbying for the twin causes of maintaining a strong national defense and keeping a wary eye on the Soviets. He spoke and wrote with authority and often with eloquence on the two most important problems of the postwar world: how to establish some sort of harmony or balance with the Soviets and how to use air power responsibly. His friend Clare Boothe Luce said: "Most military men have no writing ability whatever. General Eaker was an exception. He could express a great deal with a very few words. His columns were often nuggets of strong thought concisely and aptly written."[16] His influence became substantial. A nationally syndicated column on the responsible uses of air power he wrote weekly for eighteen years appeared in seven hundred newspapers. Forty-seven of these columns were republished in the *Congressional Record* as well as many of his speeches. Other writing appeared in a steady stream of magazine articles. In 1972, when he was seventy-six years old, he became the founding president of the United States Strategic Institute, whose quarterly *Strategic Review* became an important vehicle for the views of professional military men. He became so renowned as an oracle of air power that a wag gave him a nameplate for his desk reading AIR FORCE SPOKEN HERE. In 1977, when he was eighty-one years old, he received the Wright Trophy, given annually to a civilian for aiding the cause of aviation. The citation read: "To Ira C. Eaker for 60 years of significant public service: as pioneer flyer, military leader, industry executive and as a persuasive interpreter of aviation to the American people through the written and spoken word."

Two years later, at age eighty-three, he received the Congressional Gold Medal—an award first given to George Washington in 1776 and regarded ever since as the noncombatant equivalent of the Medal of Honor. Only five airmen had previously received it: the Wright brothers, first to fly; Charles A. Lindbergh, first to cross the Atlantic solo; Gen. William A. "Billy" Mitchell, for dramatizing the growing clout of airplanes; and Col. Charles "Chuck" Yeager, for breaking the sonic barrier. Ira Eaker's citation read:

> In the early days of flight he developed and tested procedures for aerial refueling and instrument flying that today are still indispensable to air operations. In the Second World War, General Eaker organized American and British air forces and led them in campaigns which brought victory for the Allies at a far lower cost in blood and treasure than could reasonably have been expected. Following the war's end and subsequent service as Chief of the Air Staff, he devoted himself to promoting air power and national defense. General Eaker's tireless efforts, spanning well over half a century, have benefited his country enormously and have earned for him the greatest admiration, gratitude and respect.

The medal itself has his strong face on one side and on the obverse a B-17 "flying fortress" and the phrase AVIATION PIONEER, AIR POWER LEADER.

The complete story behind those five words is the first mission of this book. But its broader objective is to shed light—through the adventures, the shrewd leadership and the forceful words of Ira Eaker—on the world's most urgent problem: how to use air power responsibly. For it is still sadly true, a half century after Winston Churchill said it to the House of Commons in 1933, that "Air power may either end war or end civilization."

Captain Eaker, Philippines, 1921.

TWO

Pioneer Aviator

2

"Managers can be trained; leaders are born"

—IRA C. EAKER IN A 1972 SPEECH ON LEADERSHIP

IRA CLARENCE EAKER was born on April 13, 1896, in Field Creek, a six-family hamlet in Llano County, Texas. He never knew why his parents chose those two names for their first of five sons. "There was no family connection with either name," he commented eighty-seven years later. "My mother just liked them, I suppose."[1] His father also had an unusual nomenclature—Young Yancy Eaker. He was a big man for that time, slightly over six feet, weighing two hundred pounds and remarkably strong. He was also stern of face, square of jaw, with piercing eyes and a cleft chin. Ira inherited his father's facial features and stamina. But it was from his mother that the boy gained his genial personality and exceptional motivation. Her name was Dona Lee Graham and she was only sixteen when she married and seventeen when Ira was born. Early photographs show a palely pretty, very slender girl, almost a foot shorter than her husband.

Ira recalled: "Neither of them had more than a grade school education. Neither of them ever had the opportunity to attend high school. But they were religious people, attended church once or twice a week and were very sound citizens by any standard in that area in those times. Each of them continued to improve their educational attainments by private study and continued reading. . . . We were as a family very poor by any modern standard, but we didn't know it.

17

We were comfortable and had plenty of food and we considered that our status enabled us to move forward and encouraged us to do so. I think I was very fortunate in my early childhood, parents, grandparents and the examples they set."[2]

This is characteristic of the positive attitude Ira Eaker always expressed throughout his adventurous life, no matter how adverse the circumstances. Aside from strong family pride, love and loyalty, many of the circumstances of his early years were indeed adverse. For Young Eaker was a cowboy turned farmer, and there was, literally, no spare money at all. The entire family worked in the fields or at any odd jobs to be found. Ruth Goodman, a classmate of Ira's in Oklahoma, where the Eakers moved in 1912, recalled that they once lived across the street from her family: "My mother knew Mrs. Eaker very well. As neighbors they visited back and forth and one day my mother noticed Mrs. Eaker making a great amount of dough and asked about it. Mrs. Eaker replied, 'Well, yes, this bread is all we ever have for our evening meal.' "[3]

The Eaker family, originally spelled Ecker and "of peasant origin," came to America in 1723 as part of the Palatine movement of Germans who fled their native land because they rejected Catholicism.[4] Ira's branch of the family, "so far as I know," he wrote in 1972, "traces from Jacob Eaker who settled on the banks of the Mohawk River early in the 18th century. He had eleven sons. Some of them settled in Pennsylvania and at least one continued on to Kentucky. One of his descendents, my grandfather, a Confederate veteran, near the close of the Civil War followed General Kirby Smith to Texas. . . . One of my earliest memories was being taken by my grandmother to visit his gravesite. The tombstone bears this inscription, 'William A. Eaker, Born 1814—Died 1874.' My father was his youngest son and he was born in 1872 and died at Eden, Concho County, Texas in 1955."[5]

It was to Eden that Young Yancy Eaker took his family in 1906 when Ira was nine. Dona Eaker's father, John H. Graham, another Confederate veteran, had moved there and done well, becoming a county commissioner and a justice of the peace. This was in the family tradition, for his father had been a judge back in Tennessee. The Eakers came to think of Eden as "home," though a drought drove them to Oklahoma in 1912 for a decade. There are sixteen Edens in the United States, but Eden, Texas, is the only one not named for Paradise, a fact unearthed by an enterprising writer in the

The Eaker Family about 1900; Ira, lower left.

New York Times in 1983. Noting that the town was founded in 1882 and named for Fred Ede, who donated land for the town square, the *Times* reported: "You'll find Eden, Texas—population 1,400—if you keep looking 165 miles north of San Antonio. Eden averages 22.28 inches of annual rainfall and enjoys a 228-day growing season. The Lions Club holds a carnival each September at Lee Pfluger Park, everybody welcome. Wool and mohair are important regional products. You couldn't do yourself a better favor than by going to Eden, Tex., for all your mohair needs. . . ."[6]

When the Eakers moved from Field Creek to Eden, a distance of about one hundred miles, it took them five days in a covered wagon. Claude Eaker, the third of the brothers, who was then three, recalled in a twenty-five-page memoir sixty years later: "A coop of chickens was tied on and our cattle and extra horses were herded back of the wagon by my brothers Ira, then nine, and Grady, seven. The procession was led by my mother driving our old canvas-topped hack. It was piled high with clothing, bedding and breakables such as the family clock. . . . We camped where night overtook us and where there was water and grass."[7]

In 1906, as nine-year-old Ira Eaker helped shepherd his family across one hundred miles of Texas in five days, it was only three years after the Wright brothers had first achieved powered flight and three years before the U.S. Army managed to make up its mind to sign the contract for "Airplane No. 1, Heavier-than-air Division, United States aerial fleet." Thirty-seven years later he would be shepherding several thousands of bombers and fighters, even the slowest going faster than 200 miles per hour, over Nazi targets in Hitler's Europe, wielding that immense power in the air as deftly as he handled his horse on the dusty road to Eden, Texas.

Y. Y. Eaker had scraped together enough money to purchase a section (640 acres) and a one-story house with five rooms and a shed. The latter became his parents' bedroom. Their farm was located about twenty miles from Eden in a community known as Hills. It had a one-teacher school to which all the boys went. The teacher, Otto Armor, boarded with them, paying $10 per month for room and board out of his salary of $25. "The 'plumbing,'" Claude Eaker's memoir continues, "was a small building some 100 feet back of the house under a large live oak tree. Face and hand washing was done at a shelf on the porch. . . . There was a water bucket and wash pan on the shelf, while above, hanging from a nail in a porch post, was an always clean towel. A comb lay on the shelf. Tooth brushes, you ask? We made these ourselves from small hackberry limbs or mesquite roots. Tooth powder was table salt. Hand lotion was vinegar with glycerine in it. If you were my mother's son, you kept clean and as well-groomed as possible, no matter how busy you were."

The biggest task for any farmer, of course, is tending the fields. Young Yancy Eaker had extraordinary vigor. Claude recalled him with open awe: "Tales of his strength were told for many years. . . . One story, told by the Green brothers, who were his contemporaries, was that he could and did plow ten acres of corn a day with a Georgia Stock walking plow. They said he had to change horses at noon for they could last at the pace a half day only, but Dad lasted all day. That made him stronger than a horse. . . ." Ira, Grady and Claude worked hard too, at the one-teacher school by day, at yard work Saturday morning. "But Saturday afternoon belonged to the boys." They fished, caught squirrels, coursed for wild bees and fended off such varmints as coyotes, rattlesnakes and, once, a rabid dog. On Sunday morning there was church, either in the schoolhouse or with readings at home. Sunday afternoon was for swimming. Most evenings Dona Eaker "read aloud to us all, not only Bible stories but many other books—*The Last of the Mohicans, Robinson Crusoe, David Copperfield* and many, many others."[8] It was a hard but happy and healthy interlude, very Tom Sawyerish.

But Dona Eaker wanted better schooling for her boys and to be closer to her parents. So, after three years in Hills, they moved much closer to Eden, selling their first farm and buying half a section about a mile out of town. There was no house, so Young Eaker, a fine carpenter, built one. Their new crops were "cotton for money and corn for the stock (no goats)," as Ira recalled—his wry way of noting that they did not contribute to Eden's mohair industry.[9] The town had a small public library, near enough to be used. It contained some fifty to sixty volumes, and Ira read them all in one summer, mostly "the fiction of the time and all the Kipling. My earliest heroes were cowboys and Indians. I grew up with them. Cowboys taught me to play poker."[10] When he sat in their laps they thought it brought them luck.[11]

All the boys attended the new Eden Public School, which had eight rooms, was made of limestone and stood two stories tall. "Grandpa Graham was on the school board and in charge of the construction."[12] It was here that Ira first displayed his lifelong knack of spotting influential leaders and associating with them. Many years later he recalled: "The Eden High School had a remarkable principal by the name of Professor Broyles. He also edited the small town weekly newspaper. He was a man of great character and he set all of us on the right road so far as thinking about problems beyond our small environment. He suggested that each of us begin, at an early date, to plan and train for careers above those normally available in that area in those times, such as farmer or rancher. He thought that we at least ought to consider an opportunity to get a higher education and extend our influence, adopt professions that would be useful to the state and the country. . . ."[13]

But the chief such influence was his mother. By then it was very clear to Dona Lee Graham Eaker that her oldest son was head and shoulders above his three surviving brothers (the youngest died at age two) in brains and promise. She repeatedly urged that the way for him to escape the hardscrabble poverty of tenant farming was to get a higher education and that the law, as exemplified by her father and grandfather, was the ideal professional goal. Early in that period in Eden, returning from his first Sunday School, Ira asked his father if he could become an Apostle. "He thought not," Eaker recalled years later with the quiet, understated humor that became his hallmark.[14] The law became his target. But active religious ceremony he dropped after he left home. "I went to church enough before I was ten years old to do me the rest of my life."[15]

About 1909 a severe and continuing drought hit southwest Texas. "It rained so little that the feed would get little over knee high, corn turned brown without making an ear, and the cotton would have only two or three bolls to the stalk. . . . The dollar a day which Dad earned as a laborer and the two dollars earned as a skilled carpenter were most welcome additions to our meagre budget."[16] So the Eakers decided to go to Oklahoma, where the climate remained benign. They chose Durant, about twenty miles north of the Texas border, where they had heard a college was being built.

This time they moved by train (newly extended to Eden). "Our best team of horses, a wagon, our clothes and household goods" went into what were called immigrant cars, accompanied by Young Eaker to feed and water the horses. Dona Eaker and her boys were in a passenger car. In Durant they unlimbered the wagon and set out to scan the country. "Work might have been found in Durant, but we were country people. . . . We saw miles of open meadow land which was covered with native grass almost knee high. It was green and lush and riffled in the breeze like water. . . . We headed south down into the Red River bottom. . . . We stopped at one of the farms and they were happy to put us to work picking cotton. . . . They even had a small one-room cabin in which we could camp. . . . We worked our way that fall up through the Blue River bottoms to the little town of Kenefic. . . . Dad rented a small house and we boys started school. Dad worked that winter hauling sand from Blue River for cement work in town. . . ."[17]

Kenefic, a few miles north of Durant, was named for the president of the Kansas, Oklahoma & Gulf Railroad. Ira attended another year of high school there. "My major interest . . . was in academics, although I did participate in putting out a student newspaper, and I went to the county track meets and joined the school's debating team. But I did not make sufficient progress, according to the principal, to get me in, at an earlier age than normal, to the Normal School at Durant, which was eleven miles away. And I began then to make an effort, and my parents supported me in every possible way, to complete a college education. I was hopeful of being able after graduation from college to go to law school at the University of Oklahoma, complete a legal education and practice law. . . ."[18]

The Eaker family stayed in Kenefic for two years, living from hand to mouth, finding accommodations wherever they worked. Dona Eaker once went back to visit her folks in Eden, leaving Young and their three older boys to fend for themselves. Claude remembered: "As a result of her training we had all been taught to cook. Ira was a fast fry cook and made good biscuits."

In the second year Ira commuted weekly to Southeastern Normal School in Durant, staying with a Miss Helen Harris and her aunt and milking a cow and doing yardwork for his board. Weekends he went home by train. In 1914 the family moved to a tiny house in Durant itself. For the first time they had running water, electricity and indoor plumbing. Also, they were within easy walking distance of the college. He was given enough leeway to devote ample time to his studies and worked only on weekends and vacations. Durant then was a sleepy farming town of about eight thousand and the normal school had a student body of about 150 in a curriculum that was part high school, part college and aimed mostly at teacher training for the Oklahoma public schools. Over the next sixty years it would gradu-

23

ally expand into the present Southeastern Oklahoma State University, with a four-year undergraduate program, several graduate schools and a student body in excess of 4,500.

But even in its small beginnings it was a stimulating environment for hungry minds, and Ira Eaker's inherent brains and evolving personality flourished in several noteworthy ways. His astonishing IQ shows in marks such as these: "Eng. Comp. 97; Eng. Lit. 97; Physics 93; Physiology 95; Latin 93; Zoology 97; Sol. Geom. 93." Only in one course did he fall below the 90 level (equivalent to "A"). That was in music; he turned out to be totally tone deaf. When he graduated he had the highest grade point average of any student up to that time.[19]

Just as he had at Eden, he found a particular mentor in Durant. This one was Professor A. Linscheid, head of the English department and later president of Oklahoma East Central College. Over the years Eaker often spoke fondly of him, recalling: "He was a remarkable individual who had come from Germany at two years of age. His family brought him over. Incidentally, they came to avoid military service. He was a very intelligent man and a tremendous influence on all of his students."[20] Professor Linscheid was also the debating instructor, and membership in the debating society became Eaker's "main interest," followed closely by reading. "They had a good library. There was much required reading—the classics. I read about two hours a day and two a night for four years. . . was on the debating team for three years and we never lost."[21] And Professor Linscheid, after his protégé became famous, said: "I remember Ira Eaker as a slender, modest young man who practiced the principle of the second mile. If we told him to read one reference book, he read two . . . always doing more than was asked of him."[22]

The steady, purposeful, eyes-straight-ahead character Eaker displayed in those early days as he worked and worked and worked at moving up in the world is not as dramatic perhaps as the more usual course of a brighter-than-average boy who zigzags, gets into occasional trouble, blows a fuse or two and finally pulls himself together to win. But it reveals an immense inner strength and self-control—a sense of discipline he got in part from his parents, in part from his teachers, but mostly, it seems, from within, from his genes. This is a quality many potential leaders reveal, but few so early as Eaker. It did not make him altogether charming or attractive, especially to girls, but it did enable him to cope with every situation that came along. Without knowing exactly where he was going or what his purpose in the world might be, he appears to have been programmed from the start to do something important and to do it surpassingly well.

The image of this sober adolescent in those formative years emerges further in the fond recollections of Ruth Goodman, his pretty classmate, neighbor in Durant and friend for the rest of their lives. She was his first sweetheart, in the innocent sense of that old-fashioned word. Sixty-six years later this gracious, eloquent lady mused about Ira Eaker as she riffled through the letters he wrote to her and the clippings and pictures about him she had accumulated: "At school the other fellows in the class weren't so very careful about their personal appearance but he always was. He was always well-groomed. He just had one suit that he wore all the time. It was always pressed and he wore a collar and a tie. . . . If he ever had any fun I didn't know anything about it. The other youngsters would have their little swimming parties and play tennis and go on hay rides and this, that and the other, but he didn't participate in any activities that way. . . .

"There were three other boys. Somehow they just didn't have the drive that Ira did. He wanted a better life-style than he had and he knew it was up to him to do something about it. His mother was very ambitious for him, and she encouraged him all she could. She recognized he was different and had more ability . . . She wanted Ira to study law and be a judge. . . . He eventually would have, if he hadn't gone into the army."[23]

But Eaker was more than a grind. He was also a leader. This comes through vividly in the pages of the *Holisso,* Southeastern Oklahoma State's yearbook ("holisso" is the Choctaw word for book). In 1914, his first year class, it records that he was elected secretary-treasurer, and a photograph shows him a member of the twenty-one-man Debating Club. In 1915, his freshman class, he is listed as vice president, and a full page devoted to the Debating Club includes these prophetic remarks: "Eaker won first place by a narrow margin; his style was logic rather than oratory; his delivery was characterized by a whole-souled earnestness that won him the day." And in his third and last year there are references to, or pictures of him on eleven pages. One, a history of the senior class, makes the fine Freudian slip of listing him as "Ira Eager." He is also on the track team, in the cast of a play called "The Pennant" and a member of the Debating Club, of course. He was the author of a page-long summary about debating, his first of what would become countless published articles over the years. It concludes with ringing juvenility: "With our able coach [Professor Linscheid] still with us, and an unbounded confidence in hard work and constant effort our slogan as a solvent for all human problems we commit our club to futurity without hesitancy or fear—IRA EAKER."

Offsetting this somber declaration—for Eaker had not yet developed the ready wit and light touch that distinguished him later on —is a spoof section, headlined: "How Would You Like To See," reading in part:

Mr. Brooks . . . . In short pants?

Marion Severance . . . Singing?

Johnnie King . . . . . . Dancing?

Mildred Goodman . . . Not hungry?

Ira Eaker . . . . Flirting?[24]

But all this hearty, wholesome innocence changed abruptly on April 6, 1917, when the United States declared war on Germany. The very next day all the boys in the college, thirty-seven in number and including Ira Eaker, went to Greenville, Texas, and enlisted. Because the seventeen male members of the senior class were about to graduate, the recruiting officer, a captain, sent them to an officer training camp.[25]

The *Holisso* that year ends with a page-per-month calendar. The page for May contains these poignant notes:

> May 1. Great excitement among students—all to enlist. . . .
> May 9. Mr. Isaacks, Marvin Shilling, Ed Battaille and Ira Eaker depart for the Officers Training Camp. Vacant seats in Assembly decorated with flags. . . .
> May 23. Final Graduation Exercises. Boys Missed.

Ira Eaker was one week short of his twenty-first birthday when he and his classmates reported to Greenville, Texas, "the nearest recruiting station we knew of. . . . A Captain Burwell, a West Point graduate whose father was then Postmaster General in President Wilson's Cabinet, was the recruiting officer. . . . He was the first professional soldier I had ever seen."[26] Burwell dispatched them to Fort Logan H. Roots, Arkansas—where the officers training camp was so new that the young recruits' first task was to help nail down some roofs.

Private Eaker was a very slight young man, weighing a mere 115 pounds and standing five feet, eight inches. A snapshot taken then shows him at attention, broad-brimmed hat on his head, rifle on his shoulder, canteen and ammo belt dangling from his waist and full pack on his back. The gear weighed more than half as much as he did. Another photo, full-face, shows a firm mouth, his father's strong, square jaw and a gentle look about the eyes—a face both purposeful and serene.

"Shortly after enlisting," he wrote forty-four years later, "I saw my first general, Robert Lee Bullard. He rode a horse; we marched afoot. It occurred to me then that this general's job was good work if you could get it."[27] As a starter, when he learned there were ten slots for "an opportunity to take examinations for the Regular Army . . . I took the exam to see how I would come out."[28] Meanwhile, on August 15 he was commissioned a 2nd Lieutenant in the Infantry Section, Officers Reserve Corps, assigned to the 64th Infantry at Fort Bliss, El Paso. Two months later his commission came through for the regular army. At almost the same time he stumbled by a remarkable series of events into being a flier instead of a foot soldier.

"I was introduced to the flying machine in 1912 when Art Smith came to Durant . . . and made a flight for a country fair. That's the first airplane I ever saw and the first airplane flight. But, naturally, I was not moved at that time to consider myself a possible participant in flying. But in 1917 . . . at Ft. Logan H. Roots the man next to me was from Mississippi, a youngster by the name of Hoy Barksdale. After the camp had progressed for some six weeks a man came to the camp, an Aviation Section, Signal Corps Captain looking for fliers, and Barksdale volunteered at once. We talked about it rather extensively. I was very anxious to do as he did, but I'd already been selected . . . to take . . . the examination for the Regular Army, and I thought that I'd better see how that went first. It always appealed to me that there might be certain advantages to joining the Regular Army unit as against the Reserve or National Guard. . . . Barksdale went on into the Aviation Section and was sent to England. I was getting letters from Barksdale about his flight training in England

Left: Private Eaker, "full-pack."
He weighed 115 pounds, his pack 75.
Right: the first five to enlist;
Eaker, lower left.

and later about his combat in the skies over France, shooting down the first German, and so forth. And, of course I was very disappointed that I hadn't gone with Barksdale. . . .

"About November of 1917 an airplane flew overhead, toward Mt. Franklin. . . . I was out on parade ground of my infantry company, my company of the 64th Infantry, and this aviator was below the level of Mt. Franklin proceeding west, and it was obvious to me that he wouldn't clear it. So he turned around, came back and landed. I was the nearest officer to where he landed, so I went over to see if I could be of any help to him. And he said: 'I can't get enough power out of this engine to climb over Mt. Franklin. I'm headed west to Deming, New Mexico, out on a recruiting drive for aviators.'

"I'd never seen an airplane engine, and I climbed up on the wheel to have a look at it. And there was one spark-plug lead that was off the spark-plug and lying on the bed of the engine. I said, 'Maybe this is your trouble.' It would reach one spark-plug and I put it back on. He said, 'Let's find out.' So he showed me how to turn the propeller

over, and he got back in the cockpit. Then we started the engine, and it ran smoothly, like a sewing machine. So I walked around the wing to tell him goodbye. He said, 'You know so much about airplane motors you ought to come into the Aviation Section of the Signal Corps.' I said, 'How do I do it?' He said, 'I told you I was on a recruiting drive.' He reached in the pocket of his leather coat and pulled out a form: 'Fill this out and send it in and you'll probably get a call to fly.'

"That afternoon I was riding a sorrel pony behind my battalion commander. I was acting as battalion adjutant,* and the major said to me on the way back from the parade, 'I saw you talking to that aviator this morning.' I said, 'Yes, sir, he gave me a form, and I'm going to fill it out and go into aviation.' He said, 'Let me see it.' I showed him the form, and he kept it and filled it out, and I was

---

*In military parlance, the adjutant is a staff officer who helps his commander with administrative matters as distinct from operational.

delayed about six weeks because I had to write for a new form. This was Major Danforth, who later became a Brigadier General in the Army Air Corps. So that's how I got started in aviation. . . ."[29]

In March 1918, Lieutenant Eaker's orders came through, putting him on detached service to get flying instruction first at ground school in Austin, then at Kelly Field in San Antonio. The first eight weeks were devoted to such basics as engine maintenance and navigation, gradually progressing to actual flying. "After about four hours with the pilot in the back seat, my pilot said to me, 'Now I think you had better take this round by yourself.' So he got out in the middle of the field and watched me take off and do a circle of the field and come back and land. It was a very thrilling experience for me but nothing happened, and after I had done this three or four times he climbed back in the plane, and he took me to what was called the acrobatic stage. He said, 'Now I will teach you some of the major maneuvers.' So we did loops and spins and rolls for the next hour, and I was then assigned to do my graduation exercises, which was a cross-country, three-legged flight from San Antonio down to Beaville, Texas, and over to Hondo and back to Kelly Field.

"As I was approaching Beaville the motor quit and I landed in a rice paddy. It was soft and I nosed over and broke my wooden propeller. Very soon thereafter a cowboy rode up who had seen the plane land, and I asked him if he would take a telegram to the nearest telegraph office. He agreed, and I wrote a telegram to the Operations Officer at Kelly Field. . . . It turned out that the nearest small town was named West, Texas. So my telegram said, 'Landed three miles east of West in a rice paddy, please send propeller.' Late that afternoon the cowboy rode out with a reply: 'Sober up and come home and all will be forgiven.' But of course this was only a bit of facetious byplay with an old friend, and early the next morning a new propeller did arrive with a mechanic. It was installed and I completed the exercise."[30] Eaker received his pilot's rating and was promoted to 1st lieutenant on July 17. In October he was transferred to Rockwell Field, near San Diego, California.

If this sort of training sounds slapdash, it must be remembered that the war in Europe was at a crisis point and no time was being wasted in getting men into action. Also, airplanes in 1918 were flimsy contraptions of wood, canvas and wire, with only the most rudimentary controls and instruments. All fliers were expected to make forced landings in any available field and to crack up too. The Beaville rice paddy was the scene of Ira Eaker's first forced landing. He would have many others and also six real crashes. In five instances he rode his plane down, in the other he bailed out so late it was a miracle he survived.[31]

His first real crack-up happened soon after he arrived at Rockwell. It taught him a lesson he never forgot and that he recounted in his 1941 book *Winged Warfare.* "I was assigned a plane for a flight. I started to climb in. The mechanic said: 'Lieutenant, I wouldn't take that ship up. The engine don't sound right to me.'

"I ran it up; it delivered full power, hit on both switches, accelerated promptly. I couldn't detect any indication of trouble. I called for the engineering officer. He ran it up and marked it O.K.

"But the mechanic still shook his head. I took off and joined a practice formation and soon forgot the warning of my mechanic as we flew out of San Diego Bay past Point Loma. Twenty minutes later, the engine quit cold without warning. I sat her down in the sea. She was a land plane and soon sank."

Eaker fastened a rope around the prop to mark the place where the plane sank and then started to swim to shore, more than a mile away. A porpoise came along. He thought it might be a shark, so he swam back to the partially submerged plane and waited to be picked up.

"While swimming around . . . I made one resolve which has remained with me through the years. When a good mechanic says an engine's bad, I don't trust my judgment. He's the doctor."[32]

At Rockwell that fall "while taking the course in aerial gunnery preparatory to going overseas, I had command of a squadron, and somewhat later I was assistant adjutant. We always had other duties than flying, but naturally we preferred flying. We averaged only two or three hours flying per day, and there was plenty of time for administrative and technical duties. Some served as supply officers, some as adjutants. All of the administrative tasks in aviation or in the military service were parceled out to the aviators, and in our squadron we approached it in that way."[33]

Then, much more suddenly than most expected in view of the huge battles of mid-1918, came the Armistice. Instead of going overseas, Eaker found himself on the receiving end of fliers coming home, most of them to return to civilian life. Eaker was tempted to get out also. But he could not do so. "I was signed up. I had a Regular Army commission. And they weren't letting any Regulars out. They were using them to process all those fellows they couldn't handle."[34]

It was at Rockwell that he met the two most important figures in his military career, Col. Henry H. "Hap" Arnold and Maj. Carl A. "Tooey" Spaatz, both back from France, where Arnold had arrived too late for any fighting but Spaatz had actually shot down three German planes. Arnold had been assistant director of the entire Air Service. Now he was appointed commander at Rockwell, in charge of 8,000 men including 375 officers and several squadrons of planes. He brought Spaatz with him as his executive. Their assignment was to demobilize as fast as possible. When the post adjutant cracked up, they picked Eaker to succeed him. Eaker was awed by both men and immediately began to note their ways of doing things and to do likewise. Again, as at Eden and Durant and as he behaved all his life, he had found key leaders to hero-worship, to follow and to emulate. He was like a sponge, constantly soaking up impressions, ideas, principles, techniques and methods—the whole panoply of behavior for becoming a leader himself. His recollections hence have a double value. They shed light and perspective on the many unusual men and women he came to know. And the comments he made about them, often in writing, reveal his own continuous self-training and growing command of words.

Of Arnold he said in 1959: "He was one of the handsomest military figures I've ever seen. He impressed me as a tremendous personality. He always had a glint in his eye, sort of a half-smile. He won your complete admiration and support just by being there. I remember a number of incidents during that period. One, during the war we had started building a hospital . . . at Rockwell. And Secretary [of War] Baker came out. He was apparently making a survey of all posts and stations and particularly construction projects. I accompanied Colonel Arnold and Mr. Baker as a sort of aide to Mr. Baker while he was on the post. We drove up to see the buildings. The foundation was just well up. And Baker said to Colonel Arnold: 'All construction must be discontinued at once. Not another pound of concrete shall be poured, not another nail driven. Stop in place. The war is over. All expenditures must stop.' "

Eaker, sitting in the back seat, was astonished to hear Colonel Arnold presume to tell the secretary of war such a policy was "absurd." But, once Mr. Baker had gone, Arnold "called in the staff and he said, 'What a tragedy because these facilities will be needed in the peacetime establishment as much as or more than they were needed in wartime. But that's the order of the Secretary of War, and that's the way it's going to be.' "

Another order came along to "select some officers to organize a squadron to go to the Philippines. . . . I said, '. . . we're going to have a hard time getting any soldiers, any enlisted men, for this job. If you will give me an airplane, I'll go over to Arizona and New Mexico to see if I can recruit some.' So I gathered up two or three airplanes and two or three officers to help me—Captain Flynn, Captain Appleby, couple of sergeants—and we took off. They went down to Tucson, I went to New Mexico. . . . We worked very hard for about six weeks, and we got 60 of them, mostly Indians, who would sign up to go. We sent in a list of 18 officers. For some strange reason the Air Service headquarters picked me—and skipped all the others. So we started out . . . for the Philippines."[35]

The 2nd Aero Squadron, Lieutenant Eaker commanding, embarked on the SS *Sherman,* which was on the way to Vladivostok to pick up the bodies of American soldiers killed by the Bolsheviks during the abortive U.S. intervention in the Russian Revolution. The first stop was in San Francisco to pick up the 3rd Aero Squadron for the Pacific. It was in the charge of two officers with whom Eaker would have long and close association—lieutenants Newton Longfellow and Charles Phillips.[36]

That was in July 1919. A month before, Arnold had moved up the coast to San Francisco to be air officer of the Western Corps area. Spaatz also had moved to another station. By then the three were fast friends. Eaker said to them, "Bear in mind, if I stay in the service, I want to come back and join you. . . ."[37]

And when Arnold left, Eaker, together with several others of the younger officer staff at Rockwell, presented their boss with a watch. It was contrary to army regulations to give one's commander something, but Arnold kept it, writing Eaker in longhand on May 30, 1919:

"When you gave me that handsome watch I was in such a big hurry that I did not have an opportunity to properly express my appreciation to Bates, Ervin, French and yourself. In addition I was slightly embarrassed. . . .

"You regular officers were the foundation upon whom my organization was built. And in any efficient, military outfit they must be the start of all organizations. Nine times out of ten a regular officer will do as he is told without question. Nine times out of ten a reserve or temporary officer will do as he pleases or thinks is right.

"I am glad that I was not disappointed in you and wish you all the best of luck in the world. If you all do not stop off in San Francisco and see me I will be disappointed.

"Again thanking you for what you did for me and assuring you that I accepted it because of my high personal regard for you all, knowing that it was wrong in principle, I am, Yours—H.H. Arnold.

"PS, If I have unintentionally omitted any names from my letter, show them it for me and explain my rush so they will understand —HHA."[38]

3

"There are no reluctant leaders. A real leader must really want the job."

—IRA EAKER IN 1975 ADDRESS

W HEN EAKER took his sixty raw soldiers to the Philippines in July 1919 it was because "I decided it might be a very useful thing to spend a little time going to see another part of the world. . . . So I decided to defer my own getting out for the necessary time to do this."[1]

Actually, it proved to be his first step, having honored the duty to sign up for World War I, toward his ultimate career choice, pointing the way to twenty years of extraordinary adventures and accomplishment before World War II brought him worldwide fame. During those two decades his pattern, part by luck, part by choice, alternated between flying, often spectacularly, and staff duty, often in direct association with national leaders. The pattern was set in the Philippines.

"When I got to the Philippines with my squadron . . . there was nobody to show us where we should go. So I moved into a vacant barracks. We hadn't had anything to eat since breakfast, coming across Manila Bay, nobody worrying about feeding us, and we got in at night in the rain at Corregidor. Nobody gave a darn. We were an Air Squadron; this was a Coast Artillery post. There wasn't anybody in the next barracks, but it was occupied, and I broke into their kitchen and got some food and took it over to my place, a bunch of cans, and got some chow for those fellows."

Lieutenant Eaker left a sign on the door of the squadron commander "whose place I'd broken into . . . saying who I was so that the next day I could make it up to him. He was a Captain of the Coast Artillery. He didn't come to see me about it at all; he went right up to headquarters. The old general had me on the carpet on the charges of breaking in and stealing and destroying property. . . .

"I told him my story and he said, 'Well, young man, I could and probably should court martial you, but you carried out one of my cardinal principles—take care of your soldiers. So I'm going to let you off this time, but my guess is you'll either wind up in the penitentiary or a general officer.' "[2]

The 2nd Aero Squadron inherited some "ancient sea planes" on Corregidor, but presently "some French and DH's from the European theatre were given us in adequate quantities." These were set up the beach at Paranaque, a suburb of Manila. Coming back one day from a practice run, Eaker's de Havilland sputtered out within reach of shore. But the street where he could have landed was crowded, so he ditched in shallow water to avoid hurting anyone and waded ashore. Heavy seas broke up the plane.[3]

After a few months Eaker was transferred to command of the 3rd Aero Squadron and ordered to set up its base at Fort Stotsenburg, sixty miles to the north. "The purpose of the squadron was to support the 9th Cavalry, a colored regiment . . . the primary regiment in the Philippines at that time. We built the first hangar there . . . that now stands in the center of the present great complex called Clark Field. We mowed a little strip out of the cavalry maneuver area and used it for a field. . . . Flying back to Manila one day I found I couldn't keep the plane under control and it fell in a spin. I recovered it by seeing the yellow water of the bay as contrasted with the darkness of the rain just in time to prevent crashing. My wheels hit the water, but I got it righted and flew it on in at jungle level, to Stotsenburg. When I landed I said to my roommate, Lt. Longfellow, 'You know, you can't fly if you can't see the horizon.' So we started experimenting the next day, trying to work out a system whereby we could fly in the clouds. We had plenty of clouds in the Philippines, and we'd pull up to about cloud level and get in them briefly; by having a plumb bob hanging down the center of our brief instrument board and by putting a carpenters level on the top long-

Captain Eaker and his DH, 3rd Aero Squadron, Philippines, 1920.

eron, you could tell by the carpenters level when you were diving and when you were climbing. And you could tell by the plumb bob when you were turning to the right and turning to the left."

Eaker and Longfellow practiced until they "could climb through 5,000 feet of cloud, come out on top and then come back through safely. That was the first demonstration that I had seen of the ability to fly with instruments. I reported this to Wright Field. And in time they sent us over, combining both these things, the bubble and the plumb bob, in one instrument. With that, with practice, we could fly through the clouds with a formation of three airplanes. . . .

"The planes were very crude. They were underpowered; they had limited range, maximum of 200 miles; and they had limited ceiling, only five or six or seven thousand feet. . . . We were largely self-taught. . . . We realized we should be able to do some bombing, but there were no bombs. . . . We practiced bombing a raft with coconuts. The ballistics were not too good but at least we developed some ideas of how we might hit something. . . . About the only thing we did grow fairly expert in was acrobatics and maneuverability of aircraft and formation flying. . . ."[4]

"We did a lot of maneuvers and a lot of practice with the cavalry

37

on locating their enemy and furnishing them information, dropping it in small, multi-colored bags with streamers so that their ground forces could pick it up and know where the enemy was and in what strength. The command structure was simple. A squadron of aviation was assigned to and generally resided near the regiment of the ground forces, Cavalry, Infantry, or whatever it might be. . . ."[5]

On July 1, 1920, Eaker was formally transferred from the infantry to the Air Service and promoted to captain. Soon thereafter, he returned to Manila to be acting air officer of the Philippine department, then headed by the redoubtable Gen. Leonard Wood, who later became army chief of staff. "I had an opportunity to deal with the senior commanders and staff in Manila. . . . Despite my youth, they gave me every opportunity to express the air view and were most cooperative in every respect. Only on one occasion did the Chief of Staff, General Rhodes, ever disapprove any request I ever made concerning air. Lieutenant Longfellow and I wanted to make a flight to China . . . and had demonstrated this practicability by putting extra tanks in a DH and flying it around Luzon on a 13-hour flight." The distance was less to China, but the risks were deemed too great. "I do not wish to be responsible for your deaths," said Rhodes.[6]

In Manila Eaker lived at the YMCA, where he made good use of the library, swimming pool and tennis courts. He was also somewhat lonely, judging from the few letters that have survived. But he kept himself too busy to brood, taking fifteen hours per semester in the evenings at the law school of the University of Manila.[7] Here his reportorial eye noted that the Philippines "had the Code Napoleon, and only two States in the U.S. had it."[8] Law was very much on his mind as he wrote his Oklahoma college mate, Eugene Faulkner, back in Durant, in thirteen pages of longhand: "I have a growing presentiment which is amounting to almost an obsession now which tells me that one of Oklahoma's most successful law firms ten years from now will be that of Faulkner and Eaker. . . . It will be pretty hard for me to quit the Army, old fellow, as I am getting along well, getting the assignments I want and have an airplane assigned to me which no one else has ever flown. But I must give up the Army as I cannot give up the plans I have worked for and dreamed of for ten years now. . . .

"I should appreciate it if you would send me a picture of yourself. You probably know that pictures of friends come to mean more to you when you're stuck off in one corner far removed from them and have not seen them for years. . . . I certainly wish you could visit here, old friend, to study with me, play basketball and swim with me. . . . Write often, Eugene. Give my best wishes to your father, mother and brother. Be careful of your own health. Good night, Partner— Ira Eaker."[9]

He also wrote long letters to Ruth Goodman—chatty, amiable and—contrary to the *Holisso*—very flirtatious. He told her about his experiences, his impressions and his continuing affection for her. When someone gave him a monkey he asked her what to name it; she suggested Tarzan. And he sent her from China a very old, embroidered robe. Looking at the beautiful garment framed on her living room wall in Durant sixty-five years later, she recalled: "It had been put away for years and years until, when Nixon went to China, Stanley Marcus went in right after him, and he bought all the Mandarin robes he could find and brought them back and had an exhibit in Dallas. . . . The prices ranged from $12,000 up to $50,000. They wanted to buy this one too but we told them it wasn't for sale. The woman there said this is really a treasure; it should be put under glass to preserve it. So that's what we did—put it under glass."[10]

Whatever romantic impulses may have occurred between Ira Eaker and Ruth Goodman did not develop. But they remained good friends through all the succeeding years. In 1923 she made a happy marriage to George C. Pendleton of Durant, who became a successful insurance broker. They dwelt in Durant all their lives and had one son, George C. Pendleton, Jr., whom Eaker helped enter the Harvard Business School and who became an eminent oil geologist in Dallas. His mother taught music at the Southeastern Oklahoma University and in 1981 was given its Distinguished Alumni Award, which Ira Eaker had received five years earlier.

Eaker had gone to "portions of China and Japan . . . in charge of a morale excursion party. Enjoyed it very much, especially Peking." But what most caught his attention, as he wrote Faulkner, were the inscrutable Japanese "habits, morals and characteristics. Here is only one small example. I rode over a hill and came suddenly upon a country school. The children wore uniforms distinctly military in cut and appearance. They carried swords as though they were guns, and as I came into view they were all marching to music with a peculiar style much like the German goose step. . . . Another illustration will tend to show their trend of thought as affected by their education. They are taught that every family must have some

Visiting China; Longfellow and Eaker.

member killed in battle or the family has a stigma attached to it which no earthly effort can remove. This makes it necessary that Japan must have a war each generation."[11]

Army tours of duty then, as now, normally had a two-year span. Eaker's tour ended in September 19, 1921. "They gave you four months leave and . . . the month that it would require to return to the States on the transport. So I had five months, and I got on a civilian Shipping Board boat [SS *Westcadoa*] with Lt. Longfellow and we continued our trip around the world. . . ." They spent a week in Saigon and Indochina, three days with the British RAF in Singapore, on to Columbo, Suez and Cairo. Here the RAF let them do some flying. Leaving their ship for a week or two, they took a train from Italy to Paris and flew to London ("first civil airliner I had ever been on"), finally rejoining the SS *Westcadoa* at Barcelona.

"So I would say that the two years in the Philippines [were beneficial] on many scores—the opportunity they gave me for travel, for seeing new peoples, the considerable time in night school studying law. . . . They had limited practical application, but I think those years from 23 years of age to 25 were a novel experience which had many rewards and compensations. They fitted me for some of the trials and tribulations of later years."[12] From the captain of the *Westcadoa* Eaker also acquired his lifelong addiction to cheap cigars.

At Mitchel Field, part way down Long Island from New York City, Eaker in January 1922 became commanding officer of the 5th Aero Squadron and, later, post adjutant. "I still wanted to go to law school. In the summer of 1923, Congress passed a law which gave a Captain a year's pay to get out. They wanted to reduce the Army. I put in for it."[14]

Soon thereafter, Maj. Gen. Mason M. Patrick, chief of Air Service from 1921–27, landed at Mitchel on the way to the Army-Harvard football game. Patrick, who was born in 1863, had been in the same class at West Point as General Pershing; Patrick ranked number two in his class on graduation, Pershing in the lower third. "Their friendship at West Point," Eaker wrote in the *Aerospace Historian* in 1973, "probably had much to do with Pershing's choice of the scholastically-brilliant Patrick as Air Chief in the American Expeditionary Forces in France, late in 1917. Again in 1921, when Pershing was post-war Chief of Staff of the Army, he appointed General Patrick as Chief of Air Service with instructions to bring some order and discipline into the upstart young Army flying branch."[15]

On the way to Mitchel from Washington, Patrick's pilot, Capt. St. Clair Street, had become ill. "I was the only pilot in Headquarters because it was Saturday. I was assigned to fly the Chief to Boston. Next day, enroute back to Washington, we stopped at Mitchel for lunch with the commander, Major Walter R. Weaver. During lunch he told the Chief that I was resigning from the Army, and he would need another Captain as adjutant. When we landed at Bolling Field, Washington, General Patrick asked me why I was resigning.

"I said I wanted to go to Law School.

"He said, 'I'm authorized to send two percent of the officers of the Army to educational institutions. I'll send you to Law School. Where do you want to go?'

"I said, 'Columbia University, Sir.'

"When I got back to Mitchel Field that night, Major Weaver said, 'The Chief's getting a little old. He'll probably forget it.' "[16]

But a week later Eaker received his orders to enter Columbia

Major Spaatz and Captain Eaker with Eaker's first wife, Leah.

University Law School for a course in contract law during the following semester.

About the same time he also embarked on an unfortunate marriage.

Her name was Leah Chase, and she was the vivacious daughter of the flight surgeon at Mitchel Field, where they met soon after Eaker arrived there in 1922. The mid-twenties were the age of the "flapper," when lively young women smoked cigarettes, drank cocktails despite Prohibition and danced the Charleston; Leah sounds very much like one. Mrs. Carl A. Spaatz, widow of the general and herself a close friend of Ira Eaker's ever after they met at Rockwell Field in 1918, remembered Leah as "very attractive, with great style, and was fun. But I don't really know what brought them together. She liked to drink and she smoked—things that Ira isn't very crazy about in a woman. She just wasn't the right wife for him."[17]

The marriage lasted seven years, first at Mitchel, while Eaker commuted to law school in New York City, then in Washington, where he was soon caught up in so many career challenges, both at a desk and in the air, that he had little time for fun. This may have been another reason for the amicable divorce in 1930. There were no children.

Still torn between law and army, Eaker went to Washington upon completing his semester at Columbia because General Patrick ordered him there "for duty in the Chief's office. . . . as assistant executive. My primary duties would involve working directly with him, preparing drafts of his speeches and his reports to the War Department and Congress. I would read the Congressional Record, marking items of Air Corps interest. I also was to read the many studies and reports which he had to consider daily and prepare briefs of their contents. . . ."[18]

This all sounded alluring, and General Patrick became his new role model, an admiring relationship he often recalled with relish. "General Patrick told me why I had been selected as his assistant— 'Your record shows that you are studious. . . .' He reminded me that he had sent me to law school and said, 'I do not require legal counsel, but I do need the assistance of a precise, legally-trained mind and the expertise in preparing briefs of a trained lawyer.'

"I learned a great deal in the three years I worked for General Patrick. Perhaps most important, he taught me to use simple words and short sentences. One day I discovered the word 'exacerbate,' and could scarcely wait to include it in his next speech. When he came to the word in his draft, he asked what it meant. I said, 'Increase, Sir.' I never forgot his response. 'We write to entertain or convince the largest number of readers. I assure you that several hundred will understand increase for every one who relates to exacerbate. When you write for me always keep to the low road; write for the great majority, not for the sophisticates.' I never used exacerbate again, until now."[19]

One reason Eaker had "not contemplated staying in the service after the First World War was that I thought it would be an unequal competition—that anyone who had had the result of four years at West Point would have a state of training that I couldn't hope to match. When I decided to stay in it was largely due to the first two years of my service. I became pretty well convinced that that was not a handicap, because I was frequently selected for command and staff assignments by West Point graduates who were my commanders in my early years in the military service, which indicated to me clearly that they didn't have any prejudices against us civilian officers who came in during the First World War. The only judgment they made about the capacity of an officer for an assignment was whether he could do the job, and whether he was properly qualified and motivated. I never in all my 30 years [of service] saw any occasion where a West Point graduate unfairly favored one of his own classmates or other West Point graduate over a non-graduate. . . .

"I had an assignment that I liked and I was given an opportunity to engage in special projects such as the Pan American Goodwill Flight and the Question Mark Flight, and when this . . . was over I had ten years of service and I was doing very well. . . . Also I had developed a great fondness for the people I was associated with, and I found that it was a challenging, responsible, worthy career. . . . I saw opportunities which I thought would justify me in continuing."[20]

4

"A flock of sheep led by a lion will always prevail over a pride of lions led by a sheep"

—ANCIENT FABLE OFTEN CITED BY EAKER

THE OTHER general besides Patrick in the fledgling Air Service was the famous William "Billy" Mitchell. That flamboyant, contentious pilot had been the outstanding U.S. air combat leader in World War I, then was the first to sink battleships by aerial bombardment, and afterwards became the nation's most outspoken advocate for an independent air force and for unified control of air power—ideas that were anathema to both the army and the navy hierarchies. He was the senior officer and leader of the "upstarts" Pershing had directed Patrick to bring into line. When Eaker reported to Washington in mid-1924, Mitchell was assistant chief of the Air Service under Patrick.

"General Patrick carried out General Pershing's directive. He did bring a measure of order and discipline into the Army's flying arm. He was a strict, sometimes stern disciplinarian, but always just and fair. . . . My office, which three assistant executives occupied, was between General Patrick's and General Mitchell's offices, and I often saw and heard the clashes of personality and method between them.

"General Mitchell believed that military aviation was being callously and dangerously neglected by the War Department. His remedy was to take our case directly to the Congress and the people, disregarding and ignoring the War Department's General Staff. General Patrick agreed that the potential in military aviation was not being properly recognized and that our budgets were inadequate, but he chose to work through the established organization, not over or around it. He sought to persuade Executive and Congressional leaders to consider the potential of air power, rather than antagonize them by appeals through the press. Despite the frequent clashes between Patrick and Mitchell, they respected and admired each other. . . ."[1]

When Mitchell's term as assistant chief ended in April 1925 he was sent to the very minor post of air officer of the VIII Corps far away in San Antonio and reduced to his permanent rank of colonel. But this stiff put-down did not stem his harangue. Indeed, it did the reverse as Mitchell deliberately sought a confrontation with the general staff. That came in September 1925 after the crash of the dirigible *Shenandoah* in a storm provoked him to accuse the War and Navy departments of "incompetency, criminal negligence, and almost treasonable administration of the national defense." He was ordered back to Washington to be court-martialed for insubordination.[2]

General Patrick, then still chief of the Air Service, told Eaker: "I want General Mitchell to have any of our files he needs for his defense, but I also want to make sure they are not lost but are ultimately returned. You are assigned that responsibility. You are the custodian of all records furnished for the Mitchell trial. You will contact Colonel White, the Mitchell Chief Counsel, and cooperate fully as I have indicated."[3]

Eaker thus became a significant participant in the Mitchell trial but a far less visible one than some of his seniors, notably Arnold. The latter was in Washington as chief of the Air Service Information Division, a job that brought him into frequent contact with Patrick and with Eaker. Patrick's relations with Arnold were frosty, but the chief tried to be evenhanded in his attitude toward both sides in the hurly-burly of the hugely publicized Mitchell trial. Though he considered Mitchell "a spoiled brat," he wanted also to protect the brightest officers in the Air Service. "He cautioned us," Eaker remembered, "not to jeopardize our careers by going overboard for Mitchell's defense. . . . Arnold, Spaatz and I were in his office. He warned us not to get the enmity of the General Staff. . . ."[4]

"We talked it over, faced up to it and decided to go ahead with it anyhow. . . . Arnold was the inspirational leader in that decision. . . . We sort of made a team, coming to Mitchell's aid . . . worked a lot together at night, getting facts and figures, making suggestions about the questions he should ask of the witnesses. . . ." Both Arnold and Spaatz testified, but "it was decided that I shouldn't."[5]

Mitchell's conviction was a forgone conclusion and came in December. He was sentenced to five years suspension from duty, rank and pay, and resigned. Arnold then became the senior flying officer and took on Mitchell's mantle as leader of the Young Turks in the Air Corps pushing aggressively for expansion and authority. He pushed too hard and was caught surreptitiously putting out derogatory material about the general staff. Since he had used a government typewriter and stationery, he was charged with misappropriating public property in a project inimical to the army. Patrick gave him a stiff dressing down from which Eaker saw Arnold emerge with flushed face. As an alternative to a court martial he was demoted and sent "into exile" in Fort Riley, a Kansas cavalry post with one squadron of ancient airplanes. But Eaker, a captain on the regular list, could not be demoted, and his actions in the trial and after had been sufficiently discreet to avoid the spotlight. Finally, his position as assistant defense counsel had been the result of a direct order from General Patrick. Eaker continued as assistant executive in the chief's office.

From his unusual vantage point in the Mitchell trial Eaker drew conclusions about method that governed his own career for the rest of his life. He was, to be sure, a strong admirer of Mitchell and supporter of his philosophy of airpower. But he also noted that Patrick's procedures gained more for these causes in the long run: "General Patrick became in time our most respected and effective advocate of air power. His erudite and impressive testimony before the many boards and commissions formed to consider the organization, status and budget for military aviation often turned the tide in our favor. He was as responsible as any other individual for raising the status of Army aviation from a Service to a Corps and for the Defense Act in 1926 which created the post of Assistant Secretaries for Aviation in the Commerce, Navy and War Departments."[6] Eaker decided that persuasion was better than confrontation and deliberately set out to become army air's most persuasive spokesman.

Gradually he learned to suppress the quick reactions that leapt to his agile mind, never to raise his voice or lose his temper and always to couch his arguments against an adversary in amiable, low-key style. It was the same procedure that won him recognition as the best poker player in army air. Whether at cards or at war, he was not as exciting or colorful as such flamboyant contemporaries as Mitchell, MacArthur or Patton. But to those who observed him regularly or for long there was great drama in the quiet, well-oiled efficiency with which time after time after time he raked in the pot at poker, won his battles in the air or gained his point in debate.

In later years Eaker commented often on the Mitchell trial and its consequences, as in these excerpts from his testimony for the Columbia University Oral History Archive: "[Mitchell] invited the court martial . . . as one of the methods of bringing before the people at large the neglect of military aviation. . . . His trial was highlighted by the suppressions of the General Staff in those days against aviation. . . . The collapse of his military career was a sacrifice, deliberate, to accomplish his purposes, and he accomplished just exactly the purposes he visualized. . . . I don't know that it had a favorable effect on the Army, but it had a tremendously favorable effect on public opinion.

"There wasn't any possibility of anybody doing anything with the General Staff at that time favorable to aviation. They were hostile to it and all its works because it was taking some of their hard-to-get funds for artillery, coast artillery, cavalry, ordnance. . . . We were looked upon as upstarts, unmilitary, non-military, much too outspoken for our own good and making dramatic claims for aviation and its possibilities—military—that had no basis in fact. The General Staff of that time was absolutely over-age and archaic. . . . Had it not been for Mitchell and the little group that he inspired and assembled around him, we wouldn't have any aviation of consequence. We'd have had no training or air leaders. We would have had no logical air war plans. . . . Without Mitchell's sacrifice there would have been no military aviation. . . . We had nobody of any seniority who was a flier at that time except Mitchell."[7]

General Patrick was not a flier in the real sense; he had obtained a pilot's license at age sixty. But, Eaker resumes: "He got more for the Army Service than anyone else could have gotten because of the high standing he had in the top echelons of the military. The Secretary of War had great confidence in him, and the men on the General Staff had great admiration for him. The War Department would have given the Army Air Service a very bad time if we hadn't had General Patrick. . . .

"We would make recommendations, even signed by General Patrick, for purchase of planes, for fighters and bombers, and the

He learned to fly at sixty.

General Staff insisted that the only thing they wanted out of aviation was observation for the infantry and cavalry divisions, maybe a little photography. They didn't want us to have any fighters or bombers.

"I had an example that's typical. I was sitting on a budget committee, as an Air Force representative. I was a Captain and everybody else on the committee was a Brigadier General. I think it was

49

General Booth who was chairman of the committee. An item came up—some ambulances for the Air Service. He said: 'What's this about?'

"I said: 'These wagons drawn by horses, or even these GMC ambulances left over from the war, are too rough. We go out on unprepared ground, sometimes out in the prairies, to pick up survivors of an aircraft wreck, often badly injured, and they die on the way to the hospital, because jolting along in these wagons and ancient carriages can drive a broken bone through their lungs.' "He said: 'We have accidents in the cavalry too. Our people fall off polo ponies. Any ambulance that's good enough for us is good enough for you.' "[8]

About that same time—July 27, 1925, to be exact—Eaker almost needed an ambulance himself. Though desk hours and committee meetings were long, he always strove to get in some flying every day, either at nearby Bolling Field or on an errand. It was one of the latter that took him to Pine Camp, in upstate New York near Canada, in a DH. Returning the next day in bad weather, he had his third crack-up while attempting a forced landing. The DH was a "total wreck," but Eaker walked away unhurt.[9]

Eaker loved flying, and he noted that proficiency as a pilot was the best path to advancement in the Air Service. "We very early learned that the people who made a name or a reputation for a flying job were more likely to come to the attention of the seniors than was an officer who couldn't fly or who did some ground or administrative job. The reason we didn't use that as an avenue for promotion is that promotion was completely lockstep: I couldn't go up till the fellow above me went up. So there was no way at that time in which I could get promotion by showing any special worthiness or special usefulness. So we didn't buck for promotion. But there was a preference for tasks, military tasks, and you got them if you demonstrated ability. . . .

"When I was a captain I always wanted to get a squadron, and when I was a major I always wanted to get a group. Of course I did more administrative and air staff duty than most, but I always kept a reputation for flying. I went out on weekends and flew at night. After finishing a ten-hour day in the office I would try to get an hour of flying, every day, to keep from being tagged as a ground officer."[10]

This shrewd policy paid off spectacularly when Brig. Gen. James E. Fechet became General Patrick's assistant, replacing Mitchell after the latter was banished to San Antonio in 1925. "I became General Fechet's aide and pilot and continued with him full or part-time for the next six years until his retirement. . . . Our relationship became very much like father and son. We not only flew together, averaging an hour per day, including frequent flights to all Air Corps stations and activities, even Panama, but we often hunted, fished, shot skeet and played bridge together."

Generals Patrick and Fechet were alike in only one way—each had exceptional strength as a commander. But in all other respects they differed dramatically. Patrick was a West Pointer, Fechet not. Patrick was a ground soldier who became a flier only in a legalistic sense, while Fechet was a cavalry man who saw that the future was in the air and became an ardent pilot with a decade of experience commanding flying schools. Patrick, with his stern face and clipped mustache, looked like a college president or a corporate executive. He spoke with gravity. Fechet's face was deeply lined and weathered from the cockpit, his voice was a bellow and his humor was hearty and often maverick. He sat his desk as he would a horse—straight-backed and jut-jawed. But he much preferred to be out inspecting air stations. Eaker wrote: "Fechet was not a scholar, like Patrick, but he had a keen, practical intelligence, a personality of rare charm, and a great zest for life and leadership. . . . He had an uncanny sensitivity for military morale. He often said he could look at the soldier at the main gate and know what he would find inside the post—an efficient, clean, disciplined group, or a dirty, dispirited, inefficient mob."[11]

In the mid-twenties "we got some very disturbing reports—by we I mean Washington, the political and military community—about inroads the Germans were making in South America [with Junkers planes, some on floats]. Somebody said: 'The only way we can stop this and keep the Germans from sending their airplanes into South America is for us to send a flight down there and interest these people in our programs. . . .' We felt, even at that early time, that there ought to be some community of weapons between all the peoples of this hemisphere. It would be ridiculous to get into a war, defending the Western Hemisphere, and have the Brazilians armed with rifles that our ammunition wouldn't fit. . . . They would have had European equipment, and they would have been cut off in a war situation from the source of it. That's no good."[12]

When the plan for the Pan American Goodwill Flight was approved, Fechet included Eaker in the list of twenty-six officers he nominated to Patrick for the ten positions specified. Patrick appointed Maj. H.A. Dargue as commander, plus three captains, of whom Eaker was one, and six 1st lieutenants. One of the latter, Muir Fairchild, became Eaker's copilot. Fairchild, a sober, scholarly pilot who had flown bombers in France in WW I, was destined, like Eaker, for greater distinction: he would become a general and, after WW II, first commandant of the Air University. He was known as "Santy" because he had once gotten out of a cockpit in winter with his head, mustache and uniform solidly frosted with snow. The Pan American flight, begun in America's sesquicentennial year, captured world attention and ranks as one of the great feats of early military aviation. Captain Eaker and Lieutenant Fairchild won particular glory, for their plane, the *San Francisco,* was the only one that completed the entire 23,000-mile journey, making every scheduled stop. It is now in the Air Force Museum at Wright-Patterson Air Force Base, Dayton, Ohio.

The Pan Am flight was widely publicized at the time, with front-page coverage almost every day for five months in all major U.S. newspapers and many foreign ones. The *National Geographic* devoted fifty-one pages to it in October 1927. But the most succinct report of all was the one prepared by Eaker fifty years later for *Air Force Magazine.* Substantial excerpts are quoted below, both because of their first-person verity and because the writing sheds light on the author's character and his way with words.

"The idea for the flight came from Major General Mason Patrick, then Chief of the Army Air Corps, who earlier had planned the round-the-world flight by four Douglas World Cruisers—a 26,000-mile flight that took 175 days in 1924. . . . Our relations with Central and South America needed attention (a condition that seems to recur periodically). The purpose of the flight was to further friendly relations with Latin American countries, to encourage commercial aviation, to provide valuable training for Air Corps personnel, and to give an extensive test to the amphibian airplane. President Calvin Coolidge sent a goodwill letter to the President of each of the 23 Pan American countries, to be delivered by the flight. Working out the organization was charged to . . . General James E. Fechet, who . . . selected the plane, the equipment and the flyers. . . ."

The plane was the OA-1 amphibian, newly designed by Grover Loening for observation work. Its canoe-shaped hull was duralumin over wood, with fuselage on top and two wings spreading forty-five

Major Dargue (left), commander, and Captain Eaker studying route of the Pan American Goodwill Flight before its December 1929 start. In pacifist America, military officers were instructed to wear civilian clothes when not on duty.

feet. The engine was a water-cooled Liberty of four hundred horsepower mounted upside-down so that the three-bladed aluminum propeller could clear the hull's up-turned beak. Fully loaded, the Loening amphibian weighed nearly three tons and could cruise at eighty-five to ninety mph.

"Mounting the engine upside down created most of our maintenance problems. Unless the piston rings were perfectly fitted, oil leaked past, fouling the spark plugs. It was normal at each stop to remove the 24 plugs and clean and replace them before starting the next leg of the journey.

"Another time-consuming, laborious task was refueling. Gasoline in steel drums had been stored along the route. It had to be hand pumped through a chamois-covered funnel into the tanks, at a normal rate of 60 gallons an hour. The Loening had a full capacity of 200 gallons.

"The plan called for five planes, each crewed by two officers, a pilot and an assistant pilot, one of whom should be an experienced engineer and maintenance officer. This was especially important because no mechanics could be carried. . . . We were divided by Major Dargue, the flight's commander, into five flight teams and, following the example of the World Flight, the planes were named for prominent U.S. cities. . . .

"Subsequent events proved that this team pairing had special significance for the success of the mission. The two pilots had to be congenial in temperament, and they must complement each other's qualifications. 'Santy' Fairchild and I developed a plan for joint labor during the training period. We also soon learned that we shared a determination, almost an obsession, to get the *San Francisco* home safely. We agreed that we were a two-man partnership in which each would invest his total assets—his reputation, his ambition, even his life. This shared realization ensured maximum effort of our team. I have no doubt the other plane crews devised similar plans. For example, all the pilots alternated daily in flying their planes."

The flight route called for a diplomatic stop at the capitals of all the countries of Latin America except Bolivia, whose thirteen thousand-foot altitude was too high for the Loening planes, and also Great Britain's Guiana, Jamaica and Trinidad and France's Guiana and Guadaloupe. "The flight schedule included 56 flying days and 77 delay days for diplomatic ceremonies and plane and engine maintenance—a total of 133 days. As actually executed the journey took 59 flying days and 74 delay days and thus was completed exactly on schedule. . . ."[13]

Before the actual takeoff from San Antonio on December 21, 1926, Major Dargue and his nine companions worked hard for several weeks, and not just at training for the flight itself. To maximize the diplomatic value of the expedition and promote the cause of aviation generally, each plane's chief pilot was expected to set up a cosy relationship with the city for which his plane was named. In Eaker's case he wrote to the San Francisco Chamber of Commerce on December 1, 1926, outlining the purposes of the flight and how they could benefit the city and the state of California and offering to do business chores for them throughout Latin America. He also wrote the California newspapers and the *New York Times*, offering to send regular reports from each way station. Since Eaker had been designated the official historian of the flight, he wound up doing this for most of the other crews as well as his own. And from Texas he also wrote long, almost fawning, letters both to Patrick and to Fechet. To each, in different language, he invoked the father-son image.[14]

To Patrick he wrote: "I tried on several occasions to properly express my appreciation to you, not only for giving me the opportunity for this flight but in all the other ways you have helped me and mine. You have indeed been as a father to me, and I should like you to know that it has been appreciated and valued more than words can adequately express. I shall however so conduct myself as to be worthy of the example you have set. . . .

"Please tell Mrs. Patrick that I have not forgotten the matter of the Spanish shawls. She shall have the best and the most beautiful which I can find in any of the countries we visit. General, I along with the great majority of the Air Corps remember the 13th of December by the fact that it is the birthday of the Chief of the Air Corps. As this day approaches this year please remember that Mrs. Eaker and I wish for you the happiest birthday which can be imagined. I think if you could know of the love and respect we all have for you it would make your load a little lighter for you and your birthday consequently happy. . . ."

To Fechet he wrote: "General, I am afraid I was never able to tell you very coherently how deeply I appreciated your giving me this flight. Of course, although General Patrick actually did the final selecting and I could not have gone without his having selected me, never-the-less I am well aware of the fact that I never would have gotten to go without your kindness. Neither would I ever have been considered had I not had the privilege of flying with you as I did during the past year. . . . If anything under the sun ever occurs whereby I can do anything for the Little Girls or Mrs. Fechet, I will be disappointed indeed if you do not let me know of it and give me the opportunity to repay in a small measure the wonderful consideration and treatment you have always accorded me. You and Mrs. Fechet have in me one who will always be toward you as a son."

These gushy letters were the last such effusions Ira Eaker ever wrote. They seem to have marked, just as he entered his thirtieth year, the end of juvenility and the onset of maturity. In later years he always kept the warm heart, caring spirit and instinctively ingratiating impulses that these letters disclose, but he expressed them in more restrained, more polished and more effective ways. Never again did he so ardently voice the need for a father-son relationship, first visible in his school-boy days with Teacher Broyles at Eden and Professor Linscheid at Durant and then enunciated so specifically with generals Patrick and Fechet. The few surviving copies of letters to his own father, some of them five pages long and always addressed "Dear Dad," show no such strong sentimentality; they are, instead, merely the dutiful salutes and reports from a loyal son. Though Eaker never said so or perhaps even considered the matter, it may well be that his overt attachments to father figures indicated the lack of such leadership inspiration and solace from his own father. In any case, after the Pan Am flight was over, though he found many leaders to follow with intense admiration and loyalty, Arnold most notably, he never again was servile or submissive. The rigorous Pan Am flight turned his molten metal into flexible steel.

"It soon developed," his narrative resumes, "that, after pilot and engineering ability, the principal crew requirement was physical stamina. Usually we were awakened at 4:00 A.M. in order to begin the day's flight by 6:00, since the early morning hours provided the best flying weather. After a normal flight of four to six hours, we landed at primitive fields or in rivers or bays, then taxied onto beaches to facilitate maintenance and refueling, which normally required three to four hours. We thus arrived at our lodgings, arranged by the advance officers, late in the afternoon, discarded mechanic's coveralls and prepared for social functions.

"There was a banquet every night given by the American colony or by the officials of the country. These usually lasted, with the dancing that habitually followed, until midnight. So, to bed by midnight for four hours of sleep before the 4:00 A.M. call for a new day of flying, mechanical maintenance, and social or protocol

Captain Eaker and Lt. Muir S. Fairchild arriving in Rio de Janeiro.

events. The latter could not be avoided or slighted since, after all, the first priority of our mission was diplomatic. Captain McDaniel remarked near the end of our flight that we had danced more miles than we had flown."

The ten young men, average age thirty-two, had of course been briefed exhaustively in advance. State Department counselors instructed them not to attempt foreign languages. "Realize what we think of people who speak English ungrammatically. . . ." This, Eaker observed, "was a great relief." Flight surgeons admonished them to drink only boiled water and "to avoid native foods. An airplane on a long flight is a poor place to have diarrhea." They also received lectures on meteorology, ". . . important since we were leaving the North Temperate Zone in winter, proceeding to the Northern Hemisphere Tropics and, after crossing the equator in Ecuador, passing into the South Temperate Zone in southern Chile, crossing the high Andes, and reversing the process as we flew northward from southern Argentina. Communications were recognized as a problem, but there was little we could do about that since radios were not installed in aircraft until years later. We did work out a set of hand or plane signals. . . .

"As I relive the memories of this flight, the principal operational experiences involve a succession of aircraft accidents and mechanical problems. The first occurred when the *New York* crash-landed in Guatemala . . . shearing off its landing gear and damaging the pontoon. Through the engineering skill of Captain Woolsey and the combined effort of all of us, the hull was repaired and the plane shipped by rail to a nearby lake, from which it was flown to France Field, Panama, for complete repair. . . . The next plane to have serious difficulties was the *San Antonio* in Columbia . . . necessitating an engine change. . . . It was 19 days before the spare engine arrived and a month before the *San Antonio* joined the flight in Brazil.

"Next came the turn of the *San Francisco.* From Valdivia, Chile, we were to turn east, flying across the Andes . . . which at that point had peaks rising to 9,000 feet. Our planes, loaded with fuel for the six-hour flight, had a maximum ceiling of 12,000 feet. Since the Andes were expected to be cloud covered, we had agreed not to attempt formation flying but to negotiate this difficult leg singly.

"It was my turn to pilot. . . . There was solid cloud cover as anticipated. After about one hour, when we should have been halfway across the Andes, our engine began to lose power, and we started to settle into the clouds. I asked Fairchild if he wanted to take to his parachute. He shared my view that landing on an ice-covered Andean peak, probably with a broken leg, was scarcely to be preferred over sticking with our plane. I held the plane at 70 miles an hour, just above stalling speed at that altitude, and settled into the clouds, expecting to crash momentarily.

"At 7,000 feet we were out in the clear over a lake. Fairchild became very excited. He stood up in the rear cockpit and showed me a crude terrain sketch that contained a lake similar to the one we were over. He shouted, 'This looks like the lake on this sketch the British engineer gave me at the banquet last night. He was a member of a survey team exploring a prospective rail route across the Andes.

President Coolidge awarding Eaker the Distinguished Flying Cross, Bolling Field, Washington, 1927.

He told me the Andes could be crossed east of Valdivia at 6,000 by following the pass containing this lake.'

"In the meantime I was flying around the perimeter of the lake trying to bring our coughing engine back to normal power. When the ice in the carburetor melted, we turned east and soon came out over

59

the plains of Patagonia. Four hours later we joined our companions, who had begun to worry. . . ."

The only tragic accident happened a few days later over Buenos Aires when two of the four remaining planes, the *New York* and the *Detroit,* collided while breaking out of a diamond formation. Major Dargue and Lieutenant Whitehead escaped by parachute from the *New York,* but Captain Woolsey and Lieutenant Benton went down with the *Detroit* and were killed instantly. The two remaining Loenings, *St. Louis* and *San Francisco,* flew on to Asunción, then back down the River Plata to Montevideo where *San Antonio* rejoined. The three-plane flotilla completed the remaining ten thousand miles up around the bulge of Brazil and the Carib islands without further accident beyond a forced landing for *San Francisco.* "Waves threw us up upon the beach, and about 100 natives rushed out of the bush. They got on a rope and, like a long team of horses, helped us pull the plane up the shore." At Havana, the last foreign stop before Miami and on home, "a U.S. citizen came up to me and said, 'I am a representative of a group headed by a Mr. Juan Trippe which proposes to survey a civil aviation route over much of your Goodwill Flight. Could I borrow your maps?' A few weeks later Pan American Airways began that survey." It became the basis of Pan American's Latin American routes.

Upon arrival at Bolling Field, Washington, the eight weary fliers lined up in their rumpled coveralls to be greeted by President Calvin Coolidge, who was wearing a gray Homburg perched squarely on his brow while other dignitaries wore toppers. Coolidge gave the eight fliers the first Distinguished Flying Crosses, a medal authorized by Congress a few months before.

Eaker summed up as follows: "There can be little question that the Pan American Goodwill Flight accomplished its mission. At an estimated cost of about $100,000, it had aroused the aviation interest of Latin American nationals and heads of state. Many of them had never seen an airplane before . . ."[15]

"The more mechanical become the weapons with which we fight, the less mechanical must be the spirit which controls them."

—FIELD MARSHAL ARCHIBALD P. WAVELL

T HROUGHOUT the twenties and early thirties the Army Air Corps was very small, averaging 15,000 men and 1,500 officers. The officer group was about the size of a small college, and, as in small colleges, they all knew each other. Though scattered at a dozen stations across the U.S., they kept in touch through job rotation and constant flights back and forth. Those officers with exceptional leadership potential quickly became visible. Leadership in a small men's college first shows in athletics, followed more slowly but with longer duration by scholarly or extracurricular brilliance. In the Air Corps skill in the air took the place of athletics, while staff work could be compared to the classroom or politics. Both paths could lead to high rank and command positions. Of the 1,500 Air Corps officers, about 50 displayed that leadership potential, and it was from those 50 (the ones who survived) that all the top Army Air commanders of World War II emerged.

In Eaker's case: "I very early decided that my career specialties would be flying and command. . . . Despite my earnest and ardent effort to qualify for and obtain command roles, my 30 years of active duty were divided equally between command and staff assignments. In retrospect I can now say that both contained career satisfaction but the command side offered greater opportunity to influence major events. It also entailed more hazard and heartburn."[1]

While waiting for command opportunity, Eaker spent the four years following the Pan Am flight mostly in Washington doing high-level staff work while fitting in as much flying as possible. "We had a thing going for us that's impossible now: we could take planes and go on cross country flights of our own volition, between stations and cities. There was no difficulty in getting a plane to go someplace— to a football game or to go fishing. And of course we defended it on the basis that it improved our capability. . . . In addition we were engaged in a very profitable enterprise. We were making friends with the civilian populace, visiting every little village and town in the country and meeting the mayor, meeting the leaders and enlisting their interests and their concerns in an adequate air arm. . . ."[2]

But adequacy in the air was not always measured just by the plane; human error cropped up all too often, sometimes for reasons as elementary as taking off without a rudder or with the controls locked. Even the best fliers could be guilty of pilot error. Eaker was, on March 16, 1926, for the only time on his record. He came in to the harbor of Minatitlán, Mexico, on the way back from Panama in the familiar Loening amphibian and neglected to retract his wheels. The plane sank.[3]

On many flights Eaker acted as pilot for General Patrick or General Fechet and for the first assistant secretary of war for air, a patrician New Yorker named F. Trubee Davison who hobbled from cracking up in a fighter while training for World War I. Soon becoming Davison's executive, Eaker also "went with him to the Congressional Committees and heard his testimony and helped him prepare a number of his papers on the aviation requests and requirements, both for the General Staff and the Congress—a very useful experience. Mr. Davison was one of the outstanding young men of his time. . . . I believe he did as much for military aviation in those years, '26 through '32, as any other individual."[4]

It was with Fechet, however, that Eaker spent most of his time in those years, both in the air and at a desk in the outer office of the chiefs in the old Munitions Building (long since gone, it stood about where the Vietnam Memorial now is on the Washington Mall.) It was Fechet who ordered him to take his first parachute drop— something Fechet himself had recently done. Fechet continued to be an Eaker role model: "He taught leadership by example. Those of us

Captain Eaker and General Fechet, 1929.

who were on his staff or unit commanders under him, nearly all of
whom became generals in World War II, unanimously acknowledged his beneficent influence on our own careers.[5]

"He once said in those early days at Kelly Field, 'You can't
control fliers by fear of punishment. How can you deter men by fear
who have demonstrated daily that they are not afraid to die? Such
men can only be disciplined by teaching respect for authority by
leadership and example. . . .'

"It early became a Fechet hallmark that he hated office routine,
paper work and the tedium of administration. He spent most of his

63

time on the flying line, in the hangars and machine shops, and he often inspected warehouses, kitchens and mess halls. His standards of measurement were flying accident rates, engine failures and morale of flyers and mechanics. . . . He often said, 'Take care of the little people and they'll take care of you. . . .'[6]

"One time, after overhearing me berate a careless civilian mechanic, whose sloppy work might have jeopardized the Chief's safety, he said to me privately, 'As you grow older you will be surprised at how many stupid people you meet; you can never hope to educate and Christianize all of them. Besides, it is often more effective to chide gently, with a sympathetic smile, rather than blaspheme or berate in a rage. For example, instead of calling a miscreant an SOB, say to him, when you go home tonight, throw your mother a bone.' This kindly advice lengthened my fuse and increased my tolerance. . . .

"One of the principal problems I had with General Fechet (captains had problems with generals then as now) concerned my vain effort to get him to make a speech. Having been accustomed to listen with pride to General Patrick, his predecessor as Chief of Air Corps and perhaps the finest military orator of his time, save Douglas MacArthur, I was keenly disappointed with General Fechet as an indifferent speaker. . . . His favorite slogan was, 'I want the people to read about what we are doing instead of what we are saying.'[7]

"He often said to us, 'My job is to make the major decisions. There'll only be one or two of those each day. If you guys do your staff work properly my decisions should be fairly obvious.'

"When someone would send him a voluminous report, he'd ask, 'What is it about? What does it say?' If he didn't get a satisfactory response, he would ring my buzzer, hand the report to me, and demand a brief. I learned early that a brief must never be more than one page. The next leader I came in contact with who had that well-known penchant was Winston Churchill. . . .[8]

"Fechet also had the first requisite of a sound commander. He could and would make a decision. His decisions often seemed to have clairvoyance. . . . A good example was his school policy. For some years the obligatory school quotas (officers sent to service schools— the Tactical School, Engineering School, Command and General Staff School, the War College, etc.) had previously been filled by those officers who could be spared, not those who were in squadron, group and station commands, or in key positions on the Air Staff in the Chief's office. The best officers were kept off the school lists and retained in positions of greater responsibility. About 1930, General Fechet altered this policy abruptly. The school lists were thereafter made up of the best officers, 'his boys.' There was naturally some grumbling. . . .

"One day during this period General Fechet, Major Tooey Spaatz and I were engaged in a three-handed bridge game, the General's favorite indoor sport. The General seemed mellow and happy, so one of us had the temerity to say, 'General, we are wondering where you got this school bug. We can't remember any schools you attended.'

"His eyes changed from kindly gray to icy blue; the smile left his face; his lips compressed into a slight line. It was already clear we had made a mistake, but it was too late to retreat.

" 'I always knew some simpleton would screw up his courage and ask me that, but I am surprised it was you two. I thought you were smarter.

" 'I'll tell you something. They didn't have schools when I was your age. You are not as lucky as I was; the competition will be a lot stiffer when your time comes. When they pick the generals for the next war, I'm not going to see the city slickers pass over the Air Corps officers because they can't speak the language, don't belong to the fraternities or wear the old school tie. But enough of this guff; whose deal is it?' "[9]

Davison and Fechet divvied up their duties in a pattern so effective it was continued until after World War II between succeeding chiefs and succeeding assistant secretaries of war for air. Davison took care of major contacts with the administration and Congress, and Fechet ran the Air Corps; when it seemed expedient, they joined forces. Eaker, as executive for Davison and pilot for both, was in the center of the action both ways and found it a rich and rewarding experience. It put him in touch with dozens of congressmen and other dignitaries, both on the Hill and also ferrying them back and forth to see Air Corps activities or, often, just to reach their home constituencies.

Of Davison Eaker recalled: "We now had, in the War Department's highest councils, a representative; and we had someone of stature. There were many instances of the Assistant Secretary's intervention, ameliorating some of the dire things the General Staff was constantly doing. We also had, at the highest budgetary level, a way of getting our facts and figures presented to the Secretary. In those years our principal problem against the accomplishment of our objectives was budgetary. We couldn't get enough money to buy the planes to demonstrate what we were talking about adequately. He helped us a lot. . . . His personality was ideally suited to the time. . . . The only thing against him was his youth; he was only 35."[10]

Among the many friends Eaker made in those years were three especially glamorous ones—Orville Wright, Charles Lindbergh and Douglas MacArthur.

Wright was a member of the National Advisory Committee for Aeronautics and almost always came to its monthly meetings. Forty years later Eaker recalled: "He did not like to fly from his home in Dayton, Ohio, an uncomfortable four-hour flight in an open cockpit, but took an overnight train ride instead. I was assigned to meet his train at 7:00 A.M. and conduct him to the Army & Navy Club for breakfast with General Patrick. I cherished this opportunity to spend an hour each month in the company of the first man to fly, and the memories still persist."[11]

After Lindbergh returned to America from his solo flight across the Atlantic, it was Eaker who was assigned to pick him up at Mitchel Field and fly him to a water landing in New York Harbor for the start of his ticker-tape parade up Broadway. "He was generously appreciative for my assistance, but seemed uncertain and slightly apprehensive of what awaited him. I felt that, if left to his own devices, he would have preferred to spend the day flying the Loening amphibian and becoming acquainted with what was to him a new and interesting type of flying machine."[12]

MacArthur had been a junior member of the Mitchell court-martial jury. He and Eaker had first met then. After the trial, as Eaker recorded: "I went over with Hap Arnold and Tooey Spaatz to an apartment on Q Street with General and Mrs. Mitchell. . . . And Mitchell said, 'I don't believe General MacArthur voted for my conviction.' This was in 1925. In 1945, 20 years later, I had the confirmation [when I saw him in the Pacific] and he told me he didn't."[13]

In 1928 MacArthur had risen to chief of staff of the army and had an office four doors away from Davison and Eaker. He seemed friendly to the Air Corps (though he did not really understand it) and was widely admired by the fliers. But "he didn't like to fly. It was not for lack of courage, because we all know he had the courage of a lion. He said to me one day . . . 'Will you take me up to Boston on Saturday?' I said, 'Yes, surely, if my superiors will approve.' General Fechet . . . said, 'I'll not only approve it, but I'll go up with you. I'm very fond of MacArthur. . . .' We were having a great air maneuver on the East Coast, the first time 300 planes had ever assembled for a maneuver. They were coming down from Boston to Washington and MacArthur was going to review them in Boston and witness their take-off. . . .

"So we flew up in a high-wing monoplane called the Iron Horse. General Fechet said, 'It's pretty rough. I think you'd be better off sitting beside the pilot.' We had scarcely taken off than General MacArthur turned green. . . . We had a bag for him. He was very ill and very embarrassed. He was one of those people who were susceptible to air sickness. . . ."[14]

Eaker was the only pilot with whom MacArthur flew during the years while he was chief of staff of the army—"about four times."[15] Eaker recalled, "He got green or very pale but wasn't sick again."[16]

Army regulations specified that no officer could remain at the same post or station for more than four years. Eaker's Washington tour ended in mid-1928 and he arranged, with the connivance of Fechet and Davison, to transfer five miles away to Bolling Field, where he became operations and maintenance officer. This freed him from a lot of paperwork, but he continued to pilot Fechet, Davison, MacArthur and others. And he now had time for a seemingly endless series of test flights and aerial adventures.

Lindbergh's feat and the other transatlantic, transpacific and transpolar flights that followed with daredevil frequency in the late 1920s and early 1930s enthralled the public and gave it a fixation on "firsts" and "world records." The Air Corps had pioneered this sort of semi-stunt with its round-the-world flight in 1924 and the Pan Am flight in 1927; now it set out to capitalize on public enthusiasm and to demonstrate by its own continuing achievements the progress and the potential of military aviation. It also sought to establish army air's claims over the oceans as well as the land in the face of the navy's growing but not yet clear-cut flying concepts. Davison of course supported this policy, but he found fault with War Department restrictions on publicity, caused in part by lack of understanding with the Air Corps point of view or direct opposition to it. He thereupon hired an Albany, N.Y., newspaper man named Hans Christian Adamson, who was also an officer in the Air Reserve, and paid his salary out of his own pocket. Adamson's task, chiefly through writing, was to polish up the Air Corps image through speeches, testimony, conferences or proposals for aviation spectaculars. Eaker was instructed to supply the basic information.[17]

The two young men hit it off well and presently took an apartment together (Eaker and Leah having now separated). They worked hard and had little else they could afford to do. "We were on very tight money rations," Eaker remembered. "The salary of a captain in those times was around $300 a month. . . . You had to be careful. There was no wild night life . . . a little bridge and a little poker and an occasional week-end party. Arnold played golf. . . ."[18] But Eaker's favorite recreation was in the cockpit, which was also, happily, in line of duty. When there was a spectacular flight to make he wanted to make it. And if none was scheduled, he would suggest something.

An opportunity came along without warning in April 1928, and led to a hair-raising adventure that now sounds utterly hare-brained as well but then seemed to make sense in view of the public's rapt attention to record flights. A German low-wing Junkers plane named *Bremen* with a three-man crew had accomplished the first east-west flight across the Atlantic, but landed one thousand miles off course on little Greenly Island, near Labrador. The next morning, a Saturday, Trubee Davison called Eaker in to talk with a representative of the Junkers Company, which thought its chief pilot, Frederick Melcheor, who was in Washington to receive the flight, could get the *Bremen* into the air if he could be taken to Greenly Island. Junkers sought Air Corps help.

Eaker looked at a map and commented that ice would make a water approach impossible; would Melcheor be willing to parachute? The Junkers representative said yes. Davison and Eaker went off to see Fechet. They decided the risks involved required a back-up plane and they would use two of the trusty Loening amphibians. Eaker recommended Muir Fairchild as the second pilot, while he would fly the lead ship. Fechet summoned Fairchild from Langley Field, Virginia. By the time he got to Bolling, Fechet had decided the trip would be too much fun to miss and that he would go also.

The small expedition took off that same Saturday afternoon and flew without incident to St. John, New Brunswick, where Fairchild came down with appendicitis. To replace Fairchild, Eaker suggested 2nd Lt. Elwood R. "Pete" Quesada, a very nimble, very verbal pilot he had observed at Bolling. It being Sunday morning, Quesada was horseback riding. But he was found and sent off in a DH to Boston, whence another Loening took him to St. John.

The next morning, Monday, the two planes headed for a refueling stop at Pictou, Nova Scotia. But a gathering storm forced them down in the Bay of Fundy. None of them was aware of its stupendous tides, but a fisherman rowed out through the whitecaps to warn them. Eaker got his amphibian off in time, but Fechet and Quesada found themselves stuck in rocks and mud as all the water raced out to sea. With a borrowed shovel Quesada and the chief of the Air Corps dug out, got off the bottom of the Bay of Fundy and landed on a nearby field. By dawn, Tuesday, the weather had lifted and they made it on to Pictou, arriving with almost no fuel left. There was no sign of Eaker and Melcheor, and their hearts sank.

Next day, Wednesday, the weather was again foul. Fechet and Quesada spent the day patching their Loening and huddling for warmth in a store on the small town's waterfront. At 3:00 A.M. Thursday there was a rap on the door, and there stood Melcheor, who reported that Eaker had landed Monday evening "back in the hills," not far away but on a slope too steep to permit a normal takeoff. They had spent all day Tuesday building an earth mound, like a ski jump, at the bottom of the slope that Eaker hoped would catapult the Loening into the sky Wednesday morning. To lighten the plane, they had loaded everything movable into a wagon borrowed from an obliging farmer, and Melcheor had brought it along with him to Pictou. The threesome nervously awaited the dawn. Presently, out of the mist came Eaker and his Loening, none the worse for wear.

By Friday both planes were over Greenly Island, which was indeed packed by ice floes. The *Bremen*'s crew waved, Melcheor leaped from five hundred feet, landing close by, and the two Loenings turned for home. They made it all right but, once more, narrowly escaped disaster—this time at Portland, Maine, landing with only a few drops of fuel in their tanks.[19]

Despite all this endeavor as well as several other highly publicized rescue missions, the *Bremen* never did succeed in taking off from Greenly. So little would seem to have been accomplished by the Fechet-Eaker-Quesada heroics except headlines. However, their series of narrow squeaks put an important idea in Eaker's and Quesada's heads. This was the need for an effective way of refueling in midair. The *Bremen* episode led directly to the famous *Question Mark* flight ten months later. As Quesada recalled it, he raised the problem of fuel supply as he and Eaker and Fechet were playing cards that night in Portland after they had found a hole in the solid overcast and landed with fuel almost gone. "It would have been nice to have had a gas station up there," he said. "Some one to come up and give you ten." Eaker said, "You mean like Smith and Richter," referring to two lieutenants who had flown for thirty-seven hours in 1923 without landing by getting gas in a pipeline from another plane. "Something like that," said Quesada, "only with a bigger plane. Why don't we conduct a refueling flight with a crew on board and stay up as long as we can?" Quesada remembered Eaker as grunting thoughtfully and Fechet muttering, "Not a bad thought."[20]

Upon their return, Fechet appointed Quesada as his pilot, giving Eaker more time to devote to Davison and to the duties of operations officer at Bolling. But the two young men continued to brood separately about the challenge of in-flight refueling. Quesada mused: "My recollection is that a fellow named Ed Pue, who was a Marine Corps pilot, and I conceived the idea of doing this privately. And Eaker, who was a person quick to grasp any opportunity he thought would help the Air Force, turned it into a military endeavor. He became the ramrod behind getting it organized. . . . He was a captain, a very, very much admired captain. People above him admired him, people below did not. They were jealous of him. He was a controversial type. He had the ability to make himself indispensable for whom he worked. . . . I always thought he was—and still do—a very fine officer. But even in those days we had our petty jealousies. . . ."[21]

That sounds snippy, but Quesada, who was a retired lieutenant general when he said it, did not mean it that way. Rather, in his jocular fashion he was simply acknowledging that it was Eaker who deserved the credit for jockeying the *Question Mark* idea into reality. Like so many Air Corps projects, it took a mixture of imagination, political savvy, opportunism and zeal, all of which Eaker had in abundance. At Bolling he spotted two suitable aircraft, a trimotored Fokker and a Douglas C-I left over from the round-the-world flight.

Then he enlisted Major Spaatz in the planning and suggested to General Fechet, who greatly admired Spaatz, that the latter be designated commander of the project. Eaker would be chief pilot. Further, to conciliate the chief, Eaker recommended Quesada as copilot.[22] Others in the crew were 1st Lt. Harry Halverson and Sgt. Roy Hooe. To man the other plane Spaatz and Eaker chose Capt. Ross G. Hoyte and two lieutenants named Woodring and Strickland. Large tanks were put in both aircraft. In the Fokker, which they named *Question Mark* since they did not know how long they could keep it up, they cut a hole in the top for the nozzle end of a hose borrowed from the fire department. Inside they installed a small stove and some crates as makeshift cots. Since they knew they would have to do some refueling at night, they put a spotlight on the wheels of the C-1. Beneath its fuselage they cut a trapdoor for the hose.

They were about ready for the final tests of this Rube Goldberg apparatus when engineers pointed out to them that static electricity, building up in the two planes in different amounts, could cause a spark that might ignite the gasoline flowing out of the hose. This problem was solved by wrapping the nozzle with copper wire and also putting a sheet of copper on top of the Fokker near the funnel. The copper sheet was grounded to one of the motors. As soon as the hose was lowered and before any gasoline flowed, the two copper terminals were brought together to equalize the electric charge in the two planes.

At last, both planes took off for San Diego, where good weather could be counted on. And on January 1, 1929, they began their actual flight. For six days they droned back and forth at seventy mph between San Diego and Los Angeles. The whole nation, alerted by the Air Corps Information Office and Hans Adamson, watched avidly through the newspapers. Ruth Spaatz and her older daughter, Tattie, then about seven, happened to be in San Diego and watched from the ground. Mrs. Spaatz said: "That's Daddy, dear. Daddy's been up there longer than anybody in the world. Isn't that wonderful?"

"No, I think it's dumb," said Tattie.[23]

Quesada recalled "the whole damn thing as Keystone comedy." And indeed some of the incidents were on the hilarious side. Since there was no radio aboard, the C-1 would fly up with urgent messages scrawled in whitewash on one side of its fuselage. At night the crew was cold for they had brought only six blankets, and the stove had

The *Question Mark* refuels over southern California during its record flight.

With radio not yet available, a "flying blackboard" was used to communicate with the *Question Mark.*

been removed to make room for a reserve gas tank, so they huddled together in one disheveled heap and shivered. Because of the rough and dirty nature of their work, the five men wore any old clothes they happened to have handy (plus fours in the case of Spaatz, Eaker and Quesada) and when they finally landed, unshaven for six days, they looked like golfers caught in the rain or rumrunners (1929 was a Prohibition year) caught with the goods. The peak of black humor came when, inevitably, the hose slipped loose one day and soaked Spaatz with 72-octane gasoline. That could burn, so he stripped away his clothes, and the others wiped him off and swabbed him with oil. He had not dried before another refueling was due; undaunted, the doughty major stood up, naked, in the hatchway and pulled in the hose.[24]

But the trip was also dangerous as the smaller C-1 hovered twenty feet above the Fokker, sometimes at night and sometimes in turbulence. Captain Hoyte, pilot of the C-1, reported: "I pick a landmark ahead for a straight course. The *Question Mark* dips beneath us and is lost to sight from me, although it is within 20 feet. . . . Sometimes it comes as close as ten feet, and then I can see its tail. Lts. Woodring and Strickland lower the hose from the fuselage and Major Spaatz

The *Question Mark* crew, just landed and scruffy after a week in the air. L. to r.: Sgt. Roy Hooe, Lt. Elwood Quesada, Capt. Harry Halverson, Capt. Ira Eaker, Maj. Carl Spaatz.

fits it in the funnel and the refueling proceeds at 75 gallons per minute. All I do is fly a straight course. My only signals come from Woodring by a rope attached to my arm. One long pull means 'slow up,' two pulls 'speed up,' a constant jiggle means the refueling is over. . . . The delivery of oil in five-gallon containers and food and supplies is simple. Woodring lowers the package on a rope . . . into Major Spaatz's arms."[25]

Finally, on January 7, the Fokker's left engine sputtered to a halt. The plane could stay up on two engines but not maintain the 5,000 feet deemed wise. After 150 hours, 40 minutes and 15 seconds, or more than 6 and a quarter days, the *Question Mark* touched down. It had flown about 11,000 miles, and its endurance mark would remain unbeaten for many years.

Press comment was adulatory. The *Literary Digest,* then America's leading news magazine, gave the story two pages, noting "it was only 25 years ago that Orville Wright in a heavier-than-air flying-machine remained in the air for 59 seconds . . . and at the time the world almost refused to believe this feat possible." The *Richmond Times-Despatch* chimed in: "Nothing is any longer incredible to the people of this incredible age . . . perhaps the most significant of any achievement in aviation since Lindbergh." The *Washington Post* said "this flight marks the beginning of a new era in commercial and military aviation." And the *San Diego Union* proclaimed the plane "should be renamed the Exclamation Point."[26]

President Coolidge promptly approved the award of the Distinguished Flying Cross to Spaatz and his crew (in Eaker's case this meant an Oak Leaf Cluster for the DFC he won on the Pan American flight). The key words in the accompanying citation were: ". . . demonstrated future possibilities in aviation which were heretofore not apparent."

Besides the obvious one of refueling in flight, these "possibilities" included:

- If a plane with the engines of 1929 could fly 11,000 miles without stopping with five men aboard, it was clear that, with the new engines already on the drawing boards, regular nonstop transcontinental flights would soon be practical. The world was shrinking.
- Hence, American bombers could soon seek distant targets, and the United States itself would be vulnerable.
- Oceans were no longer the barrier they had always been, and the navy's wartime role was forever altered.

Thirty-six years later Eaker ruminated about these lessons: "In our report to the War Department after we returned from the *Question Mark* flight we said in about three-quarters of a page, we think we have made these discoveries: We have found out what parts of airplane engines fail first by a week's continuous flying of three airplane engines. We know now what parts need to be improved and beefed up, and the requirements for better lubrication and that sort of thing. And we gave them as an enclosure a list of technical things we had discovered. . . . We said we think we may have demonstrated that it might be possible to transfer bombers overseas, refueling in flight. And it was not beyond the realm of possibility that you could do this with fighters. . . .

"Well, this report went into the archives of the War Department and lay there unused or un-noted for many years. And some people have suggested to me—Is this not a further indication of the stupidity of the Army General Staff? I've given it great thought and I'm convinced that it was not the fact that the General Staff did not get the idea of extending the range of aircraft by refueling, although few of them at that time had visualized any further effort of ours overseas.

"What primarily held up the use of refueling from 1929 . . . to post-World War II was the [kind of] power plants [available]. Refueling was really not practicable until technology reached the state where [planes] could carry the extra gear required without too much sacrifice of the bomb load. . . . The thing that made refueling-in-flight was the jet engine. You see, when you have those great propellers grinding away out in front of the plane, bringing down a hose and sending it through was the difficulty. We managed to do it by putting the refueling apparatus in the rear in the *Question Mark*. But there was always considerable hazard. Also, the power was so limited that when we in the *Question Mark* would take on 200 gallons of fuel, the weight of that fuel would pull our plane away from the refueling plane. By the loss of the refueling plane's 200 gallons, or 1,200 pounds, it would tend to rise. [The planes] would tend to separate. . . . But when you had the power of the jet engine, it was no longer a factor.

"So I think the main thing that the *Question Mark* accomplished was to call the attention of our public and our Congress to the fact that there was an Army Air Corps, that we were experimenting, and trying, and doing things. It did demonstrate the possibility of refueling-in-flight, which ultimately occurred. I heard a Strategic Air Command briefer say several years ago that in the SAC today, somewhere in the world, day and night, a bomber is being refueled every five minutes. And fighters now cross the Pacific and the Atlantic without landing as routine. It all goes back to those embryo times. Somebody had to start it, and I do feel we were fortunate to have that opportunity."[27]

While airborne in the *Question Mark,* Eaker had found time between stints at the controls to scribble letters to high-placed friends. One went to Congressman Frank Clague from Minnesota and read in part as follows:

> On Board the Question Mark
> over Southern California
> January 4, 1929, fourth day of flight
>
> Dear Mr. Clague: Here's wishing for you and Mrs. Clague the best of everything for 1929. Hope you are both well and happy. Our endurance flight is still enduring. . . . We are learning some very valuable things for aviation, both military and commercial. . . .

Congressman Clague read Eaker's letter into the *Congressional Record* after the flight was over, commenting among other florid remarks that ". . . the United States have reason to be proud of the men who made this great flight. . . ."[28] This was the first of sixty-two occasions when speeches, articles or other comments by Ira Eaker would be published in the *Congressional Record.*

In Oklahoma City the state legislature had him come to address them, and in Durant at the town's cow-pasture airport, which was already named Eaker Field, he dropped in to accept a set of silver flatware that a local craftsman named Bill Sandefeur engraved with a question mark.[29] It was still in daily use in the Eaker household forty-five years later.

6

"Napoleon's first question about a prospective new general was, 'Is he lucky?' "

—FROM A 1975 ARTICLE BY EAKER

HAVING enjoyed two spectacular aerial successes and won two DFCs, Eaker now endured a highly publicized aerial fizzle. This was the proposed "Dawn to Dusk" flight from Brownsville, Texas, to Panama in the new P-12 fighter, last of the biplane fighters. To dramatize its military potential, Eaker suggested the seventeen-hundred-mile hop. Refueling arrangements were set up in Mexico, and Brownsville was chosen for the takeoff because the airport there was new, and scheduled airline service to San Antonio was to begin on March 15, 1929.

That morning the Brownsville airport was crowded with 150 planes and several hundred spectators and officials, including Fechet, his wife, and their twelve-year-old daughter, Mary. Out of the bright sun swooped Eaker in the very first P-12, its wings yellow, tail-fin red, white and blue and fuselage stenciled *Pan American.* Mary Fechet broke a bottle of champagne on the nose. Next morning at dawn Eaker headed south but got only as far as Nicaragua before bad weather forced him down. Off again the following day, he reached Panama, waited overnight and once more attempted the dawn-to-dusk flight, back to Texas. But again bad weather intervened and he flew only as far as Tampico, Mexico. A muddy field there kept him grounded until the 20th, when he finally made it back to Brownsville. He was careful to say that the P-12 was in no way to blame. He flew on to Midland, Texas, to see his father, who was recovering from an operation, and returned to his desks at Bolling Field and in Washington.[1]

Eaker's dawn-to-dusk failure was followed by three more aerial mishaps, in the second of which he nearly lost his life. The first began auspiciously, with Eaker piloting the first nonstop transcontinental flight. The purpose, he explained later, ". . . was to demonstrate the possibility of carrying the mail across the continent. . . . That would be considerably faster than making . . . stops every two or three hundred miles. It was called the Boeing-Hornet Shuttle Flight . . . Boeing mail bi-plane and a Hornet engine . . . that was lent to me and Lt. Bernard S. Thompson to do a transcontinental flight, refueling in the air. I went to see Mr. Hearst—William Randolph Hearst—in order to see if he would be interested in publishing despatches that we would drop during the progress of this flight at designated points—cities where his papers were published; he made an agreement with me to pay $500 for each time we crossed the continent without landing. . . . So we started in August 1930, and we flew across the continent. We were on the way back and . . . doing a refueling over Cleveland. . . . In refueling [the pilot of the other plane, Lt. Newton Longfellow] pulled up and dropped a five-gallon can of oil on us." Though covered in the oil and "practically blinded," Eaker "got the plane down." After a few repairs he and his copilot "took off again and flew across to San Francisco."

Following some sleep, they started back east "and had just passed Salt Lake City. We were coming through Immigration Pass when the engine quit. . . . I landed it up against the side of a mountain. It turned, and it looked like it had a chance to roll down for several thousand feet but a wheel had broken off as it turned and . . . stuck in rock and soil. . . . We hung on the side of the mountain. We got out, but it was a very exciting experience. . . ."[2]

Back at Bolling a week or so later, on August 18, 1930, he went up on what seemed a routine test flight. "It is customary with us in Line Maintenance," he wrote in his official accident report, "after a plane has been out of commission for any work, to fly it on test . . . at least one roll, loop and spin. . . . In this case I had already rolled and looped P-12 No. 34. I then climbed to 3,500 feet and put it in a power spin to the left. . . . I let it make three turns, as I normally do, then reversed the rudder and put the stick fully forward. . . ." But the P-12 did not respond. Eaker tried moving the stick in every way with no luck. "During this time the plane had made at least ten to 14 turns, and I believe I was under 1,000 ft.

"Here I decided it was time to leave the plane, unfastened the safety belt and reached for the handhold in the wing. The spin sat me so low and hard in the seat I could not reach it. I then put both hands on the side of the seat and pulled myself up and back until my feet were in the seat and my body was lying on the turtle back. The plane then seemed to slip from under me and I went off on the left side slightly head down and on my back. The tail passed over my face, my right shoulder struck the stabilizer brace, and the stabilizer scraped the skin off my left shin. As soon as the tail passed me I pulled the rip cord. The chute opened promptly and, as it turned me over so I could see the ground, I was about twice the height of the house under me. I heard the plane crash at that moment just behind me. I landed at the doorstep of a house and only a few yards away from the plane. . . . As to the reason causing this failure of the plane to quit spinning I can offer no sure answer. . . . My chief reaction the whole time was one of amazement that the plane would not stop spinning. I stayed with the plane too long. There is some delay involved in leaving a plane which is spinning fast. . . ."

What Eaker did not include in this laconic summary was much more colorful. His life was saved when he bailed out at about two hundred feet over a house only because his half-opened chute came down on one side of the pitched roof and he on the other. His risers (the cords that connect chute and harness) took up the shock, and his only serious injury was a broken right ankle. As he was struggling painfully on the doorstep to get out of his harness, the lady of the house peeked out, then shut the door. Reappearing a few minutes later, she explained that she had paused to call the local newspaper: "They give five dollars to the first person who calls on an ambulance case."[3]

The third accident in the series—and the last crash on Eaker's record—took place at tiny Tolu, Kentucky, on March 10, 1931. This time he was flying a "one of a kind" Lockheed made of aluminum and attempting a nonstop transcontinental record. The plane, officially designated YIC-17, had a side-door and a glass-covered cockpit. Sergeant Hooe, Eaker's trusted mechanic from *Question Mark* days, speculated as the YIC-17 was readied for takeoff from Long Beach,

Having broken his ankle in a forced parachute drop from only 200 feet, Eaker hobbles around Bolling Field, 1930.

California, that it "would be hard to get out if the plane flipped over." He gave Eaker a hatchet.[4]

Everything went well until Eaker was over southern Illinois, averaging 240 miles per hour at 16,000 feet and "well in front" for the record when the motor began to sputter, "probably due to ice in the carburetor." After it stopped completely he glided over the Ohio River and, per his accident report, "saw an unplowed meadow-like patch of ground which was the only possibility." He hit the ground

at 75 mph, rolled through a fence into "soft, wet, plowed ground and turned over very fast. . . ."

Eaker found himself "upside down with my head resting on the broken glass of the cockpit cover." He had little worry about fire because the engine "had been cold for quite a while," but he "could smell the battery acid and gasoline dripping" and knew they would burn his flesh if they reached him. After about twenty minutes of wriggling, he managed to get out of his harness and in an upright position. With Sergeant Hooe's hatchet he broke through the door and set off for a farmhouse two miles away. The YIC-17 was scrapped.[5]

Thirteen years later, in July 1944, Eaker, by then a world-famed lieutenant general commanding the Mediterranean Allied Air Forces in Italy, received a letter and a snapshot from a Mr. and Mrs. Russell Oxford recalling how they had "served" him in their

Attempting a non-stop transcontinental record, Eaker took off from Long Beach, March 10, 1931, in a specially-built Lockheed (left), only to crack-up ignominiously after a forced landing in Tolu, Kentucky (right), with ice in his carburetor.

drug store near Tolu while he waited for his plane to be hauled away. Eaker replied personally at once, as he always did with such mail, saying in part: "I was vastly pleased to get your letter. . . . I recall that day very well indeed and have often told the anecdote to my friends as an example of how nice casual acquaintances can be to an airman in distress."[6]

In the midst of these ups and downs of derring-do, Eaker's romantic life suddenly blossomed. Soon after a Reno divorce from Leah he went to a big Thanksgiving dinner in 1930 at the Washington quarters of Lieutenant Longfellow and his wife, Laura. Among the guests was a sparkling, dark-haired girl of unusual beauty named Ruth Huff Apperson. Eaker was captivated, saying to Hans Adamson as they walked home that night, "That's the girl I am going to marry." Daughter of a housing contractor who had begun his career in North Carolina and moved to Washington, Ruth Apperson was twenty-two years old, halfway through George Washington University and working to earn tuition money part-time and in the summers at the Washington School for Secretaries, where she taught business English and typing. She lived at home and had two brothers and one sister.[7]

Because she had one-thirty-second Indian blood Eaker called her Little Brave. She called him Chief. "He courted me for a year—very hard, I might add," she twinkled fifty-three years later.[8] He finally brought the courtship to a head as he was driving her downtown in Washington. "Miss Apperson," he said in his no-wasted-words way, "if you are ever able to muster any affection for me, I hope you will let me know." Ten minutes later, as they reached their destination, she said, "Captain Eaker, I think the time has come."[9]

They were married on November 23, 1931, at the Fifth Avenue, New York apartment of Eleanora Carr, aunt of Hans Adamson, who was best man. "My father," Ruth explained, "was in a Washington Hospital after an accident; Eleanora offered an elegant alternative for the ceremony." It was a small wedding because Eaker's divorce was so recent. She wore a long white bridal gown and Eaker his uniform with pilot's wings, DFC ribbon and the four other ribbons from the Pan Am flight. They were a handsome pair—she an elegant beauty and he the trim figure of a dashing aviator. For their honeymoon they went on a longer than dawn-to-dusk cruise to Panama.

It was a good beginning for what became a great marriage in all respects but one: they never had children. Ruth Eaker did not finish college. Over the next half-century she devoted herself to being her husband's loving and invariably gracious helpmeet wherever military duty called. They moved, of course, to many army air stations. "I've never counted them," she said, "but there were at least 20. I liked every one of them. We've had lovely quarters and wonderful friends. I tell you—this military life is just a great one."[10]

Ruth Eaker's quick mind, warm personality and unfailing sense of humor complemented her husband's sometimes overly earnest manner and won her the admiration of everyone they met. Her winning poise showed, for example, at the dinner General and Mrs. Fechet and their two daughters gave them at their home soon after the Eakers returned from their honeymoon. The main course was roast duck, which General Fechet stood to carve. His knife slipped and the duck flew off the platter and into Ruth Eaker's lap. Fechet blushed, his wife and daughters sat with mouths agape and Ira Eaker was speechless; Ruth broke into a merry laugh and handed the duck back.[11]

At thirty-five Ira Eaker had changed markedly from the lean, intense young man who had reported to Mitchel Field nine years before. Then, with his high cheekbones, square jaw, dark and piercing eyes and a two-year accumulation of Philippine sun, he looked very much like one of the sixty Indian recruits he had taken there with him. All his life, in fact, when his strong face was in repose and particularly when he wore a flying helmet, he would resemble an-

Ruth Apperson Eaker soon after their marriage, 1931.

other Hawkeye. But when he and Ruth married, his chest and face had filled out (his hair was doing the opposite) and he looked every inch the mature man and able executive he had become. His low-keyed voice and carefully chosen words conveyed quiet assurance without swagger. And when he smiled, which was often now, his deep-seated kindliness and geniality dominated his expression. It was clear to everyone in army air that he would be one of their leaders.

So his next military assignment—journalism school—came as a surprise to many of his associates. But not to Arnold. He and Eaker had kept in close touch and were more and more in accord that army air needed to know more about the arts of public persuasion. Eaker, with his natural writing talent and strong promotional sense, was the obvious officer to study journalistic techniques. Arnold had become commanding officer at March Field near San Diego, so southern California seemed a good place to do it.

Accordingly, when Eaker's tour at Bolling neared its end and Trubee Davison said: "You may select your next station now that the new administration is coming in and the Hoover administration is going out and I'm going out . . . " Eaker replied: " 'Mr. Secretary, I want to go to the University of Southern California and get a degree in journalism.' He said: 'Prepare a memorandum from me to General MacArthur requesting such orders.' So I prepared the memorandum, and on the third day back came his memorandum, and there was no endorsement on it. I turned it over and in MacArthur's handwriting was this expression: 'Dear Trubee, I have the same regard for Eaker that you have. He's my pilot as he is yours. I'll send him to any educational institution in the country to take any course connected with aviation, but for Christ's sake not journalism.' Signed 'Mac.'

"I took it into Trubee, and he said, 'Well, I guess that's that!' I said, 'Yessir, if you didn't mean what you said to me, that is indeed that. But I remind you that you are today Acting Secretary of War. Mr. Davis, the Secretary of War, is over in England at the Davis Cup matches in London. Hanford MacNider, the Under Secretary of War, is at the American Legion Convention in Kansas City. You are the Acting Secretary of War.' He got the point, hobbled out to MacArthur's office and came back with my orders to the University of Southern California. And I did take a course in journalism for a year and a half and got a degree in journalism."[12]

At USC the Eakers lived near campus. He found the studies

interesting and not demanding and was able frequently to get away to March Field. Arnold, Spaatz and Eaker often flew P-12s "to Tucson, all around . . . because we liked to fly together."[13] Arnold felt free to treat him as on call in emergencies, one of which came with the heavy earthquake of March 10, 1933. The Eakers were picking up pieces of broken china in their kitchen when Arnold telephoned and asked him to go to Long Beach and survey the crisis in that city, the epicenter, where 112 people had been killed. He told Arnold that massive help was needed at once. Arnold sent food, medicine and blankets without getting orders from up the chain of command. This nearly got him a court-martial, but Eaker was not involved.[14]

A bigger involvement came when they started writing their first of three books—*This Flying Game*—published in 1936. "I don't remember which of us suggested originally that we team on these books. I rather think I did . . . I couldn't find what I needed for the speeches we were writing for the Army Air Corps. 'It seems to me there is a big gap here.' He said, 'Well, I know a publisher. . . .' So we started out doing it. We sat down together and drew up a list of chapter headings, and we divided these up between ourselves. He would write a rough draft of one chapter and then turn it over to me for comment or modification, suggestions, word changes. I would do the same. We would take them home at nights. . . . It wasn't much work."[15]

As the title suggests, *This Flying Game* was written before the imminence of another world war was apparent to its authors. It was a utilitarian, almost "how to" sort of book aimed at telling a broad public audience what military aviation was all about and at prompting enlistment. Its matter-of-fact, homey tone can be judged from a sentence on page 106: "Your boy, any boy, can take the first stride toward making an Army airman. . . ." But there are a number of passages of longer-term validity. For example, in a chapter on air power, the two authors made comments that would prove apt in Europe eight years later.

> The long range of modern bombers makes it possible for them to be based many miles from the boarders of the nation to be attacked. Such dispositions give the advantage of having a wide choice of points for crossing the border, and give little opportunity for spies or observers to send information of movements of the attacking planes. With their 2400-mile flying range such planes could easily leave bases at distances as great as 600 miles from the

border, penetrate hostile territory for an additional 600 miles, and have plenty of gasoline in the tanks to return to their starting point.

There are few sections of the civilized world today 600 miles in extent in which there are not large industrial areas, railroad centers, switching points, docks and bridges of importance, mobilization points for troops, navy yards, dams and aqueducts for water supply, army depots or military airports. Any or all of these installations present excellent targets for bombing aircraft, and their destruction would have a considerable effect upon the ability of the military forces to carry out their plans. . . .

During past centuries, the nations which exerted the greatest influence in the world had, if they were continental with vast land frontiers, insured this influence by the provision of the great armies. If they were insular they secured their position and domination by the provision of preponderant navies.

It appears a safe forecast that the nation of the future which will exercise the greatest national influence will be the country that has the foresight and the wisdom to provide a predominant air force. . . .

This Flying Game was well-received and went through five editions, the final one a revision published in December 1943.[16]

Upon the receipt of his B.A. from USC in September 1933, it naturally followed that Eaker would be assigned to March Field, where he commanded under Arnold, first, the 34th Pursuit Squadron and then the 17th. This put him in place for his next really important aerial challenge and accomplishment—participation in the agonizing eight weeks in early 1934 when army air took over national airmail delivery from private carriers.

Back in 1918 army pilots in a few Jenny biplanes had pioneered airmail service with flights between Washington and New York. Commercial service began in 1925 when the Kelly Act authorized the postmaster general to issue contracts. This in turn undergirt the scheduled airline business, providing enough revenue to encourage investors to form operating companies. These embryo firms at first carried only the mail and no passengers, who were regarded as a nuisance. When Congress changed the basis of payment from weight alone to the space needed for mail, the contractors began buying larger planes and adding seats. Inevitably, bidding for the airmail contracts, which provided about 70 percent of airline revenues, became highly competitive. Under the Hoover administration the postmaster general consistently favored those airlines with the strongest financial backing, provoking angry protests from the many smaller lines. The lid blew off this bubbling pot when a congressional investigating committee found indications of "a wholesale conspiracy to defraud the Government."

This was just the sort of thing to arouse President Franklin D. Roosevelt, who had already pushed through major reforms of Wall Street, the utilities industry and other enclaves of big business. Postmaster James A. Farley brought the airmail contracts controversy to Roosevelt's attention on February 8, 1934. Next day, a Friday, the second assistant postmaster asked Maj. Gen. Benjamin D. Foulois, the spunky gamecock who had succeeded Fechet as chief of the Air Corps, "If the President should cancel all contracts, do you think the Air Corps could carry the mail to keep the system operating?" Foulois took only "a moment before answering. . . . 'Yes, sir. If you want us to carry the mail, we'll do it.' " Asked how long it would take for army air to get ready, Foulois suggested "a week or ten days."

This was very hasty, as Foulois came to realize. He assumed, he wrote later in his *Memoirs,* that the post office would give him time to formulate and present a plan before the actual orders were issued. Instead, Roosevelt acted instantly. After conferring with his cabinet that very evening, he ordered Farley to cancel all the contracts as of midnight, February 19. Simultaneously he directed the War Department to take over.[17]

Two days later, on Sunday morning, Colonel Arnold and Captain Eaker were playing golf when a messenger on a motorcycle brought word that Major Spaatz, then on the Foulois staff, was calling from Washington. The two officers returned to March Field, where Spaatz told Arnold he would be in charge of the western division—the three routes from Los Angeles, San Francisco and Seattle to Salt Lake City. Arnold acted as fast as Roosevelt. Assembling his officers as soon as they could be found, he gave Maj. Clarence Tinker the route from San Francisco, Capt. Charles Phillips the one from Seattle and Capt. Ira Eaker Route CAM-4 from Los Angeles. "Move out and get ready to go," ordered Arnold, who moved his own headquarters to Salt Lake.

With only a week to get ready, Tinker, Phillips and Eaker were in the same fix as two dozen other squadron and group commanders scattered across the nation and faced with a task for which they had no specific training and equipped with planes inadequate to do it. Eaker's 34th Pursuit Squadron had "eight or ten P-26s." It was an open-cockpit single-seater with no cargo space, no radio and no instruments or lights for night flying. Nor were his pilots trained to fly in the dark. They had to because the post office wanted early morning delivery. He moved planes and men to Burbank, then the main Los Angeles airport, which had been the base for "the CAM-4 people, civilians who had been carrying the mail. They were entirely cooperative. . . . We measured our ships to see how much mail in little penny packets we could scatter into this airplane. We found we could carry about 50 pounds. . . ."

But by February 19, when operations were to begin: ". . . the philatelists had gotten busy. At 8 o'clock that evening, when the Post Office turned over to me the mail I was to carry, it was 1,400 pounds. . . . I called Arnold and told him my problem. He said, '. . . I'll give you a bomber.' So I flew over to March Field about 9 o'clock in the evening, picked up a bomber, an old B-2 bomber, went back to Burbank, picked up the 1,400 pounds and headed for Salt Lake. Well, none of my pilots had ever flown a bomber. So the first week of that effort, I would fly with these young pilots as co-pilot, up and back, giving them the necessary training until I felt they could go by themselves."[18]

Meanwhile there was nationwide hullaballoo. Lindbergh, now an airline executive, released an angry letter to Roosevelt protesting that airmail cancellation condemned "the largest portion of our commercial aviation without just trial. . . ." Will Rogers cracked, "It's like finding a crooked railroad president and then stopping all the trains." And Eddie Rickenbacker, America's top ace in World War I and now an airline officer, moaned, "The thing that bothers me is what is going to happen to these young Army pilots. . . ." Rickenbacker's worry very quickly proved accurate. Even before actual army mail deliveries began on February 19, three army pilots died in flights to assembly points.

Other deaths followed, and a storm of protest broke over the White House. Roosevelt summoned generals MacArthur and Foulois to his bedside early on the morning of March 10. Scowling, the president asked Foulois, "General, when are these air-mail killings going to stop?"

"Only when the airplanes stop flying, Mr. President," the Air Corps chief replied.

"For the next ten minutes," Foulois wrote, "MacArthur and I received a tongue-lashing which I put down in my book as the worst

I ever received.. . ." But the same day a letter from the president to the secretary of war carried the Canute-like command, ". . . continuation of deaths in the Army Air Corps must stop. . . ." and went on in diffuse language to direct him to exercise extra caution on the mail deliveries until new contracts could be obtained with civilian carriers.

Foulois accordingly halted all airmail deliveries on March 11 while plans were drawn for reduced service and greater use of bombers. Service resumed on March 19 and continued until mid-May with only one fatality. During the ordeal army air flew 1,590,155 miles with 777,389 pounds of mail at a cost of $2,767,355.22, 57 accidents and 12 deaths. Eaker's CAM-4 was the only route not to have a fatality.[19]

The airmail "fiasco" had several important fallouts. Roosevelt skillfully managed to put most of the blame on Postmaster Farley, who was bitter but philosophic. Not until 1942 did the Court of Claims render its decision finding that the postmaster general was justified because there had indeed been collusion between three companies. But the court denied the government's claim for over-payments. Foulois was jubilant, saying, "It was from this tragic experience that the first giant step was made toward the creation of an independent Air Force."[20]

7

*"Not to have an adequate air force in the
present state of the world is to compromise the
foundations of national freedom and
independence. . . ."*

—WINSTON CHURCHILL, HOUSE OF COMMONS,
MARCH 14, 1933

G ENERAL FOULOIS was jubilant after the airmail episode for
two reasons. First, he felt, as did all the Air Corps participants, that they had performed remarkably well under wild
circumstances. To be sure, twelve deaths was a sorrowful price to
pay. But Air Corps pilots were accustomed to death in their ranks,
and only half of the twelve fatalities had occurred while actually
delivering mail. In a single accident during that same period a commercial airliner had also crashed, killing eight persons, and neither
the public nor the Congress paid much attention—airliners cracked
up frequently in the early thirties.[1] Second, the airmail crisis led,
through a painful sequence, to the formation of something with a
complicated name—the General Headquarters Air Force. That label
carried little meaning to the public, but it was what Foulois meant
in his 1960 memoirs about "a first giant step toward an independent
air force."

During the airmail spasm the general staff had reluctantly allowed the Air Corps to issue orders directly to the personnel involved
instead of going through the established army channels. This sim-
plification, made necessary by the urgency and the unprecedented

character of the operation, was quickly rescinded when it ended. But awareness of the logic of direct operational control remained, both in the Air Corps and with its friends in Congress, some of whom were openly demanding complete Air Corps independence well before the airmail crisis broke. But a bill to that effect quickly perished in an ugly fracas as a major effort developed on Capitol Hill to make a scapegoat of Foulois. His relief was unanimously recommended by a subcommittee of the House Military Affairs Committee, while Maj. Gen. Hugh Drum, deputy chief of the general staff under MacArthur and an infantryman who had served on the Mitchell court-martial board and professed little use for aviation, denounced Foulois as "not a fit officer to be Chief of the Air Corps."

But Secretary of War George Dern refused either to relieve Foulois or to subject him to a court-martial. Instead all the contestants awaited the verdict of a committee Dern had appointed in March, under the chairmanship of former Secretary of War Newton D. Baker, to study the airmail operation, to conclude whether the Air Corps were "a good military air force or not," and, if not, to make recommendations for its improvement. Over a three-month span the Baker committee interviewed 105 important witnesses, including Arnold, and considered many variants for making the Air Corps more effective and giving it more freedom of action. Arnold, to the surprise of many, did not recommend complete independence at that time. He urged a separate Air Corps budget and promotion list, as well as many detailed considerations such as rank commensurate with duty. But his major thrust—a skillful bit of politics—was to support the proposal of another recent board, one headed by none other than Hugh Drum. It had advocated a GHQ Air Force.

This nomenclature went back to 1918 when General Mitchell organized scattered army air tactical units into a single striking force during the final campaigns in France. It was then termed the General Headquarters Air Service Reserve. In the following years variations of this concept were often voiced. They boiled down to a device for setting up a separate arm within the Air Corps, leaving to the latter its established function of air support for ground action but providing a procedure for handling operational emergencies of a different sort, such as the unexpected challenge to deliver the mail.

The Baker board was the fifteenth such group in sixteen years to study what to do with military aviation. Its 4,283-page report, delivered in July 1934, only five years before the onset of World War II, foresaw none of the war's cataclysmic lessons. Instead it took the remarkably shortsighted position that "the limitations of the airplane show that the ideas that aviation, acting alone, can control sea lanes, or defend the coast, or produce decisive results . . . are all visionary, as is the idea that a very large and independent air force is necessary to defend our country against attack." As for a separate Air Corps budget, the Baker board found that to do what the visionaries sought would be too costly for any nation to afford, though it did urge more funding for instrument flying equipment. It saw no need for basic change in the existing command structures or procedures of either army or navy air. As a sop to the Air Corps it absolved the pilots from criticism for the airmail problems. But its only concession to Air Corps ambitions was to authorize a GHQ Air Force within the Air Corps, while carefully making it very clear that both were still responsible to the general staff.[2]

In their first edition of *This Flying Game,* written that summer and published in 1936, Arnold and Eaker wrote: "Early in 1934 the War Department wisely established the General Headquarters Air Force, an organization comprising the striking force elements with their supporting fighter aviation. This was the first recognition in the United States of the need for an air force designed, equipped and trained to operate beyond the sphere of influence of either armies or navies. . . ."

In their revised edition of 1943 another paragraph was added: "Out of this General Headquarters Air Force and the lessons learned in its creation and employment grew the experience which made it possible for us to create in a very brief period of time air-task forces for many theatres and many war zones. Another product flowing directly from the General Headquarters Air Force was the training of the air leaders required in the great emergency. It is not accidental that every Air Force commander on our far-flung battle fronts today received his training and initial experience in our General Headquarters Air Force."

It was not until Christmas 1934 that the politically touchy choice was made of who would command the GHQ Air Force. It went, not to Arnold, still regarded with a suspicion by the general staff, but to another lieutenant colonel—Frank M. Andrews, who took command in March 1935 and moved up to brigadier general. Andrews was a veteran of combat in France and an expert fighter pilot whose most recent post had been command of the 1st Pursuit Group at Selfridge Field in Michigan. He had strikingly good looks and a suave manner and had not been involved, overtly anyhow, in the contention between the Air Corps and the general staff. Drum thought him "in harmony with all the War Department has been trying to do."[3] Andrews would soon prove him wrong.

Eaker meanwhile was back at March Field absorbed in flying fighters, running his squadrons and experimenting with instrumentation. This led to his first personal experience with General Andrews, who visited March Field in the late spring to inspect the newly established First Wing of the GHQ Air Force with Colonel Arnold commanding. Eaker recalled: "General Andrews immediately showed interest in a system we had devised for flying single-seaters through the overcast. . . . In our early attempts to climb through the clouds, I noted that when I looked out one side of the plane, the clouds passing the wing gave the impression that the plane was turning in that direction. I therefore tended to over-control and eventually fell into a spin. I devised and built a baby-buggy top for the cockpit of the P-26. . . . I then discovered if I covered the cockpit shortly after take-off and began a slow, climbing turn to the left, I was able to climb through several thousand feet of overcast without difficulty. The next step was to have additional planes flying formation on me. It was found they could do this easily. The best formation was in two-plane elements stepped down. Eventually, we were flying six-plane formations without difficulty. General Andrews, who had a reputation as one of the best instrument pilots in the Air Corps, expressed the desire to participate in this exercise. After about an hour in the covered plane, he became precise in flying it and subsequently participated in all phases of the operation, both as the covered leader and a member of the following formations. He later made this system standard in the GHQ Air Force. . . ."[4]

Another instrument problem involved the development of air-ground radio for communications and navigation. As Arnold recalled in his memoirs, *Global Mission*: "Our radio operators had to be selected with great care, for our radio equipment, though terribly expensive, was intricate and unreliable. If there was any sort of mountain in the way, reception usually failed. I remember the surprise of Eaker and myself when we were fishing in the Sierras with some U.S. Foresters who had brought a radio along on the back of a mule so that Ira and I could keep in touch with the outside world. . . . We were so busy making camp that night that I forgot all about communications. Then a ranger who had been wrangling mules all day and who was, for the moment, cooking trout, suddenly said, 'My God! I forgot the radio!' He rushed to a beaten-up box, took out the antennae, ran a wire between two trees, opened up the set and called into the transmitter: 'Hello there, Porterville, is that you? This is Bill talking. Have you got any messages for the boss?' The answer came through immediately, although there was a 10,000-ft. mountain between us and Porterville. Eaker and I sat there with our mouths open. 'How much does that thing cost?' I asked. The old mule-skinner said it cost about $600. The Air Force sets cost $2,500 apiece and were supposed to be the finest money could buy! Neither Ira nor I could understand it. . . ."[5]

Eaker often went fishing or hunting with his boss, and he and Ruth developed almost a family relationship with the colonel and his wife, Beatrice. Over the years Eaker exchanged many chatty letters with Mrs. Arnold, addressing her as "Mama B." She wrote back, "Dear Papa." Close though they were, Eaker invariably addressed Arnold by rank—a practice he followed all his life with senior officers, a notable exception being Spaatz, whom he called "Tooey." West Pointers had another usage, calling each other by their last names in informal talk, regardless of seniority. Thus, Spaatz, although also junior to Arnold, called him that in conversation and in letters, only rarely slipping into "Hap." Arnold used first or nicknames freely down the line, invariably calling his two chief associates "Tooey" and "Ira." Fechet called Ira "Iree." But Eaker, even when, in World War II, he came to outrank Fechet, always addressed him as "General."[6]

In April 1935, after fifteen years a captain, Eaker was appointed a temporary major, getting the permanent rank that August while on detached duty for two months with the navy aboard the carrier *Lexington* to observe air operations. The Pacific Fleet was engaged in "a war game against the Japanese. . . . What they had in mind . . . was the possibility that in a future war we might want to fly our airplanes off their carriers, and it actually happened . . . the Doolittle Tokyo Raid. It never became common practice in World War II because the Navy had planes built to accommodate their missions, while our planes were not built primarily to fly off carrier decks. We had other things to do. But I developed a lot of friendships with Navy officers and a lot of admiration for their morale and for their operational characteristics. . . ."[7]

More useful connections came Eaker's way in the next two years, both spent largely back at school, first the Air Corps Tactical School at Maxwell Field, Alabama, from September 1935 to June 1936, then the Army Command and General Staff School at Fort Leavenworth, Kansas, until June 1937. As foreseen by Fechet, all the rising stars in the Air Corps were sent to the first, while graduation from the second was virtually mandatory for any army officer to qualify for the star of a general officer. At Air Tac Major Eaker already knew most of the other sixty-eight students. The assistant commandant, for example, was his former commander on the Pan American Goodwill Flight, H. A. Dargue, now a lieutenant colonel. Among the eighteen instructors was one of special significance—a thin-lipped, hard-bitten major named Claire L. Chennault.[8]

In the years between 1926 and 1935 a great controversy on doctrine raged at the Air Tactical School and generally throughout the Air Corps between the "fighter boys" and those who believed that the bomber would be the dominant weapon in any new war. Chennault was the leader of the fighter enthusiasts, and by 1935 he had lost his battle.[9] As Eaker put it: "The prima donna service in the Army Air Corps was the pursuit. Nearly everybody put his preference when he went to flying school for pursuit. That grew up of course from the first World War, the ace sort of thing. Bombardment was sort of looked down upon because the planes were slow, they were big, and you had to have a crew to fly them. But in pursuit, one man could do his stuff, and he could do acrobatics."[10] Eaker himself had opted for pursuit.

But in the early thirties the extraordinary inventiveness and manufacturing skill of American industry developed a line of big, speedy, long-range airliners and bombers that surpassed anything else in the world and put the future of fighters in doubt.[11] These big planes, of which the B-17 "flying fortress" was the best-known military example, could fly so fast that few fighter planes could keep up and none could go as far. A new doctrine took root in the best Air Corps minds that heavily fortified bombers would no longer need fighter escort. In 1934 at West Coast maneuvers Arnold tested P-26s against B-12 bombers, which were not as advanced as the B-17, and concluded that existing pursuit types were inadequate. Col. Oscar Westover, later to be chief of the Air Corps, went a step further, saying they were "useless."[12]

Chennault protested bitterly. After another set of maneuvers, this time at Fort Knox, he insisted on two premises that were largely dismissed then but came back to haunt army air, and particularly generals Arnold and Eaker, in World War II: "1) Pursuit could intercept bombardment if furnished timely information and if the defense had sufficient depth to allow for necessary time factors; 2) Bombers, flying deep into enemy territory, required friendly fighter escort to prevent heavy losses if not utter failure."[13]

But the prevailing belief in engineering circles was that it was impossible to produce a fighter plane that could keep up with the bombers without losing its ability to fight. Since money was, as usual, tight, the emphasis swung increasingly toward putting the chief investment behind the bombers. When the Norden and Sperry bombsights came into being in quantity in 1933, the growing doctrine of bomber invincibility merged with the novel concept of precision bombing by day, when precise targets could be seen, instead of area bombing by night, which had previously been the principal tactic.[14]

"Doctrine," be it noted, is not the same as "dogma," though they tend to blur in the public's mind as well as in those of inflexible or doctrinaire commanders. Doctrine in military usage amounts to presently held beliefs as to the best strategy or tactics.[15] Doctrine is also something the great commanders of battle tend to flaunt, as General Patton showed with his tanks and General LeMay with his B-29s in World War II. Doctrine necessarily changes too with the invention of new weapons or new tactics for using them, from the crossbow to the machine gun to the guided missile. In the Air Corps doctrine was taught and sometimes refined by the Air Tactical School, but it was not formulated there, despite the claims of some of its articulate teachers. Eaker explained: "We worked out tactics by having annual or semi-annual maneuvers . . . two pursuit groups, an attack group and two bomber groups. And for a week or ten days or two weeks they would have exercises against each other in the field, and upon those tests we based our doctrine. And the school came along and picked it up. . . . It was all decided by people in the field; the Chief or Assistant Chief commanded those maneuvers, and the lessons learned were first approved by the Chief and then issued as Air Force manuals to the squadrons and groups. . . . [The Air

Tactical School] just had to codify it and modify it with advanced ideas as we learned more and more from our own experience and from foreign influence."[16]

The decline of emphasis on fighters at the Air Tactical School shows in the summary of the thirty-one subjects Eaker studied there. He tallied a total of 722 hours of instruction, of which "Air Force" accounted for 84, "Logistics" 54, "Attack Aviation" 46, "Bombardment Aviation" 43, and "Pursuit Aviation" only 10. He also studied such matters as "Maps & Photographs" 19, "Combat Principles" 3, and "Preparation of Efficiency Reports" 2. And he absorbed the nine principles of war as applied to air: the objective, the offensive, mass, economy of force, movement, security, surprise, simplicity and cooperation. Choice of objectives was the primary responsibility of the higher air force commanders.[17]

In between he kept up his flying, as all pilots were supposed to do. And the very day after his graduation on June 2, 1936, he was off on another precedent-breaking aerial adventure. This was the first "blind" (i.e. instruments only) flight across the nation, using a P-12 equipped with a baby-buggy canopy. To validate the feat, he brought along one of his Air Tac classmates, Maj. William E. Kepner, as wingman. They took off from Mitchel Field in Long Island and made eight stops before landing at March Field, Los Angeles four days later. Kepner reported: "Major Eaker was under a hood in his P-12 for the entire distance, covering up at the beginning of each leg and remaining covered throughout each leg until over the field where the landings were made; throughout the entire trip I was in touch with him by radio and flew just off his wing in formation, where I was able to observe that he was under the hood and flying blind. . . ."[18]

In the summer after the Air Tactical School, Eaker was again at work in the chief's office in Washington, now occupied by Maj. Gen. Oscar Westover. The assistant chief, elevated at last to brigadier general, was Arnold, "back in Washington in triumph," as Eaker put it, "just ten years after he had been banished in disgrace! He saw World War II on the horizon more clearly than any of us and worked us unsparingly to be ready, and to have Army Aviation ready, to play a significant role. He followed closely the Spanish Civil War and watched with special interest the latest weapons and tactics as that war unfolded between the German and Russian air forces. He selected air attachés with great care and put them in sensitive spots in the European capitals. He arranged to have selected aircraft and

The first "blind" flight across the U.S., 1936. Eaker is under his "baby-buggy" hood, with Kepner's P-12 flying wing to verify the feat.

engine manufacturers . . . visit England, France and Germany to bring back the latest in aircraft and engine design."[19] And he sent Eaker to the Army Command and General Staff School at Fort Leavenworth, Kansas, in the fall of 1936 because "he wanted to be sure that I was in line to be made a general officer."[20]

Hoary with history and tradition, Fort Leavenworth was founded by Col. Henry Leavenworth in 1827 to protect white traders and keep the peace among the Indian tribes. Following the Civil War it became best-known as the site of the army's only jail. But in 1881 Gen. William Tecumseh Sherman, then the army's commanding officer, started it on the path to a major educational center; he established the School of Application for Infantry and Cavalry. "Thoughtful Army officers," explained the School's 1983 history pamphlet, "had sought such a school for years because of the poor state of professional training in the officer corps. The majority of Army officers had been commissioned directly from civilian life, Civil War volunteer units, or the enlisted ranks. Even graduates of the U.S. Military Academy stagnated intellectually during service in small, isolated posts. Army officers became experts in small unit administration and operations necessary at such posts, but had little grasp of large unit tactics, strategy, or even English composition. Thus, some type of post-commissioning training was necessary to prepare the Army for future wars. . . ."

The brief fights with Spain over Cuba and the Philippines and in Mexico chasing Pancho Villa punctuated the early years of the original one-year course, which was renamed the School of the Line in 1907. Other small schools grew alongside—for engineers, for field service and for medicine. Added too was a second year for a select few called the Army Staff College. But it was World War I that established Leavenworth's value: "Although fewer than 700 officers had graduated from the schools between 1904 and 1916, these graduates dominated the staffs of the American Expeditionary Force in France during 1917–1918. Twenty-three out of twenty-six divisions in France had Leavenworth-trained chiefs of staff, while five out of the twenty-six had Leavenworth products as commanders. . . ." In consequence, the School of the Line in 1922 was renamed the Command and General Staff School, continuing to be the most important element in the Army War College. In 1923 an airfield was added. But throughout the complacent twenties and well into the thirties small attention was paid to the growing Air Corps. In those days Fort Leavenworth was widely known as "horsey." The stables and indoor riding ring "loomed as important buildings." On Sundays breakfast was held at the Hunt Lodge, and on that day as well as twice weekly riders in pink coats chased foxes with hounds.

Even in 1936, when Eaker entered, this cavalry influence was very evident. The schedule for 1936–37 called for 1,309 1/2 hours of study. Of these 349 1/2 were allocated to "Infantry," 94 1/2 to "Cavalry," and 54 1/2 to "Mechanized," the transitional word for what was happening to the horse. Aviation was not mentioned at all in the hourly allocations, though the daily classes, usually an hour long, included a handful under such headings as "Observation and Balloon Squadrons," "Troop movement by Air Transport," and "Air Force in Attack." There were twelve "Aviation" classes, "Cavalry" had twenty-three, and "Equitation" no less than thirty-nine.[21] This helps explain why Eaker, by his own cheerful admission years later, "wasn't a very good student. I didn't work very hard." Ruth Eaker chuckled: "As a matter of fact, we had lots of fun. We went ice-skating and rode and went into Kansas City to night-clubs. I just can't remember having such a good time."[22]

There were, of course a number of lectures and exercises he found interesting and useful, particularly those under the broad category of "Tactics and Techniques of the Separate Arms" (41 1/2 hours). And he again met many interesting men and made many good friends. There were 237 in his class, of whom only thirty-five were Air Corps. The air contingent included Quesada and Halverson from the *Question Mark* crew, Kepner and two officers who would reach high positions under Eaker in the Mediterranean seven years later, Maj. Nathan F. Twining and Capt. John K. Cannon. The Eakers also made special friendships with Maj. Harold L. George and his wife, Violet, destined also to be close associates in years to come. The non-air contingent included two of special note—Capt. Anthony C. McAuliffe of the field artillery, who gained fame at Bastogne with his one word reply, "Nuts!" to the German demand for surrender, and Capt. Alfred M. Gruenther, also artillery, who would become commander of the North Atlantic Treaty Organization. Eaker graduated in June 1937, placing 141 out of the 237 in his class but with a "very satisfactory" recommendation for "the General Staff Eligible List." His overall academic average was 86.93 percent.[23]

He and Ruth returned to Washington, where Eaker became chief of the public relations section of the information division. While at Leavenworth he had kept his Washington contacts alive. One of these was President Roosevelt's press secretary, Stephen Early. To Early Eaker sent a "cover" from the Pan American Goodwill Flight to which he attached the stamps of all the countries visited and which he thought the president, a fervent collector, might like to have. This brought an immediate letter saying, in part: "It is indeed a unique cover and one which makes a distinct addition to my collection. I am most grateful. . . . Incidentally, I have heard with much satisfaction of the fine work you have done in aviation, especially in developing the technique of cross-country flying. Very sincerely yours, Franklin Delano Roosevelt."[24]

Arnold, Harris and Eaker on the lawn of "Springfield," the Harris house, High Wycombe, England, 1943.

THREE

Night vs. Day Bombing

8

"Air Power is the means by which a nation exerts its will directly through the air. Air Power is the strategical weapon that can reach beyond the range of surface arms and strike at the foundations of an enemy's strength. Air Power consists of airplanes of great range and great power that can strike blows alone and unaided by the surface arms. And Air Power consists of the specialized organization required to design, produce and operate such airplanes."

—WILLIAM BRADFORD HUIE,
THE FIGHT FOR AIR POWER, 1942

THE FIVE-YEAR suppression of army air by the general staff from 1935 to 1940, with the full cooperation of the navy, ranks as the most stupid and frightening interlude in American military history. It was in large measure responsible for the disaster at Pearl Harbor, where long-range land-based air patrols could have thwarted the Japanese surprise. It almost cost the United States its ultimate victory in World War II, through lack of enough air power. It is a classic example of doctrine becoming dogma.

In defense of the ground generals and ocean admirals, it should be noted that the U.S. public and its government were adamantly isolationist for two full decades following World War I. The stated mission of both army and navy was entirely committed to defense. Forgotten was the old military lesson that the best defense is an offense. Any talk of war action outside the American hemisphere was taboo.

The army general staff clung to the view that aviation was a useful observation facility and a sort of extended artillery for the support of regimental ground action. The navy took refuge in two phrases that became cliche—it was "the first line of defense" and airplanes were "the eyes and ears of the fleet." In 1935, for example, Rear Adm. Yates Stirling declared: "The airplane has a definite function in the gunnery organization of every ship. . . . Information obtained from air scouts will have a far-reaching effect upon the tactical disposition of the ships of the fleet. . . . A united air force would in time become mostly a shore-based air force which can function only in narrow waters. The Navy wants a ship-based force. The oceans that carry our trade and communications will remain free from the influence of a land-based force." And as late as May 1940, a week before Germany smashed France and only eighteen months before Pearl Harbor, Secretary of the Navy Charles Edison said, "The Navy still considers the battleship the backbone of the fleet."[1]

Neither army nor navy saw much merit in the big, long-range bomber best exemplified by the B-17 "flying fortress," test flown in 1935. Why put many dollars into one big and as yet unproven plane when the same expenditure would purchase two or three smaller ones? The navy still did not believe long-range bombers were needed to stop an invading fleet; it could do that, it said, on its own. And the army general staff, concentrating only on defense, saw no reason to attack distant enemy industrial sources. It fell to General Andrews as commander of the GHQ Air Force to lead army air's increasingly desperate contest against the two "senior services." And, as in the court-martial of General Mitchell a decade before, Ira Eaker was an active participant in a relatively inconspicuous role that did not bring down general staff wrath upon him, though it fell on Andrews and most of the key officers in the GHQ Air Force.

Immediately upon his appointment as GHQ AF commander, Andrews had made his objectives clear by his choice of Col. Hugh Knerr as his chief of staff. Knerr was as much the leading exponent for the bombardment concept of air power as Chennault was for fighters. And, like Chennault, he was thin-lipped, hard-bitten and very outspoken. Knerr had commanded a bombardment group in the late twenties and then, from 1932 to 1935 was chief of the field service section of the Air Corps at Wright Field when it developed the initial plans for the B-17 and other four-motored bombers. Knerr, as much as any one man, was responsible for the Air Corps doctrine that bombardment was the basic weapon of air power and that the B-17 was, at last, the ideal plane to prove it. And so it seemed when the first B-17 electrified the aviation world in July 1935 with a nonstop, two thousand-mile flight from Seattle to Dayton, Ohio, at an average speed of 235 mph. But only two months later, when Boeing's test pilot took off at Dayton without releasing the control locks and the one and only B-17 crashed and burned, the general staff's reaction was to refuse to authorize funds for any more. Only by adroit juggling of existing funds for other equipment was the GHQ AF able to get approval, first, for three more B-17s, then twelve. On this slender thread hung the fate of what would become the dominant weapon of World War II in Europe, as its lineal descendant, the B-29 "super fortress," would be in Japan.

Eaker first became involved in these great issues when he returned to Washington in the summer of 1936 for three months duty in the office of Maj. Gen. Oscar Westover, chief of the Air Corps, with Arnold as his assistant. Westover and Arnold worked closely with Andrews in the effort to persuade the War Department to approve further B-17 funding. But Secretary of War Harry Woodring gave an emphatic no. Instead, said he, "What is desired is a light, responsive, less expensive type of bombardment plane capable of going not more than 300 miles beyond the coast line."[2] Eaker recalled: "I had been able to fly Louis Johnson, the Assistant Secretary of War, to some of his dates—public speaking in other cities and that sort of thing. So had others of my contemporaries. In holding our council of war, Arnold, Spaatz, Weaver, Kilner and myself, we said what to do? It occurred to us that Louis Johnson might be the method of saving the situation. So we went to him and explained what the cancellation of the B-17s could mean. . . . He caught the vision that we hoped to inspire in him, and he went personally to see Mr. Roosevelt and had them put back in the budget."[3]

At that point Roosevelt had still not made his philosophy about air power clear. Perhaps he had not yet arrived at it, for he had a strong navy bias as a result of having been assistant secretary of the navy in 1913. He had not, for example, seen fit to pick another

assistant secretary of war for air following Trubee Davison. Instead
he let aviation duties fall into the hands of an across-the-board
assistant secretary of war—Louis Johnson. The president remained
aloof from the growing contention between army air and the general
staff.

The next time Eaker entered the fray was in 1937 when he returned to Washington from Leavenworth to serve for two years as
assistant chief of the Air Corps Information Division and was promoted to lieutenant colonel. By then General Andrews was fast
falling out of favor with the general staff because of his insistant
assertion of the big bomber strategy. Andrews had accomplished
wonders in the eyes of the Air Corps in terms of new air bases,
organization, training and enthusiasm, plus major progress both in
bomber and fighter equipment. But this counted for little in the eyes
of the general staff. They regarded his attitude as close to outright
rebellion, though not overt enough to warrant the court-martial with
which Mitchell had been dispatched. The issue was brought to a head
when Rep. Mark Wilcox of Florida introduced a bill in Congress, not
for an independent air force but for a "United States Air Corps" that
would operate within the War Department on an equal basis with
the ground forces. Andrews testified politely and eloquently in favor
of the Wilcox Bill, but President Roosevelt sent word to postpone
action. The bill then died in committee and the general staff counterattacked by ordering the top officers on the Andrews staff into
scattered "exile" posts and telling Andrews that the general staff, not
Andrews, would select their replacements. Knerr was sent to the
small assignment of air officer at Fort Sam Houston, San Antonio,
Texas, in 1928 and retired a year later. Andrews was allowed to
complete his four-year tour as commander of the GHQ AF and then,
in 1939, was reduced to his regular rank of colonel and sent to Fort
Sam Houston to replace Knerr. Fort Sam, by deliberate irony, was
where Mitchell was "exiled" in 1925.[4]

In the tense summer of 1938, the last one of Andrews's tenure at
the GHQ AF, calamity glared around the globe. In Spain Franco's
fascism was nearing victory. In Germany Hitler was threatening war
with Czechoslovakia over the Sudetenland. In Asia Japan had swallowed all of Manchuria and large chunks of China itself. In the
United States the fleet was on maneuvers in the Pacific involving "an
Asiatic Power" and the GHQ Air Force was on maneuvers from
Harrisburg, Pennsylvania, to Schenectady, New York, fending off a

The famous 1938 interception of the Italian liner *Rex* by three B-17s, 700 miles off New York.

hypothetical aggressor seeking to capture industrial areas in the Northeast. Three hundred planes, nineteen airports and three thousand officers and men were involved, with headquarters at Mitchel Field, Long Island. Eaker was there as G-2 (intelligence) and as information officer, handling the press.[5]

He had brought with him a very bright second lieutenant in the reserve named Harris B. Hull, who was a Washington reporter when not on military duty and who would become a close and lifelong associate of Eaker. Hull noted that the racy Italian liner *Rex,* then about one thousand miles offshore, was inbound to New York. Eaker recalled: "He suggested to me that this would be a wonderful opportunity to gain publicity. If we flew a flight of B-17s to intercept the *Rex* 400 or 500 miles at sea and photographed it, these pictures would probably be featured in all the New York City newspapers. I submitted the idea to General Andrews, who approved it. . . ."[6]

Additional approval was needed from the Italian steamship line, which was understandably delighted, and from Maj. Gen. Malin

Craig, who had succeeded MacArthur as chief of the general staff. Craig also concurred, mindful apparently only of the publicity and forgetful of the "300-mile rule" under which the Air Corps was not supposed to fly more than that from the coast. The result was a publicity bonanza and an explosion of navy anger.

The flight of three B-17s was guided by a black-haired first lieutenant known as "the best navigator in the Air Corps." His name was Curtis LeMay and his skills were needed, for the weather over the Atlantic was very bad. They flew low, in line abreast, and broke through heavy clouds into bright sun directly over the ship 756 miles out. While passengers waved, a photographer in one B-17 took a stunning picture of the other two slender bombers streaking by the *Rex* at mast height. It appeared on the front pages of eighteen hundred newspapers and magazines. The *New York Times,* whose military editor, Hanson W. Baldwin, had gone along, called the flight "one from which valuable lessons about the aerial defense of the United States will be drawn . . . a striking example of the mobility and range of modern aviation."

But the next day as Eaker was sitting with Andrews in a staff meeting, the phone rang. It was General Craig, calling from Washington. He said, Eaker reported, "that he had received complaints from the Secretary of the Navy and the Navy's CNO, stating that the *Rex* flight was in violation of the Navy's prerogatives of controlling the sea approaches. He concluded the conversation by telling General Andrews that his B-17s henceforth were restricted to operations no further than 100 miles from shore. General Andrews asked him if General Craig would put this order in writing, and he subsequently received a letter to that effect."[7]

This was a minor rebuff, however, compared to the decision late that summer, just before Munich, when the War Department and general staff refused any further allocation for building B-17s. The Air Corps had put in for 108. The new thumbs down meant that when the European war began a year later, in September 1939, army air possessed only nineteen of its most important weapon. Most of these were quickly given to the British.

But Munich brought the decisive upward turn in army air's fortunes. For the shabby agreement that Prime Minister Chamberlain made with Hitler, justified by some as buying time for Britain to start rearming, convinced Franklin Roosevelt to come out strongly on the side of the big plane strategy. In the same month as the Munich Declaration, Westover crashed to death piloting his own plane and Arnold became chief of the Air Corps.

During 1938 and 1939, Eaker and Arnold teamed on a second book, called *Winged Warfare*, to be published in 1941. Their first one, *This Flying Game*, had sold well but was primarily utilitarian. Now they set their sights higher, with their eyes on the war in Spain and their growing conviction that a bigger conflict was in prospect. But Arnold was so busy that Eaker did most of the work. This was just as well, for Eaker was the better man with words, though Arnold too could write effectively when he had time to do so.

But life was not all just serious duty in those prewar years in Washington. General Westover wanted an Air Corps song and Eaker was assigned to get one. "We came up with the idea of enlisting the help of Bernarr McFadden in New York, the publisher of *Liberty Magazine*. I contacted McFadden in New York, who agreed to run a song contest in his magazine and provide a prize of $1,000 to the winner. General Westover presented the check to Mr. Crawford, who had been declared the winner, with the present Air Force Song ["Off we go," etc.], and Mr. Crawford sang it at the Cleveland Air Races in 1937, the first public rendition. . . ."[8]

Then there was the continuing file of fliers setting new world records of one sort or another. An exceptional case was Howard Hughes who circled the earth in 1938 in a record ninety-one hours, fourteen minutes. He was treated to lunch by Westover, Arnold and Eaker, all of whom wore civilian clothes, as army officers were directed to do most of the time in the twenties and thirties in pacifist, isolationist America. It was Eaker's first meeting with Hughes, then still debonair, charming and brilliant—eccentric yes, but far from the drug-sodden recluse he became.

In the gracious Georgetown section of Washington, not far from the Munitions Building, Ruth Eaker, blooming and happy in army life, found them a pretty house—their first home off a military base[9] —and displayed a flair for interior decoration. She was decorative herself. Soon after the Eakers returned from Leavenworth the *Washington Times* devoted a quarter-page to her photograph in a full-length summer dress "on the terrace of her newly-acquired Georgetown home." Another society page described her as "easily the Army's most beautiful wife." They were a popular pair. In particular they saw a lot of the Arnold and Spaatz families and were known to the Arnold and Spaatz children as Uncle Ira and Aunt Ruth.

Eaker's first meeting with Howard Hughes, in New York, after Hughes set a round-the-world flight record in 1938. L. to r.: Eaker; Maj. Gen. Oscar Westover, chief, Army Air Corps; Hughes; Brig. Gen. H.H. Arnold.

There were evenings of bridge or dancing at the Army and Navy Club. We "partied around" said Ruth.[10]

With Arnold himself, Eaker, who became his executive in 1940, continued in the role of admiring protégé. There were never any of the father-son overtones that had warmed his teamwork with generals Patrick and Fechet. Arnold was a powerful mentor, a somewhat overpowering one at times. Robert Lovett, the brilliant New York banker who became assistant secretary of war for air when Roosevelt reconstituted that post, thought Eaker was "over-awed" by Arnold, who, he said, was "often a bull in a china shop."[11] With Spaatz, the other member of this trio that came to dominate army air for the next decade, Eaker enjoyed true, relaxed friendship. The trio's teamwork, like that of the three musketeers, remained constant. Arnold was always dominant, Spaatz number two and Eaker number three. Eaker, who never aspired to change the order, described it in the context of Douglas Freeman's Civil War book, *Lee's Lieutenants*. "Whereas Lee had three Lieutenants, General Arnold had only one, relying on Spaatz more than he did on any other individual."[12] When General Arnold was chief in 1938 Colonel Spaatz was his operations officer, while Lieutenant Colonel Eaker was executive. And, as they moved up the ladder in World War II and after, their teamwork was always in that same one-two-three order and always with mutual trust, loyalty and candor. Spaatz and Eaker were unfailingly respectful with their boss but never hesitated to speak up when they disagreed with him: The Air Corps, full of fierce individualists, had little use for yes-men. But when Arnold overruled them, he usually, they found, proved right and when he gave an order, they obeyed. In those prewar days he was far less choleric than he became later under war pressure and heart disease. But he was often peremptory and always ruthless—"tough as an old boot," as Eaker once put it, despite his genial outward personality.[13] "He'd have fired his own mother if she didn't produce," Eaker said another time.[14] And when Spaatz went abroad in 1942 and Ruth Spaatz was tearful about the expected long absence, her husband replied, "Don't worry. Hap'll fire me in six months."[15]

Eaker repeatedly described Arnold as a "genius." Noting that Arnold was a "non-conformist throughout his career," Eaker concluded, "that was the reason he was such a tremendous success. . . . His leadership, drive, experience and imagination were the primary factors in [his] unprecedented accomplishment." And another time Eaker added: "General Arnold proceeded with the wisdom of a genius. He began building the French and the British planes, incorporating the techniques they had discovered in the early days of the war, that the Germans and the Russians had developed in Spain. And he used that money for research and development to be sure that we would at the earliest possible time have prototypes of proper bombers and fighters. Without his judgment and wisdom, and often complete disregard for regulations and authority . . . this lack of preparedness . . . which was very prominent in 1939 and '40, would have continued indefinitely."[16]

Spaatz was quite different. Where Arnold was voluble, Spaatz was terse. Eaker wrote that "he was a miser with words. If he had brought down the Ten Commandments from Sinai, there would have been only one, 'Always do the right thing.' "[17] He was fond of saying, "I never learned anything while talking." But though gruff in manner, Spaatz was warm at heart, always mindful of the well-being of the people working for him. His humor was sardonic, his attitude toward sanctimony irreverent. At the christening of a battleship he asked, "How are we going to get it up in the air and drop it on Tokyo?" When taken on a two-hour tour through St. Peters after the capture of Rome he commented that it "would make a fine dirigible hangar." On hearing of the project to land men on the moon he cracked, "Who's the enemy on the moon?" At poker, his favorite pastime, he enjoyed playing much more than just winning. He admitted that he often chose "the luck game," as he put it, instead of "the skill game," which he could play well when he wished.[18] So he often lost, which did not bother him in the least, though it did his wife. Lovett, who admired Spaatz greatly as a commander and as a friend, called him "a scamp if I ever saw one."[19] Eaker's ultimate accolade was "the only General who never made a major mistake."[20]

In the critical years 1938 and 1939, when army air still had no more than 1,700 officers and 17,000 men, two other developments besides the gathering storms in Europe and Asia contributed greatly to its progress from the bottom of the military heap to the top in Roosevelt's thinking. One was the solid friendship Arnold made with Harry Hopkins, FDR's closest advisor and an early convert to the importance of air power. The other was the solid friendship Andrews made with a then little-known brigadier general who had been added to the general staff to take charge of plans. He was George C. Marshall. In 1938 Andrews had taken Marshall on a tour of air stations and the Boeing factory in Seattle. Marshall was much impressed, both with the potential of American air power and by the character of Frank Andrews. One of Marshall's first actions after he succeeded Craig as chief of the general staff was to bring Andrews back from his Texas exile in August 1939, raise him to brigadier general and appoint him G-3 (assistant chief for operations) of the general staff—the first air officer ever to achieve such a high post. Presently the GHQ Air Force nomenclature was dropped and its units gradually merged back into becoming the operating arm of the Air Corps, which presently became the Army Air Forces. Arnold, now clearly in charge of all army air activities and with Marshall's strong backing, threw himself into the enormous problems of creating all the airplanes, facilities and crews the president had promised.

These logistics had little appeal either to Spaatz or Eaker, who craved action. The former was the first to escape from Washington paperwork. Arnold sent him to Europe from May to September 1940 to observe the fall of France and the Battle of Britain. Eaker lingered longer, partly because he and his boss had embarked on a third book, to be called *Army Flier* and to be published in 1942. They discussed the idea and briefed out the contents on a ten-day inspection flight to Alaska in the summer of 1940. But Eaker kept pestering Arnold about a command position. Finally Arnold released him, saying: "You get out and get yourself a tactical command. There is a war coming. . . ."[21] In November 1940 he was given command of the 20th Pursuit Group at Hamilton Field, just north of San Francisco. He and Ruth went by ship through the Canal; this was partly to give him time to scribble away on *Army Flier.*

"I had there 100 planes, P-40s, and 100 pilots. We were fully equipped for war, having gunnery training and all other phases of pursuit warfare training, working 14–16 hours a day, getting ready for the war we were certain we were going to be in shortly." But talk of war had been forbidden by the president. "He was under such pressure from isolationists that he would not aggravate the anti-war sentiments. We all knew his sentiments were with the British. . . . I was invited down to Bakersfield to make a talk to a luncheon club. In answer to a question I made a remark that I thought we'd be at war at a fairly early time. I'm training my 20th Pursuit Group in everything they need to stay alive, and I think they'll see combat soon. The U.P. carried it. Headlines: Col. Eaker predicts war in six months. Arnold telephoned me and said, 'I'll save your neck if I can, but how in hell did you ever make a mistake like that?' I told him my speech contained nothing like that, but someone asked me the question and I foolishly gave him an honest answer."[22]

Army Flier, like *This Flying Game,* was utilitarian, as announced in its preface. "It was evident America must train in the immediate years to come many thousand airmen if she were to survive in a dictator-harassed world. These hastily trained young officers, it seemed, should be provided a primer to their new profession outlining their new responsibilities, their new sacrifices—their lives as army flying men."

Army Flier served its purpose on Air Corps training fields, and its sizable royalties went to the Army Air Forces Aid Fund.[23] But *Winged Warfare* is by far the best of the three books by Arnold and Eaker and the only one of enduring importance. It contains many clues to their strategic thinking and also much eloquence. As an example of the latter, here is Eaker on his favorite flying topic at that time—fighters.

> The pilot in general, and the fighter pilot in particular, tends to be an individualist. The fighter pilot is a throw-back to the knights of King Arthur. His safety, his success, his survival lie in his own keen eyes, steady arm and stout heart. He gains no moral support from the close-packed ranks; he cannot be held up or shamed forward by comrades, shoulder to shoulder. He cannot hear the shouted command, he hears only the roar of the thousand horses he drives. No soldier is ever so alone as the pilot who sits with eyes glued to dimly lit instruments and climbs through wet clouds to the battlegrounds above. There is no one to applaud or reprimand; no one but he may know whether he is a hero or a coward. The fighter pilot must be a lone fighter. Here the principles of mass warfare have broken down, we are back to the tournament joust, to the mailed knight on the great charger.

Or on bombing:

> Despite the knowledge that the fighter under certain circumstances may be the superior of the bomber and capable of shooting it down, it is nonetheless a fact that the bomber is the essential nucleus of an air force. The fighter is a defensive type of aircraft strategically, but the bomber is distinctly offensive in character. Battles are won by vigorous offensive and seldom, if ever, by the defensive.
>
> Two things have served to retard the development of the bombing plane in this country. One is the feeling that the bombardment airplane, being a weapon of offense, brought into our war machine a device which operated in a manner contrary to our national military policy, which we have stoutly maintained for more than a century as defensive, and mainly for the protection of our shores. The other reason lay in the fact that the bomber, like the snake in the grass, is a particularly unpleasant fellow. He was unpopular with all and sundry because of his ability to drop high explosives, not always well aimed, at some establishments and peoples heretofore believed safe from molestation in warfare. The vision of the bomber dropping his deadly cargo on defenseless women and children, in crowded streets, on the seats of government, on the banks, the factories, the railroads, was provocative of unpleasant emotions.

Or on a subject that would prove critical in the daylight bombardment campaign that Eaker would be launching against Germany only two years later—the need for fighter escort for bombers:

During daylight in good weather, when pursuit aviation is present in strength in an area, it can pretty nearly bar the air to the bomber.

Finally, here are Arnold's and Eaker's skillfully politic views on the sensitive subject of an independent air force:

> Many feel that eventually the defensive air component of the nation will be given a status co-ordinate and commensurate with that of the Army and Navy. . . . We shall be fortunate if our time for that reorganization comes in the relative calm of peace or at worst, in the preparatory and not in the fighting stage. . . .
>
> The separate air force idea is not something to be rushed at pell-mell or hell-bent-for-leather. It must not be approached with the state of mind that everything now in existence, or which has been done, is wrong. The Army and Navy, the older services, deserve great credit for the tremendous strides they have made in the development of military and naval aviation. There are many essential services which the older and established bureaus, departments, or subdivisions of the Army and the Navy now perform for the air arm. These include supply, ordnance—arms and ammunition—signal equipment, food, shelter, clothing, and the protection of air bases. . . .
>
> It may be that eventually air forces for all countries will be separated from land and sea forces for the same reasons that sea and land forces were separated more than a century ago. There is as much diversity in equipment, strategy, technique and leadership between the air and land or sea operations as between land and sea fighting. It requires a different type of fighting man operating in a different type of vessel, differently equipped, differently trained over a long period of time, and instilled with different ideas of technique, tactics and strategy.
>
> This long step should be taken, if it is taken at all, only after careful planning and mature thought and not with a zest for radical reform. There should be a stage of gradual evolution as against an overnight cutting of binding ties. . . .

This balanced, dispassionate statement near the end of *Winged Warfare* is preceded by several pages of equally dispassionate and balanced summary of the arguments on both sides of the question of independent status. Arnold, Spaatz, Eaker and all the army air commanders carefully followed that tactful line until World War II was over. Then the arguments again became hot and heavy. Though Arnold, weary and ill, had retired, the other two musketeers, Spaatz and Eaker, guided independence into being in 1947.

Sales of *Winged Warfare* were less than twenty thousand copies —not many in a nation of 150 million people—but its impact upon publication in 1941 was substantial. Harris Hull, still in civilian clothes, was instrumental both in enhancing that impact and measuring it. As an assistant vice president of the Sperry Gyroscope Company in New York, he was strategically well located to promote *Winged Warfare,* which he did by personally carrying copies around to 150 book reviewers, columnists, radio commentators and miscellaneous "thought leaders." His secretary at Sperry kept a clipping file and tabulated from *Editor & Publisher* and its statistics of newspaper circulation a tally of the number of references, short or long, the book prompted. Hull recalled: "She put it in a loose-leaf notebook, and she'd say that *Time* magazine carried this review and then down at the bottom she put a figure of its estimated circulation; *NY Times* carried this, *New York Herald Tribune* carried this, *Los Angeles Times* carried this, and so forth. . . . She ran it through an adding machine and came out with a fantastic figure that there had been about 15,000,000 mentions of that book . . . that the airplane is here to stay and we can fly over water and do all kinds of things. . . ." Eaker asked Hull to show the notebook to Arnold. "Arnold sat there for at least 15 minutes thumbing through it. He said, 'You know, this gives me reason to understand why a book should be written.' "[24]

The 20th Pursuit Group was one of the only two in the entire Air Corps that was fully equipped in 1940. So it was heart-wrenching to Eaker and his men when orders came to box all the planes for shipment to China, where Claire Chennault, back in service as a brigadier general, was enjoying well-earned success against the Japanese with his Flying Tigers. "I knew what this would do to the morale of these pilots if they had no airplanes. So I called them in and read the telegram and told them we were going to put these planes in these crates in first class condition and in the earliest possible time. But I reminded them we also had our trucks and that I was going to conduct a maneuver and take them on a march up in Oregon on the Rogue River. We would spend a couple of weeks there doing our pistol practice, and we were going to take the two airplanes, which were AT-6s, we had left. All of us would complete our instrument flying and see if we could fly these planes about 22 hours a day. . . ."[25]

To make the arrangements for their camp in Oregon Eaker dispatched redheaded Capt. Cecil P. "Brick" Lessig to Medford, an exceptionally pretty town surrounded by orchards and set beside the

Rogue River, one of the nation's best fishing streams for steelhead trout. Lessig and an accompanying lieutenant asked for the mayor and learned he was "at Glenn Jackson's house." They went there and found the town council in session. Jackson, a lean, dynamic entrepreneur who was known as "Mr. Oregon" when he died in 1980, at once arranged for Lessig to present his proposal, which was enthusiastically approved. The Elks Club playground beside the Rogue River was provided. Jackson asked for exact details on how many tents, how much plumbing, etc., were needed and then said, "Let's go fishing." Lessig demurred, saying he had to get the job done. Jackson said it was "all arranged." So they went fishing, and Lessig returned to Hamilton four days later. Eaker greeted him with surprise, alarm and outright disbelief when Lessig said the camp was "all set up." "It'd better be," snorted Eaker, "or you'll face a court martial!" The 20th went to Medford by train, taking trucks, tents and other gear, and found their camp in elegant, streeted array, complete with showers, mess halls and even a bandstand. Eaker thanked Jackson profusely and, as was his wont on meeting an eager beaver, made a mental note of his address. Three years later Lessig, on his way to becoming a brigadier general, and Jackson, on his way to a colonelcy, were roommates at Eaker's English headquarters.[26]

Eaker himself went to England, on leave from the 20th, on August 30, 1941, to replace Spaatz as an observer. His mission was threefold: to study communications equipment for fighters either under American control or "checker-boarded" with the British, to investigate the use of searchlights on airplanes and to "obtain, so far as possible, the best thought now prevalent on fighter escort protection." He was there only one month, all of it occupied with a whirlwind of meetings, inspections and flights. His summary, thirty-eight single-spaced pages, three inches thick with its attachments, prompted Arnold to write him. "It is one of the most all-inclusive reports that I have seen from any official observer returning from abroad. . . . Heartiest congratulations."[27]

In England Eaker had called on the handful of American officers in the U.S. military mission in London and all the top British air officials, including the Air Minister and Air Chief Marshal Sir Charles Portal, visited a dozen RAF bases, flew their latest model Spitfire and talked tactics with such aces as Wing Commander Stanford Tuck, who was credited with shooting down twenty-nine

German planes. He also had some typical Ira Eaker aerial adventures.

One happened when Tuck, mustachioed, lean and battle-hardened, took him to see a late-model Spit and commented condescendingly to his chunky, balding, innocent-looking companion from America, "I don't suppose you'd care to fly it, sir?" Well, of course there was nothing Eaker would rather do. He climbed in, fingered the controls and took off into a typical cloudy English sky polka-dotted with blue. Swinging up nimbly through one of the blue dots, he stooged about for twenty minutes enjoying a fighter much better than the P-40 he was used to and then looked for a hole to come down. He found one, saw a grass airstrip with hangars and came in for a landing. Just as his wheels rolled to a halt an RAF sergeant ran up hollering: "You can't land here, sir. This is a dummy field." It was, in fact, too short for a takeoff; Wing Commander Tuck had to send a truck for it.[28]

Most of Eaker's report dealt with highly technical matters such as radio direction finding, mine-laying by aircraft or use of motion pictures for pilot instruction. Two sections have broader interest, one, dealing with "Employment of Women in War Tasks," because it is so enlightened and was quickly adopted by all the American forces, the other, on "Escort Fighters," because the need for them became a make or break crisis in the daylight air war two years later. On women, Eaker wrote:

> An observer in England is immediately struck with the universal employment of women for the majority of military tasks. They are being used in operations rooms, filter rooms and in RDF stations of all types, almost to the exclusion of men. Commanding officers of all units and establishments without exception told me women do a better job than men. A common expression was heard on every hand, "The women are the best damned soldiers in England."
>
> Tasks which have been taken over include: truck and passenger car driving, search light crews, gun truck crews, factory laborers, laborers for building runways, street car operators, communications equipment operators, RDF operators, street cleaners, airplane mechanics, airplane engine mechanics, clerical duties.
>
> At a field I visited in Scotland I noted 117 women laying runways. I asked the engineer in charge how they were coming along and he stated that they were better than the men he had employed on an adjoining field. One depot commanding officer told me that he formerly had eleven men wiring generators—this crew of eleven turned out but eleven generators a day. He now has this work being

done by women—six women were required to turn out twelve generators per day. . . . An RDF station I visited had been bombed—there were six women and two men in the RDF crew. The women, the commanding officer told me, were calmer under bombing than the men. . . .

One of the important considerations in connection with employment of women in war lies in their greater reliability. As one commanding officer told me, "They do not get drunk at the Pub on Saturday night and talk too much." He said they were much more seriously impressed with the necessity of keeping military secrets than the average man. At the operations rooms both at groups and sectors, and in war game rooms, a large majority of operational personnel are women.

In regard to escort fighters, Eaker reported that "without exception all the flight leaders and principal staff officers expressed a keen desire for an escort fighter which could protect bomber aircraft on long range trips." But there was also unanimous agreement that British efforts to accomplish this with "heavy" fighters such as the Typhoon, Tornado and Mosquito were failures, having "definitely demonstrated their inability to stand up against planes of the Spitfire and Messerschmitt class." Nor were the top British leaders "optimistic about their ability to build proper escort fighters." Air Marshal Portal thought the only "proper escort fighter will be a ship exactly like the bomber it is going to escort. If you are going to furnish us B-29 bombers, then we would like to have a number of B-29s built as escort fighters . . . equipped with guns as heavy as any fighter can bring against them. . . ."

Eaker devoted ten pages to summarizing views on all aspects of the problem—maneuverability, pressurization, armament, range, altitude. He flew a Typhoon and examined a captured Messerschmitt, noting many technical aspects of both as well as comparisons with existing American fighters. He perceived no existing solution and concluded with the recommendation "that a carefully selected committee lay down operational requirements for the fighters of the future and these be transmitted promptly to the technicians for accomplishment." This is ironic because the solution to the problem already existed in prototype and was an American design being built for the British but not yet delivered—the P-51, later famous as the Mustang.

Most American military planes during "the phony war" period of 1940–41 were built for either the British or the French. Because of the intense pacifist attitude of the American public, Roosevelt could only justify his program for fifty thousand planes by insisting they were for traditional allies whose backs were to the wall against nazism, fascism and aggression. The U.S. was the "Arsenal of Democracy," and the manufacture of war planes was not, directly anyhow, for American use. Arnold played along, knowing that the Air Corps could use some of the same aircraft and that meanwhile the nation's capability to produce planes was expanding at top velocity. The budget for the Air Corps itself was, to be sure, increased substantially, but most of it was allocated to the heavy bombers. And many of these initially were ticketed for the British, even though designed for daylight operation.

As for fighters, the RAF wanted a better escort for its own Whitley, Wellington, Halifax and Lancaster bombers, all of which were for night attack. Much of Eaker's study of fighters in England was shaped by this immediate need. And when Arnold appointed the fighter board Eaker had recommended, a night fighter was its top priority. The board of seven, including Eaker, was chaired by Spaatz and met for two weeks. Out of their deliberations came the plan for a highly successful night escort fighter, the Northrop P-61 Black Widow. But their recommendations for a long-range escort for use by day reflected Air Marshal Portal's concept of a heavily armored, multi-place fighter similar in size and performance to the bombers it would escort. They gave this hybrid the working title of "convoy defender" and recommended development of a prototype while simultaneously noting that "the feasibility of this project is a matter of considerable doubt." Such indeed proved the case over Europe when a number of B-17s were converted to convoy defenders: they were a fizzle. Of greater interest in retrospect is the board's further comment that "only with the assistance of such an airplane may bombardment aviation hope to successfully deliver daylight attacks deep inside the enemy territory and beyond the range of interceptor support."[29]

This view from a fighter board ran contrary to the continuing conviction of Andrews, Arnold, Knerr and most of the bomber enthusiasts that the bombers could succeed without an escort. And the belief persisted among American as well as British aeronautical engineers that no fighter could be built that would have both long range and top combat performance. It was not that efforts were abandoned. Plans for the P-38 Lightning and the P-47 Thunderbolt (money for which came only from England) were far along and both these fine aircraft proved very valuable as bomber escorts in Europe and the Pacific. But neither had adequate range to go all the way with the B-17s, B-24s or B-29s. Nor did the P-51 originally appear to have it. Designed by James H. "Dutch" Kindelberger of North American Aviation along the lines of a bigger Spitfire, it was ordered in quantity by the British but with a water-cooled engine. "It was sidetracked by Wright Field," Eaker recounted years later. "Too much plumbing. It can't survive in combat. You get a water or oil line broken and you're out of business. They favored the air-cooled engine. They said, you've got that big hunk of metal up in front of the pilot and the pilot will survive a lot of combat."[30]

So American use of the Mustang as an escort languished until, eighteen months later, in mid-1943, with the air battles over Germany approaching a climax, imaginative leadership and engineering made the P-51 into the dominant fighter of the war, able to go all the way to Berlin with the bombers and shoot down any fighters the Luftwaffe could put up against it.

But that is getting ahead of the story.

In November 1941, as soon as the fighter committee finished its work, Arnold sent Eaker off to North Carolina on a big maneuver General Marshall had ordered to "test out the colonels and see who our leaders should be for the great expansion coming up in the war that seemed to lie ahead. General Arnold said, 'I want you to have your opportunity.' "[31] Eaker was fighter commander on the white side and his teammate from the blind flying exploit, Kepner, was in command of the red. An RAF observer was none other than Wing Commander Tuck. Just before the maneuvers began Tuck made a forced landing in a cornfield.

"Why didn't you bail out?" Eaker asked.

"You didn't jump; I didn't figure I would," Tuck replied. Unlike Eaker's in England, Tuck's plane was able to fly out.[32]

In the maneuvers, Eaker, using what he had learned observing the RAF, flew rings around Kepner. One trick he used was to infiltrate into Kepner's daily staff conference a "spy" who radioed the red plans to Eaker from a transmitter in the nearby woods. At the conclusion of the five-day games Eaker's 141 planes had flown 170 missions with over two thousand hours in the air and a two-to-one margin of victories over Kepner. Arnold told Eaker he had "heard nothing but compliments."[33] And Marshall, who had spent thirty-six hours at Eaker's headquarters, developed a strong admiration for him that never abated.

After the maneuver, Eaker was sent at once to the Republic plant in Long Island to test the first P-47. "I went up on a Saturday and flew it about an hour and a half to two hours . . . made a number of landings, took it up to maximum altitude and tried out its maneuverability, and I came back to Washington the next morning. My wife was with me and we were staying with her mother." After a Sunday morning brunch, Eaker was "a bit worried about all this high-altitude flying I had been doing." He lay down for a nap.

"She came in after a few minutes and said, 'The Japs have attacked Pearl Harbor!'

"I said, 'You'll have to think of a better story than that to get me out of bed. . . .'

"She turned on the radio to such a loud volume that I could hear the observer in Honolulu describing the attack. So I jumped up and called General Arnold's office and Colonel Spaatz answered. I said, 'I think I'll catch a civil airliner tonight and get back to the West Coast and join my old 20th Pursuit Group.' He said, 'I think you're headed in the right direction. Get going.' "[34]

The first thing Eaker did in California was test fly the first P-51. He "thought it was the best fighter plane I had flown. It was somewhat underpowered, but I knew it was possible to correct that with the bigger engines coming along."[35] Then he was given command of the fighter defenses for the West Coast. "I put a squadron at Portland, a squadron at Seattle, one at Los Angeles and one at San Francisco . . . then set up the radar and started the fighter center in San Francisco. . . . We were . . . suspecting that the Japanese might strike the West Coast." In the near-hysteria one American plane shot at another, mistaking the red circle that was then the centerpiece of the army air insignia for the rising sun of Japan. Eaker called Arnold and the red disks were painted over.[36]

There was also, as some degree of calm returned, an increasing flow of airmen headed out into the Pacific, then the only area where American fighting was in progress. One of them was Eaker's former commander from the Pan American Goodwill Flight, Bert Dargue, now a major general and on the way to replace the hapless army commander in Hawaii, Lt. Gen. Walter C. Short. Dargue was flying to Hamilton Field from the East and ran into heavy fog. Eaker, also flying there on the way back from Los Angeles, was the last man to talk with him, reaching him by radio to warn of zero-zero conditions. Eaker turned back, Dargue did not. The wreckage of his plane was found three months later.[37]

In between his substantial flying and command duties on the Pacific Coast that frantic month of December 1941 Eaker continued scribbling at *Army Flier*. But his heart was elsewhere. On December 20, four days before he was promoted to full colonel, an increasingly impatient Eaker wrote to his old friend, Maj. Gen. Walter Weaver, acting chief in Arnold's temporary absence: "Most of our news this week has been bad. We have been searching for General Dargue and have learned that General Krogstad suffered a fatal accident at El Paso. . . . I have been working about eighteen or nineteen hours a day. It is interesting and I am anxious to stay this close to the war front in the hope that I may get to the scene of the hostilities. There have been several people passing through here headed West. General Emmons, General Tinker, Monk Hunter, etc. I hope General Arnold has not decided to save me for the Junior Prom. . . ."[38]

His letter came back, with a scribble on the back in Arnold's hand. "Keep your shirt on, son."[39]

9

"The strategic air offensive is a means of direct attack on the enemy state with the object of depriving it of the means or the will to continue the war."

—SIR CHARLES WEBSTER AND NOBLE FRANKLAND
THE STRATEGIC AIR OFFENSIVE AGAINST GERMANY, 1939–1945

THE TELEGRAM from the adjutant general of the army in mid-January 1942 said only: "Report to the Commanding General, Army Air Forces, immediately, prepared for early duty overseas."

"When I walked into General Arnold's office on a Saturday morning, I think about January 18th, I said, 'What's up, Boss?' He said, 'You're going over to understudy the British and start our bombardment as soon as I can get you some planes and some crews.' And I said, 'Bombers, hell! I've been in fighters all my life.' He said, 'Yes, I know that. That's what we want, the fighter spirit in bombardment aviation.'"

Arnold added: "There are only a small number of Air Force officers who can be used for Air Force command and similar responsibilities—responsibilities of similar size in logistics and operations. You assemble some bright young civilians who have prospects for executive ability and you train them; and I will commission them in any grade you ask, within the limits, of course, of my authorizations from the War Department. You can take a smart executive and make a fair Army officer out of him in a few months. You can never take a dumb Army officer and make a good combat leader out of him."[1]

That evening, at Arnold's request, Colonel Eaker, still not quite accustomed to the new eagles on his shoulders, and Ruth, who had remained in Washington when he rushed to California on Pearl Harbor Day, were guests at a dinner for Air Chief Marshal Sir Charles "Peter" Portal, the RAF's leader, and Air Vice Marshal Arthur T. "Bert" Harris and his wife at the home of Maj. Gen. Walter Weaver, Arnold's deputy. The Eakers were close friends of Walter and Elizabeth Weaver, and Ira had talked with Portal in London four months before and had met Harris casually in Washington. But this was his first real talk with Harris, with whom he was destined to be linked in literally earthshaking partnership for the next two years and enduring friendship for the rest of their long lives. For Harris had just been appointed to head the British bomber command, having spent the months since June 1941 in Washington as chief of the RAF delegation. His wife, whose given name was Therese but who was known to all as Jill, like Ruth Eaker, was young, lovely and elegant. The two women became chums also.

During the long, ebullient dinner and over brandy afterward, Eaker was brought up-to-date on the still-evolving Allied strategy resulting from the first of the great wartime conferences, code-named ARCADIA, which had just been concluded at the White House between President Roosevelt, Prime Minister Churchill and their top advisors. First—Germany's defeat remained the top priority despite the recent catastrophes in the Far East. Second—the first major offensive against Germany would be expansion of the strategic bombing campaign based in England. This would require close collaboration between the existing RAF organization and very large, new American elements. Third—Eaker would be in command of the American bombers, which would have their own bases and not just be merged with the British. Fourth—Eaker's bomber command would be the first establishment in Britain of the new Eighth Air Force. The Eighth Air Force itself would be headed by Maj. Gen. Carl A. Spaatz, who would remain in the States for five months organizing a fighter command, an air support command, a service command and all the men and material involved.

When it became clear in the talk that evening that daylight precision bombing was what the Americans intended, not night area attacks like the RAF, Harris, who was noted for bluntness, snorted:

"I bloody well don't think you can do it. We've tried it. We know. We've even tried it with your Fortresses."

"Sure," replied Arnold. "You tried it with one or two B-17s at a time. We don't plan to do it that way. We're going to send them out in mass formations."

"It doesn't matter a tinker's damn what you send them out in," Harris hit back. "The Boche have too many fighters, too much flak, too much bloody power against that West Wall to make it worth the losses. God knows, I hope you can do it, but I don't think you can." Turning to Eaker, he said: "Come join us at night. Together we'll lick them."

Eaker replied with a concept he was to make famous. "Yes. We'll bomb them by day. You bomb them by night. We'll hit them right around the clock."[2]

His sudden assignment was, on the face of it, an immense challenge. It turned out to be the biggest logistical, operational and diplomatic task in the entire Army Air Forces. To prepare for it he had exactly two weeks before flying off for England on February 4. Unloading his West Coast duties was the easiest part, for the established succession procedure of army air took care of major matters. But he still had numerous loose ends to tie up as well as the courtesies of departure. In addition there were the twenty-five thousand final words of *Army Flier* to write. These he did night after night, often from midnight to dawn, delivering the final manuscript to Harper & Bros. in New York the same day he flew to Europe.[3]

But his biggest urgencies were to study the details of his assignment, to learn when his planes and crews might come and to pick the handful of key people to take with him. The plan called for a total of 3,500 aircraft and 200,000 men by April 1943, with the first elements supposed to arrive in April 1942. This was a far bigger force than the combined total of all RAF units then in the United Kingdom.[4]

The post called for higher rank, and Arnold gave him his next rung up the ladder on January 25, only a month after he had become a colonel. With one of the gracious, warm gestures of which the imperious commanding general of the Army Air Forces was capable, Arnold wrote him: "Herewith a couple of stars for you to wear. Incidentally, they were my original stars as Brigadier General and perhaps they will bring you luck. I don't know whether they have brought me luck or not—they certainly have put a lot more stars on my shoulders but that does not always mean luck. Anyhow here's wishing you the best in the world."[5]

Arnold also gave him a directive that stipulated that until the arrival of Spaatz he would be "under the supervision of" Maj. Gen. James E. Chaney, commander of all U.S. forces in the British Isles. His five "immediate objectives" included establishing a bomber command headquarters; "preparation of fields and establishments for the first units which arrive to insure their effective combat; understudy British Bomber Command to insure competent and aggressive command and direction of our bomber units in England; prepare training schedules for American units arriving in England;" and "submit recommendations for any changes in training methods or equipment."[6]

As a trailbreaker to Chaney, who reported not to Arnold but to General Marshall, chief of staff, Arnold sent Lt. Col. Claude E. Duncan, a taciturn flier who had worked for him at March Field. Chaney was army air too, but was known to be extremely cautious and general staff oriented. Neither Duncan's words nor Eaker's directive, which Arnold also forwarded, made much of a dent on Chaney, as Eaker discovered when he reached London. This became his first roadblock.

For his initial staff Eaker chose six officers, two of them regular army, three reserve, plus one newly commissioned civilian. He relied on old connections and his experienced judgment, plus finding people who were "available." One who met all three of these criteria was Lt. Beirne Lay, Jr., both a reserve officer and a fine writer whose 1940 book *I Wanted Wings* had brought him to Eaker's attention. Passing Lay in the corridor, Eaker called, "Beirne, you want to come with me?" "Yes, Sir!" said Lay instantly, not knowing where it might be. He became senior aide and historian. As junior aide Eaker recruited Lt. William S. Cowart, Jr., a young fighter pilot who had flown for him in the 20th Pursuit Group. The other regular officer was Col. Frank A. Armstrong, Jr., who had flown for Eaker during the air mail crisis. He became A-3 (operations). Lt. Harris B. Hull, the reserve officer and newspaperman Eaker had found useful in the *Rex* episode, was A-2 (intelligence). Hull had been working lately as an assistant VP for Sperry Gyroscope and suggested another Sperry officer, Frederick W. Castle, a reserve captain who had gone to West

Point and was a management specialist. The civilian, who signed on initially as A-4 (supply), was a Lockheed Aircraft executive, Maj. Peter Beasley.

Hull and Castle wasted no time recruiting on their own—entirely from civilian ranks. Hull sought journalists and lawyers, for their investigative talents form a good basis for intelligence work, and lined up a dozen men, including Eaker's editor at Harpers, a *Saturday Evening Post* editor, and the author, then at Time, Inc. We were all expedited to commissions "through channels" and got to England in two or three months. Castle similarly recruited, among others, the comptroller of Vick Chemical, an executive from General Motors, a Stone & Webster engineer, two men from Bell Telephone and another from DuPont. Though known derisively in England at first as "Eaker's amateurs," this bright group quickly shaped into a first-class headquarters staff, just as Arnold had predicted. Three of the original six became generals (Armstrong, Castle and Hull) and one (Castle) won the Medal of Honor while losing his life.[7]

Before Eaker and his six-man party left for New York to catch the Pan American Clipper to Bermuda and then Portugal, a Washington friend of scant perception asked him: "Why do you want to go off to war? You have a pretty wife, a reputation and plenty of brains. You could land a good administrative job in Washington." In curt reply Eaker said: "This is what I have been waiting for all my life. This is what I have been training for for 24 years." When he kissed Ruth good-bye at LaGuardia she concluded that it was the happiest day in his life. "I'll never forget his face as he climbed aboard the Clipper," she said. "There was an expression on it that I have never seen before or since."[8]

In New York, while waiting for the four-engined Boeing flying boat to lumber off to Bermuda and then Lisbon, Eaker wrote to Arnold about the publishing plans for *Army Flier,* adding: "General, before departure, I want to thank you again for all the things you have done for me. Again I want to say how much it means to me to be wearing your stars. Here's looking forward to the time when we can go to that village in Oregon and begin doing some things we have neglected for so long. In the meantime please remember that it is going to be my aim to show you that you did not pick the wrong guy on this job I am about to undertake. . . ."[9]

In Bermuda bad weather stalled them for twelve days; the water was too rough for takeoff. This was frustrating but also beneficial, for

Eaker badly needed a rest. Then they flew to Lisbon, which was known to be a nest of German espionage. Nonetheless, it was startling to the Americans to see Luftwaffe planes parked at the airfield alongside those of the RAF. Portugal was neutral and the Dutch airline, KLM, now in the hands of the Germans, as was Holland itself, flew regular flights in and out of occupied Europe plus chartered ones to neutral Ireland. This helped the Nazis keep an eye on who was going where, and they occasionally shot down one of the flights when they thought it carried important passengers. One such attack, not long after Eaker passed through, cost the life of the English actor Leslie Howard.[10]

In Libson for one night they wore civilian clothes. "Waiting for the KLM DC-3 to take off the next morning, we went out to dinner. We had been cautioned that we were to carry no secret papers and that we could expect our clothing and other personal effects would be searched. . . . So we had a little game; each of us prepared his suitcase in a particular manner. . . . When we came back from our dinner it was quite evident that all of our baggage had been carefully searched. . . ."

When the Dutch pilot led them aboard a chartered DC-3 with all its windows covered, "We were a bit apprehensive because we realized the Germans knew that this group was there. . . ." Saying he wanted to confuse any monitoring of their flight, the pilot made an unscheduled landing at Porto, Portugal, an hour out of Lisbon, and waited an hour and a half. When he headed for England he flew well out to sea to avoid interception. "At one point in this exercise," Eaker recalled, "he asked me to come up to the cockpit. I went up and he showed me a JU-88 that was flying across in front of us. One of its engines was smoking very badly and it evidently was hurrying home. It did not follow us to attack. . . ."[11]

This low-key comment was typical of Eaker. Armstrong's memory of the episode was strikingly different. "Army," as he was called, became one of the great combat commanders of the army air—leader of the first U.S. heavy bomber mission from England a few months later, and in January 1943 the first against Germany itself. As he recalled that encounter with the JU-88 far out over the Bay of Biscay: "The German came in fast from quartering astern. The transport pilot jockeyed slightly from one side to the other in an effort to throw off the aim of the German if he opened up on us. At that opportune time Lady Luck took a hand in the affair. One engine of the German plane belched a blob of smoke, cutting off and on pilot's power and swinging him off course. The fighter bomber passed under us at about 800 yards and headed for land and a place of safety. Our pilot came out of his compartment, turned his coat collar up high under his eyes and peeped at the passengers. For the next few seconds everyone was silent—silent in prayer of thanksgiving. Some hours later we landed in England. The aircraft log of the day read, 'Arrived at destination: flight uneventful.' "[12]

They reached London via Ireland in the late afternoon of February 21, the day before Air Marshal Harris took charge of RAF Bomber Command. He greated them warmly, which was more than could be said of General Chaney. He and Eaker were old friends, and Chaney was of course courteous. But he wanted no part of Arnold's plan to set up a separate air force command under Spaatz and Eaker, with Chaney continuing as theater commander. Chaney's concept was wedded to earlier strategy, envisioning American ground and fighter forces in the United Kingdom as token and primarily for defense, while any U.S. bombers would operate with the RAF. He expected Eaker and his men simply to become a new adjunct to Chaney's existing staff of thirty-five officers, only four of whom were airmen. Eaker outflanked him for the moment by pointing out that his immediate task was to "understudy" RAF Bomber Command, which he could hardly do from London. Harris had already invited Eaker and his staff to share space at RAF Bomber Command, and Eaker and his six original companions, plus Duncan and another fourteen officers who arrived in driblets in the next few weeks, moved in at once.[13]

They found themselves in surroundings both fascinating and fruitful. "Southdown," as RAF Bomber Command was known in code, was situated in a bosky, residential section of High Wycombe, a homely industrial town whose mostly brick, mostly laboring class buildings sprawl through deep valleys in the steep, verdant Chiltern Hills about an hour's train trip northwest of London on the line to Oxford. From the air Southdown looked only like a scattering of private houses—an impression the RAF of course wanted any snooping German reconnaissance plane to take home. The heart of the headquarters was the operations block ("Ops Block" in parlance or "The Hole" or "the Brain Room" in RAF slang), a concrete box of four or five rooms buried under a mound of dirt that was planted with hay and reached by a winding path through the trees. The headquarters staff lived in the various houses, some of them a half-mile away. Air Marshal Harris, newly dubbed Sir Arthur, and Lady Harris occupied a two-story brick named "Springfield" (the Americans were surprised and charmed to learn that Britons name their houses). They insisted that Eaker live with them and also Harris's deputy, Air Vice Marshal Robert Saundby. This was not just friendly hospitality. "There was a practical reason too," as Eaker recalled. "It not only gave us a chance to spend more time in conversation but they got just so many rations, and the more rations you got the better mess you could run. So Bert Harris explained to me and so did she that we were really doing their household a favor by coming to join them." The fifth mouth at the mess was four-year-old Jacqueline Harris, a perky sprite who had difficulty pronouncing the letter "r." She called Eaker "Genewal Ila."[14]

The others in Eaker's team were billeted nearby, adjusting happily to the British custom of hot tea in bed each morning, briskly brought to each of them by an RAF WAAF (Women's Auxiliary Air Force). Each went quickly to work with the appropriate "opposite number" in the RAF. Eaker was amused by the British use of the label "Air Officer Commanding," abbreviated as "AOC." Capt. Carl Norcross, previously the editor of *Aviation Magazine,* who joined the group as an intelligence officer in mid-March and whose final assignment three years later would be managing editor of the aircraft section of the *United States Strategic Bombing Survey,* remembered that "Ira would point to one of us, such as Jack Glidden, who had worked for General Motors, and say 'You're AOC Motor Pool.' One night I had described the Norcross Automatic Chicken Feeder, a Rube Goldberg device worked with an alarm clock at a farm we once rented between Mamaroneck and Scarsdale. Ira pointed at me and said, 'If Air Marshal Harris has a fresh egg from his chickens every morning, I want one too. So you're AOC Chickens.' "[15]

Eaker's principal AOCs in those early days were Armstrong (operations), Castle (logistics), and Hull (intelligence). On the cold, gray morning of February 25 they joined Eaker and Harris in the operations block for the latter's first day of duty in his new command. The fortunes of war for both Britain and America were as bleak as the weather as they set about making plans to cripple Hitler's war machine from the air. RAF Bomber Command that day mustered no more than four hundred operational aircraft, of which fewer than half could be classified as heavy bombers.[16] The command's record had been anything but impressive in two years of effort, and it was under heavy criticism that month in particular after three German cruisers, the *Scharnhorst, Gneisenau* and *Prinz Eugen,* had steamed unscathed up the English Channel.

Britain had entered the war in 1939 with a purist philosophy about strategic bombardment. There would be "no indiscriminate bombing of civilians," only genuine military targets such as the German navy. A suggestion that the RAF bomb the Ruhr was vetoed indignantly by the air minister, Sir Kingsley Wood, on the grounds that factories were private property. And when the RAF courageously did go after the German navy in daylight in harbors such as Wilhelmshaven, both at low level and high, they were slaughtered by German fighters and inflicted only minor damage on the ships. Meanwhile the ruthless Nazi blitz of Warsaw, Rotterdam, Coventry and other civilian targets prompted a loosening of British moral standards about bombing at the same time that the RAF was realizing it simply could not endure the losses incurred in bombing by day. And at night, though losses were then at acceptable levels, Britain's bombers, still without the radar devices Britain's scientists invented later, could not see, nor hit, any target smaller than a city. After the Germans bombed central London on August 24, 1940, Churchill ordered a reprisal attack on Berlin. Thus the huge British program of destroying Germany's cities came inadvertently into being.

Portal, the Air C in C, believed in precision bombing and fathered a campaign against Germany's synthetic oil plants, on which its economy was tremendously dependent. Synthetic oil plants remained the top priority until mid-1941, but as Portal ruefully realized the RAF could not hit them he swung over to the area bombing concept. A 1940 memorandum to bomber command squadrons had pointed out that "in industrial areas there are invariably a very large number of targets. In view of the indiscriminate nature of the German attacks, and in order to reduce the number of bombs brought back . . . every effort should be made to bomb these." Webster and Frankland, the RAF's official historians, interpreted Portal's change of attitude as follows: ". . . if there was to be any strategic bombing at all, civilians would be killed. . . . Portal now believed that this by-product should become an end-product. He believed that the time had come to launch a direct attack on the German people themselves. . . ." Portal's biographer, Denis Richards, was more charitable, writing: "Portal was not at this time, however, nor did he ever become an advocate of killing civilians. He became, while it was the

Jackie Harris with two high-flying American friends, High Wycombe, 1943. She called Eaker "Genewal Ila."

most practicable policy, an advocate of destroying industrial towns."[17]

But the RAF could not even count on hitting cities, as soon became apparent to the few who set policy, though it was not of course disclosed to the general public. Before Germany declared war on the United States, American military attachés in Berlin had reported that the much-touted British bombing attacks were doing very little important damage. This became brutally clear to Churchill and the British war cabinet when they received a report in August 1941 by Mr. D. M. Butt of the war cabinet secretariat. Butt had been instructed by Lord Cherwell, Churchill's most influential scientific advisor, to study RAF bomber operations for the months of June and July 1941. The Butt report stated that only a third of their bombs had come within five miles of the aiming point; in the Ruhr it was only one-tenth.

The RAF hierarchy thought the Butt report overly negative, especially with the new electronic guiding device called "Gee" about to be introduced. And Churchill, despite his serious doubts, continued to push the bomber offensive with his habitual bulldog persistence. Bombing was, after all, the only way Britain then had of hitting Germany, and Churchill was determined to hit the Germans somehow. This was only partly in order to damage Germany's war-making capacity. Of equal importance was the shot in the arm the bomber campaign gave the weary British public. Hearing the planes droning out night after night and reading about their missions the day after, the angry British man in the street found grim satisfaction in "giving it back to the Jerries." Further, the prime minister never forgot Britain's historic policy of seeking alternatives to land battles on the continent of Europe. His ambivalence is well put in a late 1942 comment: "In the days when we were fighting alone we answered the question 'How are you going to win the war?' by saying, 'We will shatter Germany by bombing.' Since then the enormous injuries inflicted on the German army and manpower by the Russians, and the accession of the manpower and munitions of the United States, have rendered other possibilities open. . . . We look forward to mass invasion of the Continent by liberating armies. . . . All the same, it would be a mistake to cast aside our original thought—which, it may be mentioned, is also strong in American minds, namely, that the severe, ruthless bombing of Germany on an ever-increasing scale will not only cripple her war effort, including U-boat and aircraft production, but will also create conditions intolerable to the mass of the German population. . . . We must regard the bomber offensive on Germany at least as a feature in breaking her war-will second only to the largest military operations which can be conducted on the Continent until that war-will is broken. . . ."[18]

Accordingly, in September 1941 Churchill approved the air staff's proposal to create a force of four thousand heavy bombers for the area bombing of German cities. This called for the allocation of a full one-third of the British war economy—a bigger slice than went either to the army or the navy. It was a very bold decision, coming not only in the face of the Butt report and other damning evidence of operational failure but also with a rising trend in RAF losses. For the clever Germans, always nimble to find new weapons, had developed night fighters, radar and tactics that cost the RAF losses as high as 21 percent on some missions that fall. Churchill also agreed with Portal that bomber command needed new direction.

This, in brief, was the glum situation Sir Arthur Harris faced that February morning with Gen. Ira Eaker looking over his shoulder. Eaker knew about the RAF Bomber Command's quandary, which was another reason besides U.S. Army Air doctrine why he was determined to maintain an arm's length relationship with his new partner in the bomber offensive.

Harris and Eaker were remarkably alike in some respects and markedly different in others. They shared a birthday—April 13—but the air marshal was four years older and two grades higher in rank. They had arrived at directly parallel commands on virtually the same day, though the RAF had a two-year head start in operations. Both men had enlisted in World War I. Both had been ardent pilots, flying every type of plane as they moved steadily up through the ranks. Both believed wholeheartedly in the validity of strategic air war, but differed as night from day in their ideas on how to apply it. And both airmen that February day in 1942 shared the problems of unproven prowess and the courage of unshaken optimism.

In physique and personality the two men were not alike at all. Raymond Daniell of the *New York Times* aptly sketched this duality.

> Harris, who had been a gold miner and tobacco planter in Rhodesia, is a hulking giant of a man—tall with shoulders to match—having a lusty, mordant sense of humor. He is bluff and hearty for an Englishman—a provocative, stimulating conversationalist. He has the appearance of a successful Middle Western farmer and the manner of a rather crusty county judge who has seen much of life and has enjoyed every minute of it.
>
> Eaker is a soft-spoken Texan with an agile, athletic body. His features, like those of so many men who have devoted most of their lives to flying, have set themselves into sharp, firm lines that make one think of an eagle. He is modest and retiring almost to the point of shyness and he has that unconsciously thoughtful courtesy usually associated with the antebellum South. . . .
>
> Of the two Harris is the more studious. He likes to read history and books on farming, to which he hopes to return after the war. Eaker is restless and fidgety unless he is doing something. He is a confirmed believer in the value of exercise. He spends his few spare

moments of daylight playing golf, tennis and softball, and after dark
he enjoys a game of gin rummy, bridge or poker—a contest at which
he is so expert that he sometimes has trouble finding any one to
gamble with him. Harris likes cocktails and highballs but Eaker
hardly ever touches anything but a glass of sherry for sociability's
sake.

General Eaker arrived with only one preconceived notion about
Britain—namely, that it was his job to get along with the British.
He has found that to be an easy and pleasant task. . . . And the
British have found that they like this cool, efficient American general who is as different from the traditional caricature as Air Marshal Harris is unlike the American conception of a monocled
upper-class Englishman. . . ."[19]

Harris had no doubts whatever about the new plans, approved in
a February 14 directive, to smash Germany's cities, and he set about
executing them at top speed. Nor was he squeamish about killing
civilians; he relished it. Stopped one night for speeding by a police-
man who warned that "You might have killed someone, sir," Harris
growled, "Young man, I kill thousands of people every night!" He
was "convinced," he wrote, "having watched the bombing of London, that a bomber offensive of adequate weight and the right kind
of bombs would, if continued for long enough, be something no
country could endure."[20] Furthermore, this view won the blessing,
a month after Harris took over RAF Bomber Command, of the eminent Lord Cherwell, who wrote Churchill: "We know from our
experience that we can count on nearly fourteen operational sorties
per bomber produced. The average lift of the bombers we are going
to produce over the next fifteen months will be about three tons. It
follows that each of these bombers will in its lifetime drop about forty
tons of bombs. If these are dropped on built-up areas they will make
4,000–8,000 people homeless. In 1938 over 22 million Germans lived
in fifty-eight towns of over 100,000 inhabitants, which, with modern
equipment, should be easy to find and hit. Our forecast . . . of heavy
bombers between now and the middle of 1943 is about 10,000. If even
half the total load of 10,000 bombers were dropped on the built-up
areas of these fifty-eight German towns the great majority of their
inhabitants (about one-third of the German population) would be
turned out of house and home. . . . There seems little doubt that this
would break the spirit of the people. Our calculation assumes, of
course, that we really get one-half of our bombs into built-up areas.

On the other hand, no account is taken of the large promised American production (6,000 heavy bombers in the period in question). Nor has regard been paid to the inevitable damage to factories, communications, etc., in these towns and the damage by fire, probably accentuated by breakdown of public services."[21]

Many times during the ensuing weeks and months of 1942 Harris tried to persuade Eaker to join in "de-housing" the Germans—the antiseptic word by which this ruthless policy became known. If you can't hit the works, hit the workers was his repeated theme. He told Eaker "it took only a year or less to build a tank or a plane but it took 20 years to build skilled workmen, and skilled workmen in short supply would affect war production as much as loss of their factory."[22]

Eaker was always careful not to sound skeptical. Instead, he steadfastly replied to Harris, Portal or other British leaders that his orders from Arnold were to bomb by day when precise military targets could be seen; that American planes were designed and their crews trained for those tactics and not for night attacks; that he believed the daylight program would work; and that he was going to give it a thorough trial. In response the British continued to be openly skeptical but also marvelously supportive in helping the newly hatched Eighth Air Force get into the air.

In part this was because that policy had been promised at the ARCADIA Conference. But there was a deeper reason. All of England, from the brass hats at Whitehall down to the average man in the street, was touchingly grateful at last to have an ally actually on the scene—men they could see and talk to and who spoke the same language—not like the far away Russians. Early 1942 was one of the darkest periods of the war for Britain and there was widespread despair as the German army in North Africa drove almost to Suez, three of the best British battleships were sunk and sixty thousand men surrendered at Singapore. Nothing was too good for the arriving stream of American soldiers, almost all of whom belonged to the Eighth Air Force. They were invited into British homes, offered free beer at pubs, kissed by the girls. And at the command level, the Eighth became the first recipient of "Reverse Lend-Lease." Whatever Eaker asked for was given and much more he had not thought of was proffered. The biggest need was for air bases, and Harris turned over five long-established ones in East Anglia to the Americans, while air ministry undertook to build another sixty. They also provided food until American rations began to arrive, clerical help, office space, motor vehicles (including a Humber limousine for Eaker), maps, projectors for briefing, photo equipment, miles of telephone wire and endless bits and pieces such as escape kits.

Norcross observed years later: "I often think if the RAF had arrived in Alaska to help us out against the Japanese, it would be most unlikely that we would be as generous with our materials and help as the British were with us. When I visited RAF stations to learn about their intelligence operations, briefings, de-briefings, etc., they never held anything back. It was always, 'Don't do this, but do such and such because it will work better.' The A-3 people had the same whole-hearted help when they went out to study RAF operations."[23] Eaker summarized: "They turned over to us all of their experience; they kept no secrets. I don't believe there was ever a more thoroughly cooperative effort in warfare than the RAF—in fact, the whole British government from the Prime Minister on down—and our tiny but growing U.S. air effort out of the United Kingdom in the years '42 and '43."[24]

One urgent requirement was to find a suitable location for the American bomber command. General Chaney's staff was talking about putting the early American arrivals into tents, but Eaker managed to scratch that idea and also to convince the theater commander that bomber command headquarters should be in High Wycombe, no more than five miles from the RAF. He and Harris had agreed that officers from each command would attend each other's daily operations meetings and cooperate in many other ways that necessitated closeness. They drew a circle with a five-mile radius based on Southdown, and Eaker and Castle scouted the entire area. The only place they could find that had the requisite buildings and area was the beautiful Wycombe Abbey School for Girls, a sixty-acre park of historic buildings and elegant grounds almost in the center of the town. It would be ideal, Harris agreed when Eaker came back from his first inspection on March 15, "but I'm afraid you'll have difficulty getting that school. Too many of our Ministers' wives are graduates. . . ." But Eaker "put in to the Air Ministry for it. Within a day or two a Lord who was a member of the Air Staff . . . came down to see me and said unfortunately they were not able to provide that building. . . . He said 'Our girls from the colonies, Australia and

Canada, are in that school, and we have to keep them here. We can't send them home due to the submarine menace. . . .'

"I said, 'If you're more interested in educating your daughters than in winning this war, I'm glad you told us.'

"He said, 'That's putting it harshly. Let me go back and talk to my confreres, and I'll advise you tomorrow.'

"He called the following day and said, 'The school is yours. We've decided we can move it up to Oxford.' "[25]

But it would be several weeks before the move could take place, so Eaker and his staff remained at Southdown, where his major activity was completion of a plan for beginning operations from Britain. Though written only three weeks after his arrival, it ran to 104 pages with attachments and exhibited extraordinary prescience. Mentioning the British campaign to switch the Americans to night operations, he summarized the established arguments he had already offered to Harris for continuing to fly by day but added: "There are some disadvantages to daylight bombing. They are: Losses due to enemy fighter action will be higher. Losses due to enemy A.A. action may be higher." At the peak of the day battles eighteen months later this did indeed become briefly true. Noting the British had spent "a large proportion of available effort on sea targets," which was "understandable since Britain is a maritime power," he said: "We should not make this error. Let us always keep before us the German war industry as the primary target. . . ." British intelligence he described as "truly remarkable" and "worthy of emulation in toto." To cope with British mud he asked that "rubber boots be issued to all troops on arrival." And he recommended that post exchanges be provided at all installations "so that our soldiers can buy American tobacco, candies, sandwiches, coffee and toilet articles. The foregoing recommendations do not mean that I intend to coddle the U.S. soldier, show him special consideration, or emphasize the disparity between his standard of living or scale of pay and the British. It does mean that I recognize the paramount importance of morale for air combat and maintenance crews and appreciate some of the more important factors in keeping it high."[26]

Just after he dispatched this hefty document on March 20, Eaker moved out of his room with the Harrises to share quarters with his officers in a double-room barracks the RAF provided down the road a bit. He shared his own room with Lt. Col. Charles B. B. "Jingles"

Bubb who arrived March 22 via the Bermuda-Lisbon route. Bubb, whose nickname came from his habit of jingling coins in his right pant pocket, was a friend from early days in army air who had retired for health reasons and then rejoined when the war began. Eaker appointed him deputy chief of staff under Col. Claude Duncan. Bubb's pass to "the Brain Room," was number 169, "which means," Bubb noted in his diary, "that only 168 people have passed through the portals. . . . The place is in constant operation, with three shifts who stand watches of about eight hours each. The Operations Room functions as a central point to which all information pertaining to planes, enemy action, etc., is sent. The Chief of the Bomber Command has a meeting with his staff every morning and decides 'the target for tonight' and also any daylight operations that are to be conducted. Aerial photographs of different target areas in the Axis countries and photographs of the preceding day and night operations are available. It is very interesting. Both Ira and I attend unless we are away from the station. . . ."

The day after that entry Bubb wrote: "Ira left this noon to join Group Captain Sharp, and he is going on his first mission. I tried to talk him out of it but without success." But two days later Bubb wrote, "Weather was bad the night of the 23rd, so Ira did not go on a mission. . . ."[27] This non-event is worthy of note only because it introduces a subject of importance and sensitivity—i.e., should higher commanders go on missions. Harris did not approve of it, saying to Eaker: "It has taken me many years to get to know the things I should know to be a bomber commander. Peter Portal and the Secretary for Air would relieve me if they knew I contemplated it." But Eaker felt strongly, as he put it on another occasion. "No man should plan air battles who has not fought in a flying machine. No leader should ever send airmen to battle unless he knows by personal experience their problems and the limitations of their equipment and the opposition they will meet. Great leaders in the air and on the ground do not send men. They lead them."[28]

However, he and Spaatz finally "agreed that whereas we thought the Group and Wing Commanders should go on occasional missions, yet for the same reason [Harris expressed] we didn't want them to lead all the missions. We didn't want to lose them. And we said the Bomber Commander should go on an occasional mission. But General Spaatz reluctantly agreed that the Eighth Air Force commander, who was in charge of all air effort in Britain, should not. . . ."

During the war Eaker went on five missions, Spaatz none. A major reason Spaatz did not—in fact could not—go on combat missions was his having been briefed on ULTRA, the remarkable British achievement in breaking the top German code. Anyone let in on ULTRA could not risk being captured. Eaker refused an ULTRA briefing, saying he would rely upon his intelligence officer to keep him posted on what ULTRA divulged but not how it was learned. He felt much more strongly than Spaatz about the importance of participating in the air battles. This was more than the inevitable itch of a lifelong pilot to get into the action. He also wanted all his key staff officers to do so, issuing a directive to that effect a few days before he personally accompanied the first heavy bomber mission. It began, "It is my desire that the members of the Eighth Bomber Command Staff do sufficient operational missions in order to be cognizant of the problems facing combat crews and sympathetic with their effort." Most of us did.[29]

The same week Eaker clinched possession of his headquarters Harris began busting cities. He carefully chose a target he was sure he could destroy—ancient Lübeck. It was not a major industrial center, but its narrow streets and many wooden buildings made it easily combustible by incendiary bombs. And it was on the Baltic coast and therefore easier to find in the dark than towns further inland. To find it Harris made use of the new Gee device. It was one of the earliest of a string of electronic inventions British scientists introduced in what came to be called "the Wizard War" and all of which they at once offered to the Americans too.[30] Gee worked with a cathode-ray tube picking up radio pulses from three transmitters and helped a trained navigator to pinpoint his position closely, though not enough for "blind bombing;" those inventions would come later. The British expected the Germans to devise ways to jam Gee in a few months, and the new directive told Harris to make maximum use of it quickly. Luckless Lübeck was the first convincing demonstration of Gee's potential, though it had been used over the Ruhr and Cologne in the preceding fortnight in tests that helped Harris to develop major refinements in night-bombing tactics.

RAF night bombers flew one at a time, not in formation. This made takeoff and departure simple but left each bomber entirely dependent upon its own navigator. At first Harris used his few Gee-aircraft as pathfinders guided by specially trained navigators. The pathfinders dropped flares on the target as a beacon for the rest of the stream of bombers, which came along at the established rate of approximately 100 per hour. But over the Ruhr in those first tests the flares went out before enough of the main force arrived to set the city ablaze. It became evident that the first bombers after the pathfinders should carry incendiaries and that the entire bomber stream should be closed up to get there faster and achieve more concentration over the target. On March 13 over Cologne, by using Gee in all the aircraft, Harris achieved a concentration of 120 bombers in 20 minutes. The damage was severe, but Cologne was too big to be "eradicated" by that small a force. Its turn would soon come. Meantime little Lübeck, "Coventry-sized," as Harris put it, was ideal for a force of two hundred bombers.

Lübeck was somewhat beyond the 350–400 mile range of Gee, but the RAF found it easily. "Yet another asset of Gee," Group Capt. Dudley Saward explained in his *Bomber Harris,* "was that when attacking targets beyond its . . . range, aircraft could operate accurately to the system's maximum range and then fly the additional distance for a definite plotted position. Without Gee the errors of navigation had invariably been cumulative after passing across the southern shores of England." Over Lübeck and its approaches, clearly marked by the Baltic shore, the moon that night shone brightly and the pathfinders precisely unloaded their flares for the stream of 224 heavy bombers that followed. First came a wave of 40 loaded with incendiaries to light the city for the main force, which carried a mixture of incendiaries and high explosive bombs, some of the latter weighing 4,000 pounds. Of the total dispatched, 191 bombers claimed to have attacked, at a loss of twelve—6.2 percent. The center of Lübeck was almost wiped out, with 1,425 houses destroyed, 1,976 severely damaged and 312 people killed. Harris claimed a major victory, and few disagreed.[31]

Eaker was, of course, impressed with the feat and praised his host heartily. But he still was not swayed toward night bombing for the Americans, nor ever would be. Besides again citing his own directive, he pointed out to the air marshal and other RAF policymakers some of the benefits to both air forces in "bombing around the clock." It would make the Germans maintain their antiaircraft defenses all twenty-four hours. It would separate the RAF and AAF attacks and thus free the limited air space over the cramped area of southeastern England during takeoff and landings. It would face the Germans with two very different kinds of attack and force them to divide their fighters into two different type of aircraft, thus doubling the German manufacture and pilot training requirements.

The air marshal, not blind to logic though extremely inflexible, quickly granted all those benefits "if you can do it." If not, he made it clear, he assumed the American planes would be diverted to night action. Eaker agreed that this was the logical alternative but pointed out that neither U.S. planes nor crews could make such a switch without vast changes, which would waste much time. Harris and Eaker did share one view—that strategic air power *could* win the war on its own. But Eaker went on to say: "It would be desirable from many points of view to sit back, put all our effort into the air and destroy [the enemy's] weapons-making production. But that's day-dreaming. . . . In our case the elder service is the Army, and then the Navy has always in our country had great public popularity. There's no possibility in our country that we're going to get the Army and Navy to stay out of it and let the fledgling young Air Force win the war."[32]

This conservative philosophy—the same attitude he and Arnold had expressed in *Winged Warfare*—stood Eaker in good stead in early April when General Marshall and Harry Hopkins arrived in London with several urgent missions. One was to brief General Chaney on the sweeping reorganization of the American armed forces then going into effect, including Arnold's having direct command over all overseas air forces. But the bigger task was to convince the British that an invasion of Europe from England must be mounted that very year to open the "second front" Stalin was demanding. The German army was less than forty miles away from Moscow and poised to renew its offensive when the winter weather broke. It seemed all too likely the Germans would succeed unless there were maximum intervention from the western allies. The British, though already convinced that a 1942 invasion was impossible, did not come right out and say so, and the small American party returned home after a week in England thinking Marshall's policy would be accepted. Eaker knew nothing of this grand strategy at that time.

However, he saw a lot of Marshall and Hopkins, in London, at Southdown and at his first visit to Chequers, the prime minister's residence. One of the three staff officers who came with Marshall was an army air colonel who tipped Eaker off that the bombers he was awaiting would be delayed: further crisis in the Pacific was forcing diversion of forces, and the first two bomber groups for the Eighth could not be expected before July. This was of course disappointing, but everything else was upbeat. Marshall came to Southdown, met all twenty-two of Eaker's staff and gave them a strong talk about their important task. Then he and Portal joined Eaker and Harris for lunch, during which he made "many searching inquiries."

But it was at Chequers that the sense of partnership and momentum impressed Eaker most strongly. The prime minister was at his jovial, confident best and the rest of the party brilliant and glittering. The many distinguished British and American guests besides Marshall and Hopkins included Lend-Lease Ambassador Averell Harriman, Air Marshal Harris and Adm. Sir Dudley Pound, the British navy's chief. The last two were somewhat at loggerheads, for Pound still wanted RAF Bomber Command to give priority to antisubmarine warfare, while Harris was gung ho for the new city target program, speaking proudly of leveling Lübeck. Harriman asked when Eaker expected bombers of his own. Learning they were not expected until July, he suggested borrowing some from the British. Eaker replied that the British had given him everything else he could want but "Air Marshal Harris is using all the bombers he has available for his own operations." There was much talk around the dinner table and over whisky later about when and how to take the offensive against Germany and Japan, but no mention of a timetable for invasion.[33]

Of all the views exchanged between Marshall and Eaker during that busy week, only six weeks after Eaker's arrival in England, the words that firmly cemented their understanding and teamwork came when the chief of staff said while at Southdown, "I don't believe we'll ever successfully invade the continent and expose that great armada unless we first defeat the Luftwaffe."

Eaker replied: "The prime purpose of our operations over here, aside from reducing their munitions capacity, is to make the Luftwaffe come up and fight. If you will support the bomber offensive, I guarantee that the Luftwaffe will not prevent the cross-Channel invasion."[34]

Both men lived up to this bargain—one of the most important policies of World War II.

10

"Victory, speedy and complete, awaits the side which first employs air power as it should be employed. Germany, entangled in the meshes of vast land campaigns, cannot now disengage her air power for a strategically proper application. She missed victory through air power by a hair's breadth in 1940. She missed it then only through faulty equipment and the tactical misdirection of an Air Force barely adequate for the purpose. . . . We ourselves are now at the crossroads. . . ."

—OPENING OF LETTER FROM AIR MARSHAL SIR
ARTHUR HARRIS TO PRIME MINISTER WINSTON
CHURCHILL, JUNE 17, 1942

O N APRIL 15 Eaker and his little band moved into PINETREE, the code name for the transformation of the Wycombe Abbey School for Girls into VIII Bomber Command headquarters. Simultaneously their operations moved into high gear. No longer were he and his twenty-one officers just understudying the RAF; now they could begin to build their own parallel organization.

Rarely, if ever, has a military command been blessed with such a remarkable headquarters. It was historic, it was beautiful, it was sumptuously structured for their needs. The first deed to its 250 acres

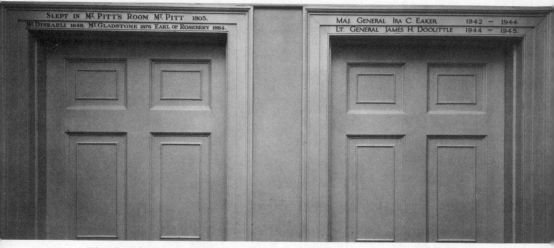

The five famous names inscribed over the twin doors to the Head's apartment, Wycombe Abbey School (PINETREE).

recorded their purchase in 1604 by Richard Arsdale, a vintner whose grandson, John Arsdale, became governor of Carolina (1695–97), introduced rice to southern U.S. agriculture and, upon his return to England, became the first Quaker member of Parliament. When he refused to take the oath because of religious differences, his seat was turned over to his son Thomas. The latter sold the property in 1700 to Lord Shelburne, whose guests included Samuel Johnson, David Garrick and John Wesley, founder of the Wesleyan faith. Wesley's journal in 1775 comments: "What variety in so small a compass! A beautiful grove, divided by a serpentine walk, conceals the house from the town; at the side . . . runs a transparent river with a smooth walk on each bank. Beyond this a level lawn. . . ."

In 1789 Robert Smith, a financial advisor to the younger Pitt, purchased the estate and presently became the first Lord Carrington. He rebuilt the old manor house into the pseudo-Gothic structure that stands today, whose crenellated stone walls, miniature turrets and mullioned windows justified the name he gave it—Wycombe Abbey. Four prime ministers—Pitt, Disraeli, Gladstone and Lord Roseberry —had slept in the bedroom the headmistress took over when the Girl's Education Society purchased the estate in 1896.[1] It was into that room, with their names neatly lettered over the door, that Eaker now moved. His staff took other second-floor bedrooms while the top floor was set aside, with chuckles, for the junior officers then on the way across the Atlantic. That floor was a windowed attic the size of two tennis courts, divided into small cubicles, each with a green curtain, bed, bureau, wash basin and brass plaque reading, "Ring Bell for Mistress."

On the first floor the large, vaulted and marble-floored lobby remained unchanged except for a reception desk. A corridor to the left led first to the commanding general's suite—also once that of the headmistress—consisting of a corner office for him and an adjoining one for his aide and secretary. Next was a large room ideal for operations; beyond that an even larger corner room with a twenty-foot ceiling that had been the library. Stripped of books and with its carved oak paneling carefully covered with beaver board (fine for maps), it became the war room, where Eaker, his staff and a steady parade of VIP visitors were briefed daily on the war news, the Luftwaffe order of battle, U-boat losses and so forth. The whole elegant layout made Southdown seem very primitive.

Another corridor led to the dining hall, which came equipped with furniture, tableware, cooks and civilian waitresses, all bequeathed by the school. Further along was the gymnasium, which Castle cut into cubicles for A-4 offices while he and his growing staff set about the first priority task of arranging the construction of the 106 installations (airfields, supply storage and repair depots) the Eighth would need, plus intricate communications connecting them all with PINETREE and many RAF stations. Nearby were a chapel and several brick dormitories that would quickly be filled. And atop steep Daws Hill was another array of buildings reached by macadam walks through stands of beech, oak and chestnut trees. The elaborately landscaped gardens had of course gone to seed. But the tennis courts, both clay and grass, were in fine shape, as was the great lawn running from the abbey beside the "transparent river" and a large pond with several pair of nesting swans. In the long evenings as spring became summer the staff used the lawn for touch football and volleyball. All officers were under Eaker's order to exercise an hour every day, and he often joined them, usually with a cigar in his mouth.

He had brought from Southdown three RAF enlisted men who would stay with him until the end of the war—Sgt. Leslie Stroud, his secretary; Sgt. Richard Searle, his driver; and Leading Aircraftsman Alfred Govier, his batman (the British word for valet). He also had the loan of twenty-four WAAF girls as clerks to handle the increasing flood of paperwork. They would provide a colorful foot-

Wycombe Abbey.

note to his continuing struggle with General Chaney after General Arnold came over for a week on May 23.

Meanwhile Eaker continued his daily attendance at RAF Bomber Command target sessions and watched closely while Harris laid on his second "eradication attack" on German cities. This time it was the turn of ancient Rostock. Though it too was well beyond the range of Gee, the RAF pathfinders found it on April 23 and the main force of three hundred heavies hit it four nights in a row, burning out large chunks of the town and provoking shrieks from Dr. Joseph Goebbels, Hitler's propaganda chief. Reassured by this second success in the "de-housing" campaign, Harris continued to urge Eaker to join the night bombing tactic. A new argument he listed was damage to morale. "I asked him," Eaker recalled, "if the bombing of London had affected the morale of the British. He said it made them work

152

harder. In the case of the Germans, however, he thought the reaction was different because they were a different breed from the British." But Eaker remained unconvinced. "I never thought morale bombing made any sense," he recorded after the war, though he refrained from such bluntness with the air marshal.[2]

In footling retaliation the Germans sent small forays of their puny bombing force over portions of England once or twice a week in this period while husbanding the Luftwaffe for the decisive attacks in Russia about to begin. The blackout was rigidly in effect throughout England, and rules called for taking cover in bomb shelters whenever the air-raid sirens howled a "red alert." At PINETREE there were no shelters but there were slit trenches into which orders said everyone must go wearing steel helmets. Norcross was duty officer one such night. "It was my job to make sure that all the male officers got up and went out to the trenches. I had to wake up the commanding general, and I was not sure just how to do it. I did wake him up. Hardest to get to move were the RAF liaison officers, who thought the whole thing was damn silly. After a few nights of it Ira decided the RAF people were right. One girl had broken an arm falling into a trench. And the morning after a German raid everyone was sleepy and could not work efficiently."[3]

From the start Eaker gave priority to maintaining good relations with the British at all levels. He quickly endeared himself to the residents of High Wycombe. The mayor, the police chief and other leading citizens were invited to the American mess at PINETREE. When he went to the town barber he sat quietly like any villager awaiting his turn. When American rations began to arrive he urged his officers to take a gift of some kind if invited to British homes, pointing out that canned peaches, for example, were available in British stores but required so many coupons that few people bought them; a can of Del Monte fruit, easily available to the Americans, cost the British a month's coupon ration. When driving in his Humber limousine on inspection trips to the new bases he would tell Searle to pick up any British soldier he saw trudging along the highway, often on the way home on leave. This kindly courtesy was widely noted. One hitchhiker remarked, "British officers would never do this."

But the episode, extensively reported in the British press and in the *Readers Digest* at home, that most captivated the public, both high and low, was the impromptu speech he gave in High Wycombe very soon after moving into the abbey. The mayor invited him to dinner with the city council. Eaker went reluctantly, saying how busy he was and extracting a promise there would be no speeches. But when the Spartan meal was concluded in about an hour he was dragged across the street to a large armory-type building where, said the mayor, "the men and women [serving in the armed forces] are being given a ball. A member of Parliament from our district will be there, so I think you ought to go over." He found about two thousand people standing around a dance floor and a dais from which the MP had just spoken. The mayor got up and talked for fifteen minutes about High Wycombe's great honor as the home of the first increment of the American bomber forces and then called on Eaker. The general said only: "We won't do much talking until we've done more fighting. After we've gone we hope you'll be glad we came."[4] These deft words became his most quoted statement, setting the tone for the entire American air effort in the British Isles.

On May 11 the advance echelon of the Eighth Air Force, having crossed the Atlantic in convoy, docked in Liverpool, bringing 1,850 officers and men, among them the author. A second shipload came in three days later. Included were elements of Eighth AF headquarters, VIII Bomber, Fighter and Service Commands and the 15th Bombardment Squadron. The various headquarters personnel went to PINETREE, while quartermaster and depot people dispersed to some of the early AF bases in small towns with ancient names like Molesworth, Grafton Underwood and Wickstead Heath.[5] All these men and their various units reported to Eaker, not Chaney, and their variety of assignments dramatized several significant aspects of the air force buildup. Though Eaker's formal role was bomber commander, he was actually "on the receiving end," to use his phrase, of all air force elements and thus additionally responsible for setting up the headquarters and base for fighter command, air support command and service command plus finding a suitable location for General Spaatz himself and Eighth AF headquarters. It was Spaatz who was responsible for organizing the units back in the States and sending them overseas, the ground personnel by ship and the fliers by air in their own planes. The sea transit was hazardous but orthodox, that by air unprecedented and considerably more dangerous. Both bombers and fighters faced harsh weather and long over-water hops in a route that ran through Maine, Greenland, Iceland and Northern Ireland. A 10 percent loss ratio had been estimated, but the actuality came in at 5.2 percent and most of these made forced landings on the Greenland ice cap or similar hard-to-get-to spots and their crews were rescued. Only a handful were lost at sea.[6]

All the bombers came by air, but most of the fighters after the first few squadrons came across in crates aboard ship. The enormous forces involved and the complications of training the men and keeping the units fit to fight offer statistical yardsticks of the unique logistical demands both Spaatz and Eaker faced. Building the Eighth Air Force itself, as well as the Twelfth Air Force spun out of it to invade North Africa, and finally the other army air elements spawned by the Eighth to support the invasion of France, was roughly equivalent to creating from scratch in two years an enterprise as big as a combination of General Motors and all the United States airlines, plus a slice of the Massachusetts Institute of Technology. To be sure, Spaatz and Eaker did not manufacture airplanes nor hand out diplomas. But they did have to set up bases and depots in a strange land, modify and repair their bombers by the thousand, assemble their fighters and push most of their officers and men through intense training courses in arcane technology.

In 1942 General Motors was the largest U.S. corporation, with 314,000 employees in 112 major plants making motor vehicles and equipment. In 1942 all the U.S. airlines together had only 39,000 employees and 254 airplanes. M.I.T. was graduating 700 yearly out of a four-year program. The Eighth Air Force grew from 6 officers and no planes in February 1942 to 185,000 officers and men and 4,000 planes by December 1943. Six months later, including the squadrons set aside for the invasion, army air in the United Kingdom reached a total of 400,000 officers and men and 8,000 planes.

Each of the 43 airfields eventually in use for the Eighth's bombers took 60 days to build, and contained 165 barracks housing 3,000 men, with all sorts of special structures like bomb dumps, maintenance shops, mess halls, hospitals, patrol supply tanks and "sea marker & flame float stores," plus, of course, a triangle of three concrete runways, each a mile long. All together they used 40,000 acres of good English farmland at a time when food was so short that many city parks were converted to gardens and vegetables were even being grown at the foot of the Albert Monument next to Buckingham Palace.[7] In addition there were another 40 major installations further north in England or over in Ireland for stockpiling and repairing airplanes and all their components. Bombers and crews did not just fly over from America and go into combat. The crews first had to be trained in the special problems of formation flying in appalling weather and against opposition not found in any other war theater. And they had to be educated in the newfangled techniques and technology, mostly British, of long-distance navigation and, quite often, bombing through overcast at targets discernable only through such devices as H2X or Oboe.

Each B-17 or B-24 had a crew of ten, and each crew member was a specialist—gunner, navigator, radio operator, bombardier, pilot. Each had to be taught procedures not included in the flying schools of Texas. How, for example, to take off along with as many as 2,000 other planes from 43 airfields crammed in an area the size of Rhode Island, spiral up through as much as 10,000 feet of heavy clouds with constant risk of collision, then assemble above the overcast behind their own squadron and group commanders, rendezvous with fighter escort over the Channel and proceed in huge formations in pre-scribed sequence to assigned targets and back, a trip often requiring ten hours in the air, much of the time on oxygen.

Communication in the air between group commanders and their squadrons and with the accompanying fighters was vital. It called for VHF installations in the bombers and fighters—something not con-templated at home. A VHF set weighted seventy-five pounds, com-plained the chairman of the Weight Review Board, and "why did the bombers have to talk to the fighters anyway?" U.S. radio operators when they arrived in England usually had a code speed of only two words a minute, which was not fast enough. That was corrected with intensive practice. But installation of VHF sets required a full-scale production line at the depot at Burtonwood, near Liverpool. In-volved was more than simply hooking up the sets; they also had to be modified to suppress the noise originating from the commutator of the bomber's motor-generators.

Other technological problems concerned improving the IFF (iden-tification, friend or foe) in all the planes to meet United Kingdom requirements; ILS (instrument landing system) installations at all the fields; radio-controlled bomb release; new maps showing how targets looked from oblique angles from all points of the compass as well as from directly above; and modification of aircraft antennae so an SOS could be sent from a plane about to ditch (an unknown number of American airmen drowned before this problem was identified).[8]

Few men who are thought of as industrial giants ever put a major organization together as fast as the Eighth was formed. And there was the added element of inspiring the crews to risk their lives; it was not just getting a large factory ready to make and sell automobiles.

How, it was often asked in later years, could a forty-five-year-old pilot and staff officer, whose biggest previous command was a prewar pursuit group of fifteen hundred men, have developed the ability to handle such a huge and complex mixture of executive, parliamentary and public relations responsibilities? One thinks of Eaker as a combat commander, which was indeed his favorite role. But he was in reality an instinctive executive and born leader, whose exceptional innate talent had been honed by years of stern self-discipline and hungry absorption of the lessons to be learned by watching the many leaders under whom he had served. His own overly modest explanation, years later, said in part: "While it was necessary . . . to supervise the introduction of nearly 100 groups into combat, I still look back upon logistics as having been the biggest problem. In the first place, it was a cooperative problem with the RAF; the combat problem was not. We could introduce these units to combat pretty well on our own initiative. . . . The management techniques used . . . were very largely those that we had learned in coming up through the Army Air Corps in the pre-war years and from the Air Tactical School, the Command and General Staff College and the Army War College. In other words, we (by we I mean the leaders and the principal staff officers) had had a requisite training. It was only by the fact that General Arnold had properly and carefully selected the commanders and staff officers that the exercise did succeed. . . . The mistakes in planning were rather rare, as the later results indicated. Most . . . were due to shortages and changes of program. For example, we would get word that six bombardment groups were to arrive in July. In the meantime the Combined Chiefs of Staff would decide to send three of these groups to the Pacific so only three would arrive. Then we would have three unused stations for a period. The next month, in August, they would tell us three were arriving and six would arrive. . . . These changes of program were not always predictable and not always somebody's fault. . . ."[9]

A major program confusion appeared in the difference between the directives given to Eaker and to Spaatz. The latter's, which controlled the planning and despatch of combat units to England, was built around BOLERO, the first plan for invading France. It called for many medium and light bombers (not suitable for strategic bombing in Europe as Eaker would soon make clear) as well as heavies. The first bomber group headquarters to arrive, the 15th, was light. Eventually, of course, the invasion did take place, but two years later and after a major diversion to North Africa and Italy. All these changes of high strategy were beyond Eaker's or Spaatz's control as well as Arnold's, though he could influence them, but they had the effect of enormously complicating and delaying the growth of VIII Bomber Command and the strategic bombing offensive.

Air Marshal Harris, well into his city-busting campaign, was also of course only on the edge of these cross currents. On April 22, the day before he began the four-nights-in-a-row attack on Rostock, the next on his list, he wrote Arnold a letter brimming with his special gusto. "Come on over and let's clean up!" he began, "1,000 bombers per raid, instead of 2–300 as now, and we've got the Boche by the short hairs. . . . Ira will have sent you the Lubeck and other photos by now. He and I see eye to eye in all such matters—and indeed in all matters. He's a great man. I do not thereby infer that I am also! But I find myself in invariable agreement with him—except perhaps that I think he will find it necessary to go easy with the daylight stuff until he has felt his way. . . . Ira has a grand bunch of lads with him and has certainly gotten (note the American verbiage) himself a fine H.Q. at Wycombe Abbey. As you may know, it was a famous girl's school before Ira walked in. I understand they took all the girls away just as soon as they saw Ira coming along with his lads. . . . Extraordinary how many people can think of ways of employing air power except the right one! I know you have your problems too. Frightening codfish all over the wide ocean spaces will never win a war. Bombing Germany and Japan will win this one—or else. . . ."[10]

A month later, on May 23, Arnold did come over, but with far more urgent matters on his mind than the pleasure of seeing Harris and Eaker and inspecting PINETREE. He squeezed in one day at both bomber commands, but most of his time was spent in London conferring with Prime Minister Churchill and other British leaders. The urgent issue was allocation of aircraft. Facing continued crisis in turning back Japanese approaches to Australia, the navy had persuaded Roosevelt to transfer large air force elements to the Pacific. Marshall was vehemently opposed, arguing that this would prohibit BOLERO. Another alternative occurred to Arnold—to reduce the aircraft shipments previously promised to the British—and it was that unpalatable proposal he had to shove down the throats of

Churchill, Portal and Admiral Pound. A secondary mission was to size up Chaney's fitness as theater commander. To help Arnold with that part of the task, Marshall sent along Maj. Gen. Dwight D. Eisenhower, then chief of the war plans division of the general staff and his assistant, Maj. Gen. Mark Clark. Eisenhower also discussed the promise of the two and a half divisions of American troops Marshall proposed to send to England at once for the modification of BOLERO known as SLEDGEHAMMER with which he hoped to establish a bridgehead in France in early fall.[11]

The British agreed unhappily to let Eaker have U.S. bombers previously allocated to the RAF; decision on SLEDGEHAMMER was again stalled; Chaney's fate was sealed, though his relief did not take place until three weeks later. Eaker later summarized the case against him: "He was too short-sighted. He knew a lot of reasons why you couldn't do something, but too few reasons why you could. He was an impediment. . . . I'll cite you one example, and I won't dwell upon it because it's not my habit to be critical. General Arnold . . . was very surprised to see we had some WAAFs. . . . I said to Arnold, 'We're building up very rapidly, and these people Bert Harris has given us are right out of his hide and he'd like to get them back. I think you ought to make an early plan to tell Hobby [Oveta Culp Hobby, first Director of the U.S. Women's Army Corp] to get us a company of our own WACs.' He went up to London and I joined him that night for dinner. He said, 'Chaney won't have any WACs in the Theatre: He said it will create a morals problem.' I said, 'General, if I were you I would get some. . . .' "[12]

The WACs were, of course, only a small symptom. Eisenhower saw the many other big ones and, upon his return to Washington early in June, recommended Chaney's replacement. Arnold and Clark went one step further, recommending that Eisenhower be Chaney's successor. Marshall agreed, making the change on June 11 while simultaneously expanding the job description from commanding general, U.S. Army forces in the British Isles to CG, European theater of operations.[13] But Eisenhower did not arrive until June 24, and in the interim there was a cascade of great events worldwide in impact and both good and bad.

The first of these came on the night of May 30 while Arnold and Eisenhower together with others in their party as well as Eaker, Harriman, Portal and U.S. Ambassador Winant were dining with Prime Minister Churchill at Chequers. By coincidence (weather being the controlling factor), it was the night that Harris was able to execute the first "thousand-bomber" attack, smashing the truly big and important city of Cologne and producing worldwide recognition for the first time of what could be accomplished by strategic air power in sufficient force. At a cost of 40 aircraft (3.8 percent), 45,000 Cologne residents were dehoused and an estimated 300 factories destroyed or damaged. But Harris had been able to assemble a total of 1,046 bombers only by throwing into the air miscellaneous aircraft of many types, largely taken from training fields. He was able to mount only two more equivalent attacks (on Essen with 956 planes and Bremen with 1,006) before the inflated force dispersed. Not until 1943 would he reach the magic 1,000 figure again. Arnold called the Cologne attack "the real beginning in the world's eyes and in Germany's eyes . . . of round the clock destruction of Germany from the air."[14]

But of more immediate importance to Eaker was Churchill's remark to Arnold that evening at Chequers. "Your program apparently will provide an aerial striking force equal to, or in some cases larger than that provided and planned by us. Perhaps your program is too ambitious. You are trying to do within a few months what we have been unable to accomplish in two or more years."[15] Eaker had no way of knowing that the wily prime minister, always leery of a cross-Channel invasion, was tilting toward North Africa as an alternative to SLEDGEHAMMER. Arnold, one of the Combined Chiefs of Staff, did know that North Africa was number four on the list of strategic options air staff planners had formulated following the ARCADIA Conference in December. The bomber offensive from England was number three, while number two was defense of South Pacific ferry bases and number one heavy bombers for Australia.[16]

In North Africa that June, Rommel was pushing the British back to the Egyptian border, and in the Crimea the Russian army was surrounded in the great fort of Sevastopol, soon to fall. Both situations presented the gravest possibilities—one that Rommel would take Egypt and cut off oil from the mideast, the other that the German offensive in the Caucasus would complete a huge pincer with the same goal. At that intense moment American code breakers learned the Japanese were crouched to pounce on Midway. This threat hit Eaker at once: four groups already poised to take off for England were abruptly about-faced to the West Coast. Just as quickly they returned to the eastern staging areas after the Japanese fleet was shattered near Midway on June 3–6 in one of the war's turning points. But their arrival in England was delayed at least a month.

Despite the uncertainties and the delays, Eaker felt buoyed by Arnold's visit. His boss had brought him not only a box of cigars but also high praise for his handling of the British and his rapid progress in getting VIII Bomber Command organized. More important, Arnold assured him that eventually he would get the aircraft he had been promised. The arrival of the ground echelon of a heavy bomb group, the 97th, on June 10 augured well, though his first B-17 still had not touched down on English soil. Eaker continued his long days, often eighteen hours, making policy decisions with Armstrong, Hull and Castle, giving assignments to new staff specialists such as quartermasters, doctors and weather forecasters, wangling this or that from air ministry, huddling with Harris, choosing and setting up headquarters such as one for General Spaatz at Bushy Park, near Hampton Court Palace up the Thames from London, and playing an occasional game of poker. He was given a puppy, half bull and half mastiff, and named it, inevitably, Winston.

On June 13 VIII Bomber Command had its first wingding—"a curious blend of forced sentiment and genuine fun," as I wrote in my diary that night. A wingding is a compulsory get-together of all officers of a command "where the social intercourse of a stag dinner and smoker could be bound with certain solemn ceremonials historically inherent in military establishments."[17] The custom began with George Washington's dinners for his staff, leading to "Regimental Nights" in the Colonial army. In army air the custom was revived by Arnold when he was still a colonel and in command of the First Wing at March Field. Eaker had been present. At PINETREE the first Wing Ding (the name was changed to "Bomber Night" for the second) was attended by 150 officers and began with a toast to the president, followed by the *Star Spangled Banner,* then a toast to the king, followed by *God Save the King.*

The dishes cleared, Eaker rose gravely and said it was customary for an officer of each rank to sit at the head table and for the general to leave the head table at the end of the meal and exchange places with a junior officer at another table. Another custom was to read the names of officers whose work had been especially notable during the preceding month. He did so. Finally he spoke somberly about another officer who had been present at the first wingding at March Field and who had just been reported missing while leading his bombers against the Japanese at Midway—Maj. Gen. Clarence L. Tinker. "I want General Tinker to know, wherever he is," said Eaker, "that all of us here realize that he went the way he would have

Eaker at PINETREE with "Winston."

wanted." That may seem sententious and trite in cynical America forty years later, but it fit the innocent American mood of 1942 and was effective to an audience of revved-up fliers yet to be bloodied in combat.

Eaker then changed places with Flight Lieutenant Aholt, one of the RAF liaison officers, and the "entertainment" began. Skits at stag parties are usually as dull as they are broad, but this one turned out quite clever and quite clean. It was stage-managed by Col. Edward Gray, formerly of AT&T and now heading the signals section of A-4 in charge of communications. In appointing Gray, Eaker told him "rank can be ignored in the party festivities," and Gray's committee took the commanding general at his word. There was ample talent —Capt. Beirne Lay, for example, a skilled writer, and Lt. Gene Raymond, Hollywood star and singer. The show was all satire about army life in Britain. One feature was the award of the "Herman Goering Iron Cross of the Order of Shicklgruber" to the officers who had made "the greatest contribution to the German war effort" in the preceding month. One went to a pilot who roamed the English sky for ten hours looking for an airport one hour's flight away, another was to a quartermaster who had canceled sewage disposal after concluding the local contractor was charging too much; he won the Herman Goering Cross for "seriously interfering with the movements of U.S. troops." One song, belted out by Raymond, had as its theme the refrain, "Whatever it is I'm against it: That's the function of the Chief of Staff." The whimsies climaxed with the presentation of a toupee to Eaker. As the general, grinning broadly, returned to his seat, he was recalled and given a comb. About to sit down again, he was once more summoned to the microphone and handed a piece of chewing gum to hold the toupee in place. Next day the chief of staff apologized for the impertinence. "Why shouldn't I take it," Eaker replied, "the same as anyone else."[18]

Spaatz and several of his staff reached England on June 20, flying in a B-24 Liberator, the other heavy bomber besides the B-17 in the American arsenal. Eaker met his old friend with delight and brought him to PINETREE at once for a first look. The next three days were spent escorting his commander to see Ambassador Winant and Harris and many of the top British leaders, and to an off-the-record meeting with the press. Spaatz began to move into WIDEWING, the code name for the Eighth Air Force headquarters in Bushy Park while his aide, Maj. S. S. "Sy" Bartlett, a Hollywood film writer in civilian life, scouted for a residence. WIDEWING had none of the glamour of PINETREE, being nothing more than a huddle of one-story cinder block buildings painted gray and erected originally as barracks. But it was only a quarter-mile from the Teddington rail station and a good deal closer to London than Eaker's bomber command. Spaatz cared little for show in any case and was content also with the gloomy Victorian residence named Park House Bartlett found for him on Wimbledon Common.

Eisenhower arrived four days later, taking over from Chaney, and was at once swept up in high strategy discussion with the British about SLEDGEHAMMER. That same week Churchill was in Washington pleading with Roosevelt to switch American policy to GYMNAST, the invasion of North Africa. His pleas were fortified by the devastating news that Tobruk with its twenty-five thousand British soldiers had fallen to Rommel. Roosevelt began to yield, much to Marshall's distress. But it would be several weeks before the big change would be formally approved. In London Eisenhower continued to press the planning for SLEDGEHAMMER, and Eaker was asked to draw up an air plan for the support of a two or three division assault on the Cherbourg Peninsula. His handwritten draft, running to eighteen pages, was remarkably similar, except for the size of the Allied forces involved, to the plan for the actual invasion, OVERLORD, two years later. The second paragraph began, "The purpose of the combined operation is to establish a second front in Western Europe, relieving pressure on Russia, encouraging the peoples of Axis-occupied territory, and initiating a series of events which shall result in the land invasion of Germany and eventual Axis defeat and collapse. . . ."[19]

One day Eisenhower came to PINETREE, where he met all the officers and was briefed by the author, who had been put in charge of the war room. The new theater commander and Eaker were well acquainted but they had never before served together. Spaatz, on the other hand, had known Eisenhower intimately since West Point, where they were one class apart and Spaatz had been Eisenhower's file closer (i.e., he marched directly behind him in parade formations). Eisenhower and Eaker had many similarities. Both were born in humble circumstances in small Texas towns, both had warm, considerate personalities and instinctively courteous manners, both were pragmatic in philosophy, adapting easily to change in military concepts or circumstances. But Eisenhower was far more of an extrovert and with a sharp temper he did not always, like Eaker, keep

Two years before Normandy, Eisenhower and Eaker confer in London.
Behind: William C. Bullitt, former U.S. ambassador to France.

under control. The two men quickly reached a level of comfortable frankness and became close friends. It was a refreshing change from Chaney.

None of them knew that Arnold had written to Churchill on June 10 promising "we will be fighting with you on July 4th." But orders came through to Spaatz on June 28 to begin combat operations on Independence Day. He and Eaker were aghast and protested—to no avail. The desire in Washington for some sort of dramatic stunt, such as Doolittle's April raid on Japan by B-25s, was emphatic. Eaker argued that a quickie out of England would accomplish no real damage, risk heavy losses and hurt the morale of his tiny command. Arnold of course knew that Doolittle's attack had done no damage and that his tiny force of twenty-five B-25s (all withdrawn from the Eighth AF) lost all his planes and 10 percent of his crews. But the impact on both American and Japanese public opinion had been immense. To produce headlines about American air action against Germany having at last begun might have similar benefits.

The Eighth had no planes at all. But the 15th Bombardment Squadron (light), planned for eventual use by the air support command, was in training with RAF Squadron 226, flying twin-engine Douglas A-20s out of Swanton Morely in Norfolk, not far from the North Sea coast. Arrangements were quickly made to borrow six of the British planes, paint over their RAF roundels and replace them with the AAF's white star and bar. The American flight would be commanded by Capt. Charles C. Kegelman and accompanied by another six manned by British pilots. Targets, to be hit at tree-top level: four Luftwaffe fields on the Holland shore.

Eisenhower, Spaatz and Eaker all visited Swanton Morely, and VIII Bomber Command intelligence officer Harris Hull went there on July 3 to perform his first combat briefing. Sweeping low across the sea to avoid radar in four flights of three each the next morning, the 15th happened to fly directly over German "squealer" ships that flashed a warning. The flak and small arms fire was very heavy as the planes split for their assigned targets. Kegelman's wingman went down in flames approaching De Kooy airfield. Kegelman's own A-20 lost the propeller for the right engine, which began to flame, and the right wingtip scraped the ground as he struggled to stay airborne. Jettisoning his bombs, he managed to get back to Swanton Morely. Eaker was there to congratulate him and the other survivors, and Hull handled the debriefing. Eight Americans were missing—one-third of the force—seven dead and one, Lt. Marshall Draper, gaining the dubious distinction of being the Eighth Air Force's first POW. Of the six American bombers four had failed to drop their bombs anywhere near their targets. The mission was, in short, the shambles Eaker had predicted. The loss became even more painful when a surviving American flier committed suicide three weeks later.

But the publicity harvest was what Washington had hoped for. In London the *Express* headlined: U.S. BOMBERS IN ACTION— FIRST RAID FROM ENGLAND and averred that "bombs were seen to burst on hangars, administrative buildings and dispersal points." American press reports were grossly exaggerated. The AP claimed that 150 German airmen had been caught flat-footed; the *Washington Post* gave equal front-page billing to the headlines YANKS RAID NAZIS IN HOLLAND, BRITISH DRIVE AGAINST ROMMEL and REDS FALL BACK ON KURSK FRONT. The *New York Times* was most off the track, asserting "the attack was no holiday stunt."

Reading the full mission report, brought to him by Hull, and noting in particular the details of Kegelman's miraculous return, Eisenhower penciled across the page, "This Officer is hereby awarded the Distinguished Service Cross." Then, shaking his head, he asked Hull, "Are all of the reports going to be like this one?"[20]

*"Be circumspect in your choice of officers.
Take none but gentlemen; let no local
attachments influence you; do not suffer your
good nature (when an application is made) to
say yes, when you ought to say no. Do not take
old men, nor yet fill your corps with boys—
especially for captains."*

—GEORGE WASHINGTON, 1777

IN MID-JULY, two and a half months behind schedule, the Eighth
Air Force at last received some airplanes—180, of which forty
were heavies. The first B-17s went to the 97th Bomb Group (H),
whose ground echelon awaited them at two adjacent bases, Polebrook and Grafton Underwood, two hours drive north of PINETREE.
The 97th thus became the spearhead of VIII Bomber Command,
destined for distinction as the first group of U.S. heavies to attack
across the Channel. But there were sudden problems first.

In preparation for the 97th and other heavy groups expected at
once, Eaker had begun to organize VIII Bomber Command down
the line in the established AAF pattern of three wing headquarters,
each to be in command of three groups, with each group consisting
of three or four squadrons of six bombers apiece. He appointed
Claude Duncan as CO of the 1st Wing, replacing him with Bubb as
chief of staff at PINETREE. CO of the 2nd Wing became Eaker's old
friend, Col. Newton Longfellow, newly arrived, and the 3rd went to
Col. Charles T. Phillips, with whom Eaker and Longfellow had gone

to the Philippines in 1919. CO of the 97th, who had flown over with his planes and skeleton crews, was a genial, easygoing old-timer who had been a pilot on the famous interception of the *Rex*—Col. Cornelius Cousland.

Eaker directed Duncan to prepare the 97th for a gunnery display in which the gunners of a selected squadron would fire at tow targets, and he brought Eisenhower and Spaatz to Polebrook to watch on August 1. It was a wretched performance, though Eisenhower, who had never seen that sort of a demonstration, did not realize how bad the marksmanship was and wrote Spaatz effusively, "Everything I noted . . . was highly pleasing in its promise that our future bomber battle tasks would be skillfully fulfilled . . ." particularly "the intimate acquaintanceship of General Eaker himself with every detail of his organization."[1]

But Eaker was furious and embarrassed, doubly so, for two days previously he had sent Spaatz his recommendation for the promotion of Duncan, as well as Bubb and Longfellow, to brigadier general. Now he gave Duncan a blistering reprimand and went back to Polebrook himself to see what was wrong. He learned that the 97th's gunners had never fired at tow targets before, the crews had done little flying at high altitude, the pilots were inept at formation flying and the whole outfit was lackadaisical, loose-jointed, fun-loving and in no sense ready for combat. As became his policy when he discovered that a group needed overhauling, he sacked the CO, Colonel Cousland, giving him a temporary job as RAF liaison officer until he went home. To replace him Eaker scanned his meagre stock of senior flying officers and appointed one on whom he knew he could count, Frank Armstrong. That restless, pugnacious officer had done well as A-3 at PINETREE but he would much rather fly an airplane than a desk, as he had indicated to Eaker more than once. Now Eaker simply said: "I have asked you to do many things for me. This time I am putting a real load on you. . . . You are going to complete the training of our new heavy bomb group and fight them in 16 days." Armstrong went out in PINETREE's sedate halls "whooping and hollering." Bubb jumped to his feet and asked, "What in hell is wrong?" "I'm going to combat!" Armstrong replied. "Fool!" said Bubb, sitting down.[2]

Arnold was spurring Spaatz and Eaker to get into action fast. This was no surprise to either of them, for their boss was always in a hurry. But this time he had a special reason to be impatient, something he could not yet confide to his two commanders in England because of security. Marshall, Hopkins and Adm. Ernest J. King, chief of naval operations, had returned from London empty-handed from a final effort to sell SLEDGEHAMMER to the British, and the switch to GYMNAST, renamed TORCH, was agreed upon by the combined chiefs on July 24 in broad policy terms but with all details to be settled. It was a deep, deep secret. Arnold of course knew about it and he desperately wanted the Eighth to show its mettle at once so he could salvage something for the strategic bombing offensive and continue to send reinforcements.

In addition, American and British newspapers were beginning to voice skepticism about the long-awaited heavy bombers from America. On August 8 the *New York Times* headlined: "British Rifts On Planes Holding Up Air Offensive." On August 16 Peter Masefield, aviation editor of the *London Times,* wrote a long, critical analysis of the B-17 and the B-24, saying: "American heavy bombers . . . are fine flying machines but not suited for bombing Europe. Their bomb loads are small, their armour and armament are not up to the standard now found necessary, and their speeds are low." Arnold was so fussed by the Masefield piece that he sent Spaatz a wire demanding a full explanation.

Under all these pressures Eaker continued unflappable. He had word daily that Armstrong was forcing the 97th's training pace with long hours of formation flying, first at low level, and then high, plus hours of gunnery practice at tow targets.[3] Eaker went up for another inspection at Polebrook and was pleased with the 97th's progress. He scheduled a first mission for August 9 but bad weather intervened. So he sent Arnold the first of an eighteen-month series of long letters that always stressed the positive and reiterated his abiding confidence in accomplishing the Eighth's imposing task. He wrote:

"The tempo is stepping up as we approach the zero hour. Tooey's and my theory that day bombardment is feasible is about to be tested where men's lives are put at stake. . . . You have two zealots in Tooey and myself that . . . daylight bombing can be done without irreplaceable losses. . . . The crews now here are bombing and shooting during all the hours of daylight, when the weather is flyable, and there is a lot of daylight in this latitude at this time of year. We have very high standards for them before we send them to combat and I am certain at least eleven of them, the first to arrive, can now meet our standards. We are having a test today of bombing from 25,000 ft. and mass firing from formation at three sleeve targets flown past them at all angles . . .

"It was a peculiar coincidence, but the British got the Spitfire 9 ready to go just at the moment we are ready to undertake high altitude bombing and they are most enthusiastic to have a crack at the FW-190 between 25,000 and 30,000 ft. so they are going to be alongside in our early missions in adequate quantity.

"Thanks for all the good people you have sent to this theatre. We not only have the best collection of officers I have ever seen assembled in one place, but they are all working like one congenial, happy family. Your solution has been perfect; from the higher echelon to the lowest there is complete accord and harmony and the fiercest enthusiasm I have ever seen. . . .

"Amid all the discouragements—slow arrival of equipment; small numbers available; bad weather and necessity for more training —one thing stands out brightly. Our combat crews have the heart and the stamina, the keenness, the will to fight and the enthusiasm which will make them the toughest fighters which have been seen in this theatre, and some mighty able fighting men have worked in these parts before. . . ."⁴

But Arnold was not placated. Incorrigible in his impatience, he sent a testy letter to Spaatz that began, "I am personally gravely concerned over the apparent extension of the time period which you had anticipated necessary to complete the training of our units prior to their actual entry into combat. . . ." Arnold continued at great length in his best I-know-better-than-you tone of voice, "Where doubt exists as to the ability of our units to acquit themselves adequately, I urge that you do not be over-conservative." And he hinted at the urgency behind his pressure when he wrote, "The strategic necessity for the immediate or early initiation of effective, aggressive American Air Force offensive operations becomes more and more apparent daily here."⁵

In reply Spaatz pointed out that since his arrival in England seven weeks before there had been only a half-dozen days when accurate bombing from twenty-five thousand feet had been possible. But Arnold never did come to understand the erratic nature of the weather over England and Europe. Nor would he ever be directly responsible for sending men into battle. Spaatz and Eaker steadfastly refused to bend to his orders beyond what they considered prudent. Eaker was determined to wait for good weather and both knew they could not sensibly maintain regular operations without a continuing flow of replacement crews. Spaatz told Arnold he expected losses to average 5 percent on the first five missions and pointed out that there were not yet enough replacement crews in England to fill the gaps. This Arnold-Spaatz-Eaker trialogue was the first indication of a pattern that continued with brief lapses throughout the war. Arnold regarded Spaatz as his chosen and trusted number one deputy and never criticized him, telling him as the war unfolded that "I want [Eisenhower] to recognize you as the top airman in all Europe."[6] But with Eaker Arnold now began questioning, doubting, needling and puppeteering. Again and again he would flout the basic rule of a good executive—to delegate authority as well as responsibility. Equally stubborn, Eaker would not budge from positions and policies he believed in, always courteously and eloquently writing back to Arnold at great length to explain. Spaatz, the buffer between the two, backed Eaker time and time again, for the policies Eaker espoused usually represented ideas he and Spaatz had already agreed upon. But the strain on Eaker nonetheless eventually became immense, and only his stoic strength and unfailing sense of humor would enable him to maintain his calm assurance.

On August 16 the weather forecast at last looked good and Eaker approved a mission for the following day. Brick Lessig, last mentioned in this narrative as the hero of the Medford, Oregon, episode and now a lieutenant colonel, had replaced Armstrong as A-3. He despatched the preliminary orders to the 97th and then went duck-shooting with the general beside a small lake ten minutes up the road at West Wycombe Park, the ancient seat of a hereditary lord, Sir Francis Dashwood. The baronet was overseas for the Foreign Office, but Helen Lady Dashwood, a vivacious, good-looking brunette with a saucy wit, had made her sumptuous Palladian manor, once visited by Benjamin Franklin, into a sort of informal country club for the officers of VIII Bomber Command. "After tea," Lessig recalled, "we were assigned our respective shooting positions. General Eaker and I were given the best spots, but to get there we had to cross a meadow, then crawl under, go over or through a barbed wire fence. We chose to crawl under, and the General rolled right into a large hornets nest. In a matter of seconds he was attacked by scores of angry hornets." Lessig tried beating them off with a branch, while the general rolled back under the fence. Watching him roll from afar, "Lady D," as all the Americans called her, thought to herself, "He probably thinks it would not be dignified for a General to run."[7]

By the time Lessig got Eaker back to the PINETREE dispensary, "The General was in pretty bad pain. . . . The doctor administered a heavy dose of anti-bee sting and a shot of sedatives. . . . (We) counted the stings and found 27 arrows in the General's neck and face, enough to kill. . . . I ordered the doctor to keep the General sedated and to have a 24-hour watch over him. I returned to my office where I rechecked the Ops order, weather, etc. and returned to the dispensary where I found the General asleep. . . . I made sure the medical personnel understood that he was not to be disturbed and that he was to remain in bed until the following day. This was difficult since I knew how much he had planned on flying the first mission, but with 27 poison arrows in him it appeared a matter of life or death. Early the next morning I rechecked the Ops order and gave the go-ahead to the 97th . . . and then took off to visit the General in the infirmary. When I arrived the bird had flown. He had called his driver . . . and driven to Polebrook just in time. . . ."[8]

The target was the Sotteville railway marshaling yard at Rouen, chosen for several reasons. Railway yards, where freight cars are assembled into trains and repair shops are concentrated, made a good place to interrupt transportation while destroying whatever the assembled cars contained. Further, they were clearly defined and easily spotted from four or five miles up. Their simple dimensions, usually twenty to forty parallel lines of track funneled at each end and with few if any buildings between them, made it easy also to plot bomb damage from photo reconnaissance planes the next day. The yard at Rouen was one of the largest in northern France and it was near the coast (a "shallow penetration") where it could be reached with full protection from the short-range Spitfire 9s provided by the RAF. For Eaker, despite the bomber doctrine that the B-17s could fend for themselves, always sought fighter cover. "As it was explained to me what my mission in England was to be," he said, "I . . . began enthusiastically to reorient myself toward bombardment. I also, very early . . . became convinced that it would be greatly to our advantage and reduce our losses significantly if we could have fighters to protect us. . . ."[9] This time the RAF provided four Spitfire squadrons, and they at once demonstrated the validity of Eaker's judgment.

That day the 97th despatched 23 B-17s. Twelve took off from Polebrook early in the long British afternoon and rendezvoused with some of the Spits in mid-Channel, heading east in a diversionary feint from which they turned back before crossing the French Coast. The deception worked, for a British radio monitor heard a German defense controller announce that "twelve Lancasters" were on the way. The other 11 bombers took off from Grafton Underwood 15 minutes later. Leading the first flight of 6 was a B-17 named *Butcher Shop* piloted by the mission's commander, Frank Armstrong. His copilot was Maj. Paul W. Tibbets, who would win enduring fame three years later piloting the *Enola Gay* and dropping the first atom bomb on Japan. The lead plane of the second flight of 5 was named *Yankee Doodle* and piloted by Capt. Rudy Flack. Eaker rode with him as an observer. The departure was watched by Spaatz, many high American and British officers and about 30 correspondents, including Peter Masefield, whose condemnation of the B-17 had been published the day before. At 23,000 feet over the Channel the two flights rendezvoused with their Spit escort and assembled in formation for the short run in to Rouen, 87 miles northwest of Paris. Visibility was good, flak sparse and the Sotteville yard was found without difficulty. The B-17s unloaded 36,900 pounds of general purpose bombs, of which 9 of 1,100 pounds each were aimed at a locomotive repair shop while the others, all 600-pounders of British manufacture, sought rolling stock repair sheds. Peering down through *Yankee Doodle*'s bomb bay, Eaker watched the mushrooming explosions and considered the bombing encouraging for a first try, with about half of the bombs in the target area. Of course a mere 12 bombers could not inflict major damage, but the accuracy augured well for what could be done with bigger formations and was the first real proof under combat conditions of the American concept of precision bombing. The Spits kept enemy FW-190s and ME-109s mostly at a distance, shooting down 2 and losing 2 of their own in exchange. One Flying Fort, *Birmingham Blitzkrieg,* was hit with a sprinkling of flak.[10]

Back at Grafton Underwood the ground crews and crowd of waiting dignitaries were fidgety and understandably nervous. The British officers in particular remembered how their few sorties with B-17s had been clobbered a year before. After three hours some specks loomed low in the southwestern sky. Everyone counted silently until it was clear that the 97th was back with no losses, home free. Eaker waved at Spaatz as *Yankee Doodle* touched down and then doffed his flying clothes and oxygen bottle, put on his regular tunic and hat, lit a cigar and emerged beaming to meet the press.

The official history of the AAF in WW II commented, "This first combat mission flown by the Fortresses of VIII Bomber Command could not have been more fortunately timed." Instead of just rebutting the Masefield criticism, Spaatz was able to wire Arnold that the Rouen attack "far exceeded in accuracy any previous bombing in the European theatre by German or Allied aircraft" and that he would not exchange the B-17 for any British bomber in production. Spaatz telephoned the good news to Eisenhower, whose diary for that day, kept by his aide, Cmdr. Harry C. Butcher, recorded: "Raid had been led by Major General Ira C. Eaker. Ike much worried about this, for he regards Eaker as an extremely valuable man. . . ." From Harris the next day Eaker received a message couched in the air marshal's ineffably hearty phrases. "Congratulations from all ranks of Bomber Command on the highly successful completion of the first all American raid by the big fellows on German occupied territory in Europe. *Yankee Doodle* certainly went to town and can stick yet another well-deserved feather in his cap."[11]

Eaker was of course jubilant but also cautious in his immediate remarks. Yes, he told the assembled journalists, "All the bombs hit in close proximity to the target. There was a little ack-ack bursting at our level and I saw three Focke-Wulfs, one of which started to attack from our right but pulled away. I guess they've got a lot of respect for our fire."[12] He reminded them that "one swallow does not make a summer." But he could not conceal his delight at being finally in action. *Life* correspondent Lincoln Barnett caught that note, writing: "In this curiously divided personality the flier is always dominant. . . . Eaker's mantle of aloof and cosmopolitan dignity parted briefly and disclosed for an instant the tempestuous, wind-driven airman within. In that moment it was Ira Eaker of Llano County, Texas, who cried happily, 'Why, I never got such a kick out of anything in my life! When I saw that old, snub-nosed Focke-Wulf comin' up at us I said to myself, Boy, this is the life!' "[13]

The next day Eaker returned swiftly to his other personality as cool executive, drafting a five-page letter to Spaatz in which he summarized in minute detail all his observations and recommendations. He noted the need for more intensive training with such spe-

Ever-present cigar in hand, an elated Eaker chats with newsmen just after returning from the first B-17 mission against occupied Europe, August 17, 1942—Ruth Eaker's "favorite picture" of her husband.

cifics as crews "must be cautioned against being too blasé. . . . Oxygen lines were too short" and "the radio operator does not have free movement for his gun. . . . The photographer in one of the planes became unconscious for lack of oxygen. . . . Station keeping can be improved. A better defensive formation is required. . . . Air discipline for take-off and landing can be improved. . . ." The "critical items" he saw included "split-second timing for rendezvous with fighters . . . navigation to the target . . . better gunnery . . . better bombing . . . better pilotage." On bombing he concluded: "The hits I plotted on the target, which have since been verified by photograph, indicate that 56 of the bombs were in the target area and 11 of the 12 planes' bombs were within a half-mile circle. One load was short about 1,000 yards. These are excellent bombardment results for that altitude for a first effort. There is reason to believe our high level bombing can and will be sufficiently accurate for the destruction of small point targets." On pilotage he concluded: "Our pilots must be able to . . . maneuver since it is quite evident that the accuracy of German anti-aircraft fire will bring about losses unless there is considerable formation maneuvering to include changes of altitude. It was quite evident to me that the four-minute run in a straight line on the bombing approach would have been fatal in this case, had there been intense heavy flak. . . ."

But his most important conclusion was: "It is too early in our experiments in actual operations to say that [the B-17] can definitely make deep penetrations without fighter escort and without excessive losses. I can say definitely now, however, that it is my view that the German fighters are going to attack very gingerly. . . ."[14]

Though VIII Bomber Command's mission of August 17 was a stunning achievement for daylight aerial bombardment, the hit and run raid on Dieppe two days later by 6,000 Canadian and British commandos plus 50 American rangers was a stunning setback for conventional ideas of cross-Channel attack by sea. Almost 4,000 of those brave but untested men were killed or captured and all their tanks lost in two days at negligible cost to the Germans. The Allied defeat confirmed Churchill's worst fears about a real invasion and made the TORCH decision seem altogether wise. TORCH would soon hobble VIII Bomber Command, which Eaker did not yet realize. But, blessed with a rare spell of continued fair weather in nearby France and Holland, he wasted no time in nailing down confirmation of the capabilities of his force, tiny though it still was.

In the next three weeks VIII Bomber Command mounted bomber operations on ten days, all escorted by British Spitfires. The first hit a German airfield in France in support of the Dieppe landings, the rest an assortment of airfields, aircraft factories and railway marshaling yards. Though the force available gradually grew to fifty-four B-17s despatched on September 6, the formations were still too small to wreak important damage. But the accuracy, especially in the light of new groups getting into action for the first time, was impressive. What most caught the world's attention, however, was the fact that no American bombers went down until the tenth mission, when two were lost. It began to seem that the Flying Fortress was all its name implied.

But this was somewhat deceptive, for it was only with the VIII's tenth mission that the Luftwaffe began to muster real opposition. Against earlier attacks, the Germans, seeing how small the American formations were and how little the damage they achieved, did not bother to deploy fighter squadrons specifically to counter them. They did, however, snoop around the edges of early flights, studying the formations, noting the limitations of Spitfire cover and estimating the weak spots in the B-17's defenses. On the 6th, when 41 Flying Forts of the 97th Group struck the Avions Potez aircraft factory at Meaulte accurately, the Luftwaffe pounced, with FW-190s making an estimated 45 to 50 passes. For the 2 Forts lost, the 97th's gunners claimed 5 FW-190s down, 13 probably destroyed and 25 damaged. The next day when a formation of 15 from the 97th hit a shipyard in Rotterdam while another 14 B-17s from the 301st BG, flying its first mission, hit a "target of opportunity" near Utrecht, there were again strong German fighter attacks. Reporting no losses, the two American formations claimed another high score: 12 German fighters destroyed, 10 probables and 12 damaged.

Not until October did weather allow bomber operations to resume. On the 2nd 62 B-17s went out, but only 36 attacked two familiar targets in France, with strong Luftwaffe opposition but no losses. On the 9th Eaker despatched 115 heavies, of which 69 hit the primary targets, a steel and engineering factory and nearby locomotive and freight-car works in Lille, with excellent results and the loss of 4 bombers. Once again the gunnery claims were large: 56 fighters destroyed, 26 probables and 20 damaged. The Lille mission was significant for several reasons: B-24s saw action for the first time, flown by the 93rd BG; another new group was the 306th, flying B-17s; because of the priority about to be given to TORCH, Lille was the biggest mission Eaker would be able to launch that year; and it was big enough to be "conducted on a really adequate scale," wrote the AAF historians, "[marking] the formal entry of the American bombers into the big league of strategic bombardment." Eaker dubbed Lille "the end of the first phase" of his bombardment plan.[15]

The RAF of course watched this dramatic seven-week period closely and with growing, if somewhat grudging, admission of its accomplishments. Eaker wrote Arnold on August 27 that the British "acknowledge willingly and cheerfully the great accuracy of our bombing, the surprising hardihood of our bombardment aircraft and the skill and tenacity of our crews."[16] Spaatz reported a growing acceptance of the daylight doctrine. The British press also changed its tune. A London *Daily Mail* columnist on September 1 wrote, "So remarkable has been the success of the new Flying Fortresses operated by the USAAF from this country that it is likely to lead to a drastic resorting of the basic ideas on air warfare which have stood firm since the infancy of flying." Even Peter Masefield slowly backed away from total negativism, writing after Lille that the question "Can we carry day air war into Germany?" needed reassessment. He again raised the problems of long-range fighter escort and also the terrible winter weather over Germany, but ended his October 18 article, "The Americans have taught us much; we still have much to learn—and much to teach."[17]

Among the arrivals in England that critical summer was a wiry, intense and imaginative colonel named Haywood S. Hansell, Jr., who was known to all in army air as "Possum" because of his scoop nose and wily mind. He and Eaker had been friends since 1931 when, still a second lieutenant, he had bailed out of a P-12 in a spin over Bolling Field a few months after Eaker nearly lost his life doing so. Hansell plopped into the frigid Potomac and almost drowned before "I was hauled off to the hospital to have large quantities of salty water pumped out of my bilges. . . . I had a telegram from Ira Eaker welcoming me to the Caterpillar Club. He went on to say that he was pleased and flattered to find me following in his footsteps, but it wasn't really necessary to follow so closely or to be so literal about it. As I came to understand later, the message was typical of Eaker: a quick extension of sympathy and understanding for a fellow flier, wrapped in slightly sardonic humor."[18]

Hansell became distinguished in part as a combat commander of B-17s against Germany and B-29s against Japan but chiefly as a planner of air operations. He had been one of the four officers in a 1941 committee headed by Col. (later Lt. Gen.) Harold L. George that put together AWPD-1, the initial strategic plan for World War II of the Air War Plans Division. When Eisenhower came to England to be theater commander he asked for Hansell to head an air planning section in his headquarters and promoted him to brigadier general. Hansell was also designated deputy theater air officer under Spaatz. The sudden decision to mount TORCH, with Eisenhower in command both of the invasion and also of operations out of the

Ruth Eaker, 1942.

British Isles, made AWPD-1 obsolete. President Roosevelt on August 24 requested a new study of the needs for "complete air ascendancy over the enemy" including Japan. The navy, always pushing hard for the Pacific, succeeded in diverting another fifteen heavy bomber groups from the forces allocated to VIII Bomber Command and asked for 1,250 heavy bombers in addition for its own use. Marshall decided to call Hansell back to begin work on a new plan that would become famous as AWPD-42. His August 26 cable requested that Hansell bring all the data about the current VIII Bomber Command bombing efforts and concluded, "Results of the work of this group are of such far reaching importance that it will probably determine whether or not we control the air." Hansell asked Spaatz for approval to take with him Harris Hull, Eaker's A-2 and now a major, and Group Capt. Robert S. Sharp, a top RAF planner. Spaatz, also wily and seeing an opportunity to mend fences between Arnold and Eaker, ordered Eaker to go along too. Spaatz wrote Arnold, "In our discussion with Ike this a.m. I emphasized the vital necessity of continuing our operations in this theater with HBS and P-38s. . . . Eaker's ideas exactly parallel mine."[19]

Thus it was that Eaker, much against his wishes, flew home for five days right in the middle of his first major campaign to demonstrate the case for daylight bombardment. Spaatz took capable charge of bomber command while his chief henchman was gone. Arriving in Washington after a tedious, all-night flight with almost no sleep, Eaker went at once to see Arnold. It was some hours before he telephoned Ruth. First things first. Then he and his beautiful wife had a happy reunion, fitting in visits with a few pals between all the military demands. He also, with his unfailing touch for the thoughtful gesture, found time to telephone the families of some twenty of his key officers in England.[20]

Eaker, Sharp and Hull made a polished presentation to Arnold and the air staff, using the latest photographs and intelligence reports to describe the first five heavy bomber attacks (three more successful missions took place without losses while Eaker was in Washington, greatly reinforcing the impact he made). He met with Stimson, Marshall, Lovett and other top strategists and policymakers, and Arnold took him to the White House to talk with the president. It all went very well. Arnold wrote Spaatz: "Ira has made a very valuable impression on everybody with whom he has talked here, and in accordance with your recommendation, I am forwarding his nomination for Major General. I hope it goes through."[21]

It did. Eaker got his second star on September 7, about the same time that Spaatz awarded him and Armstrong Silver Star medals for the Rouen mission.

12

"We have to make war as we must and not as we would like to."

—LORD KITCHENER

"THE BLACKEST day in history" was Eisenhower's exasperated first reaction when TORCH was decided upon.[1] He of course tackled his new assignment with brisk and cheerful efficiency, but there remained much ambivalence in his thinking for the next several months. Like Marshall, he was convinced that a cross-Channel invasion was the only route to triumph over Germany. The invasion of North Africa, whatever its benefits in meeting Russia's demands for opening an immediate second front and in cleaning up the Mediterranean, remained a diversion. He believed North Africa could be won in a few months and that he would return to England early in 1943 to mount the invasion of France. Plans for that effort, code named ROUND-UP, remained the top priority goal until Hitler's fanatic insistence on holding in North Africa, plus continued British caution, made it impractical. "I said to Ike," Eaker ruefully remembered, adding that his comment "gained some unpopularity, this is a diversion. You, Arnold, even Marshall know it.

But Ike said to me rather testily, 'When the heads of state make a decision I carry it out, and I expect you to carry it out too.' "[2]

For a time Eisenhower contemplated switching the Eighth Air Force entirely to the support of TORCH. But Arnold and Spaatz, backed stalwartly by Marshall, persuaded him that was too categoric. Instead, on August 18, day after the Rouen raid, the Eighth was directed to spin off and train a new air force, the Twelfth, appropriately code named JUNIOR, with Doolittle in command. That spirited officer had been scheduled to serve as commander of a 4th Bombardment Wing (medium) for the Eighth. New headquarters staffs for the Twelfth AF and its main branches were hastily put together in America while Doolittle came to PINETREE to talk with Spaatz and Eaker about which units and personnel of the Eighth should go to North Africa. Eaker and Doolittle had met at Rockwell in 1918 and had competed in setting transcontinental records, but this was the first time their careers had intersected.

During his five days in Washington Eaker had been briefed on every aspect of TORCH and was assured both by Arnold and Marshall that VIII Bomber Command would retain enough planes to continue some sort of strategic offensive. For the present, however, his bombers were ordered by Eisenhower, through Spaatz, to swing their attention to the Nazi submarine pens on the Bay of Biscay side of France.[3] The first such attack took place on October 21 against the small port of Lorient, beginning one of the most bitter, but also, from an experience point of view, most useful campaigns VIII Bomber Command would undertake. Its immediate objective was to keep the U-boats in their concrete cabins while the TORCH convoys steamed past from England and from America for the landings at Casablanca, Algiers and Oran, scheduled for early November. But the longer-term goal, desperately demanded by both British and American navies, was interdiction of the submarine attacks on the main transatlantic convoys. From mid-1942 to mid-1943 those attacks were so successful as to threaten all operations out of the British Isles (in the month of October 1942 alone 119 ships were sunk in the North Atlantic).

Eisenhower's air force "requirements" for TORCH were 1,698 planes, of which 454 were from the RAF Eastern Command in the Mediterranean, the rest from those allocated to the Eighth, including Eaker's two most experienced groups of heavies, the 97th and 301st. Since North Africa obviously would lack all training or repair facilities, Arnold suggested that England (i.e., the Eighth) serve as a continuing base. Eisenhower agreed. Then, since TORCH was still regarded as under the European theater of operations (ETO) and Eisenhower was in charge of both, Arnold suggested that he should have a theater air officer in the person of Spaatz. Eisenhower at first demurred, then agreed on October 29, six days before his departure for the Mediterranean.[4]

Down the line at PINETREE all these wrenching rearrangements initially were noticable only in the form of total cessation of letters from home (for security reasons mail was cut off, both ways, for six weeks). Then came stirrings atop Daws Hill, where the Twelfth AF was beginning to take shape. We underlings assumed that JUNIOR would be for the support of the SLEDGEHAMMER landings in France. Rumors then floated that winter clothing was being issued to Twelfth personnel, prompting gossip that Norway would be the objective. Even someone as close to the center of things as the author, just appointed Eaker's aide and promoted to captain, was in the dark. I saw all the papers except those marked "Eyes Only" that crossed his desk and noted many mentions of something designated TORCH and also its euphemism, "a certain operation." But security was preserved intact, contributing greatly to the complete surprise achieved by the actual landings on November 8.

Eaker was of course disturbed by the new delay in the Eighth's promised buildup. On the other hand, he had always recognized that the air force responsibility in England was primarily to make invasion possible, and he understood the rationale for TORCH even though he disagreed with it. He was reassured as well by seeing a copy of Eisenhower's message to Marshall on October 7 saying in part: "The future air program is certainly as important as is the ground. To date we have only developed one real weakness in the daylight bombing program. This is the extreme dependency . . . upon good weather. . . . Aside from this . . . the high-level bombing program has been rather well justified and I believe that the basic effort should remain as a principal U.S. objective."[5] On the other hand, Eaker was dismayed, as were both Spaatz and Portal, by the loss of the 97th and 301st. To keep what he always recognized as the real key to success—good leaders—he carefully cut orders relieving Armstrong as the 97th's CG and reassigning him to A-3 at PINETREE. But he had no objection when Washington chose Claude Duncan as the Twelfth's bomber commander. Similarly motivated, Spaatz carefully arranged the transfer of the 97th and 301st as on loan, still officially assigned to the Eighth, and to be sent back to England when the immediate urgencies in Africa were over.[6]

Meanwhile global events were at turning points in the Pacific, in the Middle East and in Russia, all neatly coinciding with TORCH. Midway had brought the first major defeat to the Japanese in June; on August 7 the U.S. took the offensive in the Pacific when the marines landed on Guadalcanal. In Russia the Germans had reached the Volga north of Stalingrad on August 23 and south of it on September 3, but the triumphant Russian counterattack to encircle the Germans in Stalingrad itself began October 1. In the Middle East the new British team of Alexander and Montgomery, appointed August 6, launched the great battle of Alamein on October 23, with victory over Rommel on November 4, just four days before the Allied assault at the other end of the Mediterranean. World-wide, things were looking up. Even at VIII Bomber Command, struggling to keep a mere 100 heavies operational, there was cause for some satisfaction but also for growing concern. The satisfaction came from executing eighteen more missions before year's end with losses on only ten, the concern from a slow but clear increase in the losses per mission, averaging a total of 6 percent for the period but reaching 8 percent and 7 percent on the last two.[7] Damage to the targets was minimal, especially to the subpens, whose twelve-foot-thick roofs were impervious to any bombs then in existence, but American gunnery claims for German fighters shot down continued very high —so high that they presently were recognized as grossly inflated.

Hansell was back in London in mid-September, having completed AWPD-42 in ten days—a virtuoso performance. To be sure, he had AWPD-1 to build on. But the new plan was substantially different both in estimates of force requirements and in strategy. Destruction of German war industry was still top priority, but explicitly designed to make invasion from England possible. The estimates of the number of planes of all types the U.S. would need to produce in 1943 went up from the 60,000 budgeted for 1942 to 139,000 worldwide. Of these, 63,000 would be combat aircraft for the AAF, organized into 281 groups, of which 78 would be needed for operations from Britain.

In the European theater there were several important changes in target priorities. AWPD-1, prepared before Pearl Harbor, had specified 154 targets in four systems in what was then perceived as order of importance—30 aircraft and light-metals industries, 50 electric power plants, 47 transportation centers and 27 petroleum and synthetic oil industries. Awpd-42 left German aircraft factories at the top of the list but put submarine building yards second, transportation third, electric power fourth, petroleum fifth, followed by aluminum and rubber works.[8]

Eisenhower, Spaatz and Eaker, to whom Hansell brought copies, were gratified, and so was the RAF, though major doubts still lingered

In the PINETREE war room, the author briefs Eaker on the Luftwaffe order of battle. L. to r.: Eaker, Hull (A-2), Lessig (A-3), Lt. Col. Charles Kirk (Exec., A-3), and Sq. Leader Frederick Cockburn (RAF liaison), September 1942.

about daylight bombardment. One doubter was the suave secretary of state for air, Sir Archibald Sinclair, who wrote querulously to Air Marshal John C. Slessor, assistant chief of air staff and widely regarded as having the best mind in the RAF, asking: "What are the Americans doing? What do they intend to do?" and was it not the case "that they have not dropped a single bomb on Germany, outside the range of our single-seater fighter cover?" Slessor replied on September 25 saying in part: "Gen. Spaatz asked me to come up to his Hq. this afternoon to see the new plan. . . . Hansell, who has just got back, told me in confidence that Harry Hopkins was going full out for it, and that the President was extremely impressed by it and also that General Marshall has approved it together with the consequen-

From the war room Eaker would go to the operations room to "lay on" the day's attacks, if any. L. to r.: Hull, Lessig, Kirk, Lt. Col. Cordes Tierman (weather), Eaker, Bubb (chief of staff, back to camera), Lay (historian) and Capt. Travis Hailey (A-2 staff), September 1942.

tial production and manpower implications. . . . The plan involves the provision in this country by 1st January 1944 of 2,016 Heavy Bombers, 960 Medium Bombers and 1,500 fighters. . . . The flow of aircraft is just starting. . . ."

The following day, answering questions raised by Portal, Slessor wrote again to Sir Archibald, reporting: "The Americans have six Heavy Bomber (B-17) Squadrons [sic*] operational and twelve Pursuit Squadrons (six on Spitfires, six on P-38). They are preparing these for a certain operation which severely restricts the rate at which they can now operate. . . . Spaatz has to start at the beginning breaking in the new units as they arrive. . . . The USAAF in U.K. and Northern Ireland as of 21st September amounted to 54,644 officers and men. . . . They intend to do precision bombing in Germany by daylight. This is the basis of their air policy in this theatre. They believe that with their good defensive armament they can do this when they get sufficient numbers. Their early operations lend some support to this belief—the B-17 has shown that it can defend itself and take an enormous amount of punishment. It has yet to be proved whether it is possible to carry the war into Germany by day. But they believe they will and I personally am inclined to agree with them *once they get really adequate numbers.*

"On the President's instructions they have just produced a most detailed and comprehensive plan for the destruction of German war economy, based on the assumption that we shall continue area bombing by night, aimed at devastation, dislocation of normal life and undermining morale while they single out the vital war industrial targets one by one and destroy them by high altitude precision bombing by day. I have seen this plan—while in some respects academic and unduly optimistic, it is a very impressive bit of work and, always assuming it *is* possible to bomb Germany by day, I believe it is a war-winner. . . .

"Meanwhile they are, quite rightly, feeling their way. They keep in the closest touch with us and we have a weekly meeting to discuss current operational problems. They are dividing their operations into three Phases, (1) short-range raids with British fighter protection, (2) longer-range raids using the longer-range American Fighter escort, (3) the long-range raids, including those into Germany, developing

*The RAF used the term Squadron for what the AAF called Group; RAF Group was equivalent to AAF Wing.

the techniques and tactics of getting the bombers in through the enemy fighter crust with fighter collaboration and 'scooping them out' on their return. . . . No, they have not yet bombed outside our Fighter cover because they have not yet passed through Phase I. But they have had several notable fights without fighter escort, in which they have given a good account of themselves, taken a lot of punishment with very little loss and shot down a number of enemy fighters. Unfortunately they have now got to start afresh. . . .

"I think Generals Spaatz and Eaker are good sound Commanders who know their business. Through no fault of their own it is taking longer to get going than they had hoped. But when they do get going they will, I believe, show good results. The whole thing of course depends on whether we shall be able to bomb in Germany by day, which, I think, is still a bigger 'if' than the Americans imagine. . . . Their ultimate policy is to launch 1,500 to 2,000 sorties on each of the 5 or 6 days a month which they think, after careful analysis, will be fit for day operations. If they ever do reach this figure I do not believe the losses will be as great as we now experience at night, fighting the weather and the darkness as well as the enemy. . . .

"If they find their day losses are so severe that they cannot continue to sustain them . . . I think those Heavy Groups already in this country would probably be modified and trained for night work. . . . This would involve a substantial readjustment of American air policy . . . and it might well involve a sharp swing away from this theatre towards the Pacific. . . ."[9]

This astute analysis and accurate forecast put in a few succinct words all the complex problems and questions that would bedevil the Eighth Air Force throughout the crucial year of 1943. At the end of his own copy Slessor penciled, "Portal made no comment on this— JCS." But Portal remained in doubt, as, more importantly, did Winston Churchill. "My own prophecy," Portal wrote Sinclair the next day, ". . . is this: The Americans will eventually be able to get as far as the Ruhr, suffering very much heavier casualties than we now suffer at night, and going much more rarely. . . . If it can be kept up in the face of the losses (and I don't think it will be) this will of course be a valuable contribution to the war, but it will certainly not result in the elimination of the enemy fighter force and so open the way to the free bombing of the rest of Germany. . . ."[10] In the interim the prime minister initially expressed optimism in one of his almost daily communications to the White House. On September 16, for example, he wrote Roosevelt that the first AAF missions had been "most encouraging," but, he added, not "very deep." He went on to urge that VIII Bomber Command be built up so that "together we might even deal a blow at the enemy's air power from which he could never fully recover. . . ." He did not then offer any doubts about the daylight precision doctrine but expressed "some concern" that eight hundred British and American aircraft had been withdrawn from TORCH and suggested special construction priorities for heavy bombers and fighters "for keeping up and intensifying the direct pressure on Germany. . . . The Fortress and the long-range fighter are indispensable."[11]

The PM's words were momentary grist for General Arnold and the basic American bombing concept. But a month later, on October 16, Churchill, reflecting Portal, wrote to Harry Hopkins urging American development of a night bomber, adding gloomily, "I must also say to you for your eye alone and only to be used by you in your high discretion that the very accurate results so far achieved in the daylight bombing of France by your Fortresses under the most numerous Fighter escort mainly British does not give our experts the same confidence as yours in the power of the day bomber to operate far into Germany. . . ."[12] A week later, on October 22, in a memo to the British Chiefs of Staff, the prime minister was even more emphatically negative, saying American day bombers would "probably experience a heavy disaster" when they flew beyond protecting fighters. "We must try to persuade them to divert these energies (a) to sea work, beginning with helping TORCH (including bombing the Biscay ports), and (b) to night work."[13]

Eaker of course was well aware of these somber British doubts. Though he never said so to Portal or Harris, he was himself by no means certain the daylight concept would work once his bombers went beyond fighter cover. Nor did he ever express doubts to the group commanders down the line, for, he said to me, "It would never do for the leader of a military gamble to betray any sign of lack of confidence." The best documentary evidence of his thinking appears in a long memorandum to Spaatz on October 9, 1942, on "the subject of night bombing." Its three closely worded pages reviewed his plans for the day offensive in four phases. "The first, which has largely been completed—demonstration that day bombing can be done without excessive losses and with great efficiency, with close fighter support;

the second phase, upon which we are about to enter, is the demonstration that day bombing can be economically executed using general fighter support and merely with fighter help in getting through the German defensive belt, and to help our cripples home through this same belt; the third phase will include deeper penetrations into enemy territory, using long range fighter accompaniment of the P-38 type in general support only, and continuing the use of short range fighters at critical points . . . the fourth phase will be a demonstration that bombardment in force—a minimum of 300 bombers—can effectively attack any German target and return without excessive or uneconomical loss. This latter phase relies upon mass and the great fire power of large bombardment formations. . . ."

Eaker concluded with three "Recommendations: We continue our experiments along the lines and in the phases indicated above. . . . We adhere to the principle of day bombardment as long as it proves most effective and most economical. . . . We complete our experiments with the flame dampers . . . provide them for all our heavy bombardment aircraft, installing them for any mission which, according to the tactical situation, calls for a night approach, a night return, or a complete sortie under cover of darkness."[14]

The VIII Bomber commander thus kept his options open. Crews were trained for night operations and actually participated in a number of night attacks with the RAF a year later. By then there was no longer any thought of converting the whole U.S. offensive to night; rather, these night efforts were good training exercises for H2S, the blind-bombing device invented by the British and used by the Americans by day when cloud cover made it impossible for the navigator's eyes to see the target.[15]

In the meantime, however, Sinclair had dug further into the subject, coming down to PINETREE to spend a morning with Eaker. He also huddled with Spaatz. And on October 23, the day after the PM's mordant memo, he sent a strong rebuttal. "According to our information," he told Mr. Churchill, "your pronouncement would be decisive in its influence upon American deliberations at this critical juncture. American opinion is divided . . . some want to concentrate on the Pacific; others against Germany; some want an Air Force which would be mainly ancillary to the Army, equipped with Army Support aircraft and employed (no doubt in extravagant numbers) in the theatres of land operations; others want to build up a big bomber force to attack Germany and want to do it by building up an overwhelming force of bombers in this country. Instead, however, of uniting those schools of thought . . . for a decisive attack upon Germany in 1943 and 1944, you will throw these forces into confusion and impotency if you set yourself against their cherished policy of daylight penetration." He added that this policy had, "in the opinion of the Air Staff and my own inexpert judgment . . . a chance of success. . . . It would be a tragedy if we were to frustrate them on the eve of this great experiment."[16]

Air Marshal Harris had also been whittling at the prime minister. He enjoyed ready access to Churchill, both by phone and letter and utterly outside the standard "military channels," though he sometimes shared his communications with Portal. In mid-September Harris somehow obtained and at once passed along to Churchill (with copy to Portal) a gushy memorandum Arnold had written to Harry Hopkins bemoaning the scatteration of American airpower around the globe and concluding, "Little by little our Air Plan has been torn to pieces and today we find that instead of being able to send 2,000 or 3,000 airplanes against Germany from bases in England, we end up with less than 1,000 bombers if present plans are consummated, and if this continued dispersion is not stopped."[17] Churchill had realized for some time that Harris, in the words of Dudley Saward, his biographer, "was now supporting the American day bombing policy."[18] But the PM aimed his fire on Arnold's arguments, replying: "Thank you for sending me General Arnold's paper. I agree about strengthening the Air attack on Germany and also that the Pacific should be regarded as a secondary theatre. Apart from this, I think the paper a very weak and sloppy survey of the war, and I am surprised that with his information he cannot produce something better. . . . The wearing down of the enemy's Air Forces can be achieved from several different directions, just as batteries are dispersed the better to concentrate their fire. . . . It is a great pity that General Arnold does not try first to send us two or three hundred of his big American bombers to expand our Bomber Command, after they have been adapted to night fighting. Failing this, he should send us as many American squadrons as he can to operate from this country, and teach them to fly by night. So far, his day bombing operations have been on a very petty scale. I see he does not approve of the important operation which is pending, which certainly shows him lacking in strategic and political sense, as it is the only practical step we can take at the present time, and one which, if successful, will produce profound reactions."[19]

Such sarcasm was manifestly unfair to the American bombing effort, small though it indeed still was, and Harris was "clearly upset," to quote his biographer again. Never one to hold his tongue, Harris returned to the attack on October 25, the same day Sinclair was writing Portal, and wrote another letter full of grandiloquent language to Mr. Churchill. It began, "My American air friends are despondent," trampled hard on diversions elsewhere and concluded: "You will please pardon my frankness. . . . My information is that matters have now reached so critical a stage that unless you come down personally and most emphatically on the side of throwing every bomb against Germany . . . the Bomber Plan, in so far as U.S. assistance is concerned, will be hopelessly and fatally prejudiced within the very near future for an unpredictable period, if not for keeps. . . . I hope therefore that you will see fit to press your previous demand for U.S. bombers to get on with bombing Germany. . . ."[20]

Churchill did not reply. But Portal, disturbed by the mounting squabble within the air staff and with the prime minister, "subjected his views upon daylight bombing," in the words of the official RAF historians, "to radical revision." Though still far from confident about the American program, he agreed that continued RAF opposition could indeed jeopardize the buildup of the heavy bomber forces in England that they all agreed was imperative. Accordingly, on November 7 he wrote Churchill endorsing the American doctrine. "The probability of success may not be high," he told the PM, "against the results of success if it is achieved. If success could only amount to a tour de force having no real military value, I should be entirely with you in trying to ride the Americans off the attempt altogether. Actually, however, success would have tremendous consequences." Among these he listed wastage of the Luftwaffe, continuity of attack around the clock and air superiority. "It is solely because of the great prizes that would be gained by success that I am so keen to give the Americans every possible chance to achieve it."[21]

But this about face, graceful and cogent though it was, came too late to change the PM's dogged point of view, as all the airmen would discover two and a half months later at the Casablanca Conference. Denis Richards, Portal's biographer, reviewing the controversy from the perspective of four decades after, mused: "Portal *did* have moments of doubt about the American daylight plan during 1942 when the planes were first established here and were not able for some time to hit properly at Germany. These doubts, which were entirely put behind him by November 1942, were communicated to Churchill for information and possible warning, but not in the sense of urgency for alternative courses. Characteristically, Churchill, ever impatient for action, bit more deeply on them than Portal could have intended."[22]

The American leaders, both in America and England, were largely oblivious to this gathering storm. In any case, Spaatz and Eaker were too busy to think about much beyond day-to-day duties, which continued very heavy for them both. Though VIII Bomber Command could be left in Eaker's capable hands, Spaatz had to get three other commands into readiness—fighter, air support and supply, each headed by an army air veteran. Fighter command's boss was Brig. Gen. "Monk" Hunter, who had flown in France in World War I and looked the part, having a heavy black mustache that bent like the wings of a Spad. Brig. Gen. Robert R. Candee, in charge of air support, was different, a quiet, balding officer whose resemblance to an accountant was offset by a bright wit. Supply was under an officer senior to all but Spaatz, Maj. Gen. Walter H. Frank, who regarded his assignment as not big enough and soon moved on. The VIII commanders met weekly with Spaatz to concert operations. But these were much reduced by TORCH. Hunter's few fighters, for example, were Spits piloted by Americans; the P-38s assigned to the Eighth had barely arrived when they were transferred to the Twelfth. Eaker set aside one day a week to inspect his bomber groups, both those going to Africa and the new ones coming in from the States. But most of his time was spent at PINETREE coping with logistics and a stream of important visitors.

One of these was Eleanor Roosevelt, the president's peripatetic wife. She shook hands with each of the three hundred Eighth and Twelfth officers then crammed into PINETREE and was taken to inspect a B-17 at Bovingdon, a nearby field that had been converted by Eaker into a CCRC (Combat Crew Replacement Center) where neophyte crews were taught, among other things, about British weather and communications. Entrance to a B-17 was through a small door near the tail. She nimbly shoehorned her lanky body inside, noted the two gunnery ports further forward and the ball turret beneath, asked searching questions in the compartment shared by the navigator and radio operator and then gamely insisted on tottering on high heels up the narrow steel catwalk through the bomb bay to the pilot's and bombardier's stations in the nose. On the way back down the catwalk her eye was caught by a black rubber funnel and hose clamped to the rear bulkhead. "What is that?" she asked. Told that it was for "the convenience of the crews during long flights," the First Lady declared, "How clever!"[23]

Back at PINETREE she was the guest of honor at a reception attended by a number of British dignitaries and American officers of the Eighth and Twelfth. Among them was the astringent Lady Astor, very much Mrs. Roosevelt's British equivalent as an outspoken and aggressive champion of feminism. She was also a rigid teetotaler. When Eaker offered her a cocktail that afternoon, she snorted: "Certainly not. You people will lose the war if you don't stop drinking."[24]

Another PINETREE visitor, twice, was Eisenhower. He spoke admiringly of the short khaki jacket, gathered at the waist, Eaker was wearing. It had been made for him in London after he noticed the sensible and good-looking battle jacket that was standard dress throughout the British armed forces. (American commanders above a certain level were allowed variations from the standard army olive-drab tunic and "pink" trousers—General Patton's ivory-handled pistols being another example.) A few days before Eisenhower left for Gibraltar he sent Eaker two autographed photographs. Eaker responded with a handwritten note saying he was having one framed for his PINETREE office and "keeping the other for my personal use in office or den when this war is over." He went on to say that he was sending him the jacket Eisenhower had admired. "I hope it fits. If so, please wear it for us. It will save your blouses and be much more comfortable when flying." It did fit and the TORCH commander wore it constantly. This was the origin of the famous "Eisenhower jacket" eventually adopted throughout the American army.[25]

On November 4 Eisenhower, Doolittle and others of the top staff flew to Gibraltar, setting up the interim Allied Force headquarters in its tunnels and caverns. AFHQ's three-pronged invasion of North Africa began on the 8th and went so well at first that a vast sense of relief and success pervaded America and Britain. It was in that calm mood that King George VI set forth on the 13th for his first inspection of American heavy bomber stations. The visit was only ceremonial in purpose, but it led to a significant development in VIII Bomber Command.

That morning Spaatz and Eaker drove up into Norfolk in Eaker's

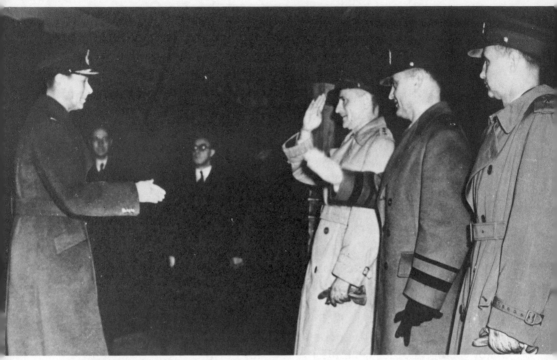

Spaatz, Eaker and Longfellow meet King George VI at the Huntingdon railway station for his first inspection of U.S. bomber bases, November 1942.

Humber, Sergeant Searle at the wheel, while Major Bartlett, Spaatz's aide, sat on one jump seat and I on the other. We rendezvoused at Huntingdon, a small railway station northwest of Cambridge with a dozen British and American staff officers and a gaggle of war correspondents on a typically bleak English winter day. Presently the king's special train pulled in, he descended and all the officers saluted and shook his hand. Then his high-sided, royal red Rolls-Royce brougham was rolled off a flatcar, and we drove away in a cavalcade with Eaker's car in the lead to inspect three bomber bases, all of them B-17s. One, the 301st, was about to leave for Africa. It had executed eight missions out of England for a loss of only one Flying Fortress. The other two were later in action, the 92nd with three missions and one loss, and the 306th, with five and five.

At the first two bases, the 92nd at Alconbury and the 301st at Chelveston, the approach driveways were lined with MP's who stood smartly to attention as our cavalcade drew up to the headquarters entrance, where the respective commanders and key officers of their staffs awaited. Despite English mud, there was a great deal of spit and polish. All went well as His Majesty looked into operations rooms and strolled around a B-17 or two. Only one episode was out of the ordinary.

Among the war correspondents was Margaret Bourke-White, the renowned *Life* photographer. This dashing lady habitually washed her handsome gray hair with a blue rinse. That particular morning she had overdone it, and the hue of her locks was almost robin's-egg. The king caught sight of Maggie, stopped dead in his tracks and was heard to say, "Who is that *extrawdinary* woman with the *extrawdinary* hair?"

When we drove on to Thurleigh and the 306th, whose commanding officer, Col. Charles B. "Chip" Overacker, and Eaker were old friends, no MPs were in sight. Rather, we passed two GIs with unbuttoned jackets, cigarettes dangling from their lips, strolling down the driveway. Neither saluted. Nor was anyone at the door as the general's car came to a stop. I, as the junior aide, nipped out and found Colonel Overacker just as the king's Rolls-Royce pulled in. Thereafter the inspection went pretty much like the others. But there was a notable absence of spit and polish.

We escorted the king back to the railway station, saluted as he entrained and then set off on the two-hour return drive to PINETREE. Bartlett and I remained on the two jump seats, with the two generals behind. Conversation was sparse. General Spaatz was taciturn by nature. Eaker seemed lost in thought as he smoked his habitual cigar. After about twenty miles he spoke up. "Tooey," he said, "I think I'd better relieve Overacker." To which Spaatz replied at once, "Ira, I don't think you'd be making a mistake."[26]

This may sound like a hasty decision based on superficial evidence, even though the 306th's losses were higher than the other groups. But Eaker was relying on a knack he learned while General Fechet's executive years before and that he mentioned in a 1973 magazine article about Fechet: "He had an uncanny sensitivity for military morale. He often said he could look at the soldier at the main gate and know what he would find inside the post—an efficient, clean, disciplined group, or a dirty, dispirited, inefficient mob."[27]

In the case of Overacker and the 306th Eaker waited six more weeks during which the group's record, measured by number of bombs on target and by B-17s lost, became the worst in VIII Bomber

Command. On January 4 he asked Frank Armstrong and Beirne Lay to accompany him to Thurleigh. "Things are not going well there," he said, "and I think we ought to take a look." Arriving at the gate in his Humber flying the red flag with two white stars of a major general, they were waved through by a sentry who failed to salute. Overacker showed them around. "As we visited hangars, shops and offices, I found similar attitudes as seen at the front gate. The men had a close attachment to their commander and he to them. But there was a lack of military propriety and I could not help feel that this might be a part of the problem that was being revealed in combat."

Returning to Overacker's office with the three men, Eaker closed the door, for he always tried to keep unpleasant matters as private as possible. "Chip," he said, "you'd better get your things and come back with me."

"Frank," he said to Armstrong, "You're in command. I'll send your clothes down."[28]

In the next forty days Armstrong's strong, steady, disciplinary hand turned the 306th around completely, making it the best group in the VIII Bomber Command and the first to drop bombs on Germany itself. Promoted to brigadier general, Armstrong handed on command of the 306th to his operations officer, Lt. Col. Claude Putnam, and returned to PINETREE and Eaker's next assignment for his favorite pinch hitter. All of this became the basis for the bestselling postwar book and film, *Twelve O'Clock High,* written by Bartlett and Lay.

About the time King George was making his first VIII Bomber Command inspection, General Arnold returned to his role of fretful critic. He was unhappy about the command's reduced frequency of operations, seeming to feel that the new groups, often incomplete, that he was sending over could go into battle at once. He ignored the need to train them in British communications, in new American formation procedures and, most difficult of all, in coping with British weather. Spaatz sent Arnold a blunt response demanding "a full understanding of conditions of operations in this theater. . . ." Eaker as usual was more explicit in his own replies. Spaatz, more nearly Arnold's age and long his heir apparent, could be terse and categoric. Eaker, more articulate and more diplomatic by nature and distinctly junior in age and status, had to be deferential. He wrote in one letter: "The weather during the past month has been, by long odds, the

In a post-war ceremony, Eaker awards the Distinguished Service Medal to Frank Armstrong.

most prominent reason for the small number of missions. . . . The directive under which we have operated limited target selection to one small geographical area. . . . Units of the Twelfth Air Force have been given first priority on organizational equipment, spare parts, personnel replacements and aircraft replacements. . . . No single aircraft or combat crew has been received as replacement. . . . Nearly 100 of the heavy aircraft now available in this group are in the hands of units not yet operational. . . . The 44th Group has been here three weeks and it has not yet received any of its transport or bomb handling equipment. . . ." In another letter Eaker told his impatient boss that, yes, it would be possible to send newly arrived bombers into action at once but that it would be suicide for them and fatal to the daylight bombardment program. "Please don't let anyone get the idea we are hesitant, fearful or lazy," he asked. "Every human thing is being done every day to make this pace as fast as possible."[29]

Arnold abated the criticism for a while but found another way to keep up the pressure on Eaker. On November 18 he sent over a newly uniformed first lieutenant named Reagan "Tex" McCrary, a vigorous, self-confident young man who had been editorial chief of the New York *Daily Mirror.* Arnold described him, accurately as it turned out, as "capable of writing up and presenting to the American people the true potentialities of air power which are factually supported by operations in your theater. . . . These facts can best be presented by news stories originating in London or the African theater. . . . You personally, Ira, can do this job from your theater much better than anyone else here in the United States. . . . For example, once a week you might broadcast to America a consolidated round-up of the air war as being fought all around the globe. . . . Such a broadcast, I am sure, would rapidly attract an audience far larger than that of any news commentator. . . . Understand that my sole desire is to present facts, or conclusions that are borne out by facts. Extravagant claims will not engender the confidence in us which is justified and which the people are entitled to have. . . . For obvious reasons, please treat this letter as one of strict confidence between you and myself. I am sure you can realize the effect of its misinterpretation."[30]

Eaker made good use of McCrary in public relations. But he himself refrained from trying to be another Edward R. Murrow, sticking to his pledge "not to do much talking until we've done more fighting."

Spaatz, in his own still unclear position as air officer for the ETO, decided on a quick trip to the Mediterranean to clarify it with Eisenhower and to inspect the Twelfth. He took with him his WW I combat associate and now chief of staff, Brig. Gen. Asa N. Duncan, and also Hansell and another key figure in air war planning just in from Washington, Brig. Gen. Laurence S. Kuter. On November 17 the party departed on the flight out around France and Spain to Gibraltar in a squadron of the 97th. Spaatz and Hansell flew in one B-17, with Hansell carrying a thick batch of secret papers in a weighted briefcase attached to his wrist. Duncan, with a duplicate set, was in a second B-17—Kuter in a third. About an hour and a half later, far at sea, the number three engine in Duncan's B-17 began to smoke and then burst into flame that engulfed the whole right wing. As the others in the formation watched helplessly, the engine fell off and Duncan's B-17 crashed while attempting to ditch. Kuter's plane circled low over the tossing water and he saw a few bodies and a yellow raft with, perhaps, someone in it. He broke radio silence to alert British Air Sea Rescue, but no survivors were found.[31]

In Gibraltar Spaatz and Eisenhower came to some tentative conclusions on organization during their first day together. Then Spaatz flew off to see Doolittle and get the feel of air operations in the Mediterranean, leaving Hansell and Kuter to work out the details. Returning to Gibraltar three days later, he found Eisenhower still hesitant about the concept of a unified air command bridging both the forces in England and North Africa. But another message from Arnold was insistent. Spaatz, Hansell and Kuter were back at WIDEWING on November 23 for a meeting with Eaker at which the immediate arrangements were explained and new assignments given.[32] Spaatz would return to North Africa to set up a new theater air force headquarters, taking with him as his new chief of staff Col. Edward P. Curtis, a vice president of Eastman Kodak who had flown fighters in World War I. Hansell and Kuter both wanted combat command opportunities, and Eaker gave Kuter the 1st Bomb Wing (H), replacing Claude Duncan, and Hansell the 3rd Bomb Wing (M), just being activated. Eaker would be acting commander of the Eighth Air Force "until formal orders are published." He appointed Longfellow to be his successor at PINETREE.

The "formal orders," recommended by Spaatz and Eisenhower and approved by Arnold and Marshall, arrived on December 1, the same day Spaatz left for North Africa, to be Eisenhower's "deputy for air operations," as the allied commander defined the assignment in a December 3 message to the British Chiefs of Staff, adding: "His position is not repeat not that of a commander because there is no time to set up separate communication systems, staff arrangements and so on. Major General Ira Eaker is simultaneously being directed to take temporary charge of U.S. air operations in England. This arrangement is to meet an emergency and does not repeat not in any way interfere with the prerogatives of the Combined Chiefs of Staff to decide upon an eventual organization that will provide the greatest flexibility and efficiency in the operation of air forces throughout the Mediterranean. I should like to point out that in connection with that broad question the related one of coordinated employment of U.S. air forces in the U.K. and TORCH must be simultaneously considered. We have already derived great benefit from my control, as a U.S. commander, over all these units. Both questions in my opinion must await the successful outcome of the current battle."[33]

13

"... in the course of action circumstances press for immediate decision and allow no time to look about for fresh data, often not enough for mature consideration."

—CLAUSEWITZ, *ON WAR*

W HEN EAKER formally took command of the Eighth Air Force on December 1 he of course had to leave his beloved PINETREE and the close-knit staff of 150 officers he had woven together in the nine months since he and his initial party of six had arrived in England in February. They were all devoted to him and found his brief, extemporaneous farewell talk in the abbey's oak-paneled mess very moving. In addition to complimenting and thanking them all and acknowledging the bigger responsibilities he now faced, he put his chief emphasis on the regret he felt at moving further away from the fighting outfits where his heart would always remain. He asked them all to give his successor as bomber commander, Colonel Longfellow, their full loyalty and support.

Behind him he left his chief of staff, Bubb, and all the general and special staff department heads, taking with him to drab, sprawling WIDEWING only four officers—Lay, historian; Lessig, assistant A-3; Beasley, A-4 specialist; and the author, his aide. Spaatz had offered Park House in Wimbledon for his personal residence but Eaker despatched me to find something more cheerful and big enough for a half-dozen officers, to qualify it as a mess. He foresaw that his new assignment would call for a lot of entertaining.

Elaborate entertaining at a time when the bitter war was far from won may sound rather like Nero fiddling while Rome burned. But Eaker knew he still had two other campaigns to wage besides the strategic offensive against Germany. He had to maintain close and cordial relations with the British at all levels from the king down. And he had to keep on persuading the river of high-level visitors that the still unproven concept of high-level precision bombardment by day would work beyond the fringes of France he was already attacking with encouraging results.

It was to the Royal Air Force that the small U.S. Army Air contingent in those early days turned for help for such major facilities as airports and many minor ones too. The RAF was superbly generous and efficient; among its services was a subdivision of air ministry in charge of housing, supervised by Air Marshal L. G. Hollinghurst, director general of organization. He promptly delegated an amiable former civilian, Squadron Leader Selwyn Lezard, to help me scout. In only a day or so Lezard turned up what was described in the realtor's leaflet as, "A remarkably fine, medium-sized house of character and great charm, built and equipped regardless of cost and in exquisite taste." Known as Castle Coombe, it was located in a fashionable, beautifully landscaped section of Kingston Hill named Coombe Warren where Eisenhower's hideaway, Telegraph Cottage, was a block away. There were two acres of gardens and a tennis court plus a gate directly onto the eighteenth tee of the Coombe Hill golf course, where Eaker often played in the long English twilight when summer came. The house was a three-story Tudor design with "handsome lounge, fine reception suite (4 rooms), 12 bedrooms, 4 bathrooms." It even had "central heating," a rarity in England. And there was a bomb shelter we never bothered to use. Castle Coombe was empty of furniture, and this also the RAF provided in another week—nice furniture too! But the walls were devoid of pictures. So I trotted around to the Tate Gallery, most of whose great collection was in storage in the country away from the Blitz, and borrowed about fifty paintings and prints of reasonable chic. The final requirement was staff, and here too the RAF put on a virtuoso performance. We were provided with a Welsh housekeeper named Gwyneth Jones, a cook, two serving maids and an upstairs maid who did our beds. These were on the second floor. On the third were rooms for Miss Jones and the maids plus two of the three British enlisted men General Eaker took with him from bomber command —Govier, his batman, and Searle, his chauffeur. Stroud, his secretary, was billeted in an RAF barracks.[1]

This of course took some time. So Eaker parked at Park House while getting installed at WIDEWING and meeting the staff he inherited from Spaatz as well as establishing relations with the three other commands now in his charge. One new appointment had to be made at once—his chief of staff. He chose a quiet, self-effacing, older brigadier general he had known for many years and who was in Ireland running one of the dozen operational training units (OTUs) Eaker had set up to receive the new groups from America and sharpen their talents. His name was Charles C. Chauncey and he turned out to be ideal for the job, staying with Eaker until the war was over. The role of a chief of staff varies with the character and strength of the general he serves. Some generals treat a chief of staff as almost an alter ego. Eaker, being exceptionally decisive, energetic and knowledgeable, regarded the post as more that of an executive assistant—not a yes-man, which he could not condone in anyone under him, but a cautious, careful paper shuffler who could be counted on to get orders distributed with a minimum of fuss and then followed up with gimlet-eyed scrutiny.

TORCH continued to preempt center stage in the ETO's operations, with every day bringing new requisitions from Spaatz for units or officers. Claude Duncan, for example, had not lasted long as the Twelfth Air Force bomber commander (he took to the bottle) and was relieved by Doolittle on November 23. To replace him Spaatz asked for Eaker's close friend from the trans-Pacific voyage in 1919 —tall, red-headed Col. Charles T. Phillips, who was showing promise in VIII Bomber Command as CO, 3rd Wing. Hansell took his place in England while Phillips took over from Duncan in Africa on December 11 only to be killed four days later while bombing El Aouina airport near Tunis.[2]

The shortage of senior commanders for the Eighth throughout 1942 and well into 1943 was an even more difficult handicap than the shortage of airplanes and crews. Seniority counted in the army, as always, and the senior officer in a unit ordinarily commanded it. But none of the handful of seniors available to Eaker had battle experience. Peacetime experience in flying, in discipline and in mastering air doctrine was immensely valuable, to be sure. But only in the cauldron of combat could the real commanders emerge. Some, like Asa Duncan or Charlie Phillips, perished before they could be fully tested. Others, like Cousland and Overacker, quickly failed and were sent home. Either way the gaps were filled by whoever was both senior and handy. Longfellow had a smattering of combat when Eaker chose him as his successor at bomber command and he had shown himself to be a brave leader in the few, small missions he accompanied as commander of the embryonic 1st Wing, once saving a gunner's life by putting on a tourniquet. But the chief reason for his appointment was his seniority.

Hansell and Kuter, both new brigadier generals, outranked Longfellow when they returned from Africa to wing commander positions—one reason Eaker wanted Longfellow to get his star also. Coming along that fall and winter with new groups were many young, able and ambitious colonels or lieutenant colonels, some of whom proved to be the leaders indispensable to the Eighth's eventual huge success. The one destined for the greatest fame was thirty-five-year-old Col. Curtis LeMay, he who had navigated so skillfully to the *Rex* in 1938 and, in late November 1942 arrived in England with the 305th Bomb Group of B-17s. But he too had to prove himself as a group commander before moving to bigger assignments, and Eaker was forced to rely during that lean winter on Longfellow, Hansell and Kuter to carry on with VIII Bomber Command. Eaker of course kept an eye on the striking arm of the Eighth, but he had also to supervise fighter command, air support and supply as well as administer the large WIDEWING staff. Hardly had he begun when, twelve days after the change of command, he was ordered to North Africa himself—not to stay, but for urgent conferences with Spaatz and Eisenhower.

After a fast start, Operation TORCH had stalled in its dash for Tunis, further east on the Mediterranean shore, and the North African campaign bogged down for a weary winter of ground action through German fire, mountains and mud, and of air action, including the heavy bombers, largely in support of the troops. This in turn stalled Arnold's and Eisenhower's concept of unified air command of British and American elements. Spaatz continued as Eisenhower's air officer but without command authority except over the American

Just back from an attack by 97 B-17s, of which three were lost, against a German airfield in France, May 13, 1943, Brigadier General Hansell stands with Colonel Curtis LeMay, CO of the 305th Bomb Group.

units, which still included the Eighth. With the battle in Africa unwon, Spaatz was obliged to draw still more from Eaker's already diminished force. The two generals, in short, had much to consider and review.[3]

Expecting to be away less than a week, Eaker flew out of Bovingdon in a B-17 on December 13, taking me along and also Col. Leon Johnson, the young A-3 he had inherited from Spaatz. We were joined by Maj. Gen. Frederick Browning of the British airborne army, who was hitchhiking. But a heavy, continent-covering storm forced us to land almost at once, at Portreith, a coastal command station near Land's End and just south of Tintagel, King Arthur's legendary last castle. We were grounded for a full week and took refuge at the Red Lion Inn on the stone-faced main street of the drab town of Truro, snug in a nook of the bare Cornish hills. The delay would have made most men fretful with frustration, but Eaker simply said: "I've been grounded by weather before. There's nothing we can do about it, so we might as well relax." There was little else to do, and there was no heat in the Red Lion aside from one fireplace on the ground floor that was not lit until evening. We spent most of the time fidgeting in twin beds in our upstairs room reading whatever we could find. Every afternoon Eaker insisted on an hour's hike through the continuing downpour of drizzle or sleet. The only real pleasure each day was the evening meal, for the Red Lion's food was surprisingly good, especially a local fish—Dover plaice. And the conversation at table was exceptional, for General Browning's wife was Daphne du Maurier, the novelist, and she came down to share the time with him.

Finally off on December 20, we completed the 1,400-mile hop to Oran without incident, met Spaatz and Doolittle and flew on the next day to Biskra, "the oasis to end all oases," as I wrote in my diary that night. Here were now stationed the 97th and 301st with two groups of P-38s some 200 miles south of Algiers on the very fringe of the Sahara, where the hard-packed sand made a natural airdrome big enough for all the airplanes in the world, with perfect weather in addition. The oasis, about a mile square, stood up green and fresh-looking from the sand as we flew in. The dispersed airplanes were a mechanized oasis of their own about a mile to the south. We landed in a cloud of dust, jumped into the omnipresent jeeps and rattled off to the nearest clump of palms, about an acre in size and separated from the main part of Biskra. In the center of this little patch of trees stood a box of plaster with a Byzantine door—the headquarters. All around were the pup tents of the men, dry and neat in the crisp and breezy air. The jeeps paused but a moment before continuing into the main oasis, which was parceled into sections separated by head-high mud walls through which the road twined. Dozens of filthy Arabs, wearing an assortment of rags, sprawled in the dust along the roadside for their noon-day siesta while others packed dates in cellophane-covered boxes ("No more dates for me," was Eaker's reaction). A rubber-tired jitney pulled by two boney horses moved out of our way—the local bus line. A bare, stinking acre on our left proved to be the Arab cemetery, where the dead were just laid out and covered with gravel. In front of a police booth an unshorn Poilu leaned on his rifle. We turned into a gateway marked Hotel Atlantique and found ourselves in a lovely garden with an ornate, four-story tiled building at the end. It all looked straight out of Hollywood, and I said as much. "This is where Marlene Dietrich and Charles Boyer came to make *The Garden of Allah,*" commented our driver casually. "They stayed at this hotel."

After a lunch of Algerian white wine (good) and British rations (poor), we returned to the airfield to present medals to the men of the 301st for the missions out of England. General Spaatz pinned them on as I passed them up to him in the proper order and read aloud the individual citations. With generals Spaatz, Eaker, Doolittle and Gordon Saville and three trim French officers standing at attention, a huddle of Arabs looking on, and a formation of planes circling overhead, it made a picture suitable for the frontispiece of a modern *Beau Geste.* My diary recorded that "the men all looked healthy and happy, keyed up by their almost daily missions against Tunis and Bizerte. Biskra offers them little enough in entertainment. There are no movies and but one whore house (two French and four Arab girls). Curfew is at six each night. Out of the 13,000 inhabitants of Biskra only 1,000 are white, and the rest are devoted to the Arab habit of stealing. So a pretty constant guard has to be maintained."

Just before we left there was a brief council between the two group commanders and the three U.S. major generals—Spaatz, Eaker and Doolittle. The group commanders asked when they could be allowed to ignore their orders and go for a better target encountered on the way—a ship concentration in a small harbor, for example. Doolittle replied: "It's always your privilege to go after a target of opportunity just so long as you're sure it's a worthwhile one. But be careful you don't hit something of no importance—laid up French ships, for example."[4]

As Eaker noted later in long talks with Spaatz, air operations in North Africa resembled touch football when compared with the big league operations out of England. There was negligible German fighter resistance and much less need for tight defensive formations. Flak was the only real hazard, forcing bombers to stay high. Battle damage was minimal, but even normal maintenance was a problem because of minimal servicing facilities. Spaatz was obliged in consequence to retain first option on replacement B-17s for the Twelfth instead of the Eighth. Neither officer approved of using heavy bombers for essentially tactical purposes, though they recognized there were few other targets available until the north shore of Africa had been cleared.

Eaker by now was fully reconciled to the reality that TORCH demanded priority for the time being. He explained later: "I was personally unsympathetic with the business of Africa. . . . But the decision was made to the contrary, and after that decision was made I didn't quarrel with it. If, after I'd made a decision, I'd had a subordinate who didn't do everything to carry it out enthusiastically, I'd have fired him. I'd have expected the over-all commander to do the same with me. . . . [Spaatz] was the fellow who decided how to divide the forces up. . . . His view was the same as mine. He would have been much happier to continue the war against the Germans in Europe, as against Africa. But the essential decision was made, and he had to go along with it. He carried it out enthusiastically. But I know we saw eye-to-eye. . . . It was a great relief to me to know that he felt as I did."[5]

From Biskra we flew to Casablanca, mostly to check on the airfield, where our B-17 sank to its hubcaps in the mud as we tried to take off, delaying us a full day while six two-ton trucks and two hundred men took hours to pull it out. On Christmas Eve we returned to Algiers and the startling news that Admiral Darlan, the devious French turncoat, had just been assassinated. We were billeted at the house Spaatz had requisitioned on the ridge above the city—an elaborate Moorish villa with red brocade walls, glass bead curtains in the arched doors and an original Rosa Bonheur painting of a cow. In the evening there was a buffet supper for six—three generals, Spaatz, Eaker, Doolittle, two colonels, Ted Curtis, now firmly ensconced as chief of staff for Spaatz, and Bradford Gaylord, who had been aboard the submarine that had just enabled French Gen. Henri Honoré Giraud to escape from Vichy France; and one captain, me. After dinner Spaatz said, "Well, what about some poker?"

But Doolittle did not play poker, and the game is no good with fewer than five at the table. Spaatz turned to me and said, "Jimmy, you play poker, don't you?"

I had participated in a little penny ante at PINETREE, so I recklessly allowed that, yes, I could play poker. Two generals, two colonels and one captain then sat down at a round, felt-covered table that looked as if it had frequent use, and I, as the junior officer, was given the task of being "banker," handling the distribution of chips and keeping the score. I gulped when I saw that the smallest round chip was for a dollar, with others of different colors for $5 and $25 as well as narrow salmon-tinted rectangles valued at $100 each.

As luck would have it, I began getting unbeatable cards and, after about an hour, had a big stack of chips in front of me while the score I kept showed the others in debt to the bank for well over $200 apiece. Horrified that this unseemly behavior would poison my military future, I deliberately set out to lose by such foolhardy steps as betting heavily on two pair or drawing to inside straights. But each time my last card would be the one I needed, and my stack of winnings kept on growing. By midnight, when we were interrupted by a brief German air raid, I began to realize that none of the others took my winning amiss and that such high stakes were normal for them. Every now and then Eaker would wryly say, "I'll bet another salmon." We paused to go out on a balcony to watch the tracers make patterns in the sky above and hear the bombs thud, without much damage, in the port below. The ack-ack made a wonderful din going up and a soft rustle as the shrapnel fell back on the bushes in the garden.

After the Luftwaffe went away we returned to the poker table and played until about two in the morning, when Spaatz, the senior officer present, said: "I guess we'd better stop. What's the score, Jimmy?" Eaker and Gaylord by then were about even, but I collected over $1,000 from Spaatz and Curtis. Whereupon Spaatz turned to Eaker and said, "Ira, you've brought a ringer with you!" To me Spaatz gave an order. "Jimmy," he said, "you are hereby appointed banker for all the command poker sessions from now on." It was a role I did indeed fill and that led to many mighty tussles and close observation of many colorful people in revealing circumstances. For Spaatz and Eaker, destined from then until 1945 to be whacking at German military muscle from opposite sides of Europe, made it a policy to meet every six weeks on one side or the other, often on the occasion of the capture of a major city. Each general would bring key staff officers for genuine "command sessions" by day, followed by informal ones around the green-baize table until late hours at night.

For two days following Christmas Eaker was busy at the new AFHQ in the St. George's Hotel in Algiers conferring with Eisenhower, Spaatz and others. Eaker was quietly sizing up Leon Johnson during these talks and liked what he saw. He also encountered an old friend, an army air colonel named Frederick L. Anderson who had a football line-player's frame and easy manner, a genial face and a strong, quick mind. Eaker had known him since the twenties, when Anderson was a first lieutenant who cracked up in San Francisco

Bay, caught tuberculosis from the cold water and was retired. Back in uniform, he had lately been head of the Bombardment School in the States and was overseas briefly on an "inspection trip" that actually cloaked his search for a combat assignment. Eaker took a shine to him at once, offering him a ride back to England and a spot in the Eighth. He had in mind replacing Kuter, who was requested by Spaatz for staff work in the Mediterranean. That was alright with Eaker, for he had sized up Kuter as a crack intellect and administrator but more interested in command than in combat. Kuter had not gone on any missions out of England in his brief stint as commander of the 1st Wing, and that was no way to win Eaker's confidence.[6]

We flew off on the 27th, heading first for Gibraltar at low level over the languid Mediterranean and spooking a German sub, which crash-dived, about an hour before Gibraltar's great bicuspid bit through the skyline ahead and we banked into the single airstrip between the fortress and Spain. Three battleships and two aircraft carriers were tied up at the mole while Spits tumbled playfully through the cloudless sky. Shrouded in the hot haze of tropic distance, the Spanish mountains rose ten miles away across the Bay of Algeciras with, so it was widely believed, German guns crouched on their summits.

On the 28th Eaker found time for a sad session with Claude Duncan, still under him because the 97th and 301st Bomb Groups were still part of VIII Bomber Command, telling him there was no spot for him in England and he should go home. Then we were shown all through Gilbraltar's tunnels, peaks, gun ports and pillboxes by the governor, British Maj. Gen. Frank Mason-MacFarlane, a ruddy, lean old boy who wore shorts, carried a swagger stick and led us at a trot whenever we piled out of the three cars in the caravan to inspect caverns full of ammunition or offices or, in one instance, a huge reservoir of water. There were stalactites on many ceilings, and water dripped steadily through the porous stone, making the air dank and the footing slippery. It looked impregnable, but not a pleasant place for a fight.[7]

The flight back to England as 1942 neared its end was routine, except that the bomb bay was full of oranges. There was one exciting moment off the Brest peninsula when I spotted four planes in formation coming at us from dead ahead and sang out on the intercom. Everybody jumped to the guns, but the formation turned out to be

U.S. reinforcements on the way to Africa—three P-38s and an escorting A-20. They passed below and a mile to the left, looking especially deadly above the leaden sea. On January 2 Eaker was back at his desk and as a first order of business got off a three-page letter to Maj. Gen. George E. Stratemeyer, chief of the Air staff in Arnold's office. He touched on many operational matters concerning both the Eighth and Twelfth Air Forces and asked for Anderson, who had gone back to the U.S. at once, to take Hansell's place as CG, 3rd Bomb Wing (M), not yet ready for action. He said he had given Kuter's key spot as CG, 1st Bomb Wing (H) to Hansell, adding: "There is a great dearth here of suitable Group Commander, Wing Commander and senior Air Force and Bomber Command staff personnel. We are doing the best we can with what we have. . . . It is now perfectly apparent that a Bombardment Group is as good or as bad as its Commander. The success of bomber operations is almost completely dependent upon this key individual. . . ."

Eaker then introduced a new subject of great and growing importance—how long should combat tours of duty last? He wrote: "Within the next sixty days we shall face a very critical period. We will arrive at the time when many of our combat crews will have to be relieved by reason of having completed their operational tours. They will be tired, war weary and punch drunk and they will have to be relieved whether there are replacements or not. As Tooey cabled you, he, Doolittle and I went over the situation very carefully and decided that the operational yardstick should be 30 missions and 200 hours maximum, with 25 missions and 150 hours minimum, giving the tactical commanders leeway within these limits. On the mission before the last, while I was away, we sent out 1,000 combat crew members and lost 100 of them, killed, wounded or missing. It is quite evident, therefore, that a combat crew must be very good or very lucky to complete an operational tour by the above yardstick. We cannot expect them to do more efficiently. Our losses would be on a much lower percentage if we had a larger operating force."

In closing Eaker put the finger even more specifically on the shortage of aircraft. "Tooey decided that the first 28 B-17 replacements would be kept by the Twelfth Air Force in North Africa and the next 46 sent to us here. In view of this it appears that our Groups operating from the theater will be down to about 18 planes per Group or less before the replacements begin to arrive so that they can be built back to 35. . . . Please rush replacement aircraft and combat crews as fast as you can."[8]

While in Africa Eaker had kept close track of the Eighth's operations out of England and saw that the 306th was still faltering, as was the 44th, equipped with B-24s. Before flying to Africa he had told Johnson, "I have got to get a new commander for the 306th." Johnson, though he had no experience with either the B-17 or B-24, had asked for consideration for the post. Like most high-ranking officers with wings, he too itched for combat command. But Eaker had replied: "No, I can't let you go here. I am going to send [Frank Armstrong] up there," which, as already recounted, he did in person on January 4. On the previous day, January 3, both the 306th and the 44th were clobbered, the 306th losing two bombers out of seventeen over the target (St. Nazaire subpens) and the 44th losing three out of eight, not over the target but ignominiously through crash landings in Wales after poor navigation on the way home. That afternoon Eaker called in Johnson and gave him the 44th.[9] As with Armstrong at the 306th, though the details differed, Johnson mastered the assignment. He went on to lead the 44th to distinction and to win his first of four stars as well as the Medal of Honor.

In making these two brilliantly successful changes at the group level Eaker was, in effect, usurping Longfellow's role as bomber commander. The latter was, to be sure, brand new in the post at PINETREE that Eaker had left in person but not entirely in habit. And Longfellow had no way of spotting an Anderson or a Johnson, not to speak of a Kuter or a Hansell. It was, therefore, temporarily logical for Eaker to treat him less as a commander than as an operations officer. But it became increasingly clear that Longfellow did not have the stuff to be a good bomber commander, and his appointment remains a clear blemish on Eaker's record—one compounded by his stubborn refusal to relieve his old friend more promptly than he finally did.

Longfellow got off to a bad start at PINETREE on the occasion of the first bomber night he hosted, back in August when Eaker returned to Washington for five days and Longfellow had to pinch-hit for him. The hapless colonel called in the three officers who had managed the first bomber night and told them: "We are going to have another bomber night and it's gotta be good. Kirk, you will do the organization; Raymond, you will do the script; Gray, you will lead the spontaneous singing. Dismissed." Gray recalls, "We decided right then to name the show, 'It's Gotta Be Good—by Command Of.' "[10]

Thin-faced, tense and irritable, Longfellow, in Hansell's words, "had the general attitude of a British Sergeant Major . . . constant criticism and domineering demand." The PINETREE staff referred to him behind his back while he was still a colonel as "The Screaming Eagle," and after he became a brigadier general, "The Shouting Star." Hansell commented further. "Longfellow was a poor choice. . . . [Eaker] kept him in that position too long. But one of Ira's great strengths was also an occasional weakness, and that was his loyalty to his subordinates. He had a fine loyalty both upward and downward and he realized, I think, some of the problems that Longfellow was wrestling with since he had had to deal with them himself, and I think he went all out to give support to Longfellow in the prosecution of an extremely difficult operation. . . . When Kuter arrived with Arnold's blessing to receive a command, Eaker put him in command of the 1st Bomb Wing. Kuter was probably senior to Longfellow at that time, as I was. Eaker asked me if I had any objection to subordinating myself to an officer who was junior to me. I was so anxious to be in Bomber Command I would work for anybody. I said sure, I would be glad to do that. Perhaps Kuter felt the same way. I suspect that Kuter wanted to become Bomber Commander when Ira left to become Air Force Commander. . . ."[11]

If that was so, it replicated a wish Kuter had felt a year before, when, according to Robert Lovett, assistant secretary of war for air, he had hoped to be the original VIII bomber commander and was passed over by Arnold and Marshall.[12] Be that as it may, there were stiff relations between Eaker and Kuter that had repercussions later when Kuter returned to Washington in mid-1943 to be one of Arnold's key assistants for the duration of the war. He was a tall, cerebral, haughty man whose brilliant abilities at staff work and planning had caught Marshall's eye and led to his becoming, at age thirty-six, the youngest general officer in army air. In Africa after leaving England Kuter distinguished himself on Spaatz's staff, particularly in helping refine AAF structure into strategic and tactical formations, and rose, following the war, to four-star rank, higher than either Eaker or Hansell. But he never proved himself in combat.

The new year brought occupancy of Castle Coombe and a pat-on-the-back letter from Arnold. Eaker, though grimly aware of how skimpy his force was, looked toward to a few weeks of concentrating

on tactics, including such imperatives as more guns in the nose of the
B-17, which the Luftwaffe had discovered to be its weak spot. But his
intentions were abruptly altered by a signal from Eisenhower on the
night of January 13. It came just as Eaker was beginning dinner with
the first guests to be entertained at his new house—Sir Louis Greig,
and his two daughters. Sir Louis, once equerry to the duke of Wind-
sor when he was Prince of Wales and then briefly King Edward VIII,
was a neighbor, very jolly, and also well-connected throughout the
English hierarchy. His two girls, both in uniform, had the peach
complexion and beautiful manners so characteristic of well-born
British women. "Midway through the soup," my diary records, "the
General was called to the telephone, but not until our guests had left
some hours later did he reveal the bomb-shell message—return to
Africa at once!"[13]

Eisenhower's message read: "Proceed at earliest practicable time
to Casablanca for conference, reporting there to General Patton.
Conference involves method of air operations from United Kingdom."[14]

14

"Victory smiles upon those who anticipate the change in the character of war, not upon those who wait to adapt themselves after the changes occur."

—GIULIO DOUHET, *THE COMMAND OF THE AIR*

THE CASABLANCA Conference, called at Churchill's request and snubbed by Stalin, turned out to be one of the war's most decisive, especially in regard to the use of air power. But Eaker had no knowledge of it whatever prior to Eisenhower's short signal, whose second sentence of course instantly alerted him that the Eighth Air Force was again in danger. The threat could be a revival of the idea that all American strategic bombing should be switched to the Mediterranean, where weather allegedly would be more favorable, or a new plea from the navy on behalf of the Pacific. He did not suspect it would be a renewal of the British attack on daylight precision tactics, for he had learned informally from his close friends in the RAF that Sinclair, Portal, Slessor and Harris were now supporting him. Slessor had, in fact, drafted a "Note on Air Policy" for Sinclair to send Churchill on December 18 that included the statement: "The view of the Air Staff is that the Americans and the RAF will be able to bomb Germany in daylight. Given sufficient strength to saturate the defenses, they think it quite possible that our losses on the aggregate will be no heavier than by night, and that the results, combined with night attack, should be doubly effective. No one can say for certain until it has been tried—and tried repeatedly.

216

It can however be said with confidence that it would be a profound mistake to try it prematurely, with insufficient numbers and with crews inadequately trained. . . ."

Slessor continued: "Americans are much like other people—they prefer to learn from their own experience. If their policy of day bombing proves to their own satisfaction to be unsuccessful or prohibitively expensive they will abandon it and turn to night action. . . . But they will not do this until they are convinced of the necessity. And they will only learn from their own experience. In spite of some admitted defects—including lack of experience—their leadership is of a high order, and the quality of their aircrew personnel is magnificent. If, in the event, they have to abandon day bombing policy, that will prove that it is indeed impossible. I do not believe it will prove to be so. . . ."[1]

To arm himself for all contingencies, Eaker told me to lug along to Africa three brief cases filled with a new report prepared by Hull: "The First 1,100 Sorties of the VIII Bomber Command." Hull's document, complete with statistics, photographs and intelligence analysis, was the first significant body of data on the efficacy of high-level daylight bombardment of pinpoint targets in the face of stiff antiaircraft and fighter defenses. The report was encouraging in many ways but weak in one. For it had taken the Eighth AF four months to accumulate a total of one thousand heavy bomber sorties over nearby targets in France whereas the British had put as many as one thousand heavies over a target in Germany in one night as early as May 1942. The American effort looked puny by comparison.[2]

Before starting south the next day Eaker telephoned Portal's office for some clues about the "conference." He learned that Portal was already at it and thus knew that it was "high-level" indeed. He was not surprised to have no further background, saying later: "If you didn't need to know something, then you weren't let in on it. . . . That's how carefully security was kept." He called Longfellow and asked for a B-17 to meet us at Portreith, and we set off in the Humber in late afternoon to drive again the weary way to Land's End. Though only some three hundred miles, it was slow going through the blackout and took until five A.M. This time the trip out around the Bay of Biscay was uneventful. We arrived midday, January 15, and were driven to the Anfa Hotel and a compound of nearby villas about five miles south of Casablanca on a bluff with a fine view of the magnificent Atlantic surf. But not until dinner that night with

Eaker and Harriman could Arnold escape from meetings to disclose the startling news that, as I wrote in my diary, "the President is under pressure from the Prime Minister to abandon day bombing and put all our bomber force in England into night operations along with (and preferably under the control of) the RAF."[3]

For once Eaker lost his customary aplomb. "General," he snorted, "that is absurd. It represents complete disaster. It will permit the Luftwaffe to escape. The cross-Channel operation will then fail. Our planes are not equipped for night bombing; our crews are not trained for it. We'll lose more planes landing on that fog-shrouded island in darkness than we lose now over German targets. . . . If our leaders are that stupid, count me out. I don't want any part of such nonsense!"

Arnold chuckled and replied: "I know all that as well as you do. As a matter of fact, I hoped you would respond that way. The only chance we have to get that disastrous decision reversed is to convince Churchill of its error. I have heard him speak favorably of you. I am going to try to get an appointment for you to see him. Stand by and be ready."[4]

Another powerful AAF figure entered the fray at Casablanca a day after Eaker—Frank Andrews from Cairo. Andrews, last mentioned in this narrative when Marshall put him on the general staff in Washington as G-3 in 1939, had gone from there to Panama to command its defenses after Pearl Harbor, when it was widely thought the Japanese might attack the Canal. After that worry abated, real trouble developed in the Caribbean with highly successful U-boat forays against Allied shipping. Andrews, in conjunction with the navy, had ably set up bomber patrols and then, in November 1942, was shifted by Marshall to Egypt as CG, U.S. forces in the Middle East. Marshall now wanted Andrews's advice on how to structure unified command in the Mediterranean and in the ETO, and Arnold at once got him into the day vs. night crisis as well. Eaker spent most of his second day at Casablanca conferring with Arnold and Andrews. He did not get to see Eisenhower immediately but did talk with Commander Butcher, his aide, whose diary for January 17 records: "Eaker wanted [Ike] to know that he was fearful the British would want to emulate Ike's policy of a unified command in North Africa for air by having the same in England, but under Air Marshal Harris. Eaker said he could work very happily with Harris, but the

Eaker, still a two-star, and his four-star boss during one of Arnold's
early 1943 visits to PINETREE.

change was much more fundamental. Our daylight bombing was at
stake."[5]

After he had made other requisite courtesy calls and gotten the
feel of the problem at hand, Eaker returned to our villa, number
fourteen, aptly named Le Paradou, and went to work. We sat at one
end of the dining table while he roughed his thoughts in pencil on
lined paper, occasionally asking me to fish out facts from Hull's
"1,100 Sorties" file. Though facing preparation of the most important
presentation of his life, he showed no sign of fatigue or nerves as he
calmly scribbled, stopping every now and then to say hello to brass
hats like General Patton, who strolled in wearing his pistols. Patton
was not a conferee but was in command of the two battalions of spic
and span troops (all helmets and boots were polished) protecting the
Anfa Hotel and adjacent villas. About four acres in extent, the site
was surrounded by a barbed wire fence strung with tin cans of
pebbles every two feet and armed sentries nearly as frequent. Gen.

Harold L. Alexander, Montgomery's boss in the Desert War, was another visitor. So was Harry Hopkins, recently married and looking relaxed ("Marriage has done him good," said Eaker). At the other end of our table Robert E. Murphy, the lanky State Department expert who had been America's chief secret agent in North Africa, huddled with Harold Macmillan, the British minister resident, trying (fruitlessly as it turned out) to evolve an "understanding" between generals De Gaulle and Giraud. Murphy referred to the latter as "Papa Snooks."[6]

Eaker's paper, the first draft of which he completed with journalistic fluency in about three hours the evening of the 17th, was entitled "The Case for Day Bombing," and began without any wasted words, "American bombers should continue to bomb by day for the following reasons. . . ." He listed seven on one page for the prime minister's eye but prepared another sixteen pages of supporting arguments for Arnold to use in the CCS meetings that would follow whatever broad decision Churchill reached. The seventh reason concerned cooperation around the clock with RAF night attacks; its supporting paper concluded ringingly:

> Day bombing is the bold, the aggressive, the offensive thing to do. It is the method and the practice which will put the greatest pressure on Germany, work the greatest havoc to his war-time industry and the greatest reduction to his air force. The operations of the next 90 days will demonstrate in convincing manner the truth of these conclusions. We have built up slowly and painfully and learned our job in a new theater against a tough enemy. Then we were torn down and shipped away to Africa. Now we have just built back up again and are ready for the job we all cherish—daylight bombing of Germany. Be patient, give us our chance and your reward will be ample—a successful day bombing offensive to combine and conspire with the admirable night bombing of the RAF to wreck German industry, transportation and morale—soften the Hun for land invasion and the kill.[7]

Eaker left me to get the document proofed and typed. The next morning he edited it for final typing and we then flew off to Algiers to spend the night of the 18th with Spaatz in his Byzantine villa. My diary records that "he and Col. Curtis at once sought revenge at poker and nearly got it from me. . . . I barely scraped through on the plus side—$25. But General Eaker . . . upheld our poker legend by winning another $1,000."

Spaatz accompanied Eaker back to Casablanca on the 19th for

more staff talks and the word from Arnold that Spaatz, Eaker and Andrews all had short appointments with Churchill the following morning in that order. My diary records Andrews quoting the PM that Eaker "nearly convinced me." Eaker's own recollection of the historic meeting was more detailed: "He came down the stairs resplendent in his Air Commodore's uniform. I had been told that when he was receiving a naval person he wore his navy uniform— the same for the other services—but this was the first time I had seen him in Royal Air Force uniform. This struck me as a good omen.

"The PM said that he understood I was very unhappy about his suggestion to our President that my Eighth Air Force join the RAF Bomber Command in night bombing, abandoning daytime bomber effort. Without awaiting my response he continued, 'Young man, I am half American; my mother was a U.S. citizen. The tragic losses of so many of our gallant crews tears my heart. Marshal Harris tells me that his losses average two percent while yours are at least double this and sometimes much higher.' "

Carefully avoiding the temptation to correct this claim (the actual figures for the preceding three months were 2.54 percent U.S. losses vs. 4.7 percent British), Eaker later wrote: "I had learned during the past year while serving in Britain that he always heard both sides of any controversy and for that reason I wished to present a brief memorandum, less than a page long (it was well known that he seldom read a 'minute' of greater length, having it 'briefed' instead) which I hoped he would read. Mr. Churchill motioned me to a seat on the couch beside him and began to read, half aloud, my summary of the reasons why our daylight bombing should continue. . . . At one point, when he came to the line about the advantages of round-the-clock bombing, he rolled the words off his tongue as if they were tasty morsels. . . ."

After the PM had finished Eaker's memo the two of them chatted informally, for they were good friends who liked, trusted and respected each other. Eaker once more stressed the benefits of round-the-clock attacks. Finally the PM handed his memo back to him, saying: "Young man, you have not convinced me you are right, but you have persuaded me that you should have further opportunity to prove your contention. How fortuitous it would be if we could, as you say, bomb the devils around the clock. When I see your President at lunch today, I shall tell him that I withdraw my suggestion that U.S. bombers join the RAF in night bombing and that I now recommend that our joint effort, day and night bombing, be continued for a time."[8]

Churchill was as good as his word. "I decided to back Eaker," he wrote in his history of the war, "and his theme and I turned around completely and withdrew all my opposition to the daylight bombing by the Fortresses." Noting that Eaker had given him the credit for saving the daylight program just as it was coming into its own, Churchill added, "If this is true, I saved them only by leaving off opposing them."[9]

Persuading Churchill to change his stand (even though the PM still did not believe the Eighth Air Force could achieve its goals) ranks as Eaker's greatest single accomplishment. Arnold noted: "We had won a major victory, for we would bomb in accordance with American principles, using the methods for which our planes were designed. After that I had a talk with the President and with General Marshall on the same subject and, as far as they were concerned, the matter was settled. Everyone said, 'Go ahead with your daylight precision bombing.' "[10]

The decision had far broader implications than air tactics alone. It also had immense influence upon the entire prosecution of the war and upon the postwar situation. Hansell commented: "If [Eaker] had bowed to the RAF and British requirements to go in for night bombing the whole course of the war would have been changed. It would have been quite impossible to defeat the German Air Force, for instance. And ultimately, of course, the German Air Force built up night defenses that were just as strong as their day defenses. . . . If it had not been for Ira's tremendous strength of character in persevering I think the war would certainly have taken a very different course."[11]

Almost certainly the Normandy invasion would not have been attempted or would have failed. Without the second front and its drain on German arms, Hitler might have stabilized the Russian front. Or, if he failed to stop the Russians, they would not have stopped at the Elbe or perhaps even at the Rhine. Russia would then have had total domination of the European continent. Similarly, if air war fanatics like Harris had had their way and succeeded in knocking Germany out of the war without an invasion, there would have been nothing to stop the Russian armies from sweeping all the way to the English Channel. It is arguable, in short, that support of daylight bombing was not only the Casablanca Conference's most important military decision but also that it had vast geopolitical consequences.

At the time, other decisions were more immediately significant. There were many of them. Sicily (code name: HUSKY) was chosen, to Marshall's woe, for invasion in 1943 instead of ROUNDUP across the English Channel. Eisenhower was relieved as commander of ETOUSA and appointed CG of the newly constituted North African Theatre of Operations (NATOUSA). Andrews was given Eisenhower's old post at ETOUSA, which delighted Eaker and all airmen. Air Marshal Arthur Tedder, a brilliant success in the Middle East, was designated Air C in C, Mediterranean, with Spaatz under him as commander of the North African Air Force, comprising the U.S. Twelfth and the RAF Desert Air Force and Eastern Air Command. Spaatz did not want the post, asking to be returned to England as CG of the Eighth. But Arnold insisted, pointing out that it was only a transitional situation and a step toward the unified air command Arnold had long sought. The Eighth was freed of any further major obligation to the Mediterranean, and Eaker ceased to report to either Spaatz or Eisenhower, though he of course maintained close liaison with both.[12]

The Casablanca Directive to Eaker and Harris began, "Your primary object will be the progressive destruction and dislocation of the German military, industrial and economic system and the undermining of the morale of the German people to a point where their armed resistance is fatally weakened," thus neatly straddling the different objectives of Eaker and Harris and between day and night. Both forces claimed to seek military or industrial targets, but only the RAF regarded morale as a valid objective. A later paragraph was more explicit and more directed to Eaker. "You should take every opportunity to attack Germany by day, to destroy objectives that are unsuitable for night attack, to sustain continuous pressure on German morale, to impose heavy losses on the German fighter day force and to contain German fighter strength away from the Russian and Mediterranean theaters. . . ."

Everybody at the Casablanca Conference concurred that two arms of German military might posed alarming immediate danger to the entire Allied effort—the U-boats and the Luftwaffe. They were designated the first and second priority target systems for both Eaker and Harris. Third came transportation, fourth oil plants, fifth other targets in war industry. Choice of individual targets was left much more to the wishes of the two commanders. Eaker, for example, was no longer obliged to pour bombs on the impregnable concrete sub-pens in France but could go after submarine assembly yards wherever they existed. Overall supervision of the two commands was carefully left vague and not, as some Americans had feared, given to Harris. The directive said American bombers would be under the operational direction of the British in target selection but that their tactics would remain entirely under Eaker's jurisdiction. Though not precisely saying so, the language left the top strategic air authority in England in the hands of the chief of the British air staff—Portal.[13]

"Peter," as his intimates called Marshal of the Royal Air Force Sir Charles Portal, was tall, lean, with a somber face and an inordinately long cleaver of a nose, which from the profile looked like the bow of an Arctic icebreaker. He was a direct thinker and very strong-willed. Arnold, his opposite number, said of Portal: "He was one of the most brilliant of the British Chiefs of Staff. He had a remarkably agile and logical mind. He was far-sighted in his military planning, and on the many problems we had in common we worked extremely well together."[14] Portal was less generous in his appraisal of Arnold, saying: "He had trouble following the strategic arguments: he never talked except on air. He had trouble holding the interest of the group. He was a grand fellow; never had any trouble with him. The American battled effectively but quietly for his Air Forces, often relying on the affability that had won him the nickname 'Hap' to get his way."[15]

This was not entirely fair. Arnold had remarkable strategic foresight insofar as air operations were concerned and made a deliberate point of staying aloof from ground or naval controversies. As Forrest Pogue, Marshall's biographer, put it just before quoting Portal's criticism, "Arnold, although given increasingly greater freedom by Marshall to control air operations, was content for the most part to remain in the Chief of Staff's shadow." On a later page Pogue elaborated, "In 1943 and 1944 recurrent efforts were made to make the Army Air Forces an independent service. The Chief of Staff depended on Arnold, and some of his assistants who had served on Marshall's personal staff, to help block this move until after the war. To quiet the demands of strong Congressional partisans of the independence move, Marshall gave Arnold increasing autonomy. The airman carefully followed the Army's line at Allied conferences and refrained from divisive statements to the press, and Marshall saw to

Eaker and his strongest supporter, Air Chief Marshal Sir Charles
Portal, RAF chief of staff, 1943.

it that Arnold got nearly all he wanted. Soldiers complained of
preferential treatment given airmen—but Marshall backed the Air
Forces' commander. In return Marshall felt that he received Arnold's loyal support."[16]

Portal, who had been the RAF bomber commander in 1940, had
been a steadfast proponent of a strategic bombing offensive against
Germany from the beginning of the war. When the U.S. became
belligerent Portal strongly supported the buildup of the Eighth Air
Force. But he had temporized until the last minute in 1942 in his
support of the daylight effort, yielding "with some mental reservations," as Slessor wrote, to the official views of his Air staff "by the
time of Casablanca that the Americans *would* be able to bomb Germany by day." Slessor explained further: "Portal, of course, did not
believe that long-range fighter escorts were practicable and was assuming that the American day bombers would be unescorted. . . . I
was wrong in my belief that they would be able to do so before the
escort fighter came on the scene. But somehow I was always convinced that they would pull it off. I admit I was only backing a very
strong hunch—which one must sometimes do in war. Perhaps it was
just as well that I did. Some who have studied the contemporary

records far more carefully than I have had an opportunity of doing think it possible that, if I had not taken that line at the time, the American bomber offensive in Europe might have been still-born."[17]

Once having swung behind Eaker's campaign, Portal never wavered. He became the Eighth's strongest British advocate throughout 1943, both in England, where he and Eaker saw each other a great deal and became fast friends as well as military partners, and also at subsequent conferences of the Combined Chiefs, where it was often Portal, not Arnold nor Marshall, who was able to plead most effectively for more heavy bombers for the Eighth against the demands of other theaters. There is much irony in the paradox that Eaker, whose biggest problem in 1942 had been to fend off British efforts to divert American heavies into night action, in 1943 found that his biggest problem was to get the U.S. to send him enough airplanes and men to be able to carry out the daylight campaign at all. Portal, somewhat in the role of devil's advocate, could speak up more freely on this topic in the CCS meetings than either Arnold or Marshall. Arnold, as cited above, was careful to take his guidelines from Marshall. Lovett, always a powerful participant, added another slant: "Whenever the Chiefs of Staff got together and started to make things tough for Marshall, Hap would rush in as a running guard and blast out interference for him. He liked doing it and Marshall respected him for it."[18] But on other occasions the shrewd American chief of staff found it expedient to let Portal run the interference— particularly when the question under discussion involved a British sphere of influence. Portal, like Marshall, never forgot that striking directly at Germany was the prime objective.

Meetings of the chiefs themselves were accompanied by many other meetings of subcommittees and advisors, involving many generals, admirals and lesser ranks along with civilian specialists from the heads of state on down to clerks. In many ways the meetings resembled those of a university board of trustees. The business sessions were very businesslike. But in between and especially in the evenings there was casual camaraderie and relaxed jollity, helping materially to cement the hearty Allied teamwork. Casablanca meals took place in the Anfa Hotel, often followed by evening strolls on the beach, with, as one example, Arnold and Churchill chatting as the latter paddled along in his blue jumper, otherwise known as his "zoot suit." The Anfa was new, starkly white and surmounted by a terraced restaurant with tables for six to eight apiece. It had previously been occupied by the German Armistice Commission, which supervised relations between the German conquerors of France and its not-quite-conquered North African colonies, and had blackout curtains that still bore the bold German imprint of their origin. The curtains were pulled across because Casablanca was well within range of any Nazi bombers that might be based in Spain or southern France—a possibility that bothered Eisenhower. The setting, the exciting daily tasks and the heady sense of victory ahead made for happy spirits and served to knit the two Allies in bonds of personal friendship as well as military partnership. Nobody pulled rank. Almost everyone disclosed his lighter side.

One night, for instance, a major (whose name I failed to note) and I were sharing a table for six with Arnold, Eaker, Tedder and Slessor. Someone pulled out his "short-snorter," and there was much banter when the major was caught without his. The "short-snorter," a wartime fad, consisted of bills from each country you visited pasted together end-to-end. The game was to collect as many signatures as possible on your own roll of bills. Anyone who had forgotten to bring his had to fork over a dollar to everyone present. Portal and Mountbatten at once jumped up from the next table to claim their share of the major's forfeits. Shortly after, as we were having coffee, Colonel Bean, who was in charge of Casablanca's Medouina airport, wandered by and paused to talk about the difficulties of building a ramp for Roosevelt, known as "A-1" in the Anfa code, to descend from his C-54 without being seen. It was the first airplane the president had been aboard since he flew to Chicago in 1932 to accept the Democratic nomination. Bean recounted also the impossibility of concealing Churchill's arrival. They halted his plane at the far end of the runway, intending to whisk him into a sedan. Not at all! He insisted on inspecting the plane and talking leisurely to a swarm of mechanics. When Secret Service men sidled up to him he trumpeted, "Scoo! Don't bother me!"[19]

Winston Churchill's frequent unpredictable behavior was often deliberate and wise and sometimes capricious and foolish. What then explains the great fuss he made about day bombing after his own air staff had come out in support of it? Partly, no doubt, it reflected Portal's recently abandoned uncertainty. But there must have been more to it than that. Could it have been a grandstand play to help divert Marshall and the Americans from concentrating on a cross-Channel invasion instead of the further drive in the Mediterranean that Churchill wanted? Eisenhower was nonplussed, sending an "Urgent Cable" to Marshall on January 13, the same day he ordered Eaker south, which began: "All of us here are at a loss to explain difficulty hinted at by Arnold over the phone this afternoon. All U.S. bomber policies in the United Kingdom were carefully coordinated with the British. . . ."[20] Denis Richards, Portal's biographer, probably put his finger on it. In his biography he concluded that: "Churchill in fact was in one of his moods of periodic reaction against the whole bombing offensive, British and American, which he had helped to launch. Knowing the current difficulties, he had been irked by the whole-hearted reliance still placed upon it by the Chiefs of Staff. Possibly he had been irked, too, by Harris's pressure upon him to 'reassert' to the Americans that 'our War Plan is to bomb Germany soft as the first step to victory.' He was also presumably unsettled by Portal's own doubts about the Americans' ability to bomb Germany effectively. But still more, the Prime Minister's mind was now captivated by the opportunities opening up for campaigns on land. . . . It was no longer true that 'the Bombers alone provide the means of victory.' . . ."[21]

To this Richards later added pungently: "You must always see Churchill as the heir of Marlborough and a would-be deviser and master of great military movements. These only became possible with the availability of U.S. forces, and TORCH showed the pattern of what would be his future preoccupation. Thereafter his heart was in Italy and OVERLORD (as long as Marshall didn't rush us into disaster in 1943) and strategic moves in the Far East, and this is basically the pattern to which everyone, including Arnold and Portal, adhered after Casablanca, with the air used primarily as the softener for OVERLORD—indirectly for most of the time, directly later. Only Harris, I think, seriously thought that, in 1944, bombing alone might bring a decision. Churchill knew the bombing had to go on, but it was no longer his prime hope or concern, and he was quite prepared—unfairly—to distance himself a bit from it at moments when it incurred odium, as at Dresden. . . ."[22]

With the presentation to the PM accomplished, Eaker's task at Casablanca was complete and we left within the hour, flying that afternoon to Marrakesh, the new departure point for the run to England. And there we sat for the next four days waiting for weather. It was, however, very different from the similar wait at Truro, for

Marrakesh is a fabulously interesting spot. The ancient seat of Moorish kings, it sits in the desert at the base of the fourteen thousand-foot Atlas Mountains, whose snowy crests make a beautiful backdrop for the adobe wall and tiled minarets of the city. We had rooms at the Hotel La Mamounia, a vast, modern building that, I noted in my diary, "in pre-war days was to French Morocco what Palm Springs is to California." Just inside the twelve hundred-year-old city wall, the hotel's red clay bulk was crowned with lovely, terraced bedrooms whence we looked out over orange groves to the snow.

Each morning Eaker and I ate oranges and eggs in bed while the hot African sun poured in upon us. Then he would usually go off to the American consulate or the airbase to catch up on messages, after which we would wander through the town afoot or in a carriage, seeing the strange sights in the marketplace (snake charmers, tumblers, dancers, mosques, palaces, tombs) or haggling in the narrow, wattle-covered alleys of the bazaar (leather goods, slave bracelets, silver poniards, cloth of gold, jewels, rugs, fruit). One day we called upon a local *sherif* of great wealth. The old Arab sat on his leather hassock fingering his white whiskers while his veiled wives brought in gorgeous five hundred-year-old velvet robes, fists full of jade, emeralds, crystal and ambergris, and chests full of gold and silver trinkets, all at very low prices. We bought many things. His house was a typical Moorish palace—a square around a patio with tiled walls, rich rugs, low tables inlaid with ivory, colored glass lamps and, in the front hall, a cow and her droppings.

We finally took off one morning at 2:30, briefed for a ten mph wind from the NW. Actually we encountered a sixty mph wind from the SE, and, since the plane was above the thick overcast, there was no way to realize the drastic change. The consequences were nearly fatal. Only the fact that our B-17 had two extra tanks of gasoline in the bomb bay (along with the usual crates of fruit) saved us from going down in the drink. The peril was discovered when it came time to change course to the east to head into Land's End. The radio operator could not get any response, and there were no holes in the clouds to come down through for a quick survey. The pilot did not dare head due east very long for fear of running clear into France and the Germans, so he presently gritted his teeth and headed down, not knowing what land, or how high, might lie beneath. I stood behind him in the nose as we eased down into the murk—3,000 feet;

2,500; 2,000; 1,500; 1,000 and still no clearing. Not until the needle indicated 500 feet did we emerge over whitecaps and an angry sea.

Turning east again, we flew on the deck for an hour and a half (at least 300 miles) before we saw land ahead—and then no one knew what land it was. After we circled for 20 minutes over its neat farms and low hills Eaker decided it could not be France since no one shot at us, nor England since there were no landing fields. That left only Ireland. We turned north and flew up the west coast under the low ceiling in very rough air while the gas gauge dropped. Eaker then took over. Having flown over Ireland before on visits to the OTUs, he remembered the general location of the nearest airport, whereas our navigator not only had never been to Ireland but lacked a map. Under the general's calm hand the B-17 at last touched down at Eglinton, a fighter field on the far northern shore of Northern Ireland. We had been in the air nearly 12 hours and had but 30 minutes gas left.[23]

Back at Castle Coombe and WIDEWING on January 26, Eaker at once lived up to his promise to Churchill by sending the first U.S. heavy bomber mission into Germany. With good weather predicted over Germany for January 27, orders went out the night before for a "maximum effort" against a truly important target—the submarine-building yards at Vegesack, near Bremen and about 20 miles inland. So puny was the Eighth that only 91 bombers from six groups could be dispatched, led by Armstrong and his 306th BG. To minimize interception they flew low and far east over the North Sea soon after dawn from five bases—Thurleigh, Molesworth, Bassingbourn, Chelveston and Shipdham—before climbing to 25,000 feet and heading for the enemy coast. By then the weather had gone to pot and it became evident that it would be impossible to see, much less hit, Vegesack. Armstrong swung to the alternate target—the naval base at Wilhelmshaven, on the coast itself, which was thinly veiled with cloud. But only 58 of the heavies were able to find their target and drop their bombs. Opposition was surprisingly ineffective by comparison with the Luftwaffe over France. An estimated 50–75 German fighters attacked, of which U.S. gunners claimed 22 shot down for the loss of one B-17 and two B-24s. The actual German fighter losses turned out to have been only seven fighters, and the bomb damage was skimpy. Nonetheless, Americans had at last bombed inside Germany, their loss percentage of bombers dispatched was only 3.3 percent and the bombing had been accurate enough to prove that, with more planes and a bigger bomb pattern, important damage would have been achieved. It was encouraging. Eaker called the mission "fairly successful."[24]

But the sense of euphoria and clear skies ahead (at least in terms of policy) he had brought back from Casablanca was short-lived indeed. Two days after the Wilhelmshaven attack he wrote a three-page letter to Spaatz to report its success and to comment morosely on other developments. "When I reached the office," he said, "I received the sad blow that you had decided to take all of our P-38s. We had the 78th Group ready to accompany our bombers by about February 1, if this had not happened. Obviously, our bombers will have to go alone for at least another six weeks. I think this . . . the most serious blunder we have made in a long time, and I have a sneaking hunch that you agree. However, when we get a bad order, we carry it out with the same diligence we would a good order.

"The other blow I received on return was an order from ETO to ship the 91st and 303rd Groups at an early date. Since you had not mentioned this in conversations I had had with you, I was led to believe you had no such intention. . . .

"We are bombing Germany now with less than a hundred heavies —something you and I both agree should not be done. . . . I am still hoping that you can avoid a further depletion of our little Air Force here. . . ."[25]

15

"No army produces more than a few great captains."

—GENERAL GEORGE C. MARSHALL

W HEN ANDREWS arrived in England on February 4, 1943, to take command of the European theater of operations in place of Eisenhower he was astonished and appalled to learn how small Eaker's air force actually was and how slow the flow of reinforcements. Like Eaker he had taken it for granted that the forthright Casablanca Directive endorsing daylight bombardment would be matched with the support to carry it out. The next day he cabled Marshall: "Please transmit message to Arnold important he visit this headquarters for discussion on build-up of Eighth Air Force. . . . Bomber strength deteriorating rapidly to point where raids cannot be made in sufficient strength to disperse anti-aircraft strength of enemy. Unless better results can be obtained US Air Forces adversely involved. Improved results are possible with more general support from fighters and larger sorties in my opinion. Press conference today showed marked interest in night versus day bombardment. . . ."[1]

Arnold was in China conferring with Generalissimo Chiang Kai-shek and generals Joseph W. Stilwell and Claire Chennault. In his absence and after talking with Stratemeyer, Marshall sent Andrews a message (drafted by Stratemeyer) notable for flat-footed bluntness and seeming insensitivity to the broader issues involved. It read: "We concur fully with your viewpoint to employ present insufficient forces on daylight missions deep into enemy territory is too costly and accomplishes too little. Any decision either to postpone effort until adequate forces become available or to use present force against targets in France and low countries or to try out night bombing will be supported here. Bombers have been allocated as directed by the Combined Chiefs of Staff. Bulk of force which was set up for England and Joint U.S., British agreement resulted in sending to North Africa. Since further diversion to Africa, Asia, Pacific is considered necessary and has been agreed to, many months will elapse before sufficient force for deep penetration against objectives in Germany can be built up."[2]

This devastating statement put Eaker and Andrews in a real bind. Both knew that it was utterly impractical to "postpone" attacks against Germany, for that would lead to further skepticism and disillusion about the validity of the daylight program and could well provoke the British to reclaim all the airports and facilities they had turned over to the Eighth and to force its conversion to night bombing under the RAF. For Harris's "de-housing" campaign was going strong and the Germans were howling. Nor did either of the two veteran American fliers have any real interest in night action, even though Eaker continued to train a few squadrons of his tiny bomber force for night attack and to develop flame dampeners and other modifications of the B-17 and B-24 needed for operations under the cover of darkness. So they continued to make daring, small raids against Germany when weather permitted, while putting the bulk of their offensive against the German U-boat pens and adjacent facilities on the French coast as the Casablanca Directive had prescribed.

It was a very risky procedure, revolving not so much around choice of targets as around the hallowed military doctrine of "preservation of force." Eaker explained in a postwar interview, "It became my duty to make certain that we did not, through any unwise or careless or hasty action, sacrifice our whole force. We could have taken, say, our first 100 bombers out at such a rate and against such distant targets that we would have lost them all in ten days, because on some of those targets we lost 10% on a mission. But I always said and reported to General Arnold that I would never operate that force at a rate of loss which we could not replace. If he would send us a bomber group each week of 18 planes, I would make certain that we lost only 18 planes that week or as nearly to that as I could. I always made it clear to him that I would never completely destroy the force because then we would be out of business and our effort would have been condemned as a failure. There was some criticism in Washington because we did not operate at a faster rate, but, by and large, I think General Marshall and General Arnold eventually understood the concept and felt that it was proper. . . ."[3]

In another postwar interview Eaker amplified this line of thought. "We knew we had to prove our case gradually. We had a pretty good idea of German defenses, and we knew we could lose our whole cause by some imprudent act. . . . A number of people thought we ought to go out every day. They just weren't acquainted with English weather. They weren't acquainted with the type of target weather we had to have to do accurate bombing. I kept saying, and General Spaatz supported me, that we wouldn't suffer heavier losses than our rate of build-up. We were not going to see that force get smaller; we were going to see it get bigger. . . . We had another thing to deal with which most people didn't understand. . . . We had to build up confidence in the crews that the operation we planned and visualized was a wise, practicable operation. If the commanders had been foolhardy and had issued orders which the crews knew were unwise or unsound, we'd have had a bad morale situation—and morale was one of the big elements in the operation. If the crews believed in their mission and thought they could accomplish it, they could do it. If they lost confidence, all was lost. . . ."[4]

Arnold and his staff in Washington were slow to accept this rationale, but the Eighth Air Force combat crews caught on very quickly. As Eaker's best and most distinguished combat commander, Curtis LeMay, recorded:

> Morale sagged in late January and early February. Then all of a sudden everybody bounced back to normal and started working hard. . . . All the combat crews had been sitting around, figuring out what their chances were. And the chances weren't very good. They got their statistics together, crudely but with terrible effect, and discovered that we were averaging an 8% loss on each mission. The tour of duty (then) was 25. Taking it from there, a 4% loss would still leave any theoretical crew completely shot down—or shot up —with the completion of their specified 25 missions. If there were a 2% loss on every mission, a crew at the start would have a 50-50 chance of finishing their tour and going home. Beyond that, the ratio declined speedily. . . . In the end everybody was going to be shot down.
>
> This kind of talk wasn't lamenting on into the still watches of the

days or nights solely at Chelveston. It was all over. Every commander in the Eighth was reporting the same thing. Someone sat down there at WIDEWING, General Eaker's headquarters, and told him that it was on the graph: the last B-17 would take off for its last mission early in March.

General Eaker said, "O.K. I'll be on it."

This impressed those who heard it, although that wasn't what Ira had in mind especially. There could be no upsurge, no new invigoration throughout our Bomber Command, until it happened *within the Command*. That was the way it did happen.

The psychology went like this: "Well, we're going to get killed anyway. What's the use of worrying about it?"

People shook themselves as if they'd been a little tired or groggy, and were properly ashamed; and then they got up and said, "Let's get cracking. It might as well be this mission as the next mission. So—what the hell?" Thus it didn't make any difference any more. Everybody stopped worrying and everybody got back into the act.[5]

LeMay became the greatest fighting leader in the AAF, going on so many missions that his men called him "Old Iron Ass." He was very tough and very demanding, but the crews quickly saw that this stern discipline was keeping their losses low and achievement high, so they respected and followed him without question. He was also an inspired innovator, largely responsible, as one example, for the "combat box" formation that became standard for the entire Eighth Air Force. Aerial formations, unlike naval, can be staggered vertically as well as horizontally. LeMay evolved a group formation in which the lead squadron of six heavies would approach the target at, say, 24,000 feet with the second squadron slightly behind and to the right at 25,000 feet and the third squadron to the left and behind at 23,000. In sharp turns away from the target after bombing, the entire group would pivot on the lead squadron while the other two crossed over from right to left and from left to right, corkscrew fashion. The next step was to stagger three such groups similarly into what became known as a "combat wing box." In addition to greater mobility it increased defensive strength by maintaining close formation at all times and providing clear fields of fire for the six gunners in each bomber.

LeMay was also responsible for evolving another tactic that became standard operating procedure (SOP)—"salvo bombing" on radio signal from the lead bombardier instead of each plane dropping

LeMay, CG, 3rd Bombardment Division, Eighth Air Force, briefing his wing and group commanders, June 5, 1944, the day before Normandy. Nearest the camera in the front row is Col. Frederick Castle.

its bombs as its own bombardier thought best. And he demanded that formations fly straight and level during the tense final approach to the aiming point despite the great temptation to weave and thus, some thought, avoid flak. Before leading the 305th Bomb Group's first mission (against the U-boat pens at St. Nazaire on November 23, 1942) LeMay spent many hours studying an old ROTC artillery manual and basing his

> calculations on probability of hits from a French 75-millimeter cannon at a target the size of a B-17 at a range of 25,000 feet (four to five miles straight up) for the Jerry flak gunners with their roughly comparable 88-millimeter flak batteries. The answer came out to 273 rounds fired per hit on a B-17. By golly, I told myself, those are pretty good odds. I am going to fly straight and level on the bomb run even if it takes *minutes* instead of seconds. Otherwise

236

we might as well stay home. . . . The bombs landed on target. No losses to flak. It worked. . . .[6]

But flak, though it caused a lot of damage, was never as mortal a threat to the Eighth's bombers as the German fighters. From their first cautious probings in late 1942, the Luftwaffe pilots developed many skillful and courageous methods of attack. The most effective of these in the first half of 1943 was head-on, sometimes one at a time but also in flights of three or more. For the B-17s with which the Americans began operations in Europe, though vastly improved over those the British had tried out two years earlier, were skimpily armed in the nose, having only one or two 30-calibre machine guns poking through sockets in the plexiglass screen, behind which the gunner had to compete for space with the bombardier. It was a hair-raising experience for B-17 or B-24 pilots to see FW-190s or ME-110s boring in at them from straight ahead and above ("twelve o'clock high" in gunner talk) at a closing speed of 600 or more mph with their guns winking brightly from each wing. Swooping past as close as 15 feet, the Germans were hard to hit as they came in, though they offered a very brief target to many guns as they darted through the center of a combat wing box. But by then they were likely to have knocked out an entire lead squadron.

The obvious cure was what became known as the "chin-turret" —an ugly, jutting lower jaw with two 50-caliber guns. But when Eaker urgently requested this modification for replacement B-17s and B-24s he was informed that it would not be until May that the B-17G, as this latest modification became known, could be delivered. None actually arrived until August. With American do-it-yourself ingenuity the Eighth's own mechanics and maintenance crews began improvising, first with "cheeks" for gun emplacements on each side of the nose and then with crude chin turrets made on the spot. To anyone who has had a fender replaced on an automobile this sort of homemade modification may seem remarkable, as indeed it was. But the Eighth's maintenance men had become old hands at all sorts of modifications and also at repairing the incredible damage with which many heavies got back to base. For every B-17 or B-24 shot down, a dozen came back with battle damage. It ranged from scattered machine-gun holes to ruptured engines to gaps as big as grand pianos. Nothing like this had been anticipated by the planners back home —nor was there anything comparable in other war theaters. So it became standard operating procedure to fix things on each base.

Some planes, of course, were broken beyond repair. They became "hangar queens" that were cannibalized for spare parts for other heavies. Some had to be taken apart and carted off to the big repair depot at Burtonwood. But that was costly in effort and time. Better for each base to have its own stockpile of spare parts plus the heavy tools needed to "work" aluminum and steel. All this is one more example of the immensity of the logistical task Eaker and his men faced.

More and more he delegated such matters to the growing cadre of battle-tested bomber leaders now in England—group commanders such as Curtis LeMay or Leon Johnson or Stanley Wray, combat wing commanders like Frank Armstrong or Ted Timberlake, and wing commanders Possum Hansell, Jimmy Hodges and Fred Anderson, all funneling up to Longfellow at PINETREE. The latter, though often peremptory in person, still had the benefit of the crack staff Eaker had assembled, notably Castle and Hull. At least one day each week Eaker would visit one base or more, sometimes driving in his Humber but flying a twin-motor AT-7 when weather permitted. The first thing he inspected at each base was the mess hall, where he would look in the cupboards, talk to the mess sergeant and finger the inside of frying pans. By then I had become enough of a confidant to ask him why. He replied with a lesson learned from a cavalry exercise in the Philippines. "We were taught always to feed and groom our horses before we did anything else." He would also talk with the commanding officer, sit in on the debriefing of crews just back from a mission or award Air Medals and DFCs in a small parade formation after saying a few quiet words to the assembled fliers and mechanics. Andrews followed a similar pattern of visits to the combat units at least once a week. Big, handsome, speaking slowly but strongly in a Texan drawl, he commanded instant respect. Even though brand new in England, he had long carried the reputation of being "the best pilot in army air" and many of the senior officers in the Eighth had served under him in the GHQ Air Force.

Andrews had set up living quarters and a small office at the swank Dorchester Hotel on Hyde Park in London, close to the American embassy and all the British leadership, with whom he quickly established a good rapport. On weekends he usually came out to Eaker's Castle Coombe for golf on the adjacent course, where the grass was kept cut but unfilled bomb craters offered a novel hazard. Here he and Eaker could talk at length about policy problems and he could meet the assorted dignitaries invited every Sunday to brunch for about fifty. The quartermaster provided our chow. It was hearty in the American tradition and proved a great attraction to British guests, for food in England was very short and there were no eggs and almost no beef available. At Castle Coombe we did not have eggs or steaks either. But we had ample game, fowl, fish, salads, chocolate, ice cream and even, on rare occasions, oranges. And there was always chile, that air force staple, which came in quart cans and invariably astonished the British, as did Eaker's favorite vegetables —turnip greens and black peas. He was a superb host with his quiet, easy and genial style and never failed to get in an adroit word on behalf of his beloved Eighth and the U.S. concept of air war. Guests included a wide range of American officers of all ranks (not just generals) and their British counterparts, ambassadors Harriman or Winant, members of Parliament, the lord mayor of London, authors passing through like John Steinbeck or publishers like Roy Howard, war correspondents like Wes Gallagher of the Associated Press or Cyrus L. Sulzberger of the *New York Times,* lords and ladies, Hollywood stars in England to entertain the troops, English scientists and intellectuals and—once or twice—Prime Minister Churchill.

Among the many problems Eaker and Andrews faced in this difficult transition was a startling request from Eisenhower, who cabled Andrews on February 17: "We are anxious to provide a qualified American deputy commander for Tedder, who is Commander in Chief for all Mediterranean air forces, and believe that Eaker is most suitable man in sight for such position. On the other hand, Doolittle, who is essentially a man of action, has through his experience here become a highly qualified commander of an American Air Force. I believe an exchange of these two officers would work for the benefit of the whole. . . ."

Eaker was of course not at all enthusiastic about such a switch, nor was Andrews. He replied the same day that it would "be a calamity to United States air operations . . . to make a change at this time" and begged Eisenhower not to insist. Two days later the amiable allied force commander in the Mediterranean agreed to "respect your request," going on to comments of historical interest in view of the major command shift between the ETO and MTO that came ten months later and included Eaker replacing Tedder himself as Air C in C, Mediterranean. "The enormous air establishment set up here requires a skilled and experienced American in Tedder's office, and for the life of me I cannot think of another man to take the job. I will not consent to the appointment of any man to it for the moment. On the other hand, I feel that Doolittle has established himself as a commander and, although he had to learn the hard way, he has learned something of the responsibilities of high command. As long as we drop Eaker out of consideration, Doolittle will take over the bomber command here and I will wrack my brain in an effort to find a suitable deputy for Tedder."[7]

A more subtle and never fully solved problem was how to handle the exaggerated claims AAF crews were making for German fighters downed in combat. For the 28 heavy bomber missions through January 3, 1943, these claims totaled 223 fighters destroyed, 88 probably destroyed and 99 damaged. The common sense of experienced airmen, both American and British, plus intelligence gathered within Germany, made it clear that these figures were inflated. It was not deliberate. Rather, as Eaker recalled: "I knew that some of them were duplicates. In an air battle people who participate are so busy and they see such fragmentary things and the targets flash by so quickly, that it is impossible to have accuracy."[8] Nonetheless, it was clear that tighter guidelines for claims were required. Longfellow's headquarters issued meticulous new instructions on January 5 and revised the previous claims to 89/140/47. "Even so," the official AAF postwar history states, "claims continued to run excessively high."[9] In the great air battles of later in 1943 there were occasions when as many as 1,000 American gunners could fire at the same German fighter at the same instant. It was as impossible to measure their claims as it would be to estimate infantry casualties in a complicated fire-fight on the ground. For their part the Germans understandably minimized revelation of fighter losses while the war was still in progress. Scattered statistics became available afterward but no reliable totals. Only an estimated 3 percent of the Luftwaffe archives survived the war. Some were destroyed by Allied air attacks, but most were burned in the final months by the archivists themselves, following orders from up the line. Goering, Germany's counterpart to Arnold, burned his own files at Karinhall in March 1945.[10] "Arguments over exactly how many aircraft B-17 and B-24 gunners shot down in defending themselves have obscured what really occurred in these air battles," concluded Williamson Murray in his definitive book, *Strategy for Defeat: The Luftwaffe 1933–1945.*

> First it is clear bomber crews claimed many more aircraft than in fact they shot down, but the cumulative effect of German losses in these battles was impressive. In July [1943] the Luftwaffe lost 335 single-engine fighters in the west. Admittedly, a percentage of these losses was not directly attributable to combat, but the pressure of stepped-up air operations and losses forced the Luftwaffe to rely increasingly on partially trained pilots. Thus, noncombatant losses reflected the pressures of combat attrition. July's losses in the west represented 18.1% of all single-engine fighter strength on July 1, reflecting not only the impact of the heavy daytime raids but also the fact that drop tanks on the P-47s had extended escort range. . . . The escalation in the level of fighting over German airspace had an effect on all theaters. By the end of July, the Luftwaffe had put limitations on the employment of fighter aircraft on tasks other than defense of the Reich, while it pulled . . . squadrons out of Brittany and the Battle of the Atlantic to return to Germany.[11]

The successful handling of another problem about the same time reveals the value of Eaker's making a close ally of Lend-Lease Ambassador Harriman. The British found that the expansion of American airfields called for more manpower than they could afford. Instead the Ministry of Labor and National Service proposed to draft 65,000 construction workers for their armed services. Harriman went to see Churchill.

> I asked him whether he wanted to see our air force in England. . . . "Of course," he said. "Why do you ask?" I told him that he would have to reverse the call-up decision, and after a while, he agreed. The Prime Minister took it up with his Cabinet, and over the strong opposition of the armed services, it was agreed. After that I was the most unpopular man in London for a time. But the construction workers were assigned and the airfields built in time.[12]

But the underlying problem of the Eighth was one that neither Andrews nor Eaker could solve on the spot—the continuing shortage of planes, crews and supplies. Bombers could still fly across the Atlantic, but the thousands of men for replacement crews and ground echelons plus the millions of tons of munitions and specialized equipment had to come by ship. And almost all the shipping that spring of 1943 was preempted by the growing offensives in the Mediterranean, in Burma-India and in the Pacific. Back in the fall of 1942

Eaker had estimated that he would need a minimum of 300 heavies to permit deep penetration attacks into Germany, and that daily maintenance of that many bombers ready for action would require a minimum of another 300 in reserve.[13] But the Eighth's total stock of heavies in February-March 1943 was at most 200, of which half were usually laid up for repair. In one of his many letters to Arnold, Eaker pointed out that his cumulative losses as of February 26 amounted to 75 planes and crews and "to date we have received but 24 replacement crews and 63 replacement aircraft." In the same letter he wrote plaintively: "The only theory upon which the failure to build-up the force here is supportable is on the ground that they can be used to better advantage elsewhere, or there is some reason why heavy bombers are not effective from this theater against Germany. As I have pointed out so many times, drawing the conclusion from our present bomber effort against Germany that heavy bombers are ineffective against them is comparable to sending a company of infantry to attack an entrenched battalion and deciding from the result that infantry attack is ineffective. There is only one thing that we require here to do a job—the job that will hurt the enemy the most—and that is an adequate force. . . ."[14]

But there was little that Arnold could do about it, knowing, as he had written Andrews, that the shipping bottleneck would not lessen until April at best. Arnold had returned from China very weary and even more cranky than usual. He was, in fact, building up to his first heart attack, which hospitalized him for two weeks in March just as he was promoted to four-star level and as Spaatz won his third. The tension on Arnold shows in several testy communications such as a memo he wrote to Stratemeyer on February 27 saying in part: "During the Casablanca Conference I was put on the defensive by both the British and the United States for not having our heavy bombers bombard Germany. First the matter was taken up by Portal, then by the Prime Minister and finally by the President. The matter became so serious that I called for Eaker and Spaatz, both of whom gave the usual and expected reasons for not operating against Germany." This, as Arnold's diary makes clear, was inaccurate—he had sent for Eaker before meeting with Portal or any of the British delegation.[15] Now, ironically, it was Portal and also Harris who were importuning him to send daylight reinforcements. On March 1 Eaker wrote Arnold: "Yesterday I had a telephone call from Air Chief Marshal Portal concerning a message he is sending . . . the grave concern the British now feel at our failure to build up our forces in this theater according to the earlier flow charts furnished us and according to the Casablanca agreements. We are still sorely in need here of a flow chart authenticated by you or by the War Department which can reasonably be expected to be lived up to. . . ."[16]

Harris chimed in on March 5 with a characteristic letter that Eaker forwarded to Arnold. It said in part: "Our only regret is that the VIIIth Bomber Force, which we know already to be fully equal in quality to the best we can produce is still too small to take its full share of the attack. Had you the force to operate by day on the same scale as we have done and shall continue to do by night, there would be no hope for the enemy in Europe, who could not long stand against such a weight of combined offensive. The whimperings of the German propagandists at our opening blows in the campaign of 1943 show that the enemy now strives to win the sympathy of the world in his misfortunes. When the Devil is sick, the Devil a saint would be. This change of tone in itself reveals his fear of what is still to come and increases my conviction that, when you can hit him as hard by day as we can by night, the day of reckoning will set on Hitler's Germany."[17]

Marshall also made a significant contribution to the dialogue. At a meeting of the Joint Chiefs of Staff in Washington on March 14 when there was a major confrontation between the conflicting demands of the European and the Pacific theaters he "intervened," as his biographer recorded, "to say that Army Air Forces had been conducting their operations in Europe with too few planes. If they could double the number of planes for each strike, they could increase the effectiveness of the attack while reducing the percentage of losses."[18]

It was at this highly opportune moment that the Eighth struck a stunningly successful blow against a major target in Germany—the submarine building plant at Vegesack. On March 18 it was hit by 73 B-17s and 24 B-24s bombing from 22,000 to 28,000 feet and using for the first time automatic flight-control equipment (AFCE), a linkage with the automatic pilot that enabled the lead bombardier to guide his plane with his sight adjustments during the final approach. Then the entire formation salvoed on his radio signal. Vegesack was very small—an obscure rectangle of sheds and shops measuring only 2,500 by 1,000 feet alongside the Wesel River, near Bremen. Eaker wrote Spaatz the next day, sending his letter by the hand of Robert Sherwood, then the head of the Office of War Information, a "very high percentage" of the 268 1,000-lb. bombs, "were in the target area" and "the PRU photographs show the place was really messed up." Despite continuous attacks by an estimated 50 German fighters, "We lost but one Liberator and one Fortress."

"PRU" stood for Photo Reconnaissance Unit, the specialized group of stripped-down fighters (usually P-38s or the British Mosquito) that inspected a target as soon after an attack as clear weather permitted. They flew above 30,000 ft. (too high for interception or flak) and carried cameras, taking stereoscopic pictures that were often remarkably detailed, revealing just where bombs had hit and which roofs had collapsed. This of course did not always disclose just how much lasting damage had been done inside. In the case of Vegesack, photo interpretation showed that 76 percent of the bombs were within 1,000 feet of the aiming point, seven submarines in various stages of construction had been hit and it would take "months" to get the yards working again.

Everyone was jubilant. Churchill sent Eaker "all my compliments to you and your officers and men on your brilliant exploit. . . ." Portal termed it "the complete answer to criticism of high altitude, daylight, precision bombing." When Arnold returned from his sickbed in Florida he wrote: "The pictures of your strike at Vegesack were much appreciated. The results of that magnificent show are certainly encouraging. . . ." Eaker quoted these and other messages in a commendation he sent to Longfellow for transmission to the entire personnel of VIII Bomber Command. He said in part: "To my mind the Vegesack raid is the climax; it concludes the experiment. There should no longer be the slightest vestige of doubt that our heavy bombers with their trained crews can overcome any enemy opposition and destroy their targets. . . . All of us can now, I feel, look forward confidently to the next chapter in the air war, wherein we shall employ the lessons we have learned in the experiment, in an air offensive with forces of sufficient size. . . ."[19]

On the night of March 26 Eaker was host at a dinner at PINETREE in honor of Churchill. Preparing for it with his usual careful attention to detail, he sent me off to Asprey's on Bond Street to buy a thick malacca cane with a big gold knob engraved as a gift to the PM from the Eighth Air Force. He also talked to the PINETREE mess officer, Clarence O. Mason, a roly-poly captain with a knack for social niceties. Mason recalled: "The Boss told me to make certain Mr. Churchill had plenty of Scotch. So I had the best waitress at the Abbey stationed in back of him, about seven or eight feet discreetly in the background, and her personal job was to keep his glass replenished. During the course of the evening he had five double Scotches. He got up and made one of the best speeches I've ever heard."[20]

It was an altogether moving occasion. Present along with Andrews and Harris were all the VIII Bomber Command wing, group and squadron commanders. Silver Stars were awarded by Andrews and, from Air Marshal Norman Bottomley, the first British DFCs were given to six Americans. The renowned actor Ralph Richardson, in British uniform as a lieutenant commander, delivered an eloquent reading of Clemence Dane's "Trafalgar Day-1940." There were toasts and songs, in which the PM joined heartily. Afterwards he went upstairs to Longfellow's quarters for another hour or more of jollity during which he knocked off most of a bottle of brandy, signed numerous short-snorters and joked with Andrews about his decorations. And, as Eaker reported to Arnold a few days later in another long letter: "He proposed we send a cable to you saying: 'We are dining together, smoking your cigars, and waiting for more of your heavy bombers. Churchill, Andrews, Harris, Eaker.' "[21]

Eaker did not know that Arnold was in the hospital. Had he known, he might not also have sent an extraordinarily blunt condemnation of the way Washington was treating his Eighth Air Force. It comprised twenty-five hundred words filling three single-spaced legal-sized pages and was written with the impersonal tone of a legal indictment, beginning:

> The current position of the Eighth Air Force is not a credit to the American Army. After 16 months in the war we are not yet able to dispatch more than 123 bombers toward an enemy target. Many of the crews who fly this pitiful number have been on battle duty for eight months. They understand the law of averages. They have seen it work on their friends.
>
> The crews know why this command has never dared to set a limit of operational tours until recently. . . .
>
> They have seen our precision bombing improve, in bloody lessons, until they know with confidence what they can do, or could do, if they had enough planes to run the increasing gauntlet of enemy fighters. . . .
>
> This is written in no apprehension of trouble with the crews. They are American and they will pay for the mistakes of their·

superiors as uncomplainingly as the men of Wake and Bataan did. This is written as a statement of our critical need of planes and crews with which to redeem the promise of the Eighth Air Force while there is still time. The time is short. . . .

In the last 16 months the German has more than doubled the signal facilities and plane detection apparatus in western Europe. The fighter planes these watchdogs launch against us on the western front have increased from 420 to 831. The total operational strength of his fighter force have increased from 1,185 to 1,704 planes. The production facilities that have hummed without interruption beyond the reach of our bombing effort have increased their monthly output from less than 500 to an average of 763 fighter planes for the last recorded seven months.

These are formidable details but they are only parts of the whole forfeit, the whole tragic price we have yet to pay for headlines on Casablanca and delay in England. The full and sickening name of that price is Aerial Supremacy over Europe.

Some day the Navy and Ground forces are going to ask us for that supremacy. When they have mastered the uncontested parts of the earth to their hearts content, they may even give us back our planes to pave the way for their well-covered approach to the heart of the enemy.

But neither they nor anyone else can give us back the time with which the German has tightened his stubborn grip on the Aerial Supremacy over Europe. That is the rising price, the daily increasing forfeit we have yet to pay. . . .

It is respectfully requested that the Eighth Air Force be given sufficient planes to redeem its unkept promise.[22]

Arnold's reaction was mild, as Eaker thought it would be, for he knew from many years of close association with the commanding general of Army Air that Arnold would pay attention to strong statements and respected officers who stood up to him in delivering them. Arnold passed Eaker's paper along to the head of the Operations Plans Division with the comment: "From this you can see that apparently General Eaker thinks that I personally am responsible for taking all the airplanes he didn't get and sending them down to North Africa. . . ." To Eaker he wrote: "You are well aware of the fact that I have eight youngsters' mouths to feed and that we are pushing airplanes out to all eight theaters as fast as we can get them ready. . . . You are doing a good job . . . and I know you will continue to do so even though we can't send you all the airplanes you would like to have. I will do the best I can for you. . . . Washington is the same old merry-go-round with one meeting after another and new and different problems coming up every day. Generals Kenney and

Harmon were here for two weeks to work out a complete plan for the Southwest Pacific. They felt they were facing slow starvation. It will be a great day when we get all those eight youngsters well fed and fat. . . ."[23]

Arnold also sent Eaker that same week the flow chart he had requested on March 1. As of April 1 the Eighth had only seven groups of heavies, one of mediums and three of fighters. Arnold's letter of March 24 estimated a swift buildup as follows:

	June 30, 1943	Dec. 31, 1943	June 30, 1944
Heavy bombardment groups	19	37	44
Medium bombardment groups	5	10	10
Fighter groups	6	15	26

But, Arnold warned, these figures "cannot and positively must not be used as definite commitments, either in your mind or in talking to Air Chief Marshal Portal. . . ."[24] In the event the buildup lagged by about three months throughout 1943—with dire consequences for Eaker and his men.

On the same day Arnold sent these figures to England he also wrote to Ruth Eaker to transmit: "my check for $147.96, which is Ira's share for semi-annual royalties on *This Flying Game.* . . . I want to thank you for your nice letter of congratulations on my promotion —it's always a pleasure to hear from one's old friends. I have been assuring everybody that the mere fact that I got 4 stars doesn't mean that the credit goes to me. It means that all the fellows who have been working with me so loyally have been able to put across their job and thereby the Air Forces have gained a position in the sun. I hear from Ira quite frequently and he is apparently building up an Air Force which, as you know, has been doing and will continue to do wonderful things. . . ."[25]

Besides the flurry of encouraging letters Arnold despatched that busy week he also put in motion a program of enormous importance in extricating the Eighth Air Force from the doldrums and setting it firmly on course for success. His action was the culmination of a confluence of scholarly and statistical approaches unprecedented in the long history of warfare. It was a method pioneered by the British under the name "Operational Research" and best defined by C. P. Snow, who said: "The lesson to the military was that you cannot run wars on gusts of emotion. You have to think scientifically. . . ." Snow traced its origins to the testing of antiaircraft gunnery by British scientists in World War I, followed by the development of radar under the 1935 Committee for the Scientific Study of Air Defense chaired by Sir Henry Tizard. Then, just before and throughout World War II, dozens of brilliant scientific devices, both defensive and offensive, evolved under the leadership of Professor E. A. Lindeman (better known as Lord Cherwell), Dr. R. V. Jones and others. Among them was Dr. Solly Zuckerman. Though a medical doctor by training, Zuckerman never practiced, diverting instead into studies of the social and sexual lives of monkeys and becoming a research fellow in the anatomy department at Oxford. This simian background led, appropriately, into studies of the effectiveness of the German blitz—how high-velocity bomb blasts affected monkeys (and thus humans), what were the merits of one size or kind of bomb versus another, what was the relative efficacy of high explosives versus incendiaries and so on. This in turn led to consideration of the best targets for the British bomber offensive.[26]

A second scholarly approach to target selection and bombing tactics came from another colorful Briton of unusual background, Col. Richard D'Oyly Hughes, a graduate of Sandhurst and a bemedaled former officer in the British army who became an American citizen and midwestern dairy farmer. Entering army air, he helped plan AWPD-1 and went to London in 1942 to organize a new general staff section for plans (A-5) for Spaatz at WIDEWING. Something of a maverick, Hughes had a puckish wit, a slight stutter and great skill at getting things done out of standard channels. Fretful on finding that Eighth Air Force intelligence and operations research were utterly dependent upon British sources, he persuaded Ambassador Winant to set up a small Embassy Operations Unit (EOU) in the American embassy itself. The EOU staff, mostly economists, came chiefly from the Office of Strategic Services in Washington, grew to ten people and was put to work by Hughes at first on improving aiming-point reports. The objective was to spot the most vulnerable point of attack in a factory and then analyze the effect on total operations if that vulnerable point were destroyed, how long repairs would likely take and the resultant effect on German war potential. EOU produced 285 aiming-point studies, providing all sorts of valuable guidelines for "organizing intelligence for precision bombing purposes and a mode of thinking systematically and comparatively about precise targets." This of course drew EOU "into the formulation of its own concepts of target-system selection. . . . It required," continued Professor Walt Rostow, an EOU captain, then (and twenty years later a controversial national security advisor to Lyndon Johnson) in his book about it,

> among other things, taking fully into account the extent to which the military effect of an attack could be cushioned by the Germans, notably, by diverting civilian output or services to military purposes or buying time for repair by drawing down stocks of finished products or in the pipeline. . . .
>
> The EOU view was, then, both a theory of bombing policy and a related method of analysis. It insisted that targets be chosen in the light of an explicitly defined military aim, linked to the full context of war strategy and, especially, to its timing. It opposed attacks designed simply to weaken the German economy in some generalized sense or to cause political disruption, and it emphasized the possibilities of evading the military consequences of bomb damage in a mature and resourceful economic situation like that of wartime Germany. (We would have emphasized the latter point still more strongly if we had known at the time how far short of full economic mobilization Germany was down to the spring of 1944.) EOU doctrine insisted on the need to concentrate bombing attacks against the minimum number of targets whose destruction would achieve the specified military goal and on the need for perseverance and thoroughness when the attack on a target system had been launched. The EOU view was, in short, a doctrine of warfare, not of economics or politics.[27]

The third, and most important, root of what the Americans came to call operations analysis began on November 16, 1942, when Maj. Gen. Muir S. Fairchild, who had been Eaker's copilot on the Pan American Goodwill Flight fifteen years before, became a member of the Joint Strategic Survey Committee set up under the Joint Chiefs of Staff "to study and survey the major (basic) strategy of the war (past, present and future). . . ." He became deeply concerned about severe criticism of AWPD-42 and the validity of the air offensive in Europe from the Joint Intelligence Committee, which had no air member and was dominated by naval intelligence and the army's G-2. It challenged the industrial and economic intelligence upon which the air plan was based. On the afternoon of December 3, 1942, Fairchild dropped in to see Col. (later Brig. Gen.) Byron E. Gates, then assistant chief of staff for management control, one of whose tasks was to develop American operations analysis in the British pattern. With Gates when Fairchild came in were two early recruits —Maj. (later Brig. Gen.) W. Barton Leach, a Harvard law professor, and Capt. (later Col.) Guido R. Perera, a prominent Boston lawyer. Fairchild expressed dissatisfaction over the way air matters were presented to the Joint Chiefs. Information came from diverse sources in the AAF and was put together hastily by officers under other heavy pressures and, he said, "this type of activity was one for which a regular Army career did not necessarily prepare an officer." Gates offered him Leach and Perera. "All right," said Fairchild, "I have a job for you. How can Germany be so damaged by air attack that an invasion of the Continent may be made possible within the shortest possible period—say one year?"[28]

Six days later General Arnold signed a directive formalizing this assignment, which he hoped would be in hand in time for the Casablanca Conference. "You [Gates] are directed to have the group of operational analysts under your jurisdiction prepare and submit to me a report analyzing the rate of progressive deterioration that should be anticipated. . . . This study should result in as accurate an estimate as can be arrived at as to the date when this deterioration will have progressed to a point to permit a successful invasion of Western Europe."[29]

Only four days later a high-powered group was appointed and convened for its first session. The chairman was Elihu Root, Jr., a New York lawyer whose father had been secretary of war under President Theodore Roosevelt and had created the army general staff. Other members were Dr. Edward M. Earle of the Institute for Advanced Study at Princeton, and Lt. Col. Malcolm Moss, chief of the target information section of AAF/A-2, as well as representatives of OSS, the British Ministry of Economic Warfare and the American Bureau of Economic Warfare. Another major figure joined the group on January 7—Thomas W. Lamont, a distinguished partner of J. P. Morgan. They did not get their thoughts fully assembled before Casablanca, but their interim report, which Arnold took with him to the conference, concluded: "It is clear that it is better to cause a high degree of destruction in a few really essential industries or services than to cause a small degree of destruction in many. . . . It is clear that results are cumulative and that a master plan, once adopted, should be adhered to with relentless determination. It is clear that our day operations and the night bombing of the RAF should be correlated so that both may be applied to the same system of targets, each at the point where it is most effective. It is already clear that with the force available during 1943, concentrated on the right targets, very grave injury can be done to the Western Axis economic system. There are substantial grounds for hoping that the study now in hand, if pressed further, may indicate that this injury will critically impair the military strength of the Western Axis."[30]

These principles were, as noted earlier, incorporated in general terms in the Casablanca Directive. And the Committee of Operations Analysts (COA), as it came to be called, and many subcommittees worked full tilt for the next two months preparing the detailed recommendations Arnold was able to implement in late March. In the meantime, Gates had written to Eaker offering him the first statistical control unit, which he accepted enthusiastically.[31] To head it came one of Root's partners in the famous Wall Street law firm of Root, Clark, Buckner & Ballantine—John M. Harlan, who would later become a Supreme Court justice as was his namesake grandfather. Harlan, quickly appointed a major and later promoted to colonel, greeted Leach, Perera and others of the COA in London on January 26, and Eaker, just back from Casablanca, saw them the next day. Initially skeptical, for he had been told the COA proposed to "tell" the air force what to do, he listened to their lengthy presentation and then said, "Now that I see your attitude, I will be glad to cooperate in every way." All but Root returned to Washington February 4 and the COA's final report was presented to Arnold in mid-March.[32]

Arnold sent the document to Andrews (with copy to Spaatz) on March 24, conveying it in the hands of one of his personal advisory council, Col. Charles P. "Pre" Cabell. An informal covering letter contained a recommendation that went to the heart of how to assure an adequate force for the Eighth. It said: "Ever since the war began, we have, as you know, advocated building up the largest possible bomber force in the United Kingdom. We have, however, avoided specifying the number of aircraft required to accomplish our objectives. I am convinced that we have to take a different tack. The Joint and the Combined Chiefs of Staff have been willing to build up the force . . . but they have unfortunately looked upon it as a reservoir from which the demands of other theaters could be met. To change this clearly untenable view, we must design a definite program of operations from the United Kingdom, get it approved, and then allocate the number of airplanes required to carry it out."[33]

The formal directive with the report told Andrews to estimate the requirements Portal, Eaker and Harris believed needed to accomplish the COA's proposed program, which "indicates that German industry may well be paralyzed by the destruction of not more than 60 targets. . . . The destruction of the ball-bearing industry would apparently have the most far-reaching effects upon German industry of any of the targets studied. . . . We believe it to be within the capabilities of the Allied Nations, by coordinated use of the Royal Air Forces and the American Bombing Forces, virtually to paralyze this industry in one, two or three attacks. . . ." Here was the genesis of the two greatest air battles ever fought, those over Schweinfurt that August and October.[34]

The COA report listed nineteen target systems in order of priority, with the German aircraft industry first and ball bearings second, followed by petroleum, grinding wheels and abrasives, nonferrous metals, synthetic rubber plants and submarine yards and bases. It pointed out the particular vulnerabilities of each category and estimated the number of bomber sorties each category necessitated. Petroleum eventually turned out to be Hitler's Achilles' heel, but the calculations on ball bearings were more detailed and more immediately persuasive. They included estimates that 86 percent of the Axis ball-bearing works could be destroyed by the destruction of ten targets; 57 percent by the destruction of five; and 43 percent by smashing just three targets in the tiny town of Schweinfurt. To dramatize other reasons why ball bearings were such an attractive objective, the report noted that every American four-engined bomber had 3,000 of them, the average American aircraft had 1,000 and a torpedo used by submarines had 162 "of such fineness that a practice torpedo must have ball-bearings replaced after two trial runs."[35]

With the blessing of Andrews and Portal, Eaker set up a joint AAF-RAF team at WIDEWING chaired by Hansell. American members included Anderson and Hughes and two other staff officers, with Cabell sitting in. British members included the director of bomber operations at air ministry and a representative of the Ministry of Economic Warfare. In ten days of intense discussion they expanded the target list from 60 to 76, left the German aircraft industry at number one and pushed ball bearings down to number three. Submarine construction yards were put back at number two—"doubtless," as the official RAF history concluded, "because the Board realized that, in the precarious condition of the Battle of the Atlantic, no plan was likely to be accepted by the Joint or Combined Chiefs of Staff unless an attack on the German submarines were given a prominent position." And, by what the same history called "an ingenius device," the German fighter force was set up as an intermediate objective, which, like Abou Ben Adhem, led all the rest. The heavy bomber forces required were specified as 800 by July, with depth of penetration limited to range of escort fighters; 1,192 by October, with depth of 500 miles; and 2,702 thereafter with depth limited only by operating radius of action of the bombers.[36]

Portal gave the revised plan his "full support," in a letter to Arnold April 15, as did Harris the same day. Portal commented: "The plan includes an estimate of the rate at which the strength of the Eighth Air Force must be developed in order to achieve the planned effect. I believe this rate of build-up and the time factor generally to be of primary importance. The German Fighter strength is increasing and every week's delay will make the task more difficult. . . . We cannot afford to miss the good bombing weather which will soon be due. We cannot exploit to the full the great potentialities of the daylight bombing technique if the requisite numbers are not available."[37]

Andrews also went over the report with meticulous care after listening to Hansell present it at the Dorchester on April 8. He directed that a letter be prepared for his signature stressing several points, but in particular that the proposed force was the minimum needed. Then he decided the matter was so important that Eaker himself should return to Washington to make the presentation. On the Coombe Hill golf course that weekend they talked it all over again on the fairways. Eaker flew back to Washington and made what everyone who heard it agreed was a fine presentation to the Joint Chiefs on April 29, speaking without notes and with compelling command of his subject. Questions were of course raised, and final decision was reserved for the meeting of the Combined Chiefs known as TRIDENT, scheduled for May 12.[38]

While Eaker was in the Pentagon he winced at the news of the first really bloody nose his bombers had taken—16 lost out of 115 despatched (14 percent) against a factory in Bremen, with 46 more bombers damaged. But there was solace in the long letter Harriman sent Lovett on April 20 that included the comment: ". . . the Prime Minister, in spite of early advices to the contrary and his own prejudice, has accepted the effectiveness of daylight bombing without reservation. This has been a tough job but Ira has finally done it. This goes too for the Air Staff—and Harris, of course. . . ."[39]

Eaker also pulled off a poker player's coup by playing what he termed a "dirty trick" on Lt. Gen. George Kenney, MacArthur's air chief in the Pacific. "I walked into Arnold's office," he related, "and he gave me the bad news that some 50 B-24s that I had expected to get he was going to have to divert to the Pacific. As I came out with the bad news I met George Kenney going in. He said, rubbing his hands with glee, 'I'm going to get your B-24s, 50 of them.' I said, 'George, that doesn't make me as unhappy as you suspect it does. As you may not know, they are turning out a new bomber that's bigger and better called the B-32.' Well, he pricked up his ears and went into General Arnold's office. I saw Arnold later that afternoon, and he said, 'I suspect you in this plot. Kenney came in to see me this morning and relinquished the B-24s. He wants the B-32s.' Well, the B-32s were about six months away from delivery of the first ones. I got my B-24s, and since then Kenney has always given me a hard time."[40]

Leaving Bolling Field on May 4, Eaker brought with him letters for Andrews from Marshall, Arnold and others and also two close friends of the ETO commander—Maj. Gen. Follett Bradley and Col. Hugh Knerr. The latter, a victim of the general staff vendetta in 1938, was back in uniform and on his way to two stars and a significant part in the maintenance aspects of the bomber offensive. Bradley, inspector general of the AAF, was under orders from Arnold to draft a final plan for the Eighth Air Force buildup. When the three landed at Prestwick after eighteen hours on the way they were greeted with the news that Andrews, "best pilot in the Army Air," had been killed the day before in the crash of a B-24 he was piloting and that hit a fog-shrouded mountain on a routine inspection trip to Iceland. It was a shattering blow to them all—for personal reasons first but also because of the new uncertainty it implied for the future of the bomber campaign.

"He was always marked as one of the future leaders of Army Air," Eaker sadly remembered. "I always felt certain that he would have been picked by Marshall to command our forces in the invasion. . . . I don't know of anybody that I had a closer friendship with and a greater admiration for than Frank Andrews."[41] On another occasion he mused about the rivalry between Arnold and Andrews, who was Arnold's senior by one year at West Point and always Arnold's chief rival for the leadership of army air. "They were entirely different. They weren't as competitive as it might have seemed, due to their similar age and rank, because they had different capacities. Arnold was always more of a staff officer type, and Andrews more of a troop command type. . . . [He] tended to be a little less tolerable of opposition—Army, Navy—that sort of thing. Andrews was more like Mitchell than Arnold was. He was just a crusader, and he didn't care who he opposed, and he was sometimes very intolerant of stupid people who opposed him, whereas Arnold always had his political eye cocked in the right direction. He would bend when it was time

The broken tail of Andrews' B-24 lies on the Iceland mountain, near Grindavik, where he crashed, May 4, 1943.

to bend. He was much better suited to the Washington scene than Andrews would have been. On the other hand, there's no doubt in my mind but that Andrews would have been a better overall commander than Arnold would have been. Arnold would have gone too much into detail."[42]

Andrews's biggest admirer was the army chief of staff, Gen. George C. Marshall, and it was he who delivered the eulogy at the memorial service in the crowded chapel at Fort Myers, saying of the fallen flier, "No army produces more than a few great captains."

In February 1943, Churchill welcomes handsome Lt. Gen. Frank Andrews, newly appointed CG of the European Theater, and soon to perish. Harris is next to Andrews in front row. Rear row, l. to r.: unidentified; Mary Churchill, the PM's daughter; Eaker; and Commander Thomson, RN, the PM's aide.

FOUR

The Combined Bomber Offensive

16

"Thrice is he armed that hath his quarrel just."

—SHAKESPEARE, *KING HENRY VI*

T HE TWO-PAGE letter Eaker brought back from Arnold for Andrews and that, of course, he never saw, reveals a dichotomy in the commanding general of the AAF that would dominate the three months of May, June and July in the bomber campaign out of England. The letter began with high praise of Eaker. "His presentation was superb. As far as I can see, everyone on the Joint Chiefs of Staff is convinced that the idea is sound. Of course there are certain individuals asking questions as to where the airplanes will come from. . . ."

But in the final paragraph of his letter he sounded a heavy-handed warning, the harbinger of the most contentious controversy between Arnold and Eaker in their entire forty-nine-year relationship. "May I drop a suggestion to you," Arnold wrote, "and that is that you watch carefully the selection of officer personnel for the various top level staffs in England. These staffs will either make or break the commanders and in view of the complex and difficult job facing everyone in England, you will need the best brains you can get, and emotion and friendship must not in any way be allowed to enter into the picture."[1]

This lecture was a follow-up on a missive Arnold had sent Andrews on April 26, while Eaker was still in Washington, which contained the wildly exaggerated judgment: "I am rapidly coming to the conclusion that our bombing outfit in the Eighth Air Force is assuming a state of routine repetition of performance and perhaps finding many excuses and alibis for not going on missions, which with more aggressive leaders might be accomplished. . . . Information I received from England is . . . that our fighter pilots are looking for excuses to go to the Savoy. . . . May this not be the result of having a leader who is not sufficiently aggressive? Has Monk Hunter lost his spirit—his dash? I know he is not the Monk Hunter I used to know. He seems to be playing safe on most of his missions. . . . Is not the same thing true of the Bomber Command? Does it not lack an aggressive leader? Is the staff what it should be? . . . Let me have your frank reactions."[2]

Andrews replied, in his last letter to his boss, that perhaps the two commanders should be more aggressive, but he reserved judgment. Spaatz also was being hectored by their over-burdened boss in Washington—about all sorts of operational problems in North Africa—though Arnold had the grace to write him, "I have been impatient all my life, and probably will be to the end of my days; but that's my make-up—and that's that."[3]

At first, however, all went well for the Eighth. Though the airmen had hoped Andrews's replacement would be another flier, Marshall sent an armored force specialist, Lt. Gen. Jacob L. Devers, with a veteran airman, Maj. Gen. Idwal H. Edwards, as his chief of staff. Devers and Eaker quickly established a solid understanding and lifelong friendship, and Eaker was soon able to write Arnold: "I never have had, and never expect to have, better relations with my Commander than now prevail with General Devers and his staff. . . . He is as strong a supporter of true air force operations as I have ever seen."[4] And at the TRIDENT conference in Washington in mid-May the Combined Chiefs of Staff strongly endorsed "the Eaker Plan," as the new blueprint for the combined bomber offensive came to be called, though the chiefs made some significant changes. Arnold could not attend TRIDENT, being hospitalized with his second heart attack.[5] In his absence the new proposals were presented by Lt. Gen. Joseph T. McNarney, deputy chief, who "stated that it had been agreed with the RAF and that it would involve six precision attacks a month in clear weather backed up by RAF night bombing of the same objectives. . . ." Portal spoke up to say that "in spite of the most critical of all available experts, the Air Ministry was convinced that, if given the resources asked for, General Eaker would achieve the results he claimed," adding that he himself was "one hundred percent behind the plan." Churchill, having given Harriman his promise of support as they crossed the Atlantic on the *Queen Mary*, said there was no need to discuss the U-boat war or the bombing of Germany because "there were no differences of opinion on these subjects."[6]

The most important decision at TRIDENT was to schedule OVERLORD, the invasion of France, for May 1, 1944, a postponement that gave Eaker and Harris exactly one year to complete POINTBLANK, code name for the combined bomber offensive. Their attacks were authorized by the CCS in four phases, with elimination of the Luftwaffe as the over-riding priority—a task assigned primarily to the Eighth Air Force. Harris was advised: "This plan does not attempt to prescribe the major effort of the RAF Bomber Command. It simply recognizes the fact that when precision targets are bombed by the Eighth . . . in daylight, the effort should be complemented and completed by RAF bombing attacks against the surrounding industrial areas at night."[7]

Lest there be any doubt about the strategic objective of the combined bomber offensive, the TRIDENT conferees added a significant sentence to the goal as defined at Casablanca. The Casablanca Directive, it will be recalled, said only that the purpose was Germany's "progressive destruction and dislocation . . . to a point where their capacity for armed resistance is fatally weakened." The CCS added, "This is construed as meaning so weakened as to permit initiation of final combined operations on the Continent." That strategy was all right with Arnold and Eaker, for both had long recognized its logic. But it grated on Harris and some of the American bomber commanders such as Hansell, who clung to the view that strategic bombing could defeat Germany without an invasion being necessary.[8]

Even as Eaker's overall policy was being resoundingly seconded, the undercutting of the Eighth continued, a spectacular example being the diversion of two groups of B-24s already in England, and another that was on the way there, to North Africa for a single attack on Ploesti, Germany's most important source of oil, in faraway Rumania. When Eisenhower recommended the operation to the Combined Chiefs of Staff on April 30 he estimated that "the air echelons of these groups, with only a minimum of ground personnel," would be needed for only six weeks. Marshall told Eaker it would be "for a period not to exceed 15 days."[9] They were actually gone for four months. Their widely publicized, low-level attack by 177 B-24s dispatched cost 54 bombers downed (30 percent) and did heavy damage. But the refineries were substantially back in operation within a month; the Americans had not yet learned that targets had to be hit again and again to keep them "out." The Ploesti raid was a prime example of what Harris sneeringly tabbed "panacea targets." Eaker protested the loss of his B-24s, but to no avail, writing Arnold, "I imagine you fight these things as hard as you can, but I believe it is fair for me to state now that if these diversions are to continue it will be impossible to accomplish the result anticipated, simply because the force required will not be furnished."[10]

But Arnold was in an unreasonable frame of mind. Unquestionably his unstable health had accentuated his habitual impatience. He was agitated too about continuing in his own post—only a personal ruling by President Roosevelt had prevented his being relieved after his first heart attack six weeks before. In addition he was receiving reports, not always correct, from some of his staff, as well as advice that was sometimes self-serving; colonels in Washington were often ardent for an overseas assignment and one way to get it was to call attention to a weak spot abroad. Longfellow and Bubb were weaklings, and sour remarks about them inevitably percolated to Arnold's ears. So too did inexpert diagnosis of operational problems in distant England. A major example was the urgent need for jettisonable gas tanks for the new P-47 fighter in order to extend its range, involving an enormously complex mixture of logistics and tactics. The "drop-tanks" that hung under the fighters used in crossing the Atlantic were made of resinated paper and could not be flown at altitudes calling for pressurization; unable to get appropriate ones from the U.S. quickly, Eaker, Harriman and the RAF cooperated to improvise manufacture of a new design in England, with inevitable modifications before they became operational; and General Hunter, CG of fighter command, expressed a view popular down the line that it was unrealistic to expect fighter pilots to go into action carrying tanks that made them "flying blow-torches" if they were hit. Word reached Arnold that the VIII Fighter Command P-47s were dropping their tanks before they reached the enemy coast and when the tanks were still half full. But when he was given that report on June 12 the tanks had not yet been tried in combat.[11]

Hunter, whose neck joined Longfellow's on the implacable Arnold's chopping block, was an old friend of the commanding general of Army Air and had been a WW I ace. Along with his elaborate mustache this gave him a reputation for flamboyance that his orthodox philosophy as CG, VIII Fighter Command, did not sustain. He followed the air tactical school doctrine that the primary mission of fighters in offensive action was to fly formation with the bombers and fend off attacks by enemy fighters. This was just what the VIII Bomber Command leaders also wanted as they prodded into German defenses in the spring of 1943. He pursued, in short, defensive tactics that were reinforced by his difficulty—even greater than that of VIII Bomber Command—in getting adequate forces.[12]

When Hunter arrived in England in June 1942 with Spaatz he took over the three Eagle Squadrons of the RAF—so-called because their pilots were Americans who had gone to war before Pearl Harbor. They flew the short-range Spitfire V and then the better Spit IX, which enabled them to escort U.S. bombers part way to targets in France and meet them on the way out. Hunter was scheduled to get three groups of the longer-range P-38 in the fall of 1942, but these were all siphoned off to North Africa. Then the P-47, known as "the Jug" because of its radial engine and beer-bottle shape, began to reach England but turned out to have serious deficiencies in radio communication—it could not "talk" to others in its formation or to the bombers being escorted, and this was an absolute must in the European theater. That took time to solve, time that the U.S. pilots used to good advantage in getting accustomed to flying the new plane. But it was not until April 1943 that the P-47 at last saw combat, and July when drop-tanks became available in quantity. Meanwhile, Hunter's handful of Spits made "sweeps" up and down the Channel and short-range escort missions of the bombers, where their presence clearly deterred German interception. In one of Eaker's letters to Arnold (April 16) a month before their controversy became heated, he reported: "The first combat of the P-47s in this theater. Yesterday, 54 P-47s made offensive sweeps and they succeeded in destroying three FW-190s for the loss of three P-47s. Definitely one, and we believe another of these, was not due to enemy combat but to engine trouble. The pilots' reports concerning the P-47s in these combats was that they could turn inside the FW-190s and outdive them at high altitudes. I think we may say, therefore, that the initial skirmish of the P-47 against the FW-190 has been in our favour."[13]

Meanwhile, however, the Germans had been making radical changes in their fighter tactics. Discouraged by the firepower of tight formations of B-17s and the "umbrella" of fighters that escorted them partway, the Luftwaffe, as Eaker reported in a May 18 letter to Arnold, "now has two squadrons of FW-190s equipped with 37 mm. cannon. Yesterday they stood off at 1,500 yds., outside our effective range, and knocked down three of our bombers with this long-range cannon fire. At Kiel, and again yesterday, a considerable number of large bombs, 250–300 lbs., were dropped on our formations by pursuit aircraft. At Antwerp, 23 FW-190s in a fairly tight formation dive-bombed our formation with large bombs, and two of our aircraft are believed to have been destroyed this way." Only one of these tactics proved to be a substantial hazard—the cannon fire from points out of reach of the B-17's fifty-caliber guns, soon expanded to include twin-engined ME-110s and JU-88s shooting cannon and rockets from behind the bomber formations. These attacks, Hansell noted, "constituted a very real menace. If the formation loosened up to provide a target of less density, the single-engine fighters closed in on the exposed flank airplanes. Against these attacks, the bombers had no satisfactory defense. Escort fighters were needed to prevent the Luftwaffe fighters from taking up these positions."[14]

In the same letter about the P-47's first combat, Eaker also reported "our greatest disaster to date"—the 100 percent loss of a mission of ten medium bombers (B-26s) sent to attack two power stations on the Dutch Coast. Eaker's reaction to the B-26 "disaster," the only occasion in the war when an entire air force mission was lost in action, displayed him at his best, both in decisiveness and in consideration for his fliers. As originally structured, the VIII Bomber Command was allocated a full wing (the 3rd, commanded by Hansell) of mediums, trained for the zero-level attacks that had proven very successful under Kenney in the southwest Pacific, where Japanese defenses were negligible. The planners in Washington had high hopes for similar success in Europe against coastal targets even without fighter support, which was impractical at zero level. The first B-26 mission on May 14 had been inconclusive, with no damage done and no losses, though some planes were hit by flak. Three days later when eleven took off to attack the same two targets, one B-26 returned in a few minutes with engine trouble, but "Possum Hansell would never forget the feeling of waiting with others at the field in the fading light, knowing they were never coming back." The next day Eaker flew to the B-26 base at Bury St. Edmunds, taking me along and also Col. Harold McGinnis, the Eighth's air inspector

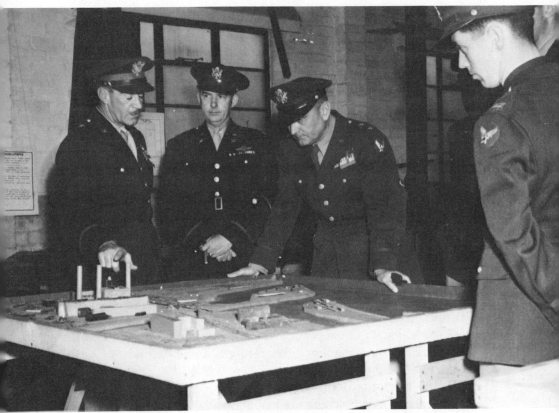

The informal inquest at Bury St. Edmunds following the 100 percent loss of the second B-26 mission, May 1943. Eaker (center) studies a model of the Dutch coastal target, attended by Col. F. M. Brady, base CO; Col. Harold McGinnis, air inspector, Eighth Air Force; and the author.

general. We stood around a table model of the targets while Eaker talked quietly with Col. F. M. Brady, the group CO. Then he instructed Brady to "tell your man there will be no more zero-level missions. They are stood down. We'll retrain them for medium-altitude missions with fighter cover."[15]

Ten days later he wrote Maj. Gen. Barney M. Giles, who had succeeded Stratemeyer as Arnold's chief of staff and was holding the fort in Arnold's absence: "Two members of a B-26 crew who participated in this attack were picked up in a dinghy in the Channel a week after the mission. . . . Our Inspector General is now engaged in piecing out the story and the full report will be along shortly.

... As nearly as I can make out the preliminary report ... four planes were knocked down by flak; two collided, probably resulting from injury to crews through flak; two were destroyed by fighters on the way home; and two ... were lost due to unknown causes. ... I am now convinced that we must discontinue low-level attack except for that against surface vessels. ... I am going to put the medium bombers in the Air Support Command and give them maximum training as part of the tactical air force to support any ground forces invading the Continent." A year later the B-26s proved invaluable during OVERLORD but at the time Eaker's command decision served to reinforce Arnold's *idée fixe* that the Eighth was overly cautious.[16]

In that same pregnant letter, one of many four-pagers Eaker sent Arnold or Giles that month, he covered other urgencies, three of which are quoted here in part. "We now have five new Groups here with both their air and ground echelons, and they have already executed five of six missions. Their operational use is greatly restricted, however, because their organizational equipment has not arrived. We have raked and scraped from every source, including the British, all the tools, the bomb-handling equipment, gas trucks and so forth which we could lay our hands on. Obviously, however, these units will not be at maximum operating efficiency until their organizational equipment arrives. ...

"The P-47s are doing all right. We are well pleased with their performance in combat and are having much less engine trouble. The fighter pilots assure me that they believe they can cope with the FW-190 at any altitude, but they well know, of course, that they really come into their own around the 30,000-ft. The P-47 is, of course, of little more use than a Spitfire IX to accompany long-range bombers until the long-range tanks are provided. These tanks are of no use until they are perfected to the point where they will be usable at high altitude. ...

"Operations during the past ten days went off very well. We have obtained the approval of the Combined Bomber Offensive program, and we have made approximately 1,000 sorties of the 2,800 we have to do prior to July 1. Of the six missions executed within a period of eight days, four were highly successful. The loss rate ... is well under 5%. ..."[17]

As soon as the TRIDENT Conference ended, Castle Coombe became the home for six weeks of a uniquely influential guest, Robert A. Lovett, assistant secretary of war for air. He came, not because

Eaker and his brilliant ally, Assistant Secretary of War for Air Robert
Lovett, 1943.

Arnold had asked him to, but because he wanted to see for himself
just how the Army Air Forces' most important arm was doing. His
visit brought enormous benefits to the Eighth. Tall, thin, bald, aqui-
line of face and elegant of dress, Lovett looked a bit forbidding but
had wisdom, warmth and wit that won everyone at once. He has
come down through the years by unanimous acclaim as one of the
most brilliant and effective of all the World War II policy makers.
John F. Kennedy provided the best evidence of that judgment when
he became president fifteen years later and offered Lovett his choice
of the three most important posts in the cabinet—secretary of state,
defense or treasury, all of which Lovett refused because of poor
health. While a Yale undergraduate in 1917 he had joined, and then
flown in France with, a naval fighter squadron formed by Trubee
Davison. After ww I Lovett moved into the world of Wall Street
finance and north shore of Long Island residence from which Davison had come. It was when Davison flew back to Long Island for
weekends in the late twenties with Eaker as his pilot that the future
Eighth Air Force commander and the future assistant secretary of

war for air met. "We became very fond of him," Lovett recalled. "Adele [Mrs. Lovett] and I both thought that way about Ruth and Ira almost instantaneously. It's unusual for me to make friends that way. It usually takes me a little time, but this was a complete capitulation almost on introduction."[18]

After Davison stepped down when Roosevelt was elected president in 1932, the post of assistant secretary for air lapsed until 1941. Then the growing threat of war led Roosevelt to bring two Republicans into his cabinet—Henry L. Stimson as secretary of war, and William F. Knox as secretary of the navy. Stimson, a Wall Street lawyer and former secretary of state, at once recruited Lovett. He had become expert on logistics as a director of the Union Pacific Railroad and was on a railway inspection trip in California in 1941 when he next saw Eaker, then CO at Hamilton Field. "Ira was happy as a clam there. We talked about the P-40 for a long time. How the hell he ever got that plane to fly I don't know. Worst pile of junk. . . ."[19] Through the Union Pacific Lovett had become close to Harriman, whose father had built it, becoming a partner of the august Wall Street banking house of Brown Brothers, Harriman. From London in 1943 both Harriman and Eaker had been urging Lovett to come over. When at last he did so, on May 17, while Arnold was still in the hospital and then on a quick fishing trip to Oregon, Eaker moved out of his own suite at Castle Coombe to make it available for the distinguished visitor, but carefully avoided telling Lovett about it for he knew his friend would be embarrassed.

At dawn the day after Lovett arrived, a cuckoo took station in a larch tree outside his window and returned every morning during his visit to serenade him noisily and derisively with "Cuckoo! Cuckoo!" This produced much merriment at Castle Coombe, which was heartily shared by Lovett. At the bottom of the garden was an AA battery manned ("womanned," said Eaker) by a jolly squad of English farm girls and a female lieutenant. Eaker had made chums of them all and took Lovett down to get acquainted. "One of the them," Lovett recalled, "said, 'I do hope that our constant firing doesn't bother you at night,' and I said, 'No, the only thing that bothers me at night is that big black and white cuckoo. Perhaps you could be good enough to correct that problem by putting a few shells through that larch tree.' " The secretary's repose was not always interrupted, for he spent much of his time in England visiting all the bases and talking with all ranks. He also, of course, saw Devers,

Bradley, Knerr and Winant as well as Portal and many British leaders.[20]

Lovett brought Eaker the news of Arnold's second heart attack, and the Eighth Air Force commander at once wrote him a long, amiable and newsy letter of consolation, beginning, "I am greatly concerned . . . by the news Bob Lovett brought about your indisposition," and concluding, "Don't worry about us; we are doing all right and all of us are pulling for you to be back on the tightrope with your big umbrella again in the very near future."[21]

But when Arnold did return to his Pentagon desk early in June his mood was anything but amiable. Instead of noting the series of successful missions of growing size since TRIDENT, he sent Eaker several gruff cables asking why so few heavy bombers had been in action in view of the substantial reinforcements he had just been sent. He also suggested several officers for consideration as replacement for Longfellow. Background came in a letter from Giles dated June 11, saying: "General Arnold is back in the driver's seat. . . . I pointed out to him that a large number of your groups were very new and that a number of your combat crews had recently arrived. General Arnold believes that you are especially weak in your Chief of Staff and your Bomber Commander. As a matter of fact he flatly refuses to OK Bubb for promotion. I tried to sell him on the idea that a Theater Commander has a job to do and he should know more about how to employ the officers available than anyone else. Suggest that you write General Arnold a personal letter on Bubb's promotion and in case you do not get what you want believe that it would be a good idea for Bubb to be given another job or returned to the States. . . ."[22] But before Eaker received that temperate advice he had another sharp cable from Arnold, beginning, "Further relative to low percentage of airplanes your organization has been able to keep in commission," and going on to suggest that the Eighth might "not" be able to "handle the supply and maintenance problems which will greatly increase with the very large additional number of airplanes being assigned your theater within the next few months." Arnold added that he was "reserving full decision until the return of Colonel Knerr," and concluded, "Your frank comments are desired."[23]

Eaker, acting with the full support of Knerr, Devers and Lovett, volleyed back with a stiff cable the next day. He faulted Arnold's calculations on aircraft available for combat because Arnold had not included the training time needed for new crews and the lack of ground equipment. There were indeed 664 heavy bombers in the ETO, but only 385 were at Longfellow's disposal for operations against Germany. As for replacing Longfellow, Eaker said none of the suggested officers "has yet had any experience in this theater or a command and combat experience in any other theater to justify his immediate assignment as Bomber Commander with the exception of Hansell and the possible exception of Anderson. . . . Hansell has been carefully considered for eventual Bomber Commander. He is nervous and highly strung, and it is very doubtful whether he would physically stand the trials and responsibilities. . . . Anderson has but recently arrived and was without experience either as a group commander or a wing commander in this theater. Immediately upon his arrival he was given wing command and he has been gaining valuable experience in that regard. . . . Hope to have Anderson ready to relieve Longfellow by July one. This makes it necessary to relieve Hansell at same time, replacing him with LeMay. Urge earliest possible promotion of LeMay as recommended about two months ago by me and Theater Commander. . . . Conclusion with frankness as you suggested: You are not satisfied with conditions here. Neither am I, and I am not satisfied with the support I have had. . . . Understand reasons and credit you with doing all you can to help us. Neither of us has been able to accomplish ideal for reasons both should appreciate. We get nowhere with recriminations. I can do this job if I get the same support from you I am getting from Theater Commander. Nobody can do it without that."[24]

Arnold hit back on June 15 with a letter beginning: "Your cablegram relative to the maintenance of your airplanes and the number being operated was not entirely what I expected. I am perfectly willing to take the blame for anything, but that does not correct the existing situation." He followed with two pages of detailed, querulous paragraphs that in effect cast doubt on most of Eaker's assertions about crew shortage and maintenance, concluding: "I am willing to do anything possible to build up your forces but you must play your part. My wire was sent to get you to toughen up—to can these fellows who cannot produce—to put in youngsters who can carry the ball. . . . In any event, a definite change seems to be in order but you have to be tough to handle the situation. This has been a long letter but I am writing it because I want you to come out of this a real commander. You have performed an excellent job but there are times when you will have to be tough—so be tough when it is necessary and pass out the bouquets when they should be passed out. I hope you will accept this letter in the spirit in which it is written."[25]

While the main controversy swirled over bomber command's leadership, maintenance and shortage of crews, the parallel storm over fighter command came to a head as well. It was precipitated by a June 12 memorandum to Arnold from one of the bright young colonels on his advisory staff—Emmett R. "Rosie" O'Donnell, Jr., who later achieved distinction and high rank as a B-29 commander in the Pacific. O'Donnell, on the basis of "combat reports" and "talking with several pilots who have recently returned from the U.K.," declared that "fighters are not escorting our heavy bombardment to the full extent of their capabilities. They have been in very little combat, have few operational losses and have knocked down very few enemy aircraft. . . . Recommend that the attached wire or something akin to it, be sent to General Eaker."[26] As noted earlier in this chapter, O'Donnell's verdict was based in large measure on inaccurate data about the use of drop-tanks. But in a broader sense he was correct: Hunter was keeping his planes on a short leash, tied to bomber escort and not free to seek out the Luftwaffe and provoke a fight. As Eaker phrased the issue later: "The real argument was whether the fighters would clear an area and the bombers would go through that area, or whether the fighters would fly in proximity to the bombers, in formation with them, above, to each side and below, to keep the German fighters off them as they progressed toward the target. I suppose there were some who supported each of those ideas even late in the war."[27]

Arnold, hair-trigger as ever, followed O'Donnell's suggestion and fired off a caustic, three-page cable that reached Eaker about the same day as his letter about "being tough." "What is the reason for the short escort?" he asked. "I hesitate to ascribe it to the range characteristics of the P-47. . . . Desire you give this subject your personal attention and forward me your comments as soon as possible."[28] Eaker had already, in long letters, outlined the problem of getting the drop-tanks needed to increase the P-47's range and had also suggested his old friend, Kepner, now a major general, as Hunter's replacement.

Now he patiently drew up a five-page response both to Arnold's letter and the cable. As always he put a velvet glove on his iron hand. The letter began: "Averell Harriman talked to me the day after his return about his two conferences with you. His conversations, plus your own recent letters, lead me to make the following comment quite frankly and after careful consideration. Regarding our personal relation, I have always felt the closest bond of friendship between us as two individuals. I have never thought that you placed quite the confidence in me officially as an officer as you did as a friend. I sometimes thought that you were tough on me officially in order to make certain that nobody had a feeling that I got the positions I held through our personal friendship, and to make doubly sure that you did not allow that friendship to influence you unduly toward me officially. . . ."

Eaker went on to "set down some comments flowing from recent events." He would relieve Longfellow and Bubb as of July 1 and replace them with Anderson and Col. John A. "Sammy" Samford, "a very able officer who has been Deputy Chief of Staff here. . . . Anderson especially asked for him. . . . This Bomber Command job of ours is a man-killer. It will break anybody down in six months unless he be a very unusual fellow. I shall continue to give it closest scrutiny. . . .

"I believe Kepner will make a good man in Fighter Command, but I cannot put him into the job without some experience and indoctrination in this theater. I have talked the whole situation over with Hunter and he understands the position thoroughly. . . . He still insists that it was absolutely necessary, having new men and a new plane, to break them in gradually. I thought, along with Tooey, that the situation was so critical for fighter support for our bombardment effort that we should have taken more of a chance with our fighters, and I have continually urged Hunter to greater boldness in this regard. I must admit, however, that Hunter's system is now paying results. His fighter pilots have high morale; they are enthusiastic about supporting the bombers and they have complete confidence in their ability to beat the Hun, using the P-47 against his best fighters. The principal handicap, of course, to full and thorough support of the bombers, has been the lack of long-range tanks. This position is rapidly clearing up. . . .

"One of my principal worries now is that our official supporters in the highest levels, and our supporting public, may not be able to stand our losses in combat. I want you to know that we can stand them and that we are doing everything possible to keep them at a minimum. . . . It is perfectly evident now that the Germans admit that our daylight bombing against their industry is the principal

The head table at a PINETREE "Bomber Night" in 1943 after Anderson became commander. Facing camera, l. to r.: Spaatz, Portal, Anderson, Eaker and Harris. Back to camera, l. to r.: Slessor, Kepner and unidentified colonel.

threat, and they are marshalling their strongest and best defenses to cope with it. We may as well frankly admit that it is going to be a bloody battle. The side will win which can make good its losses. In other words, the side which has the most reserve strength. . . ."

Eaker then gave the coup de grace to the YB-40—the heavily armored B-17 with extra gun turrets Portal and others believed to be the only feasible "escort fighter" for the bomber formations. He wrote: "The plain truth of the matter is now, that we do not want any more YB-40s as such. We want all our bombers to be able to carry bombs. . . . The main reason why the YB-40 has proved unsatisfactory in its present form is because it did not have the same flight characteristics as the other bombers. It required two inches more manifold pressure, additional RPM in order merely to hold formation, and it

was too heavy to have the same rate of climb as other bombers.
. . . Bomber Command put these planes in as a unit. Naturally, the
Germans recognized the difference in type and, while showing some
curiosity, they did not take on these planes. We then put YB-40s one
on each side of the leader in each wing. This had been the man the
Germans had been trying to knock out. It was here that the difference in flight characteristics showed up and the difficulty of maintaining formation became apparent. There was definitely a
depreciation in morale of the YB-40 crews, which I think is understandable. They were in the hot-seat all the time and they did not
carry bombs."

After touching on a variety of other tactical and public relations
matters Eaker closed this long letter—clearly one that risked his own
neck on the Arnold chopping block—with a respectful but very
strong punch. "I shall always accept gladly and in the proper spirit,
any advice, counsel or criticism from you. I do not feel, however, that
my past service which has come under your observation indicates
that I am a horse which needs to be ridden with spurs. I think you
know that I will do my best, not only for you but because I realize
the importance in this War and to our Air Force of the job I have
to do here. Naturally, I am working pretty hard and under considerable strain. I am endeavoring, however, to maintain my calmness,
good health and good judgment, and to exercise soundly the functions of command which devolve on me. I cannot tell you how happy
I am at the thorough support I have had from General Devers.
Naturally, the presence of his Chief of Staff, Idwal Edwards, here is
a very fine thing for me and for this Air Force. We have been through
a dark period and we are not entirely out of the wood yet, but I think
we will make the grade in one of the toughest spots imaginable if I
can maintain your confidence and support."[29]

The day before Eaker dictated this long, show-down statement
his boss addressed two short letters to him that dramatize the ambivalence of Arnold's attitude. One was positive, beginning: "Your boys
are doing a great job over there. During the past several days the
tempo has been stepped up considerably. This has been noted by
everybody in authority here in the United States. The newspapers
have commented on it time and time again. I hope we will be able
to settle the replacement problem soon. . . . Give my regards to
everybody over there and tell them that we over here are mighty
proud of the fine work they are doing." The negative letter—obvi-

ously drafted by one of his staff because the file copy in Arnold's papers at the Library of Congress bears the hand-written inscription at the bottom: "As rewritten in Gen. A's Office"—said: ". . . . there are too many headquarters in our organization. This is probably because we have too many people trying to make and trying to be Generals. Now I am not criticizing you or your method of doing business personally. I am criticizing all of us and the American way of doing business wherein we compound one headquarters upon another just to get promotions. With the above in mind, I am withholding the promotions of Colonels LeMay and Timberlake. . . ."[30]

When Eaker received this rebuff he patiently wrote a low-key, factual explanation of the combat wing commander role. "It is exactly parallel with the brigade commander in the ground forces. He has but a small staff as his is not an administrative headquarters, neither is he in the channel of command for correspondence, supply and similar subjects. He has under his control three heavy bomber groups . . . and a striking force of 148 heavy bombers. I submit that this task is worthy of the grade of Brigadier General and think it can be best performed only by that rank. I do not agree, and I think it is unjust to say or to infer, that we created this Combat Wing merely to get additional Brigadier Generals. Since Anderson became Bomber Commander, LeMay has commanded our 4th Wing, now including six heavy bombardment groups which are operational, and which, with its supporting services, totals more than 15,000 officers and men. He has proved by successful group command over a period of many months that he is an able combat leader. Timberlake has likewise proven thoroughly capable of Wing Command and he now has a provisional wing of three Liberator-equipped heavy bombardment groups on temporary duty in Africa. While the success of his mission [Ploesti] is not entirely dependent upon his promotion, I think the chances of its success will be enhanced thereby. . . . The primary consideration in this matter, it seems to me, is the fact that the Theater Commander, myself and all the experienced Air Force Officers who have examined conditions here, agree that the proposed organization is needed for our efficiency in doing our job. . . ."[31]

By this time, with letters and cables flying back and forth across the Atlantic in epistolary similarity to combat box formation, it began to look as if generals Arnold and Eaker were devoting more time to fighting each other than to defeating the Germans. Other senior people intervened. To an Eaker cable that stressed the need

for a "higher flow of crew replacement" and said "ten groups maintained at full operational strength can bring more pressure on the
enemy than 20 emaciated groups where battle casualties are not
promptly replaced," Devers added, "I concur in Eaker's recommendations. His requirements for replacements are the barest minimum.
. . . Most damaging to the fighting spirit of our combat units are
empty places at the mess table." And Harriman, after clearing the
text with Eaker, got off a cable saying: "Find Eaker and Harris in
complete agreement that outcome of battle over Germany both day
and night hinges largely on success of our Fortresses in destroying
strength and vitality of German fighter air force before possible new
German tactics in defense are developed. The decision will be
affected by number of planes we can get into the battle during the
next two or three months. Controlling factor at present is availability
of crews, now out of balance with airplanes. . . ."[32]

But the most effective calming voice was that of Lovett. He had
returned to Washington in mid-June and at once, of course, conferred with Arnold, giving him very strong reassurances about
Eaker's command competence and also the justice of Eaker's pleas
for "more replacement crews. . . . Better trained crews. . . . Delivery
of operational equipment and ground echelons prior to, or concur-
rent with, the arrival of combat groups. . . . Planes should arrive with
necessary modifications completed in this country, particularly with
respect to mounting 50 calibre guns forward. . . . If these urgent
needs are promptly met the operational efficiencies of the Eighth Air
Force will, in my opinion, increase by at least 50 percent."[33]

On July 7 Arnold called it a truce with his equally strong-willed
subordinate in England. "You were quite frank in your discussion
of our relationship, and I want you to get this firmly in your mind
that had I not had confidence in you—confidence in your ability, I
would never have built you up for the job that you now have. I give
you full credit for having the inherent ability—the knowledge and
judgment that goes with the command that you now hold. That being
the case, I see no reason in the world for any fears or suspicion as
to our relationship entering your mind. But you must know me well
enough by this time to know that I am very outspoken. I say what
I think and do what I think best, so when you hear these rumors,
comments, criticisms or what-have-you, always remember that if
there is anything serious you will be the first one to hear of it and
it will come from me direct. I hope that . . . will be reassuring to you

and will eliminate any doubt or apprehension that you may have as to your status with me. . . . Saw Ruth last night for the first time in a long time and she looks grand. . . ."[34]

Forty years later Lovett mused: "It was clear from the start that Hap had been making wild statements about what the B-17 could do. It couldn't do everything. It needed a nose turret above everything. They put this chin on it. That helped. Another thing it needed was fighter escort in deep penetrations. I think Hap transferred some of his acrimony to Ira because of the failure of the B-17 to perform as he said it would. . . . There was some acrimony, but as far as Ira was concerned, it made no difference. It certainly never affected him in his loyalty to Hap. . . . I pushed hard on Hap. His hands were tied by his mouth. He said our only need was Flying Fortresses, that's all; very few fighters could keep up with them. . . . The Messerschmidts had no difficulty at all."[35]

Lovett's "push" on Arnold immediately speeded up the flow of crew replacements, drop-tanks and a variety of intricate improvements for the B-17s, B-26s and P-47s. But his chief thrust was insistence on the "immediate need for long range fighters. This may be met by proper tanks for P-47s, but ultimately P-38s and P-51s will be needed. . . . Fighter escort will have to be provided for B-17s on as many missions as possible in order particularly to get them through the first wave of the German fighter defense, which is now put up in depth so that the B-17s are forced to run the gauntlet both in to the target and out from it. The P-47s can serve as top cover if satisfactory tanks are developed for them. The ideal plane, however, now in production is the P-38 for long range escort duty. . . . It has been used in over water escort duty on operations with a radius of slightly over 400 miles. However, the moment it drops its wing tanks it must turn back. High hopes are felt for the P-51 with wing tanks."[36]

Belatedly persuaded, Arnold bucked the problem to Giles in a June 22 directive that was yet another specimen of his standard I-don't-care-how-you-do-it-but-get-it-done method. "Attached, are Mr. Lovett's comments on the P-47 situation. . . . About six months remain before deep daylight penetration of Germany begins. Within this next six months, you have got to get a fighter to protect our bombers. Whether you use an existing type or have to start from scratch is your problem. . . ." Arnold made no mention of the P-51 but did express the belief that the P-38 was too slow. Giles, a much more decisive chief of staff for Arnold than Stratemeyer had been, at once flew west to see J. H. "Dutch" Kindelberger, president of North American Aviation in California and the sole manufacturer of the P-51 Mustang, which he was making primarily for the British. With its original Allison engine changed to the Rolls-Royce Merlin, it now had the performance to match the Messerschmidt but lacked the range for long escort duty. Instead of wing tanks, Giles suggested: "Take out the radio set behind the pilot and put in a 100-gallon tank. Then open up the wings and put in bullet-proof tanks the entire length." Kindelberger protested that the wings and landing gear were not strong enough for the increased load. But Giles insisted, and tests showed that the sturdy Mustang could indeed take off with the extra three hundred gallons of gas. It became the wonder weapon of the bomber offensive. But it would be January before the Eighth Air Force could get the P-51 in quantity—too late for Eaker's immediate combat challenge.[37]

Craven and Cate, the official air force historians, pronounced in 1948, "The failure to have developed such a plane was the most serious flaw in the AAF's program, and it is difficult to account for."[38] When this was called to Eaker's attention in 1959 he snorted: "No. That isn't the truth of it at all. . . . I am surprised that an historian would make such a statement. All the Air Force knew the answer. . . . It took the pressures and exigencies of war, and all the manufacturers that came in to help in the war, to push the state of the art of building to where you could get an airplane that could go a thousand miles and deal acceptably with the Messerschmidt ME-109s. It was the state of the art we were up against. It had nothing to do with controversy. There wasn't a man on the Air Force staff, from General Arnold on down, who wouldn't have given his neck for a long-range fighter. . . . We were experimenting with the P-38 Lightnings. . . . They attempted to accompany the bombers several hundred miles inside Germany, and then they would drop their wing tanks if they were called upon to fight. They couldn't tarry long, however, because their fuel would just get them back. . . . [It] is just like saying you can't understand why we didn't have a great big Cadillac in 1910: the state of the art just hadn't developed to that point.

"You will find that the best tacticians, the best strategists . . . deal with what they know to be the possibilities of weapons. . . . It would be a serious weakness on the part of a commander . . . to plan some conflict or strategy with weapons which couldn't be produced for several years. That would be stupid. You have to plan to use what weapons you have and can visualize as being available in your time span. We didn't have long-range fighters then. Nobody here, or abroad, or even in Germany, which was ahead of us in fighter development, even suggested the possibility of long-range fighters."[39]

To Lovett, in several long exchanges of letters after the powerful assistant secretary of war for air returned to Washington, Eaker expressed his immense gratitude. "I have noted a great change," he wrote, "all on the improvement side, in our relations with the 'Home Office.' This I attribute almost entirely as an aftermath of your visit here and to your very hard work on our behalf after your return."[40]

And, in one of those deft gestures at which Eaker was so adept, he dispatched his supply-side troubleshooter, Col. Peter Beasley, to search London for a stuffed cuckoo. One was found, handsomely mounted beneath a glass bell jar, and was sent off to Lovett with a brass plaque as a "memento of Castle Coombe." Lovett replied: "I have seldom been given the bird in a more enjoyable fashion than that devised by you and your colleagues. My delight is doubled by the thought that the infernal racket raised by that extremely bad tempered bird is silenced temporarily and I don't care how many shots the anti-aircraft batteries . . . had to fire to get on the target. I am discussing with the Wild Life Section of the Department of the Interior the most appropriate steps to take to keep this cuckoo from laying eggs in my nest. If there are going to be any eggs laid around here I am going to do it myself. . . ."[41]

17

"Hitler built a fortress around Europe, but he forgot to put a roof on it."

—FRANKLIN D. ROOSEVELT

C ARL NORCROSS, whose intelligence assignments took him home to the States several times in 1942 and 1943 for lengthy periods, observed: "The time cycle of the air war was three months. If an officer left the UK for three months, he would come back to find it a different war. Either we had changed or the Germans had changed. We had new targets, new priorities, new kinds of equipment (in radar, communications, bombs), different fighter escort, changes in formation, changes in the way we worked with the other wings, new rules about crew behavior if shot down. Or the Germans had become stronger or weaker in their fighter planes, in their flak, in their radar or other communications, in their air-sea rescue, in their treatment of prisoners, in building V-1 or V-2 sites, in camouflaging targets, in operating trains during daylight, etc., etc."[1]

At no time in all of World War II were such fluctuations more marked than in the spring and summer of 1943. Consider, as a first example, the U-boat crisis. The year had begun with near hysteria in the high commands in Washington and London over the continuing huge Allied shipping losses in the North Atlantic. If these could not be stopped that summer or greatly reduced, the UK would have been throttled and any conquest of the Continent made impossible. There were an estimated 240 U-boats operational in the Atlantic,

with another 120 training in the Baltic. New ones were being produced at a rate of between ten and fifteen per month, while sinkings
averaged between five and seven. It was clear that bombing the
U-boat building yards, such as Vegesack, while the most efficient way
to eliminate the underwater boats of Admiral Doenitz, could not be
effective quickly enough to reduce the operating fleet in time to
permit the vast buildup of forces for the UK and North Africa; hence
the top priority orders to the Eighth Air Force to keep banging at
the concrete submarine sheds on the Bay of Biscay side of France and
to the RAF to obliterate the surrounding French towns. Both air
forces complied, though neither Eaker nor Harris believed their raids
did much to handicap the operating U-boat fleet at sea. In the first
quarter of 1943 63 percent of the Eighth's bombs were against submarine facilities, 30 percent of the RAF. In the second quarter the
Eighth's percentage fell to 52, while the RAF stayed at 30. Then, so
abruptly the airmen involved found it hard to believe, the crisis was
over, the battle of the Atlantic won.[2]

The victory came from a mixture of strict convoy discipline,
improved radar and very long range (VLR) aircraft, primarily B-24s,
prowling the sea lanes from bases in North Africa, England, Ireland,
Iceland, Greenland and North America and keeping the U-boats
submerged. Doenitz gave the air attacks at sea the primary credit.
The subpens, as he commented during the heat of the battle, continued to function though "the towns of St. Nazaire and Lorient have
been rubbed out as main submarine bases. No dog or cat is left in
these towns. Nothing but the submarine shelters remain." After the
war the U.S. Strategic Bombing Survey concurred, saying, "strategic
bombing can at best be considered only an incidental contributing
factor."[3]

Eaker and all his fliers were happy to be allowed to turn their
backs on the subpens along the Bay of Biscay coast. Sorties to "flak
alley," as the men called it, fell in the second half of the year to 16
percent. But there had been useful by-products of the otherwise
fruitless U-boat campaign. One was the improved combat technique
that evolved there—tighter formations, better bombing method and
discovery of the B-17's vulnerability to head-on attacks. Another
benefit could be labeled "opportunism." The relative nearness of the
subpen targets made them a less dangerous objective than industrial
targets in Germany itself. Since the Eighth was functioning on a
shoestring basis, it was something of a blessing in disguise to be

obligated to make attacks in France instead of the much more desirable ones in the Reich. After the opening shot at Wilhelmshaven on January 27 Eaker managed to sneak two more shallow raids into German terrain in February, three in March and one in April. Not until May did the Eighth begin to get strength adequate for its mission. In February its daily combat strength averaged only 74 operating combinations (combat crews and planes). In March it managed to put up missions of 100 on three occasions. On May 29 it set a record of 279 to three targets in France.[4]

To the leaders of the Luftwaffe this obvious American timidity and slow growth added up to weakness. As with Doenitz and the U-boats, Goering and his Luftwaffe henchmen were trying desperately to rearrange their dwindling squadrons of planes to meet the bomber offensive from England, most of it at that point being British. RAF Bomber Command between March and July, in addition to its huge onslaughts on the French ports, dispatched 18,506 sorties in 43 major attacks on German cities, including 34,000 tons of bombs on the Ruhr. In Wuppertal-Barman, for example, a fifteen-minute blitz ruined the heart of the city and killed 2,450 people. After an April attack on Essen Goebbels wrote in his diary, "The damage is colossal and, indeed, ghastly. . . ." General of night fighters, Joseph Kammhuber, had managed to increase his night-fighter Gruppen to 18, which was five more than in 1942, but they totaled only 500 planes, of which a third were still in the Mediterranean or in Russia. Flak, also under Kammhuber, had been doubled to about 400 heavy batteries, 40 percent of Germany's total, most of them taken, as Air Marshal Harris liked to point out, from the Russian front. In May Kammhuber, buttressed by estimates of American aircraft production obtained from Germany's OKW, put in a plea to increase his command to 2,160 night fighters, saying he was fearful the U.S. bombers would soon be committed to night action. Goering took him to see Hitler, who shouted: "If the figures of 5,000 a month were right, you would be right too. In that case I would have to withdraw from the Eastern front forthwith and apply all resources to air defense. But they are not right! I will not stand for such nonsense!"[5]

Not until July, a month in which Eaker was able to send his bombers into Germany all of ten times, including two deep raids (to Kassel and Oschersleben), and helped the RAF set off the awful fire storm that devastated Hamburg and killed 50,000 people, did Goering approve an increase in fighter defenses. But Hitler balked again, insisting that a change from the offense to the defense was out of the question and that any increase in aircraft production should go into bombers, not fighters. Eventually the Luftwaffe did manage to push through a ruling for more fighters, but it was too late to make any real difference. What they could, and did, do at once was redispose their defense structure, thereby signaling their recognition that the daylight threat was hitting their vitals.

Instead of some 300 day fighters spread in a thin screen along the south shore of the English Channel, the Luftwaffe pulled back and staggered its Gruppen in depth on all the major approach routes to the Ruhr and the big industrial targets, with control from a central point. This was precisely what Chennault had predicted at the air tac school in 1935. Next the Germans found themselves obliged to bring back virtually all of their fighters from the Mediterranean to protect Germany's heart. Russia was a far more decisive theater to the Nazis but that front also was stripped of fighter defense. By the end of 1943 the Eastern Front of 1,650 miles was defended by only 425 German fighters, while the Reich itself was guarded by 1,650, 68 percent of the Luftwaffe's front-line strength. Even so, there were not enough day fighters in existence; as early as April 1943 an ULTRA interception revealed that the Luftwaffe was also using its night fighters for day-time defense. This shortsighted expedient was a catastrophe, for the night fighters represented a heavy cost in special equipment and in crew training that was thrown away in planes not designed to compete with American day fighters or with B-17 gunners. On August 17 alone, over Regensburg and Schweinfurt, the GAF lost 21 night fighters in day operations. In the month of July (worst of the year) the GAF's total fighter losses amounted to an estimated 335 in the West, 245 in the Mediterranean and 210 in the East.[6]

Eaker and the others at the top in the AAF and RAF did not, of course, know all these details at the time. But enough of them trickled through—from photo-reconnaissance, from spies, from code intercepts—to make them all certain that Germany was being hurt and hurt hard by the bomber offensive, both American and British. The British damage was more visible and vastly bigger in extent. It was the bludgeon. Eaker's rapier thrusts were less easy to measure, but it was reassuring to intercept a message in which Goering told his fighter pilots "the Fortresses must be destroyed regardless of everything else," going on to order them to stop attacking stragglers and to focus, under threat of court-martial, on the formations, which

Churchill and Eaker talking with 2nd Lieutenant McFann at a British army exercise, 1943.

must be prevented at whatever cost from reaching their targets.[7] And Eaker knew from the Eighth's own experience with battle damage and crew shortage that, even if his gunners were not knocking down as many ME-109s and FW-190s as they claimed, normal attrition was taking its toll. Miscellaneous radio traffic between the Luftwaffe bases during and after big American attacks gave clear evidence of what Lt. Gen. Johannes Steinhoff, inspector general of the German air force, confirmed when the war was over:

"In the course of this defensive battle against the four-engine enemy bombers the number of German fighter pilots remaining, most of whom were not very experienced anyway, was enormously depleted. With the battle going on, morale continued to go down. . . . A bad problem facing each pilot was the return to base after a mission. Very frequently fighting took place over long distances above cloud cover, and the completely disoriented fighters had to go below the deck and attempt to land wherever they could. Together with insufficient navigational aids, this resulted in many additional losses and a wide scattering of our aircraft. . . . Those who like myself have flown these attacks and have maneuvered through the stream of innumerable bombers will never be able to forget this picture, and I am sure there is not one who could claim that he did not feel relieved when he landed back home in one piece."[8]

With his supplies of planes and crews at last growing fast and, for a time, on schedule, and with mounting evidence that the Luftwaffe might indeed be defeatable in 1943 if the pressure were kept up, Eaker of course set out to maximize the Eighth's blows against the targets specified in POINTBLANK. He had not forgotten Schweinfurt and its concentration of ball-bearing works, and he knew there were only two or three months when clear weather deep inside Germany could be counted on for perhaps a third of the days. But first he had to rearrange the commands of both his bomber and his fighter arms. Bigger forces called for a stronger echelon of operational and administrative headquarters below bomber command itself. He created the first air divisions—four of them—in place of the previous wings. Three divisions were allocated to bomber command and one to air support command in preparation for OVERLORD. Under bomber command each of its divisions was in command of three combat wings, and each of the latter in command of three groups. The groups themselves were expanded gradually to an authorized force of four squadrons of 13 airplanes each plus a squadron reserve of five, giving a group strength of 72 (it was 18 when Eaker came to England). All reported to Anderson, who took over at PINETREE in June. His appointment necessitated relieving not only Longfellow but also Hansell, who was Anderson's senior and had many qualifications for the bomber command post, as noted by Eaker earlier.

Hansell took the bad news with grace after a two-hour session with Eaker at WIDEWING, from which he emerged with face pale and lips pursed. He did, however, prevail on Eaker not to send him back to Washington for duty on Arnold's staff as Arnold wanted. Instead Eaker arranged for Hansell to be deputy to Air Marshal Sir Trafford Leigh-Mallory, former head of RAF Fighter Command, who was designated the chief planning officer for the air aspects of OVERLORD. That would have been an ideal position for Hansell but for the fact that Leigh-Mallory managed to offend virtually all the other top commanders involved in the OVERLORD preparations and was gradually shunted aside. Hansell found himself unhappily back on Arnold's staff in a few months, escaping again to become, briefly, CG of the first B-29 bomber command in the Pacific, where LeMay shouldered past him. Though Hansell never quite made his mark as a top commander, his brilliance at planning did make a very significant contribution to the success of the strategic bombing concept both in Europe and the Far East.

Dismissing Longfellow, his oldest friend, was difficult for Eaker, but he handled it with poker-faced calm and always thereafter stuck to his assertion that Longfellow had been the best officer available to him at the time and had never gotten as much credit as he deserved. Thirty years later Eaker added: "There was disagreement between Longfellow and the Wing Commanders. One of them was LeMay. . . . Kuter and Hansell as wing commanders always had trouble with Longfellow. In their opinion he was too tough. And I had known that aspect and thought it would be very useful. . . . I had a very high regard for Longfellow. But I could understand where his personality would not be agreeable with some of the others. And I told him so and he understood it."[9] In a letter recommending Longfellow for the training command, Eaker wrote to Maj. Gen. Davenport Johnson, commander of the Second Air Force in Colorado Springs, "I really believe Longfellow will be a great help to you, as he was to me while here. He understands better than anybody I know the whole problem of bombardment operation in this theater. He is a tireless worker, and despite the fact we almost killed him off here working, or carrying the responsibility, for 24 hours a day, 7 days a week, I believe he will spring back after a few weeks' rest and do a tremendous job for you and your Air Force. There never was a more loyal officer than Newt. The further I go in this business, the higher I place loyalty among the officer requirements."[10]

Johnson did give Longfellow a job, but he was reduced to his regular rank as colonel.

Hunter was luckier. When Kepner arrived to replace him at fighter command Arnold happened to be in England also and his mustachioed friend from World War I cornered him after a dinner at Castle Coombe to protest fiercely that the switch was unfair and that he had done a good organizing job in England. Persuaded, Arnold gave him a medal and sent him home to be CG of the First Air Force, whose role was primarily antisubmarine patrol.[11]

Bigger command changes were also in the making. The concept

of "air support" as a command designation had become obsolete in North Africa, primarily because of the precedent-setting RAF experience with Gen. Bernard Montgomery and the Desert Army. Air Vice Marshal Arthur Coningham, a feisty New Zealander known to all as "Maori" (pronounced "Mary"), had satisfied Montgomery that air support of ground forces worked much better when under unified command by an airman than by the traditional scattered command from battalion or company units of foot soldiers. Spaatz quickly persuaded Eisenhower likewise, and Kuter drew up new AAF regulations defining U.S. air forces as either strategic or tactical. They were at once rearranged that way in the Mediterranean. In England that summer Arnold decided to do the same, leaving the Eighth as solely strategic and using its air support command as the nucleus of a new air force to be solely tactical. On July 31 he chose Maj. Gen. Lewis H. Brereton to head it. Brereton had been CG of the Ninth Air Force in the Middle East. With the successful conquest of the Mediterranean the various air forces there were being consolidated, and the Ninth's planes and crews were going to Doolittle's Twelfth (tactical). Instead of deactivating the Ninth and its rich tradition, Arnold decided to redesignate it for OVERLORD whenever Brereton and his headquarters staff could get to England. For security reasons there were no public announcements, but Eaker was kept fully posted and also informed that he would be in administrative command of both the Eighth and the Ninth when the time came.[17]

Undergirding both air forces was the plan Gen. Follett Bradley completed in England in April, cleared with Arnold and brought back to Devers and Eaker in late May. It called for the buildup of the Eighth to 254,000 officers and men and 230,000 for the Ninth— a grand total of 485,000. This was quickly cut back to 415,000 when Arnold decided once again to deplete England in favor of the Mediterranean. He diverted 15 groups of heavies from the Eighth to a new strategic air force, the Fifteenth, formed from the heavy bomber elements of the Twelfth. (Doolittle became CG. His place as CG of the Twelfth was taken by Maj. Gen. John K. Cannon.) Even so, the Eighth's growth during the balance of 1943 was very large—from 11 heavy bomber and 3 fighter groups in May to 21 and 11 at the end of December. Total U.S. combat aircraft in the theater rose from 1,671 in June to 2,619 in September, 3,061 in October and 4,242 in December. By the end of the year deliveries were almost up to the totals called for under the POINTBLANK directive. But there was a serious lag in between in the arrival of heavy groups—3 in June; 2 each in July, August and September; none in October; 1 in November; and 5 in December. New fighter groups were also slow to appear, reflecting bottlenecks in the expanded manufacture of the P-51, more drop-tank complications and other logistical problems already recognized by both Eaker and Arnold. What neither of them had expected was, in the bland words of the official air force historians, "a serious lack of balance between combat and service units," reflecting "faulty planning" and inadequate shipping reserves. There turned out not to be enough trained service units in the entire United States to meet the demands specified in the Bradley Plan. Eaker, who had noted sourly in April that "our Air Service Command is our weakest single factor in the Eighth Air Force," now, in July, just as his air battles were at their hottest, faced the irony of at last having what appeared to be enough bombers and crews for the task but not enough service men to keep them flying.[13]

Throughout his army career Eaker had become accustomed to making do with less than he needed. Now, however, he was up against the implacable demand of a target schedule he himself had specified in his presentation of "the Eaker Plan" in Washington in April. Its four phases promised to demolish the seventy-six key targets listed in the POINTBLANK directive in methodical progression and with completion no later than April 1, 1944. About the first phase he had said: "Experience in the European Theater to date indicates that at least 800 airplanes must be in the theater to dispatch 300 bombers on operations. Hence, until the level of U.S. bomber strength in this theater reaches approximately 800, it will not be feasible to sustain a precision bombing offensive against the German fighter factories. It is estimated that we will be able to accommodate and train a force of this capacity by July. . . ."[14]

In June Eaker's stock of bombers briefly did reach the level called for, as indicated by the dispatch of formations almost at the 300 figure six times in the last week of the month. But in the second phase, which began July first, the combination of slowed deliveries of new planes and the inability of the service command to repair battle damage as fast as expected began to cut sharply into the Eighth's ability to meet its schedule of POINTBLANK targets to be hit. By mid-August, when the plan called for a total of 1,068 operational bombers on hand, the Eighth had 921, of which 105 were still in North Africa, leaving the actual force at 816.[15]

Nonetheless, using the forces available, Eaker managed to send out a number of dramatic and highly successful missions, some of them deep into Germany and most against POINTBLANK targets. On seven occasions in the six weeks beginning July 1 he and Anderson dispatched more than the magical 300 heavies. The bombing was for the most part excellent. But the cost was high. On July 28, for example, successful attacks on an aircraft factory in Kassel and against other industrial targets in Oschersleben, both near the center of Germany, cost 22 bombers (7.2 percent) downed and three times that many damaged, with claims of 56/19/41 against the Luftwaffe. There was also the first instance of a new kind of diversion—orders from Washington to attack non-POINTBLANK targets. Four days before the missions to Kassel and Oschersleben the Eighth sent the same groups of heavies more than one thousand miles northeast into central Norway to hit a plant making "heavy water"—a key ingredient in German efforts to develop atomic bombs. Because defenses were slight losses were low—one B-17 crash-landed in Sweden. There would be many other such diversions from POINTBLANK, particularly against the V-1 and V-2 launching sites Germany began building along the Channel.[16]

The Eighth was very active, too, testing and training for something known in layman's language as "bombing through the overcast" or, in British scientific terms, "H2S." Eaker wrote Arnold about this on July 20 in a letter that also reported that he had been sitting up "generally from the hours of 11 P.M. to 1 or 2 A.M." doing a revision of *Winged Warfare*. He continued, "We have had a lot of weather during June and July when the overcast bombing devices could have been used to good advantage." But Portal had demurred, saying, as Eaker went on: "If we lose some of these devices now, the counter measure would be at once apparent to the Germans and when we need it in force for the bad winter weather we should not have it. The reason why we are more likely to lose this device is because it would be in the lead of our bomber formations in daylight, where enemy fighters habitually work on the leader. The reason the RAF can use it is because they install it in Mosquitos which habitually fly at 30,000 feet and have a greater normal cruising speed than any night fighter the Germans can bring against them." He added that the Eighth would eventually use an American improvement of H2S known as HZX but would for the present make do with the British "Oboe." It was "not as good," but "we are looking for a considerable degree of accuracy, sufficient at least so that we can dump our bombs in the heavily built-up industrial areas."[17]

Plans were also well along for bigger and more immediate objectives. Under the rules laid down at Casablanca, Portal was Eaker's immediate boss in terms of POINTBLANK target choice, as he was also for Harris. In mid-July Portal urged that Eaker work out a joint operation with Spaatz against the two biggest German fighter factories, both far down in the south, just above the Alps, and the source of 48 percent of all GAF fighter planes. One of these was at Wiener-Neustadt, near Vienna, the other at Regensburg. Portal undertook to write Tedder in the Mediterranean, while Eaker wrote to Spaatz. The concept evolved for Doolittle's Fifteenth Air Force (including Anderson's B-24s) to bomb Wiener-Neustadt while the Eighth hit Regensburg and then shuttled on to sanctuary in North Africa. The plan was completed in all details, including LeMay going down to North Africa in advance to scout the landing arrangements and confer with Spaatz and Doolittle, and was scheduled at least twice, only to have bad weather in England scrub both missions. When Doolittle eventually went ahead on his own to hit Wiener-Neustadt, Eaker and Anderson turned to a substitute effort—one in which two separate but coordinated missions from the Eighth on the same day would attack two major targets very deep in southern Germany, one of them Regensburg, after which the attackers would fly on to Africa, the other nearby Schweinfurt, from which the bombers would fight their way back to England—thus the origin of what became the first of the two greatest air battles ever fought.[18]

The increased momentum of the Eighth after the Casablanca Conference had not escaped the attention of the press. Dealing with intricate public relations problems became a substantial concern of Eaker's throughout 1943. He had allowed war correspondents to accompany the heavies for the first time on February 26—six on a mission of ninety-three B-17s and B-24s to Wilhelmshaven. One of them was Walter Cronkite, then representing the United Press. Another was Robert B. Post of the New York Times. He was killed on one of the two B-24s lost that day.[19]

Women war correspondents were dauntless also. One of them—Dixie Tighe of International News Service—asked permission to go on a heavy bomber mission too. Eaker referred it to the theater commander (still Andrews), noting that "present regulations from the War Department" were unclear "whether duly accredited women war correspondents are to be given operational flights on the same status as men. . . ." Andrews characteristically had no doubts and assumed full responsibility. Eaker then endorsed the file to bomber command, ordering an investigation down the line to ascertain: "Will the presence of women reporters on missions jeopardize in any way the successful performance? . . . Can arrangements be worked out aboard the aircraft whereby the use of toilet facilities for women reporters can be made with propriety and decency as they are, for example, aboard an air liner? What is the attitude of combat crews?" The record is unclear whether Ms. Tighe did in fact ever go. But *Life*'s intrepid Margaret Bourke-White wangled her way onto at least one B-17 mission in the Mediterranean.[20]

A different kind of public relations problem was provoked by Sy Bartlett, the screen writer who had been Spaatz's aide in 1942 but had remained in England when Spaatz went to North Africa. Bartlett was assigned to operations research and analysis at PINETREE under Harlan—a staff function of growing importance as scientific thinking was applied to military operations. In a top secret room at PINETREE charts were maintained showing the comparison between groups in, for example, number of planes assigned versus number operational; percent of airplanes reaching target versus number dispatched; percent of bombs on target; number of rounds of ammo per Luftwaffe plane claimed; ratio of men out ill to percent of bombs on target; relationship between crew illness and diet. This last emphatically reinforced Eaker's long-held view that the mess hall was an important key to operational effectiveness. Bartlett, nimble-minded and verbal, was good at summarizing these lessons learned, and it was both brave and appropriate for him to go, as he did one night late in March, as an observer with an RAF attack on Berlin. Over the Nazi capital he persuaded the RAF bombardier in his plane to let him toggle the bomb drop when the right moment came. Then Bartlett's show-business instincts toggled him. Back in London before breakfast, he called a press conference at Claridge's Hotel that led to large headlines in the afternoon tabloids proclaiming him as "First American to Bomb Berlin."

Next morning at WIDEWING, Eaker and most of the headquarters officers assembled in the war room for the daily briefing. This was conducted by several officers, with the RAF news reported by Squadron Leader J. Roland "Jack" or "Robbie" Robinson. He was an exceptionally suave and witty speaker who had been an MP before the war, then intelligence officer of the Eagle Squadrons, and, upon their transfer to the American fighter command, intelligence liaison to Eighth AF headquarters. After the war he returned to Parliament as Sir Roland Robinson, rose to party whip for the Tories, moved to the House of Lords as Lord Martonmere and ended his career as governor general of Bermuda. He became a favorite of Eaker's and was especially useful on matters of public relations. That morning, however, he brought a flush to Eaker's cheeks and a hoot of laughter from the assembled officers when he gravely related, "Last night Major S.S. Bartlett of the United States Army Air Forces bombed Berlin—escorted by 1,000 bombers of the Royal Air Force." Unamused, Eaker sent Bartlett a reprimand: "The unfortunate publicity . . . has jeopardized our relations with the RAF and discredited us with the British public with whom we have worked so hard for joint British-American relations. . . . I have directed the Commanding General, VIII Bomber Command, to acquaint you with the proper channels for releasing publicity in the future and to take the necessary steps to insure that you follow these channels."[21]

Several other colorful individuals also became involved significantly in Eighth Air Force public relations in this period. One was John Hay "Jock" Whitney, the New York financier and polo player who would, fifteen years later, become U.S. ambassador to Great Britain. He had arrived in England as a captain assigned to intelligence at fighter command. Lovett arranged for him to meet Eaker, who promptly reassigned him to the Eighth Air Force public relations office, located in Grosvenor Square, London, where he quickly made his presence felt and moved up to a colonelcy. Another was the world-renowned star from silent film days, Ben Lyon, who in 1930 had played the boyish RAF pilot attacking a zeppelin about to bomb London in Howard Hughes's "Hell's Angels." He and his equally renowned actress wife, Bebe Daniels, had not done well in films after the "talkies" took over and had moved to London in 1936, where, as the *New York Times* put it, they "began a second career as unofficial American ambassadors of good will." Because they stayed on in spite of the blitz, though their studio was bombed out three times, they and their show, "Hi Gang!" became immensely popular with the British public. At the Lyons townhouse on South-

wick Street, just behind Marble Arch, Eaker met many British nota-
bles such as A. V. Alexander, first lord of the admiralty, as well as
Hollywood stars Clark Gable and Burgess Meredith, who had joined
the army as enlisted men. He brought Ben Lyon into uniform as a
lieutenant colonel to work alongside Whitney.[22]

Another Hollywood star—at a different level—who arrived in
England as a major was America's most distinguished motion picture director, William "Willie" Wyler. Eaker sent him back to the
States in June 1943 with, he wrote: "approximately 10,000 ft. of
Kodachrome 16 mm. film, most of which he has shot personally,
depicting our combat mission and activities on the ground. The crew
of the *Memphis Belle* has been used as a central theme. The reason
this footage has not been sent back in small batches is that its news
value would have been slight if incorporated piecemeal into news-
reels. . . ." Eaker, who had Wyler draft the letter's technical details,
asked that he be given full facilities to make a "documentary film of
powerful impact . . . a whole of far more potential value than its
separate parts." The famous result, early in 1944, was shown to FDR
in the White House with Wyler present and then nationwide to
crowded theaters. Eaker also sent the *Memphis Belle* itself and its
crew home for "morale and training purposes." It was the first B-17
to complete twenty-five missions.[23]

On June 10 Eaker held a press conference—"the second one
I've had in 17 months," as he wrote Arnold the same day. "I am
still following the policy of talking more about what we have done
and boasting less about what we intend to do." About seventy British and American journalists attended, "and they showed friendship to our cause." To Lovett Eaker explained: "It was designed
. . . to break down the present tendency of the press here to divide
into two schools: the first, to pan the War Department for not
giving us the aircraft we need to do the job; the second, to pan us
for not using to the best advantage the tremendous numbers of
aircraft the War Department had undoubtedly given us. My theory
has always been that if we do not play fair with the press and give
them some idea of what goes on, in so far as the interests of security will permit, we cannot expect them properly to present our
view to the people. . . ."

One thing Eaker said that day pointed up a bigger lesson than
simply numbers of planes and crews available. "Armies and navies
do not fight every day, but for some reason the general public has

come to expect air forces to fight daily. This is an erroneous impression which you can help us to correct. An air force which fights ten major battles in any month, with the same planes and crews, has done an outstanding job."[24]

Four days later Devers received a "for his eyes only" cable from Marshall saying: "Reference Eaker's recent statement regarding rapid growth of the bomber command in England: Put him on his

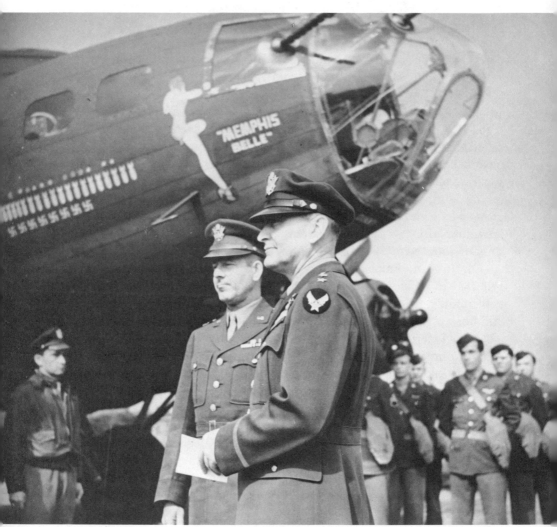

Devers, new CG, European theater, and Eaker bid the crew of the *Memphis Belle*—first B-17 to complete twenty-five operational missions —bon voyage as they head for home, June 9, 1943.

guard against such statements because the immediate result was a heavy drive for more planes for the Pacific. . . . If Eaker understands that he is selling out his organization he will be more discreet."

Devers sent the message to Eaker, who responded the next day with a memorandum to Gen. Idwal Edwards, chief of staff for Devers, saying in part: "The Marshall wire would not have been clear to me if I had not this date received General Arnold's cable indicating that no more new groups are coming for some time. . . . They have, therefore, in the War Department, changed the base. They have departed from their announced plan as presented to us. That is why the Release has served to embarrass them. Some day there will be an opportunity to answer the careless charge of indiscretion which I feel is wholly unwarranted in view of the careful check I made with the Theater Commander prior to this Release. In the meantime, I regret exceedingly if it has caused General Devers any worry or embarrassment. . . ."[25]

"It seems to me," Eaker wrote to Lovett two days later, "I am damned if I do and damned if I don't!" In that same letter, he added, with the mixture of whimsy and cold blood so often evident in his exchanges with the sophisticated assistant secretary of war for air: "Our little pup, which you predicted would wind up with mustard and between the halves of the bun, has passed away. Miss Jones is heartbroken. . . . We had a ferocious fight over Kiel our last time out. The 4th Wing got pretty badly beat up. . . . I visited them immediately and am delighted to tell you that they were all for going out the next day, battered as they were. Their fighting spirit is absolutely superb. The weather prevented. . . . We lost 26 bombers, or a little over 10%. Our overall percentage of losses is still, however, less than 5%. We feel quite certain that the new 'do-or-die' group the Germans have been assembling, as you know, were after us over Kiel."[26] This was a reference to the intelligence, via intercepts, that specially armored Focke-Wulfs were being dispatched with orders to ram the B-17s if all else failed. A number actually did so.[27]

How to live up to the great expectations of the CCS and quiet down those of the public continued to nag at Eaker as the fighting got more and more intense at the end of July, a month in which the Eighth's loss ratio averaged 7 percent and replacements were at a low ebb. Lovett had written him that "the Press had been filled . . . with inquiries as to whether or not we can take the increased rate which our deeper penetration into Germany has occasioned. . . . There is also a very disturbing wave of optimism surging throughout the country, the general tone being that the Allies will knock Germany out by Christmas . . ." while Arnold cabled testily at the end of the month on "the necessity for full data on the progress of the Combined Bomber Offensive with particular reference to July operations." Eaker decided to send back a party of five officers, three of them American and two British, with the dual purpose of a presentation to Arnold and his staff on the progress of the CBO and, secondly, "to try to open up the pipeline on PR and get a proper coverage on press, radio and pictures of Eighth Air Force activity." Because the joint attack on Schweinfurt and Regensburg was now set for the first break in the weather in August, neither he nor Anderson could lead the party to Washington, though Eaker felt he "should." Instead he selected Air Commodore A. C. H. "Bobby" Sharp, who had been attached to the Eighth as deputy chief of staff and was one of the ten officers who shared Castle Coombe with Eaker—two devices by which Eaker maintained and dramatized the close liaison between RAF and AAF. He told Arnold: "You will find that Air Commodore Sharp is a very keen fellow and practically a disciple when it comes to talking about the Eighth. He . . . has been on our operational missions, has been Chairman of the Operational Planning Staff and is thoroughly familiar with our operational system. He has another advantage as the presenter of our case, and that is that he can be presumed to be impartial, being an RAF officer, and he is also familiar with the RAF side of the CBO."[28]

The others in the party were Whitney, Lyon, Robinson and myself. We had put together a forty-five minute sequence of talks, slides and charts that were well-received in the Pentagon air room on August 10. Arnold ordered us to put on the show before large audiences of officers at West Point, at the intelligence school in Harrisburg and at other major training bases around the country. I had double duty, having been designated by Eaker to chair a committee in England to prepare "an anniversary book," as he wrote Arnold, "depicting the Eighth Air Force activities during the past year, serving the same purpose as RAF Bomber Command's book, *Bomber Command,* of which 2,000,000 copies were distributed in England with very good effect." While the Eighth's book, *Target Germany,* was being written in four months time by two talented journalists, captains Arthur Gordon and Richard Thruelson, one on leave from

Hearst Magazines, the other from the *Saturday Evening Post,* I was to line up publication in the U.S. It was published at year-end by Simon & Schuster along with a fourteen-page excerpt in *Life.* Sales of the American, British and Danish editions (the last one postwar) passed the 3 million mark.

Punk weather over Europe stalled Eighth attacks until August 12 when two missions totaling 330 B-17s hit targets in the Ruhr and at Bonn, losing 25 (7.5 percent). Similar size forces hit several targets in France and the Low Countries on the 15th and 16th, losing two and four. At last, on August 17, the anniversary of the first B-17 attack on Europe, good weather was forecast over southern Germany and the daring plan to hit both Schweinfurt and Regensburg was set in motion.[29]

An immediate ominous factor—one that threw the plan far out of kilter—was very bad weather over the American bases in England. The plan called for a task force of 146 B-17s under LeMay to take off first, followed ten minutes later by a second force of 230 under Brig. Gen. Robert B. Williams. Both would fly identical courses out of England and deep into Germany, with most of the German fighters, it was hoped, trying to stop the leading task force on the way in and expecting to beat it up on the way back. But LeMay's force would fool them: he would not turn back to England, but fly on to North Africa. During the time when the Luftwaffe would be on the ground refueling behind LeMay, Williams's force was expected to turn off to the east, swat Schweinfurt with much less opposition and scoot for home. LeMay's seven groups, having been rigorously trained in instrument takeoffs, made it up through the murk on schedule and headed for Germany. But it was almost an hour and a half before the fog lifted and the Williams task force got the final go-ahead from Anderson at PINETREE. By then, as Anderson well knew, the diversionary benefits of the plan were gone. He could have scrubbed the mission, but, as he explained later, "Inasmuch as the importance of these targets increased almost daily, the risk involved in dispatching the two bomb divisions individually was felt to be commensurate with the results which the destruction of these two targets would achieve."[30]

Nor did he check the question with Eaker, knowing the decision was entirely his. And he knew too the pressure of the CBO timetable as well as some of the arm-twisting that had come from Arnold. For

Eaker's part, he sat at WIDEWING chewing his cigar and waiting quietly for the "strike report," first from LeMay, then from Williams. This was the short radio message sent at the apex of each mission. Eaker had wanted to go to Schweinfurt, but Devers, having been given his cue by Arnold, forbade it. When Eaker asked, "Couldn't you just look the other way?" his theater commander replied, "If you go, when you get back (if you get back), you'll be on the first plane to Washington."[31]

There have been many fine descriptions of the long, brutal battle that day, the most vivid being by Beirne Lay, one of the original six to come to England with Eaker in 1942 and who rode as copilot in one of LeMay's B-17s. For this book it suffices to list the key outcomes: 1) despite the timing failure of the diversion and the hordes of German fighters that were able to work over both air divisions at leisure while they were far beyond their own fighter cover, the bombers got through to their two targets and hit them with spectacular accuracy; 2) the damage at both was immense; and 3) the losses in both American and German aircraft set new records in the history of air war. It was the last fact that caught the attention of the press and led to widespread speculation—in the public but not the military —that the daylight campaign deep into Germany would have to be suspended until long-range fighters were available. That day at WIDEWING Eaker learned that LeMay's division had lost 24 B-17s and Williams's 36—making a total of 60 (15 percent). And heavy battle damage to the ones that returned had still to be fully assessed —especially in North Africa with its limited repair facilities. American claims totaled 288/37/99, which was gratifying even if you assumed, as the Eaker plan did, that claims should be reduced by 75 percent. Eaker's concern that day was on ascertaining just how much of his bomber force he still had in being. He decided to fly to North Africa at once to see for himself.[32]

Through Anderson he arranged for a B-17 piloted by Capt. William R. "Smitty" Smith, a clean-cut Pennsylvania coal miner's son with a college degree who had flown to Schweinfurt with the 351st Bomb Group and returned with no crew injuries but his plane full of holes. He was asleep next morning, for the entire group had been stood down, its planes inoperable until repaired. The only plane available was named *Spareball* and had not gone to Schweinfurt because one of its engines had a habit of spewing oil. Three hours later Smitty picked up Eaker, General Hodges and Colonel Hughes

LeMay's B-17s (146 dispatched) leaving the badly battered Messerschmitt works at Regensburg to fly on to North Africa instead of back to England, August 17, 1943—anniversary of the initial raid by 12 B-17s against Rouen a year before.

and droned on to Land's End to pause for dark before the long flight that night out around France and Spain. *Spareball* arrived at Marrakesh at 7 A.M. on the 19th with oil all over one wing.

By then Eaker knew that both targets had suffered major damage and that the force that had hit Schweinfurt, in addition to the 36 B-17s MIA (missing in action), had another 27 so stove in they probably would never fly again as well as 95 others with lesser damage. But he still knew nothing explicit about LeMay's force except the tally of 24 MIA. As soon as *Spareball* was refueled he insisted on continuing for the eight-hour flight across North Africa to Tunis, where he was met by Col. Elliot Roosevelt, FDR's son and CO of a photo-reconnaissance unit under Spaatz. They drove off to see Spaatz while Smith and his crew, weary from thirty hours of continuous flight and no sleep, looked for the mess hall. It was closed, but a sergeant gave them a gallon can of marmalade, some bread and fruit juice. This they were munching as evening fell when orders came to fly on another hundred miles to LeMay's temporary headquarters, set up in a tent at the desert airfield of Telergma. By now the party included Spaatz, Doolittle, Roosevelt and Col. Lauris Norstad, who was Spaatz's assistant chief of staff.

LeMay was laconic, as usual. When Eaker asked, "Curt, when will you be able to go back?" LeMay drawled, "As soon as we can hang some bombs and put some fuel in these crates."

But the damage situation at first looked so bad that Eaker thought the original plan to hit a German air base at Bordeaux on the way back should be scrubbed. Besides the 24 B-17S MIA at least 20 more of LeMay's original 146 dispatched were broken beyond repair and another 40 seriously shot up. As it turned out, the indomitable LeMay was able to take off with 85 B-17S on August 27, bomb Bordeaux and return to England with the loss of another three. But it was very clear to Spaatz and Eaker that shuttle missions to North Africa were impractical. They would have to await the capture of the Foggia area in Italy and the establishment of real repair facilities.

Eaker lingered only a day, chiefly to give Smitty and his crew some sleep, getting back to England on the 22nd. He was so favorably impressed with Smith that he invited him to serve as his command pilot. This Smith did for the rest of the war. But first he insisted on completing his combat tour of 25 missions; he had done only 24. When Gen. Chauncey, Eaker's chief of staff, suggested, "Forget that," Smith thought it over for a day and said: "Sir, I came over here to finish a tour, and I don't want to have to explain to people for the rest of my life why I didn't finish it. I may regret it, but I've got to fly that last mission." He did, over Emden, on October 2, with 349 B-17S, of which two were lost.[33]

While the Schweinfurt-Regensburg battles were in progress, QUADRANT, the next meeting of the CCS, was taking place in Quebec from August 14–24. Arnold was well enough to attend, but said very little, being quoted briefly only three times in those minutes dealing with Europe and the Mediterranean. However, POINTBLANK received a great deal of attention from others. It was number three on the agenda, following "Strategic Concept for the Defeat of the Axis in Europe," and "OVERLORD." The strategic concept, as drafted by U.S. Chiefs of Staff declared, ". . . the successful prosecution of the Combined Bomber Offensive is a prerequisite to OVERLORD." To execute OVERLORD in May or June of 1944 was unquestionably QUADRANT's most important decision. The British made a last-ditch effort to switch to ARMPIT, the proposed landing at the head of the Adriatic, but Stimson and Marshall insisted on the cross-Channel strategy with an American in command. In a strong memorandum to the president before the conference opened, Stimson urged, "we must put our most commanding soldier in charge of this critical operation . . . General Marshall." In another paper, Stimson, who had just completed a long swing through England and the Mediterranean, commented: "General Eaker and his men . . . were all confident. . . . Eaker's losses are approaching the margin of safety and his continuity of operations is greatly interfered with by the weather. On the other hand, our air forces in the south are able to operate almost every day and their percentage of losses had been a mere fraction of those incurred by Eaker's forces in the north. If we could establish air bases in Italy. . . ."[34]

On the opening day of QUADRANT, August 14, Gen. Sir Alan Brooke, British chief of staff, presented a resume of "the present situation in the European Theater" and called on Portal, who began by saying, as reported in the third person style of the minutes: "The German air force was now completely on the defensive. . . . The United Nations Air Forces, on the other hand, were everywhere on the strategic offensive." He gave only a brief nod to RAF Bomber Command, which only a year before he had tried to persuade Eaker to emulate, saying: "The night offensive was steadily increasing. Radio aids to navigation had proved immensely effective. Certain steps were now being taken to baffle the defenses which had resulted in a decrease in casualties from five-to-six percent to only three percent." Portal then turned to the AAF with the first of many glowing tributes and emotional pleas, "The daylight bombing—the most important phase of all—was being extraordinarily effective. The first object of POINTBLANK was to knock out the fighter factories and to destroy fighter planes in the air to achieve complete mastery in the air over Germany. The forces available to the Eighth Air Force had done remarkable work but the program was behind schedule for reasons, however, which are quite understandable. The targets were being hit, the enemy aircraft were being shot down and a high percentage of the aircraft were returning safely, but it was a great battle which hung in the balance. . . ."[35]

Arnold chimed in to say "it was difficult to confine a discussion on the war in the air to Europe since available resources must be spread between all theaters. Early estimates, based on British experience, of the replacements of men and machines had proved too low in the case of the operations of the Eighth Air Force. In addition, there was the problem of the 'war-weary' crews. General Eaker at present had some 800 aircraft, but only 400 crews. . . . Finally, he questioned the possibility of obtaining the maximum use of heavy bombers in England during the winter months. In this connection North Italian bases would prove valuable. . . ."

Portal instantly said "he agreed with General Arnold's view as to the importance of Northern Italy." At that point, however, the Allied armies in the Mediterranean were three weeks away from their invasion of the Italian boot in September and it was clear that strategic air bases would not be available anywhere in Italy during 1943. Portal then moved to the key point. "The battle against the German fighter forces was a vital battle. . . . If German strength was not checked in the next three months, the battle might be lost, since it was impossible to judge the strength which the German fighter forces might attain by next spring if our attack was not pressed home."[36]

At a conference attended by both Roosevelt and Churchill as well as all the top military policy makers of the two allies—a conference where the main theme was the assertion of American military primacy in prosecuting the war—it is curious to find that the chief spokesman for the U.S. Army Air Forces was the head of the Royal Air Force, Sir Charles Portal. Over and over again the tall, saturnine air chief marshal came back to the same theme, either through his own powerful phrases or a "British Intelligence Appreciation" he inserted in the proceedings. "On the one hand," he said, "German fighter strength was stretched almost to the breaking point, and in spite of their precarious situation on the Russian and Mediterranean fronts, they had found it necessary to reinforce their fighter forces on the Western Front from these sources. On the other hand, the expansion of German fighter strength was continuing and had increased 13 percent during this year. It had been hoped that this expansion would by now have been stopped. The Eighth Air Force, who were achieving a great task with their existing resources, believed they could achieve even greater successes if their strength was increased.

"He asked the Combined Chiefs of Staff to take action to make a victory in the battle of the air as certain as possible before the autumn. If this was not done, the Germans, by conservation of their strength and by the development of new methods of defense, might be in an unassailable position by the spring. To achieve our object diversions from the Eighth Air Force should be stopped, loans of aircraft from the Eighth Air Force to other theaters must be returned and the bomber command of the Eighth Air Force must be built up and reinforced to the maximum possible. . . ."[37]

Portal spoke even more strongly about the latest British Intelligence Appreciation, commenting: ". . . in spite of some short-falls in the build-up, Germany is now faced with imminent disaster if only the pressure of POINTBLANK can be maintained and increased *before* the increase in the GAF Fighter Force has gone too far. . . . The daylight 'Battle of Germany' is evidently regarded by the Germans as of critical importance and we have already made them throw into it most, if not all, of their available reserves. If we do not now strain every nerve to bring enough force to bear to win this battle during the next two or three months but are content to see the Eighth Bomber Command hampered by lack of reinforcements just as success is within its grasp, we may well miss the opportunity to win a decisive victory against the German Air Force which will have incalculable effects on all future operations and on the length of the war. And the opportunity, once lost, may not recur."[38]

The British Intelligence Appreciation he circulated stated flatly that: "The doubling of the German S.E. fighter force on the Western Front and the allocation of this increase to Belgium, Holland and Northwest Germany are attributable solely to the development of Allied day bombing of Germany. The defense of Germany against these attacks has in fact become the prime concern of the GAF. . . . There can be no doubt that Germany regards the defense of the Reich against daylight air attack as of such supreme importance that adequate support for military operations in Russia and the Mediterranean has been rendered impossible. . . ."[39]

The first dividend from Portal's vehemence at QUADRANT was Eisenhower's return of the Eighth's three groups of B-24s. Another was Arnold's decision to bring Knerr back to England to seek a solution to the acute shortage of service units. They flew over early in September and concluded that "the only answer seemed to be that of shipping immediately large numbers of personnel as casuals for organization and training in the theater." In army parlance "casuals" were officers or enlisted men without immediate assignments, accumulated in replacement depots ("repple-depples," as the GIS called them). The first shipment of 17,000 enlisted men and 3,000 officers arrived in October, and the total reached 45,000 by December—all of them greenhorns as far as repairing heavy bombers were concerned. Eaker's total stock of heavies remained stalled at the 800 mark in September and the operational level was far lower. It would be the end of the year before the service situation began to click, reflecting in large measure the skill of Hugh Knerr, who was designated commander of the air service command, succeeding Maj. Gen. Henry S. F. Miller, who was moved to the Ninth AF.[40]

Arnold was jolly and upbeat during his week in England, enjoying visits to a few group headquarters and long talks with Eaker at Castle Coombe. He expressed no particular fret about the increased rate of loss at Schweinfurt and Regensburg, following much the same line as Lovett, who had written: "We know that you have taken heavy losses but I, for one, can not get too disheartened about it when you consider that a 15% loss over Schweinfurt is actually only the equivalent of three days operations at 5%. . . . We are all enormously impressed with the jobs just done and the guts the outfit has shown." Arnold's visit to England coincided with what Eaker described to Lovett as "the most disgusting weather, from a bombing point of view, which has been experienced during any summer of the war." It was possible to make attacks into Germany only twice, and the first of these, September 6, was a complete fiasco. Two divisions totaling 333 B-17s took off for targets in Stuttgart, but found them cloud-covered. They then sought scattered targets of opportunity and, by breaking up their tight defensive formations, gave the Luftwaffe an opportunity the Germans quickly grabbed—35 bombers (14 percent) were lost with no U.S. accomplishment except large claims—98/20/50. Conversely, the next venture into Germany—308 B-17s and 24 B-24s to Emden—came back with only seven bombers lost. The drop in losses was due to the mission's being the first to bomb through the overcast with pathfinder B-17s equipped with H2S (Portal having relented on its use).

The expanding medium (B-26) bomber attacks—limited to nearby France and the Low Countries and escorted by Kepner's fighters—had better hunting, going out on eighteen days during September to hit German airfields and transportation targets. Several such attacks, in which the heavies also participated, constituted another diversion from POINTBLANK. It was Operation STARKEY, "the support of a sham invasion on the Continent" as reported in one of Eaker's letters to Lovett. "On the final day of this effort we put out more than 1,300 sorties [including mediums] . . . the first time the Eighth had exceeded 1,000 sorties on one day. The Germans did not accept the challenge and there was no air battle of any consequence. On that day they had some 360 planes airborne but they were very careful to avoid combat. The intensive operations against airfields in occupied territory were not by any means wasted. Many aircraft were destroyed—more than 90 on one mission. Repair establishments with a capacity of more than 500 planes a month have been destroyed or very seriously damaged. For the first time, the estimates of German air strength . . . showed a decline."[41]

As Arnold departed for home, Brereton came through from Egypt for three days before going on to the U.S., from which he would return in October to take command of the Ninth. Eaker reported this to his boss in Washington in a letter that began, "We all wish you could have stayed with us longer . . ." and went on, as was Eaker's wont, to cover operational items of special interest, in particular the latest evidence of the Luftwaffe's pinch. "The Germans will not fight unless targets in Germany are attacked." The same day (September 11), he wrote Spaatz that Arnold had again brought up his pet subject—"having a supreme Strategical Allied Air Force Commander to coordinate the heavy bombardment of Axis objectives . . . from any and all European bases." Eaker said, "I suggested to Portal that you and Tedder, Harris, Portal and myself should get together and talk this over." Their discussion never took place, but Arnold stuck to his goal, as all of them would learn with various degrees of surprise three months later.[42]

Eaker's desk work had now reached such a heavy volume that he needed additional secretarial help beyond trusty RAF Sergeant Stroud. Col. Oveta Culp Hobby, director of the Women's Army Corps, had begun sending companies of the trim American women in uniform abroad. Remembering Eaker's stand in the hassle with Chaney fifteen months before, she sent the first overseas WAC Company to the Eighth. Eaker appointed one of them, Sgt. Mary Weiler, as his second secretary. Shrewd, meticulous and invariably gracious, she worked for Eaker along with Stroud until the end of the war and then, for many years, was secretary to Clark Clifford, the eminent Washington lawyer, presidential advisor and secretary of defense 1968–69.

One of the first things Weiler typed, on September 13, was Eaker's note of appreciation to Devers for his promotion to lieutenant general. His third star reminded him, he chuckled, of the dinner in his honor earlier that year at the English Speaking Union, where an aged, titled lady remarked, "I think a gentleman of his importance should wear more things on his shoulders."[44]

18

"The real importance of the air war consisted in the fact that it opened a second front long before the invasion of Europe. That front was the skies over Germany. . . ."

—ALBERT SPEER, *SPANDAU, THE SECRET DIARIES*

THE BITTER BATTLES over Schweinfurt have come to symbolize the daylight bombing campaign against Germany, just as the firestorms over Hamburg and Dresden have come to characterize the night. In both instances this oversimplification has led to exaggeration and misinterpretation. The ball-bearing factories at Schweinfurt, producing 43 percent of the Reich's war needs, were the single most important target on the POINTBLANK list, causing some experts to believe that knocking them out completely would end the war. But Air Marshal Harris sniffed that Schweinfurt was another "panacea." Oddly enough, both views were correct.

When Eaker went to interview Albert Speer, Hitler's brilliant minister of armament production, in Heidelberg in 1976, Speer said, "If you had repeated your bombing attacks and destroyed our ball-bearing industry, the war would have been over a year earlier." But Speer also told Eaker: "The fire bombing of Hamburg, Dresden and the like were great disasters locally. It would have been better if you had been able early in the war to have abruptly increased the size and weight of these bombing raids." When Eaker asked him, "Which of the target systems—shipbuilding, fighter plane and engine factories,

Target Germany—an Eighth Air Force combat wing on the way, 1943.

oil, ball bearings or transportation—was most decisive?" Speer replied, "It was the combination."[1]

There were several reasons Eaker did not send the Eighth Air Force back to Schweinfurt at once after the August 17 attack. One was the need to recuperate and to replenish his battered B-17s and crews. Another was the weather. A third was the initial belief that the damage done to the ball-bearing works was greater than turned out to be the case. The bombing that day had not been as concentrated as the simultaneous attack at Regensburg (where every important building in the Messerschmitt fighter factory was hit), but it was very good, with 88 direct hits on two of the three ball-bearing plants.

310

At Kugelfischer, one of the three, for example, 663 machines were destroyed and production of ball bearings dropped from 140 tons in July to 69 in August and 50 in September. Overall, said Speer, production fell 38 percent. But most of the bombs were high-explosive, set with fuses to go off on impact. They smashed the top floors of the five-story buildings, causing them to collapse onto the ground floor, where the ball-bearing machines were located. Because only a few incendiaries were dropped, there was little fire and the ball-bearing machines could be salvaged. This the Germans, with Teutonic efficiency and zeal, promptly set about doing. And Speer, who had long worried about Schweinfurt's vulnerability, also began dispersing these vital machines to many obscure places. Even so, the shortage of bearings was so acute that he sent emissaries to Sweden to preempt its ball-bearing output and to Switzerland to buy more.[2]

One reason there were so few incendiaries in the American bomb load was the expectation that Harris would send RAF Bomber Command with many incendiaries to Schweinfurt that night. But Harris did not do so, disagreeing with the idea in principle and protesting that the town was too small for his bombers to find, even with the aid of any fires set by the Eighth. Besides, he had another top priority objective to hit that same night—Peenemünde, the German rocket center on the shores of the Baltic north of Berlin. From ULTRA and other intelligence the British knew the rocket attacks on which Hitler pinned such hopes were on the verge of being launched against London. In one of the most effective raids of the war—one that demonstrated that the British too could use precision tactics—Harris dispatched 597 heavies, which flew in low over the Baltic and had little trouble spotting tiny Peenemünde because its waterside location was clearly visible by radar. They lost 40 bombers but slew over 130 German scientists and engineers as well as smashing many laboratories and putting the "v-weapon" program an estimated four months behind. An extra dividend was the suicide of Gen. Hans Jeschonneck, Arnold's counterpart as chief of the German air staff, who had already that day been "harangued" by Hitler over the American successes at Regensburg and Schweinfurt. He put a bullet through his head.[3]

Though Portal was of course delighted with the RAF's exploit at Peenemünde, he and the air staff felt "a creeping suspicion that the Bomber Command assault on German cities was not actually proving as decisive as Sir Arthur Harris believed." And they were also increasingly irked by Harris's failure to pay more than lip service to the POINTBLANK directive. "The Schweinfurt episode," as Denis Richards, Portal's biographer, put it, "highlighted a growing divergence." Under the CBO directive, first from Casablanca and reinforced by "the Eaker Plan" approved by the CCS, RAF Bomber Command was supposed to blast areas around the pinpoint targets the Eighth was hitting. Harris did lay on a few such attacks, but they were minor efforts, and he made no secret of his belief they were a waste of time and a divergence from the city-busting he deemed so imperative. "He believed," wrote the RAF historians, "the bombing offensive was the ultimate and decisive campaign. He was convinced that it could be the prelude not to an invasion but to an occupation." The air staff view was well put by Air Marshal Bottomley, Portal's deputy, who wrote Harris, "Your night bomber forces would make the greatest contribution by completely destroying those vital centres which can be reached by day only at heavy cost; examples are Schweinfurt, Leipzig and centres of twin-engined fighter industry." Bottomley then cited an intelligence report that said that "whereas the German people feared the night attacks, Hitler and the German High Command feared the daylight precision attacks on individual factories. Hitler openly boasted that he could, by means of his party organizations, control the morale of the population for some considerable time—certainly over the critical year 1943." But Harris delayed any raid on Schweinfurt on one pretext or another. It was not until Portal gave him a direct order that he finally, on the night of February 24, 1944, sent 734 heavies to lay waste the town, following a day attack by the Eighth of 266. By then, however, Speer had successfully dispersed the ball-bearing machines. Shortage of ball bearings never became a crucial problem for the Germans, and Schweinfurt itself, as Harris took glee in saying, had indeed become a "panacea target."[4]

The Portal-Harris controversy grew steadily worse and persisted until the end of the war, with the stubborn bomber commander insisting on area targets, notably Berlin, and the chief of the air staff pressing him to switch to precision targets, notably oil refineries. They exchanged no fewer than thirty letters or memoranda, some of them four thousand words long and all impeccably polite, arguing their different views. Portal almost relieved Harris but concluded, "His good qualities as a Commander far outweighed his defects and it would have been monstrously unjust to him and his Command to have tried to have him replaced on the ground that while assuring me of his intention to carry out his orders he persisted in trying to convince me that different orders would have produced better results."[5]

For his part, Eaker, ever loyal, never once criticized either Harris or RAF Bomber Command's strategy, though Arnold, ever blunt and ever more critical of Portal's direction of the CBO, on his visit to London in September 1943, suggested to Portal that a single commander (American and, presumably, Spaatz) be put over both forces. Eaker's attitude is indicated by a letter he sent Lovett on October 9 reporting: "We had a great fight yesterday over Emden and Vegesack [near Bremen] . . . and engaged at one time or other more than 300 German aircraft. Harris's RAF boys followed up our attack on Bremen last night with 119 bombers and lost but three. The opposition against them was negligible. As has often been pointed out, when they follow into an area where we have had a hot battle in the afternoon, they get away almost unscarred. This is to be contrasted with the fact that Harris sent 400 to Hanover last night and lost 30. It points very clearly to the value of our cooperative effort."[6]

Within three weeks after hitting Schweinfurt on August 17, Eaker and Anderson realized they would have to send their bombers back. From diplomatic and business sources in Sweden and Switzerland they learned about the frantic German search for ball bearings. Photo-reconnaissance revealed intensive repairs at the Schweinfurt factories. And ULTRA intercepts made it clear both how worried the Germans were about follow-up attacks and how urgently they were now building up their fighter forces. From other intelligence they determined that more incendiaries and different fuse settings were required. But not until October 4 did the skies begin to clear over Germany and at first this was true only in the north. On the fourth, eighth, ninth and tenth VIII Bomber Command dispatched important missions of more than three hundred heavies against POINT-BLANK targets in Germany, doing major damage each time and also suffering large losses. Two targets were notably deep penetrations— Anklam, the Arado engine works on the Baltic shore somewhat east of Berlin, and Marienburg, the Focke-Wulf fighter factory far further on into East Prussia, while diversionary forces hit the Polish ports of Danzig and Gdynia. At Marienburg 58 percent of the bombs fell within 1,000 feet of the aiming point and 83 percent within 2,000 feet. The factory was almost completely destroyed in what Eaker described as "the classic example of precision bombing." But losses that second week of October added up to 95 B-17s and nine B-24s, a total of 7.3 percent of bombers dispatched. Almost a third of the losses (30 B-17s) fell in the one attack directly toward the heart of Germany—to Münster, just north of the Ruhr, on October 10.[7]

At last, on October 14, the weather was clear over Schweinfurt and Eaker and Anderson dispatched their heavies on what became the biggest and most spectacular air battle ever fought. They had planned to send 319 B-17s and 60 B-24s. But weather over England was, as usual, poor, and the B-24s, only recently back from North Africa, were not yet adjusted to assembling above an overcast.

The Focke-Wulf plant at Marienburg, near Danzig, October 9, 1943— "the classic example of precision bombing."

Only 29 were able to make formation; they abandoned the mission and went instead on a diversion toward Emden. The B-17s flew on, accompanied as far as Aachen in the Ruhr by P-47s, of which 196 were dispatched. But they too were hampered by the weather and many missed their rendezvous with the heavies over the Channel. This made little difference, for the German fighters as usual stayed distant until the American escort turned for home. Then the carnage began, with 28 B-17s downed on the way in and another 32 on the way home, when fog in England prevented fighter escort from meeting them. A total of 60 heavies (19 percent) went down. But the Luftwaffe could not stop the B-17s from reaching their target. In fact, never throughout the war did the heavies turn back because of enemy action.[8]

Eaker and Anderson had expected a fierce fight, as had the crews. At the 385th BG the briefing officer concluded: "This is a tough job and I know you can do it. Good luck, good bombing and good hunting." A gunner in back added loudly, "And goodbye!" As Roger Freeman's *Mighty Eighth War Diary* continued this anecdote: "The tension was broken by loud guffaws. The apprehensive gunner and all 385th Group bombers returned safely." Eaker spent the long day and most of the following night with Anderson at PINETREE.[9] The next morning he sent a remarkable cable to Arnold:

"Yesterday the Hun sprang his trap. He fully revealed his final counter measure to our daylight bombing. It was not unexpected since he has revealed single acts in the play from time to time in the past as he practiced and trained. Yesterday he ran off the full scale dress rehearsal prefectly timed and executed as follows: a screen of single-engine fighters flew in from the front very close firing normal 20mm cannon and machine guns. These closely followed by large formations twin-engine fighters in waves, each firing large numbers of rockets suspended under wings. Firing began at long range and twin-engine planes broke away further back than single-engine planes. Rockets were lobbed in barrage quantities into formations. The very effective rocket attack points very strongly to use proximity fuses. Single-engine fighters than refueled and attacked from all directions to engage our gunners. These followed closely by reformed formations of twin-engine rocket carriers attacking principally from front and rear. There was complete concentration on one formation, one combat wing, until rockets expended. Then all enemy aircraft concentrated on our cripples with gunfire. The whole operation was perfectly timed and coordinated and skillfully executed. More than 300 enemy fighters participated in attack; more than 700 attacks made on our formations during the principal battle.

"One of our combat wings was practically wiped out. The others were not seriously engaged or damaged and did excellent bombing. Strike photos just seen indicate all three large factories . . . destroyed. Ninety-nine enemy fighters were destroyed, 30 probably destroyed, 14 damaged. Sixty of our bombers were lost. Of these all believed lost to enemy fighters. Five returned to England but were so badly damaged crews elected to bail out and are safe. Rocket damage to individual aircraft was not more severe than in past and in most cases was not mortal. It did cause many planes to fall out of formation, where they were finished off by single-engine fighters. Rockets also damaged engines and fuel tanks, making impossible the long journey home.

"This does not represent disaster; it does indicate that the air battle has reached its climax. . . . Here is what you can do to help:

"1: Rush replacement aircraft and crews. We have thus far this month received 143 planes and 143 crews; we must have minimum of 250 planes and crews this month and we must grow bigger, not smaller.

"2: Send every possible fighter here as soon as possible. Especially emphasize earliest arrival of additional P-38s and Mustangs.

"3: Give us 5,000 110-gallon and 3,000 150-gallon auxilliary droppable tanks for fighters as soon as possible and continue at that rate monthly.

"We must show the enemy we can replace our losses; he knows he cannot replace his. We must continue the battle with unrelenting fury. This we shall do. There is no discouragement here. We are convinced that when the totals are struck yesterday's losses will be far outweighed by the value of the enemy material destroyed."[10]

Arnold sent Eaker's cable to Field Marshal Sir John Dill, senior British representative in Washington to the CCS, who returned it with a handwritten note reading: "Dear Hap. Many thanks. This is a damned good 'airmanly' telegram." Arnold also called a press conference at which he proclaimed, "Now we have got Schweinfurt!" This was an exaggeration. Speer set the loss at "67% of our ball-bearing production." Press reaction to the loss of sixty bombers was, on the whole, low-key. *Time Magazine,* for example, commented on October 25: "Suddenly the cost of victory loomed large. . . . The price

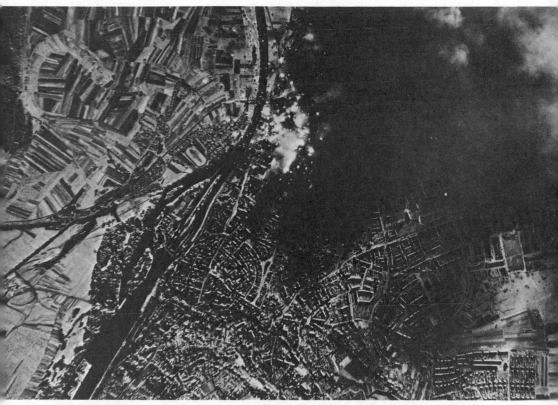

The incendiaries take hold at the ball-bearing works, Schweinfurt II, October 15, 1943.

was not exorbitant: without bearings the mechanized German war machine would be helpless." But Arnold imprudently announced that losses as high as 25 percent on some missions might be expected and could be accepted. This provoked protests from Eaker, who reminded his boss that this sort of talk did not sit well with his crews, even though the Eighth's fliers had now become battle-hardened. Eaker recalled: "The reaction of the whole air force was entirely different from the August raid. . . . [It] left the participating crews in a sort of stunned condition. But the October raid didn't. And the reason . . . was because there was no longer any question of our being able to cut it. Everybody in the Eighth Air Force believed by that time that we were getting sufficient support. . . . We were well aware that we were going to be able to send up by the end of the year 500 bombers and 400 fighters on a single mission."[11]

317

Arnold's most important reaction was to expedite the flow of fighters to England in ways beyond those already in train—steps he could have taken earlier had he not been so wedded to belief in the B-17's defensive ability. He cabled Kenney in the Pacific that all the P-51s and P-38s he had been expecting in November and December would go to England instead and he would get P-47s as substitutes. A similar message went to Spaatz in North Africa. To Eaker he cabled about shipping fighters as deck load on tankers. "We realize that you need the airplanes badly. We also realize that General Knerr would like very much to get them as deck load rather than in crates due to the man-hours lost in assembling the crated planes." Finally Arnold began the touchy process of cutting back the agreed levels of P-51 shipments to the RAF. There was no sign of recrimination or defeatism either from Washington or from London. Marshall told Eaker he was "tremendously impressed," adding: "I like the tone of your message. No great battle is fought without heavy fighting and inevitable losses." Portal wrote: "I believe your attack in Schweinfurt will be worth many times its cost. In fact, it may well go down in history as one of the decisive air actions of the war."[12]

Arnold also sent several messages of praise, but they were intermingled with querulous doubts. He asked Eaker to commend all the crews and to tell them on his behalf, "The cornered wolf fights hardest, and the German Air Force has been driven into its last corner." But he also cabled Eaker: "It appears from my viewpoint that the German Air Force is on the verge of collapse. We must not (repeat) must not miss any symptoms of impending German collapse. . . . Can you send any substantial evidence of collapse?" Eaker first replied with a long letter saying in part: "There is much evidence pointing in the direction you are inquiring. Yesterday's effort was not, as might at first appear, contrary thereto. I class it pretty much as the final struggles of a monster in his death throes. There is not the slightest question but that we now have our teeth in the Hun Air Force's neck. . . . Nothing more clearly indicates the defeat of the German Air Force than its absolute unwillingness to mix with our fighters. . . . Your commendations have been placed in the hands of the air combat crew members and have done untold good. It is amazing what a pat on the back will do for a hard-fighting, battle-weary fellow."

This hasty and somewhat flamboyant letter was an example of Eaker's calculated effort both to bolster Arnold's support and to fend off potential criticism. He followed it a few days later with a more detailed and more judicious assessment. It began, "There are no definite indications yet that the German Air Force is on the verge of collapse but there exists evidence of severe strain and some signs of eventual cracking." There followed a list of many specific examples of decline in fighter strength and of less effective pilots, ending: "CONCLUSION: It is believed that the German Air Force is straightened to uttermost. . . . It can now be stated with certainty that completion of POINTBLANK as scheduled will produce the result desired. German Air Force will be reduced to point where it will be ineffectual in opposing allied bombing effort and unable to defeat our landing."[13]

Eaker knew all too well how mercurial the Army Air Forces commander was—a bouquet one day, a brickbat the next. Only a month before, Arnold had been peppering him with complaints during the bad weather period in September about "why we do not use massive flights of aircraft against a target now that we have planes and pilots in sufficient quantity to put over 500 planes in the air. What is the answer?" This sort of thing was often drafted for Arnold by his eager-beaver staff. On September 28, for example, Kuter sent Arnold drafts of "three radios and a letter, all building a fire under General Eaker." Nor was Eaker the only target of such needlings. In early October Kuter sent another staff officer the draft of a letter to Portal referring to "not employing our forces in adequate numbers. . . . I am pressing Eaker to get a much higher proportion of his force off the ground and put them where they will hurt the enemy." Kuter wrote: "General Arnold wants early action in the preparation of a letter of the general tone and content of the enclosed quick draft. He knows it will make Air Chief Marshal Portal mad, and that is what he has in mind." Now, in response to a congratulatory cable on October 16 from Portal about the second Schweinfurt mission, Arnold again stuck in a needle about mustering "the total weight of our combined bomber forces against the installations mutually selected for destruction. Such measures will require immediate scrapping of some outmoded tactical concepts, closer coordination between all elements of command, and more effective use of our combined resources."[14]

Eaker rarely let such needles from Arnold get under his skin. "You see," he told a postwar interviewer, "he had great pressures put on him from higher levels—from the Joint Chiefs of Staff, the Com-

319

bined Chiefs of Staff, the President and also the public. And so, whereas there were times when I thought he was partial and unjustly critical, I was also cognizant of some of the pressures he was under and didn't take it to heart as much as I might have had I not been somewhat acquainted with what he was going through."[15]

Hansell, who returned to Arnold's staff during this period and accompanied him to subsequent CCS meetings, as did Kuter, was much more outspoken. "Arnold," he said, "was terribly impatient. He just did not understand air combat. His crews, led by Ira, were doing a simply astonishing job. I marvelled at their willingness to keep on fighting. I think Ira probably did too. . . . Ira met the ultimate test, he and Fred Anderson. Going to Schweinfurt and losing 60 B-17s is a tremendous loss, and then going back two months later and doing it all over again. The first one took enormous tolls, and the second one, following that experience, took tremendous courage and will power and an unswerving adherence to the objective. . . . I think that Arnold treated Ira very badly. He never understood the tremendous contribution that Ira's stamina had made to the conduct of the war. . . . He was not creating the miracles that Arnold wanted to report. Arnold just never understood what Eaker was up against. . . . I understand a little of that misunderstanding because I had a 7:30 meeting every morning with General Arnold. He had an 8:30 meeting with General Marshall. He had to repeat what we told him about the previous day's operations. Marshall would say, 'What did the Eighth Air Force do yesterday?' and Arnold would have to say, 'Nothing.' And Arnold was not the type of personality who could stand up under that kind of thing. I think it was infuriating to Arnold to have to keep repeating that statement. And yet most of those missions . . . were held up by the weather."[16]

The middle of October 1943 was significant for Eaker for more reasons than the second Schweinfurt battle. His friend and ally Averell Harriman departed for Moscow to become U.S. ambassador to the Soviets. On October 15 Eaker officially assumed command of all U.S. Army Air Forces in the United Kingdom, comprising both the Eighth and Ninth Air Forces. The post had been assigned to him by Marshall on September 7, but activation awaited Brereton's arrival to take charge of the Ninth. And King George VI summoned Eaker to Buckingham Palace for a forty-five-minute talk and one of Britain's highest honors. The usual decoration for important Americans was an OBE (Order of the British Empire). Eaker was given the KBE

Three-star Eaker presents the Air Medal to his pre-war boss, two-star Fechet, Castle Coombe, England, 1943.

(Knight of the British Empire). That night at Castle Coombe he was teased with toasts to "Sir Ira!"[17]

Castle Coombe was also enlivened by a visit from Major General Fechet, Eaker's early mentor and now back in uniform with a sinecure overseas assignment he received largely because of Eaker's suggestion. Arnold directed his predecessor as chief of Army Air to review the awarding of decorations in the war theaters. Very grizzled, very hearty and still with the erect carriage of an old cavalry officer, Fechet, now wearing one star fewer than his protégé, enjoyed himself enormously visiting the bases and playing poker with Eaker and the rest of us at Castle Coombe. He still called Eaker "Iree," and Eaker always addressed him as "General."

Castle Coombe was also the scene of the only occasion in the author's forty years of close association with Eaker that he was observed to lose his temper. The provocation began with the gift of a dozen steaks—first we had seen in eighteen months overseas—sent

321

by C.R. Smith, the tall Texan best known as president of American Airlines and later secretary of commerce and who was in two-star uniform in WW II helping run the Air Transport Command. They were brought over packed in dry ice, and Eaker invited two high-ranking pals from the British military to share them with him and his eight messmates. I, as mess officer, carefully instructed Miss Jones to broil them rare, or "underdone," as the British called it. At dinner that night after suitable preliminaries it came time for the main course, and Miss Jones appeared proudly at the door from the pantry carrying a silver platter with the twelve steaks, all cooked rare but also slathered in cream sauce. Eaker fixed her with a glare and snapped, "Miss Jones, take those steaks back and wash off that God-damned sauce!" I slipped out with her and made sure this ablution was performed and the meat put back briefly into the oven to regain some degree of charred exterior.

On November 1, despite Eaker's continued pleas, Arnold formally activated the Fifteenth Air Force with the fifteen groups originally promised the Eighth plus Doolittle's heavies from the Twelfth. Eaker had argued, in a five-page memorandum on October 1, that the Eighth had "the primary task of destroying 113 key targets in the six primary systems of German industry," and "that but 10% of these targets are closer to heavy bombers based in Italy." He also pointed out that, although weather at the bases in Italy was no doubt better than in England, it was weather in the target area that really mattered. Blind bombing devices, such as H2X and Oboe, now coming into real use by the Eighth, could be operated out of England and not out of Italy. The problems of maintenance could be solved better in England than in the Foggia area of Italy, where not even airfields suitable for heavy bombers existed, much less repair facilities. And getting back to Italy in damaged condition, perhaps on only two motors, would be much harder for the heavies over the Alps than "down hill" across the Channel to England. Finally he cited the "Principle of Concentration of Force." The Luftwaffe, he said, "faces West. In order to overcome it and beat our way through to our industrial targets in Central Germany, we must employ the largest possible force. It is axiomatic that our loss rate goes down as the force builds up. The movement of several groups out of the UK leaves a diminished force which must face the concentration of defenses in Western Europe. It can be expected, therefore, that our losses will be heavier. . . ."[18]

But Arnold was not to be swayed. Viewing the war and the future of army air with the perspective of broad strategy as distinct from immediate operational urgencies, he remained convinced that strategic air power needed to be separated from theater dominance as well as from close support of ground forces. Though the shuttle missions to and from North Africa had proved to be impractical, he was already contemplating similar shuttles to and from Russia. And he wanted to have two substantial strategic air forces, widely apart, to justify the single strategic air commander for all of Europe he continued to regard as imperative. Finally, he could argue, quite rightly, that there were top-priority POINTBLANK targets in the Balkans, Ploesti being the most obvious, which were clearly out of reach from England alone.

The heart of Eaker's problem remained the continuing lag in the buildup of his forces, bombers in particular. On October 12 he forwarded to Washington a summary by Anderson of the combined bomber offensive for the period April 1 through September 30, reporting attacks against 13 U-boat yards responsible for 82 percent of U-boat construction; 8 of the 11 U-boat bases; 7 assembly plants producing 84 percent of German single-engine fighters; 2 component plants; 41 percent of dive-bomber assembly; 12 of the 23 aircraft and aero engine repair depots in occupied territory; 60 percent of the ball-bearing production; 29 percent of synthetic rubber; 40 percent of aero tires, 30 percent of truck tires and 30 percent of tank treads; one-third of metal propeller production; and three of the largest producers of motor trucks. This had taken 9,603 aircraft to 83 CBO targets with 835 aircraft on diversions; 57 of the 83 attacks "were considered successful," a 69 percent record of success, which "agrees well with the CBO plan, which estimated that two out of every three attacks would be successful."

The 69 percent mission accomplishment also, the report pointed out, "agrees well with the percentage of planes and crews asked for under the CBO plan which were actually in the theater." Between April 1 and September 30 the plan called for an average of 676 heavy bombers, but the actual average had been only 526, or 78 percent, while operational crews averaged 265 versus 423 planned, or 63 percent. "Thus 69% of the mission has been accomplished with 78% of the planes and 63% of the crews considered necessary, and in addition 4,513 of these crews and planes have been dispatched on targets which were not considered in the CBO plan." As of October

10, the report added, the Eighth had a total of 911 bombers (including mediums) versus 1,246 planned (73 percent) and 825 crews versus 1,039 planned (79 percent). These figures were changed, of course, by the losses at Schweinfurt, but Eaker still had enough bombers and crews to continue the CBO. Two questions hung unanswered: Would he get enough force to complete the CBO by May 1? And would the weather cooperate?[19]

The added force did arrive. But the weather did not cooperate. In his postwar book *Global Mission* Arnold summarized what the daily operations reports gave in detail. "In mid-October the weather shut down foggily on southeast Germany for most of the remainder of the year. Until January 1944 the only missions we were able to send into Germany were within range all the way of our longer-legged P-47s and P-38s. (Two exceptions, uneventful as far as enemy fighter interception was concerned, were long hauls in November to special targets in Norway.) By the time the weather let us get back to central and southeast Germany it was January and we had P-51s."[20]

Eaker very much wanted to hit remote POINTBLANK targets at once. On October 22, just a week after Schweinfurt II, he wrote Arnold another three-page letter that included the following: "We plan, at an early date, a) A maximum effort of more than 500 heavy bombers on an important target—a concentrated attack to headline to the Germans 'the biggest force the Americans have ever sent against a German target.' This is the complete answer to their propaganda that we cannot take the losses they are able to inflict. b) A simultaneous attack with a minimum of 100 aircraft each on four remaining principal aircraft factories. c) An attack with eight combat wings of 54 aircraft each simultaneously on eight different targets in the Combined Bomber Offensive scattered through an arc of 90 degrees." But the weather did not permit such a mission for many weeks, and it would have been folly to seek such pinpoint objectives when they could not be seen. Bombing through the overcast with H2X, Gee or Oboe made it possible to hit industrial areas but not particular factories.[21]

Ironically, the AAF, so firm in its dedication to precision bombing, found itself in those months more and more forced into RAF-style area attacks. On October 20, for example, five days after Schweinfurt II, Eaker sent 282 heavies above the clouds to Düren in the Ruhr (the first U.S. use of Oboe), losing only nine bombers, though three gunners in one B-17 died from the failure of oxygen equipment. In

November, VIII Bomber Command was able to go into Germany seven times, several of them with formations of more than 500 heavies. But all the missions were shallow penetrations often forced as high as 30,000 feet to get above the overcast. This usually prevented enemy interception but was fearsomely hard on the crews. Temperatures fell below minus 50 degrees, ice two inches thick formed on windows, hands froze in seconds if gloves were removed. And very little damage was done in terms of POINTBLANK goals. The MIA figure rose on the few occasions when the Luftwaffe was able to intercept, as over Bremen on November 26 when 29 heavies were lost. But since the force dispatched totaled 633, this was only 4.5 percent, a statistic of little solace to those who died, but far below the 25 percent Arnold had announced he was willing to spend. The same pattern held throughout December, with eight missions into Germany, virtually all shallow and through the clouds, and climaxed on December 30 when 710 heavies bombed with inconclusive results through the clouds over Ludwigshafen, as far south in Germany as Schweinfurt, losing 23 (3 percent), in part to enemy interception but with many bombers falling because of mechanical troubles.[22]

Eaker often said in later years that he and Anderson would have gone right back into the heart of Germany, even without the long-range fighters, if weather had permitted. He believed that, had the Eighth had gone back to Schweinfurt with 600 heavies instead of 300, the Germans would still have shot down 60, but that would have been a replaceable 10 percent loss. Hansell noted that "a large portion of the B-17s were sent to the Mediterranean, at the expense of the Eighth. If the Schweinfurt missions had been launched with 1,000 bombers instead of 300 the losses would probably have been the same, 60 bombers, but the percentage would have been 6% instead of 20%, and the targets would have been destroyed. . . . The plans for these missions initially contemplated massive attacks—2 to 3,000 bombers. When we carried them out with 300 the losses were inordinate. The Germans used all the fighters they had in attacking those 300. If there had been 300, and 300 more, and 300 more, they probably would not have taken any appreciable losses at all on the succeeding waves."[23]

Such thoughts are, to be sure, suppositions and not provable. But their conclusions were reinforced by the actual experience in Germany when the weather finally broke on January 11, 1944, and the Eighth dispatched 663 heavies deep into Germany, against POINT-

BLANK targets in Oschersleben and Brunswick, escorted this time all the way by P-38s and P-51s. The loss once more was 60 bombers, but this was 10 percent, not 20 percent. In a postwar interview Eaker added a further slant on the importance of mass. "A great many said we should have waited until we had a thousand bombers. . . . But that's absurd. The crews would not have been properly trained. We would not have had the background or experience. We would not have known how to do the job. It was those earlier years that made it possible for us to accomplish the results that we did when we got adequate forces."[24]

Eaker was once asked, "What does it do to your guts when you know you have to send men out, and by the thousands they're going to be killed?"

He replied: "Well, you know that you yourself are not going to be there long unless you get control of any failure due to fear—that you've got to expect losses. And you'll have disastrous losses at times due to weather, operational conditions, and enemy concentrations. You have to be prepared to take that without changing your plan or changing your morale, or you'll be sent home. . . . There are two types of fear. One is physical, one is mental. And the physical can be much more easily coped with than the mental. The physical will have an effect, and I've had it many times during my flying career, when death appeared imminent, and it would have no effect other than to spur me to quick action and decision, such as getting out of a plane in a flat spin at 200 feet, and there would be reaction of fear during the progress of the operation. But there would be such things as nightmares afterward for a brief period.

"But on the mental fear, there are two principle phases. One is making a decision that will cost men their lives. The other is making a decision, and so conducting yourself, as to be a factor in the failure of a significant military operation. And those two things will wear you down. You don't ever show the physical characteristics you do with physical fear, but it will keep you from sleeping well at night; you're thinking about every possible aspect of it and anything you might do. After an important mission like Schweinfurt you wonder if you might have taken other courses of action that would have prevented heavy loss of lives. So I would say, on the subject of fear, of the two, physical and mental fear, the first affected me up to the time I got an important command and was a very minor factor. I always flew more rather than less after disasters or near disasters in the air. But the mental fear has to be combatted very carefully. I always said to myself, if I worry too much about the past, it will decrease my ability to deal with the future. So when I would get morose over a past decision or a past engagement like one of the great raids, I would change my attitude by thinking about what I should do in the future. That's the way I coped with it."[25]

Down through the decades since Schweinfurt II the conventional wisdom has been that a) the mission was "a disaster;" b) "no air force could sustain such losses;" c) hence there could be no further deep penetrations into Germany until the long-range fighters became available at year end; and d) "the Eighth Air Force had for the time being lost air superiority over Germany." These conclusions, first enunciated in 1948 in Volume two of Craven & Cate's officially-sanctioned history of *The Army Air Forces in World War II,* have been picked up and regurgitated by dozens of subsequent journalists, pundits and historians of one level or another. In fact, however, all four conclusions are either greatly exaggerated or downright wrong.[26]

Victory in battle is measured first by achievement and second by cost. Disaster is defined as "total failure"—hardly true at Schweinfurt. There the achievement was threefold: first, by demonstrating that, even without escort, the bombers could not be stopped; second, by inflicting great damage on a major target; and third, by producing final evidence that POINTBLANK strategy was sound. The 19 percent cost was high—60 bombers down and 600 officers and men eliminated, about one-third of whom were killed, the rest captured. By comparison, the capture of Tarawa in the Pacific a month later cost the marines one-third of their attacking force, with 991 dead and 2,311 wounded. Tarawa is rated "a victory." Capture of terrain is, to be sure, more definitive than bombing an industrial target that can be repaired and so must be hit repeatedly (Schweinfurt was bombed twelve more times). With his usual vivid phrases Harris remarked: "A successful air offensive is an abstract proposition. You just go out, come back, and go out again, one day here, next day there, and there is nothing to show for it on the map. No columns of prisoners to photograph, no captured fieldpieces to mount in the village square. All you have to show is a photograph of a ruined city, taken six miles up, which the newspapers, with the best intentions in the world, reproduce as a blur." As Portal said at the time, the strategic air commanders considered the price of Schweinfurt II well worth the effort.[27]

And such costs could indeed have been "sustained," as Arnold's announced willingness to accept 25 percent losses on occasion indicated and as the growth of the Eighth Air Force demonstrated. In June Eaker had written Arnold: "We may as well frankly admit that this is going to be a bloody battle. The side will win which can make good its losses. In other words, the side which has the most reserve strength." That side was clearly the Allies. Heavy losses such as Schweinfurt could be swallowed so long as the average remained low. For the year 1943 the Eighth's average came out at 5.2 percent.[28]

What halted deep penetrations from October 15 to the end of December was not the lack of long-range fighters, though these were much desired and would have reduced the losses, but simply the atrocious run of bad weather. No orders were ever issued by Eaker or Anderson to refrain from deep attacks. Nor is there any indication in the hundreds of operational papers exchanged during that period that such a deliberate holdback was considered. The statement that air superiority over Germany had been lost can only be chalked up to ivory-tower superficiality. Neither side had superiority in 1943. Their fight for it was the dominant issue of the war in Europe and not fully settled until it was achieved in the renowned "Big Week" in February 1944, then demonstrated over Normandy in June and, finally, exploited in the last twelve months of the war, when both American and British air forces could roam at will over Germany. Control of the air in the two and a half months after Schweinfurt II belonged to the clouds.[29]

19

"To remove a General in the midst of a campaign—that is the mortal stroke."

—THE DUKE OF MARLBOROUGH IN A LETTER QUOTED BY CHURCHILL
IN THE HOUSE OF COMMONS, MAY 25, 1938

"**I**T IS A nuisenza to have the influenza. McIntire says I need a sea voyage. No word from U. J. yet," was the playful way President Roosevelt began a cable to Prime Minister Churchill on October 25, 1943—one of many on the very serious subject of planning the next CCS conference and persuading Stalin to attend. McIntire was FDR's doctor, and "U. J." stood for "Uncle Joe," their code for the Russian dictator, who was being very coy and suspicious about leaving Soviet soil. Eventually he agreed to come out as far as Teheran. Roosevelt and Churchill would hold the CCS meetings (code name: SEXTANT) not far away, in Cairo, beginning November 22, with Generalissimo Chiang Kai-shek a participant for the first time. Once the discussions with the Chinese were completed, November 27, the American and British parties would fly to the capital of Iran for five days with the Soviets and then return to Egypt for a second session at Cairo, concluding December 7. Following his doctor's advice, Roosevelt went to North Africa on the battleship *Iowa,* taking along most of the American contingent, including Hopkins, Marshall and Arnold.[1]

SEXTANT followed QUADRANT by only three months, but "in these 90 days," as Churchill expressed it in another preliminary cable to Roosevelt, "events of first magnitude have occurred. Mussolini has fallen; Italy has surrendered; its fleet has come over; we have successfully invaded Italy and are marching on Rome with good prospects of success." But, Churchill went on, "Our present plans for 1944 seem open to very grave defects. . . . The disposition of our forces between the Italian and the Channel theatres has not been settled by strategic needs but by the march of events, by shipping possibilities, and by arbitrary compromises between the British and American. The date of OVERLORD itself was fixed by splitting the difference between the American and British view. It is arguable that neither the forces building up in Italy nor those available for a May OVER-LORD are strong enough. . . . If we make serious mistakes in the campaign of 1944, we might give Hitler the chance of a startling comeback. Prisoner German General von Thoma was overheard saying, 'Our only hope is that they come where we can use the army upon them.' All this shows the need for the greatest care and foresight in our arrangements, the most accurate timing between the two theatres, and the need to gather the greatest possible forces for both operations, particularly OVERLORD. I do not doubt our ability in the conditions laid down to get ashore and deploy. I am however deeply concerned with the build up and with the situation which might arise. . . ."[2]

Churchill was here expressing traditional British interest in the Mediterranean as well as the centuries old British doctrine of avoiding massive involvement in land fighting on the Continent. He was also painfully conscious of how drained Great Britain had become, both of money and manpower. How different the American attitude was shines through many papers prepared by the U.S. Chiefs of Staff aboard the *Iowa* as well as in their talks with the president. They were confident to the point of sounding cocky.

For example, in a nine-page "Estimate of Enemy Situation," dated November 18, the U.S. Chiefs of Staff commented: "Germany is now on the defensive on all fronts. She has no decisive offensive capabilities. Her military resources are inadequate to meet all of her defensive requirements. The German Air Force is unable to ward off destructive Allied strategic bombing. Its concentration to resist such bombing leaves Germany's land fronts in the east and south inadequately supported. . . . Out of an overall fighter strength of 2,422 in operational units, 1,686 are concentrated in Germany, the Low Countries, and France. . . . In addition to general destruction of German industrial capacity and dislocation of civilian life, the German Air Force itself has suffered direct and indirect damage which tends to impair its ability to maintain the present scale of defense. Heavy combat losses have been inflicted on it, single-engine fighter production has been substantially reduced, the percentage of serviceability has been lowered, and the flow of replacements has been seriously interrupted. The growth of the German fighter force has been checked; attrition and production are now approximately in balance; and, if the attack is pressed, and resisted at current intensity, a decline in strength may be expected, opening the way to further progress in the effectiveness of the attack. Assuming continued growth in the strength of the Allied air offensive, the results achieved may be expected to increase progressively. The cumulative effects may so weaken German's capacity for armed resistance as to accelerate greatly the collapse of her will to continue the conflict. . . ."[3]

On the same day the U.S. chiefs also submitted a memorandum calling for "Integrated Command of U.S. Strategic Air Forces in the European-Mediterranean Area," and recommending establishment on January 1 of "The U.S. Strategic Air Forces in Europe" (USSTAF) with Spaatz in command. He would "be charged with the strategic direction of the U.S. Strategic Air Forces," would "assign missions to them, keeping the appropriate theater commanders informed." And he would "be charged with the coordination of the operations . . . with those of the RAF Bomber Command, through the Chief of the Air Staff RAF." Headquarters would be in the United Kingdom.[4]

Here was the penultimate step in the structural change Arnold had been pushing, despite repeated rebuffs by Marshall, Portal and others, ever since he had first proposed it in a letter to Spaatz in England almost exactly a year before when Spaatz was still CG of the Eighth and Eisenhower was still operating out of Gibraltar. Arnold wrote: ". . . air operations in Europe must be controlled and planned by one man. . . . Unless we are careful, we will find our air effort in Europe dispersed the same way we are now dispersed all around the world. We will find as many different bases of operations operating under as many different directives and commanders as there are land commanders. This must be prevented. We should take advantage of the ring of air bases with which we are now surrounding Germany so as to secure maximum striking power. This, of course, takes into consideration the question of weather, the question of location of targets, and the question of priority of targets. Quite obviously, with one man in command of all the air, he can move the mass of his air where it will be most effectively employed and use the rest of it to support the ground arm."[5]

In planning the creation of USSTAF Arnold had brought Spaatz back to Washington in October to brief him privately on the proposal to be presented at SEXTANT. It was generally expected then that Marshall would be in command of OVERLORD and that Eisenhower would take his place in Washington. Spaatz wanted to keep the USSTAF headquarters in Africa or Italy, but Arnold overruled him. Aboard the *Iowa* all these interwoven matters were discussed in exchanges of lengthy position papers and also in meetings with Roosevelt. A related but far bigger question than the unity of command for the strategic air forces was that of unity of command at the very top. The Americans wanted a single supreme commander bridging both the European and Mediterranean theaters, but the British insisted on maintaining the old structure, noting they had more forces in the Mediterranean than the Americans, though the reverse was true in England itself. Other urgent topics included how to arrange for strategic air bases inside Russia itself, how to get Turkey into the war against Germany and how to get Russia into the war against Japan. As the *Iowa* began its passage, Secretary of State Cordell Hull, Harriman and a high powered group of advisers were completing a conference in Moscow with Stalin, Molotov and other top Soviet figures. Hull cabled Roosevelt on November 2 that Stalin "promises to get in and help defeat the enemy in the far East after German defeat." But no answer was forthcoming at once on the shuttles.[6]

At Cairo itself the first conference was devoted largely to geopolitical issues and military planning with the Chinese. The projected new central control of strategic air power was, however, strenuously opposed by the British in a four-page position paper arguing that the existing arrangements under Portal were working well and a change "would not secure any advantage." But no action was taken prior to the switch to Teheran. There, at the first meeting between Stalin and Roosevelt, the President pressed "U. J." for a decision on the shuttle bases. Stalin took the matter under advisement. The next day, November 30, at a plenary session with twenty-six attending, Roosevelt opened the talks by introducing General Brooke, the British chief of staff, who pledged OVERLORD during May with "a supporting operation in southern France." Stalin pledged a big Soviet drive at the same time to hinder the transfer of German troops. Roosevelt then promised that the appointment of a C in C for OVER-LORD would be announced "within three or four days or immediately after he and the Prime Minister had returned to Cairo." The minutes do not record it, but Churchill reported in his postwar history that he informed Stalin he was "almost certain" it would be Marshall. Thereafter there were no discussions of particular relevance to the uses of air power. Stalin was effusively courteous to Roosevelt but "industrious," to use the adjective applied by Charles Bohlen, first secretary of the American embassy in Moscow, "in his attacks on the Prime Minister." For example, at a dinner at the British legation that happened to coincide with Churchill's birthday, and where the event was toasted, Stalin spoke of the president and the prime minister as his "fighting friends," adding, "if it is possible for me to consider Mr. Churchill my friend." The British returned to Cairo with no illusions about the Soviets, but the Americans continued optimistic.[7]

Back at Cairo on December 2 the CCS swiftly got down to the hard decisions of policy and strategy, while the president faced up to the particularly hard decision on who should command OVER-LORD. On December 4 the control of strategic air came close to acrimony as Portal again expressed the RAF's objections, saying he "could not undertake to subordinate the operations of the RAF to those of the Eighth Air Force" and that the latter's record was "as satisfactory as was possible without the full resources envisaged in the bomber plan. General Eaker had only some 75% of his full resources and was . . . therefore achieving only some 54% of the results expected. The program was, in fact, some three months behind. He realized the reasons which had caused this and would like to say that he felt that the Eighth Air Force had done everything that was possible under the circumstances. General Eaker had done his utmost to keep the plan to schedule. In spite of his smaller resources, he had penetrated deep into Germany and had accepted the consequent losses. Air operations in Europe and the Pacific could not be compared. In no other part of the world were our bomber forces up against some 1,600 German fighters over their own country."

Arnold interrupted aggressively that "the proposals he had put forward were designed in part to overcome the lack of flexibility in the operations of the U.S. bomber forces in Europe. They had not changed their technique. He had sent a series of inspectors to the

333

United Kingdom to try to probe into the reasons for this. In other theaters 60 or 70% of available aircraft were used in operations. In the UK only some 50% were used. . . . He could see no reason why at least 70% of the planes available should not be regularly employed. The failure to destroy targets was due directly to the failure to employ planes in sufficient numbers . . . nor was the proper priority of targets being followed. . . . Training, technique, and operational efficiency must all be improved. Only a new commander divorced from day to day routine could achieve this."

Portal, dignified though deeply indignant, began to reply, saying that "if a commander were appointed who insisted on keeping the bomber force rigidly to the program, it would undoubtedly be found that, in fact, less sorties were flown, and he, for one, could never permit his own fighters to escort bombers on a mission he did not believe to be sound. . . ."

But Marshall intervened. "It had always proved the case," he said, "that a combat commander was loath to release any forces in his possession lest they should not be returned to him. As far as the air forces were concerned, there was required a commander for the strategic air both in Italy and in Europe who, by reason of his position, was not affected by this very human weakness. . . . The U.S. daylight bombers were being operated from bases all over the world and in some of these planes were achieving twice the results obtained in the UK. . . . Whether the Eighth and the Fifteenth Air Forces were integrated or not, he still believed that a commander in England was required who could give full consideration to the many problems involved and impart the necessary drive. He suggested that action be deferred in order to provide additional time to consider the views put forward by Sir Charles Portal and General Arnold." This was agreed.[8]

Also on December 4 Roosevelt made his famous decision to keep Marshall in Washington and give command of OVERLORD to Eisenhower. This great surprise of course dominated the remaining CCS sessions. On the 7th when command of strategic air came up for decision, Portal said quietly that "the British Chiefs of Staff could not signify their approval of the proposals, but recognized the right of the U.S. Chiefs of Staff to issue such directives to their own air forces as they saw fit." He was prepared to carry out his part of any final directive but suggested that, "before implementing the new policy, General Arnold should, if possible, hear the views of General

Eisenhower, General Wilson and Air Chief Marshal Tedder." The proposal was approved with those amendments. Finally, after ruling on many other matters on this last day of SEXTANT, the CCS agreed that unification of command in the Mediterranean would take effect December 10; Eisenhower would hand over command on January 1 or earlier; and that whenever public announcement of his appointment as supreme commander, Allied Expeditionary Force, was made, there should also be announcement of the new supreme allied commander, Mediterranean Theater. That post went to Sir Henry Maitland Wilson, and both announcements came on December 24.[9]

Arnold was delighted by Eisenhower's appointment. For one thing, the commanding general of the Army Air Forces knew he had much to gain from Marshall's retention in Washington, since he was very much a protégé of the chief of staff. For another, Eisenhower's designation greatly smoothed the bumpy path to USSTAF. Arnold lost no time in setting elaborate rearrangements in motion, operating at the trip-hammer pace he preferred, "slap dash," as Sir John Dill described him.[10]

On the 7th, directly after the CCS meeting, Arnold's diary records: "Lunch with Tedder. Discussed personalties and new organization." That afternoon he flew on to Tunis, followed by Roosevelt, Hopkins and others, for a dinner with Eisenhower, Spaatz and their key staff officers. He "talked to Beadle Smith and Eisenhower. Both agreed that Spaatz was man for job. Wouldn't take anyone else, not even Tedder. . . . President asked about Marshall's trip and I told him. He seemed surprised and wanted to know when it was decided." (The chief of staff, though as calm of face and manner as usual, was, of course, deeply distressed and returned to Washington the other way around the globe to give himself extra time for reflection.) On the 9th Arnold flew to Foggia where he "discussed with Spaatz, Doolittle, House, Cannon, and O'Donnell implications of Cairo-Teheran Conference and what it meant to them." On the 12th he flew to Marrakesh and back to America by the south-Atlantic route, arriving on the 15th in Washington, where the first message to Eaker, the next day, read: "Ruth ill with pneumonia. Will keep you informed. Condition not critical."[11]

Spaatz's diary for the meeting on the 9th adds major clues to what became—quite unnecessarily—the most painful transition in Eaker's career. He wrote: "Discussed [with Arnold] personnel to be utilized in new set-up. Presented to him my ideas of moving present staff to UK with me when assume overall command of Fifteenth and Eighth. (Had been told earlier that headquarters would have to be in UK, and I repeated again that I do not want it.) Recommended that Eaker be brought to Mediterranean Theater to be overall Air Commander, Doolittle command Eighth Air Force, Brereton remain with Ninth, Cannon remain with Twelfth (as well as Tactical Air Force Commander). No decisions made."[12]

Back in London Portal on the 14th asked Eaker to come in and told him about Arnold's sharp criticisms and the Spaatz appointment. Portal informed Arnold: "I found Eaker thoroughly alive to the need for earliest possible attack on POINTBLANK targets and to importance of using maximum force available. I am confident you will see great achievements as soon as weather gives him a chance." Cables to Eaker from Arnold on the 16th reported Ruth had been "taken to Doctor's Hospital. . . ." and on the 17th "Ruth very much improved. Temperature gone." Eaker was reassured about his wife and not perturbed about Spaatz returning to a command above him, something he had long expected and several times suggested.[13]

So it was an absolute bolt from the blue when he received an eyes-only cable on the 19th saying: "Conference at SEXTANT provided for changes in command Mediterranean Theater and a commander for OVERLORD. If existing slate goes through there will be a vacancy in the Mediterranean Air Command. It has been decided that an American will take over Command of the Allied Air Force in the Mediterranean position now held by Tedder. As a result of your long period of successful operations and the exceptional results of your endeavors as Commander of the Air Force in England you have been recommended for this position." The message went on to list other changes "tentatively" set up, with Spaatz as head of U.S. Strategic Air Force in Europe, Doolittle of the Eighth, Cannon the Twelfth and Gen. Nathan F. Twining of the Fifteenth. It concluded, "Who would you like to have as your Deputy for all administrative matters for the U.S. Air Forces in that Theater, if the above goes through?"[14]

Had Arnold been thoughtful or considerate enough to send a personal letter explaining the positive reasons behind all this, Eaker would have obeyed without cavil, even if unhappy. As it was, following Portal's report of Arnold's faultfinding at Cairo, the cold wording of the cable struck him as equivalent to dismissal. After their long controversy a few months earlier Arnold had promised him that, if

When Eaker chose to show displeasure he left no doubt about it.

he were ever dissatisfied, "you will be the first one to hear of it and it will come from me direct." That had scarcely been the case this time, and Eaker thought it was grossly unfair, that he had been "let down." Since the cable was "tentative" and full of "ifs", he bitterly resolved to dig in his heels.[15]

First he carefully phrased an eyes-only response to his boss. "Believe war interest best served by my retention command Eighth

337

Air Force: Otherwise experience this theater for nearly two years wasted. If I am to be allowed my personal preference having started with the Eighth and seen it organized for major task in this theater, it would be heart-breaking to leave just before climax. If my services satisfactory to seniors, request I be allowed to retain command Eighth Air Force. Reference your proposed slate, if I leave Eighth Air Force recommend Edwards assume command of it. Also recommend Doolittle retain Fifteenth. To do otherwise loses value of prior training and experience for their tasks in their respective theaters and at the most critical time. Specifically to answer your last question and if you do not follow foregoing recommendations, request Major General I. H. Edwards as Administrative Deputy new task."[16]

Then he talked to Devers, who did not yet know he too would be going to the Mediterranean, and the ETO commander at once sent a cable to Arnold urging that Eaker remain at the Eighth and praising his accomplishments and abilities. Eaker also spoke to Portal, who was shocked but could not intervene, though he did pass the news to Churchill. Eaker then dispatched similar cables to Spaatz and Eisenhower, each beginning, "Arnold proposes new assignment for me," and going on to express his hope of retaining the Eighth and to ask their advice. Of Spaatz he asked "whether I am agreeable to you . . . or do you prefer change?" To Eisenhower he concluded his appeal: ". . . will be governed of course entirely by your desire." All these messages went out on the 19th.[17]

Spaatz drafted a reply that he cleared with Arnold before transmitting it to Eaker on the 21st. It read: "In view of command assignments, importance of having an American in command of Mediterranean Allied Air Forces, and establishing U.S. Strategic Command in UK, believe best interests in overall conduct of war effort makes necessary your assignment as Air Commander in this theater. Because of close relationship with other services and other nationalities in both theaters and for most effective integration of effort I consider it essential that American air rank and experience be distributed between two theaters. Believe that command of an air force is of relatively less importance compared to overall requirements and particularly since Eighth Air Force under new setup will function as an operating headquarters more nearly approximating VIII Bomber Command."[18]

Eisenhower's reaction was to ask Spaatz to meet him at Tunis for discussion. But this meeting could not take place until Christmas

Day, and by then much more had transpired. Arnold replied to Devers on the 20th: ". . . all the reasons that you have given me are those that have been advanced as reasons why [Eaker] should go down and be commander of the Allied Mediterranean Air Forces. I am duly appreciative of his splendid cooperation and loyalty to me and have enough confidence in him to be sure that regardless of the job to which he may be assigned his loyalty and cooperation will be unquestioned. . . . This move is necessary from the viewpoint of world wide air operations." Next day Arnold replied to Eaker. "No one knows better than I do the difficulties encountered leaving an organization that has been build up and most successfully operated under one's personal direction. This is particularly true when the loyalty from top to bottom is unquestioned and the commander has complete cooperation from all of his personnel. Such is your position at this time. The dictates of world wide air operations necessitate major changes being made. This effects you personally and while from your point of view it is unfortunate that you cannot stay and retain command of the organization that you have so carefully and successfully built up, the broader view of the world wide war effort indicates the necessity for a change. I extend to you my heartfelt thanks for the splendid cooperation and loyalty that you have given me thus far and for the wonderful success of your organization, but I cannot see my way clear to make any change in decisions already reached."[19]

Two days later, on the 23rd, the formal orders came through relieving Eaker as CG of the Eighth and appointing Spaatz to command USSTAF, both to be effective January 1. Eaker replied on Christmas Eve: "Orders received will be executed promptly Jan. one. Am in communication Spaatz discussing staffs and matters of mutual necessity."[20]

That would appear to be the end of an unseemly, if militarily correct and entirely private, dispute. But Marshall, just back in Washington as the dust was settling, was decidedly unsettled. Having expected to be in charge of OVERLORD, he had long been thinking about who he would choose as its key commanders and had strong convictions on the subject. Before getting back to Washington, the chief of staff, on December 21 had wired Eisenhower some of his suggestions, not yet having seen the proposed changes the supreme allied commander designate had sent him in a letter dated December 17, including Devers to Mediterranean Theater commander, and

Tedder to be "my chief airman and with him I would have Spaatz." Disturbed by the chief's views and not realizing his own letter had not been received, Eisenhower sent Marshall a long, defensive explanation of the reasons behind his own choices. This awaited Marshall's arrival in Washington just before Christmas along with word of Eaker's relief. Marshall on Christmas Eve hastily sent Eisenhower two stiff replies, one accusing Tedder and Spaatz of being "selfish" in pushing Eaker out of England, the other expressing his own "concern" about the transfer of Devers and Eaker and the apparent tendency "to gut the Mediterranean headquarters and leadership." These troubling messages reached Eisenhower just as he and Spaatz were about to hold their meeting in Tunis to discuss Eaker.[21]

Bedell Smith, Eisenhower's powerful chief of staff, had already informed Spaatz, as the latter's diary confides, that "strong objections were being raised to the transfer of Eaker from UK, and I told him that unless this was done I would not consider the overall strategic command with headquarters in UK. . . . Feel that Arnold has slipped from his original decisions so that he has not stated them firmly to Marshall but has thrown it all into the lap of Eisenhower. My original estimation of Eisenhower's fairness has been strengthened by the way in which he is taking this, and the way he is standing by me in my decisions."[22]

At Tunis on the 25th, as the Spaatz diary continues: "Met General Eisenhower. . . . He told me that message would go to Marshall this afternoon, giving my views as his views in respect to transfer of Eaker. Asked me to come down to Algiers tomorrow to see answer from Marshall, but until we hear anything different, for me to make plans to proceed to the UK on 28 December. . . . He is firm in his decisions and I consider him one of the finest men I know." On the 26th the Spaatz diary goes on: "In C-47 flew to [Algiers] discussing following points with Gen. Eisenhower and Gen. Bedell Smith: 1) Message from Marshall pointing to me as selfish and ambitious in asking for Eaker's release and transfer to this theater. Told Eisenhower that I would write letter to Gen. Marshall—but do not think I will—believe best plan to ignore it. 2) Am definitely set to go to England on 28 December. 3) Told Eisenhower that I felt sure that the old cat fight would develop between 8th and 9th Air Forces unless an organization were set up there similar to that in this theater. Told him that it is most necessary to designate an over-all Air Commander in the theater. Told Gen. Eisenhower that I proposed dealing through the over-all Air Commander in this theater [Eaker] but that I would not deal direct with the 15th Air Force."[23]

Christmas 1943 was a very busy day for Eisenhower. Prior to his talks with Spaatz he had met with Churchill for final decision on the prime minister's newest brainchild—the landing at Anzio. This was one of the topics Eisenhower included in his very long message to Marshall that afternoon. But the first topic was Eaker. "His proposed transfer to this theater has from time to time been suggested as a possibility ever since I heard that Spaatz is to be the commander of the American Strategic Air Forces. To be perfectly frank, this assignment for Spaatz leaves me somewhat puzzled both as to purpose and as to the position of such a command in an American organization, since we always, in each theater, insist upon a single commander. However, General Arnold and General Spaatz proposed the Eaker transfer to me specifically when I met them briefly at an airport in Sicily sometime back and I agreed. It is necessary to find a good man for the post of Air Commander in Chief of the Mediterranean. It would appear to me to be something of a waste to have both Spaatz and Eaker in England. . . . You will note that I am assuming that an American is to have command of the air here. In fact, at a conference at Tunis this morning Spaatz definitely proposed that if Eaker is to remain in England, he, Spaatz is the logical man to leave here as Air CINC of the Mediterranean instead of assigning him as commander of Strategic Air Forces. What I am trying to say is that Eaker is completely acceptable to me. . . ."

Eisenhower then added a paragraph that clearly indicates, if not said in so many words, his ground officer bias toward tactical vs. strategic air power and his consequent preference for Tedder and Spaatz. "With regard to air command for OVERLORD I am anxious to have there a few senior individuals that are experienced in the air support of ground troops. This technique is one that is not (repeat not) widely understood and it takes men of some vision and broad understanding to do the job right. Otherwise a commander is forever fighting with those air officers who, regardless of the ground situation, want to send big bombers on missions that have nothing to do with the critical effort."[24]

Simultaneously Eisenhower cabled Eaker: "Your personal message reached me en route to my base headquarters, which accounts for the delay. As you well know, I would be more than delighted to have you with me. I note that your orders have already been issued but the fact is, as I have just informed General Marshall, your transfer was proposed to me specifically by General Arnold in a brief conversation in Sicily and I agreed because of the absolute necessity of finding an outstanding man for the post of Air CINC of the Mediterranean as I understand that an American is to succeed to that command. I have told General Marshall that you are completely acceptable to me but that it would be a waste to have both you and Spaatz in England. I have the highest regard for you both and feel quite frankly that if Spaatz goes to England as commander of the American Strategic Air Force, an assignment which leaves me somewhat puzzled both as to purpose and position, then you should come here. On the other hand, if Spaatz remained here as Air CINC of the Mediterranean, you should remain in England. We do not (repeat not) have enough top men to concentrate them in one place."[25]

Three days later, on the 28th, Marshall closed the discussion with a gracious message to Eisenhower beginning, "I followed a confused trail while traveling the Pacific." He blessed all of Eisenhower's recommendations, including Devers and Eaker to the Mediterranean, and concluded, "In other words, you list your final desires and so far as I can see now they will be approved."[26]

Spaatz arrived in England December 29, was met by Eaker and taken at once to Castle Coombe, "where," Spaatz's diary wryly notes, "too many people did not help recuperation from a most tiring trip." The next two days were filled with strategy meetings between the two old friends and Smith representing Eisenhower. Spaatz explained the SEXTANT conference and other reasoning behind the big switch in positions. Eaker said afterwards, "It did not make me feel any less heart-burn at going, but it made me understand it better." On January 1 Smith reported to Eisenhower that the present Eighth AF headquarters would be "reduced, becomes Hq., USSTAF, to be located at WIDEWING; VIII Bomber Command, augmented by reduction of former Eighth AF Hq., becomes new Hq. Eighth AF, located at High Wycombe." Spaatz would have two deputies: Anderson for Operations, "including POINTBLANK operation of the Fifteenth and coordination of the Ninth and RAF," and Knerr "for coordination, personnel and logistic requirements between Eighth and Ninth. . . . I have been into this carefully with Spaatz and Eaker. The above planned organization represents *no* increase in personnel and *no* increase in the number of Hq. . . . Spaatz, Eaker and myself are convinced it will work and that it is the minimum organization necessary for general control and coordination of all the elements involved. We are now looking into the possibility of placing your Hq. at WIDEWING" (as took place).[27]

To those of us who saw Eaker daily during this tense fortnight, there was no sign of the outside power struggle or his own inner torment. He was poker-faced, discussing his problem only with a very few associates—Devers of course; Chauncey, his chief of staff; Portal and Harris. At breakfast and dinner at Castle Coombe he was his habitual engaging self, as, for example, teasing Peter Beasley after several mornings in a row when Beasley explained his absence from dinner the previous night by saying, "I was seeing *Flare Path*," the latest hit on the London stage. "Flare Path" turned out to have been Winnabelle R. Coffee, an Iowa woman who was one of Jacqueline Cochran's ferry pilots. Beasley married her postwar. At night Eaker often played poker with customary nonchalance and skill. When the news broke everyone was flabbergasted. And a great majority of his close staff wanted to go with him.

Congratulations and commiserations poured in—dozens of them, including Churchill, Sinclair, Portal, Anderson, Knerr and Lord Trenchard, founder of the RAF. A December 26 letter of "heartiest congratulations" came from Arnold, who added: "Your new assignment in replacing such an outstanding RAF airman as Tedder pays tribute to your talents as an organizer and a leader. This new task, as you well know, covers an extensive and active arena. It requires the ablest leadership to effectuate close coordination and cooperations between ground and air forces, between commands within the air forces, and finally between the various nationalities that constitute this command."[28]

More in tune with Eaker's feelings was a letter from Lovett. "I write . . . to congratulate you formally on the new promotion your new command involves and to commiserate with you privately at leaving the Eighth after you have seen the baby through rickets, croup, and measles and just at the time when it grows into a strong young warrior. I suppose that's the penalty of rank under a military organization but I confess that the military system does not make a great deal of sense to me. . . . You obviously have another terrific job ahead of you. The Air Forces, of course, take a good deal of pride in having the air command in that theater go to an American and apparently the British belief and confidence in you made their acceptance of the proposal easier. One shred of comfort—and about the only one—I get from the move is the thought that because of your vast experience in the attack on Germany the operations of the Fifteenth Air Force may be made more effective and brought into play sooner than would otherwise be possible. . . . All of us here feel that the Army Air Forces and the country owe you a debt of gratitude for the patient, intelligent, and imaginative work you have done in building up a real striking force against Germany and in developing the techniques to make our efforts fruitful. I am particularly proud of the way you have handled the many difficult problems of relationship with the British and we are all well aware of the fact that the comradeship which has developed between the AAF and the RAF is in large part due to your wise handling of the situation. In a conversation with General Marshall this morning, he specifically referred to this point and to the debt which we all owe you and which I am extremely happy to acknowledge."[29]

On January 1, 1944, the *New York Times* ran an editorial half a column long, headed GENERAL EAKER MOVES UP and saying, in part, he "demonstrated that mass air attacks could be made in daylight against heavily defended enemy territory effectively and economically after the Germans and the British had given up the attempt as hopeless. His transfer . . . is a well-deserved promotion. . . . It was of supreme importance to Allied air strategy that General Eaker's experiment should succeed. . . . Whatever the invasion cost in human life may be, it will be less than if General Eaker and his friend and collaborator, Air Chief Marshal Sir Arthur Harris, chief of the RAF's Bomber Command, had not won the battle for a trial of air power first. . . . General Eaker will be missed in Britain, not only by the officers and men of his command but by the British with whom he worked so smoothly. . . . He is a soldier, not a diplomat, but for brevity and tact it would be hard to match his first speech after his arrival in Britain, 'We won't do much talking until we've done more fighting. We hope that when we leave you'll be glad we came.' " That speech was given in High Wycombe, and its Mayor now wrote him, "You did much to show the people of High Wycombe what an American gentleman was like and the example you set will not readily be forgotten."[30]

While meticulously answering all these letters, Eaker also found time to send personal notes to all his key underlings thanking them for "unselfish devotion." At Castle Coombe Miss Jones was instructed to make the house ready for Tedder and any officers he designated. She wept. As for his three RAF enlisted men, Eaker first asked them if they wanted to come with him and then arranged for RAF orders to be cut transferring them. He had brought Captain Mason up from PINETREE in mid-December to be his aide, freeing me for special assignments, the first of which was to serve as the junior member of a committee of six in preparing, per army regulations, a two-inch thick report on Eighth Air Force operations for the thirteen months he had commanded it. The Castle Coombe Mess had $1,200 left in the till (a goodly sum in 1943). Mason and I presumed it should be returned to the quartermaster. Not at all, said Eaker, explaining that it was both legal and appropriate to retain such funds so long as they were used "for the good of the Mess." He already had a postwar plan in mind. A year later, with the consent of his eight messmates, he had a silver punch bowl and nine cups (one for each of us) made by Gorham and inscribed "Lt. General Ira C. Eaker's Castle Coombe Mess, Kingston Hill, Surrey, 1943" and all our names. The bowl, ladle and five surviving cups now permanently occupy a glass case at Eighth Air Force headquarters, Barksdale Field, Alabama.

On January 7, the RAF laid on a dinner in his honor in a hall in Bushy Park, not far from WIDEWING. There were about two hundred guests, headed by air marshals Portal, Bottomley, Harris and Saundby and attended by other officers at all levels, including most of the Eighth Air Force senior staff. Some fifteen toasts and brief talks were given, with a final upbeat response from Eaker. No notes seem to have been taken. But sometime during the evening Portal told Eaker that Colonel Holt would like to see him on his way through north Africa. Who, asked Eaker, was Colonel Holt? He learned it was the name Churchill used when traveling incognito. The PM was in Marrakesh recovering from pneumonia. A few days later when Eaker arrived at Bovingdon, where Smitty was waiting with *Yardbird* (a more up-to-date B-17 than *Spareball*), he found Air Marshal and Lady Harris there to bid him farewell as well as a color guard and the entire RAF band to give him a rousing send-off.[31]

At Marrakesh in the elegant Taylor Villa Churchill was "utterly tired out. . . . I never remember such extreme fatigue and weakness in the body," he wrote. "Every temptation, inducement, exhortation and to some extent compulsion, to relax and lie down presented itself in the most seductive form. . . . However, events continued to offer irresistible distraction." He kept the communications lines buzzing with messages to Roosevelt, to Alexander, and to the British Chiefs of Staff. And he gave audiences to Montgomery on the way to London; to Benes, the tragic president of Czechoslovakia on his way back from Moscow; and to Eisenhower on his way home to see Marshall and get a breather before OVERLORD. Here too he saw Eaker for half an hour in a room with tall windows and the sun shining through the orange groves outside.[32] Churchill said: "I can understand your disappointment, young man, at having to leave the Eighth Air Force just when it's achieving its maximum effect on the war effort. But as for your new assignment, I want to remind you that we're entrusting to you two of our favorite British units, the Balkan Air Force and the Desert Air Force. If we didn't have great faith in you we wouldn't put them under your charge. You'll also have the RAF Coastal Command, the French air forces, and your own very considerable Twelfth and Fifteenth Air Forces. All in all, it will be a much larger command, with more responsibilities, then you had in the United Kingdom."[33]

This was the best sort of salve for Eaker's bruised spirits, as was the prime minister's parting remark. "The prediction you made to me at Casablanca last February about our combined bomber missions, including 'round the clock bombing,' are now being verified. I no longer have any doubt that they will prove completely valid."[34]

Cassino
March 15, 1944.

FIVE

Cassino, Ploesti, and Rift with Russia

20

"The conflict of the Present and the Past, The ideal and the actual in our life, As on a field of battle held me fast, Where this world and the next world were at strife."

—A STANZA FROM HENRY WADSWORTH LONGFELLOW'S POEM *MONTE CASSINO,* WRITTEN THERE IN 1869

THE MEDITERRANEAN Allied Air Forces (whose jaw-breaking name was quickly shortened to MAAF) came into being December 10, 1943, after the CCS agreed at SEXTANT to merge Tedder's Mediterranean Air Command in the eastern Mediterranean with Spaatz's North African Air Forces in the western. Tedder became the first Air C in C, with Spaatz as his deputy, but neither attempted any actual reorganization because they knew they were going to England almost at once. Operations continued without interruption. During the period from December 10, 1943, to January 15, 1944, MAAF flew 37,811 effective sorties, dropping 13,915 tons of bombs on targets ranging from Italy to Austria to Bulgaria. When Eaker took over on January 15, 1944, MAAF was the world's biggest air command, as measured both by personnel and planes. The Americans mustered more officers and men, 217,118 versus 104,311 British—a total of 321,429. But the RAF had more than twice as many aircraft—8,852 versus 3,746—a total of 12,598, of which 4,323 (60 percent of them U.S.) were in combat units.[1]

Flying on from his meeting with Churchill at Marrakesh, Eaker reported in Algiers to the new supreme allied commander, Mediterranean, Gen. (later Field Marshal) Sir Henry Maitland Wilson,

351

whose elephantine size and shape caused him to be known to all as "Jumbo." Eaker wrote Lovett a week later: "He is a very kindly, fatherly individual who anyone must immediately like at first sight. I am convinced that it would be difficult to find a better commander for this theater. I also spent an hour with General Devers, who had arrived the week before. . . ." Devers was Wilson's deputy on the American side. Deputy Air C in C for Eaker was his old friend, Air Marshal Sir John Slessor, who had spent 1943 as air officer commanding, RAF Coastal Command in England, earning a large measure of the credit for defeating the U-boats. Before appointing him to his new post Portal meticulously asked Eaker's approval, which was hearty. Jaunty "Jack" Slessor, despite legs hobbled by childhood polio, had been a distinguished fighter pilot in World War I and became the RAF's most articulate thinker, much as Eaker had become army air's best spokesman. They made a fine team.[2]

The alternation of American and British officers in the top levels

Slessor and Eaker, Caserta, Italy, 1945.

of command was one of two major innovations in the prosecution of air war that evolved in the Mediterranean, the other being the concept of tactical air as distinct from strategic. The latter was developed primarily in England. But the Mediterranean theater had been the primary proving ground for the use of air power in support of ground action ever since El Alamein, and it had been the crucible of joint command ever since the Allied landings in North Africa. MAAF made real advances in both these fields. The CCS directive had indicated the general framework MAAF should have. In accordance with the desire for centralized tactical control expressed by Tedder and Spaatz on the basis of their long experience in the Mediterranean, MAAF was set up by Eaker and Slessor with a single, combined, U.S. and British operational staff under the two of them, but with three separate administrative staffs headed by a deputy C in C (U.S.), a deputy C in C (British) and the A.O. C in C Middle East (British). The chart looked like this:

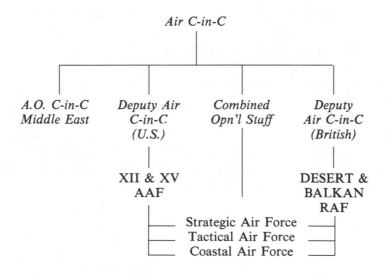

The Air C in C himself was established on a level with the naval C in C (Adm. Sir John Cunningham) and the C in C, 15th Group of Armies (Gen. Sir Harold Alexander), all three reporting to General Wilson, the supreme allied commander, Mediterranean.[3]

This relatively simple structure was complicated by the simultaneous creation of USSTAF, based at WIDEWING under Spaatz and giving him operational control over the Fifteenth Air Force in Italy as well as the Eighth in England. Before Eaker left England Spaatz and he agreed that all USSTAF operational directives would go only to Eaker, who in turn would pass them along to the Fifteenth while retaining the right to alter them as weather or other unpredictables might make necessary. This was very unorthodox, puzzling not only Eisenhower but many others in the chain of command. It functioned smoothly. But that success, as both Spaatz and Eaker often commented, was due primarily to their close friendship and total mutual trust. The month the war ended, Spaatz said: "It wouldn't have worked except for the personal relationship. . . . The thing that USSTAF brought about in getting operational control over the Fifteenth was that it created a necessity for frequent meetings between Eaker and myself, which not only insured the coordination of the Fifteenth's operational activity but the entire tie-in between the Air Forces in the Mediterranean and the Air Forces up here."[4]

In England Spaatz eliminated VIII Bomber Command and sent Doolittle and Eighth AF headquarters to PINETREE. At WIDEWING he kept a tiny personal staff for himself and divided USSTAF duties between two deputies—Knerr for administrative and service functions and Anderson for operations. In Italy Eaker set up Edwards as his deputy for administration. On the operational side he inherited three exceptional officers, all of them old friends. The well-established Twelfth (tactical) Air Force was under the command of Maj. Gen. John K. Cannon, a veteran of the North African campaign. The fledgling Fifteenth (strategic), created three months before and with only six groups of heavies operational, was under Maj. Gen. Nathan F. Twining, previously commander of the Thirteenth Air Force in the South Pacific. The third officer was handsome, young Brig. Gen. Lauris Norstad, who had been director of operations for Spaatz and would fill the same role at MAAF on the combined operational staff. It too was a mix of American and British officers, 49 of one, 69 of the other. Under Eaker and Slessor they set policy, established objectives and coordinated planning. Actual operations were then carried out by the various fighting units, all of which were structured entirely on national lines. These were predominantly American or British, but there were also squadrons from Brazil, Poland, France, New Zealand, South Africa, Australia and, later on, Russia. "Here," as Marquis Childs wrote in his *Washington Post* column, "is no less than the pattern for a United Nations air force."[5]

Much of this huge conglomeration was still scattered around

the African shores from Cairo to Casablanca when Eaker took command in mid-January. But the main action was now either in Italy or based there, and it was obvious that, as he wrote Lovett in the same letter quoted above, "there is a tremendous reorganizational task confronting us. . . ." It involved moving the 15,000-man Allied Force and MAAF headquarters to Italy as fast as possible as well as the bulk of the fighting units and service elements. However, taking priority over everything was the landing at Anzio, scheduled for the very next week. So Eaker flew to Italy at once, pausing for one night and day in Tunis to see Tedder, have a final talk with Bedell Smith and touch base with the twenty-four AAF officers who came on from England to serve with him. (With characteristic courtesy Eaker took only those who wanted to go.) Edwards was the senior; Chauncey would continue as Eaker's chief of staff, bringing along his chief clerk, Sgt. Sol Stameshkin; Hull would be A-2 (intelligence); Whitney would initially head public relations, assisted by McCrary; five of Eaker's Castle Coombe messmates had specific tasks; Mary Weiler would remain his secretary along with RAF Sergeant Stroud. We were all bivouacked for several weeks in Tunis or nearby La Marsa while Eaker went ahead to preside over the air support for the Anzio landings. He established MAAF headquarters alongside Alexander in the immense Royal Palace of Caserta. Once again we found ourselves occupying a building with unique historic and architectural characteristics as well as peculiar living conditions. The most noticeable of the last was the uncomfortable discovery that the palace's 1,200 rooms were already inhabited by a 180-year accumulation of fleas.

Eaker's positive attitude and the decisiveness with which he acted in that critical first week are best revealed by quoting again from his long letter of January 23 to Lovett. "On Tuesday [the 18th] I departed for Bari and spent the afternoon with Twining. . . . On Wednesday I visited General Cannon . . . and came in the afternoon to Caserta. . . . Slessor, Norstad and I moved in and at 8 o'clock on Thursday morning, the 20th, MAAF Hq. officially opened . . . communications having been completed to all of the Air Force subordinate commands. . . . In preparation for [Anzio] we had two conferences daily with General Wilson, with General Alexander, Admiral Cunningham and myself present—one at 10 in the morning and one at 6 in the evening. At 2 A.M. on the morning of the 22nd the landing was launched. It is now about 36 hours since two divisions went over the beaches and there has been surprisingly little enemy reaction. . . . The enemy air reaction to the landing was almost as impotent as the land effort. Yesterday two attacks were made by enemy fighter bombers with fighter protection. There were about six FW-190s in the first effort and eight in the second. They set on fire two of our landing craft, killing about 40 men. These were the only casualties suffered in the entire landing according to present reports. We had 20 fighters above the beaches at the time and we definitely destroyed two of these fighter bombers and damaged at least two of the supporting fighters. . . . It appears that the enemy was caught completely by surprise. . . . In the air in Italy the Hun is absolutely flat on his back. . . ."

Switching from such operational detail, Eaker also informed Lovett of a highly important policy understanding he reached that week with Wilson—one that both men followed until the war's end. After the creation of USSTAF by the CCS, the American Joint Chiefs of Staff kept a protective eye on the U.S. ground forces by issuing a directive to Spaatz and Eaker saying, "Should a strategic or tactical emergency arise requiring such action, the Theater Commanders, may, at their discretion, utilize the Strategic Air Forces . . . for purposes other than their primary mission." When Eaker arrived in Algiers he learned, as he wrote Lovett, "that such an emergency was to be declared" during the Anzio landings. "I advised very strongly against General Wilson's declaring such an emergency, stating that I had full authority from General Spaatz to use the Fifteenth Air Force as the situation indicated. General Spaatz had been through a year of the war in Africa and he fully understood the difficulties here and believed that flexibility must be allowed the C-in-C, MAAF. General Spaatz was further reassured in this view by the knowledge that I would take heavy bombers off the battlefield and put them on their strategic tasks to the maximum. General Wilson agreed to leave it that way and we have not declared such an emergency."[6]

Though there was no emergency, either real or declared, at the time of the Anzio landings, a genuine one developed a month later when the Germans finally counterattacked, almost overwhelming the two U.S. divisions deployed there. The Anzio landings were a last-minute improvisation, conceived by Churchill and reluctantly approved by Roosevelt, the reluctance stemming not from the concept but from shortage of reinforcements and landing craft, all of which were obligated to leave the Mediterranean immediately after the debarkation in order to reach England in time for the invasion of Normandy, then planned for May 1. The Anzio task force was commanded by Maj. Gen. John P. Lucas—no Patton—who was dubious about the task from the start, recognizing that the 110,000 men available to him might be cut off and wiped out if they headed too far inland. Furthermore, Gen. Mark Clark of the U.S. Sixth Army, to whom Lucas reported and who was no Patton either, had given him ambiguous orders. The obvious first objective, only twenty miles inland, was the Alban Hills, which Lucas almost certainly could have captured in a few days in view of the slight immediate German resistance (they were guarding fifty miles of the Italian coast with only one battalion). But Clark's orders directed Lucas to advance "on" the Alban Hills, not "to" them. Accordingly, as Clark himself recorded, "It was considered wise to make only limited advances in the first few days in order to consolidate positions about seven miles deep and fifteen miles long around Anzio, awaiting the arrival of reinforcements." About this Slessor wrily commented, "They duly arrived—on both sides."[7]

Ordered by Hitler to drive the Americans into the sea within three days "at any cost," his brilliant overall commander in Italy, Field Marshal Albert Kesselring, assembled from the north and as far away as Greece a mixed bag of reinforcements adding up to about five divisions and began a strong assault on February 16. It was met, as Churchill wrote, "by every aircraft we could fly." On the 17th MAAF dropped the heaviest bomb tonnage ever expended until then on a single day in close support of ground troops—972 tons, of which two-thirds fell from the Fifteenth's heavies. Using them then and until the crisis ended a week later put Eaker in a difficult spot, for Spaatz, blessed with several days of clear weather over Germany, was just about to launch the crucial "Big Week" air onslaught from England and wanted the Fifteenth to participate in coordinated attacks with the Eighth on such targets as the Messerschmitt factory at Regensburg. But Eaker quickly recognized that the Anzio situation deserved priority and obtained Spaatz's concurrence in a few minutes via the new "Redline" radio link that made it possible to exchange messages, automatically encoded at one end and decoded at the other, in only half an hour. On the 20th Eaker felt able to split the heavies, sending 105 to the beachhead and 126 toward Regensburg. Weather over the Alps prevented the latter force from reaching its strategic target. At Anzio the Germans were stopped, but the

surrounded Allies inside the perimeter, now commanded by Maj.
Gen. Lucian K. Truscott, who replaced the hapless Lucas, remained
stuck for nearly three months, huddling behind sandbags within easy
range of German artillery emplaced, of course, on the Alban Hills.
Both German and Allied participants gave MAAF a major share of
the credit for the successful defense, and Devers noted to Arnold that
"important new lessons in tactical employment have been evident."
But Churchill ruefully wrote, "I had hoped that we were hurling a

Truscott and Eaker at the beleaguered Anzio beachhead, February 1944.

wildcat onto the shore, but all we got was a stranded whale." The essential reason for Anzio's failure, however, was given by Kesselring. "The landing force was initially weak, only a division or so of infantry, and without infantry armor. It was a half-way measure as an offensive that was your basic error."[8]

In landing at Anzio, near Rome and one hundred miles behind the stalemated land offensive near Cassino, Churchill, Alexander and the other Allied commanders on the scene believed they could either force the Germans to withdraw from Cassino or trap them. It appeared to be a classic example of what tacticians call a flank attack but the PM, with his flare for vivid words, dubbed it a "cat's claw." To disguise it and to apply maximum pressure at Cassino, Alexander launched a vigorous attack there a week before the Anzio landings. But the Germans, though fooled by the choice of Anzio (they had expected an Allied landing further up the coast near Pisa), did not budge. Instead they shattered two foolhardy but immensely brave American attempts to bridge the flooded Rapido River in one of the war's worst U.S. defeats, leaving 1,681 soldiers dead, wounded or missing and the battle as stalemated as ever.

The Americans involved were part of the 36th Division of General Mark Clark's Fifth Army. It was manning the Mediterranean side of the line, while the famous British Eighth Army, conquerors of Rommel in Africa, tried to advance along the Adriatic. Both armies reported to Alexander. The Gustav line, as the Germans called it, was an ideal defensive position. It stretched across the narrowest and steepest section of the Italian boot, where the treeless, bare-boned, mile-high Abruzzi Mountains reached literally to the water's edge at each shore. There was only one gap—the north-south valley where the Liri River ran south to meet the little Garigliano River and form the east-west Rapido six miles below the ancient stone town of Cassino. In summer these two streams were little more than creeks, but in the winter and spring they became torrents and the surrounding lowlands so waterlogged that tanks had to stay on the few roads. Peering down from 1,300 feet above the town was the famous Benedictine Abbey, begun in 529 by St. Benedict himself. Its squat, square, four-story limestone walls covered seven acres and rose from a scarp so steep that the only approach road up Monastery Hill required seven switchbacks to climb it. Not a building of external beauty, though its inner cloisters were handsome, the abbey looked more like San Quentin prison than a shrine of religious history and the repository of significant art and an archive of seventy thousand documents and illuminated scrolls. Its blond walls, dotted with three rows of small windows, glistened in the sun above the miasma of battle, serene, aloof and somehow malevolent. The abbey became the symbol of the soldiers' frustration and the object of their hate. Slessor put it well. "It was astonishing how that towering hill with the great white building atop dominated the whole scene in that valley of evil memory, and Private Doe from Detroit, Smith from Wigan, Jones from Dunedin or Yusif Ali from Campbellpore eyed it and felt that behind those windows there must be at least an enemy observer waiting to turn the guns on him personally when the time came to attack."[9]

Repulsed on the Rapido and stalled at Anzio, Clark decided upon another head-on attack, this time up Monastery Hill northeast of the abbey. So doing, in the words of John Ellis in his *Cassino, The Hollow Victory,* Clark "activated a gruesome sausage machine that was, over the next four months, to suck in and spit out the very innards of four Allied Divisions." Monte Cassino was not a single hill; rather, it was the end of a five-mile ridge gradually rising to a 5,400-foot snow-capped peak called Mt. Cairo. The ridge was sliced with ravines and jagged with rock outcroppings and caves, all of which the Germans had skillfully fortified with concealed mines, barbed wire and steel-turretted machine gun posts, some of them only a few yards from the abbey's walls. Infantrymen could only get up in single file, sometimes on hands and knees, supplied by mules, only one in 20 of which survived the ascent. It was murderous, and it failed. The American 34th Division tried it first and was badly cut up. Then Gen. Alphonse Juin's French Corps lost 15 officers and 264 men killed, six officers and 394 men missing and 800 of all ranks wounded before abandoning the struggle. Juin wrote, "Our hearts overflowing with pity and pride, we saw them coming back, haggard, unshaven, their uniforms in rags and soaked in mud, the glorious survivors of the regiment." Then it was the turn of New Zealand. From the Adriatic, Alexander brought in the 4th Indian Division and the New Zealand Division, forming the New Zealand Corps. It was commanded by the renowned Lt. Gen. Bernard Freyberg, winner of the Victoria Cross in World War I and veteran of action in Egypt, Crete, North Africa and Italy in WW II. He was a burly six-footer, full of derring-do and assurance and packing as well a lot of political clout. His division had been sent to the Mediterranean by his home government, which had considered calling it home a year earlier to face the Japanese but left it in Italy for the time being largely because Freyberg recommended it. Alexander was, of course, aware of Freyberg's political leverage and therefore inclined to back his impetuous suggestions as the New Zealand Corps replaced the battered Americans on the gun-swept side of Monastery Hill. Freyberg in turn tended to take the advice of his new subordinate, Maj. Gen. Francis Tuker, commander of the Indian Division.[10]

Tuker, who thought the frontal attack a great mistake and wanted a far wider flanking effort (as did General Juin) was "almost shy, aloof, an intellectual" and "a professional who did not suffer gladly the fools and amateurs he detected around him." He considered Freyberg "an absolute dunce," Clark "a flashy ignoramus" and Alexander "an indolent fifth wheel." But it was Tuker, so know-it-all, who precipitated the tragic and militarily unnecessary destruction of the abbey itself. He swallowed the widespread belief that the Germans were using it for observation and recommended that "It is a modern fortress and must be dealt with by modern means. It can only be dealt with by applying 'blockbuster' bombs from the air. . . ." As for Freyberg, after his Indian troops had clambered up the slope enough to see the American corpses from the previous carnage and be bloodied themselves, he too recommended bombing the abbey.[11]

Neither Clark nor Alexander wanted to take such action. Both knew that the Vatican had passed along the word that the Germans were not making any use of the abbey. They knew too, as experienced battle leaders, that destroying the building would not materially change German control of Monastery Hill. They also had Eisenhower's December 29 directive to "all commanders," that "if we have to choose between destroying a famous building and sacrificing our own men, then our men's lives count infinitely more and the buildings must go. But the choice is not always so clear-cut as that. In many cases the monuments can be spared without any detriment to operational needs." But both Clark and Alexander were under increasing pressure from Washington and London over the lack of progress in Italy. And they were aware of the growing clamor in the press worldwide, as, for example the headline in the London *Times* on February 10: MONASTERY USED AS OBSERVATION POST. Finally—and crucially—both knew that if Freyberg's troops failed in their attack, the blame could fall on them for refusing his request

The Monte Cassino Abbey atop Monastery Hill before, during and after the February 15, 1944, bombing and subsequent artillery barrage.

to destroy what he deemed to be an "important obstacle to the success of this mission." Alexander gave the order. Through Wilson and Devers it was transmitted to Eaker. Thus it fell to MAAF to be the fourth great force to destroy the abbey, the previous ones being the Lombards around 580, the Saracens in 883, and an earthquake in 1349.[12]

"Let's go have a look," Eaker said to Devers, and the two generals took off on February 14 in an L-5 Courier plane with Eaker at the controls and three fighter bombers flying cover a thousand feet above them. Skimming a few hundred feet over the abbey, both men saw what they believed to be evidence of German use. "We clearly identified German soldiers and their radio masts," Eaker wrote later. "I could have dropped my binoculars into machine-gun nests less than 50 feet from the walls."[13]

Flying over the battlefield was just the sort of action Eaker loved. But he had no enthusiasm for bombing the abbey, sharing the views of Clark and Alexander that the ruins would make an even stronger obstacle and that any observation could be done equally well from nearby. But he recognized that this was another occasion when air support of ground action took priority over strategic objectives. He decided to do the job thoroughly. Next day, February 15, an unopposed stream of heavies, mediums and fighter bombers dropped 576 tons on the building, damaging it severely and killing an estimated 250 civilian refugees in the upper levels while the thousands of Allied troops in the valley cheered wildly. All the monks, who had taken refuge in the cellars, escaped unharmed. And the art and archives had been removed with scrupulous care by the Germans several weeks before. Artillery then demolished what was left of the abbey. But the New Zealanders on the ridge, some within two hundred yards, never captured the ruins. They remained in German hands until their deliberate withdrawal from the Gustav line two months later. No definite evidence, despite much hearsay, ever turned up to prove they were using the abbey before the bombing, though they quickly set up strong points in what was left of it afterward.[14]

At the end of February, after the Anzio crisis had subsided but while bitter battle still blazed at Cassino, Spaatz came to Caserta for three days to confer with Eaker as they had agreed to do once a month, alternately in Italy and England. They had much to discuss, the top item on their agenda being further coordination between the

Eighth and Fifteenth of the sort brilliantly achieved in the just-completed "Big Week" that brought the Luftwaffe to the brink of collapse. Both generals knew the pressure had to be maintained to keep the Nazi fliers down, for it was clear from intelligence sources that German fighter production, now dispersed into caves and forest nooks, was still substantial.

In the coordinated attacks from February 20 to 25, the Fifteenth was initially held back by Anzio. But on the 22nd bad weather over the beachhead enabled the whole available strength of the Fifteenth (248 heavies and 185 fighters) to be thrown at Regensburg while the Eighth went to four other aircraft factories north of it with 288 heavies and 596 fighters. This was the first coordinated attack actually executed. In addition to heavy damage to their targets, the two forces split the German defenses. The Eighth encountered 127 Luftwaffe fighters, claiming 76/9/49, and the Fifteenth met 127, claiming 42/17/6. The Eighth lost 41 bombers and 9 fighters, the Fifteenth 19 and 2. On the 23rd the Eighth was weather-bound, but the Fifteenth hit the Steyr ball-bearing and aircraft factories in Austria. And on the 24th both air forces were out again in mutual support, the Fifteenth dispatching 113 heavies and 173 fighters to Steyr, while the Eighth sent 542 heavies and 653 fighters to Gotha and Schweinfurt. Losses again were heavy—49 bombers (9 percent) for the Eighth and 17 (15 percent) for the Fifteenth, while the Eighth claimed 112 German fighters destroyed and the Fifteenth 100. The P-51s were now actively pursuing the German fighters, no longer just keeping them at bay from the bomber formations, in some cases shooting them up on the ground. Finally, on February 25, the grand climax of "Big Week" and the only occasion when both the Eighth and Fifteenth hit the same target on the same day, they rendezvoused over Regensburg, the Eighth with 820 bombers and 670 fighters, the Fifteenth with 176 and 166. This time the Eighth encountered only 59 enemy, but the Fifteenth 200. The latter had a terrific fight, claiming 82 enemy but losing 32 (19 percent).[15]

Not for four months (July 7) would there be another coordinated attack, the Eighth going to Leipzig and the Fifteenth to Blechhammer. Three more coordinated attacks were carried through later that month and three more in August until the advance from Normandy, the landing in Southern France and progress in POINTBLANK made joint action academic. All told in the eight month period from

January through August, ten joint attacks were executed. No fewer than 40 were specifically proposed, of which 23 were scrubbed by bad weather and 7 for other reasons. Until the end of June the Eight was the more enthusiastic proponent of joint attacks—of the 21 coordinated raids proposed in that period the Fifteenth requested only 1. This reflected the Fifteenth's preoccupation with the Italian campaign until the capture of Rome. In the summer, however, with larger forces at its disposal and fewer obligations to the ground forces, the Fifteenth suddenly became eager for the Eighth's support as it went after oil targets deep in Silesia and Czechoslovakia—of the 19 coordinated attacks proposed in July and August, the Fifteenth requested 13. At that time, however the Eighth was often forced to decline in favor of tactical targets in support of the swiftly advancing troops from Normandy.[16]

"Ten coordinated attacks in eight months are not many missions. The question arises," I wrote in the *History of* MAAF in 1945, "whether these ten were so successful in themselves as to justify the existence of an over-all air command such as USSTAF, involving two major theaters and two major fronts. Were they against important targets? Were they effective? Did they, in fact, divide and confuse the German fighter forces? The answer to the first two of these questions is a clear-cut Yes. All ten of the targets were high on the priority lists, and destruction of several of them—Regensburg for example—was an indispensable prerequisite of Allied victory; intelligence reports appraised results in almost every case as *good* or *excellent.* The answer to the third question . . . is anything but clear-cut. The only three joint attacks that took place while the Luftwaffe still had vim and vigor in the 1943 sense came before the Fifteenth was big enough to represent as big a threat to Germany as the Eighth. Conversely, when the Fifteenth was full grown, the GAF no longer had muscle or appetite for a real defense. When the coordinated attacks resumed again in July the GAF reacted strongly to the first," losing 162 fighters while the two U.S. air forces lost only 41 bombers (2 percent of the combined total dispatched). Thereafter the GAF had little sting left and both the Eighth and Fifteenth went out of their way to provoke fights. This was a complete reversal of the situation that existed at the time of USSTAF's conception.[17]

What seems clear from the perspective of four decades later is that USSTAF's value is better appraised in broader terms. It paid off markedly in the constant jockeying with the ground commanders over the right use of air power. Spaatz's backing helped Eaker with Wilson and Alexander, as already noted. Soon after the battles at Cassino and Anzio Eaker came north and was of great help to Spaatz in his struggle with Eisenhower to preserve strategic bombing and refine tactical support in France on the basis of experience in Italy. There was also the complex matter of shuttle missions to Russia and ground support of the Russian armies. Harriman on February 2 had finally obtained Stalin's reluctant consent to building an American base in the Ukraine. Arnold assigned the logistics involved in setting up Eastern Command to USSTAF, but the eventual operations involved both the Eighth and Fifteenth, with Eaker leading the first mission in June. And there were also a raft of policy rulings from Arnold that necessitated close understanding and identical follow-through by the two strategic air forces in Europe. One of these that came up for discussion while Spaatz was at Caserta was Arnold's decision to abandon the established combat tour of twenty-five missions, posing touchy morale problems for both air forces. Finally, there was the long-term goal, never far from Arnold's mind, of establishing air power on an equal footing with ground and naval. USSTAF served all of these ends and served them well.

During the three days Spaatz spent on his first visit to MAAF, the palace of Caserta was the setting of the marathon poker session of the war, beginning a year's tournament between "the Spaatzwaffe" and "the Minions of MAAF." It was held in a gloomy, high-ceilinged room, once part of the royal suite, and went on until after midnight three nights in a row. The USSTAF commander had brought with him only one associate, Elliot Roosevelt, who had gone to England to be CO of a photo-reconnaissance unit based at PINETREE. MAAF mustered four contestants—Eaker, Whitney, General Bartron of the air service command, and myself in my usual role as banker. A guest participant was Cyrus Sulzberger of the *New York Times,* just back from the Cassino front. Because the bombing of the abbey had become one of the most publicized events of WW II and the battle of Cassino was still raging, Caserta was clogged with correspondents, some of whom, Ernie Pyle and Martha Gellhorn for example, wandered around the edges of the poker match, as did members of the MAAF staff while Tex McCrary took snapshots. It was, I imagined, rather like the way courtiers may have sauntered through the royal

The marathon poker match in the palace: Elliot Roosevelt deals draw, with a pair of "jacks or better" needed to open.
Sulzberger, with poor cards, passes, but Eaker, with two pair, bets while leering at Spaatz on his left.
Spaatz, with four hearts, stays, as does Whitney, with a low pair.

bedchamber when the palace was completed in 1774 for Don Carlo, King of Naples.

Sulzberger's story about the bombing had appeared in the *New York Times* under a six-column headline and alleged extravagantly that the abbey had "crumbled into ruins beneath vast clouds of dust as the German soldiers who had violated all civilized codes by employing the sanctuary for military purposes met their day of wrath. . . ." His poker was more precise, and he wound up a winner. Another, modestly, was Spaatz. But Roosevelt lost heavily—$3,000. He of course did not have that much cash with him and he preferred not to pay by check. Instead he eventually sent me, with extraordinary carelessness, out around France and Spain via the APO, a bulging brown manila envelope out of which tumbled a pile of the old, white, English five-pound notes, big as cabbage leaves, which had miraculously escaped the greedy paws of any censor who might have opened it.[18]

As March began Eaker could look back on his tumultuous first six weeks in the Mediterranean with justifiable satisfaction. He was never one to boast, but his gradual adjustment and then enthusiasm for his new task show clearly in his replies to many letters of mixed condolence and congratulation. On January 23, for example, he wrote to Artemus L. Gates, Lovett's opposite number as assistant

368

Parton (back to camera), with a pat straight, doubles Eaker's bet. After drawing replacement cards everyone drops but Parton and Spaatz, who raise each other several times before Spaatz runs out of chips and calls. Parton shows his straight, but Spaatz won—he had drawn a fifth heart, and a flush beats a straight.

secretary of the navy for air: "You evidently sensed that I was a bit forlorn. . . . You were quite right and your letter cheered me greatly. This is going to be an interesting job in a very interesting section of the war. It is unfortunate that I had to be in England when everything was subordinated to the operations in Africa, and now have to be in Africa when everything is subordinated to operations in England, but that cannot be helped. Somebody had to hold these jobs and I am thankful for any war assignment as long as the war lasts."[19]

To Portal he replied on February 8: "I cannot say that I am as happy in this assignment as I was in England, for such is not the case. However, this is certainly a tremendous task and you have my personal assurance that I shall devote every ounce of energy to it."[20]

From Arnold that same week came an amiable letter about the latest edition of *This Flying Game,* concluding: "By this time you have been able to settle down more or less in your new job. It is an entirely different kind of job and requires different technique for the employment of your aircraft. It also requires a different kind of technique on your part in your relationships with the various commanders. I am of the opinion it will do you a considerable amount of good. It will increase your experience and give you a reputation along other lines than that in which you were engaged in England. In other words, you should come out of this a bigger man by far than you went into it. . . . I would like very much to have you write me from time to time as you have in the past—tell me about your troubles, how you are getting along, and wherein I can be of help to you."[21]

Eight weeks later, following another stage in the escalating battle for Cassino and after giving Arnold's son "Hank" some fatherly advice at the Anzio beachhead, where the young man was an artillery officer, Eaker wrote: "With each passing month I see additional evidence to support the Command change you made. I also fully agree that this job will be a very useful experience for me. It is a tough one but I have no inferiority complex about it."[22]

Pamela Churchill, separated from the PM's son Randolph, wrote to thank Eaker for some fruit, adding: "Life has not been the same here without you all. But we still plod along. . . . Baby Winston is staying at Chequers for the moment. He has a model of a Fortress, which he refers to as 'General Eaker's plane!' All his own idea. . . . I have seen the Harrises several times. I think they miss you terribly. . . ."[23]

Of all the letters the MAAF C in C received in that transition period none pleased him more than a note from Brig. Gen. Curtis LeMay, still in England but soon to go to the B-29s in the Pacific. ". . . you are missed here. While you may be absent in body, the spirit of Eaker rides in every bomber to Germany."[24]

21

"I hope we shall have learnt by the time we attack again that five hundred casualties today often save five thousand in the next week."

—AIR MARSHALL SLESSOR REGARDING THE MARCH 15, 1944, ATTACK
ON CASSINO

WITHIN a few days after the abbey was smashed on February 15 it became clear that the New Zealand Corps' effort to capture the ruins and break through into the Liri Valley had failed. "Now," wrote Lt. Gen. Fridolin von Senger und Etterlin, the very able German commander on the spot, who was also a Rhodes Scholar and a gentleman, "we would occupy the Abbey without scruple. The Germans had a mighty, commanding, strongpoint which paid for itself in all the subsequent fighting."[1]

It would have been smarter for the frustrated Allies to wait for good weather before trying again to breach the Gustav line. But pressures from London and Washington were immense. The capture of Rome, now many months behind schedule, remained the ostensible goal, though the Holy City had only symbolic value and no military importance. The chief strategic objective of the Italian campaign had already been accomplished with the capture of the Foggia plains on the Adriatic and the establishment there of the Fifteenth Air Force. But Clark had his heart set on Rome, while Alexander, much the wiser of the two, sought to destroy the German armies in Italy. So the ground force philosophy of bludgeoning ahead through the mountains prevailed. Once again generals Alexander and Clark chose head-on attack, this time against the town of Cassino itself at the foot of the mountain. And once again Freyberg demanded a preliminary heavy air bombardment, "designed," Alexander afterward claimed, "to knock the Germans out of Cassino. . . . The ground troops of the New Zealand Corps were merely to follow up and mop up."[2]

Freyberg was not the only advocate of using air power to "blow a hole through the opposition." Those were among the words used in a petulant, two-page letter from Arnold to Eaker beginning: "We are all very greatly disturbed here by the apparent 'bogging down' of the Italian campaign. . . . If we in the Air Forces accept this situation, I have reason to fear that we will be dragged down to the level and outlook of the Ground Forces. . . ." Why not, Arnold went on, assemble all available airplanes and crews, "including those in rest camps," and "establish a force which, for one day, could really make air history. Withdraw our Ground Forces temporarily . . . and, utilizing all this assembled air power, break up every stone in the town behind which a German soldier might be hiding. When the smoke of the last bombers and fighters begins to die down have the ground troops rapidly take the entire town of Cassino." Arnold continued with complaints about "the lack of ingenuity in the air action" and concluded: "In order to break this stalemate I believe it depends upon the initiative of the Air Forces. Am anxiously awaiting reply from you."[3]

Eaker did not agree. He had already pointed out to Freyberg that bomb craters would make it impossible for tanks to operate, but Freyberg had insisted that bulldozers would quickly clear a path. Plans for a temporary withdrawal, air attack and ground follow-through were drawn by February 24, but three weeks of rain and snow halted all action until March 15. On March 6, nine days before that fateful ides of March, Eaker replied to Arnold. "Little useful purpose is served by our blasting the opposition unless the Army does follow through. I am anxious that you do not set your heart on a great victory as a result of this operation. Personally I do not feel it will throw the German out of his present position completely or entirely, or compel him to abandon the defensive role, if he decides and determines to hold on to the last man as he now has orders to do. . . ."[4]

The morning of March 15 brought near-perfect weather—clear sun, chill air, no wind and only a few thin clouds. By long-cut orders the ground troops quietly slipped back 1,000 yards from their small bridgehead across the Garigliano at Cassino while artillery around the desolated valley kept up the usual sporadic fire against known German posts, just as if it would be another normal desultory day. At the airfields scattered around Foggia, in Sardinia and closer to the front, eleven groups of heavies from the Fifteenth and five of mediums from the Twelfth revved up for take-offs beginning at 8:30, carrying nothing smaller than 1,000-pound bombs for the morning attacks, which would continue at ten-to-fifteen-minute intervals until noon, all directed to approach Cassino at right angles to the front so as to minimize the chance of hitting Allied troops. Fighter-bombers would keep the Anzio front busy. In the afternoon attacks were scheduled for a variety of related targets in the Cassino area to hamper reinforcements and beat up German gun emplacements, but most of these were called off by weather. From Caserta at dawn a jeep cavalcade set forth bringing sundry brass to watch the show. In the lead was Alexander, wearing his habitual polished cavalry boots and fleece-lined leather air force jacket. He looked the very model of a modern British general as the red band of rank on his cap made a bright beacon through the early morning mist on the jolting forty-mile ride to Cassino. The second jeep carried Eaker and me. Others brought various staff officers and the press. We all perched on scattered rooftops about two miles south of the target. British correspondent Christopher Buckley reported: "Sprout after sprout of black smoke leapt from the earth and curled slowly upward like some dark forest. One wave had no sooner started on its return journey than its successor appeared over the eastern skyline. I remember no spectacle so gigantically one-sided. Above, the beautiful, arrogant, silver-grey monsters performing their mission with what looked like a spirit of utter detachment; below, a silent town suffering all this in complete passivity."[5]

This carried poetic license a bit far. The 25,000 people who once lived in Cassino had long since fled. Its already-damaged stone buildings and the ancient tunnels connecting some of them were occupied only by 300 very tough Nazis of the 1st Parachute Division, with another 600 dispersed on the slope behind. About half of those in the town survived in the cellars, tunnels or bell-shaped, steel pillboxes big enough for two men. The testimony of the seventeen prisoners taken the first day (three of whom I interrogated personally) made it clear that for the first few hours "the defense system was completely broken down" while the Germans were dazed by shock and struggling to dig out of the rubble and catch their breath in the "huge clouds of smoke and dust." Then was the moment when the New Zealanders might have won the battle had they pressed their attack. But Freyberg held them back while engineer parties tried to build bridges for tanks across dozens of bomb craters, many of which promptly filled with water. In the town the infantry found the streets so full of rubble that one New Zealand brigadier estimated that under ideal conditions (i.e., no enemy fire) it would have taken bulldozers forty-eight hours to clear a single path through Cassino. These delays gave the Germans just time enough to crawl out of their holes in the rocks and take up strong sniping and machine gun positions. They stopped the diffident ground assault. Up in England Eisenhower's diary noted on March 21, "Cassino has developed into a small Verdun."[6]

The 1,172 tons of bombs completely smashed the town, as promised. Clark wrote Eaker, "The results obtained . . . were those

The first bombs hitting the town of Cassino, March 15, 1944.

predicted." But Eaker was far from happy about the operation, "Redlining" Spaatz that afternoon, "you would not have been proud of your Fifteenth Air Force if you had seen what I saw today. . . ." Several groups of heavies, he wrote Twining two days later, had not found the target at all and two of them dropped their loads on Allied positions, killing seventeen Allied soldiers and upheaving the headquarters of Lt. Gen. Sir Oliver Leese, commander of the British Eighth Army, who escaped harm though two of his caravans were destroyed and four of his men hurt. Eaker promptly wrote Leese a note of apology, which was accepted with grace and nonchalance. But the bigger lesson—one not followed in Normandy three months later when an American lieutenant general and many of his men were killed by bombs falling short—was that heavies were not suitable for close support of ground action. Eaker's letter to Twining observed: "By contrast with the mediums . . . they looked very bad and everybody commented on it. The mediums' formation was precise; they

A low-level photo-reconnaissance picture of Cassino taken just after the final bomb run.

passed over their targets exactly on time, and their air discipline was perfect."[7]

To Wilson, Devers and Arnold, Eaker wrote separate, long, "lessons learned" summaries, including these comments of longer-term interest: *To Wilson:* "The bombing of an enemy strong-point such as Cassino must be followed by a determined and vigorous ground attack. . . . Bombing cannot be looked upon as a cure-all, but as a means to an end in the capture of such a strong-point. It will have, in general, the same effect as concentrated and prolonged artillery fire. . . ." *To Devers:* "47% of the bombs located were within the target area . . . defined as within a circle with a radius of 1,000 feet. . . . The accuracy or inaccuracy of the bombing had nothing to do with the success or lack of success of the ground battle. You have to look no further in determining the reasons for the failure to take and hold the Cassino area than to look at the casualty lists of the ground forces on the three days, March 15th, 16th and 17th. On the day of the great battle when Cassino was supposed to have been taken, the New Zealand Corps lost four officers and eleven men. . . ." *To Arnold:* "I feel that the Air Forces opened the door at Cassino but that the Ground Forces did not enter. . . . This view is shared by some of the most responsible commanders, non-air, particularly General Wilson and General Devers. . . . I know two men who, had they been in command of our Ground Forces, would now be well on the way to Rome if not in Rome. One of them is Patton and the other is Devers."[8]

Eaker continued in a fine example of his clear thinking and deft words: "There are many reasons why the Ground Forces have not been able to stage a break-through and capture Rome. Many of them are good reasons: Soft ground, heavy rains, extreme cold, excellent defensive terrain, insufficient forces for offensive action, and unwillingness to accept casualties, etc. All of these, when boiled down to the final essence, merely mean that a Ground Commander who gets the same percentage of casualties that we in the Air Forces take as a matter of course might be criticized and might be called a butcher. In saying that Patton or Devers would have taken their Ground Forces through, I know very well that they would have been criticized for the losses on the day or days they went through, but the point I make is that their overall losses would not have been as great as this business of daily attrition which the present method involves and which, over a considerable period, total more than would the one sharp, fierce battle. . . ."⁹

Alexander's reactions come through as very stiff-upper-lip. When he left Cassino on the afternoon of the bombardment he was convinced that "nothing could still be alive in the town and that the enemy forces must either be dead or have to withdraw." He had told Freyberg that he "didn't want him to have heavy casualties." After the New Zealanders missed their opportunity on the 15th, it should be noted that they did press the battle courageously, losing 9 officers and 111 men on the 16th and 16 officers and 189 men on the 17th. By the 26th, when Alexander called off the offensive, they had lost 140 officers and 1,970 men in exchange for possession of about nine-tenths of Cassino and an expanded bridgehead over the Garigliano. Alexander blandly declared many years later: "The British Army has never and I know never will shirk any battle however hard it may be fought. But their leaders quite rightly want to know if the sacrifice of men's lives is worthwhile. . . . We believe in making a good omelette but not in wasting eggs."¹⁰

Alexander and Clark now had no choice but to halt their offensive, regroup and wait six weeks for the ground to dry. This unwanted pause had two benefits from Eaker's point of view—it left him free to concentrate his heavies on POINTBLANK targets and it gave MAAF the opportunity on the tactical side to display some "ingenuity" of the sort Arnold had demanded. But first he dashed to England at the end of March, urgently summoned by Spaatz. The trusty old *Yardbird* had been replaced by a shiny new B-17 named, no one recalls why, *Starduster,* stripped of most weapons and fitted with chairs, bunks and a table. Having ample room, Eaker took with him his three RAF enlisted men for a visit with their families, an instance of what Ernie Pyle called his "nice way of doing little things for little people." Smitty flew them on the weary long trip around Spain and France to WIDEWING, where Spaatz was caught in a mighty tussle with Eisenhower and others on the best way to use air power in support of OVERLORD—the Normandy landings. It had long been established that control of the strategic air forces, both U.S. and British, would pass to Eisenhower on April 1. By then the "intermediate objective" of defeating the Luftwaffe was scheduled to have been achieved, as indeed it had been. But Spaatz and Eaker as well as Portal were convinced that pressure had to be continued against the GAF lest it revive. They believed the best way to do this was to give top priority to the destruction of Germany's remaining oil resources, both real and synthetic. But another school of thought espoused by Tedder and supported by Professor Zuckerman argued that priority should be given to smashing German communications to the beachhead area. Mixed into this was a real quarrel between Spaatz and Air Marshal Sir Trafford Leigh-Mallory, who was still ticketed to be Air commander for the invasion. On April 8, after returning to Caserta, Eaker reported his share in these vital discussions in a long letter to Arnold.

"I arrived on the 25th and went with Tooey at once to see Eisenhower. . . . We discussed mainly the command set-up for the air in the UK and the directive for air operations in support of OVERLORD. . . . Tooey favored the oil plan as a second priority after the German Air Force, whereas Tedder favored the communications plan. Eisenhower asked for my view, and I stated that I was certain of one thing: that the German Air Force must be first on the priority. I was also certain that if communications were attacked prior to D-Day for OVERLORD, a schoolboy could tell where the Allied landing would be. I felt, therefore, the communications plan depended pretty well on timing. If I were doing it, I would not make a single attack on communications south of the Rhine before D-Day. I would then go full-out on communications to isolate the battle area. . . . I was not prepared to give a view on the oil plan and its critical and immediate effect on OVERLORD. I was emphatic, however, that nothing should be allowed to interfere with the continuous offensive against the German Air Force, particularly on airdromes and manufacturing establishments. My own view, which had been corroborated by my two months experience in Italy, was that communications attacks are of little effect unless the Army puts pressure on the enemy to make him expend supplies. . . .

"Tooey and I then went to see Tedder and spent an hour with him where the above discussions were continued. That afternoon the big conference came at the Air Ministry, with Tedder, Portal, Leigh-Mallory, Eisenhower and Spaatz present. I was not present. . . . I saw Tooey that night, however, and I have never seen him quite so jubilant and overjoyed. He had won out completely on the command set-up. The strategic British and American Air Forces were not to be put under Leigh-Mallory. Eisenhower was to have three coordinate air commanders: Leigh-Mallory, tactical; and Spaatz and Harris, strategic. Tedder was to be the coordinating staff agency, but not the air commander. The communications plan had won out over the oil plan, but Tooey was not too displeased about this, since all had firmly agreed that the German Air Force was to be an all-consuming first priority. . . .

"The day before I left I got a call from the Prime Minister's secretary. . . . I spent an hour with him. He asked me many questions about Cassino, and about the lack of aggressiveness on the ground. He told me that he was having Alexander come home to go over that situation with him. Incidentally, Alexander left here yesterday for that trip. . . . Devers has taken over the Allied Armies in Italy during Alexander's absence. . . ."[11]

Well before Arnold's demand for "ingenuity" Slessor had suggested a sweeping new approach to tactical air operations. On February II he asked Norstad, MAAF's director of operations, for a review of bombing policy. "There are now," Slessor noted, "some seventeen German divisions in Italy south of Rome. I do not believe the Army —even with our support—will move them. But I think it more than possible that the Hun, by concentrating all this force so far south, has given us—the Air Forces—an opportunity." The deputy Air C in C went on to observe that the Germans had barely been able to keep their frontline troops supplied prior to these big new reinforcements. "I find it hard to believe that . . . he has not put a load onto his communications which they will not be able to stand if we really sustain a scientifically planned offensive *against the right places* in his L. of C. [Lines of Communication]."[12]

Slessor was quick to point out that "there was nothing very original about this conception" in general terms. It had been pioneered in 1942 when Montgomery and Air Vice Marshal Coningham used their tiny Desert Air Force to nip off Rommel's tenuous and over-extended supply lines, cutting roads, sinking ships and strafing motor transport all the way from Alamein to Tunis. But two factors prevented North Africa from being a complete proving ground for the tactics of interdiction. First, the Luftwaffe was still strong and the Allied air forces were obliged to devote a large portion of their effort to counter-air operations. Second, the German rail, road and sea lines of communication were too simple and too vulnerable in North Africa to provide a real test of air potential. Not until the campaigns in Sicily and Southern Italy did the Allied air forces come to grips with a well-developed and complex communications net-

379

work. By then too the Luftwaffe was tottering, while Allied air strength soared. There was, therefore, every justification for regarding the Sicilian and Southern Italian campaigns as the first real test of what a tactical air force would do to enemy lines of supply. Zuckerman and a panel of British scientists known as the bombing survey unit were employed to study the results. Zuckerman's report, issued December 28, 1943, and at once adopted by Britain's air ministry as doctrine, drew several broad conclusions about the proper use of air power. Among them were, first, a reaffirmation of his belief that destruction of railway yards was the simplest and "best" single tactic; second, that "a far more costly air effort would be needed to achieve a tactical success, in the sense of a sudden blocking of communications at any given series of points;" and, third, "railway and road bridges are uneconomical and difficult targets, and in general do not appear to be worth attacking. . . ."[13]

But, as Allied air operations moved up the Italian boot to Rome and above, different views began to emerge. In October Brig. Gen. Earle E. Partridge, chief of staff of the XII Bomber Command, noted that "we have . . . given high priority to marshaling yards. While these yards are undoubtedly essential for handling the large volume of traffic required to support the civilian population, it appears that it may be possible for the enemy to move the relatively small amount of traffic needed for military supply. . . ." XII Bomber Command then carried out a hesitant first attempt to interdict Italy just north of Rome by cutting bridges instead. In the three weeks this was tried, using heavies alone, the three major (but *not* two minor) rail lines down Italy were severed and, according to an Italian general who had been chief of the Italian liaison staff to Kesselring and who escaped to the Allies, Kesselring actually considered abandoning Rome in consequence. This success was not perceived by the Allies, and bad weather and other commitments caused abandonment of the interdictory attacks on November 28.[14]

But the concept continued to germinate and was well-stated by a Twelfth AF intelligence proposal on January 15 just before Eaker's arrival. ". . . marshaling yards . . . are poor targets in Italy because: a) They offer the largest concentration of lines to be cut; b) they are the most easily and quickly repaired targets because they are near repair facilities, materials and crews; c) they are not of vital importance to the German because he is using principally through trains; and d) these attacks destroy rolling stock and locomotives which would be of great value to the Allies later on and which, under a plan of complete interdiction, would be useless to the Germans. . . . That leaves two possible classes of targets. The first class embraces power stations and sub-stations and the electrical installations. These targets are the easiest of all railway targets to destroy. However, the destruction of these targets will not interdict a line. The German will simply change to steam traction. . . . The second class of targets is made up of bridges and viaducts. These structures present such problems as fusing and weight of bomb to be used on each individual target; and concededly an all-steel bridge is a difficult target to destroy. However, structures of masonry construction, or with masonry piers and abutments, are vulnerable. And there are at least three distinct advantages to this class of target; a) the destruction of a bridge or viaduct is a clean and complete severance of the line; b) it presents a major and slow repair problem to the enemy accentuated by the fact that this type of target is, normally, some distance from repair facilities; and c) most of the targets will probably be free, or relatively free, of anti-aircraft defenses. . . ."[15]

Slessor and Norstad now extended this idea to *all* German supply lines, not just railways. On February 18 Eaker issued a new directive, stating that the tactical objective would be to force German withdrawal to at least the Pisa-Rimini line by making impossible the supply of his expanded armies spread along the Gustav line. Both Spaatz and Wilson quickly endorsed the plan, and on February 22 Wilson asked the CCS for a new directive, instructing him to contain the largest possible number of German troops away from OVERLORD without launching ANVIL, the invasion of Southern France that was supposed to take place simultaneously with the one in Normandy. Wilson believed ANVIL (which Clark had been scheduled to lead) was not practical until the deadlock in Italy was broken. The CCS would not agree to cancel ANVIL but on February 26 did issue Wilson a new directive establishing the campaign in Italy as top priority. The abortive Cassino battle then intervened, and the interdiction program was not given CCS blessing until March 19 when the objective was defined as "to reduce the enemy's flow of supplies to a level which will make it impossible to maintain and operate his forces in central Italy." Tex McCrary, now in charge of MAAF public relations, gave the campaign the apt code name STRANGLE.[16]

Freed, with Alexander's concurrence, of duties along the now quiet fronts at Cassino and Anzio, MAAF was able for the first time to use its two main arms precisely for the aims defined by their titles. Whenever the weather permitted, the strategic air force went to major targets deep in Germany or the Balkans. When such targets were obscured, the heavies hit railway yards from Rome to the Po Valley but no longer went for the bridges. These became the favorite game of the mediums and fighter-bombers, dramatically proving Zuckerman wrong and evolving tactics that were emulated to great advantage in France during and after OVERLORD. Slessor described this feat in lively words in a long letter to Portal on April 16. "One of the remarkable developments in the past three months to my mind has been the emergence of the bridge as a worthwhile bombing objective. At the present time, of the 25 clean cuts in the Italian railways, 16 are bridges. I have always thought the bridge a rotten objective for a bomber—and so indeed it was in the past. The explanation of the change is two-fold; first, the astonishing accuracy of the experienced medium bomber groups—particularly the Marauders [British word for the B-26] . . . secondly, the accuracy of the fighter-bomber in the low attack. I hope the value of the bridge as an objective in attack on communications is thoroughly realized by the Tactical Air Forces in the UK—it is something rather new since Tedder's day out here."[17]

Bridge busting was the most important but not the only new tactic STRANGLE dramatized. The fighter-bombers learned how to "post-hole" railroad tracks in the open by skimming them at low level and dropping a series of delayed action bombs. They also tossed bombs into the openings of tunnels. Strafing German trucks on the twisting mountain roads was lucrative by day, though trucks and wagons could still get through by night. Along the two coasts night was partial protection for barges and small craft, but these could sometimes be spotted with flares or searchlights and hit by the coastal air force. Between March 15 and May 11, when DIADEM, the ground attack on Rome was launched, MAAF flew 65,006 sorties in the STRANGLE campaign, dropping 33,104 tons of bombs, claiming 296 Luftwaffe fighters and losing 365 bombers and fighter-bombers, most of them to flak.[18]

It is harder to quantify precisely just what STRANGLE accomplished. Its influence on OVERLORD is granted by all. Exactly how much it helped win the final battle for Rome is open to question, though the statistics of roads cut, trucks destroyed and supplies delayed are mountainous, and everyone agrees the contribution to victory was major. Some postwar analysts have decried MAAF's original hopes that STRANGLE could cause the Germans to retreat all by itself. Had the Cassino front been kept active daily, forcing the Germans to expend ammunition instead of conserving it, they might have withdrawn before May. But there was a total lull, and MAAF gradually qualified its expectations. On April 7, in one of his round-up letters to Arnold, Eaker wrote, "My personal belief is that our communications attack will make it possible for the Army to move forward when they next make an effort. . . ." The air plan for DIADEM, dated April 28, described the objective as "to so reduce the supplies available to enemy forward troops that he is unable to offer sustained resistance to the assault." When the battle began with an enormous barrage on the night of May 11, von Senger's men had slightly more ammunition on hand than at the time of the Cassino bombardment (18,000 metric tons versus 17,000), but the enemy was subsisting on a total of 4,000 tons per day of total supplies, including food and fuel, which was "1,000 to 1,500 less than he would have to have during an Allied ground offensive." In some cases tanks were pulled into position by oxen. Many formations were so dispersed by the interdiction that "unit integrity was impossible." Thus the veteran Hermann Goering Division rushed down from Leghorn to the Liri Valley "where," as Slessor described the battle, "it suffered heavy losses in men and vehicles on the way in, and its morale was at a low ebb by the time it found itself in all the confusion of a fluid battle called upon to putty up a gap which, by the time it arrived, was too ragged and gaping for any putty."[19]

Alexander's armies on the other hand, refreshed and replenished, lacked for nothing and outnumbered the Germans by three to one. Within a week the Gustav line was broken and the Germans were in full retreat, which was superbly executed. German efficiency was abetted by Clark's hunger for personal glory. Determined to be first into Rome, Clark diverted his U.S. Sixth Army at Anzio, now increased to six divisions, from the direct inland thrust that might have cut off the German escape from Cassino as Alexander had planned. Instead, by Clark's direct order and over Truscott's horrified objections, the Sixth Army wheeled sharply left toward Rome itself, which was captured June 4 with Clark in the van. Von Senger's army escaped in good order, to reform north of the city and fight for another ten bloody, wasteful months. Alexander was of course furious but kept a stiff upper lip as usual. He could have preferred charges against Clark or demanded his relief but understood that preservation of good relations between the British and their bigger U.S. ally was more important. Forty years later Eaker, who thought Alexander "the best of the British Army commanders," said about this ugly episode, "It's very hard to stay in control when you're commanding forces of mixed nationality."[20]

About STRANGLE and DIADEM Slessor, on June 18, 1944, wrote a balanced summation whose major conclusions remain compelling in the light of the many wars in the succeeding forty years. "It may clear the issue to mention first the things that air power can *not* be expected to do in a land campaign of this nature: a) It can not by itself defeat a highly organized and disciplined army, even when that army is virtually without air support of its own. . . . b) It cannot by itself force a withdrawal by drying up the flow of essential supplies. . . . c) It can not *entirely prevent* the movement of strategic reserves to the battle front. . . . d) In short, it can not absolutely isolate the battle field from enemy supply or reinforcement. . . . e) It can not absolutely guarantee the immunity either of our forward formations or back areas . . . against the occasional air attack. . . . What it can do, and has done in the present battle . . . is to make it impossible for the most highly organized and disciplined army to offer pro-longed resistance to a determined offensive on the ground. . . . The converse of (a) above is equally true. An army by itself cannot, in modern warfare, defeat a highly organized and disciplined army on the defensive. The power of the defense on land has not been over-come by the tank or by improved artillery technique, but by air power. . . ."[21]

Eaker left to Slessor, Norstad and Cannon the daily prosecution of STRANGLE and DIADEM though he was of course kept fully posted. He was much more concerned about the completion of POINTBLANK and the combined bomber offensive. Whenever possible he deployed the Fifteenth's heavies on true strategic targets. It quickly became clear that operations from Italy failed to offer the release from weather restrictions Arnold had hoped for; a vast bank of clouds hung over the Alps during March, canceling missions and greatly inhibiting coordinated attacks with the Eighth, as already noted. But the Fifteenth found useful targets of opportunity on eighteen days within Italy itself in the primary task of keeping the Luftwaffe down. For example, 373 heavies on March 18 bombed five airfields at the head of the Adriatic, preceded by a low-level fighter sweep that caught many German planes still on the ground, destroying 56. In the subsequent air battle another 23 were knocked down by the bombers and 17 by escort fighters while the Fifteenth lost 7 bombers and 3 fighters. In southern France as part of the OVERLORD transportation plan the Fifteenth was assigned 14 rail centers, and MAAF's bombers, operating out of Foggia and Sardinia, swept over them with negligible interference, dropping 3,000 tons.

By far the most important strategic targets for the Fifteenth, however, were the remaining sources of German oil. For crude oil itself Ploesti was the best-known and biggest: 2 million tons were pumped from Hungary and Rumania in 1943. But the Germans also built a huge hydrogenation complex for extracting synthetic oil from coal, producing 6,180,000 tons in 1943. Many of those plants were clustered in central Germany, now well within the escorted range of the Eighth. Others were scattered through eastern Germany, Czechoslovakia, Austria and Hungary, most of them reachable only from Italy. Following his return from England Eaker made these oil targets his top priority, leaving to Twining the actual operations while he himself dealt with the complex political manipulations to fend off all other objectives competing for attention. There were many of the latter. They included the preparations for ANVIL, further support of the ground advance up Italy, supply drops to the Partisans behind German lines in Italy and to Tito in Yugoslavia, preparation for the shuttles to Russia and sowing the Danube with mines. In attacking the oil sources it was sometimes expedient, in light of the priority given to transportation, to use railway yards as the aiming points while knowing that the adjacent refineries were more significant.[22]

It would be pointless for this narrative to recite all the operational factors involved or the pros and cons of the various strategic alternatives. The onslaught against oil became the decisive one, and the 24 attacks the MAAF made against Ploesti added up to the biggest battle of the USSTAF oil campaign. It began April 5 when 146 B-24s and 90 B-17s hit Ploesti rail yards (and adjoining facilities). By August 19, when Rumania surrendered to the Russians, the Fifteenth had flown 6,186 sorties on 20 daylight missions, escorted by 3,400 fighters, and dropped 13,469 tons of bombs. These efforts were complemented by four night missions by the RAF's 205 Group. During the five-month campaign an average of only 140,000 tons of crude were refined monthly at Ploesti—38 percent of the January-March average. The total estimated reduction was 1,129,000 tons. Put together with the simultaneous blows by the Eighth and Fifteenth to the hydrogenation plants, the oil shortage crippled not only German industry but also its tanks and planes. The last fact is particularly pertinent, for postwar study by the *Strategic Bombing Survey* unearthed startling evidence that, despite all the damage done to its aircraft factories, Germany's monthly plane production had continued to rise (though not as much, of course, as it would have otherwise). But planes were worthless without fuel to fly them.[23]

Ploesti was the third most heavily defended target in the Reich, following Berlin and Vienna. During the battle approximately 59,800 airmen attacked it, losing 2,432 men (4.1 percent). Eaker and Twining flew to Bucharest as soon as the fighting ended with a team to salvage records of the damage before the Russians could get there to confiscate them. A fitting climax to the story of Ploesti was the rescue of 1,061 of the fliers by B-17s that only twelve days earlier had taken part in the last Ploesti mission.[24]

While the battling went on there was also great progress in the massive task of assembling the major Mediterranean headquarters in the drab, mercantile town of Caserta, where the palace, second largest building in Europe (after Versailles) was converted into a parody of the Pentagon. Squatting in squalid disorder at the base of the sharp hills separating the Neapolitan plain from the Volturno Valley about twenty-five miles inland from Naples, it is an enormous, neoclassic pile of brick and marble laid out in the form of a rectangle measuring 253 meters by 202 and five stories high, while the whole structure contains no fewer than 1,200 rooms, most of them huge. Once it must have been a truly magnificent sight, but the erosion of war had reduced it to shabby disarray, like a rich dowager found disheveled in the gutter. The tiled roof was broken in a dozen places by errant bombs; its once-exquisite gardens were littered with military camps and motor parks; its once-handsome chambers overflowed not only with the harassed headquarters of Alexander's Fifteenth Army Group and Cannon's Tactical Air Force but also two centuries accumulation of filth. There was almost no heat, no sanitation, and the weak electricity tended to fade out altogether at unpredictable moments each evening.

Throughout January, February, March and April, with the clearly audible cannonade at stubborn Cassino symbolizing Allied frustration, MAAF's growing headquarters lived and worked in a few

Eaker, followed by Twining, being greeted by Rumanian air force commanders at Bucharest, August 19, 1944. Arriving before the Russians, the Americans salvaged precious data about their damage to Ploesti.

crammed remnants of space scattered on four floors and three sides of the building. Life in a palace proved disillusioning. Instead of beautiful rooms full of handsome furniture, we found nothing but barnlike vacancy, with only the marble floors and frescoed ceilings to indicate where grandeur once dwelt. For the palace had long since ceased to be a royal residence, having been taken over first by Mussolini as a staff school for the Regia Aeronautica and latterly by the Germans as a headquarters. Only a few paintings and furnishings, too big for light-fingered removal, remained for the Allied occupation. Decent furniture was of course obtained for the Air C in C, but everyone else camped out on cots, sharing the few wardrobes and chairs and queuing up morning and night outside the one small bathroom, where it was usually necessary to rap the tap smartly three or four times to make the water come.

It was wet and cold in early 1944. Each morning Eaker and his small staff (no more than two dozen for the first month in Caserta)

The Royal Palace at Caserta, with the cascades and reflecting pools descending from the mountain a mile behind.

would rise and dress in shivering discomfort, gobble breakfast at a temporary mess set up in the next room and walk down the five stories of stone steps to work, dodging the bedraggled scrubwomen interminably stirring up the dust in the interminable halls. Arrived at our desks, mostly planks on sawhorses, MAAF's embryonic staff strove to conduct the far-flung air war without benefit of files, typewriters, lights or even passable communications. In the evening, alternately shivering and scratching fleabites, we clambered back to the other side of our gargantuan abode to huddle around a small fireplace and swig the small stock of whiskey Mason, ever thoughtful about such basics, had brought from England. Headquarters MAAF in those parlous days was a command post, nothing more.

It was quickly decided to convert the palace entirely to offices and set up living quarters in camps nearby for the fifteen thousand officers and men who eventually congregated there. The process went on all spring but was not completed until the capture of Cassino in May enabled Alexander's headquarters to move forward, leaving room for Wilson's to come up from Algiers. To handle MAAF's move, Eaker designated Glenn Jackson, the eager beaver he had met at Medford, Oregon, in 1940 and who had come to England as a major in mid-1943, moving into Castle Coombe. Jackson was a prodigiously energetic and talented executive—qualities that in the postwar years led to great success in newspapers, utilities and public service. When he died in 1980 he was saluted in the local press as "Mr. Oregon." In Caserta he was the first MAAF staff officer to win a decoration, the Legion of Merit, for his work as headquarters commandant, and was promoted to colonel.

On the flat, almost treeless fields just south of the palace on the road to Naples there were few buildings and a considerable drainage problem. Until Jackson's bulldozers cut ditches and boardwalks were built, the alternately dusty and muddy site was known as "Jackson's Hole." Here were erected "streets" of tents and huts for 2,637 officers and men, of whom half were Americans. A half mile further down, at the very busy Marcianise airfield, space was created for another 300 Americans, and a nearby school was converted to housing for III WACs. Much tonier was the so-called "upper camp," officially named Cascades, on the north side of the palace, which Jackson built for Eaker, 9 other U.S. generals, 9 RAF air marshals and commodores and 47 more officers, mostly colonels and all either section heads or on the personal staffs of the various generals. There were also 49 AAF and 21 RAF enlisted men. Eaker and the generals had two-room huts. A few of the colonels wangled trailers, originally designed as traveling offices and no longer needed when the palace was occupied. The rest of us enjoyed individual pyramidal tents, designed for four men, each with wood floor, potbellied stove and furniture swiped from nearby villas. There were privies discreetly off in the bushes, shower stalls and a mess hall big enough for all. Three other prefab huts lined with bamboo grown and split on the spot were arranged around a patio as a club. This miniature village was scattered prettily among magnificent plane trees and cedars in what had originally been called "the English Garden," laid out in 1782 by order of Queen Marie Caroline of Austria around a small pond with a fake ruin on an island in the middle. Jackson hired a dozen Italians to convert it to a swimming pool, providing a hilarious spectacle in the process. The pond was full of mud, which turned out to be full of eels—a delicacy in Italy. The workers were overjoyed, stumbling around in the muck, grabbing two or three eels at a time and looking very much like a ballet of miniature Laocoöns.[25]

Camp Cascades took its name from the extraordinary artificial watercourse alongside of which it was pitched. Built at the same time as the palace, a series of five cascades stretched for nearly two miles through the formal gardens behind it. The water feeding the succession of elaborate falls, pools and grottoes sprang from near the top of a steep wooded hill, having been brought there by twenty-seven miles of aqueducts and tunnels. It gushed first down the steepest part of the hill between marble statues of Diana and Acteon, the former surrounded by nymphs, the latter transformed into a stag being attacked by dogs. Four more cascades embellished with other figures from classic mythology flattened out to an enormous reflecting basin 475 meters long by 27 wide. It was big enough for Clark's pilot to land him there once in a Moth plane fitted with floats. In summer it became a swimming pool for the enlisted men. At Camp Cascades the social life of MAAF was concentrated and here the flow of visitors was billeted and entertained, not only great military figures such as Marshall, Arnold or Portal but luminaries as diverse as Eve Curie, Lillian Hellman, the king of England and Marshal Tito of Yugoslavia. In the warm summer sun it became a very pleasant spot to lounge during the luncheon break or after the offices in the palace shut down normally at five. And there was also the fabulous island of Capri, a few miles off the coast, to go to on weekends when urgencies permitted. Capri had been taken over as a rest camp for MAAF combat crews, but the exquisite Villa Vismara was reserved for Eaker and his staff. Other exceptional diversions were also close— Pompeii and the Amalfi Drive, Paestum and its Doric temples, some excellent restaurants and assorted dives in narrow-streeted Naples. Vesuvius, whose symmetry gave Naples and its bay the beauty explaining the vain-glorious old Italian proverb, "See Naples and then die" (for everything else will be anticlimax), chose March and April to erupt spectacularly. Smoke towered to the stratosphere, rivers of lava ran down two sides and a shower of clinkers the size of baked potatoes covered Cannon's Pompeii Flying Field to a depth of six inches and destroyed sixty planes—much more than the Luftwaffe could have done.[26]

And there were many times when Eaker and all of us on his staff had duties to tend to elsewhere in the first half of 1944—Algiers and Tunis often, Cairo and Jerusalem once or twice and beloved England every other month. But the main staff work, of course, took place in the palace, where Eaker now had a very large office on the fourth floor facing south. On one wall were locked cupboards behind which stat control maintained all the readiness statistics, current target data and other top secret operational detail. Behind the Air C in C's desk was an enormous canvas, perhaps ten feet high by fifteen long, depicting an agonized Prometheus chained to the fabled rock with a vulture pecking at his belly. When messages from Washington occasionally became intense, Eaker was wont to remark that the picture "really shows General Arnold pecking at me."

Actually, however, the tension between the two men, which had reached such strained extremes the year before, now was almost completely gone. They had returned to their longtime roles of revered patron and respected protégé. On Eaker's forty-eighth birthday, April 13, Arnold sent him greetings and warm words about their long association, to which Eaker replied: "I do remember our service together since 1918, in many capacities and stations, with pleasure and profit. . . . Tooey and I grew nostalgic at our last meeting, like two old soldiers, discussing our long period together with you and finally came up with the one conclusion that we must not let the Old Man down in his long fight for air power. . . ."[27]

22

"There is no truce with Adam-zad—The Bear that looks like a Man!"

—*THE TRUCE OF THE BEAR,* BY RUDYARD KIPLING, 1909

A S STRANGLE and DIADEM conquered Rome on June 4 and OVERLORD's landings in France began on June 6 still a third campaign of great significance reached crescendo on June 2 with the first shuttle-bombing flight to Russia. The shuttles were given the code name FRANTIC in wry acknowledgement of the breakneck pace with which they had to be organized in the four months after Harriman won Stalin's reluctant approval on February 2. Dispatching the heavies was no problem; the difficulties were all at the Russian end, involving an incredible array of logistic, planning and diplomatic obstacles.

Eastern Command, as the U.S. headquarters in Russia was named, was under USSTAF, so Spaatz was responsible for the logistic and strategic planning aspects while Harriman and Brig. Gen. John R. Deane, head of the U.S. military mission in Moscow, coped with the diplomatic. Eaker was a participant in all these matters both because of his close personal association with Spaatz and Harriman and because MAAF was the closest U.S. command to the advancing Soviet armies. And he soon became involved operationally with the Russians in other ways than the shuttles. To Stalin every deal with the Allies was on a tit for tat basis. As Deane commented to Marshall: "They [the Russians] cannot understand giving without taking, and as a result even our giving is viewed with suspicion. Each transaction is complete in itself without regard to past favors. The party of the second part is either a shrewd trader or a sucker to be despised." Having granted the Americans air bases in Russia, Stalin now demanded an air base in Italy, ostensibly for the Russians to fly to and from their mission to Tito in Yugoslavia. The request was granted in April. Simultaneously there arose the touchy subject of establishing a "bomb-line" dividing the Red Air Force and MAAF's spheres of activity in the Balkans and eventually in Poland. Eaker sent a colonel to Russia to work under Deane but solely on the daily bomb-line liaison with the Red Air Force.[1]

Three small cities in the Ukraine were chosen for Eastern Command. Poltava, location of the great battle in 1709 when Czar Peter the Great routed King Charles XII of Sweden and established Russia as a world power, became the headquarters. Once inhabited by 130,-000 people, it had been almost obliterated by the retreating Germans in 1943, but the airfield had two skimpy concrete runways, and one four-story building near it had not been completely demolished. The other two fields, at Mirgorod and Piryatin, were also inadequate. None of the runways were oriented toward the prevailing wind. Neither were there dispersal areas, bomb dumps, control towers nor any facilities whatever for communications, maintenance or housing. Everything had to be shipped in—personnel through Teheran by plane and heavy supplies through Murmansk in convoys running the U-boat gauntlet (the original plan assumed a 50 percent loss in transit). Spaatz wanted to send 2,050 American ground personnel, but the Russians flatly refused more than 1,200 and then held them for several weeks in Teheran haggling about group visas. For their part the Soviets provided 882 maintenance specialists and 2 labor battalions of men and women to lay steel matting at the fields. Five ships laden with 26,000 tons of essentials (12,393 tons of landing mat, 7,274 of high-octane gasoline, 1,341 vehicles, etc.) safely negotiated the U-boat peril but were held up outside Archangel by the "gorlo" or ice throat. By April 23 their cargo was safely ashore, requiring 2,100 freight cars for the long haul south paralleling the front where the Russians were readying their summer offensive (promised, tit for tat, to follow OVERLORD). But only 534 cars were available and no more than half the supplies reached the Ukraine before the first B-17s landed. By herculean effort a mile of steel mat was in place at each of the three fields.[2]

The Russians had agreed to supply bombs for the missions out of Eastern Command, but it was discovered that they made no distinction between cast and welded bomb cases. Since welded cases are ballistically unsuited to high-level precision bombing, bombs had to be shipped in (there were 2,084 tons in the first convoy to Murmansk). House-keeping equipment, rations, medicine and all the host of intricate maintenance tools and parts for American aircraft trickled from Teheran. The tightest squeeze came late in May from the last-minute decision to send P-51 fighters along with the B-17s. That required an emergency air shipment from Italy to Poltava via Teheran of 250 P-51 wing tanks and many maintenance items, while others, as well as 30 P-51 crew chiefs, were loaded aboard the B-17s on the first mission, code-named FRANTIC JOE.[3]

On April 29 Spaatz and Eaker rendezvoused in Algiers with Harriman, who was on his way through the Mediterranean from Moscow to Washington. They made several significant decisions about FRANTIC. Spaatz had intended to dispatch the Eighth from England on the first mission, but the imminence of OVERLORD ruled this out, so he said he would assign the task to the Fifteenth, specifying a wing of no more than 150 bombers since Eastern Command bases could not handle the five hundred-plus heavies contemplated in the plan. He also stressed that the first mission must be a visible success to demonstrate the effectiveness of American daylight bombardment to the Soviets and that it would be wise to pick a target that would suit Russian objectives, not just those of POINTBLANK. He observed that the three original bases, from fifty to a hundred miles behind the Russian lines, would need to be moved forward soon along with the Russian advance. And he said he was sending Anderson and three officers from England to Moscow to discuss target choice and base relocation as well as the urgent need for photo-reconnaissance from Russia and direct communication between Eastern Command and USSTAF. When Harriman remarked that involvement by high-level officers would impress the Soviet leadership, Eaker suggested that he accompany FRANTIC JOE and proceed to Moscow "to look after" USSTAF's interests. Harriman was enthusiastic, and it was agreed upon. Spaatz then accompanied Eaker back to Italy for a three-day breather at Capri, luxuriating in the Villa Vismara. There was more planning by day and a lusty poker match each night while an Italian violinist played *Lili Marlene* and other melodies in the garden. Spaatz, though outwardly dour, was a sentimentalist at heart and a lover of music, both good and bad. Eaker could not care less: he was still tone-deaf.[4]

The Villa Vismara, named for its wealthy Roman owner, perched on several terraces about three hundred feet up the cliffs above the Fragonari Rocks on the south side of the island. The Fragonari are a tourist attraction, for one of them is a natural bridge through which small boats can pass when the Mediterranean is calm. A mile to the west at the Piccolo Marina and clearly visible also were the villa and pool of British comedienne Gracie Fields. They had been converted into a club for air crews. On a nearby hilltop was a villa once owned by Mussolini's family. Out of sight a few miles to the east were the ruins of the palace of Tiberius, where he entertained guests by having slaves tossed off the two thousand-foot cliff. At the Vismara the furnishings were sumptuous. In the dining room, for example, was a circular table of blue-gray marble about four inches thick and seven feet in diameter with a two-foot hole in the center holding a copper basin filled with water lilies. This was inconvenient for poker, which was played in the large drawing room across the entrance hall. The most interesting room at the Vismara, however, was at the top, very large and with a peaked ceiling suggesting that it began as an attic. It contained only two pieces of furniture—a concert-grand piano and a huge fourposter bed. Here, so the Vismara's Italian majordomo told us, was where Leopold Stokowski and Greta Garbo had dallied during their brief but much publicized romance a decade earlier.

Back in England by May 3, Spaatz sent the initial FRANTIC JOE orders off to the Fifteenth through MAAF, and Eaker initiated with Twining the detailed planning involved. It was an assignment he relished immensely, recalling his happy days as a group commander and giving him the chance again to take direct charge of an air operation and lead it into action. The elements of the 5th Wing of the Fifteenth Air Force chosen to carry out FRANTIC JOE comprised five veteran bomber and fighter outfits. One of them was the 97th BG (H) with which Eaker had ridden in a bomber named *Yankee Doodle* on the first B-17 mission against Europe—the attack on Rouen, August 17, 1942. He of course decided to fly with the 97th again, and a B-17 was renamed *Yankee Doodle II* to accommodate him. Colonel

C. W. Lawrence, CO of the 5th Wing, was designated commander of the task force, but Eaker dominated the planning and the unusual instructions to the group commanders. He told them, for example, "not to enter into political or social discussions based on comparisons with our own institutions. The Russians do not recognize personal opinions in the armed forces. Statements made by individuals are considered official opinions of the government." In an instruction to briefing officers he said to tell "all personnel on the operation they *must not* speak disparagingly of the B-24. . . . The reason for this, not to be divulged in the briefing, is that a number of these B-24s are ear-marked on a Lend-Lease basis." Another message stated: "The ultimate objective of FRANTIC JOE is to impress the Russians with the power and capabilities of the Strategic Air Forces. To do this effectively this relatively small Task Force must be in good fighting trim. Since maintenance and supply in Russia will, at best, be relatively inferior, the Task Force must not be wilfully subjected to strong opposition with consequent possibility of heavy battle damage en route. . . ."[5] And the final predawn briefing included a careful and emphatic doctrination on how to behave.

> The Fifteenth Air Force Task Force is the first major American unit to be based on Russian soil. Impressions created will color the thinking of the entire Russian military establishment and set the stage for future relations. Every officer and enlisted man therefore has in his hands, by his conduct and actions, a profound responsibility. Our performance will be the yardstick by which the Russians will judge the fighting capabilities, the discipline, the morale and the energy of the whole of the American forces, Ground, Naval and Air.[6]

There remained the question of target. Eaker and Twining recommended German airfields in the Galatz section of eastern Rumania where some five hundred Luftwaffe planes were concentrated in support of the German defense lines. On May 26, at Harriman's request, Eaker took the plans to London for a final strategy session with Spaatz, Harriman and others at Park House. Harriman, on the way back to Moscow from Washington, brought with him Maj. Gen. Robert L. Walsh, newly designated CG of Eastern Command. Eaker brought along his intelligence chief, Col. Harris Hull, and me. Eaker wanted to schedule the first mission for June 12 to allow more time for Eastern Command to get ready, but Spaatz insisted on an earlier date because both he and Eisenhower

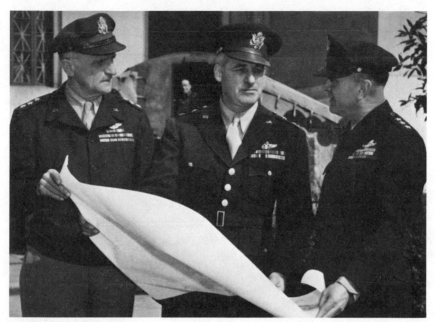

Spaatz, Twining and Eaker at Fifteenth Air Force headquarters in Bari, on the Adriatic, 1944.

hoped the first shuttle might divert German attention from OVER-LORD, then only twelve days away though no date had been picked beyond "the first week of June." Spaatz rejected Galatz as the target, saying first choice of the objective should be left to the Russians, if they would express it to Deane, and, secondly, that USSTAF goals from which the Russians might care to pick were Luftwaffe production plants in Latvia and Poland. It was decided to schedule FRANTIC JOE for the first day weather permitting after June 1, and instructions were sent to Deane to clarify the target choice with the Soviet hierarchy. Deane did so at once and ran into another wall of Soviet inscrutability. For reasons they did not choose to disclose but that later turned out to be their fear that American air activity in Latvia or Poland would interfere with their midsummer offensive, which actually began, per promise, on June 23, they refused approval of the Latvian or Polish targets. Instead the Russians suggested transportation targets further south, one of which was the railway yard at Debreczen in Hungary. Deane protested that all these targets were as near to Italy as to Russia and it was wasteful to bomb them instead of more remote objectives that made landing in the Ukraine logical. Unable to budge the Soviet views, Deane recommended they be accepted, commenting, "once started . . . we will be allowed a great deal more freedom of action, not only on the selection of targets but on all other matters. . . ." Spaatz agreed and Debreczen became the target. The night before takeoff from Foggia Eaker wrote a long letter to Arnold reviewing the entire project and saying, ". . . we know the tremendous significance you attach to this operation and are going to do everything we can to establish a relation of friendship, mutual respect, trust and confidence between ourselves and the Russians. . . ."[7]

The 130 B-17s in FRANTIC JOE and their escort P-51s took off at 6:55 A.M. on June 2, heading northeast over the Adriatic in clear weather. With Maj. Pat Nolan as pilot, Eaker rode as copilot in the lead plane of a flight of three. To his right was a B-17 piloted by the 97th's commander, Col. Frank Allen; to his left a B-17 piloted by 2nd Lt. Alfred Bond. Three MAAF staff officers were in other planes—Hull, to help with target choice and other intelligence; McCrary, to handle the crowd of war correspondents known to be waiting at Poltava; and the author, to write the formal report on the mission. Five P-51s turned back early, but from then until the target the trip was utterly uneventful, not even one enemy fighter appearing as the peaks of Yugoslavia gave way to the Danubian plain. Two other Fifteenth Air Force task forces were out of sight, flanking us on each side and headed for other targets than ours as a device to confuse any German fighters in the area. Three hours later, from altitudes ranging up to 25,000 feet, we dropped our 1,030 500-lb bombs squarely on Debreczen's undefended locomotive works and rail yards and turned away toward the Carpathians and Russia. Then came the only loss of the day. An engine in Lieutenant Bond's B-17, only a few yards from Eaker's, caught fire. It pulled out of formation, flew along under control for a minute or two (long enough for the crew to have bailed out) and then exploded. One instant there was a Fortress, the next nothing but a blob of smoke and four flaming engines meteoring toward earth. No parachutes were seen. Our escort fighters peeled away to return home while another group took their place for the long and uneventful run-out to Russia. Over the Carpathians the weather closed in as if to symbolize Soviet secrecy. When we crossed the Russo-German battle lines a few feeble bits of flak appeared above the overcast like ink blots on linen. At the Dnieper the formation let down to the deck in a drizzle, buzzing the rich bottomland of the Ukraine. At 1:20 in the afternoon the fighters landed at Piryatin, while the bombers reached Mirgorod and Poltava an hour later.

At Eastern Command, Deane wrote: ". . . the first three Fortresses, flying in a V-shaped wedge, came into sight through the overcast. They were followed by seventy more, flying in perfect formation. The sky was filled with them, and huge as they were, they seemed much bigger with their silver wings silhouetted against the black sky above. For an American standing on the field below it was a thrill beyond description. There in the sky was America at war— these few planes epitomized American power, the skill of American industry and labor, the efficiency of American operations and the courage of American youth. . . . The day our first landings were made marked the high tide of our military relations with the Soviet Union."[9]

Yankee Doodle II was the first B-17 to land, and Eaker, wearing a fatigue hat and a trench coat, was the first officer to emerge. Since he was the highest-ranking American officer yet to come to Russia, the Soviets had sent an officer of the same rank to meet him—Lt. Gen. Dimitri D. Grendal, chief of Soviet army intelligence. The Soviet party also included Maj. Gen. N. V. Slavin, the Russian general staff officer with whom Deane dealt, and Maj. Gen. A. R. Perminov, the Russian base commander. They were accompanied by a buxom, middle-aged woman in Red Army uniform incongruously wearing white, high-heeled satin pumps. Kathleen Harriman, who was there with her father as well as Deane and Walsh, explained that the woman was Perminov's aide. "Those are her best shoes, so naturally she wore them." The Russians handed Eaker a large bouquet of roses and another to Kathy. "First time you've ever been bunched?" asked Kathy. He reciprocated by distributing a handful of Robert Burns panatellas and then wowed the crowd by pulling a Legion of Merit medal from his pocket and formally pinning it to Perminov's chest, while some twenty U.S., British and Russian war correspondents milled around taking notes or pictures. Everybody then piled into jeeps for the mile drive through the rain to Eastern Command headquarters for a brief conference. An hour later Eaker took off in a Russian DC-3 to fly the five hundred miles to Moscow. The plane had bucket seats along each side. Eaker sat on one side with Grendal, Slavin and Deane, talking intensely about targets all the way. The Harrimans and we three MAAF officers sat facing them, but spent most of our time looking out the windows as we skimmed at tree-top height (apparently standard Russian practice) over a continuous panorama of smashed bridges, burned towns, zigzag German trenches and the isolated strong points the Soviet armies preferred—all empty now but scarring the fields as far as the eye could see. That night, as Deane had predicted (and as recounted in Chapter 1 of this narrative), Eaker quickly gained Soviet permission to send his bombers to the Mielec aircraft factory in Poland Spaatz had suggested, then to come back to Poltava, and to hit one of the Galatz airfields on the return to Italy.[10]

June 2 had been a long, long day for Eaker—the dawn takeoff from Foggia and the seven-hour mission to Poltava; the immediate two-hour trip to Moscow; a quick nap; followed by his post-midnight session with Molotov, Slavin, Novikov and Nikitin at the Kremlin until 4:00 A.M. on the morning of the 3rd. But he headed back to Poltava after only a few hours of sleep in order to launch the mission to Mielec. He found the assembled war correspondents feeling browbeaten and frustrated. They wanted to stay on for the first U.S. takeoff from Russian bases, but their Soviet chaperone insisted they return to Moscow forthwith. This attitude underwent a complete about-face, however, when Eaker granted the newsmen an American-style press conference—friendly, straightforward and revealing considerable off-the-record information. As the diary I kept for Eaker during this period notes: "Eaker expressed pleasure at the great help the AAF had received from the Russians, mentioned Red 'fighter support' and revealed that the targets for the shuttle attack had been chosen at Russian request and that the bombing had been good. Discussion followed as to the release of his statement and it was decided this would be done as soon as he had safely returned to Italy. He agreed to let members of the press go on missions from Russian bases, provided the Russians had no objection, and likewise approved of their making frequent visits to Poltava. . . . The Red official . . . thereupon quickly retracted his order. . . ."[11]

At this point a weather low moved in over central Europe and it became evident that Mielec could not be bombed for several days at best. Plans were therefore rearranged for hitting Galati airfield and returning to Poltava, which 104 B-17s and 42 P-51s did on June 6. The results were good and no bombers were lost. The fighters claimed 6/3/1 for the loss of two P-51s. First Lt. Callen J. Hoffman was credited with the first U.S. victory from Russian bases—a Ju-88.

Meanwhile Eaker had darted back to Moscow for lunch with Molotov and for the party at Spasso House on the eve of D-day in Normandy, returning to Poltava the next morning in time to meet the bombers as they got back from Galati. Then, for three days, he at last had a chance to unwind, doing "little," his diary records, "but talk to the men and rest." As usual, however, he got in some exercise daily, including one occasion that caused Russian jaws to drop. Some of the Soviet ground personnel at Poltava challenged the American fliers at volleyball, and Eaker nonchalantly joined the U.S. team, playing in shirtsleeves. No one could imagine a Russian general doing something like that.[12]

During Eaker's ten days in Russia almost everything seemed to be going well at Eastern Command. True, the living conditions were primitive. Most of the 1,200 permanent U.S. personnel and all the shuttle visitors were housed in tents, with field latrines, "C" rations and boiled drinking water. But the sense of adventure was exhilarating, and the Russian personnel at the bases as well as the local peasants were genuinely friendly, the overall atmosphere hospitable. At Poltava several concerts of folk songs were performed in the ruins of a hangar decked out with a makeshift stage, with dances afterward. The Americans were surprised to see Russian soldiers dancing together and startled the Russians with a display of U.S. jitterbugging. Contrary to the U.S. impression that all Russians were strapping giants glowing with health, the peasants and local soldiery tended to be shorter than the Americans and generally exhibited signs of malnutrition, bad teeth, scabies and other ailments, including venereal disease. Eastern Command's medical officer considered Soviet medical practice generally fifty years behind American. It was found that the Russians did not use soap for washing dishes, saying it caused diarrhea. Instead they used a 3 percent soda solution and a greasy towel. Flies were ignored, garbage allowed to stand around for days. Since Russian women were used perforce in the U.S. field kitchens, rigid supervision was mandatory. "If Russian kitchens may be termed bad," I wrote, "their latrines can only be called indescribable, while bathing among the local populace appeared to be at best a biennial event." But each nationality had that great saving grace—a sense of humor, exemplified in a posted memo on living arrangements:

Haircuts—2 barbers will be furnished every Wednesday. *Bath day* from 1300 to 1800 on Wednesday, or any other day 20 men are

Eaker (bald head) playing volleyball against the Russians at Poltava, 1944.

available for baths. *Sheets & pillowcases*—will be changed by the Russians every Wednesday. *Laundry*—collected every Thursday and returned following Wednesday. *Vodka*—to be ordered from Maximov in bulk and for cash. *Repairs*—will do upon request. *Rats & Mice*—Russians will supply a cat.[13]

In method and management attitudes the differences between the two nationalities were striking. A Russian worker was accustomed to being given a single task, such as one truck, one in particular, to drive; they were surprised by the flexibility of the Americans, who moved from one job to another on a moment's notice. Eaker wrote Lovett: "When we landed . . . General Perminov told off eight

402

Russians for each of our bombers to help refuel them and bomb them up. From early afternoon when these eight Russians, none of whom could speak English, were assigned to a bomber they looked upon that bomber as their personal war machine. They worked all afternoon rolling up drums and pumping gasoline. . . . When they finished about 10 o'clock at night they were told the bombs would be delivered to the plane at midnight. Those same eight men, without the slightest hesitation or question, laid down beside the bomber and had a little rest. When the bombs arrived they got down to work, without food or question, and worked willingly and cheerfully until the bombs were aboard, about daylight. Even then they would not leave their charges until they were fully assured there was nothing left to be done. Russian women, who laid the steel mat for our runways . . . showed the same spirit and singleness of purpose. They have a great pride. . . ."[14]

But the most clear-cut example of the difference in management came when Perminov was showing Eaker around the three bases of Eastern Command. All had entrance gates manned by sentries, as was the case in U.S. bases everywhere. At each gate two Soviet sentries, with bayonets fixed on their rifles, snapped to attention as the two generals approached. Eaker inquired about their standing orders and learned that they were about the same as at home—four hours on duty, admission only to those with passes, etc. "What do you do," he asked, "when you change the orders?"

"Oh!" said Perminov in surprise. "We never change the orders, we change the guards."

Touring the three bases, Eaker cast a practiced eye at many details, noting in particular the lack of any air-raid warning procedure, the skimpy antiaircraft defenses and the few YAK fighters on station, most of them far below U.S.—or German—standards. He learned there had been an increase in German reconnaissance in the past few days, and he fretted about getting his men and planes back to Italy. I wrote: "One night there was an alert and everybody piled out, grumbling, into slit-trenches, but no hostile aircraft appeared. It was obvious to all that the bases presented attractive targets though no more so than all the U.S. fields in Italy, most of which had lain unmolested, much nearer the front, for months." Dawdling for five days while the persistent low refused to move, the 5th Wing's men grew bored. "Once the novelty wore off, life was exceedingly dull. With no battle damage, only routine airplane checks and repairs needed doing. So the crews lolled in the warm sun, played soft-ball in the thick clover, ambled curiously through the ruined towns, flirted with the few American nurses, made a few tentative approaches to the somewhat meaty Russian girls, griped about the plain food and went to bed early."[15]

With Normandy at its most crucial stage, Spaatz ordered the mission to stay put as a threat to the German rear. On June 10, weather over Poland having failed to improve, he approved returning to Italy and attacking any available target on the way. Eaker went to Moscow a final time that day to attend a luncheon for Molotov honoring the second anniversary of Lend-Lease. The lunch lasted from two to five, and Eaker got back to Poltava about 8:30. Next morning at 3:30 everyone was up and took off at 6:20 in the same B-17s and P-51s to bomb Focsani airport, near Ploesti, and proceed to Foggia. I wrote my parents in New York afterward: "The flight home duplicated the shuttle out in most essentials, but we had more opposition. There was a good bit of flak over the target, and Nazi fighters made some passes. . . . All the formation watched as one Fort began to straggle, slowly dragged out of the protective formation and then was jumped by the prowling Huns. Guns flickered for a few minutes and then the B-17 slowly turned on its back, flowered in flame and smoke and broke apart. Parachutes popped from it like seeds from an overripe nut. A gut-cramping sight." Among those on the downed plane (and the only one who did not survive) was the photographic officer with all his pictures. They were scattered over the Rumanian landscape, and some of them, those showing the B-17s parked close together at Poltava in the absence of dispersal sites, quickly fell into German hands, with dire consequences ten days later.[16]

When Eaker returned to Caserta, bringing with him a case of fresh caviar from the Harrimans that was shared by all at the Camp Cascade mess, he was pleased and optimistic, writing Lovett: "My overall reaction is definitely that the Russians are friendly and will cooperate with us in any joint undertaking which makes sense. They are a very realistic people. When they turn anything down we ask for there is generally a very good reason behind it. For example, they were opposed to giving us fixed corridors across their lines for our PRU planes. . . . They had found by experience that when defined corridors are established the antiaircraft batteries relax. The Germans very quickly took advantage of this. . . ."[17] What Eaker—and few of the Americans—realized that early was that there were more sinister "reasons" behind Russian behavior than simply tactical judgment. While the brief honeymoon lasted he wrote thank you letters to Molotov, Nikitin and others in the Soviet command and received one from Perminov. Then, with no warning, the roof fell in —quite literally—at Poltava.

Late in the afternoon of June 21 the second shuttle mission—this time 137 B-17s and 63 P-51s from the Eighth Air Force in England—landed at the three Eastern Command bases, having lost three bombers and two fighters while bombing the Ruhland oil refinery south of Berlin. The distance was so long that five of the B-17s had to land at Kiev because of fuel shortage. The B-17s were shadowed part of the way by a German plane that kept a discreet distance but could accurately measure the size of the formation. Soon after the task force landed another Luftwaffe plane was observed reconnoitering Poltava. And the Germans also had some of the photographs scavenged from Focsani. That night just after midnight German bombers arrived overhead in force, to circle leisurely for two hours while dropping thousands of antipersonnel, incendiary and general purpose bombs. "Russian antiaircraft and fighter defenses," Deane wrote, "failed miserably. Their antiaircraft batteries fired 28,000 rounds of medium and heavy shells assisted by searchlights, without bringing down a single German plane. There were supposed to be 40 YAKs on hand as night fighters, but only four or five of them got off the ground. Both their antiaircraft and night fighters lacked the radar devices which made ours so effective."[18]

It was a triumph for the Germans and the worst defeat of its kind for the U.S. since the Japanese caught MacArthur's B-17s on the ground at Clark Field in the Philippines on December 8, 1941. Destroyed or damaged beyond repair were 50 aircraft, including 47 of the 73 B-17s on the field. The other B-17s and all the P-51s escaped harm when the Germans hit Mirgorod the following night, having been dispersed to other towns in the Ukraine in the meantime. The worst damage, however, was the loss of 397,000 gallons of 100-octane fuel, about half the total stored there, as well as much of the stock of bombs. Only two Americans lost their lives because Perminov refused to allow any Americans to go on the field to fight the fires. Soviet deaths totaled 30, with another 95 wounded, many of these casualties occurring during the three days it took to clear the field of the vicious little antipersonnel bombs (9,500 being removed on the third day alone).[19] The Russian method there and elsewhere when faced with minefields was to march laborers or soldiers, both men and women, in line abreast across the field, with or without mine-sweeping implements. When this was reported after the Poltava disaster, it was greeted with disbelief in Allied headquarters. But later that year, when Eaker met Marshal Tolbuhkin in Bucharest and they compared notes on comparative methods of fighting the German armies, he heard grim confirmation. Eaker remarked that "in operating against Kesselring's German armies in Italy we had found it necessary to lay down an artillery barrage to protect the engineers while they cleared the minefields. . . . Marshal Tolbuhkin responded, 'We have come through minefields too but the system you outline caused too much delay. I marched a thin line of infantry through the minefields. They destroyed the mines with their feet. . . .' "[20]

The Poltava setback could not have come at a worse time. Only a few days before, building on the success of OVERLORD and FRANTIC JOE, Harriman had climaxed months of delicate effort by winning from Stalin on June 10 an offer to provide half of the dozen air bases for heavy bombers he disclosed the Soviets were building in the Vladivostok area, adding that stockpiling of fuel and reserves for the United States could begin there at once. Stalin linked this offer to obtaining 300 B-24s and 240 B-17s for the Red Air Force. Arnold had foreseen such a gambit and had persuaded the president to allow Harriman to counter that these heavies would be "delivered after agreement had been reached regarding our operation from Soviet Far Eastern bases." (This was the only occasion FDR permitted Lend-Lease to be used as a bargaining chip with the Russians.) Harriman added that Arnold would be glad to train Soviet airmen to fly them, either in the U.S. or in Russia. Stalin preferred the latter. Arnold quickly agreed, setting aside a B-24 squadron and crews for the purpose. Since obtaining those Far Eastern bases was the prime objective of the entire FRANTIC exercise, this seemed at the time to be a major breakthrough.[21]

Six weeks elapsed before the Soviets were willing to talk about the subject again. In the interim much that happened had altered Stalin's attitude enormously. The disaster at Poltava began the decline. Deane wrote: "There were no recriminations on either side. On the contrary, every effort was made to capitalize on the misfortune by drawing closer together and redoubling our efforts. Nevertheless, the disaster sowed the seed of discontent, the Russians smarting and sensitive because of their failure to provide the protection they had promised, and the Americans forgiving but determined to send their own anti-aircraft defenses as protection for the future. Meanwhile we had invaded France and the Russian lines had moved far to the west. The bases in the Ukraine soon were too far to the east to justify the long flights over friendly Russian territory and we started negotiations with a view to moving them farther west. These negotiations failed completely."[22]

All the Byzantine twists and turns in those negotiations and the parallel ones concerning the continuance of FRANTIC require a full book to summarize. Indeed, a number of books have done so, notably those by Harriman, Deane, Glenn B. Infield and the unpublished Syracuse University thesis of Thomas A. Julian, which is by far the most detailed. A study of this "Search for American-Soviet Military Collaboration," as Julian subtitled his 368-page opus on FRANTIC, climaxed by the January 1945 Yalta Conference, is essential for any serious student of the contentious U.S.-USSR relations since World War II ended. Eaker was in the thick of the growing controversy and it shaped his thinking, as well as that of Spaatz and the other top Allied military leaders, for the rest of their lives. For the purposes of this narrative a brief survey must suffice.

The initial air force reaction to the Poltava disaster was laconic. Col. F. J. Sutterlin, Anderson's FRANTIC project officer at USSTAF, who had accompanied the mission, radioed: "Conditions regards planning abruptly altered by enemy last night. [We] are now faced with problem whether political advantage worth price of maintenance. . . ." Eaker's reaction was more positive. He wrote Arnold: ". . . we must prepare to defend our Russian bases or abandon the project. My view is that there is no place in Europe now where the hunting is as good as in that area. Our night fighters here [in the Mediterranean] have found very few German planes in recent times and our antiaircraft have no German planes to shoot at. The German reaction to the FRANTIC project has been stronger than anywhere else in recent times. Walsh advised me yesterday that some 300 German planes have been moved into that area since FRANTIC was initiated. We all want to destroy the German Air Force—where better then than in Russia where the German has indicated his willingness to fight?" Spaatz instantly informed Deane and Walsh that USSTAF would not be deterred from continuing FRANTIC, provided adequate defenses were set up first. Eaker offered a night-fighter group from MAAF, and Deane's first presentation of these proposals received a warm approval from Slavin and Nikitin as well as Perminov. Stalin gave Harriman a tentative okay.[23]

On June 27 the remnants of the Eighth AF task force (71 B-17s and 55 P-51s) flew an easy mission to Foggia, bombing an undefended oil refinery in Galicia on the way. Among those aboard was Lt. Col. Ed Gray, who had been Eaker's signals officer in PINETREE days and now had the same job for LeMay's 3rd Division. He was standing behind the pilot in the lead plane while the latter radioed the "strike report" back to LeMay in England—a standard procedure that dramatically displayed how effective air force communications had become. People generally knew the B-17 to be a powerful and beautiful airplane that could carry a lot of bombs, take a lot of punishment and put up a strong defense against attack. But few realized that it was also an enormous electric generator containing more than six miles of wiring. The generators run by its four engines turned out enough power to light a medium-sized hotel, and its radio could instantly reach any one of a hundred airfields in England, even from as far away as Rumania. It was LeMay's practice to be at a base operations room when a strike report was due. This time he spoke briefly in reply. The pilot turned to Gray and said, "Congratulations." "For what," asked Gray. "You've just been promoted to Colonel," was the answer—a thoughtful courtesy from LeMay, who was warm and gracious beneath his gruff exterior. In Italy Gray flew over to Caserta for a reunion with Eaker, who invited him to a "Promotion Party" in his honor that night. This, of course, was a poker game. Gray lost $185 to Jock Whitney.[24]

Early in July Spaatz again came to Caserta, this time to meet with Deane, Walsh, Sutterlin and Eaker and decide what to do. The initial concept as outlined by Sutterlin was to increase American personnel at Eastern Command to 18,682. But the conferees recognized that would be too much to expect the Russians to swallow, so they cut the proposal to 8,900 for the three existing fields while a fourth one was prepared in the Kiev-Vinnitsa area further west. They were unaware that Vinnitsa was where the Germans in 1943 had discovered a mass grave of 9,432 bodies slaughtered by the Russians in similar fashion to the 15,000 they slew in the Katyn Forest, unearthed about the same time. This was one reason the Soviet hierarchy showed no enthusiasm for putting an American air base there.[25]

The Caserta conferees also decided that the only practical way to keep up the FRANTIC missions during the temporary shortage of gas and supplies at Poltava was to send task forces consisting solely of fighters. When Deane returned to Moscow and presented these various ideas, the Soviet air officers were receptive, but Slavin was notably cool toward the extra personnel requested, and it took eight days to get clearance for only forty-seven specialists, as well as transport for P-38 drop-tanks, since that twin-engined fighter would participate for the first time. At last, on July 22 Twining dispatched 76 P-38s and 58 P-51s to strafe several airfields in Rumania. This force flew one additional attack out of Eastern Command and another on the return leg to Foggia, achieving marked success, with total claims of 120/18/37 for the loss of seven P-38s. On August 7 the bomber shuttles resumed, with a successful attack on a Focke-Wulf fighter assembly plant near Gdynia in Poland by 75 B-17s and 64 P-51s from England. In Washington, Arnold, ever optimistic, began the dispatch of a night-fighter squadron and its equipment direct to Russia instead of from MAAF as Eaker had offered.[26]

In the meantime, however the Russian offensive swept far further west than even the Russians had dared expect, conquering Rumania by the end of August and reaching the outskirts of Warsaw in Poland by August 1. Stalin saw victory clearly in his hands and felt much less reason to seek American aid or to be cooperative with USSTAF. But, with Muscovite wile, neither he nor his spokesmen simply said Eastern Command was no longer necessary. Instead they began a deliberate campaign of delay and sabotage. In early July, new Russian guards took over security arrangements at Poltava, Mirgorod and Piryatin and started discouraging American fraternization with Russian peasants, especially women. This took the subtle form of clubbing any woman seen walking or talking with U.S. soldiers. Some American men attempted to fight back, and there were some serious brawls. On July 15 all U.S. personnel were restricted to their working or living areas at night and instructed not to venture outside by day except in pairs. The increasingly nasty situation came to a head in early August with the uprising of the Polish "Home Army" in Warsaw in what became one of the most revolting tragedies of World War II.[27]

The Polish Home Army under Gen. Tadeusz Bor-Komorowski rose against the Nazis on August 1 after receiving what he believed was approval from Moscow. The Red Armies were at the Vistula, only a few miles away, and could have joined in the city's liberation. Instead, they halted for months while the Germans methodically extinguished the rebellion at a cost estimated at 250,000 Polish lives. Support of the Polish Home Army was a British responsibility, and Slessor dispatched seven heroic volunteer missions from MAAF's 205 Group to drop supplies by night between August 8 and 17, when they were halted as ineffective and too costly (losses were 20 percent). A promise of aid was made personally by Stalin to the premier of the Polish government in exile in London on August 9 and Stalin repeated it to Harriman the next day, as did Molotov the day after that. But no aid appeared. Churchill then requested a supply drop from England, as did Roosevelt. A shuttle was the only practical way to do it, and Russia flatly refused approval, going on to denounce the Warsaw rebels as reckless adventurers who had acted without Soviet permission. Harriman wrote Eaker on the 19th: "I am outraged. . . . It is a dirty business. The only satisfaction I have gotten so far is that they know in no uncertain terms how the Americans feel about it. I realize it is essential that we make every effort to work with them and, in spite of discouragements, I am still hopeful. But one thing is certain, that when they depart from common decency we have got to make them realize it." At last, on September 11 the Soviets gave their approval, and Spaatz sent off the final FRANTIC mission on the 18th, with 107 B-17s dropping 1,284 canisters of guns, food and medical supplies, of which only a small fraction landed within the shrunken Polish Home Army perimeter. Roosevelt ordered a repeat attempt but Stalin himself refused permission, and the gallant Poles surrendered a few days later.[28]

In the middle of that bitter and disillusioning experience, Molotov had the gall to tell Harriman that the Eastern Command bases, now hundreds of miles behind the front, had been loaned to the Americans just for the summer and Russia needed them back. Harriman, furious, blistered him with the reminder that also involved was the promise of bases near Vladivostok. Simultaneously the ambassador wrote Secretary of State Cordell Hull that the Russian leaders were men "bloated with power" who felt they could force all the world to do their bidding. A week later Spaatz again rendezvoused at Capri with Eaker, as well as Walsh and Hugh Knerr. They decided there was no alternative but to reduce Eastern Command to minimum size while still retaining possession for bargaining purposes, though none of them believed Stalin would make good on his promise of Pacific bases, and Knerr, the supply specialist, was, "convinced that the Siberian railroad will not support any sizeable force." Spaatz wanted Arnold to investigate through Deane the feasibility of new bomber bases in the Vienna area or Poland. But Eaker, shrewd poker player that he was, came up with the most intriguing idea. In an eyes-only letter to Arnold on August 26, he pointed out that the Russians now had four general officers in Italy. ". . . we have received several transport squadrons loaded with supplies destined for the Balkans and also a fighter squadron. In other words, we are breaking our necks cooperating with the Russians in this theater. Despite that, they are not helping us at all. It was suggested that we are not very smart in continuing this attitude. I said I would get in touch with you to see whether or not you would like the Supreme Allied Commander to notify the Russians . . . that we do not have facilities available for their mission and their aircraft in this theater. In other words, if they are getting tough with us, should we get tough with them? I personally feel this is the sort of thing the Russians understand. . . ."[29]

Arnold was attracted by Eaker's *quid pro quo* approach but concluded after discussion with others in Washington that threatening to withhold Lend-Lease supplies would be a stronger lever. He approved cutting Eastern Command down to one base (Poltava) and 300 men and at once stopped all supply shipments and reinforcements, including the night-fighter squadron for the Soviets. It was off-loaded in Italy for MAAF. But he authorized Harriman to renew the promise of six B-24s and issued orders for the shipment abroad of the B-24 squadron and 46 specialists to train the Red Air Force. On October 7 the Soviet Foreign Office approved U.S. retention of Poltava with a small caretaker force. By then, however, the major objective of Russian bases on the Pacific was slipping from Arnold's grasp. On September 28, two days before the six B-24s were due to fly to Russia, the Soviet government declared it was no longer interested in having its own personnel trained to operate them. And in

December Deane was informed that the Soviet would need all its Pacific bases for its own purposes and that American naval and air forces would be unable to operate from them.[30]

Thus FRANTIC failed in its major objective, though hindsight suggests the United States was lucky in that respect, for Japan was beaten speedily from the Pacific Ocean side and the evasive Soviets entered the conflict too late to get the kind of spoils they could have grabbed if American B-29s had actually operated from Vladivostok.

Nor was FRANTIC a military success in the literal sense of defeating Germany. The Luftwaffe was not diverted from Normandy, and the nineteen shuttle missions hit targets that could just as easily have been attacked directly from Italy at far less cost in time and money. The shuttle concept itself, regardless of the Russian failure to cooperate, was faulty. Gen. Leon Johnson, who won the Congressional Medal of Honor leading Eighth Air Force B-24s from temporary bases in North Africa in the famous low-level attack on Ploesti in 1943, remarked: "It [operating from auxilliary bases] always seemed easy to someone who didn't know the problems. Once you tried it, however, you found that it was impossible."[31]

"FRANTIC's historical importance," wrote Julian in the closing pages of his solid 349-page thesis, "lies chiefly in illuminating the nature of American-Soviet relations. . . . The Soviet treatment of the FRANTIC project showed earlier than perhaps any other event in the wartime relations between the USSR and the U.S. that the conception of Soviet interest held by Stalin and the other Party leaders did not involve friendship with the West."[32]

Deane, writing his perceptive *The Strange Alliance* in 1947, noted aspects of this discord that still held true four decades later: "As far as our future relations with Russia are concerned, I feel the shuttle-bombing venture will be of value in pointing to the vast difference in attitude towards Americans that exists between the rank and file of the Russian people and their leaders. Starting with Novikov, Nikitin, the entire air staff, and extending down to the women who laid the steel mat for our runways, we encountered nothing but a spirit of friendliness and cooperation. . . . Starting in the other direction and working up through the General Staff, the NKVD, the Foreign Office, and the party leaders who lurk behind the scenes as Stalin's closest advisers, we found nothing but a desire to sabotage . . . and in the end we were literally forced out of Russia by restrictions which had become unbearable. The attitude of the people may be changed by one-sided propaganda from above—the attitude of the present leaders never has changed and probably never will."[33]

Harriman went to the heart of the matter in a letter to Harry Hopkins. "I am disappointed but not discouraged. The job of getting the Soviet Government to play a decent role in international affairs is however going to be more difficult then we had hoped. . . . Ninety percent of the Russian people want friendship with us and it is much in the interest of the Soviet Government to develop it. It is our problem to strengthen the hand of those around Stalin who want to play the game along our lines and to show Stalin that the advice of the counselors of a tough policy is leading him into difficulties."[34]

23

*"In the British and American bombing of
Germany and Italy during the war, the
casualties were over 140,000. . . . These heroes
never flinched or failed. It is to their devotion
that in no small measure we owe our victory.
Let us give them our salute."*

—WINSTON S. CHURCHILL, *CLOSING THE RING*

THOUGH Anzio, Cassino and the prolonged battle for Rome captured the public's attention in the first half of 1944, the chief assignment for the Allies in the Mediterranean was the invasion of southern France, originally code named ANVIL and planned to coincide with the invasion of Normandy. MAAF was given the task of making the air plan in January, just as Eaker was arriving. The idea was entirely American in origin and vehemently opposed by the British, who preferred, as Slessor put it, "to serve OVERLORD by keeping up the pressure in Italy and intensifying the enemy's difficulties in the Balkans. . . . Eaker agreed with us."[1]

Delay in capturing Rome forced postponement of ANVIL, and, after OVERLORD made good the landings in Normandy without the diversion in southern France, Churchill and the British chiefs tried hard to get the U.S. to scuttle ANVIL completely. On June 19, when both Marshall and Arnold were visiting Italy, Eaker put on what the diary of Harold Macmillan, still minister resident in the Mediterranean, called an "immense dinner" in their honor at Camp Cascades. Previously there was a conference where, as Macmillan added, Eaker

414

supported "Alexander's plan for advancing to the Piave river and threatening an attack through the Ljubljana Pass, directed on Vienna . . . as an alternative to ANVIL. Generals Marshall and Arnold did not react as unfavorably as had been expected. But it is thought that Eisenhower will not like it."[2]

Macmillan was right. Eisenhower still had some forty divisions in America to bring into action and needed another port in France. He demanded ANVIL and he demanded it "quickly." Macmillan wrote that Churchill was "enraged," but the PM limited his expression of annoyance to the new code name he gave the landings— DRAGOON, "since I was dragooned into it." No British forces except naval were involved, but the withdrawal of ten crack U.S. and French divisions left Alexander's armies in Italy too weak to slam on through the new German "Gothic Line" from Pisa to Rimini and capture the Po Valley as a base for the Fifteenth Air Force much nearer to Germany. This was the main reason for Eaker's position, but it led Marshall to chide him, "I think you've been with the British too long."[3]

Since the plans were all in hand and the extensive preparations (such as building fourteen airfields on Corsica) largely completed, DRAGOON could indeed be launched "quickly" and the attack went in with clockwork precision on August 15. By then Eisenhower's armies were near Paris and the Russians had split the Baltic states at Riga and were poised on the boundaries of East Prussia itself. Thus the new Allied uppercut against southern France found the Germans in a situation that was already desperate. Though the Allied buildup in Corsica had been obvious for months, the hard-pressed Germans had been obliged to pull away a sizable proportion of the forces they had allocated to defend the French Riviera. Only ten Nazi divisions remained south of the River Loire and but seven were deployed along the Mediterranean coast. As for the Luftwaffe, it was estimated to have in southern France the puny total of 200 operational planes. But German defense capabilities were still considerable. The coast they were guarding is a rugged one, with rocky promontories overlooking many small beaches where the French had sited numerous coastal batteries. These the Germans strengthened while deploying another 450 heavy and 1,200 light antiaircraft guns in the area.[4]

For the invasion the Allies mustered clear-cut and overwhelming superiority. Against the Luftwaffe's 200 estimated aircraft MAAF could marshal 5,000. Against the seven weak German divisions the U.S. Seventh Army, under the command not of Clark but of Maj. Gen. Alexander M. Patch of Guadalcanal fame, could throw not only ten veteran divisions of American and French troops from Italy but commandos, special service forces and paratroops borrowed from England. Off shore lay 450 British, U.S. and Italian warships including five battleships and nine aircraft carriers.[5]

So DRAGOON became a pushover, though not without its scary moments and instructive episodes. The actual location of the landings near St. Tropez was successfully obscured by heavy bombing of other areas and sundry deceptive measures. Most of the coastal batteries and radar stations were smashed by joint aerial and naval bombardment, and on D-Day the naval task force could report that "only a few rounds of 75 mm and 20 mm fire and 60 rounds of mortar fire were directed at the boat lanes, causing no damage." MAAF's heavies and mediums expended 7,350 tons of bombs on coastal batteries, about a quarter of which were in the assault area. The navy expended "about 15,900 projectiles 5-inch and over," estimated to weigh a total of about two thousand tons. Inspection of the batteries after their capture showed many guns still serviceable and "it was evident that the neutralization of the positions had been due to the annihilation or demoralization of the gun crews by sheer weight of barrage." General Patch and General de Lattre de Tassigny, the French commander, interviewed the German admiral in command of the shore defenses shortly after his capture and asked him which of the two types of bombardment had the greater effect. He replied, "The air bombings."[6]

On D-Day itself as three divisions and a glider-borne task force led the assault, paratroops dropped on the hamlet of Le Muy, fifteen miles inland, to interdict the one road leading from the interior. These operations entailed bringing six troop carrier groups of 64 aircraft each down from the Ninth Air Force in England out around France and Spain to Italy. On D-Day the procession of 204 C-47s towing two gliders apiece stretched more than a hundred miles from the takeoff areas near Tarquinia, just above Rome, over Elba and on to southern France. Had the Luftwaffe had any muscle left, the target would have been enticing. As it was, there were no losses to enemy air action. Even so, glider casualties were heavy—approximately 3 percent of the 9,000 airborne personnel engaged. Most of the casualties came about in landing, for the Germans had studded

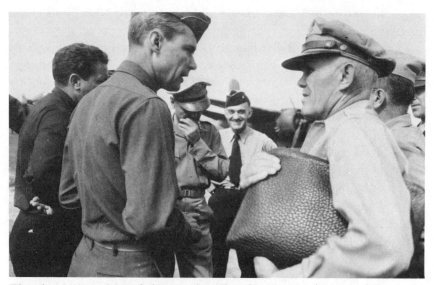

The air commanders of the two invasion fronts meet in central France, September 1944. In foreground Hoyt Vandenburg (left) talks with Joe Cannon. Behind Vandenburg's left shoulder is Quesada. In center background, hand on chin, is Eaker, with Kepner just behind in his traditional place as Eaker's wing man.

the fields of Le Muy with posts that impaled the flimsy canvas kites. Of the 407 gliders dispatched only 47 could be salvaged.[7]

Once ashore, the DRAGOON armies moved inland fast, expertly supported by Twelfth Air Force and French mediums and fighter-bombers. These were controlled from several fighter direction ships, as were the carrier planes. The battle quickly turned into a race up the Rhône Valley and landing strips were improvised along the way, with fighter control moving inland also. On September 11 the DRAGOON armies met Patton's Third Army at Somberon, near Dijon. Soon thereafter control passed to Eisenhower, as did the French Air Force and small pieces of the Twelfth. Devers left the Mediterranean to become commander of the Sixth Army Group, comprising Patch's Seventh Army and de Lattre's French and was succeeded by Lt. Gen. Joseph T. McNarney, deputy chief of staff under Marshall. Between August 10 and September 11 MAAF flew 23,830 effective sorties and lost 194 planes to flak and accident, an overall loss rate of .0081 percent. The decline of the Luftwaffe, by contrast, stands out starkly in the statistics of Allied "claims" between Anzio, seven months before, when enough Germans ventured into the air for MAAF to bag

468, and southern France, where only eight furtive Nazi pilots could be cornered.[8]

On D minus one Eaker flew to Corsica, where Fleet Adm. Sir A. B. Cunningham gave a small dinner for Churchill. The PM, though still miffed about the strategy involved, could not resist participating in the battle. Eaker sat next to him and wrote about the occasion in a long colorful letter to his father in Texas a week later. "Mr. Churchill was in rare form and obviously pleased with the way the invasions were going. . . . He referred to our meeting at Casablanca and said that the daylight bombing, about which there was considerable doubt in his mind at that time, had more than matched his fondest expectations. . . . On the day of the invasion I flew a Mustang P-51 single-seater fighter for an hour over the invasion coast. It was a great sight to see hundreds of ships, nearly a thousand of them, lined up off shore and many hundreds of small boats loaded with troops plowing relentlessly toward the shore. It was also a good sight to see the broadsides fired from the battleships and to see the bombs raining down from our heavy bombers. . . . I went to the beachhead. . . . As I was going [back] aboard the boat after visiting Seventh Army Hq just at dusk the Germans made an air attack and laid several dozen small bombs across the ship. . . . Four men were killed and 44 injured. General Devers, General Cannon and several other persons who were with me nor I were injured. It was a very thrilling experience since the antiaircraft made a great show firing at them and we could hear the whistle of the many small bombs as they fell about us. The next day I drove some 300 miles over the roads in Southern France, visiting all the Army, Corps and Division Headquarters. About noontime I came to the headquarters of the motorized column of the 45th Infantry. They had just cleared the Germans out of a village. We saw several hundred prisoners file by on the western edge of the town. A French Partisan came up and pointed to a tree 100 yards away and said there was a dead German sniper under the tree. We went over to have a look at him. He had both hands over a hole in his middle. . . ."[9]

The Air C in C and the PM were not the only staff officers who itched to participate in the fighting. McCrary jumped with the paratroops, I flew in a glider tug and Whitney prowled about the front in a jeep, getting into the biggest adventure of his life. He had been charged since February with direction of MAAF's liaison section, which consisted of being Eaker's political advisor and representing the air C in C at the Joint Rearmament Committee (training the French Air Force), the Office of Strategic Services (spying), the Psychological Warfare Branch (mostly dropping leaflets), and the Post-War Planning Committee. This mixed bag was excellent background for Whitney's appointment, thirteen years later, as ambassador to Great Britain. But on August 22 he carried his liaison duties one step too far—he got captured. He and other Americans who fell into German hands were loaded into boxcars and shipped off toward Germany. Whitney's train survived several Allied strafings and was approaching the German frontier when he bravely led the escape by some, not all, of his boxcar's occupants by prying open a door and jumping as the train slowed momentarily. They hid in a forest until the Allied front caught up with them. Whitney returned to Caserta September 12, substantially diminished in weight but unharmed and jocular as ever. Eaker laid on a poker party in his honor.[10]

Training and equipping the French Air Force—one of Whitney's liaison duties—had been a pet project of U.S. Army Air from the start of the North African invasion in late 1942. But not until April 1944 did the French begin to receive adequate supplies of American aircraft. Throughout that spring the Joint Air Commission, whose chairman, Col. (later Brig. Gen.) Robert G. Ervin, was a Castle Coombe alumnus and had met Eaker at Rockwell Field in 1918, struggled to get P-47s and B-26s to accouter the French squadrons in time for DRAGOON. Eaker took a keen interest, an early example being a letter to Lessig, who had been back in Washington since late 1943 unhappily flying a desk for Arnold and concerned primarily with theater supply and redeployment. Eaker wrote him on March 20: "I am most anxious to get six or eight intelligent, alert, keen, French-speaking young officers to do liaison duty with the French. Believe me, these French are doing a marvelous job fighting. . . . They love to fight. If you have anything to do with it, therefore, please help us to equip them on schedule. They will blow up a German or cut a German throat probably with more relish than anybody." It was done, and the French performed superbly, albeit in small totals, during the invasion, making 3,207 sorties and dropping 1,325 tons of bombs in August.[11]

One of the French pilots was Antoine de Saint-Exupéry, whose *Night Flight* is a classic of beautiful writing about aviation. He was forty-three and had been grounded by Spaatz a year before after crash-landing a P-38 at Tunis. McCrary brought to Eaker's attention

St. Exupery's passionate desire to fly in the liberation of France, and Eaker, always ardent to fly himself, authorized five more photo-reconnaissance missions. Major Saint-Exupéry took off from Sardinia on July 31, 1944 to make a mapping sortie east of Lyon. He never returned.[12]

Another famous Frenchman with whom Eaker was briefly involved at this time was Gen. Charles de Gaulle. They had met a few times in England when de Gaulle was far less powerful than he had become by August 1944. Eaker had sized him up then as "a pretty difficult fellow to deal with"—a judgment all the Allied leaders came to share.[13] On August 18, with DRAGOON at crescendo, Eisenhower's diary noted: "General de Gaulle is causing a great deal of consternation in Allied minds, as he desires to fly from Africa direct to France, using his Lockheed Lodestar. This is an unarmed ship and its fuel capacity does not allow enough margin of safety. General Devers and General Eaker have offered him full use of a Fortress or a C-54 which could rendezvous with a fighter escort over England. However, de Gaulle is adamant and desires to use a French ship and a French crew. It has necessitated a message going out from General Smith informing him—de Gaulle—that if he does not coordinate the movement and the escort, we cannot be responsible for his safety. . . ."[14]

General de Gaulle had been in the Mediterranean for a fortnight and had come to see Eaker several times about the French Air Force and about making what Eisenhower thought was to be a brief "inspection" trip to see French troops in action. The Air C in C, habitually courteous and helpful, invariably found the leader of the Free French egotistic and haughty. He had, Eaker said: "a deep-seated hatred for our leaders because he felt they had not accorded him a measure of partnership and dignity he should have had as a leader of a principal Allied nation." The last time, when de Gaulle came to the palace in Caserta without an appointment to decline Eaker's offer to provide him with his own, comfortably appointed B-17, *Starduster,* the Air C in C did not interrupt a staff meeting and let him cool his heels in the anteroom for twenty minutes. Then he radioed Arnold, ". . . I have sent it on to Casablanca anyhow to be available and in readiness if he changes his mind. . . ."[15]

But de Gaulle had something far bigger in mind than mere "inspection" and used his little Lockheed, taking off from Gibraltar on one more of the decisive steps of his astonishing career. Landing in central France on August 20 after a very risky flight, he backed French Gen. Jacques Philippe LeClerc, commander of the 2nd Armored Division, in flouting Eisenhower's strategy and heading directly for Paris. Eisenhower had planned to bypass the French capital in pursuit of the German armies, which were fleeing in disorder. He wished to avoid the delay and the drain on supplies, especially gasoline, which a Stalingrad-type siege of a major city would entail. Neither he nor de Gaulle knew that demonic Hitler had given orders to destroy the city in any case. But de Gaulle wanted Paris at once, even if it were badly damaged, in order to consolidate his hold on the French government and to forestall the strong French Communist Party from doing so. His letter to Eisenhower on August 21 demanding the city's immediate liberation was instrumental in persuading the supreme commander to change his orders. Three days later LeClerc's 2nd Armored, with support from Bradley's 4th Infantry Division, raced into the heart of Paris, capturing it after several brisk but limited battles. LeClerc accepted the German surrender "on behalf of the Provisional Government," not "the Allied Command" as he was supposed to do. The next day de Gaulle entered, occasionally under fire, and skillfully avoided any formal linkage with the other politicians who assembled to meet him, especially the Communists. On the 26th it was the tall, gawky figure of de Gaulle that led the victory parade down the Champs Elysée.[16]

With the swift and easy victory in southern France the history of MAAF and the Mediterranean theater reached its apex. This was the event for which Allied arms had been girding themselves for two long years. Among the fighter groups that patroled ceaselessly over the Riviera beachhead in late August was one (the 324th) that had fought at El Alamein. Among the U.S. divisions that swarmed up the Rhone Valley were three that had taken part in the original North African invasion. By interesting coincidence the peak of the strategic bombing offensive against oil—MAAF's other main task—came at almost the same moment. Seven days after the DRAGOON landings, the Russians forced the surrender of Rumania, thus bringing to an end the five-month campaign by the Fifteenth Air Force against Ploesti, source of 30 percent of Axis oil. From September on the emphasis at MAAF turned increasingly from the conduct of offensive operations to the cleanup of the debris of war. Not that there was a lack of major fighting still to be done. The Italian campaign had to be pushed home until the elimination of Kesselring's tough troops, and the bombardment of oil stores and refineries deep in Germany, Poland and Czechoslovakia had to be maintained with unremitting pressure. But by the fall of 1944 these were relatively routine, albeit grim and bloody, procedures from the air point of view—tasks the tactical and strategic air forces could carry on with minimum guidance from above. Eaker's attention swung more and more to the problems of redeployment, diplomacy and closing up shop—tasks calling for a nice balance between immediate prosecution of the war in Europe and long-term arrangements for movement to the Pacific, occupation of Germany and, in particular, close-harness relations with the Soviets.[17]

The rescue of over a thousand U.S. and Allied airmen from Rumania, already noted, dramatized this new phase in MAAF operations. Similar ACRU (Air Crew Rescue Units) followed quickly. Between November 8, 1942, and May 8, 1945, when fighting in the Mediterranean officially terminated, 28,178 U.S. airmen were reported missing in action (plus 3,863 killed and 4,796 wounded). It was known that many of the MIA had escaped death, but for a year and a half there was little the air forces could do about it. Aside from a few individual excapes (such as that of Beirne Lay, one of Eaker's original six to arrive in England, who became a B-24 group CO, was shot down leading his fifth mission and hid out in France), the bulk of the missing men were corralled in closely guarded prison camps deep in enemy territory. After the air forces established themselves in Italy and began concentrated operations in the Balkans, this situation began to change. Aided by Partisans in northern Italy and Yugoslavia, a sizable number of missing fliers trickled back to base. From September through January 1943, the Fifteenth processed 108 evaders and escapers. In January 1944 there was only one, in February, 11, March, 32, April, 86 and May, 176. It became clear that rescue arrangements were inadequate and Twining sent Eaker a memorandum in June recommending creation of an organization to recover escapers from Serbia. MAAF worked up plans for "a unit of twelve to 20 officers and men, to include a Flight Surgeon and medical personnel" and Eaker obtained Wilson's approval in mid-July. To head the first ACRU Eaker picked a remarkable officer.[18]

Col. George Kraigher was a Yugoslav-born American citizen who flew for the Serbian air force in World War I. Afterwards he became a chief pilot for Pan American Airways, which sent him to Africa when WW II began to set up its new route across the dark

Col. George Kraigher and co-pilot about to take off in a C-47 "work horse" to drop supplies to Tito's Partisans.

continent. When MAAF came into being, Eaker, who had known Kraigher for years, recruited him to serve, under Whitney, as liaison with Tito's headquarters. Kraigher was at Tito's mountain hideout when German paratroops attacked in an effort to assassinate the Partisan leader, and both men narrowly escaped. This was but one of a dozen adventures the grizzled and totally nonchalant fifty-three-year-old flier survived in 1944 as he personally flew B-25s or C-47s on 45 missions to drop supplies or land on secret airstrips as deep in enemy territory as Czechoslovakia. It was from such a strip that Kraigher accomplished his first ACRU mission, as Eaker jubilantly reported to Arnold. "Yesterday 70 crewmen were brought out from Mihailovic territory. Three hundred more have been located and will be brought out shortly. . . ."[19]

Yugoslavia then was split into two political groups—the Partisans headed by Tito, and the Chetniks, led by Mihailovic—hostile to each other but cooperative in succoring Allied flyers. Fifteenth Air

Force crews in missions over the Balkans were carefully briefed on the "islands of resistance" controlled by the two groups. In some "islands" there were landing strips, in others none. So it became SOP for both Partisans and Chetniks to move parties of AAF personnel from one area to another through enemy lines. More than one AAF officer or airman was killed in these moves. In several cases landing strips located near the Germans were operational one night, yet the following night, with the assembled crews sitting in the nearby hills, the operation had to be called off because of the capture of the field by the Germans. Sometimes airplanes arrived over the field and had to be ordered away; at least one rescue was completed under fire. Late in July, at the time of ACRU #1's creation, more than one hundred U.S. aircrew plus Russian, French and British fugitives had congregated at Mirovsce, in Chetnik territory, where an Allied agent had a radio in touch with Fifteenth Air Force through Bari, Italy. One of the fliers, Lt. T.K. Oliver, devised a code of nicknames, serial numbers and other references intelligible only to members of his own squadron. The first line read, "150 Yanks are in Yugo, some sick, shoot us work horses. . . ." Those last two words were AF slang for C-47s. By the time Kraigher brought his ACRU there on August 11 with 12 C-47s escorted by fighters, the party had grown to 225. They were flown to Bari along with four Chetnik stowaways, who were promptly collared.[20]

This set the pattern for other ACRUs, each tailored to fit the local circumstances. Hull led ACRU #2 into Switzerland, trucking 66 escapers back through southern France soon after its liberation. Because the Swiss were understandably touchy about their neutrality, "escapers" were defined as men forced down outside Swiss borders and who technically had been in enemy hands before reaching sanctuary. All 66 of them autographed a white chamois skin for Eaker that embellished his study for 40 years. Another 900 were classified as "internees," having in most cases landed crippled heavies behind the Swiss frontier. They were eventually released to an Eighth Air Force ACRU.[21]

ACRU activity peaked in September and October as the Germans disintegrated in France and the Balkans. Besides Rumania, Yugoslavia and Switzerland, men were recovered from Bulgaria, Albania, France, Czechoslovakia, northern Italy, Greece, Poland, Austria, Hungary, Turkey and Spain. By October 20, MAAF had records of 3,570 Fifteenth and Twelfth Air Force fliers rescued plus many from the Eighth, the RAF and other allied components.[22] By then MAAF's work was largely done. Aside from northern Italy and northern Yugoslavia with an estimated 200–400 "evaders" in each, the entire Mediterranean had been cleaned up. Only in Austria, Hungary and Germany were there remaining big concentrations of prisoners; early in October Eisenhower's command, SHAEF, took over responsibility for their recovery. MAAF had pioneered the technique, and SHAEF drew heavily on its experience.

Rescuing stranded airmen and dropping supplies to the guerillas in Yugoslavia were activities encouraged by Marshall, Eisenhower and Arnold, but after the dispute over DRAGOON Eaker was directed by Washington not to permit any fighting activities by the Americans in the Balkans; these were to be regarded strictly as a British responsibility. Thus, when the British occupied southern Greece in October 1944 to preempt the area from the Russians and asked Eaker to provide U.S. planes for a paratroop drop on Athens, he had to say no.[23] Yet the Balkan Air Force was officially part of MAAF and the distinction was a puzzling one to outsiders as well as to significant new national leaders such as Tito. As Slessor explained it in his postwar book, *The Central Blue:* "In effect, west of about longitude 20° East [the Adriatic], I was responsible through Eaker to Sacmed [Wilson] and east of that line direct to the British Chiefs through Portal. It was an odd set-up, but it worked all right, largely because I had in Ira Eaker an Allied Commander-in-Chief who was not only an old friend but a great airman and a splendid chap who stood on no dignities, trusted me to serve him loyally in the sphere where he was responsible and left me to get on with it—and gave me all the help he could—where he was not permitted by his directive from Washington to have a direct interest."[24]

Tito's Partisans eventually won out over Mihailovic's Chetniks, but when the German paratroops almost succeeded in killing him on May 26, Tito sent Eaker "a personal message . . . asking for our help," as Eaker reported to Arnold. This was promptly provided by the Balkan Air Force, as Eaker explained, "We feel it is most important . . . because of the large forces they are tying down in the Balkan area." Lieutenant General Sudakov of the Russian mission at Bari came to see Eaker on June 1. "He was greatly worried that he had lost contact with the Russian Mission with Tito. He stressed in his conversation with me his pleasure at the cooperation we have given him and his Mission and spoke with great admiration of our air effort in support of the Partisans."[25] Fleeing from the Germans, Tito unexpectedly landed in Bari on June 4 and was sent at once by the British to the Yugoslav island of Vis, which, Macmillan noted in his diary, had "already been taken from the Germans by joint action of the British commandos and Partisan troops. He will then be on Yugoslavian soil and not a refugee. . . . It may be helpful because it should increase our hold over him. . . ."[26]

Two months later Tito again came to Italy, this time securely established as head of a nation largely liberated by the Russians but greatly helped by both the British and the Americans. He arrived at Caserta swankly dressed in a dark gray uniform with black frogs on the arms and was accompanied by a large Alsatian dog, two enormous guards carrying submachine guns and a very pretty young woman who was listed as his interpreter but was actually his mistress. Eaker gave a dinner for Tito at Camp Cascades attended by two dozen high-ranking Allied officers and diplomats. Tito insisted that his two guards be there too. One stood by the door, the other directly behind the marshal, which somewhat interfered with serving his food. Soon after the meal had begun the electricity abruptly cut off, as was the wont of Italian generators. In the dark the silence was electric for perhaps half a minute before the lights came on once more. Then the two guards were observed in crouch position, their submachine guns at the ready, one still by the door, the other in a far corner, both of them tidily covering the entire party.[27]

Macmillan had Tito to lunch at his villa in Caserta that same week, along with Brig. Fitzroy Maclean, the top British liaison officer to the Partisans. Macmillan's diary recorded: "I told the latter that I was not prepared to have Marshal Tito's personal bodyguard standing in my dining room during lunch. I thought Brigadier Maclean might explain to the Marshal that this was not the custom among gentlemen in our country. A firm position proved successful. The bodyguard stood in the passage."[28]

Eaker's amiable relations with Tito and the Yugoslavs climaxed the following winter with a visit to Belgrade. First, however, he drew upon a decidedly nonmilitary talent at MAAF. This was playwright Thornton Wilder, who was in Caserta as a lieutenant colonel in A-5 (plans). The air C in C thought it would be a good idea for the Yugoslavs to see a translation of Wilder's great play, *Our Town*. Tito agreed and Eaker suggested that Wilder go along to help with the presentation, adding, "I do not believe it would be wise for you to be away from this Headquarters, in view of your own duties, for more than ten days or two weeks." Eaker himself went to Belgrade on March 10, 1945, to look at possible new sites for Fifteenth Air Force bases, lay a wreath on the tomb of the unknown soldier and receive the Order of the Partisan Star, First Class.[29]

Tito, acknowledged Communist though he was, remained cooperative with the Allies throughout the war. But the Russians did not. The deteriorating relations with the Soviet hierarchy became the major problem Eaker faced. Only a few months before, with the first of the shuttle missions to the Ukraine, those relations had gotten off to a happy and auspicious start. But the closer the Russians advanced across the Balkans, the more difficult it became to maintain a satisfactory working relationship with them. Every day seemed to bring a new problem. Besides saving its men, MAAF was curious to see what it had actually done to the many major targets now exposed to view, like wrecks on the sea bottom, as the tide of Nazism withdrew. Ploesti was the first and greatest example, and MAAF was able to get its hands on all the refinery records in the few days before the Soviets took full control of Rumania. This swift grab by Eaker and Twining turned out to be highly opportune, for the Russians soon made it clear they had little interest in assisting U.S. bomb evaluation teams. Instead they did their best to thwart them. Similarly, when the ACRU in Bulgaria revealed some horrid atrocities inflicted on American captives, the Soviets stalled any effective retribution. Eaker sent a high-powered mission to Sofia for five months to bring the culprits to justice and the beastly Bulgars were quite willing to inflict immediate severe punishment, but the air C in C insisted that they be held "in custody for disposition and trial by War Crimes Tribunal to be created under armistice terms." Though the Soviets never directly said "Niet," they steadfastly avoided any joint action with the Allies, and MAAF finally washed its hands of the matter.[30]

Vastly more important than these relatively minor issues were strictly operational questions such as bomb lines, day-to-day air support of the Russian columns, forced landings in Russian territory, air transport linkage and the Allied proposal to move the Fifteenth, or portions of it, to the Budapest area. Broached in the period of relative stalemate on the Western and Eastern fronts in the fall of 1944, the project was designed to increase the weight of the strategic air offensive on the heart of Germany itself. But, despite Stalin's personal agreement at Yalta in January 1945, no bases were ever

Eaker and Tito, with interpreter, in Belgrade, March 1945.

made available to American bombers or fighters. Eaker commented to Deane in March, "I imagine the protracted delay means that our friends hope to kill the project by delay." He was right.[31]

But the urgent need for bomb lines established daily was something the Russians could not simply "delay" or ignore, though they tried the latter tactic by insisting that bomb lines continue to be established in Moscow. That had worked all right for many months while the Russian lines were still remote, but failed utterly in the fall of 1944 when the Eastern front became fluid and bomb-line adjustments had to be made quickly. Eaker described the procedure he wanted: ". . . in a rapidly moving situation any bomb-line designated from Moscow is likely to be unsatisfactory. A much better plan would be to have air liaison officers from this theater with the forward elements of the Red Armies to keep us advised of the locations of their forward echelons from day to day, plus a general agreement that we will not execute missions closer than an agreed number of miles to these forces unless specifically requested by the Red Army commanders to do so."[32] The inevitable happened on November 7 when a Fifteenth Air Force P-38 group made a navigational error and inadvertently strafed a Russian column in Yugoslavia, killing a So-

428

viet lieutenant general and five of his men. YAKs interposed, shooting down two P-38s but losing three themselves. The Soviet general staff in Moscow at once filed a formal complaint with Deane; Eaker and others sent profuse apologies; and the Russians reacted correctly. As Eaker reported to Arnold nine days later, "An RAF Air Commodore, recently returned from Sofia, who attended the funeral of the Russian Lt. General we accidentally killed, talked with the Russian senior officers and stated 'They received it very well and said that it was clearly an error and they showed no resentment.' "[33] He also pointed out in a long cable to Marshall and Deane that "37 bombing or strafing missions have been flown by Fifteenth Air Force between 18 August and 11 November near Soviet lines in Yugoslavia and Hungary. They have resulted in destruction of 621 enemy aircraft and damage to 306 as well as destruction of great numbers of railway rolling stock and vehicles and Germans. This is the first unfortunate occasion in all that effort."[34]

But the Soviet hierarchy still would not agree to bomb-line liaison outside Moscow. After several weeks of frustrating negotiation, Deane recorded in his *The Strange Alliance*: "General Eaker took the bit in his teeth and sent a message . . . in which he asked us to inform the Russians that effective at two o'clock in the morning, Sunday, December 3, 1944, the Mediterranean Air Forces would confine their activities to the west of a line which he designated. The line [which was altered daily] was sufficiently far to the west to give full protection to Russian Air and Ground Forces but far enough to the east to include the principal roads over which the Germans were retreating. . . . The Russians' acquiescence to Eaker's arbitrary action confirmed the suspicion that had long been growing in my mind that relations with the Soviet authorities would be improved if they were characterized by a tougher attitude on our part. . . . I think the most outstanding lesson that came of our efforts to co-ordinate air operations with the Red Army was the effectiveness of positive action as opposed to negotiation. . . . They had much more respect for us and acquiesced more readily when we simply informed them that 'This is what we are going to do—take it or leave it.' There is merit in considering adherence to similar procedure in the future."[35]

In late October, when pressures in Europe were low (aside from the tiresome difficulties with the Russians), Eaker flew to the States for redeployment planning deliberations in Washington, a much-needed break from duties and a reunion with his beautiful wife, whom he had not seen for more than a year. Ruth Eaker had kept busy with good deeds in Washington and around the country such as appearing at war bond rallies, greeting returned fliers and autographing the 3,500th B-17 modified at the United Airlines facility in Denver. Her husband flew home on October 21 and spent four days huddling with Stimson, Lovett, Marshall, Arnold, Giles and Harriman. Then he and his wife flew to California to see old friends in Los Angeles and at Hamilton Field, near San Francisco, returning to New York on November 2 to stay at the St. Regis Hotel and see *Oklahoma*. They had a happy time and talked, of course, about their own plans for postwar, though the conclusion in the Pacific then looked much further away than turned out to be the case.[36]

Eaker's thoughts about the postwar era were first recorded back in April in a letter replying to Hansell, then still on Arnold's staff in Washington but destined shortly to head the effort to hit Japan with B-29s using the same high-level, precision bombing tactics he had helped make effective over Germany. After thanking Hansell for his good wishes and his speculations about the future, Eaker wrote: "I have limited personal ambitions. All I want to do is stay in the war until it is over and then retire and take up a little of the joy of living which has been so seriously interfered with for a very long time by putting military service first in all my interests and activities." He went on to express a philosophy he stuck to. "I believe that we have three categories of personnel: The old men, the middle-aged men and the young men. I want to see the old men all retired to a well-earned rest as soon as possible; I want to see the middle-aged men step out as soon as the war is over and let the young men, like Fred Anderson, Norstad, Kuter and yourself build up the subwar Air Force. There is only one job in the world I would take after the war is over and that would be Military Governor of Japan. Since there is no likelihood of anybody offering me that job, I shall apply for retirement as soon as the war is over and earlier, if the powers that be feel that there is no command job for me in this war. I may do a little writing and a little radio work if the occasion offers after the war, but the only campaign I shall ever wage is to get the old men out and the young men in. . . ."[37]

But only nine days later, in the letter to Arnold already cited (Chapter 20), Eaker made his pledge that "Tooey and I . . . came up with one conclusion that we must not let the Old Man down in his long fight for air power." Throughout 1944 he and Spaatz and

Arnold maintained a trialogue on postwar plans and it is clear from rereading those exchanges that Eaker never set the air force aside as the centerpiece of his thinking and lifelong purpose, though he did stick to his intention to get out and make room for younger men. In one letter, for example, Eaker asked Arnold if it "would not be possible for you to propose legislation to authorize an Air Academy?" But the most significant one followed another meeting with Spaatz in Caserta. Eaker wrote Arnold: "Thanks for your letter of June 29 outlining the problems the Air Forces face. . . . It is almost staggering in its implications. The main thing is, however, that if we do not realize what we are up against and prepare and organize to meet it, all will be lost and the result will be disaster for our Air Forces and waste and unpreparedness for our country.

"Tooey was here when your letter came and we read it over together and talked over its provisions paragraph by paragraph. . . ." Eaker commented at length on such specifics as Arnold's mention that "several thousand lawyers were going to be required to conclude all the contracts incident to the cessation of wartime production." Then he added "one other suggestion and it concerns the redeployment of the Air Forces at the end of the European struggle. Here again, my personal interests dictate against your adopting my proposal. It really originated with Tooey. He said in the course of our discussion that if he had the problem of redeployment, he would get on one end of the pipeline and put me on the other. As I told you when you were here, I will be very happy to retire immediately when the European war is over. . . . Despite this I feel that Tooey's suggestion makes sense, as his suggestions always do. He and I have worked together for over two years now in perfect harmony in the conduct of the air war in Europe and I believe that the best way to tear down the great house here and re-erect it most expeditiously elsewhere is for him to sit on the dispatch end and me on the receiving end, or vice versa. . . ."[38]

And that is what actually came to pass, though not quite in the orderly way Eaker envisioned. Eight months later, on March 22, 1945, he received orders from Marshall to report to Washington to be Arnold's deputy as commanding general of all the Army Air Forces and, much of the time, to run them during Arnold's recurring heart attacks.

24

"There is small risk a General will be regarded with contempt by those he leads if, whatever he may have to preach, he shows himself best able to perform."

—XENOPHON

ARNOLD'S fourth heart attack hit him in mid-January, as Lovett pungently confided to Eaker. "Hap had a recurrence of the trouble that he had a year ago and is now down in Florida where he will probably be for another four weeks. The doctors swear that there is nothing organically wrong but admit that this is a . . . warning which must not be ignored. . . . I have tried ever since I have been here to impress on Hap the necessity of delegating more and more responsibility and emulating the example of General Marshall in avoiding unnecessary speeches, dinners, and the vast number of exhausting engagements which could so easily be declined. In his penitent mood Hap agrees fully but when he begins to feel well again he hops into a plane, makes an inspection at Indianapolis, Louisville, Richmond, a speech that night before the United Bustle and Whistle Manufacturers convention, gets back here at night and then tries to clean up his desk the next day, while attending during the evenings a dinner to a visiting Mexican General, a party for three movie actresses who have come to inaugurate the March of Dimes, a session with the National Geographic Society, and a hearing on the conservation of automobile tires. Worthy as these organizations may be,

General Marshall is able to avoid them and I feel that Hap can too. . . ."[1]

But when the commanding general of the Army Air Forces returned to duty in February "he failed to slow down," as Marshall's biographer, Forrest Pogue wrote. "In the spring . . . he had trouble with his heart again, and once more Marshall scolded him."[2] But this time the chief of staff also took action: he forced through a staff shuffle in Arnold's office. It began with a command vacancy in the Pacific. This gave Marshall the chance to offer Lt. Gen. Barney M. Giles, Arnold's brilliant deputy and devoted chief of air staff, an overseas assignment, a prospect Giles of course relished.[3] Marshall then wrote Arnold in Florida on March 15 suggesting that Eaker be brought home to replace Giles after first making a quick trip to the Pacific. Arnold replied four days later in a letter both forthright and puzzling. He wrote: "Quite naturally I have been thinking about . . . any reorganization which must take place to cut down the work I have been doing. . . . Personally, I think that the fellow who goes in and takes Giles' place should be the fellow who will take my place as Commanding General, Army Air Forces. It is a job that cannot be learned over night because of the thousand and one ramifications. However, if you ask who the fellow is who will take my place, I cannot answer at once. Offhand, it looks to me like one of two, both of whom are absolutely essential in the Air Forces in the jobs they are now doing overseas, so I suppose they are both out. I like your suggestion of Eaker coming in and Giles going to the Pacific very much. Eaker has been through the mill in the War Department, knows the way the wheels turn, and will require a minimum of schooling. A short tour of the Pacific should acquaint him with that theater. . . . I will return to Washington tomorrow. . . ."[4]

Who were the two candidates for his job Arnold had in mind? The first, unquestionably, was Spaatz. The other, most likely, was Maj. Gen. Hoyt S. Vandenberg, newly distinguished as commander of the tactical air forces in France and nephew of the powerful Republican Senator Arthur Vandenberg, chairman of the Military Affairs Committee. It could not have been LeMay (who had not yet shown what he could do with the B-29) nor Kenney (no strategic air experience) nor any one of several rising stars without top command experience in combat. Obviously, however, he was not including Eaker. There seems to be no clear evidence why. Perhaps he still thought of his protégé as too junior or "not tough enough." Or it might have been his awareness of Eaker's oft-reiterated intention to retire as soon as the war ended. In any case, Marshall had not waited for Arnold's reply: he had already alerted Spaatz of his intention to bring either Spaatz or Eaker back to Washington. Spaatz signaled Eaker to meet him in Cannes on the French Riviera.

On March 16, two days before that rendezvous, Eaker, who was expecting Harriman to arrange a visa from Russia so he could fly to Moscow to dicker with the Soviets about new air bases in Hungary or Austria, had escorted his own deputy, Slessor, to the Marcianise airfield at Caserta to bid him good luck on his own new assignment —as Portal's Number Two and eventual successor in Air Ministry. For the trip to Cannes Eaker took Brig. Gen. William E. Hall, who was slated to be commander of any new airfields. Talk about the new bases (which were never made available) quickly took second place behind the news that Marshall wanted one or the other of the two old cohorts back in the Pentagon. "Well," Eaker ruefully recalled, "being the junior and knowing that General Eisenhower would not want General Spaatz to leave, I could have guessed who was coming home." Orders came through on March 22 to report to Washington no later than March 30.[5]

Eaker was unhappy but poker-faced about the switch. Once again, as when he was transferred from the Eighth just as its triumph was at hand, he was being ordered away from participation in final victory. Only seven weeks later, as Allied arms surged into the Po Valley, the Nazi forces in Italy became the first of the three fronts to capitulate. This Eaker would have relished—not so much for the obvious fruits of conquest as for the satisfaction of talking personally to the big bag of German leaders captured and incarcerated temporarily on Capri—men like Hjalmar Horace Greeley Schacht, once head of the Reichsbank, Fritz Thyssen of Krupp, or any of a dozen top commanders of the German forces against whom he had fought so long.[6] The transfer also probably cost him his fourth star, which he would have been in line to receive had he finished out the European war as air C in C in the Mediterranean. On January 14 Eisenhower had sent Marshall a long, thoughtful discussion of "four-star generals," saying, ". . . first consideration should be to accord this rank to relatively few officers and to preserve its traditional prestige in our army. . . . In this theater I think that only Spaatz and Bradley should be promoted on the first list. . . ." The supreme commander mentioned several others such as Devers as deserving and included

Eaker, remarking, "Eaker works strategically under Spaatz and should at least wait until Spaatz has held the rank for a period." It was given to Spaatz two months later. But the post of deputy to Arnold did not call for that much rank. Eaker thus lost out, as did Doolittle, until forty years later when a special act of Congress gave each of them the full title of general.[7]

With only a week before he was due in Washington, Eaker minimized the formalities of his departure from MAAF—no farewell parade or ceremony, just a quiet, casual dinner in the Cascades mess at which he said a few jocular words and thanked them all. One day he spent at the Twelfth with Cannon, who would be his successor as air C in C, another at the Fifteenth with Twining. On the 25th Smitty flew him from Marcianise to a field near Saarburg to see Devers, then on to Orly, near Paris, to hold a two-day commanders powwow with Spaatz, Doolittle, Vandenberg, Anderson and Knerr. He brought with him both Cannon and Twining. And in *Starduster* he found room not just for his aide, Major Mason, but also his three RAF henchmen, Stroud, Searle and Govier, taking them home to England for keeps. On the 27th Eaker flew on to London, staying at the Dorchester and paying calls on Portal, U.S. Ambassador Winant and Lord Trenchard, founder of the RAF. That evening he gave a dinner for nine close friends, including Ben Lyon and Bebe Daniels, Lady Dashwood, Beasley, Smitty, Mason and myself. On the 28th he breakfasted with Slessor, Lady Slessor and their daughter Judy, lunched with Air Marshal and Lady Harris at Springfield and took off for the Azores and home. Back in Washington on the 29th, Eaker was met at the airfield by generals Giles and Kuter, Colonel Lessig and wife, Ethelyn, and by Ruth Eaker, beaming.[8]

He had only a quick talk with Arnold. The impetuous AAF commander, back only ten days from his hospital bed in Florida, buzzed off on the 31st, despite Marshall's advice to take it easy, on a six-week inspection trip in Europe and Brazil. He told Eaker to see Marshall, which he did for two hours on the morning of the 30th. Marshall told him to visit the Pacific bases, China and India, then return home through the Mediterranean, adding, as Eaker recalled it: "The purpose of this exercise is to determine . . . how much of the European air forces we need to transfer to the Pacific to knock off the Japanese, and more particularly, how much can they support logistically. How long will it take you?" Eaker said he would let the chief of staff know that afternoon after talking to Gen. Harold L. George at Air Transport Command. The answer he gave—and stuck to—was twenty days. After long talks with Giles and Lovett and members of the air staff who briefed him on the other theaters, he spent Easter Sunday and three days with his sparkling wife, departing for the Pacific on April 4.[9]

In Hawaii on the 5th he had talks with many officers, flying on to Kwajalein on the 8th and Guam on the 9th, where his most important talks were with LeMay about the B-29 offensive. LeMay had replaced Hansell in January. Together they flew to Iwo Jima, where he conferred with its base commander, his old bugaboo in early days in England, General Chaney. Thence to Saipan to see Gen. Rosie O'Donnell and on to Tinian. At one base he gave a short talk to the assembled officers in which he praised LeMay as "without doubt the best man for the job here." And somewhere along the line LeMay explained his radical plan, begun on March 9 against Tokyo —one of the war's most daring and most successful—to give up the traditional high-level, daylight attacks on precise targets and to wipe out Japanese cities by low-level incendiary blitzes at night. "I told him," Eaker said later, "that it just might work."[10]

At Leyte on the 11th Eaker dined with Kenney, then flew on to Manila, where he saw MacArthur. "He put his arms around me and said, 'How's my pilot?' I said, 'Very well, Sir.' He said, 'You may remember that I had something to do with your military career. I selected you the first Army officer to take a course in public relations at the University of Southern California.' I said, 'Yes, Sir, you did.' I didn't remind him that he had first opposed it. I'm sure that he had forgotten that he first opposed it. But he did remember that he did it. I say that not critically, because General MacArthur has no greater admirer than I." It was during this talk that MacArthur also told Eaker that he had indeed voted against the majority in the court-martial of Mitchell nineteen years before.[11]

On April 13, his 49th birthday, Eaker was sleeping on the porch of Kenney's quarters at Fort Stotsenberg when Kenney woke him with the news that President Roosevelt had just died. Next morning he flew straight across the Japanese lines to Kunming and was met by Chennault, valiantly trying to fly effective missions with few planes and inadequate logistics. Thence on the 15th to Myitkyina in Burma for talks with another old friend, Maj. Gen. Howard Davison, CG of the Tenth Air Force. Davison had been the CO at Bolling in 1930 when Eaker nearly lost his life bailing out of his P-12. That

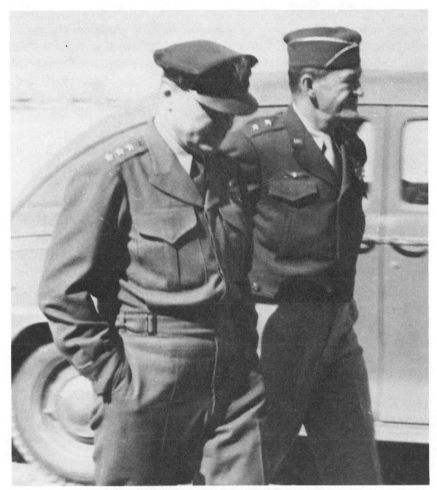

Eaker and Chennault, Kunming, China, April 14, 1945.

night he spent in Calcutta with Maj. Gen. George Stratemeyer, CG of Eastern Command. Three days later, after a day of sight-seeing far from any war front in Karachi and a pause in Cairo, the former air C in C of the Mediterranean touched down once more at Marcianise, where he was met by Cannon and a group of officers, including the author. Spaatz flew in the next day, the 18th, and there was, of course, a fine poker bash in the evening at well-loved Camp Cascades.[12]

On the 19th Spaatz and Eaker flew to Cannes to meet Arnold and to find themselves embroiled in the silliest squabble in the entire

437

thirty-two-year history of the Arnold-Eaker relationship. As Arnold wrote, "I wanted to talk with the senior Air Force officers about the reorganization of the Air Forces." In series he talked with Doolittle, Vandenberg, Cannon and Twining, climaxed with the arrival of Spaatz and Eaker. "At times the conference became very heated. One time Ira Eaker said to me: 'I didn't ask to go to Washington!' That made me explode, and I said: 'Who in hell ever did ask to go to Washington? Do you think I ever asked to go there and stay ten years? Someone has to run the Army Air Forces. We can't all be in command of combat air forces all around the world!' At that point General Spaatz stepped in with a remark that calmed us both down."[13]

The fuss over, the three top leaders of the AAF decided upon a dozen officers to be switched immediately from Europe to Washington and faced the very delicate subject of who should be in command of the B-29s in the Pacific. Arnold's journal comments: "MacArthur and Nimitz both want the Twentieth Air Force. Eaker was on MacArthur's side until I pointed out that Kenney's Air Force had never done a real strategic mission." But the problem was more complicated than that. For two years the Pacific had been split into two theaters, one headed by MacArthur and the other by Nimitz. As the two attacks converged on Japan both wanted to control the strategic bombers. LeMay could (and did) handle them operationally. But he was far junior to Kenney and to several navy fliers on the Nimitz side. So Arnold astutely took advantage of the precedent set by USSTAF in bridging two separate theaters in Europe. He sent Spaatz, who outranked all the airmen in the Pacific, to the Marianas to command the strategic offensive while reporting directly to Arnold. Thus, as Eaker had urged in his letter of the previous October quoted in the last chapter, he was at "one end of the pipeline" and Spaatz "at the other."[14]

But this was still some weeks ahead when Eaker and Spaatz flew from Cannes on April 20th in Spaatz's B-17 named *Boops* to see Eisenhower and Bedell Smith at Rheims. Next day Eaker went on to London, where he again stayed at the Dorchester. On the 22nd he talked with Winant and Jock Whitney, recently transferred to the ambassador's staff, taking off later that day for the Azores, Bermuda and Washington, arriving on the 24th, precisely twenty days after his departure. His diary noted, "Today acted as Commanding General,

AAF, in General Arnold's absence." Arnold stayed in Europe until May 3, then visited Brazil and paused at Miami for a medical checkup before resuming his duties in Washington on May 14. Meanwhile Eaker had reported his conclusions to Marshall.[15]

In sending Eaker on his "mission," Marshall was very deft. Several top staff officers, Giles or Kuter for example, could have made the same junket, but they lacked Eaker's immense experience both at building huge air forces, strategic and tactical, and then operating them against air opposition far stiffer than anything the Allies faced in the Pacific. Eaker was listened to with admiration verging on awe and provided respectfully with everything he sought by everyone to whom he spoke in the Pacific, Chinese and Indian theaters. Only Spaatz could have gotten to the heart of the strategic problem as surely. Marshall knew this and followed Eaker's recommendations to the letter. "I recommended," said Eaker, "that the effort be made not through India and through Chennault's air force but through the Marianas. I told him they could prepare a combination in time for about a third of the European air forces. I recommended that LeMay lead the bombardment forces because of his experience in the European theater and his great success."[16]

On May 6, two days before V-E Day in Europe, Lovett wrote Spaatz: "Barney is now in the Pacific, Ira has taken over and we hope Hap will be back toward the end of the week so that we can start rolling. During the past few weeks the dramatic events surrounding the utter collapse of the Wehrmacht have succeeded each other with such rapidity that everyone over here is a little bit dazed. Yesterday one of those things happened which we had all been hoping for. In a first-page, two-column story in the *Washington Post* . . . Von Rundstedt's interview was carried in which he said that he 'regarded air power as the most decisive factor in the Reich's military failure.' He went on to say that in order of importance the main factors were: first, lack of fuel—oil and gasoline; second, destruction of the railway system; third, Germany's loss of raw material areas; and fourth, smashing of the home industrial sections such as Silesia and Saxony by air attacks. In answer to a question as to the D-DAY landings in Normandy, he said that his 'reserves were so dispersed and placed that I could have met the D-DAY landing, even though it surprised us, except for the fact we had no mobility, and could not bring up our reserves . . . the unheard of superiority of your air force made all movement in daytime impossible. . . . "I am sure you must realize how terribly proud and gratified all of us are with the results of the combined bomber offensive and the magnificent job turned in by the Air Forces under your command. . . ."[17]

On May 9, the day following Germany's capitulation, Marshall characteristically found time in his immensely busy schedule to write Eaker the following sensitive letter:

> My dear Eaker,
>   In the midst of the celebrations of the European victory and the numerous messages of congratulations to the various leaders, I have felt that you, by reason of your transfer to a post of great importance in the War Department, have been denied much of the personal and official satisfaction which is your due.
>   You organized and initiated the great air attack on Germany and the Continent. You carried through those most difficult phases. In the Mediterranean theater you directed the strategical bombing operations from the bases in that region and commanded the Allied Air Forces in Italy.
>   All these duties and great responsibilities you discharged with conspicuous success and you also displayed marked efficiency in the effectiveness of your dealings with our Allies.
>   For these great services I tender you my personal congratulations and appreciation.[18]

A month later Arnold wrote Eaker in similar vein. Army air's peripatetic commanding general had tarried only three weeks in Washington before charging off to the Pacific to pave the way for Spaatz to become CG of the strategic air forces there. On June 8 he paused at Hamilton Field, near San Francisco, to dictate:

> Dear Ira:
>   As I leave on this trip I want to say to you a few things which I know, if we were together, you would probably shrug off and that would be the end of it. Accordingly, I shall put it in writing.
>   I realize fully the disappointment which you felt when, due to my illness, you received the call to return from your post in the combat zone to this Headquarters. At the time when our forces in Europe were on the threshold of victory, you were forced to lay down command of the great Allied Air Forces in the Mediterranean Theater and your long and important relationship with all the Air Forces in Europe, to which you made so tremendous a contribution. This to undertake a position in the War Department in Washington —which as we both know is never sought by any airman or soldier of your war experience—a call made necessary by my own absence. As a result, you were unable personally to direct and witness the

end-product of the effort, the skill and the courage which you brought to the war effort in the past three years.

You have played a major role in the development and employment of the air power which brought our European enemies successively to their knees. Your sure tact and inspiring understanding of people have played an outstanding part in the welding of our effort as one with that of our Allies.

Conscious as I am of these things, I want to express to you my sincere appreciation of what you have done and are doing and my recognition of the sacrifice of your own personal desires which accompanied your assumption of burdens which I was forced temporarily to lay aside. I shall go to the Pacific with the sure knowledge that the many responsibilities I am leaving with you will be more than fully discharged.[19]

In the Pacific Arnold set up Spaatz's new command at Guam over the strenuous objections of MacArthur but with relaxed acquiescence by Nimitz.[20] Meanwhile LeMay's low-level attacks were relentlessly smashing Japan's industrial centers and the atom bomb was readied for its first test, which was totally successful, as President Truman learned on July 16 at the Potsdam Conference with Stalin and Churchill's successor, Clement Atlee. Both the air force and the navy doubted that use of atomic weapons was necessary, arguing that the existing combination of air attacks and naval blockade would bring the Japanese down quickly. Arnold shared that view, but also observed, "There is a probability that if atomic bombs are not dropped and demonstrated in this war, we may, as we always do, neglect it post-war, and Russia will come along and get it first."[21] When the Japanese rejected the Allied ultimatum, Truman, still at Potsdam, made the fateful decision, confirming it in a message to Stimson on August 2. The president was partway home across the Atlantic on the cruiser *Augusta* when he received, on August 6, the message, "Hiroshima bombed."

The pros and cons of dropping the atom bomb have been examined in detail by many experts and analysts and it is not the province of this book to offer another judgment. However, it should be recorded here that the air commanders involved were scrupulous in making their positions clear. Arnold's views, noted above, were expressed in January 1945 just before he went into the hospital. In their turn Eaker and Spaatz were briefed in strict confidence when they returned from Europe. Spaatz arrived in Guam on July 5 before Truman left for Potsdam and before the bomb was tested. He had verbal orders to drop it but, as he testified twenty years later: "I insisted on written orders. That was a purely political decision, wasn't a military decision. The military man carries out the orders of his political bosses. . . . Of course, the fire bombing was just as disastrous in a way as the atomic bombing. We stuck rather rigidly, in the European war at least, to having a military target as the objective. Although a lot of the bombing was inaccurate enough— dropping through the overcast with the H2X . . . having it scattered around—so that the general effect was the same as area bombing. But the operation was directed toward a military target."[22]

Eaker filled in the story in another postwar interview. "I went as the Air Force representative with General Marshall to the conference in President Truman's office and I heard the conversation, the recommendations and decision announced by the President. [He] asked me to remain behind and when I did so, he said, 'Here is a letter to General Spaatz directing him to drop the atom bomb, and I trust you to deliver it." The written orders, transmitted to Spaatz on July 24, specified that after the first bomb was dropped others would be used as soon as they became available.[23]

A further sidebar to this story was disclosed in a 1975 interview with Robert Sherrod, who had been a distinguished combat correspondent in the Pacific and then editor of the *Saturday Evening Post.* Eaker told him: "Spaatz called me by radio-telephone . . . the scrambler, and said 'Does General MacArthur know about this?' I said, 'I don't know, but I suspect he doesn't.' He said, 'I feel very strongly that we should not drop this bomb without MacArthur being informed, since he is the theater commander.' " Eaker then called Marshall, who spoke to Truman and called back to say: "You are authorized by the President to tell General Spaatz that he may go personally to Manila and acquaint General MacArthur with his order. But no one else." Spaatz then flew to Manila, saw MacArthur and gave him the details, including the total confidentiality required. Eaker added, "MacArthur kept the faith."[24]

Following V-Day, Eaker was lionized by parades at Eden and San Antonio, Texas, and a reunion of the class of 1917 at Southeastern State College in Durant, Oklahoma. He flew to Durant in *Starduster* and was treated to "a downtown parade, assembly on the campus, a dinner . . . with his classmates, a boat-ride on Lake Texoma, a visit to the Dam, and a picnic supper at the home of Mrs. George Pendleton." A gold watch was bestowed upon him, and "Eaker Week" raised $408,358 for war bonds. Especially enjoyed were the evening with his college sweetheart and talking with many of his former teachers, notably Dr. Linscheid, of whom he said in his brief talk at the dinner: "I have been in many situations since I left Dr. Linscheid's care. I'll always remember his final words, 'Remember, the greatest quality of man is humility.' I have remembered that."[25]

The week of V-J Day he took a party of twelve, including the author, on a four-day swing through Germany, flying over Hamburg, Regensburg, the Remagen Bridge, a dozen battered cities in the Ruhr and elsewhere, and landing at specific targets of special interest, like the I.G. Farben chemical plant at Ludwigshafen. One day we spent in Berlin, inspecting the smashed Reichs Chancellery, going down in Hitler's bunker and again at Tempelhof to its underground Focke-Wulf plant. On the fourth day the party flew to Salzburg and drove to Berchtesgaden to tour "Eagle's Nest." Hitler's glamorous mountaintop chalet had been bombed flat, but the subterranean barracks and shelters were still intact, smelling musty. (They were eventually blown up lest the Führer's lair become a tourist attraction and a shrine to neo-Nazis.) Eaker then flew back to England for a few days of reunion with Portal, Harris, Slessor and others before returning reluctantly to the heavy task awaiting him in Washington —"the dismal prospect," he said, "of destroying, or being a major influence in destroying, the world's greatest Air Force, reducing it from 2,380,000 men to 400,000. And destroying it at a time when I realized that it was probably needed most, to defeat a greater tyranny than the two we had just defeated."[26]

Besides the obligatory demobilization of the army and the Army Air Forces, Arnold, Spaatz and Eaker faced the grueling duty of at last achieving air force independence. Arnold, though he did not actually retire until January of 1946, turned over virtually all these responsibilities to his two henchmen. Spaatz was always his designated successor and became the last CG of the AAF, with Eaker loyally continuing as deputy commander and chief of the air staff, though he pined to withdraw, writing Harris, who had already retired, in November 1945: "The date of my retirement has not been definitely set as yet. . . . I have agreed to stick with [Spaatz] until we get our legislation through Congress and the organization is pretty well along, but I told him I wanted to get out within a year. I shall then go to Oregon and start my own post-war plan. It will always include good fishing and salmon smoking for all of you."[27]

Truman, Spaatz and Eaker at the White House, August 1, 1946, designating it Air Force Day. It was the thirty-ninth anniversary of the inception of the Aeronautical Division of the Army Signal Corps with three men and no airplanes.

But achieving air force independence, which had seemed such a simple concept in the days of Billy Mitchell, proved remarkably difficult. This despite the full support of Truman as well as Marshall and then Eisenhower, who became chief of staff in November. Other factors had emerged from the victories of World War II. One of these was the conviction of Marshall and Eisenhower as well as almost everyone that unity of command in war was mandatory. A second was the new dominance of strategic war, which the air force leaders regarded as primarily a function of aerial bombardment. Spaatz put it: "Strategic bombardment is . . . the first war instrument of history capable of stopping the heart mechanism of a great industrialized enemy. It paralyzes his military power at the core." A third factor

444

was the last-minute appearance of atomic power on the scene. Which branch, army, navy or air, should control strategic use of the atomic weapon? Many committees set up among the services and Congress had studied these intertwining considerations, and Truman tried to put them all together in December 1945 by asking Congress to establish a single Department of National Defense in place of the existing War and Navy Departments and creation of a separate air force, coequal with the army and the navy.[28]

But the navy objected. Secretary of the Navy James V. Forrestal and the admirals feared that such a structure would cost the navy both its own air arm (as had happened in England when the RAF absorbed the British fleet's air arm) and also the Marine Corps. The navy strongly opposed a separate air force and opted for keeping the status quo, with coordination to be achieved through the Joint Chiefs of Staff and their committees, as in WW II. Months and months of hard work and contention ensued, involving layers and layers of plans and no small measure of heat. When the naval leaders argued that the task of the proposed civilian secretary was beyond the capacity of one man, Eisenhower told the Military Affairs Committee that, if such were the case, no one should be elected president.[29]

All this is too big a subject to go into extensively in this book, especially since the eventual solution was only the first of many compromises. Suffice it to say that Spaatz and Eaker captured victory for the air force, ably assisted by Stuart Symington, who succeeded Lovett as assistant secretary of war for air, and by Norstad, who had ended the war as chief of staff of the Twentieth Air Force and became the AAF's chief planning officer. Not until July 1947 was the National Security Act finally passed. It accomplished most of what the airmen wanted—unity of control (if not command) under a single cabinet officer, independence, equal status with the army and navy, and authority for all strategic air operations. But the navy kept its air arm, as did the marines theirs, and the army certain other flying elements. Eaker grumped that the act "legitimized four military air forces," to which Symington added, "I don't say this is a good book, but I do say it is a good chapter."[30]

With the requisite legislation at last on track, if not yet passed, the path was cleared for Spaatz to become the first chief of staff of the independent United States Air Force, with Symington the first secretary—appointments that took effect in September. Eaker was in line to follow Spaatz, and this was widely expected. But his mind had long been made up. At the end of February 1947 he put in for retirement in mid-June. Beforehand he called on Eisenhower, still army chief of staff, who was astonished, saying, "Ira, I thought you were going to take over after Tooey."[31] He also, of course, talked it all over with Spaatz, reiterating his firm belief that the "oldsters" should make room for the "next generation." Spaatz concurred, saying, "Okay, you do it first and I'll follow."[32] He did so a year later, turning the post over to Vandenburg in response, many thought, to political motives on Truman's part. Not so, Symington insisted, stating that he had told Spaatz the decision was "entirely" up to him and that Spaatz replied it was a choice between McNarney, an expert on logistics, and Vandenburg, a "fighting commander." They asked Eisenhower for an opinion and "Ike instantly said Vandenburg."[33]

The news of Eaker's intentions produced a deluge of letters, all offering praise and many expressing regret and surprise. With his usual scrupulous courtesy he answered them all, frequently offering insights into his motives, as, for example, in reply to the managing editor of the *Washington Post.* "I have no plan, prospect or commitment for any position in civil life. I may say that I have turned down some normally fairly tempting offers in the past few weeks. First I want to get a long and much needed rest; secondly, I want to write down a few things I have seen in 30 years of military service and particularly during the second world war that may have some interest. . . . The main reason, however, for my retirement is that I am gloomy about the future prospects for the security of our country. As I have gone about the country during the past 22 months urging an adequate security force, occasionally people have said or implied that I am an heir apparent preaching the maintenance of an empire in order to hold high rank and high command. It occurred to me that they might pay more attention to my warning when I am again a private citizen with no special or personal interest other than as a citizen. My diversions run a little more to fishing than to raising pullets or beefsteak. The locale of this weak streak will be manifested along the banks of the Rogue River in southern Oregon, perhaps in the vicinity of Medford. . . ."[34]

One of Eaker's last important actions in office was a five thousand-word lecture on June 5 to the National War College on "The Army Air Forces, Its Status, Plans and Policies." He roamed eloquently over the difficulties of disposing of "surplus property in the amount of twenty-five billion dollars, including more than 100,000 airplanes," the first steps toward rebuilding and the future of "push-button warfare," noted that "we counted more destroyed tanks and mechanized vehicles in the Rhône Valley after the invasion of southern France than the Germans used in the conquest of France," speculated about the size of future budgets and concluded:

> We wholeheartedly support General Eisenhower's oft-expressed view that it is not any one arm which wins a war but a well-balanced team composed of the three principal arms—land, sea and air—under a single leadership which wins battles and wars. We are determined . . . to cooperate with the other branches to this end. To do less would be folly in the atomic era, in these fateful times, for we agree with Mr. Lilienthal, the Chairman of the Atomic Energy Commission, who only the other day said: This [atomic energy] is indeed a great force we have in our hands. If in dealing with it we are too stupid, we may not have to worry about the ridicule of our descendants. We may have no descendants.[35]

That night at the officers club at Bolling Field he was the guest of honor at a farewell dinner where he and Ruth were given a large silver box covered with engraved signatures, and Spaatz made a wry

About to retire, Eaker receives an Oak Leaf Cluster for his Distinguished Service Medal from Eisenhower, as Spaatz looks on. Ike wrote Ira, ". . . your going will leave a gap that will never be completely filled. . . ."

and witty speech. "Back in January 1929 I saw more of Ira than I've ever seen before or since of any person. We spent 150 hours, 40 minutes and 15 seconds in the old Army plane, the *Question Mark*. Sometimes I think Ira Eaker has been trying for an endurance record with me ever since, and has given up at last. He just can't take me any longer."[36] On June 13, two days before Eaker left on his terminal leave, Eisenhower presented him with an Oak Leaf Cluster to his Distinguished Service Medal—one of the most important of the fifty-plus decorations Ruth carefully arranged in a four-drawer, velvet-lined spool cabinet. On the 14th he wrote the Civil Aeronautics Agency about getting a pilot's license, asking for his "old civil aeronautics license #126, if possible." That day the *New York Times* editorialized: "One of the great commanders of the Second World War . . . will doff his three stars tomorrow. . . . He will be sorely missed in the high councils of security. His retirement at 51, however, is the result of a deep conviction than he can be of more service outside of uniform than in. He intends to devote himself to the cause which he cherishes as earnestly—the cause of making the nation aware of the peril in which it stands if it allows itself to become weak in the air. . . ."[37]

But no award or commendation ever meant more to Eaker than the handwritten letter and four coins he received that week from Eisenhower, framed at once for his study wall:

Dear Ira

You may be entirely devoid of faith in good luck pieces. If so, the enclosed will, nevertheless, possibly serve to remind you of the days we spent together in World War II. They consist of a coin from Britain, one from Africa, a composite one from France, and a silver dollar from America, and were part of a collection I carried throughout the war. While I never accorded to them any mystic power, I never found that it hurt any to rub them a bit when the going was critical.

My best wishes will always follow you and yours. You deserve all that your fondest hopes can picture for a future life.

Your devoted friend,
Ike E[38]

Eaker in 1979 beside the Pentagon plaque displaying his portrait and those of the other five aviators who won the Special Gold Congressional Medal—the Wright brothers, Lindbergh, Mitchell and Yeager.

Mr. U.S. Air Force

25

". . . legendary, invisible, mysterious,
outrageous Howard Robard Hughes. . . ."

—*TIME* MAGAZINE

R UTH EAKER very much enjoyed Washington and the constant
stimulus of old friends and world leaders, the White House
receptions, the sense of being at the heart of things. "I didn't
really want Ira to retire or to leave," she said forty years later, "but
he was very tired and whatever he wanted suited me." On June 15
they moved out of their capacious, square, brick, two-story house,
quarters number 6 at Fort Myer in Arlington and headed for Oregon
in her brand-new Cadillac. "I cried all the way to Ohio," she added,
only half joking.[1]

Her husband had taken a shine to Medford when he brought the
20th Pursuit Group there for a "camp" in 1940 and met Glenn
Jackson. Medford is an unusually pretty town, situated in southwest
Oregon along the well-named Rogue River in a broad valley fes-
tooned with world-famous fruit orchards and girt by handsome
mountains. And it had a better-than-average small-town newspaper,
the *Medford Mail Tribune,* once winner of a Pulitzer Prize. When
Jackson joined Eaker's staff at Castle Coombe in 1943, went with him
to Italy and learned of his determination to take up journalism after
the war, he suggested that Medford might offer a good starting point.
Jackson mustered out in 1945, returned to Medford and learned that

Robert Ruhl, owner and editor of the paper, was considering selling it. Jackson and his family owned two other small papers in Oregon; to add the *Mail Tribune* would make a strong chain and power base. Eaker, a small-town boy by birth and at heart even after all his worldly experience, liked the proposal "to control the editorial policy of two or three small newspapers and radio stations and perhaps eventually get into politics." But when he and Ruth reached Medford late in June, they found that Ruhl had changed his mind.[2]

The Eakers spent a week in Medford looking for a house to buy or suitable land on which to build—all with the hope that Ruhl would change his mind again. Then they drove on to Los Angeles, planning a three-month vacation in a place where both had many friends and connections. These dated in part from days spent at Rockwell and then March Field, in part from the big concentration of aviation manufacturers (notably Donald Douglas and Dutch Kindelberger), and in part from their more recent links with the films. Willie Wyler was directing his famous war apologia, "The Best Years of Our Lives," Jimmy Stewart had been a B-24 group executive in the Eighth, Beirne Lay and Sy Bartlett were preparing "Twelve O'Clock High," and Ben Lyon and Bebe Daniels were living in a Santa Monica beach house while Ben served as casting director of Twentieth Century Fox. The author was also in Los Angeles, having been appointed West Coast editorial director for *Time, Life* and *Fortune.* Falling back into the role of aide, I rented the Eakers their first civilian residence, a humble bungalow on Veteran's Avenue in West Los Angeles. Ruth quickly found better quarters on the Santa Monica beach while her husband began work on some magazine articles and had several residual duties to perform before his retirement became official on August 31. On July 24 he flew to Oklahoma City for the unveiling of his portrait at the State Historical Society, getting chuckles from the audience in his speech afterward by saying: "Back in 1942 a certain A. Hitler promised his friends I would one day hang in Germany. But thanks to friends in the Historical Society I'll now hang in Oklahoma."[3] In August he was in and out of Washington twice. In L.A. he kept up a large correspondence, doing most of his own typing. He apologized for that in a letter to Bedell Smith, formerly Eisenhower's chief of staff and now ambassador to Russia, adding: "I have a fixed feeling that we are headed for trouble again and I am hopeful that I may be of more service beating a drum for national security out of uniform than in. . . . There is a good prospect that I may get mixed up in the country newspaper, small-town radio business. . . ."[4]

But Ruhl did not change his mind, and new opportunity knocked on the Eakers' Santa Monica door in the lanky person of Howard Hughes.

Eaker had met Hughes only twice. Once, just for lunch, was in 1938 as mentioned in chapter 8. The second time was in 1946. "One morning," Eaker recalled, "I read in the paper that Howard Hughes had crashed while testing a new photographic plane, the XF-II, his company was building for the Air Force. I called General Nathan Twining, then head of Wright Field and the Materiel Comand, and said, 'Nate, have we run out of test pilots? Why is a 40-year-old civilian, Howard Hughes, testing one of our experimental planes?' Twining said, 'I get your point. I'll take care of it.' " Some months later Sy Bartlett telephoned Eaker and asked if he would talk to Hughes, who thereupon came around to quarters number 6, Fort Myer on a Saturday afternoon to plead that he be allowed to "complete the test program. If I don't, some will say I am afraid to fly it because of my own accident. It is much safer for me to fly it than one of your young test pilots. I did many hours of taxi tests in the first article. I flew it and I know what happened." Eaker replied that he sympathized but that "it was my duty to protect the government interest, and I did not propose to alter my decision." Hughes asked if he could appeal to higher authority, and Eaker at once asked Spaatz, who lived two doors away, to come over. Hughes then announced, "If you will allow me to fly the tests on the plane, I'll sign an agreement that if I crack it up I pay for it." Spaatz replied, "If you'll do that, you can fly it."[5]

Now, in September 1947, Hughes, who lived in Los Angeles, looked up Eaker again. This time he began by saying he understood Eaker had retired, adding, "I would like you to join up with me." Eaker explained that he already had retirement plans in hand, but Hughes persisted, asking, "Will you listen to my proposition anyway?"[6]

When Eaker told him to go ahead, Hughes, who was very clever at luring any game he wished to catch, spoke in words that could not fail to appeal to Eaker's strong evangelical streak, especially when his Oregon plans had just come unstuck. "This country has been good to my father and me," Hughes began. "I think the United States is headed for dangerous times again. I believe the side with the best weapons will win the next war. I also believe the time will come again, as it did between the last two wars, when we shall neglect our defenses. It will be hard to get funds for new weapons as it was then. The most critical thing is that there will be inadequate funds for experimentation and research. I propose to take the profits from all my enterprises and establish a great laboratory, attract the most eminent scientists and give them ideal facilities with which to work. Then I'll say to the Army, Navy and Air Force, if there are any weapons they consider vital to our security and for which they cannot get funds, my laboratory will undertake the research and development.'"[7]

" 'How much,' asked Eaker, 'do you propose to devote annually to this effort?' He named a figure of several millions guaranteed and said he wanted me to assist him. . . . 'If you are that kind of a patriot,' I said, 'we'll try it for a year and see how it works out.' We shook hands and that was the only agreement we ever had with respect to employment, or ever needed, for that matter."[8]

The taproot of the Hughes fortune was the Hughes Tool Company, generally known as "Toolco," which his father, "Big Howard," had founded in Houston, Texas, after inventing the first oil-drill bit that would bore through rock. In 1924 when Big Howard died and his son, then eighteen, bought out the other relatives and became sole owner, Toolco was worth $750,000; when he himself died in 1976, a drug-sodden wreck at seventy, it was worth an estimated $2.3 billion. Since the oil drill was a simple device that earned more and more money, Hughes was happy to leave Toolco's management to others while he established himself in Los Angeles and drew capital from Houston whenever he chose—a few million to get into film making or to design airplanes and many, many millions when he bought control of RKO, the big Hollywood film studio, and 75 percent of Trans World Airlines. He was clearly gifted with an astonishing range of talents besides wealth and good looks. In films he won an Oscar within two years for a silent comedy and then produced the sensational "Hell's Angels," a WW I flying epic starring Ben Lyon and introducing a new sex goddess in Jean Harlow. As an airplane designer he created the D-1, a wooden racer in which he set a world speed record of 352 mph in 1935. And in 1938 he became a national hero with a ticker-tape parade in New York by girdling the globe in ninety-one hours and fourteen minutes in a

Lockheed he helped design, breaking the previous record by four days.[9]

But Hughes was also a maverick whose business methods drove his associates wild and whose ruthless, headstrong behavior got him into continuous trouble with the U.S. government and with the U.S. Air Force as he tried to develop his aviation activities into a meaningful role in ww II. Hughes Aircraft Company was his vehicle for this purpose, with headquarters in the Culver City section of Los Angeles. Its efforts, under a series of frustrated managers, resulted in two extravagant and utterly useless airplanes. One was the biggest plane ever built, the much-publicized "Spruce Goose," a flying boat made entirely of wood, with eight engines and a wingspread twice that of the B-29. Wood was used to save aluminum. The size was huge in order to carry as many as 700 troops into combat. It got into the air exactly once, two years after the war, when Hughes himself flew it for about a mile, 70 feet over the San Diego harbor. The other plane was the FX-II—the experimental photo-reconnaissance plane he crashed in Beverly Hills on its first test. It was an evolution of his D-I, originally made of wood, then converted to metal and long delayed by his persnickety supervision. It was beautiful looking, with twin booms flanking a short, needle-nosed cockpit. The two 3,000-HP engines each had two contra-rotating propellers positioned one behind the other. In his test run Hughes flouted the flight plan approved by the air force, taking off with twice the gas load specified and then proceeding to retract the landing gear, although that was something that was supposed to be left to a second test. The landing gear light flashed red for some time and then went off after he pushed forward hard on the controls. He could have landed quickly as the plan required but continued to circle over Los Angeles at 5,000 feet for more than an hour until the XF-II suddenly jerked "as if someone had tied a barn door broadside onto the right-hand wing." He thought it was the landing gear and monkeyed with the controls while fast losing altitude and then crashing into two houses in a swank residential section of Beverly Hills.[10]

No one on the ground was hurt, but Hughes suffered terrible injuries, chest crushed, many bones broken, left lung collapsed, extensive burns and cuts and his heart pushed to one side. The doctors did not expect him to live and gave him heavy injections of morphine to make his pain bearable. He survived, but it was the prolonged use

of painkillers that caused his eventual drug addiction, sporadic diso-
rientation and eventual madness. The air force investigating board
diagnosed the cause of the accident as pilot error, when Hughes
failed to observe that the right rear propeller, having lost oil, had
reversed its pitch. Hughes gamely test-flew the second FX-II, after
gaining Spaatz's approval, but the war was over and the air force,
never enthusiastic, canceled the contract for the remaining 98 originally ordered.[11]

When Eaker agreed to go to work for Hughes, the eccentric
billionaire had lost many millions ($7.5 million alone on the Spruce
Goose) at Hughes Aircraft, and that little subsidiary of Toolco, as
Fortune put it in a major article in February 1954, "was a putterer
on the fringes of the aircraft industry; its gross business was about
$2 million—on which it lost $750,000." Yet, as *Fortune* reported in
the same paragraph, by 1953 it "was one of the wonders of the
post-Korean industrial build-up. . . . Hughes Aircraft could be called
a major national resource, and sales were running at a clip of about
$200 million."[12]

Eaker was the chief architect of this remarkable turnaround.
Instead of taking direct command of decrepit little Hughes Aircraft
Co., he became a vice president of Toolco, specifically charged with
being its liaison officer with the aircraft subsidiary. He and Ruth
went to Houston for two months, staying at the Lamar Hotel and
trading in her Cadillac for a new Buick. Eaker quickly established
a good rapport with Noah Dietrich, the executive VP who managed
Toolco affairs, though Hughes was president, as he also continued
to be of Hughes Aircraft. As usual when faced with major new
responsibilities, Eaker focused first on finding key leaders for the
operations involved. He quickly made two superb appointments for
the Culver City plant. The first, as VP and general manager, was
retired Lt. Gen. Harold L. George, who had built and run the Air
Transport Command with huge success in WW II. Eaker was back
in Washington for a few days in November testifying at a Senate
investigation into alleged hanky-panky in the award of air force
contracts for Hughes and bumped into George, whom he had known
for years, in the Statler Hilton. They had breakfast together and
Eaker learned that George was out of a job. He had gone to Peru at
$50,000 per year to run its national airline, but the airline had run
out of capital. Eaker suggested that George join Hughes Aircraft.
George said he "couldn't imagine working for Howard Hughes."

But after some weeks of intricate jockeying with the complicated Californian, George took over as general manager, having won a flat promise from Hughes that "I will not interfere in the operation."[13]

The second, as VP and assistant general manager, was Charles B. "Tex" Thornton, who had just returned to civilian life as director of plans at Ford Motors in Detroit. As a WW II colonel in army air, Thornton had much to do with setting up its innovative and indispensable statistical control system. In June Thornton had written Eaker about his impending retirement. "I feel that I missed something during my military service in that I did not become well acquainted with you until the latter part of the war. However, it was sufficient for me to have the greatest respect for you, your ideas and your ability. . . . I would like to be one of the subscribers to your newspaper." Five months later, Thornton, disillusioned with Ford, got in touch with Eaker in Houston and switched jobs.[14] Both George and Thornton were at work in Culver City before the end of 1947, and Eaker soon moved his office there also, still in the role of liaison with Toolco and its temperamental owner. Ruth found them a white clapboard and red brick house with pretty, sloping grounds at the corner of Groverton Place and Sunset Boulevard just across from the UCLA campus. Eaker lost no time planting some avocado trees.

At Culver City George and Thornton found themselves in charge of about 800 workers doing such trivia as rebuilding a dozen used twin-engined transports Hughes himself had bought in Hawaii as a speculation plus a handful of tiny air force contracts for such things as ammunition belts and flexible feed chutes. Hard-boiled Noah Dietrich, a former accountant, told them sourly that their main task was to avoid losing money and that the best solution might be to shut Hughes Aircraft down completely. There was, however, one embryo project at Culver City that Eaker, George and Thornton quickly perceived had great promise—a small electronics lab run by two scientists in their thirties—Dr. Simon Ramo and Dr. Dean E. Wooldridge. Seeking an all-weather fire control system, the air force had given Ramo and Wooldridge and their 150-man staff two pilot studies, one to link an airborne search radar with a Sperry gunsight fitted with a computer and the other an electronic seeker for an air-to-air missile for bomber defense. Neither was urgent, and only a few hundred thousand dollars were committed. But in 1948 the air force became concerned over its lack of an all-weather intercepter and geared up for the Lockheed F-94, giving Hughes Aircraft an $8 million order for 200 of the Ramo-Wooldridge fire-control units. George said that small contract was the company's "dress rehearsal for mobilization" as the Korean war broke out in 1950.[15]

But there was more than that to the story of how Hughes Aircraft emerged in 1954 with what *Fortune* described as "a virtual monopoly of the Air Force's advanced electronic requirements." Behind the scenes Eaker played a decisive poker hand with Howard Hughes. "Shortly after we began to build up the laboratories . . . at Culver City," Eaker recounted, "Gen. K. B. Wolfe, who was then Deputy Chief of the Air Staff for Materiel, was visiting California, and he and I being old friends met for lunch. He told me an interesting story about his problems in developing radar for a series of needle-nosed fighter aircraft, to be known as the Century series since their designations were to be F-100, 101, etc." Wolfe went on to say that he had talked to all the companies that made the radar for the air force in WW II, telling them it was too heavy and would not fit into the needle nose of the new fighters and also lacked the range and other improvements "which the state of the art ought now be able to supply. . . . Each, without any collaboration and collusion, told him essentially the same thing. They said, 'We came to help you in the war years, and if you get in trouble we will help you again, but don't bother us now. We have to get back to our television sets, ice boxes and other civil consumption products. If we don't, our competitors will beat us out. . . .' " Eaker, recalling the pledge Hughes had made him, took General Wolfe to see him. Hughes listened attentively to Wolfe's story and then asked Eaker, "Do you think we can do it?" Eaker replied, "We can certainly try." Hughes then asked Wolfe what it would cost.[16]

As Eaker's narrative continued: "Wolfe said, 'Of course this is purely curbstone, but you have to build a laboratory and assemble the scientific talent, and I may tell you also that you will have to have the best radar. I can not and will not contract with you to develop it. I am going to publish specifications to the whole industry, and the company that turns out the best equipment will win the competition. I would say that you might have as much as six to ten million dollars in it by the time you have a prototype radar for test by the Air Force.'

"Howard considered Wolfe's statement for a few minutes, then turned to me and said, 'Let's do it.' That verbal directive was the only charter under which we operated during the next several years.

. . . The Hughes Aircraft Company increased from 800 people to 27,000. The new airborne radar was developed and all the fighter and intercepter aircraft developed for the next several years carried the Hughes radar and fire control devices. General Wolfe's estimate was slightly low. We spent more than 20 million dollars of Howard Hughes' money on the laboratories and in the production of the new models of radar and fire control apparatus before we received a penny of profit in return."[17]

Sales by Hughes Aircraft to the military rose from $8 million in 1949 to $197 million in 1953, while profits rose from $400,000 (after taxes) to $8 million.[18] This was more than Toolco itself was producing, and Noah Dietrich found it expedient to move his own office from Houston to Los Angeles. Hughes Aircraft in the space of five years had become the largest manufacturing facility of electronic equipment on the West Coast, with major operations in radar, in lasers, in communications satellites, in guided missiles, in computers, in propulsion and launching techniques and a raft of other arcane devices encompassed in the new word "avionics."[19] In a 1952 speech to the Air Force Association annual convention in Detroit Eaker commented that avionics had become so complex that they "must be designed into the airplane, or better still, the airplane must be designed around them. . . . We are not our own masters. The weapons race has already produced destructive devices of such speed and operating at such altitudes that the human mind and human muscular reaction is not fast enough." He warned that a pilot could no longer accomplish his mission at "transonic and supersonic speeds in all weather, day and night . . . without . . . automatic devices for . . . target finding, gun aiming, rocket and guided missile launching and control, bomb aiming, identification and navigation."[20]

During those several years of heady success from 1947 to 1952 at Hughes, Eaker, good executive that he was, carefully kept out of operational decisions at Culver City. He would go to his office there each morning, read and answer his considerable mail, study the latest reports of operations, chat with George or Thornton or the latter's bright new assistant, Roy Ash, and then go to the Bel Air Country Club for lunch and to play golf or bridge.

In the evenings there was the bright social life of Beverly Hills, with many stimulating overnight guests from elsewhere, Lindbergh being one. He took a walk through the UCLA campus and, true to his Lone Eagle persona, "expressed satisfaction that he had gone unrecognized by the thousands of students hurrying to classes."[21] Weekends in Beverly Hills Eaker often played tennis at the nearby estate of Willie Wyler. One player was his former sergeant, Sol Stameshkin, who had become a broker. Another was Sy Bartlett who once brought a personable young salesman named John Richardson to join the game. Eaker subsequently hired Richardson for Hughes Aircraft. Thirty years later, when the company was doing business in the billions annually, Richardson became its president. Contact with Howard Hughes himself was sporadic but amiable. His eccentricities were gradually worsening, but had not yet become extreme. Though often seen on the arm of a Hollywood star such as Ava Gardner and much talked about in the gossip columns as a "playboy," he was more and more devoting his attentions to a demure starlet named Jean Peters whom he eventually married. They came to the Eakers' house for dinner once and reciprocated the entertainment at the bungalow behind the Beverly Hills Hotel where Hughes was currently living. When Eaker needed to talk business with Toolco's president and owner, it was usually riding in a car at night on spectacular Mulholland Drive, which winds along the crest of the Santa Monica Mountains with the sparkling, endless spread of Los Angeles lights, fireflies on parade, to one side and those of the San Fernando Valley the other. "One reason," Eaker noted, "was un-

Among the aerospace leaders the Eakers met after their return to Washington was the Nazi-trained rocket specialist, Wernher von Braun.

doubtedly the fact that Howard could hear better in an automobile. Another was the fact that this gave complete security to his conversations. There could be no wire taps. . . ." It was, to be more blunt, a sign of his growing paranoia.[22]

"One night after we had finished several hours of conferences," Eaker continued, "Howard walked out to my car with me. We were standing under a street light and I pulled out a clipping from a gossip column which inferred that Howard had the finest stable of blondes in Hollywood and handed it to him, saying, 'It doesn't help us in our dealing with the seniors in government to have our owner represented as a playboy. Why do you permit this drivel to go unchallenged?' A tired smile traced his weary face as he said, 'In this strange motion picture world in which I operate, if they did not write that about me they might say I was queer. I would rather have it this way.' "[23]

On the average Eaker was away one day each week making a speech to an aircraft industries group, inspecting a new avionics development somewhere in the U.S. or keeping his fingers on the military pulse at the Pentagon. These were part of his assignment for Toolco, as tidily listed in a three-page memorandum insisted upon by Dietrich. For several years Eaker's writings for publication took a back seat to his speeches, but these sometimes broke into print prominently, as on March 15, 1948. That day Representative Lyndon B. Johnson, nearing the end of a decade in the House and about to become a senator, inserted a long speech on national security by Eaker into the *Congressional Record,* commenting: "General Eaker was the first one to tell us that having the second best Air Force was just like having the second best poker hand. No fighting son of Texas has contributed more tangibly to victory than General Eaker. . . ."[24] Johnson came from the same part of Texas as the Eakers and had been materially helped by Eaker's father in his first, very-close election to the House. So he was grateful. But, years later when LBJ was president and Eaker wrote a newspaper column in which he sharply criticized Johnson's handling of the war in Vietnam, the president drew him aside at the White House and asked, "Ira, why are you so critical of me?" "Because I think you are wrong, Mr. President," Eaker replied. Johnson never spoke to him again.[25]

Eaker's father died of a heart attack at seventy-nine in June, 1949. The general and his wife went to the funeral in Eden, Texas, and visited briefly with his brothers and their wives—solid, good people all, but none with anything like the breadth of accomplishment achieved by the oldest son.

Six months later the real father figure in Eaker's life, General Arnold, died as well, at age sixty-four after one more heart attack. He also had been living in California, near Hamilton Field, north of San Francisco, but the two men apparently never saw each other there despite many amiable letters back and forth and many invitations both ways. Arnold was frail physically and also financially, eking out a living beyond his pension from magazine articles, a venture in raising beef and the advance royalties of his final book, *Global Mission,* published in 1949. Hughes and Eaker jointly bought one hundred copies, got Arnold to autograph them and sent them to Churchill, Portal, Slessor, Alexander and other English wartime associates plus some of the U.S. Air Force aces mentioned in the volume. Many vivid letters came back, and one of them (from Admiral Stark) prompted Eaker's last letter to his air force mentor. He added: "As soon as I know when Tooey and Ruth can be here I will be in touch with you, and if you and Bee can come down, I will make reservations in the desert. It will be a great thing for the six of us to get together for a week or so and do a little reminiscing. . . ." Arnold replied on the 9th: "Bee and I will keep our fingers crossed for the desert reunion. That would be grand!" It was their last exchange. When the news of Arnold's death reached Culver City on the 16th Ruth and Ira Eaker sent Bee Arnold a telegram reading: "There is of course no real solace for you in this tragic time. It must be a source of great pride to you, however, as it is to all of us who worked under General Arnold's able supervision during the past 30 years in the Air Force, to know that he carved a great and unique place in American history which will always be accorded to him and grow in stature with the receding years. . . ."[26]

There were trips abroad. A cable from London to Culver City in June 1950 read, "Will you and Mrs. Eaker give us the pleasure of lunching with us on Tuesday, June 27th at 1:15 at 28 Hyde Park Gate? —Clementine Churchill." They accepted. A year later they mounted the steps of St. Paul's together to hear Eisenhower dedicate its new American chapel in a superb speech to a glittering throng that included the queen and the two princesses, the Churchills, Spaatz, Slessor, Trenchard, Mountbatten and many, many other wartime comrades.

Every spring Eaker took a week to join a dozen of the army air

One of the annual reunions held at Jock Whitney's Greenwood Plantation, Thomasville, Georgia. Front row, l. to r.: Spaatz, W.H. Stovall, Roy Atwood, Whitney. Second row, l. to r.: Hunter, Eaker, Everett Cook, Anderson.

leaders, who were stationed in Europe in WW II, for bird-shooting by day and poker by night at Jock Whitney's plantation in Thomasville, Georgia. In a 1947 letter to Fechet after one such reunion Eaker reported, "I shot 18 quail and one wild turkey and had a most enjoyable time, two days of horseback riding all day with a little of the usual pastime in the evening at which I did very well. . . ."

Between Labor Day and the first week of October for eighteen years he and Spaatz, Lessig, Jackson and a few other cronies rendezvoused in Medford "to fish, play poker and rough it." Though denied his newspaper opportunity there, Eaker built a cabin halfway down the Rogue River to the Pacific that (until a small airstrip was added) could be reached only by shooting the rapids downstream or bucking them from the ocean. It had no plumbing, no electricity, no telephone. Ruth Spaatz, who once made the jolting upstream trip to inspect the cabin, quipped that "it was not built for co-educational fun." But the men relished it, following a ritual Lessig described. "Spaatz was the senior, so we automatically took our guidelines from him each morning after breakfast. We'd sit around having coffee on the porch watching that beautiful river rush by, but not until Tooey would say, 'Well, guess it's time for a little fishing,' would any of us stir."[27]

This serene, fulfilling and important way of life began to fall apart in 1951 when the unpredictable Howard Hughes moved his own base of operations to Las Vegas, gradually accumulating large holdings of real estate and resort hotels. To duck California's heavy taxes, he suggested that the Ramo-Wooldridge lab, which was clamoring for expansion, should move to Las Vegas too. The two scientists, with George's backing, refused. When Hughes then held up approval of expansion funds for Culver City, Ramo and Wooldridge went to him to say they would have to notify the air force that the company's scheduled deliveries could not be met. For the moment Hughes appeared to yield. But bickering grew on many related issues, a major one being the demand for some sort of equity in the company itself —something he had never granted anyone. Noah Dietrich tried to take charge behind George's back, and Eaker tried fruitlessly to pour oil on troubled waters. In mid-August 1953 the controversy exploded. Ramo and Wooldridge were the first to go, resigning to join forces with small Thompson Products of Cleveland in what grew into TRW, Inc., a giant of the space industry. Sixteen senior members of the staff followed. George gamely tried to hold the company together but demanded that a five-man committee, including outsiders, be set up as a quasi board of directors to establish corporate policy. "You are proposing to take from me the right to manage my own property," Hughes snorted. "I'll burn down the plant first." "You are accomplishing the same effect without matches," was George's reply. He too resigned. Thornton and Ash went next—to found an enterprise that grew into another giant—Litton Industries.[28]

The air force became understandably distraught. Its then secretary, an aviation executive of great experience named Harold Talbott, rushed to Los Angeles with his able assistant secretary for materiel, Roger Lewis. At a Beverly Hills Hotel lunch Hughes greeted them in a sports jacket and avoided serious talk. The three then drove to Culver City where Lewis addressed the remaining scientific staff, which was threatening to quit en masse. As Hughes listened stonily, Lewis besought them to delay action while the management problems were resolved. Privately Talbott told Hughes, "You have made a hell of a mess of a great property and, by God, so long as I am Secretary of the Air Force you're not going to get another dollar of new business." Hughes replied, "If you mean to tell me that the government is prepared to destroy a business merely on the unfounded charges of a few disgruntled employees, then you are introducing Socialism, if not Communism." But he saw the handwriting on the wall and asked for—and obtained—ninety days grace. On December 17, 1953, the last of the ninety days, he transferred the entire Hughes Aircraft Company and its assets to a newly set up nonprofit corporation whose name became the Howard Hughes Medical Institute, chartered in Florida but with offices and plant to remain in Culver City. The HHMI's specialty would be "principally the field of medical research and medical education." Hughes himself would be the sole trustee.[29]

On the face of it this startling step seemed a magnanimous demonstration of public spirit and integrity by the notoriously power-hungry Howard Hughes. It made good on his pledge to Ira Eaker six years before. It went far toward palliating the jittery scientists at Culver City. It cleared the decks with the angry air force leadership. It brought hosannas from the press. And it certainly resulted in pulling Hughes Aircraft Company back from the brink of collapse or substantial decay. All that was fine. But to the sharp eyes of the Internal Revenue Service it was a pellucid ploy. The IRS refused to grant the HHMI tax-exempt status.

What Hughes had done was a skillful piece of financial slight of hand. Toolco *gave* HHMI its patents, trademarks, goodwill and stock in a donation valued at a mere $34,463. Toolco *sold* to HHMI inventories and receivables on government contracts amounting to $74,618,038. HHMI had no cash to pay for these assets, so it assumed a debt to Toolco of $56,574,738, plus a promissory note for the $18,043,300 difference. The note was for three years at 4 percent annually. Toolco also leased to HHMI the land and buildings at Culver City at a rental that would bring in $26 million over the ten years of the lease. Finally, HHMI subleased the same Culver City property to Hughes Aircraft Company for $30,600,000 for the same period.[30]

Unscrupulous and sharp though this certainly was, it was also very, very clever—yet another mark of the unquestionable genius in Howard Hughes's devious mind. It was neatly summarized by Donald Bartlett and James B. Steele in their *Empire, the Life, Legend and Madness of Howard Hughes:*

> Howard Hughes, multimillionaire, had created a charity without donating a single penny in cash or stock that paid dividends, or any real estate. The charity started life with a debt of $18,043,300 to the man who founded it, meaning that Hughes would collect millions of dollars in interest payments from his own charity. The agreements showed that Hughes had no intention of giving money to his medical research institute for at least a decade, if ever. Instead, the institute's only source of income would be payments from the aircraft company for the real estate and fixed assets subleased to [it].
>
> At the same time, the Hughes Tool Company could deduct its lease payments to the medical institute on its federal income tax return. . . . Even better, the aircraft company's cost of subleasing buildings from the medical institute could be passed along to the American taxpayer. The $30.6 million sublease represented an additional cost of doing business, a cost that Hughes Aircraft could tack on the bill it sent to the U.S. government for work on military contracts—its only source of income.
>
> In short, Hughes had created the ultimate charity: the American taxpayer was to pick up the entire bill for the Howard Hughes Medical Institute, while Hughes basked in the warm glow of testimonials to his philanthropy and quietly collected money from his own charity.[31]

When the IRS in 1955 understandably refused tax-exempt status for HHMI, Howard Hughes reacted with fury and political cunning, many lurid details of which (including payments to President Nixon's brother) are spelled out in the Bartlett and Steele book. In March 1957 the IRS abruptly reversed its original decision but refused to explain why. Once again Howard Hughes remained king of his own castle.[32]

Ira Eaker's flight plan during all this tricky turbulence makes an instructive example of his extraordinary (some would say exaggerated) sense of loyalty. He understood little about the financial shenanigans for he was inexperienced and naive in monetary matters, never having had any capital of his own nor any money to spare beyond his military pay until he joined Toolco at $50,000 a year in

1947. He did, however, have a very strong sense of duty, and hence loyalty, to anyone he was reporting to, whether it be the imperious General Arnold or the sly Howard Hughes. In both those instances, and, in fact, in every aspect of his long life, his overriding loyalty was to the air force. Hughes had backed him fully in his reorganization of Hughes Aircraft—with spectacular results. When the squabbles in Culver City broke out Eaker saw it as his first duty to preserve the company, not for Toolco or for Howard Hughes so much as for the national well-being. George had similar broad-gauge motivations, but quit in frustrated disgust. The others who quit too—Ramo, Wooldridge, Thornton, Ash and the scientists down the line—did so not solely in disgust but in order to build empires of their own. Eaker sought no new empire, nor was he hungry for more money or power at Toolco or in Culver City. His administrative boss, Noah Dietrich, stayed on too, but connived constantly to take over when the increasing mental instability of Howard Hughes gave him the chance.[33]

To run Hughes Aircraft in George's place, Dietrich found another man of exceptional talent—Canadian-born Lawrence A. "Pat" Hyland, chairman of Bendix Aviation Corp. Tall, soft-spoken and only a year younger than Eaker, he had served in WW I as a sergeant in the American army, become a naturalized citizen and a specialist in radio research, joining Bendix in 1937. He was brought to Dietrich's attention by a brilliant young aeronautical engineer named Allen E. Puckett, who was then on the scientific staff at Hughes Aircraft and rose in turn to be its president and chief executive officer in 1978. At Culver City, Hyland expanded Hughes Aircraft sales from $200 million in 1954 to more than $5 billion when he retired to chairman emeritus in 1979. The first, transitional months were very touch and go, however, and Hyland was explicit in his thanks to Eaker for surviving that period. "Ira," he said, "was one of the few that remained after the big hassle that took place in 1954 . . . when about 100 people from the topside of the management . . . together with Ramo and Wooldridge departed. He was occupying the corner office, as he should have because he was the elder statesman at the time. . . . He was particularly helpful in straightening out our responsibilities with the Air Force and the Navy, which were in a pretty sorry state because of the radical changes in management. . . ."[34]

By 1957 Hughes Aircraft was again rolling smoothly, but Hughes himself was more and more reclusive, sometimes literally impossible to reach. Increasingly paranoid, he alternated between periods of brilliance and stupor and was well aware of his vulnerability. Tipped off that Dietrich was on the verge of trying to have him declared mentally incompetent, he fired him in May. Eaker was not involved, and there is no evidence to suggest that Hughes thought he was. But the harsh fact remained that the tragic tycoon stayed walled off in Las Vegas, no longer apparently interested in Hughes Aircraft, where Hyland, at the insistance of the air force, had an autonomy never enjoyed by George. One day that summer, his patience gone, Eaker sent a message to Las Vegas, saying he had an urgent matter he must discuss with Howard Hughes and that if there were no reply he would resign. There was no reply. They never saw each other again.[35]

It would seem natural that Eaker might have been resentful. But the simple fact is that he was not. Rather, he was just sorrowful. Steadfastly over the years he avoided criticism of his former boss, acknowledging his quirks and oddball behavior in the same way one might talk about the limitations of a man who has suffered a stroke or is drifting into senility—sad medical facts but not faults of character. His interpretation may have been naive, but it was genuine. He summarized it blandly in 1962: "Knowing of my ten years association with Howard Hughes, friends often ask me about his reported eccentricities. My considered reply always is this. If as many people had worked on me trying to take money away from me as have plagued Howard, I should probably have more peculiarities than he has. If I had been subjected to his environment, to his tragedies, to his temptations and to his fabulous financial successes, and had come through the reserved, sincere, earnest, intelligent individual I always found him to be, I should be happy indeed."[36]

26

"Anybody who ever planned to fight a frugal war, lost. War is the most wasteful enterprise ever devised by man. In warfare only one thing is more expensive than victory, and that is defeat."

—EAKER IN A 1965 COLUMN

D ONALD W. DOUGLAS, founder in 1920 and still in 1957 the gentle presiding genius of the famous Douglas Aircraft Company, a few miles up the Coast from Culver City, heard the news of Eaker's resignation from Hughes and immediately made him a proposal—to become a corporate director and open a Washington office to represent Douglas Aircraft at the highest levels of the Pentagon, the Congress and the White House as the Eisenhower presidency neared its end. Eaker, ever the firehorse, was enthusiastic at once. Ruth, sorry to leave Washington a decade before, now found herself beguiled by California life-styles and her own exquisite house. But, as always, "whatever Ira wanted was all right with me." First they rented a house in Georgetown and then bought 2202 Decatur Place, NW, a narrow, three-story town house just off Massachusetts Avenue and two miles from the White House. There were no more avocado trees, but there were a small terrace and garden in back reached through glass doors from the cellar-level dining room.[1]

During World War II Douglas Aircraft had prospered, as indeed did all the nation's plane makers beneath the cornucopia of U.S. war production. But it had lost its prewar eminence as leader of the industry when Boeing's B-17 and B-29 moved to the fore. Douglas made earnest efforts to regain position but fumbled them. Both its management methods and its technology were "old-fashioned" in the brave new world of jets and avionics. Establishing a Washington office was too little a step. Eaker was not expected to lobby or to be a Douglas salesman (he would have refused either role). Rather, his assignment was to get shrewd guidance about the future trends of munitions expenditure and policy thinking. At the end of his first year, in a note to himself prior to the January 1959 board meeting he jotted down: "Concern over failure to win major competitions. . . . Prospects for the future: Grim, due to many factors, including 1) Reduced defense buying, 2) The Weapons Systems concepts, 3) Keener competition, 4) Transition to jets. . . ."

He had quickly obtained direct access to the thinking of the Pentagon leaders, all of whom were old friends and many his former subordinates. Twining, for example, had become chief of the air staff and then chairman of the Joint Chiefs. LeMay presently succeeded him. The latter told Eaker in 1960, in words he promptly passed along to Douglas, much of whose production was still geared to propeller-driven planes, that "the Air Force would buy no more propeller aircraft except over his dead body." That year too Eaker was one of a group of seventy-two executives from the U.S. aircraft industry who spent two weeks touring NATO commands in Europe. In his report to the Douglas board he noted the speed with which West Germany was rebuilding and the reverse in East Germany, observed that de Gaulle was expected to become "less contentious" and stated flatly that "the present NATO Armed Forces could not prevent Russia overrunning Western Europe without wide-scale use of atomic weapons." He concluded with a review of "the political climate in Washington," saying, "Three months ago I reported a sensing in Washington that Nixon stood a good chance to beat any Democrat likely to be nominated. Lately there has been a considerable shift. . . ." Just before the election he reported: "The next great issue in national security which will face the new administration . . . may well be labeled 'Weapons and Space'. . . . Recently the Air Force called upon several organizations, including Douglas, to make a study of weapons and space. The Douglas presentation to the Air Staff . . . created tremendous interest. The Douglas study showed that for a very modest expenditure weapons can be developed and placed in space which can completely dominate the earth." That sounds like a line from President Reagan's "Star Wars" proposal in 1984, but it was phrased in 1960.[2]

Douglas Aircraft did not succeed in its come-back struggle. In 1967 it was obliged to submerge into what became McDonnell-Douglas Corp. Eaker had left the Douglas board six years earlier, in October 1961, when he reached the mandatory retirement age of sixty-five. Douglas simultaneously gave up the Washington office, but Eaker kept it in his own name and rapidly acquired another major aerospace enterprise as his employer—none other than the Hughes Aircraft Company. This time Howard Hughes himself had nothing to do with it (he had turned his back on the Culver City plant). But Frank William Gay, who had replaced Noah Dietrich as his chief henchman, and Hughes's secretary for thirty years, Miss Nadine Henley, remained very aware of how valuable Eaker had been. So did Hyland, who recalled: "We felt that most of the things that Ira believed in we believed in too. Being a defense company, we could not directly do some of these things, but Ira did them on his own. We not only allowed him but encouraged him to do so."[3]

Eaker, in short, was at last free to revert to the journalistic goal he had dreamed about for Medford. He had learned in the interim, as all professional journalists do, that a writer, no matter how talented or persuasive, is always more effective in reaching and influencing an audience if he has a power base. The Washington bureau chief of a great newspaper such as the *New York Times* or even a small one like the *Santa Fe New Mexican* has more clout than the same reporter would on his own—clout measured in four ways: financial back-up, ready access to prime sources, recognized status as a spokesman and an established audience awaiting his wisdom. Eaker now had the first three of these attributes. He had financial independence in the form of an office and secretary plus a $50,000 annual consulting fee from Hughes Aircraft with no administrative responsibilities—this on top of generous pensions from the air force and from Douglas. He knew everybody who was anybody in the aerospace world as well as the top military and political leaders in the U.S. and abroad. And he possessed universal respect both as a war hero and as an immensely successful aviation industry expert. All he lacked was the built-in audience, and this he set about creating forthwith.

His first step was to start a weekly newspaper column on the broad themes of national security and American military strength

473

(or weakness). It began, appropriately, in Texas, where a good friend was Houston Harte, publisher of the *San Angelo Standard Times* and several other small dailies in the area. Harte had an unusual hobby —whenever a Texan general or admiral of his acquaintence appeared on the cover of *Time* magazine, Harte would buy the original art work and give it to the family of the officer. Eaker's picture embellished *Time*'s cover on August 30, 1943, and Harte at once purchased the original painting by Ernest Hamlin Baker and gave it to Ruth. Twenty-one years later, when the Eakers were visiting in Texas and the general broached the idea of a regular column, Harte offered to give it a try. The column was a quick success, and Eaker wrote it for eighteen years, missing only one week. It was syndicated first by the Copley News Service, whose client list grew from three hundred to fourteen hundred papers between then and 1974 when he transferred to the Los Angeles Times Syndicate. Most of the clients were small dailies or weeklies that bought a package of material from the syndicate and used whatever they had room for. The Copley chain estimated that "about half"—i.e. seven hundred papers—used the Eaker column. It also appeared regularly, however, in some national media—*Air Force Times,* for example, always ran it. The monetary return was minimal—$50 per column as part of the package.[4]

But Eaker was not writing for money. He strove to be a sort of Paul Revere or Johnny Appleseed, spreading the word as effectively as he could about the dire dangers he believed America faced. He had come back from Europe in 1945 deeply alarmed by his experiences with the Soviets, and nothing in the intervening years had lessened his concern. The nation had squeaked through the Korean war by a mixture of luck and Truman's courage, but without a clear-cut victory. Succeeding crises—the Berlin Wall, the Bay of Pigs and Vietnam being the most obvious—as well as the incessant jockeying among the four services for money and weapons and a coherent national defense policy, gave him endless opportunity to cry havoc and suggest alternatives. Hyland put it well: "He was occupying a position that was very badly needed in the country at that time. I happened to be chairman of the Strategic Weapons Section of the Central Intelligence Agency for about ten or fifteen years when military activities under various administrations were going downhill pretty fast. . . . During those years the whole military picture, the way in which to fight a war, was going through a radical change. . . . The enormity of the change is something you just can't comprehend. . . . The position that we were in during those years was that we were cutting back our military appropriations by 10% a year while the Russians were adding 10% a year. And those were the critical years in which Ira helped keep the spark alive throughout the country. Ira was one of those who kept stoking this little bit of a flame that kept it going until such time as it was needed. . . . He got the message across that we were losing ground in our defense policy and that it was very important we do something about it. . . . Those things are very definitely things that you can't put numbers on, but I know from the feedback that we got from various places at various times that he was heard and admired and, I think, was a very real force in the country."[5]

A weekly column appearing for the most part in minor papers could not, of course, account for that much national impact even though supplemented by many other magazine articles. In addition Eaker undertook a steady regimen of speeches and lectures—not for money (though he would accept an honorarium if it were offered) but to plant ideas in fertile ground. His audiences were rarely big or individually significant, running at the rate of about two a month in organizations such as the Wings Club in New York, the Reserve Officers Association in El Paso, the American Ordnance Association in Orlando and—frequently—the Air War College in Montgomery, Alabama. Whenever he made a speech or wrote a column he especially liked, he merchandized it shrewdly, using techniques he had learned while an army air staff officer in Washington in the hungry days of the 1930s when he observed that a few words in the right place were worth millions tossed to the public at large. His method could be likened to precision bombing. He would send a copy of something to a congressman or a senator he knew to have a particular interest in the subject, and, very often, it would wind up being inserted in the Congressional Record. Between 1957 and 1981 the Air University Index of Military Periodicals lists 329 articles by Ira Eaker. Of these or his speeches, the Congressional Record reprinted 60. Though he had never voted while in uniform, Eaker became an increasingly conservative "Eisenhower Republican." But he habitually avoided party differences by "sticking to the high ground of the national need." On both sides of the aisle he became one of the most cited and most believed outside commentators on national defense.

He was no Walter Lippmann, as he well knew. The *New York Herald Tribune,* where Lippmann got his start and which now belonged to Jock Whitney, rejected the Eaker column as "too narrowly focused to be used regularly." The column and also his speeches tended to be staccato and pungent rather than philosophic or above the battle. But he did indeed have the knack Clare Boothe Luce noted: "He could express a great deal in a few words. His columns were often nuggets of strong thought." As defense secretaries and chiefs of staff came and went, Eaker's quiet, reasoned words became a stream of continuity in Congress and around the nation, always on the side of greater preparedness and unrelenting suspicion of Soviet motives and methods. In 1977 Senator Barry Goldwater of Arizona called Eaker "one of our nation's most important military spokesmen."

Here are some examples:

1947: Not long ago I was talking on a subject which had been assigned to me—A Brief Look at Two Wars, The Last One and the Next One—when a heckler arose in the audience and said: "There you go, you military men, talking about war. That's what causes war." Although a bit taken aback by the interruption I recovered in time to say what I think is absolutely true: It had not occurred to me that when the preacher preaches about sin that he is encouraging sin; neither had it occurred to me that when the doctor talks about disease he is promoting disease. But this I can say to you— of all the men in the world, the man who hates war most is the man who has to fight it. . . .

The proposition that a military force is designed for the winning of war is an old one indeed. The theory rode with Genghis Khan, with Napoleon, and with Hitler's fanatic legions. There is a new proposition I should like to present for your consideration and that is this: let us provide military forces for the preservation of peace and not for the prosecution of war. . . .

My greatest concern regarding our military establishment in the years which lie ahead is this: I fear that we shall spend vast sums needlessly and wastefully because we are not building the right kind of military establishment and we are not providing keen, alert management and requiring our military leaders to operate their establishment in a businesslike way. . . ."

1963: May we always remember that *men* win or lose wars. There is evidence that in our weapons making and war planning we have gone overboard on science and have overlooked the importance of man power. Twenty years ago one man, Churchill, saved England. During those times one man, a madman, Hitler, lost the war for Germany. Men will always make the decisions; decisions will always be decisive. . . .

It ought to be obvious to the fuzzy-minded pacifists that Russian leadership can not be trusted. Their word is worthless. They are still dedicated to the Lenin theory that the end justifies the means. It ought to be clear also that firmness, a convincing demonstration that we will fight for our rights, is the only way to deal with Russia. . . ."

1965: The speed of present day communications and the power of modern weapons could combine as the reason or excuse for making tactical decisions, commanding troops on the battlefield, from Washington. . . . This must be resisted and avoided at all costs. Every battle of the future will be a disaster like that of the Bay of Pigs if tactical decisions are made by senior political leaders. Germany was doomed when Hitler took command of German troops in the field.

1966: An examination of the war in Vietnam reveals a strange anomaly. There is no single commander of all forces engaged there as there was against the Nazis in Europe (Eisenhower) or against Japan (MacArthur) in World War II. There was also unified command in Korea.

In Vietnam, Gen. Westmoreland commands U.S. troops plus the Marine divisions, the Republic of Korea division, the battalions from Australia and the Philippines and New Zealand. The tactical air forces supporting ground forces are also under his control.

He does not command the naval carriers in the Bay of Tonkin, the air forces engaged in attacks on North Vietnam nor the B-52 SAC bombers operating on call from Guam. These naval forces are under the command of CINCPAC (Commander in Chief, Pacific), headquartered in Honolulu, while the SAC bombers are under the U.S. Strategic Air Command. Surprisingly, Westmoreland does not command the 300,000 South Vietnamese ground forces fighting alongside his own troops, although he supplies their weapons and much of their air support. . . .

To illustrate the command complexity in Vietnam, let us suppose that a great fire rages in Baltimore—half the city is burning; Washington, Philadelphia and New York rush fire-fighting equipment to the scene but insist that their fire companies remain under the direction of their respective fire chiefs. . . .

Any fire needs a single chief for all fire-fighting forces involved, and he wants to be at the scene of the fire. War, like a fire, demands unified command and the leader should be in the war zone.

1967: The draft is not the answer to military man power requirements today because it is grossly inadequate and unfair. It is inadequate because it does not supply the type of man power required in the military services today. Weapons are now so complicated and require such technical competence and skill for their operation and maintenance that it is absurd to expect short-term trainees to man them effectively.

The draft is inequitable because it picks boys and often favors married men and college students. I am ashamed of our people and our leaders when I read that 60% of those killed in Vietnam are 17, 18 and 19-year-old boys. War is a man's job. The draft of minors makes no more sense than the Children's Crusade of the Middle Ages. . . .

The present draft system should be replaced by a professional defense force of about 1,500,000 skilled, eager volunteers to man our quick reaction defenses—air defenses, anti-submarine defenses, anti-missile systems and the strategic retaliatory forces (bombers, ICBMs and missile-firing submarines). . . .

1971: What I want, what this country must have, is a strategic force of such size and composition that no enemy will ever dare to launch that massive nuclear first strike. We have had such a force, and it has kept the uneasy nuclear truce for two decades. We have lost it. We must never cease our effort until we get it back. That is our highest national priority.

1971: In his State of the World Message to Congress on February 18th the President [Nixon] suggested a new title—'realistic deterrence.' I don't know how that translates into Russian, but I know how 'strategic superiority' translates. So do the Reds.

1971: Today there is much hopeful talk about substituting negotiation for confrontation. I think I can tell you when nations can survive without military power. When the citizens of our countries no longer need the protection of local police, when they no longer have to lock their doors against hostile intruders, when all the people of the earth have reached that happy state of education, morality and freedom from crime, then nations, which are only combinations of people, can survive without military defenders.[6]

Among those outside of Washington who took note of Eaker's crusade was the unusual Dr. Arthur G. B. Metcalf, born in Boston in 1908. In quick sequence he was a student, alumnus and teacher at M.I.T., Boston University and Harvard, test pilot, lieutenant colonel in army air in WW II, professor of physics at Boston University and inventor of a variant of the "electric eye" for controlling electronic power generation. The invention prompted him to form the Electronics Company of America in 1954 to exploit it, rapidly becoming very wealthy and enjoying such extracurricular activities as piloting his own P-51 over the New England hills and becoming chairman of the board of Boston University. In 1972, disturbed by the growing superiority of Soviet arms to those of NATO and the U.S., he "thought it would be a good thing to . . . give a voice to the professional military. I noticed that all the newspapers and most of the slick magazines gave very little opportunity in their pages for presenting

Eaker, Metcalf and Adm. Harold Baker at a U.S. Strategic Institute planning session.

the views of military men. . . . Most writing in the military and strategic field was done by academics who wrote largely for each other. . . . Many of these authorities on nuclear weapons and war waging . . . had indeed no military experience of any kind. . . ."[7]

Metcalf decided to form the United States Strategic Institute as a nonprofit activity that he himself "would fund rather extensively" and that would have as its main purpose the publication of a quarterly *Strategic Review* plus occasional *Reports* on strategic subjects. Metcalf believed the venture needed "just the right leadership if it was going to be taken seriously. I had over the years read many military journals and I always came back to the feeling that General Ira Eaker was not only the most expressive voice heard in those journals . . . but his view and understanding of the application of air power was perhaps foremost among all airmen, including people presently in the Air Force." Since he did not know Eaker, he asked a mutual friend, retired Adm. Harold Baker, to call on the general and enlist him as the founding president. Eaker was then seventy-six and commented that "he had a great many things to do." But he agreed, thus beginning an important new friendship and adding a gratifying new dimension to his role as aerospace spokesman.[8]

The first quarterly issue of *Strategic Review* appeared in April

1973, handsomely bound in glistening white kromekote and carrying 180 pages of sober articles deliberately pitched above the ken of the layman. "It was not our intention," said Metcalf, "to try to reach the general public. That was too big a job for us. We wanted to confine our list of members of the Strategic Institute to that small group of decision makers we could reach—in the military both at home and abroad, in the Congress and in patriotic institutions. We pawed over many, many lists of names that we conjured up from our own acquaintanceships. . . ." The result, after several years, was a blue-ribbon membership at $25 per year of about one thousand individuals, and some three thousand subscriptions at $18 from assorted centers of influence such as the Africa Institute, Pretoria; the Embassy of the USSR, Washington; the Ford Foundation, N.Y.; Harvard's Center for International Affairs; Institut für Internationale Politik und Wirtschaft der DDR, German Democratic Republic; Ministry of Defense, Tel Aviv; Nato Library, Brussels; the PLO, Beirut; the Rand Corporation, California; the White House; and several hundred military and foreign affairs libraries all over the globe. The *Strategic Review,* in short, was another example of seeking broad influence through pinpointing precise targets.[9]

Its editorial credo, as voiced in the first issue, was succinct: "It has been generally noted that little has been written by Armed Forces seniors, active or retired, on national strategic doctrine and the essential elements of a sound national security. Instead, most of the writing on strategy and military policy has been contributed by academicians without military education, training or experience with conflict. We believe that this can be a hazard to sound national defense and vital decision-making in the thermonuclear age. We propose, therefore, to encourage military professionals and others skilled in the military art to express their views on those strategic concepts which they believe important to our security. We propose to provide an authoritative journal . . . to ensure that these ideas reach our governmental leadership and the public, who must together make the critical decisions upon which the national future depends. . . ."[10]

The five articles that made up the first forty pages of Volume I, Number 1 fully met this description. The first three were lined up by Eaker. The lead piece was by Gen. Bruce K. Holloway, retired chief of the Strategic Air Command, on "Reflections on Nuclear Strategy and the Nixon Doctrine." This was followed by an interview with Adm. John S. McCain, Jr., recently retired CINCPAC (commander in chief, Pacific) on "Our Pacific Interests." The third article, "Technology: The Mold for Future Strategy," was a coup, for the author, Gen. George S. Brown, was appointed the new chief of staff of the air force the week it appeared. There followed two pieces, one on "The Role of the Submarine in the Strategic Balance" by retired Vice Adm. Ruthven E. Libby, and "Arms Control and Defense Spending" by retired air force Col. Francis X. Kane. The balance of the first issue (140 pages) was devoted to a "supplement" of the sort that thereafter would be published as separate *USSI Reports*. By British professor John Erickson, it was a detailed summary and analysis of "Soviet Military Power."[11]

This is clearly not the stuff to attract a wide, popular readership. How then to measure its effectiveness? One yardstick was the participation the institute won from key people. Clare Boothe Luce became a director and later a vice president. Another director was Richard V. Allen, later President Reagan's national security advisor. They and the other officers served without remuneration. Top figures in all four services (army, navy, marines and air force) and many branches of government were happy to prepare articles for a token stipend of only $200. But the most compelling evidence of influence accumulated in what Metcalf, his able editor in chief Walter F. Hahn and his staff of two editors dubbed "the St. Peter File." Anticipating the Pearly Gates, Metcalf laughed, "When we get there someone is going to say, 'Well, what did you do to justify your existence?' " So the USSI collected in one file drawer all the unsolicited testimonials, reprint statistics and other bits and pieces of data to demonstrate that the *Strategic Review* was making a far bigger dent on policy making than its four thousand distribution might suggest. Some of the items:

- Reprints. Almost from the start in 1973 the entire contents of each *Strategic Review* were republished in the Pentagon's "Current News Service," going to thousands of offices in and out of government. The Congressional Research Service of the Library of Congress in 1979 included thirty-five thousand reprints of an article on "The Impact of Foreign Military Jobs on the National Industrial Base" in a collection of material prepared for "the National High School Debate Topic for the academic year 1979–80." Adm. Stansfield Turner, head of the CIA, reprinted 450 copies of a piece on "U.S. Intelligence and the Congress" for use in a class he was teaching at the National Defense University.

- Press Coverage. Between 1977 and early 1980 the *New York Times* reported twelve *Strategic Review* articles. In 1983 the *Times* devoted a full page to a *USSI Report* on "The Nuclear Balance in Europe" while the *Wall Street Journal* quoted and praised it in a lead editorial. The *Report* was also extensively summarized in major newspapers in England and Germany. In connection with a 1979 cover story in *Time* magazine on national defense the "Publisher's Letter" up front noted the "remarkable variety of military periodicals," singling out two by name: "Reading *Aviation Week* and *Strategic Review* can be quite interesting once you have broken the language barrier."
- Testimonials. Senator Henry M. Jackson of Washington: ". . . essential reading for both specialists and informed citizens." Manfred Worner, West German minister of defense: " . . . one of the most outstanding forums in the Western world on questions of strategy. I am indebted to the journal for its substantial contributions to my thinking and parliamentary work and would not want to do without it." Drew Middleton, *New York Times* military correspondent: ". . . serves the national and global security of the United States in a manner approached by no other publication. . . . As the security position of America becomes more complex and, possibly, more dangerous, reading *Strategic Review* has become a 'must' for everyone concerned with the future of the Republic."[12]

When Eaker accepted the presidency of the Strategic Institute in May 1972 he stipulated that he would do so only long enough to get the operation going. In October 1973 when it was clear that the launch had been a success he turned the responsibility over to Admiral McCain and wrote Metcalf: "I am happy to continue on the Board and serve as your Vice Chairman. There are some, no doubt, who would agree that my principal talents lie in vice. I want expecially to congratulate you on your conduct at the Annual Meeting. Our Board contains men of strong individual personalities and opinions. Therein lies much of its strength. The fact that you were able to get essential agreement on all the major objectives and policies attests to your success as our Chairman and your remarkable ability to gain compromise without abandoning principle. . . . With every good wish to you as my favorite patriot."[13]

The two men had by now become very close friends—a relationship that surprised others for they were so very different in personality. Whereas Eaker was quiet, low-key, incisive, always wearing a velvet glove over his iron hand, Metcalf was voluble, impetuous, a driver. His short, vigorous figure with bald head and beard bristled with showmanship. But his abundant ego was balanced by a lively sense of humor and self-deprecation. "I'm a long-winded editorial writer," he confessed. "I don't have the skill to write short editorials. Ira does, Ira has the skill. . . . Clare Luce used to beat me over the head with 14-page letters in long-hand trying to teach me how to write. She said you're like all ex-professors. Woodrow Wilson is the only man I knew who wrote sentences as long as you. Sometimes you have 80 words in your sentences. Cut it out!"[14]

His reply to Eaker's letter reflected the adulation (an extreme but accurate word) Metcalf had developed toward his new associate. "You have assessed what little I did with your characteristic modesty and generosity. I am proud of my contribution and more importantly that my efforts should have received your approbation. . . . But I have no illusions. What has really catapulted our important enterprise . . . were the unique contributions of your personal prestige and sponsorship. . . . Your electricity is something that is in the air and at Colorado Springs I could sense its tingle as the guest of one whom every one from the Chief of Staff down referred to as Mr. U.S. Air Force. . . ."[15]

Over the course of the next decade the two men were in constant touch, by mail and telephone in between the "think sessions" of the institute's editorial board. They also traveled a lot, mixing fun with research. Eaker introduced Metcalf to the air force leaders and its major institutions—the Air Academy in Colorado Springs, Strategic Air Command Headquarters in Omaha, and the Air University in Alabama. In the summer the Eakers often were Metcalf's guests in Martha's Vineyard or aboard his yacht, *Veritas*. They flew frequently to Europe for brass hat gatherings and to see old friends from WW II. One of these trips included being briefed at NATO headquarters in Brussels by its then commander, Gen. Alexander Haig. Another was to join the RAF Bomber Command, renamed the Strike Command, in joint ceremonies at High Wycombe commemorating its teamwork with the Eighth Air Force. "Old Bomber Harris,"

Eaker wrote Whitney, "made a talk in his usual rare form. Although he is now 84, somewhat heavier and walks with the aid of a cane, his mind seems as sharp as ever and his satire is as beautiful as ever. . . . You would have enjoyed the fly-past of two WW II planes, the Lancaster and a B-17."[16]

The most rewarding—and newsworthy—of these trips, however, was their visit with Albert Speer at Heidelberg, October 21, 1976. The durable Nazi, freed from prison after twenty years, had become a best-seller and again a figure of importance through his remarkable books recounting his years as Hitler's architect and then minister of armaments. These skillful *mea culpas* were self-serving in the extreme, but they also provide some of the best insights into the haphazard policies followed by the Third Reich. Eaker arranged the meeting in order to fill in some of the crevices of fact and interpretation about the air war. The three men sat in Speer's garden for several hours, taping their conversations, which were published in full in *Air Force Magazine* in April 1977. Eaker began by saying: "Mr. Speer, it seems we worked at cross purposes in the last war. It was your mission to supply the weapons for the Nazi land, sea and air forces. It was my job to prevent your accomplishing that by bombing your munitions factories. . . ." He went on to ask: "Which hurt you more, the RAF night bombing or the American daylight bombing? Or was the combination, called round-the-clock bombing, the most effective Allied strategy?" Speer noted that the RAF raids began first, with "horrible loss of civilian life," and that the later, "ever-increasing" day attacks by the Eighth caused "our military leaders" to tell Hitler that "unless the daylight bombers could be stopped, the end of the war was clearly in sight." On balance Speer judged that "it was the combined air effort that destroyed our means to wage war. . . ." He went on to amplify the comment he had made in his *Spandau, The Secret Diaries* that "the real importance of the air war consisted in the fact that it opened a second front long before the invasion. . . ." Now he told Eaker: ". . . well over a million Germans were ultimately engaged in antiaircraft defenses, as well as 10,000 or more antiaircraft guns. Without this great drain on our manpower, logistics and weapons, we might well have knocked Russia out of the war before your invasion of France."

Their talk roamed thoughtfully over the merits of the ball-bearing and transportation attacks, turning then to the defeat of the Luftwaffe. Ruefully Speer said: "I was still turning out the required number of fighter planes, but by that time we were out of experienced pilots. We were so short of fuel that we could give the incoming pilots in our flying schools only 3-1/2 hours flying training per week. These poorly trained and inexperienced Luftwaffe pilots, by that time, were suffering heavy losses. A pilot only survived for a maximum of seven missions against your bombers and their accompanying long-range fighters in 1944 and '45. This was very discouraging to German pilots. It represented an attrition of 14% for each mission."

Speer wanted to know why the Eighth did not join the British city-busting campaign, and Eaker replied: "Airpower pioneers, including Lord Trenchard, General Douhet and General Mitchell, had long believed that bombardment aviation might be able to reduce the will of civilian populations to resist. Our own doctrine held that the way to reduce civilian morale was not by killing people but by depriving them of the resources for further resistance. The U.S. airpower doctrine, which covered the employment of the Eighth Air Force out of Britain, never contemplated attack on civilian populations, other than that incidental to attacking munition factories. A letter I wrote to General Spaatz in 1943 contained this often-quoted observation: 'We must never allow the record of this war to convict us of throwing the strategic bomber at the man in the street.' "[17]

During the many years in Washington the Eakers slipped easily into a busy, comfortable and happy living pattern. Weather permitting, he would always walk the two miles to his office before nine and usually back again late in the afternoon. Though moved several times, his office of two rooms and an entry was always within a block of the Army and Navy Club on Farragut Square, where he usually lunched and then savored an hour or two of bridge in the card room before returning to his never-abating pile of paperwork. In addition to his column, speeches and the growing affairs of the Strategic Institute, he was always eager to lend a hand to anyone who cared about air power. It was during this period that one of his colleagues (name now, alas, forgotten) gave him the aluminum "name-plate" for his desk reading AIR FORCE SPOKEN HERE. When Columbia's distinguished historian, Allan Nevins, pioneer of the concept of oral history, came to Eaker for advice on how to raise $40,000 to tape the memories of everyone still alive who had known General Arnold, Eaker persuaded Donald Douglas to put it up. When one of "my boys," as Eaker always called those who had served under him in the war, wrote or published a book on aviation, he would buy twenty

Doolittle and Eaker with Gen. David Jones, who was chairman of the Joint Chiefs of Staff 1978–82.

copies and mail them to twenty influential people around the nation —men like Bob Lovett and Jock Whitney, with whom he maintained a large correspondence, as he did with dozens of others of his acquaintance, high and low. Every week or so he darted off to one part of the country or another to lecture. The air force was always ready to give him a lift to Maxwell Field, Alabama, for confabs at the Air University or to Colorado Springs for sessions at the Air Force Academy. In the evenings he and Ruth often dined at the elaborate Chevy Chase Club, where he sometimes played indifferent golf on weekends. She quickly reestablished old connections in the nation's capital, fixed up their house with her tasteful touch and kept him company on their frequent trips abroad—though not when he went to inspect the mess in Vietnam.

Every year, as close as possible to February 17, the anniversary of Eaker's departure for England with six cohorts in 1942, there was a reunion of the "Castle Coombe Group," as Eaker's closest wartime teammates came to call themselves. Besides the nine of us who actually lived at Castle Coombe, these reunions grew to include other early arrivals in England such as Gray, Norcross and Hull—about fifty officers all told. We would gather at the Carlton with cocktails for husbands and wives. Ruth Eaker then took the ladies to dinner while the men repaired for a ceremonial meal at the Army and Navy Club. One fixture was a toast to Fred Castle, whose father, a retired West Point colonel, would respond. Castle is enshrined as the most heroic of the early fliers of the Eighth. After serving as A-4 at bomber command and building the indispensable bases, that quiet, earnest young man had persuaded Eaker to give him command of the 94th Bomb Group at Bury Saint Edmunds. He rose to brigadier general in command of a combat wing after LeMay went to the Pacific. On the day before Christmas 1944, at the peak of the Battle of the Bulge, he lost his life and won the Medal of Honor leading the entire Eighth Air Force, 2,034 bombers strong plus fighter escort, over Germany.

The Castle Coombe reunions always concluded with a "command session" for a select few around the poker table, with General Spaatz a frequent participant. The stakes were more sensible than in wartime, but the thrust and parry of cards and bets, wisecracks and wisdom among old friends as lively as ever. General and Mrs. Spaatz were frequent companions of the Eakers in those years. Spaatz, never one to care much about money, had very little beyond his pension when he retired in 1948. He and his Ruth lived in a rambling, old house they at first could not afford to paint. Averell Harriman, then owner of *Newsweek,* gave the first chief of staff of the United States Air Force a hand up by making him *Newsweek*'s columnist on military affairs. Spaatz could write very well when he knew what he wanted to say, but the words did not come easily to that exceptionally taciturn man, and Eaker very often helped out either with rewriting or doing the entire task. They collaborated on many air force matters too. Thus, they were responsible for founding the Air Force Historical Foundation in 1953, taking turns as its president. What finally eased the Spaatz family fortunes was also indirectly due to

Eaker and Spaatz talking with Neil Armstrong, first man to walk on the moon, at the Wright Brothers Memorial Banquet, Beverly Hilton Hotel, December 5, 1969.

Eaker. Tex Thornton, having left Hughes Aircraft to found what became the extremely prosperous Litton Industries, invited Spaatz to be a director and very early gave him generous options on the company's stock. It was this nest egg that gave Ruth Spaatz a comfortable income when her husband died in July 1974. He had fallen a month earlier and banged his head against a radiator in what was first diagnosed as a heart attack and then as a stroke. Eaker visited him daily. "I believe he only recognized me once or twice during the first 15 days. . . . The last ten days he appeared to be recovering. For example, on the 13th of July, he said to me, 'I am counting on you to get me out of here.' I said, 'Tooey, tomorrow I will bring out a deck of cards and a quart of I.W. Harper. We will start playing gin rummy and they will then know you are sufficiently recovered to go home.' He said, 'That's a deal.' Later that evening he told Ruth Spaatz to remind me of our date to play gin rummy the next day. He suffered his final heart attack at 1:30 A.M. the following morning."[18]

While the general continued to conduct his life at the pace of a man half his age, awards and honors of all sorts continued to pop over the Eaker transom. There was, for example, the charming matter of the "Eaker Horses." One, named "Ira Eaker" by his breeder, retired Col. H.B. Marcus, won a three-furlong race at Gulfstream Park in March 1959 and then six furlongs, Willie Shoemaker up, at Aqueduct that fall, with presentation of the trophy by former New York Governor Averell Harriman. "Ruth Eaker," Sam Hicks owner and trainer, appeared briefly on the racing scene two years later, winning the mile and one sixteenth in 1:48:4 at Pimlico. Pictures of both steeds briefly adorned the Eaker study, then yielded to more meaningful trophies. He was designated an honorary chief master sergeant and also an honorary logistician. The International Flight Research Corporation bestowed the eighteen-inch-high, gilded Reveredo Trophy, named for "Peru's Lindbergh," who distinguished himself by flying solo from Lima to Buenos Aires in 1937. A corporate fellowship in Eaker's name was established by the Aerospace Education Foundation. The Eighth AF Historical Society in Florida endowed the Ira C. Eaker Outstanding Airmanship Award to be given annually by Eighth AF headquarters. The Ruth Apperson Eaker Award was set up at the University of Southern California for the best editorial in the *Trojan,* the student paper. Maj. Gen. and Mrs. Robert J. Smith established the Ira C. Eaker Distinguished Lecture on National Defense Policy at the Air Academy. And Arthur Metcalf endowed an annual Ira C. Eaker essay contest at the Air University. Then, in 1977, at age eighty-one he received aviation's top prize, the Wright Trophy, "for 60 years of significant public service."

His greatest honor, however, came two years later when he was awarded a Congressional Gold Medal as "Aviation Pioneer and Air Power Leader." The ceremony took place at the Pentagon in a room full of generals, both active and retired, as well as close personal friends such as Ruth Spaatz. When the effusive citation was read and other speeches completed, General Eaker rose to respond. His once muscular frame was now stooped with age, his face gaunt, but his soft voice was clear, and the habitual twinkle was in his eye. His short talk was reminiscent of the one he had made in High Wycombe thirty-eight years before. Thanking everyone concerned, he noted that the citation, like other recent introductions before his lectures at air force gatherings, sounded "all too much" like an obituary. Smiling gently, he concluded, "I can almost smell the roses."[20]

Epilogue

EAKER'S HEALTH began to fail in 1978. He suffered no single major or terminal illness. Rather, his supple body, which had never had any ailment worse than a broken ankle or too many bee stings, slowly endured a general breakdown. It started with a prostate tumor that was removed that July. It was malignant, but the cancer did not spread. His recovery from the operation, however, was slow as other complications afflicted him, and his weight, normally 180 pounds, dropped alarmingly. One cause turned out to be a stomach ulcer the doctors concluded had been there for a decade. The general then admitted that he had often had a tummy ache, which, with characteristic stoicism, he never mentioned. "That's one reason for the ulcer," remarked Ruth.

But he continued doggedly to walk the two miles to his office and back in the late afternoon until April 1981, when he reluctantly gave up the space, retreating to his study at home for his correspondence, which continued massive and fell more and more on his devoted and able wife to handle. He wrote me then, "My weight has stabilized apparently at about 141 pounds and I am gaining strength slowly."

A moderate stroke struck in November 1981, leaving him slightly paralyzed on the right side and able to walk only with a cane. Indomitable, he continued to climb down and up the three flights of stairs at 2202 Decatur Place at least twice daily, sleeping longer and longer each day until by 1985 he was abed about eighteen hours out of each twenty-four. Twice a week, Ruth drove him to the hospital at Andrews AFB for therapy and occasional longer rests, and he ventured out to fewer and fewer ceremonies and dinners. The two disabilities that particularly distressed him were the loss of most of his hearing and memory. It was sad to see this once so-vibrant man become silent and unable to respond. But he always smiled, never complained and never lost his sense of humor. "My memory is gone," he said to me once, "but I've got a darned good forgetory."

Early in 1985 two separate events brought him new recognition and luster. Congress, prompted by Senator Barry Goldwater and spurred by President Reagan, passed special legislation awarding four-star status to Eaker and to Jimmy Doolittle. And Hughes Aircraft, the tiny company Eaker had saved from collapse thirty-five years before, was bought by General Motors from the Howard Hughes Medical Institute for $5 billion. The charitable contrivance

Presentation of Eaker's fourth star at the Pentagon, April 26, 1985. Ruth Eaker pins one shoulder while Gen. Charles Gabriel, USAF chief of staff, waits to do the other.

to which the Internal Revenue Service had stoutly tried to deny tax-free status thus became the world's biggest private philanthropy, larger than the famed foundations of Carnegie, Rockefeller or Ford.

On April 26, 1985, two weeks after his eighty-ninth birthday, Eaker donned the blue air force uniform for the first time (it was still army khaki when he retired in 1947) and went to the Pentagon to receive his fourth star. It was a touching, thirty-five minute ceremony presided over by Gen. Charles A. Gabriel, air force chief of staff, and attended by about sixty dignitaries and old friends. After Gabriel reviewed Eaker's "unbelievable career," he concluded: "I'm sorry it took so long for a grateful nation to recognize all you've done for us and finally set things right for this great air pioneer, this proven combat leader, educator, strong spokesman for national security. . . . I'm proud to put him back in uniform and make him the Four Star he really deserves."

While Eaker smiled gamely and leaned heavily on his cane, Gabriel pinned on one of the new stars and Ruth the other, stabbing herself in the process and bringing chuckles from the throng. She then spoke a few words of thanks on her husband's behalf, he sat down and the guests queued up to shake his hand. Among them were Ruth Spaatz, Barry Goldwater, Leon Johnson, Harris Hull, Pat Hyland of Hughes Aircraft, General Arnold's son Bruce, Arthur Metcalf and Ed Gray, who had come from Florida for the occasion. When Gray greeted his wartime boss he said, "Ira, you look great!"

General Eaker replied, "Ed, you are my favorite liar."

Sources

ARCHIVES

Abundant, important documents relative to General Eaker can readily be accessed in many libraries and research centers.

The biggest single collection is in the Manuscript Division of the Library of Congress, to which he gave his personal papers. These fill eighty boxes. The MS Division also has the papers of Arnold, Spaatz and many other air force associates of Eaker. In the LC's Prints and Photographs Division are large numbers of pictures of all these individuals.

The second biggest collection is in the Air Force Historical Research Center, Air University, Maxwell AFB, Alabama. For many years the HRC was named for Albert F. Simpson, an officer who came to Eaker's attention in the Mediterranean and whom he appointed the first air force historian. A third worthy collection is in the library of the Air Force Academy, Colorado Springs, and a fourth at the Air Museum, Wright-Patterson AFB, Dayton, Ohio. All the air force archives are coordinated through the Office of Air Force History, Bolling Field, Washington. It maintains microfilm of most of the papers located elsewhere and is quick to help a researcher track elusive items. The author is deeply grateful for such advice from Dr. Richard H. Kohn, Chief, Office of Air Force History; Dr. Herman Wolk; and Mr. William S. Heimdahl.

At the Library of Congress I am indebted to James Hutson, chief, Manuscript Division; at Maxwell to Dr. Robert B. Lane, director, Air University Library, as well as Mr. Cargill Hall, chief, Research Division, AFHRC; at the Air Academy to Mr. Duane J. Reed, chief, Special Collections Division; and at the Air Museum to Col. Richard L. Uppstrom, director, and Lt. Col. Jack B. Hilliard, curator.

Though military papers pertinent to the air force are well maintained and easily researched, the opposite, sadly, has been the case with photographs of air action and air force leaders. The Prints and Photographs Collection at the Library of Congress is very large, but also cumbersomely filed as well as swamped with unprocessed material. The Defense Audio-Visual Agency at the Naval Air Station, Boiling Field, is in even worse shape. It has many fine pictures, but copies are almost impossible to pry loose from the bureaucracy. Prints are readily obtainable, on the other hand, from the Air Force Office of Public Affairs (Magazine and Book Division), Arlington, provided the researcher can supply the right negative number. Unfortunately, the prints in many files or as reproduced in many books (General Arnold's *Global Mission* being one example) frequently have not been numbered. My thanks in finding pictures in this maze go particularly to Maj. William H. Austin, USAF.

Sources

The new laser-disk technique is belatedly coming to the rescue of the photographic filing problem. At the Smithsonian's National Air and Space Museum Library, with the cooperation of Dr. Kohn's Office of Air Force History, prints are now being recorded on disks—50,000 to each disk. These can be monitored on a CRT (Cathode Ray Tube), the number noted, and the original print tracked to the archive where it abides. At the Air and Space Museum the author has been greatly helped by Mr. Dana Bell.

Non-air force archives with substantial Eaker material that has been studied for this book include:

The National Archives, Washington;

The Houghton Library, Harvard, where the author's papers are on file, including many reports I prepared or supervised as secretary to the general staff, MAAF, and chief air historian, Mediterranean Theater, 1944–45;

The United States Military History Institute, Carlisle Barracks, Pennsylvania, where I am indebted to Dr. Richard J. Sommers, archivist-historian;

The Air Historical Branch, Defense Ministry, Lacon House, London, where I was shepherded by Air Commodore R. M. H. Probert, chief;

The Public Record Office, Kew, Surrey, England, with its holdings of papers from the prime minister's private office and those of the British Chiefs of Staff;

The Imperial War Museum, London;

The Broadwater Collection, Churchill College, Cambridge, to which I was graciously given access by the present Winston S. Churchill, MP;

Finally, I am beholden to the superb libraries of Dartmouth College, Hanover, New Hampshire. Besides its collection of 1,600,000 volumes, the Dartmouth Library has obtained many others for me from all over the U.S. via interlibrary loan. I have been given yeoman help by Dr. Robert D. Jaccaud, research librarian at Dartmouth. Grateful, too, am I to Miss Alison Curphey, who served as my able library researcher for three months in 1983 between undergraduate semesters at Wellesley.

ORAL HISTORY INTERVIEWS WITH EAKER

Dr. Charles H. Hildreth and Dr. Alfred Goldberg, May, 1962, AF/CHO
Arthur K. Marmor, January 1966, AF/CHO
Cadet Richard Tobin, March 1974, AF/ACAD
Donald Shaughnessy, 1959–60, COHC
Lt. Col. Joe B. Green, USAF, February 11, 1967; January 28, 1972; March 30, 1972; and April 10, 1972, USMHI

EAKER INTERVIEWS WITH THE AUTHOR

The first interviews in direct connection with this book took place March 27–28, 1983. These were followed by dozens of talks with him and Mrs. Eaker in the next two years and were preceded by forty years of intimate teamwork beginning in England in 1942, with many notations in my diary and letters, now at the Houghton Library, Harvard.

EAKER INTERVIEWS WITH OTHERS WHO KINDLY MADE THEM AVAILABLE

Thomas M. Coffey, September 23, 1973; September 9 and October 29, 1974; April 8, 9, 18 and 24, 1975; October 27, 1978; June 22, 1979; October 30, 1979.
Group Capt. Dudley Saward, RAF; December 23, 1982.
Robert Sherrod, November 20, 1975.

Sources

AUTHOR'S INTERVIEWS WITH OTHERS

Maj. Gen. Charles C. Chauncey, USAF (Ret.), August 12, 1983
Helen Lady Dashwood, May 3, 1983
Maj. Gen. Howard C. Davidson, USAF (Ret.), October 6, 1983
Lt. Gen. Harold L. George, USAF (Ret.), by telephone, December 20, 1983
Edward D. Gray, November 23, 1983
Maj. Gen. Haywood S. Hansell, USAF (Ret.), April 27, 1984
Governor W. Averell Harriman, March 6, 1984
Marshal of the Royal Air Force Sir Arthur T. Harris, May 10, 1983
L. T. Hyland, December 20, 1983
Brig. Gen. Harris B. Hull, USAF (Ret.), July 29, 1984
Gen. David Jones, USAF (Ret.), October 21, 1983
Gen. Curtis E. LeMay, USAF (Ret.), April 16, 1985
Brig. Gen. Cecil P. Lessig, USAF (Ret.) and Mrs. Ethelyn Lessig, August 11, 1983
Hon. Robert A. Lovett, December 14, 1983
Lt. Col. Clarence O. Mason, USAF (Ret.), July 26, 1983
Dr. Arthur G. B. Metcalf, September 22, 1983
Mrs. George C. Pendleton, August 9, 1983
Denis Richards, May 22, 1984
Group Capt. Dudley Saward, RAF, December 23, 1982
Mrs. Carl A. Spaatz, October 7, 1983
Hon. Stuart Symington, November 3, 1983

PERIODICALS
There have been literally thousands of newspaper and magazine articles about General Eaker as well as several hundred by him. When quoted, these are cross-referenced in the Notes.

CORRESPONDENCE
Among the many who have written the author with helpful ideas and significant perspective a dozen stand out as having been especially valuable: Thomas M. Coffey; Edward L. Gray; Maj. Gen. Haywood S. Hansell, Jr., USAF (Ret.); Mrs. Jean Peters Hough; Mrs. Cecil P. Lessig; Carl Norcross; George C. Pendleton, Jr.; Forrest Pogue; Denis Richards; Hon. Robert A. Lovett; Dudley Saward; and Mrs. John Hay Whitney, who graciously provided copies of her husband's considerable personal correspondence with General Eaker.

ENTREE
For easy access to many records and introduction to key individuals involved in the life of Ira Eaker and the growth of the United States Air Force, the author is especially indebted to the Air Force Historical Foundation and the Eighth Air Force Historical Society.

Notes

CHAPTER 1

(pages 5–13)
1 Cooper, *The German Air Force,* 232.
2 Churchill, *The Second World War,* 5:527.
3 From Eaker speech, "Some Observations on Air Power," to the Society of Experimental Test Pilots, December 5, 1978, Washington, D.C.
4 Harriman and Abel, *Special Envoy,* 314.
5 Ibid.
6 Deane, *The Strange Alliance,* 121.
7 Ibid, 107.
8 Eaker interviews with Lt. Col. Joe Green, February 11, 1967, 40, USMHI.
9 Eaker diary, Parton Papers, Houghton Library (HL), Harvard.
10 The author was present.
11 From Eaker speech, "Soviet Leaders and People," to Squadron Officers School, Air University, November 21, 1974, reprinted in *Aerospace Historian,* June 1978.
12 Ibid.
13 Harriman letter to Eaker, March 23, 1944, Eaker Papers, Library of Congress (LC), Washington, D.C.
14 Ibid. Eaker Papers contain many planning papers and letters between them and others involved.
15 Parton, MAAF Historian, 1945, *The History of FRANTIC,* Parton Papers, HL.
16 Interview with the author, Honolulu, May 25, 1983.

CHAPTER 2

(pages 17–34)
1 Eaker conversation with the author, September 13, 1983, Washington, D.C.
2 Eaker interview with Lt. Col. Joe B. Green, January 28, 1972, 2, USMIII.
3 Eaker interview with the author, September 9, 1983, Washington, D.C.
4 Letter to Eaker from Mrs. Minerva J. Eaker, Ilion, New York, July 14, 1930, and his reply, July 21, 1930, and undated clipping from unidentified newspaper reporting findings of genealogist Lorena Shell Eaker, Danville, Virginia. Eaker Papers, LC.
5 Letter from Lt. Gen. Ira C. Eaker to Mrs. Odis C. Eaker, Danville, Virginia, December 15, 1972, author's collection.

6 Roy Meador column, "16 Edens—Count 'em" Op-Ed Page, *New York Times*, August 27, 1983.

7 Claude Leslie Eaker, *About People and Places*, unpublished memoir. Eaker Papers, LC.

8 Ibid.

9 Mrs. Ira C. Eaker letter, January 17, 1984, to the author, conveying answers from General Eaker to several questions.

10 Eaker interview with Thomas M. Coffey, April 8, 1975. Washington, D.C.

11 Mrs. Ira C. Eaker letter, see 9 above.

12 Claude Eaker memoir, see 7 above.

13 Eaker, Green interview, see 2 above, 4.

14 Eaker address at Air University, March 17, 1961, published in *Airpower Historian*, 8:3, 1961.

15 Eaker interview with the author, March 27, 1983, Washington, D.C.

16 Claude Eaker memoir, see 7 above.

17 Ibid.

18 Eaker, Green interview, see 2 above, 6.

19 Transcripts from Kenefic High School and Southeastern Oklahoma State Normal School; also *The Southeastern*, Durant, Oklahoma, February 11, 1942, cited by Betty M. Sears in her thesis on Eaker at Southeastern Oklahoma State University, October 1979.

20 Eaker interview with Arthur K. Marmor, AF/CHO, January 1966, AFHRC.

21 Eaker, Coffey interview, see 10 above.

22 *The Southeastern*, Durant, Oklahoma, July 11, 1945.

23 Ruth Goodman Pendleton interview with the author, September 9, 1983, Durant, Oklahoma.

24 *Holisso*, 1914–18, Library, Southeastern Oklahoma State University, Durant, Oklahoma.

25 Eaker, Green interview, see 2 above, 6.

26 Ibid.

27 Eaker Air University address, see 14 above.

28 Eaker, Coffey interview, see 10 above.

29 Eaker, Marmor interview, see 20 above.

30 Ibid.

31 Eaker, Accident Reports, AFHRC.

32 Arnold and Eaker, *Winged Warfare*, The portions in quotes are from the book, the porpoise anecdote from Eaker conversation with the author.

33 Eaker interview with Cadet Richard Tobin, Air Academy, March 1974, AFHRC.

34 Eaker interview with Donald Shaughnessy, 1959, COHC.

35 Ibid.

36 Mrs. Ira Eaker letter to the author, January 10, 1984.

37 Eaker, Coffey interview, see 10 above.

38 Arnold letter to Eaker, May 30, 1919, Eaker Papers, LC.

CHAPTER 3
(pages 35–44)

1 Eaker interview with Arthur K. Marmor, AF/CHO, January 1966. AFHRC.

2 Eaker interview with Donald Shaughnessy, 1959, COHC.

3 Eaker, Accident Reports, AFHRC.

4 Eaker, Marmor interview, see 1 above.

5 Eaker interview with Lt. Col. Joe B. Green, January 28, 1972, 22, USMHI.
6 Ibid.
7 Eaker letter to Eugene Faulkner, September 27, 1920, Eaker Papers, LC.
8 Eaker, Marmor interview, see 1 above.
9 Eaker letter to Faulkner, see 7 above.
10 Ruth Goodman Pendleton interview with the author, September 9, 1983, Durant, Oklahoma.
11 Eaker letter to Faulkner, see 7 above.
12 Eaker, Marmor interview, see 1 above.
13 Eaker conversation with the author, October 1983, Washington, D.C.
14 Eaker interview with Thomas M. Coffey, April 8, 1975, Washington, D.C.
15 Eaker article in *Aerospace Historian,* June 1973, adapted from an address to the Squadron Officers School, Air University, June 5, 1972.
16 Eaker, Coffey interview, see 14 above.
17 Mrs. Spaatz interview with the author, October 27, 1983, Washington, D.C.
18 Eaker article, see 15 above.
19 Eaker article, see 15 above.
20 Eaker interview with Cadet Richard Tobin, Air Academy, March 1974, AFHRC.

CHAPTER 4
(pages 45–60)
1 Eaker article, "Air Chiefs Patrick and Fechet," *Aerospace Historian,* June 1973.
2 "Micropaedia," Encyclopedia Britannica, Vol. 6, 943.
3 Eaker article, see 1 above.
4 Eaker interview with Thomas M. Coffey, April 8, 1975, Washington, D.C.
5 Eaker interview with Donald Shaughnessy, 1959, COHC, and with Arthur K. Marmor, AF/CHO, January 1966, AFHRC.
6 Eaker article, see 1 above.
7 Eaker, Shaughnessy, Marmor interviews, see 5 above.
8 Ibid.
9 Eaker, Accident Reports, AFHRC.
10 Eaker interview with Cadet Richard Tobin, Air Academy, March 1974, AFHRC.
11 Eaker, "Memories of Six Air Chiefs: Part II—Westover, Arnold, Spaatz," *Aerospace Historian,* December 1973, and Eaker article, see 1 above.
12 Eaker, Shaughnessy, Marmor interviews, see 5 above.
13 Eaker, "The Air Corps 1926 Pan American Flight," *Air Force Magazine,* September 1975.
14 The letters to the newspapers and the two generals and many related items are in the Eaker Papers, LC.
15 All quotes and other facts in this interwoven narrative come from Eaker's *Air Force Magazine* article, see 13 above.

CHAPTER 5
(pages 61–77)
1 Eaker, "The Military Professional," *Air University Review,* January–February 1975.
2 Eaker interview with Cadet Richard Tobin, Air Academy, March 1974, AFHRC.

3 Eaker, Accident Reports, AFHRC.
4 Eaker interview with Lt. Col. Joe B. Green, January 28, 1972, 21, USMHI.
5 Eaker, "Maj. Gen. James E. Fechet: Chief of the Air Corps, 1927–31" *Aerospace Historian,* September 1978.
6 Eaker, "Toward the Sound of the Guns," *Aerospace Historian,* Summer 1967.
7 Eaker article, see 5 above.
8 Eaker, "As I Remember Them: Air Chiefs Patrick and Fechet," *Aerospace Historian,* Summer 1973.
9 Eaker article, see 5 above.
10 Eaker interviews with Donald Shaughnessy, 1959, COHC.
11 "Memories of Six Air Chiefs," address by Eaker to Squadron Officer School, Air University, June 5, 1972.
12 Eaker, "The Lindbergh I Knew," *Aerospace Historian,* Winter 1977.
13 Eaker interview with Robert Sherrod, November 20, 1975, Washington, D.C.
14 Ibid.
15 Ibid.
16 Eaker interview with the author, March 5, 1984, Washington, D.C.
17 Copp, *A Few Great Captains,* 73.
18 Eaker, Shaughnessy interview, 35, see 10 above.
19 The *Bremen* adventure was widely reported at the time. A colorful summary can be found in Copp, *A Few Great Captains.*
20 Ibid.
21 Quesada interviews with Steve Long and Ralph Stephenson, May 12, 1975, 3–4, 35 and 63, USMHI.
22 Ibid.
23 Talk of the Town, *New Yorker,* June 8, 1929, 12.
24 Condensation of many press reports from the time and recollections of the participants.
25 *Literary Digest,* January 19, 1929.
26 Ibid.
27 Eaker interview with Arthur K. Marmor, AF/CHO, January 1966, AFHRC.
28 *Congressional Record,* House of Representatives, 1929, 1445.
29 Clipping from unidentified magazine, "A History of Eaker Field . . . sponsored by First National Bank," probably published in Durant, Oklahoma. Eaker Papers, LC.

CHAPTER 6
(pages 78–91)

1 *Air Corps News Letter,* 13:6, April 26, 1929.
2 Eaker interviews with Lt. Col. Joe B. Green, USMHI and Eaker Papers, LC. Longfellow's participation confirmed by Eaker to author.
3 Eaker, Accident Reports, AFHRC, and Eaker interview with Cadet Richard Tobin, USAF Academy, March 1974, AFHRC. Copp's *A Few Great Captains* adds details, 94–95.
4 Hatchet anecdote comes from Eaker conversation with the author, October 1983.
5 Eaker, Accident Reports, and Green interview, see 2 above, Eaker Papers, LC.
6 Ibid.

7 Author's conversation with General and Mrs. Eaker, October 1983. See also Copp, 3 above, 96.

8 Ibid.

9 Author's conversation with Mrs. Ethelyn Lessig, wife of Brig. Gen. C. P. Lessig, San Antonio, Texas, August 11, 1983.

10 Parton, Eakers conversation, see 7 above.

11 Copp, *A Few Great Captains*, 97.

12 Eaker interview with Robert Sherrod, November 20, 1975, Washington, D.C.

13 Eaker interviews with Donald Shaughnessy, 1959, COHC.

14 Coffey, *Hap*, 6–8. See Copp also, 113–114.

15 All but the final sentence from Eaker, Shaughnessy interview, see 13 above. The last, perhaps overly nonchalant, remark from interview with the author, September 13, 1983, Washington, D.C.

16 There is much Arnold-Eaker correspondence about the book in their papers at the Library of Congress, giving royalty details, et cetera. The preface was originally supposed to be by Amelia Earhart, but, Arnold wrote Eaker in 1935, her effort was "not very satisfactory." They turned to Donald Douglas instead.

17 This brief summary of the air mail controversy, about which reams have been written, is drawn from three documents: Foulois, *Memoirs;* Tillet, *The Army Flies the Mails;* and Eldon W. Downs, "Army and the Airmail— 1934," *Aerospace Historian,* January 1962.

18 Details of the Arnold-Spaatz-Eaker teamwork during the airmail episode are drawn from many sources but primarily the Eaker Papers at the Library of Congress and his interviews for Columbia University, Eaker, Shaughnessy interview, see 13 above, the Air Academy, Eaker accident reports, Eaker Tobin interview, see 3 above, and with Arthur K. Marmor, AF/CHO, January 1966, AFHRC.

19 Airmail controversy, see 17 above.

20 Foulois *Memoirs,* 260.

CHAPTER 7
(pages 92–102)

1 From January 5 to June 1934, domestic airlines had 25 accidents, and 29 fatalities. *Air Commerce Bulletin,* no. 3 (September 15, 1934). In "Army and the Airmail—1934," *Airpower Historian* (January 1962), Lt. Col. Eldon W. Downs commented: "Most military officers discounted the fatalities, marking them up to experience as was customary in other hazardous military duty. One Western Zone route commander, Captain I. C. Eaker, summarized their views. The Army flyer, he wrote, was a 'very bewildered young man' who disliked the 'hysterical hullaballoo,' and was unaccustomed to the publicity and the controversy, and to being the 'butt for political agitation.' It would have been different, he thought, if the Army had taken an unwanted assignment, one considered unprofitable. But profit and politics kept the controversy alive and, worse still, the criticism of the military airmail caused many airmen to take unnecessary chances." Foulois said: "The Army Air Corps has casualties every year. They are simply a part of Army flying. The average is between 40 and 50 annually." *New York Times,* March 17, 1934.

2 For further details of the airmail controversy and results, see Foulois

Notes

Memoirs, Tillet, *The Army Flies the Mails,* and Downs, airline accidents, see 1 above.

3 Copp, *A Few Great Captains,* 264–266.
4 Eaker, "Lt. Gen. Frank M. Andrews," *Air Force Magazine,* September 1980.
5 Arnold, *Global Mission,* 138.
6 Eaker Papers, LC, and personal observations of the author during World War II.
7 Eaker interview with Cadet Richard Tobin, USAF Academy, March 1974, AFHRC.
8 Air Tactical School roster, 1935–36.
9 Greer, *The Development of Air Doctrine.* Of the dozens of books and articles on this theme this is by far the most comprehensive and objective.
10 Eaker, Tobin interview, see 7 above.
11 Richard K. Smith, "The Intercontinental Airliner and the Essence of Airplane Performance, 1929–1939," *Technology and Culture,* July 1982—a superb summary.
12 *The Development of Air Doctrine,* see 9 above.
13 Ibid.
14 Craven and Cate, *The Army Air Forces,* 1:598–99.
15 Merriam-Webster's *Third* puts it more ponderously: "*Doctrine* may indicate a formulated theory supported or not controverted by evidence, backed or sanctified by authority, and proposed for acceptance."
16 Eaker, Tobin interview, see 7 above.
17 *The Development of Air Doctrine,* see 9 above.
18 Kepner letter "To Whom It May Concern," June 10, 1936, Eaker Papers, LC.
19 Eaker, "Memories of Six Air Chiefs: Part II, Westover, Arnold, Spaatz," *Aerospace Historian,* December 1973.
20 Eaker comment to the author, September 12, 1983, Washington, D.C.
21 Roster, Catalog and Eaker ratings, Command & General Staff School, 1936–37, and *A Brief History of Fort Leavenworth,* Combat Studies Institute, Fort Leavenworth, Kansas, 1983.
22 Mrs. Ira C. Eaker comment to the author, February 25, 1984, Washington, D.C.
23 Mrs. Eaker comment, see 22 above.
24 Eaker Papers, LC.

CHAPTER 8
(pages 107–27)
1 Edison quote is from Huie, *The Fight for Air Power.* For a fuller understanding of the struggle of the airmen for autonomy in the cumbersome toils of the War Department general staff one should read two authoritative works: Otto Nelson's *National Security and the General Staff* and James E. Hewes, Jr.'s *From Root to McNamara: Army Organization and Administration, 1900–1963.* Both describe the WDGS historically as a mixture of yo-yo and pendulum. It began with Secretary of War John C. Calhoun's effort to assert centralized control of the War Department and the army after the War of 1812. While the army itself dispersed into geographic districts under professional military commanders, a departmental staff reported directly to the Secretary. From the start the letter was called the

WDGS, "but it was not a general staff in the modern sense of an overall planning and coordinating agency." (Hewes, 3) Instead it was made up of many separate bureaus—quartermaster, pay, ordnance, medical, etc, each with considerable autonomy.

Lincoln pulled the resultant confusion together in the Civil War under Grant's unified command. But immediately after, in a pattern the U.S. repeated following every subsequent war, "the Army was reduced to a skeleton force and scattered throughout the West." (Nelson, 10) At the start of the Spanish-American War army strength was 2,143 officers and 26,040 men stationed in 77 posts. Inevitably the military effort broke down ("embalmed beef, troops not able to land, supplies sent to Tampa, which lacked terminal facilities. . . ." (Nelson, 40). In 1903 Secretary of War Elihu Root founded the first real general staff. But it too was allowed to fractionate into bureaucratic disarray prior to World War I. The WDGS was almost forced out of existence and reduced to 36 members, of whom only 19 were on duty in Washington when the U.S. entered the war. Gen. Robert Lee Bullard, whom Eaker had noticed on horseback in 1917, "observed after passing through Washington on the way to France . . . 'if we really have a great war, our War Department will quickly break down. . . .' " (Nelson, 225) It did, and "the near collapse of the economy in the winter of 1917–18 forced the President and Congress to act." (Hewes, 23) Gen. Peyton C. March was brought back from France to be chief of staff and pushed through an immediate, effective reorganization which regrouped the WDGS into five main divisions—executive, war plans, purchase & supply, storage & traffic, and operations. At war's end the WDGS mustered 1,000 officers.

Again the pendulum swung. "The National Defense Act amendments of 1920 returned generally to the pre-war pattern of fragmented, diffused authority and responsibility with effective control at the bureau level." (Hewes, 50) Much had been learned from the WW I experience and the "WDGS usefulness was such that its desirability was taken for granted by the entire Army . . ." but "The War Department and the Army were so reduced in the economy years of the early 1930's that they were too weak to stand the strain of rapid expansion." (Nelson, 312 and 314) "The General Staff bogged down and had to undergo a radical reorganization after Pearl Harbor. . . . In the two years before Pearl Harbor the War Department staff, including the General Staff, became a huge operating empire increasingly involved in the minutiae of Army administration." (Hewes, 62 & 64) "The major item which had not been taken into consideration was the possibility that the U.S. would become involved in a war of more than one front." (Nelson, 317) "Two days after Pearl Harbor Marshall asserted that the War Department was 'a poor command post.' The decision General Marshall reached was to substitute the vertical pattern of military command for the traditional pattern of bureaucratic coordination. This centralization of executive control would enable him to decentralize operating responsibilities." (Hewes, 67)

That great achievement was "the most drastic and fundamental change which the War Department had experienced since the establishment of the General Staff by Elihu Root in 1903." (Nelson, 335) Hewes noted (336): "Brilliant managers and administrators may be relatively rare in the federal bureaucracy, but in both world wars such men arose who met successfully the challenge of the war by asserting effective control over the Department's operations. When Mr. Root outlined the administrative mismanagement of the War Department during the Spanish-American War to the Senate Military Affairs Committee, its chairman, Senator Joseph Hawley of Connecticut, a Civil War veteran who was customarily called General, suggested that General Grant could have solved the problem easily. When reminded that General Grant was no longer available, the Senator replied that 'God always sends a man like him in time of need.' "

2 Ibid.

3 Eaker interview with Arthur K. Marmor, AF/CHO, January 1962, AFHRC.

4 Huie, *The Fight for Air Power,* 71, 144–153, and Copp, *A Few Great Captains,* 374, 401, 472.

5 Copp, *A Few Great Captains,* 417 and Eaker, "Lt. Gen. Frank M. Andrews," *Air Force Magazine,* September 1980.

6 Eaker, "Lt. Gen. Frank M. Andrews, see 5 above.

7 Details drawn from many sources, chiefly Copp and Eaker, see 5 above, and LeMay and Kantor, *Mission with LeMay,* 184–193. The letter from Craig has never turned up. Eaker believed it was "removed from the files," LeMay that it was "snuck out."

8 *Eaker, "Memories of Six Chiefs, Part II: Westover, Arnold, Spaatz,"* Aerospace Historian, December 1973.

10 Clippings in Eaker Papers, LC. Personal anecdotes from the author's many conversations with the Eakers.

11 Lovett interview with the author, December 14, 1983, Locust Valley, N.Y.

12 Eaker interview with Cadet Richard Tobin, March, 1974, USAF Academy, Colorado Springs.

13 Eaker interview with Tom Coffey, April 8, 1975, Washington, D.C.

14 Eaker interview with Tom Coffey, October 27, 1978, Washington, D.C.

15 Mrs. Spaatz interview with the author, October 7, 1983, Washington, D.C. Also cited by Copp.

16 Eaker, Marmor interview, 22, see 3 above.

17 "Memories of Six Chiefs," see 8 above.

18 The author was with General Spaatz during his tour of St. Peters and also played poker with him many times when the "luck" vs. "skill" approach was laughingly described by the general. Other two quotes were recalled by Eaker in conversation with the author.

19 Parton, Lovett interview, see 11 above.

20 Eaker article, see 8 above.

21 COHC, Eaker, Marmor interview, see 3 above.

22 Eaker, Coffey interview, see 13 above.

23 Arnold Papers, LC.

24 Hull interview with the author, July 29, 1984, Washington, D.C.

25 Eaker interview with Lt. Col. Joe B. Green, February 11, 1967, USMHI, 12–13.

26 Brig. Gen. C. P. Lessig interview with the author, Ft. Worth, Texas, August 11, 1983.

27 Eaker Papers, LC.

28 Eaker conversation with the author in England, 1943.

29 Fighter Board Report, "The Future Development of Pursuit Aircraft," October 27, 1941, USAFHRC.

30 Eaker Coffey interview, see 13 above.

31 Eaker, Green interview, see 25 above, 13.

32 Copp, *Forged in Fire*, 185, and *The Air Force News Letter*, 24:15, September 1941. Eaker letter to Arnold, November 13, 1941, Arnold Papers, LC.
33 Ibid.
34 Eaker interviews with Donald Shaughnessy, 1959–60, 85, COHC.
35 Eaker, Coffey interview, see 13 above.
36 Wright, Howard J., "Changing Insignia," *Aerospace Historian*, June 1980.
37 Copp, *Forged in Fire*, see 32 above, 219.
38 Eaker Papers, LC.
39 Eaker, Green interview 15.

CHAPTER 9
(pages 128–48)
1 Eaker interview with Arthur K. Marmor, AF/CHO, January 1966, AFHRC.
2 Eaker told the author about this meeting. It is also quoted in Copp, *Forged in Fire*, 227.
3 Lincoln Barnett of *Life Magazine*, manuscript of unpublished article, 1943, Eaker Papers, LC. Also Copp, *Forged in Fire* and April 1984 letter to the author from George Jones, Eaker's editor at Harper & Bros.
4 Freeman, *The Mighty Eighth*, 4.
5 Arnold and Eaker Papers, LC.
6 "Initial Directive to Bomber Commander in England," Jan. 31, 1942, Eaker Papers, LC.
7 Many sources, but chiefly Carl Norcross letters to the author. Eaker and Hull interviews with the author. Armstrong and Castle memoirs. Copp.
8 Barnett MS, see 3 above.
9 Eaker Papers, LC.
10 Eaker interview with Lt. Col. Joe B. Green, March 30, 1972, USMHI, and Eaker Papers, LC. Also Copp.
11 Eaker Papers, LC.
12 Armstrong memoir, "So Near Heaven, Surrounded by Hell," unpublished, East Carolina University Library, Greenville, N.C.
13 Many Eaker interviews refer to his problems with Chaney—notably those in Columbia University's Oral History Archives.
14 Eaker quote is from interview with Coffey, April 18, 1975, other details from Barnett, see 3 above.
15 Norcross letter to the author.
16 Saundby's *Air Bombardment: The Story of Its Development*, says on 121: "In February 1942 . . . the daily average was 374."
17 Drawn from Webster and Frankland; Hastings, *Bomber Command;* Copp, *Forged in Fire;* Richards, *Portal of Hungerford;* plus letters and conversation with Richards.
18 Saward, *"Bomber" Harris*, 110–11, Churchill, *Second World War*, 4:783.
19 *N.Y. Times Magazine*, June 6, 1943, 3.
20 Harris, *Bomber Offensive*, 52–53.
21 Webster and Frankland, 1:331–32.
22 Eaker, Green interview, see 10 above.
23 Norcross, see 7 above.
24 Eaker, Marmor interview, see 1 above.
25 Eaker, Coffey interview, see 14 above.
26 Plan for "The Initiation of U.S. Army Air Force Bombardment Operations in the British Isles," March 20, 1942, signed by Eaker on letterhead of the

American Observer Group, High Wycombe, Bucks, and prepared in response to a directive from Maj. Gen. Charles L. Bolte, chief of staff, U.S. Army Forces in the British Isles, AFHRC, 520.168-1.

27 Bubb, Col. C.B.B., diary, Eaker Papers, LC.

28 *Current Biography*, 1942, 226.

29 First Eaker quote is from Coffey, see 14 above. Staff directive is in Eaker Papers, LC.

30 Many books cover the immense contribution to air tactics and control by British scientists, beginning with Sir Robert Watson-Watt's and Sir Henry Tizard's invention of radar in 1937. The best summary, in the author's opinion, is *The Wizard War: British Scientific Intelligence 1939–1945* by R. V. Jones. See also Saward, see 18 above.

31 Saward, see 18 above, 117–24.

32 Coffey, see 14 above.

33 Many sources: Eaker interviews, Copp, Coffey, all cited above.

34 Eaker interview with the author, December 1983. A similar quote is in Coffey, see 14 above.

CHAPTER 10
(pages 149–67)

1 Mimeographed one-page "History of Wycombe Abbey, Buckinghamshire," prepared by the Girl's School before WW II, Parton Papers, HL.

2 Eaker interview with Dr. C. H. Hildreth and Dr. A. Goldberg, May 1962, AF/CHO.

3 Norcross letter to the author, March 17, 1983.

4 Eaker interview with Tom Coffey, April 18, 1975, Washington, D.C.

5 Freeman, *The Mighty Eighth*, 5.

6 Craven and Cate, 1:645.

7 General Motors statistics from *Moody's Industrials, 1943,* and *Dun's Business Rankings, 1982;* airline data from *Aviation Facts and Figures, 1945;* M.I.T. data from Education Directory to Colleges and *Universities, 1941–42.* Eighth AF data from Craven and Cate, Vol. 2, 600–64. See also Kaplan, *One Last Look,* 43–45. Besides the 43 airfields for bombers there were 16 simpler ones for fighters. These also took up much acreage.

8 Communications detail supplied by Col. Edward D. Gray, Eighth AF signals officer, and Lt. Col. Boris Maximoff, one of his assistants, in letters to the author—1984.

9 Eaker interview with Lt. Col. Joe B. Green, March 30, 1972, USMHI.

10 Harris letter to Arnold, April 22, 1942, Air Ministry.

11 Many mentions of these discussions in Eaker Papers, LC.

12 Eaker, Coffey interview, see 4 above.

13 Copp, *Forged in Fire*, 262.

14 Arnold, *Global Mission*, 316.

15 Sherwood, *Roosevelt & Hopkins*, 581.

16 Craven and Cate, 1:560.

17 Mimeographed, one-page *"History of Air Corps Stag Parties",* distributed that evening, Parton Papers, HL.

18 Parton Papers, HL; Gray interview with the author, November 23, 1983, St. Petersburg, Florida; Barnett, see Chapter 9, note 3.

19 Eaker Papers, LC.

20 Copp, *Forged in Fire*, 266–69.

Notes

CHAPTER 11
(pages 168–81)

1 Eisenhower Papers, 449.
2 Armstrong, unpublished memoir, see Chapter 9, note 12.
3 Ibid.
4 Eaker to Arnold, August 8, 1942, Eaker Papers, LC.
5 Copp, *Forged in Fire*, 283.
6 Craven and Cate, 1:591.
7 As remembered by Lady Dashwood in conversation with the author, London, May 1983.
8 Lessig letter to the author, March 23, 1984.
9 Eaker interview with Lt. Col. Joe B. Green, March 30, 1972, 18, USAMHI.
10 Craven and Cate, see 6 above, 661–65. Freeman, *The Mighty Eighth*, 12–13, *New York Times*, August 18, 1942, front page. Armstrong memoir, see 2 above.
11 Craven and Cate, see 6 above, 665.
12 *New York Times*, see 10 above.
13 Barnett MS., see Chapter 9, note 3.
14 Eaker Papers, LC.
15 Craven and Cate, see 6 above, 209–41. Copp, see 5 above, 309–10.
16 Eaker Papers, LC.
17 Craven and Cate, see 6 above, 221–22.
18 Hansell, unpublished article for *Aerospace Historian*.
19 Marshall to Eisenhower, August 26, 1942. Eaker Papers. LC. Spaatz quote from Aug. 27, 1942, letter to Arnold. Arnold Papers, LC, Box 38.
20 The author's parents were among those he called. After his return, when thanked, he spoke of the others.
21 Eaker, Spaatz and Arnold Papers, LC. Also Copp, see 5 above, 299.

CHAPTER 12
(pages 182–201)

1 Craven and Cate, 2:60.
2 Eaker interview with Tom Coffey, October 27, 1978. In an earlier interview with Coffey, April 18, 1975, Eaker was more explicit about his temporary "unpopularity" with Eisenhower, saying, "I received considerable criticism because I . . . continued to feel we were neglecting our principal target, Germany. . . . It would have been very easy for me to say, 'Let's take the UK effort and go to Africa and let me lead it.' And then we'd have been through in UK because we'd never have gotten back. The British would have filled up our airdromes."
3 Eisenhower memorandum to Spaatz, October 13, 1942, Spaatz Papers, LC.
4 See 1 above, 60–66, 105–7, and 282–83.
5 Eisenhower Papers, #538.
6 See 1 above, 65.
7 Ibid, Table of all Eighth AF bomber missions, 841–52.
8 See Craven and Cate, especially vol. 1: 559 and 2:368. Also Hansell, *The Air Plan That Defeated Hitler*.
9 Slessor to Portal, September 25 and 26, 1942, Air Historical Branch, Lacon House, Defense Ministry, London.
10 Webster and Frankland, 1:358–59.

11 Ibid, 355.
12 Ibid, 360.
13 Ibid.
14 Eaker Papers, LC.
15 Webster and Frankland, 2:150 footnote lists eight night missions, three of them over France and the others over Germany, on which small U.S. units (three or five planes each time) went along. The U.S. lost two bombers.
16 Ibid, 360–61.
17 Saward, *"Bomber" Harris,* 171–73.
18 Ibid, 174.
19 Ibid, 173–74.
20 Ibid, 175.
21 Webster and Frankland, see 10 above, 362–63, and Richards, *Portal of Hungerford,* 310.
22 Letter to the author, January 21, 1984.
23 The author was Mrs. Roosevelt's escort.
24 Eaker interview with Tom Coffey, April 18, 1975, Washington, D.C.
25 The author overheard Eisenhower's comment to Eaker about his jacket. Photostat of Eaker's letter to Eisenhower, dated November 1, 1942, is in the Eaker Papers, LC. A year later, September 8, 1943, Eaker wrote a memo to the quartermaster about a new booklet "on the ETO Jacket, Field, Wool, O.D." that "this jacket should be furnished to Eighth Air Force crews . . . it has been represented by the Germans that they consider the leather jacket unsuitable for American prisoners in German hands since its use might aid an escape. It is important, therefore, that our combat crews which may fall into German hands wear a battle jacket which is distinctly military and which they will be allowed to wear. . . ."
26 The visit to the 306th is mostly from the author's memory or diary, Parton Papers, HL.
27 Eaker, "Air Chiefs Patrick and Fechet," *Aerospace Historian,* June 1973.
28 Strong, *First Over Germany.*
29 Arnold Papers, LC.
30 Arnold letter to Eaker, November 18, 1942, Eaker Papers, LC.
31 Copp, *Forged in Fire,* 321.
32 Minutes of the meeting and supporting documents, Eaker Papers, LC.
33 Eisenhower Papers, 790.

CHAPTER 13
(pages 202–15)
1 Parton Papers, HL.
2 Craven and Cate, 2:124.
3 Ibid, 106–9.
4 Parton diary, see 1 above, plus author's memories.
5 Eaker interviews with Donald Shaughnessy, 1959, COHC.
6 Eaker confirmed his opinion of Kuter in conversation with the author, July 29, 1984.
7 Parton diary, see 4 above.
8 Eaker letter to Stratemeyer, January 2, 1943, Eaker Papers, LC.
9 Johnson interview with Dr. James C. Hasdorff, August 1975, AFHRC.
10 Gray letter to the author, November 30, 1983.

11 Hansell interview with the author, April 27, 1984, Hilton Head, South Carolina.
12 Lovett interview with the author, December 14, 1983, Locust Valley, New York.
13 Parton diary, see 4 above.
14 Eaker Papers, LC.

CHAPTER 14
(pages 216–31)
1 Slessor to Sinclair, December 18, 1942. Air Historical Branch, Lacon House, Defense Ministry, London.
2 Hull's report, of which 50 copies were made, covered the first 23 missions, August 17, 1942—November 23, 1942. Key facts included:
   Losses: 13 by enemy action, five by flak. Total: 18.
   Casualties: Killed, 15; seriously wounded, 31; slightly wounded, 65; missing, 155; known prisoners, 16.
   Battle damage: Repairable by nearest combat unit, 170; repairable by 4th Echelon, 15; to be collected for salvage, 8; damaged beyond repair, 3. Total: 196.
   Bomb statistics: Loaded, 4,585,600 lbs.; on target, 2,619,800 lbs.; returned, 630,000 lbs.; unaccounted for, 31,000 lbs. The use of pounds instead of tons somewhat disguised the embarrassing difference from RAF statistics but brought laughter from Arnold.
3 Parton Papers, HL.
4 Eaker article, "Some Memories of Winston Churchill," *Aerospace Historian,* September 1972.
5 Butcher, *My Three Years With Eisenhower,* 236.
6 Parton Papers, HL.
7 Eaker Papers, LC.
8 Eaker article, see 4 above. Further details are from the author's memories of Eaker's comments just after his meeting with Churchill.
9 Churchill, *Second World War,* 4:678–79.
10 Arnold, *Global Mission,* 26.
11 Hansell interview with the author, April 27, 1984, Hilton Head, South Carolina.
12 Craven and Cate, 2:113–15 and 274–7.
13 Ibid.
14 Arnold, *Global Mission,* 228.
15 Pogue, *George C. Marshall: Organizer of Victory, 1943–1945, vol. 3,* 5.
16 Ibid, 5 and 71.
17 Slessor, *The Central Blue,* footnote, 432.
18 Lovett interview with the author, December 14, 1983, Locust Valley, New York.
19 Author's diary, see 3 above.
20 Eisenhower Papers, 768.
21 Richards, *Portal of Hungerford,* 311.
22 Richards letter to the author, January 21, 1984.
23 Author's diary, February 23, 1943, see 3 above.
24 Freeman, *The Mighty Eighth,* 25, and *Mighty Eighth Diary,* 35.
25 Eaker letter to Spaatz, January 29, 1943, Eaker Papers, LC.

CHAPTER 15
(pages 232–56)

1 Andrews cable to Marshall, February 5, 1943, Arnold Papers, LC.
2 Marshall cable to Andrews. Copp, *Forged in Fire,* 359.
3 Eaker interview with Lt. Col. Joe B. Green, March 30, 1972, 19, USMHI.
4 Eaker interviews with Donald Shaughnessy, 1959, COHC.
5 LeMay and Kantor *Mission with LeMay,* 278.
6 LeMay, "The Command Realities," *IMPACT, The Army Air Forces' Confidential Picture History of World War II,* 5:xi.
7 Eisenhower Papers, 959, 966 and 967. Air Marshal Philip Wigglesworth, who had been Tedder's senior staff officer, became his deputy. In a letter to Spaatz about being Tedder's deputy, Eaker made a point of further historical interest in view of the change of commands at the end of 1943: " . . . I do believe . . . that I am of most use to the Service in this theater. On the other hand, if it works out that you can come back to head the Eighth Air Force, nobody will be happier than I. I hope, however, to get my old job back as VIII Bomber Commander in that eventuality." Eaker Papers, LC.
8 Eaker, Shaughnessy interviews, see 10 above.
9 Craven and Cate, 2:224.
10 Boog, Dr. Horst, "Germanic Air Forces and the Historiography of the Air War," *Aerospace Historian,* March 1984.
11 Air University Press, January 1983, 181.
12 Harriman, *Special Envoy,* 195.
13 Eaker letter to Spaatz, October 8, 1942, Eaker Papers, LC.
14 Eaker letter to Arnold, February 26, 1943, Arnold Papers, LC.
15 Arnold Papers, LC.
16 Eaker letter to Arnold, March 1, 1943, Eaker Papers, LC.
17 Harris letter to Eaker, March 5, 1943, Eaker Papers, LC.
18 Pogue, *George C. Marshall: Organizer of Victory,* 3:173.
19 The Vegesack summary is drawn from 1) Eaker's letter to Spaatz, March 19, 1943; 2) Arnold's letter to Eaker, April 19, 1943; and 3) Eaker's Commendation to VIII Bomber Command, March 24, 1943—all in the Eaker Papers, LC. See also Craven and Cate, 2:326–27 and 344–46; Freeman, *Mighty Eighth War Diary,* 46, and *The Mighty Eighth,* 27–28; and *IMPACT,* May 1943, 16–17.
20 Mason interview with the author, Honolulu, July 25, 1984.
21 The author attended the dinner and the gathering upstairs afterward. Eaker quote is from his letter to Arnold, April 5, 1943, Arnold Papers, LC.
22 Eaker memorandum to Arnold, undated but obviously in March, 1943, Eaker Papers, LC.
23 Arnold letter to Eaker, March 26, 1943, Eaker Papers, LC.
24 Arnold letter to Eaker, March 24, 1943, Eaker Papers, LC. Also AFHRC #520.161.
25 Arnold letter to Mrs. Eaker, March 24, 1943, Eaker Papers, LC.
26 Rostow, W. W., *Pre-Invasion Bombing Strategy,* 7–8. Snow quote is from his Godkin Lectures at Harvard, *Science and Government,* 29.
27 Rostow, see 26 above, 16–24. The author knew Colonel Hughes as well as many of the operations analysts and took minutes at some of their meetings with Eaker.

28 Hansell, *The Air Plan That Defeated Hitler,* 145–49. Also the very thorough and interesting *Leaves from my Book of Life* by Perera, full of colorful detail.
29 Hansell, see 28 above, 148. Also Perera, see 28 above, 71.
30 Perera, see 28 above, 72–88.
31 Eaker letter to Gates, January 11, 1943, Eaker Papers, LC.
32 Perera, see 28 above. Also many relevant letters in Eaker Papers, LC.
33 Arnold letters to Andrews and Spaatz, March 24, 1943. Arnold Papers, LC.
34 Arnold directive to Andrews, March 24, 1943, Arnold Papers, LC.
35 See excerpts from the COA Report attached to Arnold letter to Spaatz, see 33 above.
36 Hansell, see 28 above, 157–67. Webster and Frankland, 2:220.
37 Portal letter to Arnold and Harris letter to Eaker, both April 15, 1943, Eaker Papers, LC.
38 The author was one of the foursome in the golf game between Andrews and Eaker. See Copp, *Forged in Fire,* 385–87 for other details.
39 Harriman letter to Lovett, April 20, 1943, Arnold Papers, LC.
40 Eaker interview with Robert Sherrod, November 20, 1975, Washington, D.C.
41 Eaker interview with Lt. Col. Joe B. Green, April 10, 1972, 22, USMHI.
42 Eaker interviews with Donald Shaughnessy, July 24, 1959, COHC.

CHAPTER 16
(pages 261–81)
1 Arnold letter to Andrews, May 2, 1943, Arnold Papers, LC.
2 Arnold letter to Andrews, April 26, 1943, Arnold Papers, LC.
3 Arnold, *Global Mission,* 440.
4 Eaker letter to Arnold, June 8, 1943, Eaker Papers, LC.
5 Coffey, *HAP,* see 304–7, 308–9, 312–13, 343–45, 358–63, and 381–82 for details of Arnold's continuing heart trouble and how it influenced his behavior both in regard to Eaker and in general.
6 *Foreign Relations of the United States, The Conferences at Washington and Quebec, 1943,* 24, 25, 241–53. Also see Richards, *Portal of Hungerford,* 16; Webster and Frankland, 2:23; Harriman, *Special Envoy,* 210–11. Harris had also given the Eaker Plan strong support in letters to Churchill on April 22 and to Portal April 15, per Saward, *Bomber Harris,* 202–14.
7 Ibid.
8 Hansell, *The Air Plan That Defeated Hitler,* 168–71.
9 Eisenhower Papers, 961. Marshall cable to Devers for Eaker, May 20, 1943, Eaker Papers, LC.
10 Eaker letter to Arnold, June 8, 1943. Eaker Papers, LC. Dugan, "Ploesti: German Defenses and Allied Intelligence," *The Airpower Historian,* January 1962.
11 Hansell, *The Air Plan That Defeated Hitler,* 122–24; The inaccurate report about tanks came from Col. Emmett O'Donnell (see 26 below).
12 Hansell, see 8 above, 126.
13 Ibid 123–24. Eaker letter to Arnold, April 16, 1943. Arnold Papers, LC.
14 Eaker letter to Arnold, May 18, 1943, Arnold Papers, LC. Hansell, see 11 above, 125.
15 Craven and Cate, 2:339–41. Hansell comment is from Copp, *Forged in Fire,* 399. Eaker statement to Brady was overheard by the author.

16 Eaker letter to Giles, May 28, 1943, Eaker Papers, LC.
17 Ibid.
18 Lovett interview with the author, December 14, 1983, Locust Valley, New York.
19 Ibid.
20 Eaker letter, see 16 above.
21 Eaker letter to Arnold, see 13 above.
22 Giles letter to Eaker, June 11, 1943, Eaker Papers, LC.
23 Arnold cable to Devers for Eaker, June 12, 1943.
24 Cable to Arnold from Eaker signed Devers, June 12, 1943, Eaker Papers, LC.
25 Arnold letter to Eaker, June 15, 1943, Eaker Papers, LC.
26 O'Donnell memorandum to Arnold, June 12, 1943, Arnold Papers, LC.
27 Eaker interview with Coffey, April 9, 1975, Washington, D.C.
28 Arnold cable to Devers for Eaker, June 26, 1943, Eaker Papers, LC.
29 Eaker letter to Arnold, June 29, 1943, Eaker Papers, LC.
30 Two letters from Arnold to Eaker, June 28, 1943, Arnold Papers, LC.
31 Eaker letter to Arnold, July 6, 1943, Arnold Papers. LC.
32 Eaker cable to Arnold with Devers addendum, June 22, 1943. Harriman cable to Lovett, June 28, 1943. Eaker, in approving Harriman's draft, wrote him: "I am very grateful for the message you brought back to me and for the efforts you made in our behalf while you were home. I am sure that has done much to take the load off us here. . . ." In a June 28, 1943 letter to Lovett Eaker wrote: "Averill Harriman talked to me shortly after his return. . . . He felt quite certain that General Arnold was not inimical to me, either personally or officially, and that he was keenly bent on helping us in every way. He thought, as you did, that our reporting has been defective, for it was quite certain that General Arnold did not have our picture clearly." Eaker Papers, LC.
33 Lovett memorandum to Arnold, June 19, 1943, Eaker Papers, LC.
34 Arnold letter to Eaker, July 7, 1943, Arnold Papers, LC.
35 Lovett interview, see 18 above.
36 Lovett memoranda to Arnold, June 18 and 19, 1943, Eaker Papers, LC.
37 Arnold directive to Giles, June 22, 1943. Arnold Papers, LC.
   Giles-Kindelberger details are drawn from Coffey, *HAP*, 308.
38 Craven and Cate, 1:604.
39 Eaker interviews with Donald Shaughnessy, 1959, COHC.
40 Eaker letter to Lovett, July 6, 1943, Eaker Papers, LC.
41 Lovett letter to Eaker, July 7, 1943, Eaker Papers, LC.

CHAPTER 17
(pages 282–308)

1 Norcross letter to the author, March 17, 1983.
2 Craven and Cate, 2:242–43 and 313.
3 Ibid., 315–16.
4 Ibid., 308–9; 843–45.
5 Cooper, *The German Air Force, 1933–1945,* 298–301.
6 Ibid., 302–3. See also Murray, *Strategy for Defeat,* 149 and 179.
7 Coffey, *Decision Over Schweinfurt,* 264.
8 Speech at the Air Force Academy, May 1968, cited in Hansell's *Air Plan That Defeated Hitler,* 131–35.

9 Eaker interview with Tom Coffey, April 18, 1975, Washington, D.C.
10 Eaker letter to Johnson, June 19, 1943, Eaker Papers, LC.
11 Copp, *Forged in Fire,* 434–35.
12 Craven and Cate, see 2 above, 642–43.
13 Ibid., 621 and 636–41.
14 TRIDENT Conference Proceedings, see Chapter 16, note 6, 248.
15 QUADRANT Conference Proceedings, 1019.
16 Freeman, *Mighty Eighth Diary,* 78–80 and Craven and Cate, 3:279.
17 Eaker letter to Arnold, July 20, 1943, Arnold Papers, LC. Eaker had begun
the H2S tests on March 3 with a directive to VIII Bomber Command saying
Portal had agreed to provide H2S equipment and that "I am concerned . . .
that we employ to the fullest extent as soon as possible all the late
instrument navigational devices so that we can operate in wider range of
weather than has been possible in the past." Eaker Papers, LC.
18 Eaker memorandum to Devers, July 17, 1943 and letter to Spaatz, July 19,
1943, Eaker Papers, LC.
19 Freeman, see 16 above, 41.
20 Eaker memorandum to Devers, March 9, 1943 and 2nd endorsement to CG,
VIII Bomber Command, March 16, Eaker Papers, LC.
21 The author was present at the WIDEWING presentation. Reprimand is in the
Eaker Papers, LC.
22 The author was a frequent guest of the Lyons. Quote from *New York Times*
obituary, March 26, 1979.
23 Wyler and the author worked closely together during the war and after.
Eaker letter went to Col. Milton W. Kaye, Chief, Photographic Services,
June 14, 1943. See also Eaker's directive of June, 1943 to CG, VIII Bomber
Command, regarding return of the *Memphis Belle* and crew to the U.S.,
Eaker Papers, LC.
24 Eaker letter to Arnold, June 10, 1943, Arnold Papers, LC. press conference
release, June 10, 1943 and Eaker letter to Lovett, June 17, 1943, Eaker
Papers, LC.
25 Marshall cable to Devers, June 14, 1943 and Eaker memorandum to
Edwards, June 15, 1943, Eaker Papers, LC.
26 Lovett letter to Eaker, June 17, 1943, Eaker Papers, LC.
27 Steinhoff speech, see 8 above, 134.
28 Lovett letter to Eaker, July 1, 1943. Eaker letter to Giles, August 6, 1943
mentions Arnold cable, Eaker Papers, LC. Eaker letter to Arnold, August
7, 1943, Arnold Papers, LC.
29 Freeman, see 16 above, 86–89.
30 Coffey, see 7 above, 32.
31 As recounted by Eaker to the author.
32 Freeman, see 16 above, 89–95.
33 Coffey, see 7 above, 84–89 and 271–73.
34 QUADRANT, see 15 above 412–13, 447, 474, and 496–98.
35 Ibid., 850–52.
36 Ibid., 854–55.
37 Ibid., 872.
38 Ibid., 1018–19.
39 Ibid., 1022.
40 Craven and Cate, see 2 above, 640. Eaker letter to Lovett, September 16,
1943, Eaker Papers, LC.

41 Lovett letter to Eaker, August 21, 1943 and Eaker letter to Lovett, September 16, 1943, Eaker Papers, LC. Freeman, see 16 above, 102–19.

42 Eaker letter to Arnold, September 11, 1943, Arnold Papers, LC. Eaker letter to Spaatz, September 11, 1943, Eaker Papers, LC.

43 Eaker letter to Capt. Anna W. Wilson, Grosvenor Square, London, August 1, 1943 includes comment, "We in the Eighth Air Force feel honored and very fortunate that this first unit is largely for service with us." Eaker Papers, LC.

44 Barnett, see Chapter 9, note 3.

CHAPTER 18
(pages 309–28)

1 Eaker and Arthur G. B. Metcalf, "Conversations with Albert Speer," *Air Force Magazine,* April 1977.

2 Craven and Cate, 2:703–04. Speer, *Inside the Third Reich,* 285. Hansell interview with the author concerning fuse settings, April 27, 1984.

3 Jones, *The Wizard War,* 346–47.

4 Richards, *Portal of Hungerford,* 313–16. Webster and Frankland, 2:10–15, 34–35, 43, and 53–70.

5 Richards, see 4 above, 318–30.

6 Eaker letter to Lovett, October 9, 1943, Eaker Papers, LC.

7 Craven and Cate, see 2 above, 696–99. Freeman, *The Mighty Eighth,* 67–77, and *Mighty Eighth Diary,* 120–25. Eaker quote from letter to Lovett, November 1, 1943, Eaker Papers. LC. See also Eaker interview with Coffey, April 24, 1975. ULTRA influence noted by Williamson Murray, *Air University Review,* July–August, 1984, 56.

8 Ibid., Craven and Cate, 699–701, Freeman, *The Mighty Eighth,* 78–79, and *Mighty Eighth Diary,* 126–27.

9 Freeman, *Mighty Eighth Diary,* 126. Eaker, Coffey interview, see 7 above.

10 Arnold Papers, LC.

11 Dill note in Arnold Papers, LC. Speer quote from *Inside the Third Reich,* 286. Arnold press conference discussed in Coffey, *Decision over Schweinfurt,* 34–36. Eaker quotes from Coffey interview, see 7 above. Eaker's October 19 letter to Arnold concerning the 25 percent loss comment remarked, "It seems to me well to remember that our overall losses are still below 5%. From the standpoint of maintaining crew morale I am anxious that our crews do not feel that their leaders anticipate enormous losses." Eaker Papers, LC.

12 Arnold cables to Kenney, October 28, 1943, and to Spaatz, October 29. Cutback of P-51s to RAF for reconnaissance involved British commitment to ship 150 Spitfires per month to Russia as outlined in Giles letter to Eaker, December 16, 1943, all in Arnold Papers, LC. Portal message to Eaker, October 15, 1943. Churchill to Devers for Eaker, undated. Marshall to Devers for Eaker, October 11, 1943, all in Eaker Papers, LC.

13 Arnold's two commendations and "collapse" message in Eaker Papers, LC, as are Eaker's two letters of October 15, 1943 and cable of October 22.

14 Arnold cable to Devers for Eaker, September 25, 1943, Eaker Papers, LC. Kuter memoranda to Arnold and Loutzenheiser, September 28 and October 11, 1943, are in Kuter Papers, USAF Academy, as is prior exchange with Arnold in which Kuter writes, "This will make Air Marshal Portal mad," and Arnold scribbled back, "That's just what I want to do—HAA." Arnold

cabled to Devers for Portal, October 17, 1943, Eaker Papers, LC.

15 Eaker interviews with Donald Shaughnessy, 1959, COHC.

16 Parton, Hansell interview, see 2 above.

17 Marshall to Devers, September 7, 1943. General Orders, No. 1, headquarters, USAAF/UK, October 15, 1943, Eaker Papers, LC.

18 Eaker memorandum to Devers, October 1, 1943, Eaker Papers, LC.

19 Anderson memorandum to Eaker, October 12, 1943, Eaker Papers, LC.

20 Arnold, *Global Mission*, 495.

21 Eaker letter to Arnold, October 22, 1943, Eaker Papers, LC.

22 Freeman, *Mighty Eighth Diary*, see 9 above, 131–60.

23 Parton, Hansell interview, see 2 above.

24 Eaker letter, see 21 above, 165–66. Eaker quote from undated Coffey interview with Dudley Saward, biographer of Harris.

25 Eaker, Coffey interview, see 7 above.

26 Craven and Cate, 2:703–6.

27 Harris quote from *Fortune*, "The Fleeting Opportunity," December 1943.

28 See Chapter 16, note 29. See also Arnold's *Global Mission*, 495. "We had the planes and the replacement crews by then to maintain the loss rate of 25% which I had originally determined must be faced."

29 LeMay concurred in this judgment. Asked by the author in an interview, April 16, 1985, "Was there ever a directive from anyone saying let's wait for deep penetrations until we have the P-51?" he replied, "No, I don't think anything like that ever occurred. . . . I don't think there was ever definite waiting for fighters. There's a lot of muddled thinking by writers on this subject. Everyone seems to say that we got over there and, lo and behold, we woke up to the fact that we always had to have fighters to penetrate. The doctrine was that we would always have fighters to accompany the bombers on a mission. . . . Those had long since fallen by the boards due to budget considerations and we not only didn't have any but we didn't even have any drawings. . . . We had to depend only on what fighters were available."

CHAPTER 19
(pages 329–46)

1 *Foreign Relations of the United States, Diplomatic Papers: The Conferences at Cairo and Teheran 1943*, GPO, 1961, Roosevelt quote, 39.

2 Ibid, 110–11.

3 Ibid, 214–21.

4 Ibid, 228–29 and 231.

5 Arnold letter to Spaatz, November 15, 1942, Spaatz Papers, LC.

6 See 1 above, for references to Russia see 43, 70–71, 130–33, 141–48 and 152–55; to unity of command see 150–51, 195, 203–9 and 246–55; for Marshall as likely supreme commander see Churchill message to Roosevelt, 131, "Can you give me a firm date when Marshall will be available? . . . Press this morning publishes reports from Washington correspondents that Marshall will be succeeded by Eisenhower and Eisenhower by Alexander. . . ."; also, minutes of meeting of U.S. Chiefs with Roosevelt, November 15, 195, when FDR said "it was his idea that General Marshall should be the commander in chief and command all the British, French, Italian and U.S. troops involved. . . ."

7 Ibid, 432–35, 529, 576–77 and 836–38.

8 Ibid, 681–86.

9 Ibid, 734, 756–57, 761 and 819.

10 Dill comment cited in footnote, Webster and Frankland, 2:86.

11 Arnold diary, Arnold Papers, LC. Five cables about Ruth Eaker, December 16–19, Spaatz Papers, LC.

12 Spaatz's diary was sporadic, sometimes in his own hand, sometimes recorded on typewriter by Harvard Professor Bruce Hopper, who was Eighth Air Force Historian. Entries quoted here are Hopper version, AFHRC. See also Hopper's own "Journal," Spaatz Papers, LC.

13 Portal letter to Arnold, December 15, 1943, Arnold Papers, LC.

14 Arnold message to Devers for Eaker, December 18, 1943, Eaker Papers, LC.

15 Arnold comment, see Chapter 16, note 34.

16 Eaker message to Arnold, December 19, 1943, Eaker Papers, LC.

17 Eaker messages to Spaatz and Eisenhower, December 19, 1943, Eaker Papers, LC.

18 Spaatz message to Arnold, December 19, 1943, copied in Spaatz diary, AFHRC. Spaatz message to Eaker, December 21, 1943, Eaker Papers, LC.

19 Eisenhower message to Spaatz, December 24, 1943, Spaatz Papers, LC. Arnold message to Devers, December 20, 1943, and Arnold message to Eaker, December 21, 1943, Eaker Papers, LC.

20 Adjutant Gen. Ulio message to Eaker, December 23, 1943, and Eaker message to Arnold, December 24, 1943, Eaker Papers, LC.

21 Eisenhower messages to Marshall, December 17 and 23, 1943, nos. 1423 and 1426. Marshall message to Eisenhower, December 21, 1943, no. 5585. See also Pogue, *George C. Marshall: Organizer of Victory,* 370–76.

22 Spaatz diary, see 12 above.

23 Ibid.

24 Eisenhower message to Marshall, December 25, 1943, EP no. 1428.

25 Eisenhower message to Devers for Eaker, December 25, 1943, EP no. 1429.

26 Marshall message to Eisenhower, December 28, 1943, no. 5810.

27 Spaatz diary, see 12 above. Eaker quote from interview with Tom Coffey, April 24, 1975. Smith message to Eisenhower, January 1, 1944, is copied in Spaatz diary.

28 Arnold letter to Eaker, December 26, 1943, and others mentioned, Eaker Papers, LC.

29 Lovett letter to Eaker, December 28, 1943, Eaker Papers, LC.

30 A. L. F. Haynes, Lord Mayor of High Wycombe, letter to Eaker, January 8, 1944, Eaker Papers, LC.

31 Coffey interview, see 27 above, plus author's recollections. Eaker directive to Chauncey concerning Eighth Air Force report, December 27, 1943, Eaker Papers, LC.

32 Churchill, *Second World War,* 5:438–60; quote is from 450. Years later Eaker remembered their meeting as happening in Casablanca, but his memory was faulty, for the prime minister was too ill to leave Marrakesh until he headed for home January 14.

33 Over the years Eaker often mentioned or wrote about this meeting, sometimes with variations of phrasing. This is the version used in Coffey, *Decision over Schweinfurt,* 348.

34 Quoted by Eaker in a speech published in *King's Cliffe Remembered,* 20th Fighter Group newsletter, May 1983.

Notes

CHAPTER 20
(pages 351–70)

1 The chief source for this paragraph and much of this chapter is *The History of M.A.A.F., December 10, 1943–May 9, 1945,* prepared by the author of this book in his part-time assignment as MAAF Historian. In some instances I have picked up or closely paraphrased portions of its 420 pages or the accompanying 53 volumes of supporting documents but have not always indicated them by quotation marks since I am quoting myself. Figures used in this paragraph are on 3 and 5, Parton Papers, HL.

2 Eaker letter to Lovett, January 23, 1944, Eaker Papers, LC.

3 *MAAF History,* see 1 above, 14.

4 Ibid, 14–18. Spaatz quote is from his interview with Bruce Hopper, May 20, 1945, Spaatz Papers, LC.

5 Childs quote from *Washington Post,* February 3, 1945.

6 CCS Directive of December 4, 1943, creating USSTAF was amended by the JCS on January 5, 1944. *MAAF History,* see 1 above, 18. Eaker letter to Lovett, see 2 above.

7 Slessor, *The Central Blue,* 561–67. Blumenson, *Anzio: The Gamble That Failed,* 45–47, 50, 57 and 66–68. *MAAF History,* see 1 above, 151–72.

8 Craven and Cate, 3:346–61. Devers message to Arnold, March 10, 1944, Eaker Papers, LC. Churchill quotes from *Second World War,* 5:488, 5:490. Memorandum, March 4, 1944, headquarters, Fifth Army on "Influence of Allied Bombing Operations in the Anzio Beachhead" by 1st Lt. Charles N. Bourke, assistant adjutant general, lists bomb statistics and the POW comments about them, Eaker Papers, LC. Kesselring quote cited in *The Italian Campaign,* Time-Life Books, 139.

9 Slessor, see 7 above, 578.

10 Ellis, *Cassino: The Hollow Victory,* 114. Hapgood and Richardson, *Monte Cassino,* 114, 115, 143 and 148–50.

11 Hapgood and Richardson, see 10 above, 151–54.

12 Ibid, 31 and 155–72.

13 Ibid, 185–86.

14 Ibid, 202–44. See also Craven and Cate, 3:355 and 362–64.

15 *MAAF History,* see 1 above, 142–50.

16 Ibid.

17 Ibid, 147–48.

18 Parton Papers, HL.

19 Eaker Papers, LC.

20 Ibid.

21 Ibid, February 7, 1944.

22 Ibid, April 7, 1944.

23 Pamela Churchill letter to Eaker, March 10, 1944, Eaker Papers, LC.

24 Ibid, January 28, 1944.

CHAPTER 21
(pages 371–91)

1 Von Senger und Etterlin, *Neither Fear Nor Hope,* 202–3.

2 Alexander interviews with Dr. Stanley Mathews, January 10–15, 1949, USMHI.

3 Arnold letter to Eaker, undated, but obviously in late February 1944, Eaker Papers, LC.

4 *MAAF History*, 175. MATAF operations order P.TAF/69/Air, March 13, 1944, AFHRC.

5 Ibid, 175–85. Buckley quote cited in *The Italian Campaign*, Time-Life Books, 145.

6 *MAAF History*, see 4 above. POW Interrogation Report, headquarters, C.S.D.I.C., A.A.I., to the author, March 23, 1944, AFHRC. See also Ellis, *Cassino: The Hollow Victory*, 221–25.

7 Eaker Redline to Spaatz, March 15, 1944. Eaker letter to Twining, March 17, 1944. Eaker letter to Leese, March 16, and his reply, March 18, 1944—all in Eaker Papers, LC.

8 Eaker memorandum to Wilson, April 12, 1944. Eaker letter to Devers, April 6, 1944. Eaker letter to Arnold, April 4, 1944—all in Eaker Papers, LC.

9 Eaker letter to Arnold, see 8 above.

10 Statistics on casualties in hand-written note from Maj. Gen. Alfred M. Gruenther, Clark's chief of staff, to Eaker, April 5, 1944, Eaker Papers, LC. Alexander quotes, see 2 above.

11 Eaker letter to Arnold, April 8, 1944, Eaker Papers, LC.

12 Slessor, *The Central Blue*, 568.

13 Ibid, 569. *MAAF History*, see 4 above, 187–89.

14 Ibid, 189–90. The Italian general was B. A. Venceslas D'Aurelio.

15 Ibid, 191–92.

16 Slessor, see 12 above, 569–70.

17 Ibid, 572.

18 Statistics from MAAF pamphlet, *Air Power in the Mediterranean*, February 27, 1945, prepared by the Historical Section, which was headed by the author, AFHRC.

19 Among the skeptics of STRANGLE are Sallager, F.M., *Operation Strangle* and Ellis, John, *Cassino: The Hollow Victory*. The first cites my *MAAF History* as a major source but, in my opinion, misinterprets the evidence. The second is superbly expert on ground action but betrays a shallow understanding of the capabilities and limitations of air power. Craven and Cate, 3:373–84, give a more balanced summary. Air Plan for DIADEM cited in *MAAF History*, 198.

20 Clark's actions in DIADEM have been discussed by many historians—most fully in Ellis, see 19 above, 165 *et seq.* Eaker quotes from interview with the author, October 1983.

21 JCS 1794, June 18, 1944. Cited in *MAAF History*, 214–15 and in Slessor, see 12 above, 580–84.

22 *MAAF History*, 132, 134 and 138–39. Craven and Cate, 172–79.

23 Pamphlet statistics, see 18 above, 10–11.

24 Ibid.

25 The preceding five paragraphs are drawn, in some sentences verbatim, from the author's *MAAF History*, 49–60.

26 Ibid. Cannon memo to Eaker, April 16, 1944, summarized Vesuvius damage as then tallied—80 planes hit, 60 of them irreparably, AFHRC.

27 Eaker letter to Arnold, April 19, 1944, Arnold Papers, LC.

CHAPTER 22
(pages 392–413)

1 Deane quote cited in Pogue, *George C. Marshall*, 3:530. Other details from *The History of FRANTIC, American Shuttle-Bombing to and from Russian*

Bases, 26 October 1943–15 June 1944, prepared by the author in his role as MAAF Historian, July 12, 1944, Parton Papers, HL.

2 Ibid.

3 Ibid.

4 Ibid. See also the most comprehensive postwar study, Thomas Anthony Julian, *"Operation FRANTIC and the Search for American-Soviet Military Collaboration,"* (Ph.D. diss., Syracuse University, 1968), 175–78.

5 FRANTIC, see 1 above, 20. See also Infield, *The Poltava Affair,* 59 and 63.

6 FRANTIC, see 1 above, 21.

7 Ibid, 18–20. *Operation FRANTIC,* see 4 above, 197–2. Eaker letter to Arnold, June 1, 1944, Arnold Papers, LC.

8 FRANTIC, see 1 above, 21–22.

9 Deane, *The Strange Alliance,* 119–21.

10 Eaker diary, Parton Papers, HL.

11 FRANTIC, see 1 above, 22–23.

12 Ibid, plus author's recollections.

13 Ibid, 10, 11, 15 and 16.

14 Eaker letter to Lovett, June 13, 1944, Eaker Papers, LC.

15 FRANTIC, see 1 above, 24.

16 Parton Papers, HL, contain all the author's wartime correspondence.

17 Eaker letter, see 14 above.

18 Deane, see 9 above, 122.

19 *Operation FRANTIC,* see 4 above, 226–29.

20 Eaker speech to Squadron Officers School, Air University, November 21, 1974, published in *Aerospace Historian,* June 1978.

21 *Operation FRANTIC,* see 4 above, 214–20.

22 Deane, see 9 above, 122.

23 Sutterlin message to Spaatz for Anderson, June 22, 1944, Spaatz Papers, LC. Eaker letter to Arnold, June 26, 1944, Eaker Papers, LC. See also *Operation FRANTIC,* 4 above, 230–37.

24 Gray interview with the author, November 1983, St. Petersburg, Florida.

25 *Operation FRANTIC,* see 4 above, 241–42 and 248–50.

26 Ibid, 243, 251–55 and 259.

27 Ibid, 268 and 271.

28 *Operation FRANTIC,* see 4 above, 276–88. See also Craven and Cate, 3:316–17. Harriman letter to Eaker, August 19, 1944, Eaker Papers, LC.

29 *Operation FRANTIC,* see 4 above, 289–95. Eaker letter to Arnold, August 26, 1944, Eaker Papers, LC.

30 *Operation FRANTIC,* see 4 above, 300–2, 308–10, 327–29 and 339.

31 Ibid, 343.

32 Ibid, 345 and 349.

33 Deane, see 9 above, 124–25.

34 Harriman letter to Hopkins, September 10, 1944, Julian thesis, see 4 above, 306.

CHAPTER 23

(pages 414–31)

1 Slessor, *The Central Blue,* 585.

2 Macmillan, *War Diaries,* 469.

3 Slessor, see 1 above, 586–88. Macmillan, see 2 above, 476. Marshall comment from Eaker interview with Tom Coffey, October 27, 1978.

4 *MAAF History,* 123 and 216–48, Parton Papers, HL.
5 Ibid.
6 Ibid.
7 Ibid.
8 Ibid.
9 Eaker diary and letter to his father, August 22, 1944, Eaker Papers, LC.
10 For the full story of Whitney's capture and escape see his 17-page "Statement" after his return, Eaker Papers, LC, and Kahn, E. J., *Jock.*
11 *MAAF History,* 37–38, 291–18. Eaker letter to Lessig, March 20, 1944, Eaker Papers, LC.
12 Cate, Curtis, *Antoine de Saint-Exupéry,* 524–27.
13 Eaker comment to the author.
14 Butcher, *My Three Years with Eisenhower,* 648.
15 Eaker comment, see 13 above. Eaker message to Arnold, August 18, 1944, Eaker Papers, LC.
16 Collins and Lapierre, *Is Paris Burning,* 83–320, gives elaborate detail on de Gaulle's coup. See also Eisenhower message to CCS, August 15, 1944, Eisenhower Papers, 2069–70.
17 *MAAF History,* 249–51. Much of this paragraph and succeeding ones in this chapter are picked up, close to verbatim, from this *History* the author wrote in 1945.
18 *MAAF History,* 319–40.
19 Ibid. See also *New York Times* obituary of Kraigher, September 18, 1984. The author accompanied Kraigher on two B-25 supply drops over Yugoslavia.
20 Ibid.
21 Ibid.
22 As of May 8, 1945, the date the war ended, MAAF had recovered 6,267 fliers, of whom the 5,718 men of the Fifteenth Air Force were 25 percent of its total MIA of 22,753, and the 549 men of the Twelfth were 10 percent of its total MIA of 5,425.
23 Butcher, see 14 above, 549 records on May 28, 1944 ". . . an emissary of Marshal Tito visited Ike. . . . Ike wrote Gen. Marshall . . . to increase the flow of supplies to Tito. Now the Chief of Staff has replied that General Eaker has temporarily assigned an additional troop-carrier group from southern Italy and has seven B-25s, 30 heavies of the RAF and 40 Italian bombers engaged in delivering supplies. . . ." See also Eaker letter to Arnold, October 1, 1944, reporting his decision on Greece, Eaker Papers, LC.
24 Slessor, see 1 above, 558 and 623.
25 Eaker letter to Arnold, June 1, 1944, Eaker Papers, LC.
26 Macmillan, see 2 above, 454.
27 The author met Tito at the time and heard the dinner anecdote from Eaker.
28 Macmillan, see 2 above, 500.
29 Eaker diary. Translation of Tito's letter to Eaker, February 5, 1945 and Eaker's reply and memo to Wilder, both February 13, 1945. Cables from Belgrade, March 8 and 9, 1945. All in Eaker Papers, LC.
30 *MAAF History,* 252–53 and 341–9.
31 Ibid, 379.
32 Eaker memorandum to Wilson, November 22, 1944, Eaker Papers, LC.

Notes

33 Eaker message to Arnold, November 16, 1944, Eaker Papers, LC.
34 *MAAF History*, 385.
35 Deane, *The Strange Alliance*, 137–39 and 141.
36 Eaker diary, LC.
37 Eaker letter to Hansell, April 10, 1944, Eaker Papers, LC.
38 Eaker letters to Arnold, July 11 and October 9, 1944, Eaker Papers, LC.

CHAPTER 24
(pages 432–48)
1 Lovett letter to Eaker, January 28, 1945, Eaker Papers, LC.
2 Pogue, *Marshall*, 3:72.
3 Giles Oral History 814, AFHRC.
4 Marshall letter to Arnold, March 15, 1945, and Arnold's reply, March 19, both in Marshall Library, Lexington, Virginia.
5 Harriman wrote that his visa request for Eaker on March 15 "was not even answered," *Special Envoy*, 422–23. See also Eaker diary, LC. Eaker quote is from his Oral History 626, AFHRC, and his "Conversations," AWC, both given many years later. In them he recalls that Marshall himself came to Cannes for the meeting. But this must be an example, so often found in oral histories, of memory playing tricks, for Marshall's diary, at Lexington, makes it clear that the chief of staff was in Washington for the entire month of March. Possibly Spaatz and Eaker did talk with him about Arnold's illness, etc., in Marseille earlier that year when Marshall paused on the way home from Yalta.
6 The author did interview Schacht, Thyssen and others, at Capri on May 12, 1945. The talks produced a few tidbits of valuable intelligence, the only thing worth quoting here was the unexpected touch of humor supplied by the proverbially dour head of the Reichsbank. Told that there were rumors Hitler was dead, Schacht said, "I wouldn't believe it if he told me so himself." Parton Papers, HL.
7 7Eisenhower Papers, nos. 2426–27.
8 Eaker diary, LC. Stroud and Searle wrote Eaker touching letters of affection, gratitude and pride. Bebe Daniels wrote a long letter ending, "You've made hundreds of friends over here who are going to miss you like the devil, and I'm one of the hundreds."
9 Eaker diary, LC. Also Eaker conversation with Lt. Col. Joe B. Green, February 11, 1967, AWC.
10 Ibid. Eaker speech quoted from Narrative History, headquarters, XXI Bomber Command, Twentieth Air Force, AFHRC. Eaker quotes from interview with the author, October 27, 1983. LeMay quotes from interview with the author, April 16, 1985.
11 Eaker interview with Robert Sherrod, November 20, 1975, Washington, D.C.
12 Ibid. Also Eaker diary, LC.
13 Arnold, *Global Mission*, 549–50.
14 Arnold Journal, Box 272, Arnold Papers, LC. Also his *Global Mission*, 563 and 565.
15 Eaker diary, see 8 above.
16 Eaker, Sherrod interview, see 11 above.
17 Lovett letter to Spaatz, May 6, 1945, AFHRC.
18 The original, framed, hung in Eaker's study for forty years.

19 Arnold letter to Eaker, June 8, 1945, Arnold Papers, LC.
20 Arnold, *Global Mission*, 565 and 569.
21 Eaker interviews with Herman S. Wolk, August 7, 1974, and Tom Coffey, October 27, 1978, both in Washington, D.C.
22 Spaatz interview with Dr. Arthur Goldberg, Office of Air Force History, May 19, 1965; see also his interview with Noel Parrish, February 21, 1962, both at AFHRC. For a crisp and measured consideration of the broad factors involved as perceived then, see Henry Stimson, "The Decision to Use the Atomic Bomb," *Harpers Magazine*, February 1947.
23 Eaker, Green interview, see 9 above.
24 Eaker, Sherrod interview, see 11 above.
25 *The Southeastern*, Durant, Oklahoma, July 11, 1945.
26 Itinerary from "Inspection of Selected Areas of Germany, August 15–20, 1945," 519.152–3, AFHRC. Eaker quote from interview with Arthur K. Marmor, Office of Air Force History, January 1966, AFHRC.
27 Eaker letter to Harris, November 26, 1945, Eaker Papers, LC.
28 Wolk, *Planning and Organizing the Postwar Air Force, 1943–1947*.
29 Ibid.
30 Ibid.
31 Harris Hull was with Eaker and overheard Eisenhower's remark.
32 Eaker interview with the author, October 13, 1983.
33 Symington interview with the author, November 4, 1983.
34 Eaker letter to Alexander F. Jones, March 14, 1947, Eaker Papers, LC.
35 Spaatz Papers, LC.
36 Eaker Papers, LC.
37 *New York Times*, June 14, 1947.
38 Eisenhower also sent Eaker a more conventional but glowing letter on June 13, 1947, saying, in part: "I must say that the thought of your impending departure fills me with a special feeling of regret, even sadness. In war and in peace you have served the Air Forces, the whole Army and the country so well that your name will always be synonymous with the soldierly qualities that have brought our nation victory in all its wars. All of us in the War Department have come to count with such certainty upon your staunch loyalty, wisdom and energetic performance that your going will leave a gap that will never be completely filled. . . ." Eisenhower Papers, nos. 1754–55.

CHAPTER 25
(pages 453–70)
1 Ruth Eaker interview with the author, October 12, 1983, Washington, D.C.
2 Eaker interview with Lt. Col. Joe B. Green, March 30, 1972, 43, USMHI.
3 Minutes, board of directors, Oklahoma Historical Society, July 24, 1947. The painting is by Boris Gordon, Washington, D.C.
4 Eaker letter to Smith, August 15, 1947, Eaker Papers, LC.
5 Eaker unpublished article, "Howard Hughes, As I Knew Him," written in 1962, Eaker Papers, LC.
6 Ibid.
7 Ibid.
8 Ibid.
9 *Time Magazine* cover story obituary on Hughes, April 19, 1976.

Notes

10 Bartlett and Steele, *Empire, The Life, Legend and Madness of Howard Hughes,* 136–44 and 156–57.

11 Ibid, 153.

12 *Fortune Magazine,* February 1954, 116.

13 George telephone interview with the author, December 20, 1983. Also talk with Ruth Eaker, February 4, 1985. Hughes pledge to George is quoted in *Fortune,* see 12 above.

14 Thornton letter to Eaker, June 3, 1947, and latter's reply, June 9, Eaker Papers, LC. Thornton hiring in Houston confirmed in Eaker interview with the author, September 13, 1983, Washington, D.C.

15 *Fortune,* see 12 above.

16 Eaker article, see 5 above.

17 Ibid.

18 *Fortune,* see 12 above.

19 Undated (but probably 1950) spiral-bound brochure, "Research and Development Laboratories, Hughes Aircraft Company," author's collection.

20 *Aviation Week,* October 6, 1952, 52, 56 and 59.

21 Eaker "The Lindbergh I Knew," speech in St. Louis, Missouri, April 22, 1977, published in *Aerospace Historian,* December 1977.

22 Eaker interview with the author, March 5, 1984, Washington. Stameshkin interview with the author, 1984, Los Angeles. Ruth Eaker interview, see 1 above. Eaker article, see 5 above.

23 *Op. cit.,* #5.

24 Copy of the Dietrich memorandum, undated but obviously 1954, author's collection. Johnson remarks in *Congressional Record,* 94, March 8–May 10, 1948, appendix, 1626–27.

25 Eaker comment to the author, 1983.

26 Eaker and Arnold Papers, LC.

27 Eaker letter to Fechet, February 24, 1947, Eaker Papers, LC. Ruth Spaatz interview with the author, October 7, 1983. Lessig interview with the author, August 1983. Eaker interview with the author, March 28, 1983.

28 Bartlett and Steele, see 10 above, and *Fortune,* see 12 above.

29 Ibid.

30 Bartlett and Steele, see 10 above, 199–201.

31 Ibid.

32 Ibid, 202–4.

33 Details on Dietrich plot, Bartlett and Steele, see 10 above, 228.

34 Hyland interview with the author, December 20, 1983, El Segundo, California.

35 Details of the Eaker resignation from interview with the author, 1957, Washington, D.C.

36 Eaker article, see 5 above.

CHAPTER 26
(pages 471–89)

1 Ruth Eaker telephone talk with the author, February 14, 1985.

2 Eaker's notes, minutes and other papers concerning his directorship at Douglas, author's collection.

3 Hyland interview with the author, December 20, 1983, El Segundo, California.

525

4 Syndicate details from letters to the author from Charles Ohl, editor-general manager, Copley News Service, December 12, 1983, and Lt. Gen. Victor H. Krulak, USMC (Ret.), former president, December 14, 1983, and January 5, 1984, author's collection.

5 *Op. cit.,* #3.

6 Eaker quotes in order: 1) Speech, Alumni Association, Los Angeles, May 10, 1947; 2) Speech, Air War College, December 6, 1963; 3) Eaker column, March 22, 1965; 4) Eaker column, October 31, 1966; 5) Speech, California Chapter, Air Force Association, Santa Monica, California, March 27, 1967; 6) *Ordnance Magazine.* January-February, 1971; 7) *Ordnance Magazine,* July-August, 1971; 8) Speech, Inter American Defense College, October 13, 1971.

7 Metcalf interview with the author, September 22, 1983, Winchester, Massachusetts.

8 Ibid.

9 Ibid. Also membership roster, USSI, 1982–83, author's collection.

10 *Strategic Review,* 8, no. 1, April 1973, 2–3.

11 Ibid. Metcalf letter to the author, September 26, 1983, credits Eaker for arranging the first three articles.

12 "The St. Peter File," USSI.

13 Eaker letter to Metcalf, October 10, 1973.

14 Parton, Metcalf interview, see 7 above.

15 Metcalf letter to Eaker, October 15, 1973, USSI.

16 Eaker letters to Metcalf, April 24, 1974, October 26, 1976, and March 7, 1980, USSI. Eaker letter to Ed Gray, May 31, 1977, author's collection. Eaker letter to Whitney, October 1, 1976, Estate of J. H. Whitney.

17 *Air Force Magazine,* April 1977. Eaker's observation, "We must never allow the record of this war to convict us of throwing the strategic bomber at the man in the street," was in a letter to Spaatz, Jan. 1, 1945 (Box 20, Spaatz Papers, LC), vehemently objecting to proposals, chiefly from Harris but augmented by Soviet requests, to blitz Berlin, Leipzig, Dresden and other German cities as the Russian armies approached. Eaker cited his words in the Preface he wrote to David Irving's widely read 1964 book *The Destruction of Dresden.* That ancient center of German culture was destroyed by a fire storm created by the RAF on the nights of February 13 and 14 with help from an Eighth AF daylight attack aimed at railway yards in the city. Eaker had no part in the actual operation but defended it in the preface with words the *New York Times* quoted in its editorial on the fortieth anniversary of the bombing: "I deeply regret that British and U.S. bombers killed 135,000 people in the attack on Dresden, but I remember who started the last war and I regret even more the loss of more than 5,000,000 Allied lives in the necessary effort to completely defeat and utterly destroy nazism." (The actual death toll at Dresden has since been recalculated as closer to 30,000.)

18 Based on the author's regular contact with the Eakers during this period. Eaker report of Spaatz death from letter to the author July 29, 1974.

19 Data on the Eaker horses from clippings, Eaker Papers, LC.

20 The author was present.

Glossary

AAF	Army Air Forces
ACRU	Air Crew Rescue Unit
AFCE	Automatic Flight Control Equipment
AF/CHO	Air Force—Chief Historical Office
AFHRC	Air Force Historical Research Center
AFHQ	Allied Force Headquarters in the Mediterranean
ANVIL	First code name for the landings in southern France
AOC	Air Officer Commanding, an RAF usage.
ARCADIA	Washington CCS Conference, December 20, 1941–January 14, 1942
AWC	Army War College
ARMPIT	Code name for the proposed landings at the head of the Adriatic
AWPD-1	Air War Plans Division Plan at the start of World War II
AWPD-42	Revised Air War Plans Division Plan, 1942
BG	Bomber Group, AAF
BOLERO	Build-up of American forces in the United Kingdom for the invasion of France
CBO	Combined Bomber Offensive
CCS	Combined Chiefs of Staff, American and British
CG	Commanding General
CO	Commanding Officer
COA	Committee of Operations Analysts
COHC	Columbia Oral History Collection, Columbia University
CRT	Cathode Ray Tube
DFC	Distinguished Flying Cross
DH	De Havilland

DIADEM	Code name for the campaign to capture Rome, March–June, 1944
DRAGOON	Final code name for the invasion of southern France, previously called ANVIL
EOU	Embassy Operations Unit, the analytical committee at the U.S. embassy in London, 1943–44
EP	Eisenhower Papers
ETO	European Theater of Operations
FG	Fighter Group, AAF
FRANTIC	Code name for the shuttle-bombing operations to and from bases in Russia
FRANTIC JOE	Code name for the first shuttle-bombing mission to and from bases in Russia
GEE	British radio-navigational device, 1942
GHQAF	General Headquarters Air Force
GYMNAST	Code name for the capture of Casablanca, 1942
HL	Houghton Library, Harvard.
HUSKY	Code name for the invasion of Sicily, 1943
H2S	British radar navigation and blind-bombing device, 1943
H2X	American improvement of H2S, 1944
IFF	Identification Friend or Foe device used on British radar
ILS	Instrument Landing System
JCS	Joint Chiefs of Staff, U.S.
JUNIOR	Code name for Twelfth Air Force while in formation in England
LC	Library of Congress
MAAF	Mediterranean Allied Air Forces
MASAF	Mediterranean Allied Strategic Air Force
MATAF	Mediterranean Allied Tactical Air Force
MIA	Missing in Action
MTO	Mediterranean Theater of Operations
OBOE	British blind-bombing device controlled by ground stations
OKW	Oberkommando der Wehrmacht (German High Command)
OTU	Operational Training Unit
OVERLORD	Code name for the invasion of France, June 6, 1944
PINETREE	Code name for VIII Bomber Command Aq. and, subsequently, Eighth Air Force Hq. at High Wycombe, England
POINTBLANK	Code name for the Combined Bomber Offensive
PRU	Photo-reconnaissance Unit

Glossary

QUADRANT	CCS Conference at Quebec, August, 1943
RAF	Royal Air Force, Great Britain
REDLINE	Code name for automatic encoded and decoded messages between MAAF and USSTAF
RDF	Radio Direction Finder
ROUND-UP	Plan for possible invasion of France, 1943
ROTC	Reserve Officer Training Corp
SEXTANT	CCS Conference at Cairo, November–December, 1943
SHAEF	Supreme Headquarters, Allied Expeditionary Force, 1944–45
SHINGLE	Code name for the landings at Anzio, January 1944
SLEDGEHAMMER	Code name for possible invasion of France, October–November 1942
SOP	Standard Operating Procedure
SOUTHDOWN	Code name for RAF Bomber Command Hq. at High Wycombe, England
STARKEY	Code name for proposed attack on Pas de Calais area, Aug.–Sept. 1943
STRANGLE	Code name for MAAF interdiction campaign in Italy, March–June, 1944
TOOLCO	Abbreviation for Hughes Tool Company
TORCH	Code name for the invasion of North Africa, November 1942
TRIDENT	CCS Conference, Washington, May 1943
ULTRA	Code name for the British breaking and intercepting of the top German code
USAAF	United States Army Air Forces
USAAF/UK	United States Army Air Forces, United Kingdom
USAF	United States Air Force
USAFHRC	United States Air Force Historical Research Center, Air University, Maxwell AFB Alabama
USMHI	United States Military History Institute, Carlisle Barracks, Pennsylvania
USSI	United States Strategic Institute
USSTAF	United States Strategic Air Forces
VHF	Very High Frequency
VLR	Very Long Range
WIDEWING	Code name for Eighth Air Force Hq., Bushy Park, England, subsequently Eisenhower's Headquarters for TORCH
YAK	The basic Soviet fighter plane

Bibliography

Books, Theses and Major Documents

Air Ministry. *The Rise and Fall of the German Air Force, 1933–1945.* London for internal use only: Air Ministry, 1948. Reissued in New York: St. Martin's Press, 1983.

Alexander, Earl. *The Alexander Memoirs, 1940–1945.* New York: McGraw-Hill, 1962.

Ambrose, Stephen E. *The Supreme Commander: The War Years of General Dwight D. Eisenhower.* Garden City, New York: Doubleday, 1970.

Arnold, H.A. *Global Mission.* New York: Harper & Bros., 1949

Arnold, H.A., and Eaker, Ira C. *This Flying Game.* New York: Funk & Wagnalls, 1936. Revised 1943.

———. *Winged Warfare.* New York: Harper & Bros., 1941.

———. *Army Flier.* New York: Harper & Bros., 1942.

Babington-Smith, Constance. *Air Spy: The Story of Photo—Intelligence in World War II.* New York: Harper & Bros., 1957.

Bartlett, Donald L., and Steele, James B. *Empire: The Life, Legend, and Madness of Howard Hughes.* New York: W.W. Norton Co., 1979.

Blumenson, Martin. *Anzio: The Gamble That Failed.* Philadelphia: Lippincott, 1963.

———. *Bloody River: The Real Tragedy of the Rapido.* Boston: Houghton Mifflin, 1970.

Bond, Harold L. *Return to Cassino: A Memoir of the Fight for Rome.* New York: Doubleday, 1964.

Boylan, Lawrence B. *The Development of the Long-Range Escort Fighter.* Ph.D. Thesis, University of Missouri: 1955.

Bryant, Arthur. *The Turning of the Tide, 1939–1943.* New York: Doubleday, 1957.

———. *Triumph in the West, 1943–1946.* London: Collins, 1959.

Butcher, Harry. *My Three Years With Eisenhower.* New York: Simon & Schuster, 1946.

Chennault, Claire. *Way of a Fighter.* New York: G.P. Putnam's Sons, 1949.

Churchill, Winston S. *The Second World War, 6 Vols.,* Boston: Houghton Mifflin, 1948–1953.

Classic Aircraft of World War II: London, Bison Books Ltd., 1982.

Coffey, Thomas A. *Decision Over Schweinfurt.* New York: David McKay, 1977.

531

————. *HAP.* New York: Viking, 1982.

Collins, Larry, and Lapierre, Dominique. *Is Paris Burning?* New York: Simon & Schuster, 1965.

Cooper, Matthew. *The German Air Force, 1933–1945: An Anatomy of Failure.* New York: Jane's Publishing, 1981.

Copp, DeWitt. *A Few Great Captains.* Garden City, New York: Doubleday 1980.

————. *Forged in Fire.* Garden City, New York: Doubleday, 1982.

Craven, Wesley F., and Cate, James Lea. *The Army Air Forces in World War II.* 7 vols. Chicago: University of Chicago Press, 1948, 1949 and 1951.

Davis, Larry. *B-17 In Action.* Carrollton, Texas: Squadron/Signal Publications, 1984.

Deane, John R. *The Strange Alliance, The Story of Our Efforts at Wartime Cooperation with Russia.* New York: Viking, 1947.

Douhet, Giulio. *The Command of the Air.* Translated by Dino Ferrari. New York: Coward-McCann, 1942.

Ehrman, John. *Grand Strategy.* vols. 5 and 6, London: His Majesty's Stationery Office, 1956.

Eisenhower, Dwight D. *Crusade in Europe.* Garden City, New York: Doubleday, 1948.

————. *The Papers of Dwight David Eisenhower: The War Years.* 4 vols. Baltimore and London: Johns Hopkins Press, 1970.

Ellis, John. *Cassino, The Hollow Victory.* New York: McGraw-Hill, 1948.

Foulois, Benjamin D. *From the Wright Brothers to the Astronauts: The Memoirs of Major General Foulois.* New York: McGraw-Hill, 1960.

Forrester, Larry. *Fly for Your Life, The Story of R-R. Stanford Tuck, D.S.O., D.F.C., and Two Bars.* New York: Bantam, 1978.

Freeman, Roger A. *The Mighty Eighth.* Garden City, New York: Doubleday, 1970.

————. *Mighty Eighth War Diary.* London, New York, Sydney: Jane's Publishing, 1981.

Goldberg, Alfred A. *A History of the United States Air Force, 1907–1957.* New York: D. Van Nostrand, 1967.

Green, Joe B. *Ira C. Eaker.* Maxwell AFB, Alabama, Thesis, Air Command and Staff College, Air University, 1967.

Greer, T. H. *The Development of Air Doctrine in the Army Air Arm, 1917–1941.* Montgomery, Alabama, USAF Historical Division, Research Studies Institute, Air University, 1955.

Hansell, Haywood S., Jr. *The Air Plan That Defeated Hitler.* Atlanta: Higgins-McArthur/Longino & Porter, 1972.

Hapgood, David, and Richardson, David. *Monte Cassino.* New York: Congdon & Weed, 1984.

Harriman, W. Averell. *America and Russia in a Changing World.* Garden City, New York: Doubleday, 1971.

Harriman, W. Averell with Abel, Elie. *Special Envoy—to Churchill and Stalin, 1941–1946.* New York: Random House, 1975.

Harris, Sir Arthur. *Bomber Offensive.* London: Collins, 1947.

Hastings, Max. *Bomber Command.* New York: Dial Press-James Wade, 1979.

Hauptmann, Hermann. *The Luftwaffe, Its Rise and Fall.* New York: G. P. Putnam's Sons, 1943.

Herbert, Kevin. *Maximum Effort: The B-29's Against Japan.* Manhattan, Kansas: Sunflower University Press, 1983.

Bibliography

Hewes, James E., Jr. *From Root to McNamara: Army Organization and Administration, 1900–1963*. Washington: Center of Military History, 1975.

Huie, William B. *The Fight for Air Power*. New York: L. B. Fischer, 1942.

Hurley, Alfred F. *Billy Mitchell, Crusader for Air Power*. New York: Franklin Watts, 1964.

Infield, Glenn. *The Poltava Affair: A Russian Warning, An American Tragedy*. New York: MacMillan, 1973.

Irving, David. *The Destruction of Dresden*. New York: Holt, Rinehart & Winston, 1964.

Jones, R. V. *The Wizard War*. New York: Coward, McCann & Geoghegan, 1978.

Julian, Thomas Anthony. "Operation *Frantic* and the Search for American-Soviet Military Colleboration, 1941–1944," Ph.D. Dissertation, Syracuse University, New York: 1967.

Kaplan, Philip, and Smith, Rex Alan. *One Last Look: A Sentimental Journey to the Eighth Air Force Heavy Bomber Bases of World War II in England*. New York: Abbeville Press, 1983.

Kennett, Lee. *A History of Strategic Bombing*. New York: Charles Scribner's Sons, 1982.

Killen, John A. *A History of the Luftwaffe*. Garden City, New York: Doubleday, 1968.

LeMay, Curtis, and Kantor, McKinley. *Mission with LeMay: My Story*. Garden City, New York: Doubleday, 1965.

Lewin, Ronald. *Ultra Goes to War*. New York: McGraw-Hill, 1978.

Loening, Grover. *Amphibian: The Story of the Loening Biplane*. Greenwich, Connecticut: New York Graphic Society, 1973.

MacCloskey, Munro. *Secret Air Missions*. New York: Richards Rosen Press, 1966.

Macmillan, Harold. *The Blast of War, 1939–1945*. New York: Harper & Row, 1968.

———. *War Diaries: Politics and War in the Mediterranean, January 1943–May 1945*. New York: St. Martin's Press, 1984.

Morrison, Wilbur H. *Fortress Without a Roof*. New York: St. Martin's Press, 1982.

Murphy, Robert. *Diplomat Among Warriors*. Garden City, New York: Doubleday, 1964.

Murray, Williamson. *Strategy for Defeat: The Luftwaffe, 1933–1945*. Maxwell AF, Alabama: Air University Press, 1983.

Nelson, Otto. *National Security and the General Staff*. Washington: Infantry Journal Press, 1946.

Orpen, Neil. *Airlift to Warsaw, The Rising of 1944*. Norman, Oklahoma: University of Oklahoma Press, 1984.

Osur, Alan M. *Blacks in the Army Air Forces During World War II: The Problem of Race Relations*. Washington: Office of Air Force History, Government Printing Office, undated.

Parton, James. *The History of "FRANTIC", American Shuttle Bombing to and from Russian Bases, October 26, 1942–June 15, 1944*. Parton Papers, Houghton Library, Harvard.

———. *The History of MAAF, Dec. 10, 1943–May 8, 1945*. Parton Papers, Houghton Library, Harvard.

Perera, Guido R. *Leaves from My Book of Life*, 2 vols. Boston: Privately printed, 1974.

Pogue, Forrest C. *George C. Marshall: Organizer of Victory, 1943–1945*. 3 vols. New York: Viking Press, 1973.

Richards, Denis. *Portal of Hungerford.* London: Heineman, 1978.

Rostow, W. W. *Pre-Invasion Bombing Strategy, General Eisenhower's Decision of March 25, 1944.* Austin, Texas: University of Texas Press, 1981.

Sallagar, F. M. *Operation "STRANGLE" (Italy, Spring 1944): A Case Study of Tactical Air Interdiction.* Santa Monica, California: Rand Corporation, 1972.

Saundby, Sir Robert. *Air Bombardment.* London: Chatto & Windus, 1961.

Saward, Dudley. *'Bomber' Harris.* London: Cassell/Buchan & Enright, 1984.

Schmidt, Matthias. *Albert Speer: The End of a Myth.* New York: St. Martin's Press, 1984.

Sears, Betty M. *General Ira C. Eaker, Oklahoma's Pioneer Aviator.* MBS Thesis, Southeastern Oklahoma State University, Durant, Oklahoma, 1979.

Seversky, Alexander P. *Victory Through Air Power.* New York: Simon & Schuster, 1942.

Sherwood, Robert E. *Roosevelt and Hopkins: An Intimate History.* New York: Harper & Bros., 1948.

Slessor, Sir John C. *The Central Blue: Recollections and Reflections.* London: Cassell & Co., 1956.

Snow, C.P. *Science and Government.* The Godkin Lectures at Harvard, 1960. Cambridge: Harvard University Press, 1969.

Speer, Albert. *Inside the Third Reich.* London: Weidenfeld & Nicolson, 1970.

———. *Spandau, The Secret Diaries.* New York: Macmillan, 1974.

Strong, Russell A. *First over Germany, A History of the 306th bombardment Group.* Russell A. Strong, Kalamazoo, MI, 1982.

Sulzberger, Cyrus L. *A Long Row of Candles.* New York: MacMillan, 1969.

Tedder, Lord Arthur. *With Prejudice: War Memoirs.* Boston: Little, Brown, 1966.

Tillett, Paul. *The Army Flies the Mails.* Tuskaloosa, Alabama: University of Alabama Press, 1955.

Truscott, Lucian K. *Command Missions: A Personal Story.* New York: Dutton, 1954.

USA. *The Conferences at Cairo and Tehran 1943.* (Operations SEXTANT and EUREKA), published in *Foreign Relations of the United States, Diplomatic Papers.* Washington: Government Printing Office, 1961.

USA. *The United States Strategic Bombing Survey.* Washington: Government Printing Office, 1945–1946.

USAAF. *Target Germany: The Army Air Forces' Official Story of the VIII Bomber Command's First Year over Europe.* New York: Simon & Schuster, 1943.

USAF. *An Aerospace Bibliography.* Washington: Office of Air Force History, 1978.

———. *U.S. Air Force Oral History Catalog.* Washington: Office of Air Force History, 1982.

———. *The Army Air Forces in World War II, Combat Chronology, 1941–1945.* Washington: Office of Air Force History, 1973.

Von Senger und Etterlin, Frido. *Neither Fear Nor Hope.* New York: E.P. Dutton, 1964.

Watson, Mark Skinner. *United States Army in World War II: The War Department: Chief of Staff: Prewar Plans and Preparations.* Washington: Historical Division, United States Army, 1950.

Webster, Sir Charles, and Frankland, Noble. *The Strategic Air Offensive Against Germany, 1939–1945.* 4 vols. London: Her Majesty's Stationery Office, 1961.

Winterbotham, F. W. *The Ultra Secret.* New York: Harper & Row, 1974.

Wolk, Herman S. *Planning and Organizing the Postwar Air Force, 1943–1947.* Washington: Office of Air Force History, 1984.

Acknowledgments

Grateful acknowledgment is made to the following for permission to reprint previously published material:

Aerospace Historian: excerpts from "Air Chiefs Patrick & Fechet" by General Ira C. Eaker, June 1973. Copyright © 1973 by the Air Force Historical Foundation; excerpts from "Some Memories of Winston Churchill" by General Ira C. Eaker, September 1972. Copyright © 1972 by the Air Force Historical Foundation; reprint of "Eaker Speech to Sg. Officers School" by General Ira C. Eaker, Air University, June 1978. Copyright © 1978 by the Air Force Historical Foundation. Reprinted with permission. No additional copies made without the express permission of the author and of the editor of *Aerospace Historian.*

Air Force magazine: excerpts from "The Pan American Goodwill Flight" by General Ira C. Eaker, September 1975. Copyright © 1975 *Air Force* magazine; excerpts from article recording full interview by General Eaker and Dr. Arthur Metcalf with Albert Speer, April 1977. Copyright © 1977 Air Force magazine. Reprinted by permission from *Air Force* magazine, published by the Air Force Association, Washington, D.C.

Air University Press: excerpts from *Strategy for Defeat—The Luftwaffe, 1933–1945,* by Williamson Murray, 1983. Air University Press. *Strategy for Defeat—The Luftwaffe, 1933–1945* is a government publication published by the Air University Press. It was written by Dr. William Murray while he was serving as a Senior Visiting Research Fellow with the Airpower Research Institute, Center for Aerospace Doctrine, Research, and Education at Maxwell Air Force Base, Alabama.

Lt. Gen. Frank Armstrong: excerpts from unpublished memoir, "So Near Heaven, Surrounded by Hell." Reprinted by permission of the estate of Frank Armstrong.

Doubleday and Company, Inc.: excerpts from *Mission with LeMay, My Story* by Curtis E. LeMay and MacKinley Kantor. Copyright © 1965 by Curtis E. LeMay and MacKinley Kantor; excerpts from *America and Russia in a Changing World: A Half Century of Personal Observation* by W. Averell Harriman. Copyright © 1970, 1971 by W. Averell Harriman. Reprinted by permission of Doubleday and Company, Inc.

Acknowledgments

Fortune: excerpts from "The Fleeting Opportunity" by Charles J.V. Murphy, December 1943. Copyright © 1943 Time Inc.; excerpts from "The Blowup at Hughes Aircraft" by Charles J.V. Murphy, February 1954. Copyright © 1954 Time Inc. All rights reserved.

Harper & Row, Publishers, Inc.: specified excerpts (approx. 925 words) from *Winged Warfare* by Major General H.H. Arnold and Colonel Ira C. Eaker. Copyright © 1941 by Harper & Row, Publishers, Inc.; specified excerpts (approx. 500 words) from *Global Mission* by H.H. Arnold. Copyright © 1949 by H.H. Arnold. Copyright renewed 1977 by Eleanor P. Arnold; specified excerpts (approx. 500 words) from *This Flying Game* by Brigadier General H.H. Arnold and Major Ira C. Eaker (Funk & Wagnalls, Co.). Copyright © 1936 by Harper & Row, Publishers, Inc. Reprinted by permission of Harper & Row, Publishers, Inc.

William Heinemann Limited: excerpts from *Portal of Hungerford* by Denis Richards. Copyright © 1977 Denis Richards. Reprinted by permission of William Heinemann Limited.

Historical Times, Inc.: excerpts from *The Command Realities* by Curtis LeMay, *Impact,* vol. 6, page xi. Reprinted with permission of Historical Times, Inc.

Houghton Mifflin Company: excerpts from *The Hinge of Fate,* Volume IV of *The Second World War* by Winston S. Churchill. Copyright 1950 by Houghton Mifflin Company. Copyright © renewed 1978 by The Lady Spencer Churchill, The Honourable Lady Sarah Audley and The Honourable Lady Soames; excerpts from *Closing the Ring,* Volume V of *The Second World War* by Winston S. Churchill. Copyright 1951 by Houghton Mifflin Company. Copyright © renewed 1979 by The Lady Sarah Audley, and the Honourable Lady Soames. Reprinted by permission of Houghton Mifflin Company.

William B. Huie: excerpts from *The Fight for Air Power,* 1942. Copyright © 1942 William B. Huie. Reprinted by permission.

Dr. Thomas A. Julian: excerpts from "Operation FRANTIC and the Search for American-Soviet Military Collaboration, 1941–1944," unpublished Ph.D. dissertation, The Maxwell School, Syracuse University, 1968. Copyright © 1968 Thomas A. Julian. Reprinted by permission.

Macmillan, London and Basingstoke: excerpts from *The War Diaries: Politics and War in the Mediterranean, January 1943–May 1945* by Harold Macmillan. Copyright © 1983 by Harold Macmillan. Used by permission of Macmillan, London and Basingstoke.

Macmillan Publishing Company: excerpts from *The Central Blue* by Air Marshal Sir John Slessor. Copyright © 1956 Sir John Slessor. Used by permission of Macmillan Publishing Company.

The New York Times: excerpts from "16 Edens—Count 'Em" by Roy Meador, August 28, 1983 Op-Ed. Copyright © 1983 by The New York Times Company; excerpts from "The Team that Harries Hitler" by Raymond Daniell, June 6, 1943 *New York Times Magazine.* Copyright © 1943 by The New York Times Company;

Acknowledgments

excerpts from "General Eaker Retires," Editorial, June 14, 1947. Copyright © 1947 by The New York Times Company. Reprinted by permission.

St. Martin's Press, Inc.: excerpts from *The War Diaries: Politics and War in the Mediterranean, January 1943–May 1945* by Harold Macmillan. Copyright © 1983 by Harold Macmillan, and reprinted with permission of St. Martin's Press, Inc.

Simon & Schuster: excerpts from *My Three Years with Eisenhower* by Harry Butcher, 1946. Copyright © 1946 Harry C. Butcher. Reprinted by permission.

USAF Historical Division: excerpts from *The Development of Air Doctrine in the Army Air Arm, 1917–1941* by T.H. Greer, 1955. Reprinted by permission of the Office of Air Force History.

United States Strategic Institute: excerpts from "A Message from the Directors," *Strategic Review,* vol. 1, #1, pp. 2–3, April 1973. Copyright © 1973, United States Strategic Institute. Reprinted by permission.

University of Texas Press: excerpts from *Pre-Invasion Bombing Strategy: General Eisenhower's Decision of March 25, 1944* by W.W. Rostow (Austin, 1981). Copyright © 1981 by the University of Texas Press. Reprinted by permission of the University of Texas Press.

Viking Penguin Inc.: excerpts from *George C. Marshall: Organizer of Victory* by Forrest C. Pogue. Copyright © 1973 by the George C. Marshall Research Foundation; excerpts from *The Strange Alliance* by John R. Deane. Copyright 1947, renewed © 1974 by John R. Deane. Reprinted by permission of Viking Penguin Inc.

W.W. Norton & Company, Inc.: excerpts from *Empire, The Life, Legend, and Madness of Howard Hughes* by Donald L. Bartlett and James B. Steele, 1979. Copyright © 1979 Donald L. Bartlett and James B. Steele. Reprinted by permission of W.W. Norton & Company, Inc.

Unless otherwise noted, the photographs are courtesy of the United States Air Force, coming from many repositories. Grateful acknowledgment is also made to the following sources for permission given:

Averell Harriman: 11.

Houghton Library, Harvard (Parton Papers): 8; 314; 317; 348; 368–69 by Tex McCrary/USAF; 374; 375; 402.

Brig. Gen. Harris B. Hull: 111.

Imperial War Museum, London: 225, 286.

Library of Congress: 74, 104, 165, 417, 444.

Life Picture Service: 186 by Margaret Bourke-White, *Life* © 1942, Time, Inc.; 187 by Margaret Bourke-White, *Life* © 1942, Time, Inc.; 362 bottom, U.S. Army/Bettmann Archive; 362 left, U.S. Army; 363 top by George Rodger, *Life* © 1944, Time, Inc.

Acknowledgments

Arthur Metcalf: i.

National Air and Space Museum (to which the Eakers gave their extensive picture collection): 14, 19, 28, 29, 37, 40, 84, 206, 236, 462.

National Archives: 59, 137.

Group Captain Dudley Saward: 258.

U.S. Military Institute, Carlisle Barracks, Pennsylvania: 358.

Mrs. John Hay Whitney: 465.

Wycombe Abbey School, High Wycombe, England: 152.

Index

A

Adamson, Hans Christian, 68, 83, 84
Adriatic, landings at head of. *See*
 ARMPIT
Aerospace Education Foundation,
 489
Air Corps, 46–47
 advancement in, 61
 Eaker on, 61–62
 in airmail controversy, 92–94,
 503n
 image building, 67–68
 prewar development, 116
 song, 113
 suppression by general staff,
 1935–40, 107–108
 in twenties and thirties, 61
Air Corps Tactical School, 98–99
 Eaker at, 97
Aircraft. *See also* Fighters; Japan,
 B-29 bombardment of;
 Russia, American heavy
 bombers for
 in 1918, 30–31
 allocation. *See* Aircraft
 development and
 procurement; Eighth Air
 Force, aircraft diversions
 from
B-12, 97
B-17, 5, 97, 108, 109, 168, 170, 173,
 175, 177, 188, 190, 194, 212, 215,
 233, 279, 283, 297, 394, 408,
 472
 conversion to convoy defenders,
 124
 crew, 156
 nose, vulnerability, 237
 number at start of WW II, 112

B-24, 163, 170, 178, 233, 237,
 263–264, 283, 396, 406, 411
 crew, 156
B-25, 166
B-26, 268, 279, 306–307, 382
 disaster, 266–268
B-29, 109, 123, 179, 472
B-32, 254
C-1, 70
C-47, 424
communication in air, 156
convoy defenders, 124
D-1, 456, 457
de Havilland, 36, 38
Douglas World Cruiser, 52
Flying Fortresses. *See* Aircraft,
 B-17
Focke-Wulf
 factories, bombing of, 313–314
 ramming B-17s, 297
Fokker, 70
FW-190, 178, 265, 266
FX-11, 455, 457–458
Iron Horse, 67
Lockheed F-94, 459
Messerschmitt, 123, 279, 280
 factories, bombing of, 310,
 357
Mosquito, 123
Mustang. *See* Aircraft, P-51
OA-1 amphibian, 52–54
P-12, 78, 87, 99
P-26, 89–90, 95, 97
P-38, 124, 191, 194, 231, 279, 316,
 318, 409
P-40, 270
P-41, 280
P-47, 124, 126, 241, 264–265, 268,
 273, 274, 279, 318

P-51, 5, 123, 125, 126, 279, 290, 316, 318, 324, 365, 394, 516n, 517n
P-61, 124
in Philippines, in 1919, 37
prewar manufacture, in US, for allies, 123–124
Spitfire, 121, 122, 194, 265, 516n
Spitfire 9, 171
Tornado, 123
Typhoon, 123
YAKs, 403, 429
YB-40, 275–276
YIC-17, 80–82
Aircraft development and procurement
for fledgling Air Service, 48–50
prewar, 109–110, 116, 124
wartime, 147–148, 158–159, 170
Air Crew Rescue Units, 422–425
Air force, independent, 119
Arnold and Eaker on, 119, 443
establishment of, 443, 445–446
Air Force, postwar, Eaker on, 431
Air Force Day, 444
Air Force Historical Foundation, 487
Airmail, military involvement in, controversy over, 88–93, 503n
Air offensive, successful, Harris on, 327–328
Air Officer Commanding, Eaker's amusement at term, 135
Air power
Churchill on, 13
Eaker and Arnold on, 87–88
Eaker's early views on, 47–48
Eaker's writings on, 12
Huie on, 107
in land campaigns, 289, 384
Mitchell's advocacy of, 45–46
Patrick as advocate of, 47
Roosevelt's philosophy of, 109–110, 116
strategic, Eaker on, 147
strategic vs. tactical, 108, 341, 353
Russian use of, 8
tactical, Slessor's views on, 379
von Rundstedt on, 439
Air Service
advancement in, Eaker on, 50
ambulances, 50
early years, 45
Air War Plans Division, 179
Alamein, battle of, 185
Alexander, A. V., 295
Alexander, Sir Harold L., 220, 353, 355, 359, 361, 364, 367, 371-

373, 377, 379, 381, 383–384, 415
Allen, Frank, 398
Allen, Richard V., 481
Anderson, Frederick L., 210–212, 238, 252, 272, 274, 275, 277, 287, 291, 299, 300, 315, 320, 323, 325, 342, 343, 354, 394, 435, 465
Andrews, Frank M., 116, 124, 218, 221, 226–227, 232, 242, 245, 252, 253, 262, 293
assertion of big bomber strategy, 110
as chief of GHQAF, 94–95, 110–112
death, 254
and prewar Air Corps, 108
and prewar B-17 funding, 109
rivalry with Arnold, 254–256
visits to Castle Coombe, 238–239
visits to combat units, 238
Anfa Hotel, 219, 226–227
Anklam, 313
ANVIL, 381, 385, 414–415
Anzio, 341, 355–359
ARCADIA, 129, 141, 160
Armor, Otto, 20
ARMPIT, 303
Armstrong, Frank A., Jr., 131–133, 135, 161, 169, 170, 174, 181, 184, 198, 199, 213, 230, 238
Armstrong, Neil, 488
Army Air Corps. See Air Corps
Army Air Forces, 116
claims for German fighter losses, 240–241
Group, definition, 188
losses, compared to RAF, 221
strategic and tactical forces, 289
strength, in 1943, 351
Wing, definition, 188
Army Command and General Staff School, 101
Eaker at, 97, 100, 102
Army Flier (with Arnold), 117, 127, 130, 132
Army Staff College, 101
Arnold, Beatrice "Bee" (Mrs. Henry H.), 96, 464
Arnold, Bruce, 493
Arnold, Hank, 370
Arnold, Henry H. "Hap," 32–34, 66, 68, 86, 87, 98, 104, 113, 114, 119–121, 124–127, 132, 141, 147, 152, 160, 166, 170, 178, 190, 192, 205, 214, 218, 221, 226, 227, 232, 234, 242–243, 245,

250, 253, 264, 267, 287, 288, 290, 298, 305, 315, 328, 329, 367, 376, 384, 390, 391, 406, 407, 409, 411, 414–415, 419, 420, 425, 429–431, 439–441, 485, 514*n*, 516*n*
aid to earthquake victims (1933), 87
in airmail episode, 89
assigns Eaker overseas duty in 1942, 128
assistant chief of Army Aviation, 99–100
on atomic bomb, 441
and buildup of Eighth, 246–247
chief of Air Corps, 113
criticism of Eighth Air Force, 169–172, 198, 261–262, 271, 319–320
death, 464
Eaker on, 32, 115
on Eaker's accomplishment with Churchill, 222
on Eaker's job in Mediterranean, 369–370
Eaker's relationship with, 96, 114–115
on ensuring force of Eighth, 252
gives Eaker his Brigadier General stars, 130–131
Global Mission, 95, 324, 464
goal of unified air command, 223, 307, 313, 323, 331–332
handling of Eaker's takeover of Mediterranean Air Command, 336–341
heart trouble, 242, 262, 271, 432, 513*n*
and independent air force, 119, 443
on Italian campaign, 303–304, 372
meeting with Spaatz and Eaker at Cannes, 437–438
in Mitchell trial, 46–47
on Portal, 224
postwar plans, 430–431
and prewar B-17 funding, 109
at QUADRANT, 303–306
response to Schweinfurt bombing, 316–318
rivalry with Andrews, 254–255
at Rockwell Field, post WW I, 32–33
service in WW I, 32
support of central control for strategic air power, 333–334
testimony to Baker board, 93

thank-you to officers at Rockwell, 33–34
on Vegesack bombing, 244
visits PINETREE, in 1943, 219
visit to England in 1942, 158–159, 161
wartime relationship with Eaker, 172, 199–200, 272–279, 391
work habits, 432–433
Arsdale, John, 150
Arsdale, Richard, 150
Arsdale, Thomas, 150
Ash, Roy, 461, 466, 469
Astor, Lady, 195
Atlee, Clement, 441
Atom bomb, 441–442, 445
Atwood, Roy, 465
Australia, heavy bombers for, 160
Automatic Flight Control Equipment, 243–244
Avionics, 461
AWPD-I, 179–180, 185–186, 248
AWPD-42, 181, 185–186, 249

B

Baker, Ernest Hamlin, 474
Baker, Harold, 479
Baker, Newton D., 32–33, 93
Baker board, 93–94
Baldwin, Hanson W., 112
Balkan Air Force (British), 5, 425
Balkans, targets in, 323. *See also* Ploesti, Rumania
Ball-bearing works, German. *See* Schweinfurt
Barksdale, Hoy, 27–28
Barnett, Lincoln, 175
Bartlett, Donald, and Steele, James B., *Empire, the Life, Legend and Madness of Howard Hughes,* 468
Bartlett, S. S. "Sy," 163–164, 196, 197, 293–294, 454, 455, 462
Bartron, H.A., 367
Battle of Atlantic, 283
Bay of Biscay, subpens, bombing of, 183, 283–284
Beasley, Peter, 132, 202, 281, 343, 435
Benes, Edvard, 346
Benton, John W., 60
Berlin, bombing of, 293
Big Week, 328, 357, 365
Birmingham Blitzkrieg, 174
Biskra, Algiers, 207–208
Blechhammer, bombing of, 365
Boeing-Hornet Shuttle Flight, 79
Bohlen, Charles, 333

BOLERO, 157–158
Bolling Field, Eaker's service at, 67
Bombers. *See also* Aircraft
  day, Churchill on, 190
  development of, 97–98
  night, Churchill urges
    development of, 190
  prewar, 108
  transoceanic hops, 154–155
Bombing. *See also* Salvo bombing;
    Target systems area,
  British use of. *See* Cities, German,
    British bombing of
  day
    effect on German aircraft
      allotments, 305
    German countermeasure to,
      315–316
    Eaker on, 118
    precision, 313–314
    precision (daylight) vs. area
      (night), 98, 129–130, 136, 141,
      143, 146–147, 179, 187, 189, 190,
      192, 216–217, 225, 233, 250,
      263, 312, 324
    Eaker on, 170
    Speer's evaluation of
      effectiveness of, 484
  pursuit, 97
  round-the-clock, 146–147, 220
    Churchill's view of, 221, 346
  strategic, 444
    British philosophy about, 136
    of sub bases, importance of,
      283
Bombing missions, commanders
    going on, controversy about,
    144
Bond, Alfred, 398
Bordeaux, 302
Bor-Komorowski, Tadeusz, 410
Bottomley, Norman, 245, 312, 345
Bourke-White, Margaret, 197, 293
Bovingdon, 194
Bradley, Follett, 254, 271, 289, 434
Brady, F. M., 267
Bremen, bombing of, 160
Bremen, rescue episode, 68–70
Brereton, Lewis H., 289, 307, 320,
    336
Bridges, as targets, 381–382
British, American relations with,
    Eaker's promotion of, 203
British Eighth Army, 359
British Intelligence Appreciation,
    304–305

British scientists, contribution to war
    effort, 508n
Brooke, Sir Alan, 303, 332
Brown, George S., 481
Browning, Frederick, 206
Broyles, Professor, 22
Brunswick, bombing of, 326
Bubb, Charles B. B. "Jingles,"
    143–144, 168, 169, 187, 202,
    264, 271, 274
Buckley, Christopher, 373
Budapest, 427–428
Bulgaria, atrocities in, 427
Bullard, Robert Lee, 27, 505n
Bullitt, William C., 165
Bury St. Edmunds, 266–267
Bushy Park
  Eighth Air Force headquarters at,
    161, 163. *See also*
    WIDEWING
  RAF honors Eaker at, 345
Butcher, Harry C., 175, 218
Butcher Shop, 174
Butt, D. M., 137–138

C

Cabell, Charles P. "Pre," 252
Camp Cascades, 389–391, 414
Candee, Robert R., 194
Cannon, John K. "Joe," 102, 289,
    335, 336, 354, 355, 384, 418,
    435, 437, 438
Carr, Eleanora, 84
Casablanca, 209
Casablanca Conference, 193, 215, 216,
    222–223, 250
Casablanca Directive, 223, 232, 251,
    263
Caserta, Royal Palace of, 355,
    367–368
  July 1944 conference at, 408–409
  MAAF headquarters in, 355,
    386–391
Cassino, Italy, 359–377, 381, 383. *See
    also* Monte Cassino Abbey
  lessons learned at, 376–377
Castle, Frederick W., 131–132, 135,
    142, 161, 236, 238, 487
Castle Coombe, 203–204, 214, 238,
    344
Castle Coombe Group, 487
Cavalry, influence in army, in
    thirties, 101–102
CCS conferences. *See* ARCADIA;
    QUADRANT; SEXTANT;
    TRIDENT

Chaney, James E., 131, 134, 142, 147, 152, 159, 166, 307, 436
Chase, Leah, 42–43
Chauncey, Charles C., 204, 302, 343, 355
Chennault, Claire L., 97, 98, 108, 120, 232, 285, 436–437
Cherbourg Peninsula, Eaker's plan for invasion of, 164
Cherwell, Lord, 138, 140, 248
Chiang Kai-shek, 232, 329
Childs, Marquis, 354
China, Eaker's trips to, in 1920, 39, 40
Chinese theater, Eaker's visit to, 436–437
Chin-turret, 237
Churchill, Clementine, 464
Churchill, Mary, 258
Churchill, Pamela, 370
Churchill, Winston, 13, 64, 129, 136, 137, 139, 158–160, 166, 216, 220, 226, 241, 258, 263, 286, 304, 329, 330, 333, 341, 343, 356–358, 410, 415, 418
    advised by Sinclair on bombing policy, 191–192
    on American bombing missions, 189–190
    dinner at PINETREE in honor of, in 1943, 244–245
    Eaker convinces of merit of round-the-clock bombing, 221–222
    Eaker's meeting with, at Marrakesh, 345, 351
    on Eaker's transfer to Mediterranean, 346
    on Eighth's air superiority at Normandy, 6
    support of invasion of North Africa, 160, 164
    on Vegesack bombing, 244
    views on bombing policy, 138, 192–194, 218, 221, 227–228, 253–254, 346
Cities, German, British bombing of, 136, 138 140, 145, 152, 160, 233, 311, 312
    Eaker on, 485
Clague, Frank, 77
Clark, Mark, 159, 357, 360, 361, 364, 371–372, 374–375, 377, 381, 383–384
Clark Field (Philippines), 36
Clifford, Clark, 308

Cockburn, Frederick, 186
Coffee, Winnabelle R., 343
Cologne, bombing of, 146, 160
Columbia University, Eaker's studies at, 41–42
Combat box formation, 235
Combat Crew Replacement Center, 194
Combat tour of duty, length of, 212, 367
Combat wing commander, role of, 277
Combined bomber offensive, 262–263. See also Eaker Plan; POINTBLANK
    air statistics, 268
    Eaker's summary of, 323–324
    July 1943 operations, 297–298
    in late 1943, 324–325
Combined Chiefs of Staff. See Arcadia; Quadrant; Sextant; Trident
Committee of Operations Analysts, 249–252
Congressional Gold Medal, recipients, 13, 450
Congressional Record, Eaker quoted in, 12, 77, 463, 475
Coningham, Arthur, 289, 379
Cook, Everett, 465
Coolidge, Calvin, 52, 59, 60, 75
Cousland, Cornelius, 169, 205
Cowart, William S., Jr., 131
Craig, Malin, 111–112, 116
Craven, Wesley F., and Cate, James Lea, *The Army Air Forces in World War II,* 327
Cronkite, Walter, 292
Cunningham, Sir A. B., 418
Cunningham, Sir John, 353, 355
Curie, Eve, 390
Curtis, Edward P. "Ted," 201, 209–210, 220

D
Danforth, [Maj], 30
Daniell, Raymond, 139
Daniels, Bebe, 294, 435, 454, 523n
Danzig, 313
Dargue, H. A. "Bert," 52–54, 60, 97, 126–127
Darlan, Jean, 209
Dashwood, Lady, 172, 435
Dashwood, Sir Francis, 172
Davison, F. Trubee, 62, 64–65, 67–68, 70, 86, 110, 269–270

Davison, Howard, 436
Dawn to Dusk flight to Panama,
    78–79
Deane, John R., 7–8, 392–393,
    397–400, 405–408, 411, 412,
    428, 429
  The Strange Alliance, 412, 429
Debreczen, Hungary, bombing of
    rail yards, 8–9, 397–398
Defense Act (1926), 47
de Gaulle, Charles, 220, 420–421
de Lattre de Tassigny, [Gen], 416
Demobilization, 443
Dern, George, 93
Desert Air Force (British), 5, 379
Detroit, 60
Devers, Jacob L., 262, 270, 271, 276,
    278, 289, 296, 297, 300, 308,
    338–340, 342, 343, 352, 358,
    364, 376, 379, 417, 418, 420,
    434, 435
DIADEM, 382–384, 392, 520n
Dieppe, bombing of, 177
Dietrich, Noah, 458, 459, 461, 466,
    469, 470, 473
Dill, Sir John, 316, 335
Distinguished Flying Cross
  to aviators of Pan American
    Goodwill Flight, 59, 60
  to *Question Mark* crew, 75
Distinguished Flying Cross (British),
    first given to Americans,
    245
Doctrine, military, 98, 107
Doenitz, Karl, 283
Doolittle, James H. "Jimmy," 5, 166,
    183, 195, 201, 204, 207–209,
    239–240, 289, 292, 302, 322,
    335, 336, 338, 354, 435, 438,
    486, 493
Douglas, Donald W., 454, 471,
    485
Douglas Aircraft, 471–472
Douhet, Giulio, 485
Downs, Eldon W., 503n
Draft, Eaker on, 477–478
DRAGOON, 415–417, 421
Draper, Marshall, 167
Dresden, bombing of, 309, 526n
Drum, Hugh, 93, 95
du Maurier, Daphne, 207
Duncan, Asa N., 200–201, 205
Duncan, Claude E., 131, 134, 144, 168,
    169, 184, 204, 211
Durant, Oklahoma, 22–23
  commemoration of *Question Mark*
    flight, 77

Eaker Field, 77
Eaker's return to, after war, 442
Düren, bombing of, 324–325

E

Eaker, Claude (brother), 20, 21,
    23
Eaker, Dona Lee [née Graham]
    (mother), 17–18, 21, 22, 25
Eaker, Grady (brother), 20, 21
Eaker, Ira C., xi–xii
  in Air Corps, in late twenties to
    thirties, 62
  in airmail episode, 89
  appearance, 85–86, 139–140
  on Arnold's impatience, 319–320
  Arnold's opinion of, 433–434
  on atomic era, 447
  attachment to father figures, 55–56
  attacked by hornets at West
    Wycombe Park, 172–173
  awards and decorations, 488–489
    Congressional Gold Medal, 13,
      489
    Distinguished Flying Cross
      (1927), 59, 60
    Knight of British Empire,
      320–321
    Oak Leaf Cluster for DFC
      (1929), 75
    Oak Leaf Cluster for DSM,
      from Eisenhower, 447–448
    Order of Partisan Star, First
      Class, 427
    Silver Star, 181
    Wright Trophy, 13, 489
  on bomber commanders going on
    missions, 144
  bomber command in England
    AOCs in early days, 135
    assignment to, 128–129
    goals of, stated by Arnold, 131
    plan for beginning operations
      (1942–43), 143
  on bomber crew training, 175–176
  on bombing missions during war,
    145, 174–175
  on bombing of Rouen, 177
  on bombing strategy, 173
  in *Bremen* rescue attempt, 68–70
  brothers, 20, 463–464
  in Bucharest, in 1944, 386, 387
  case for day bombing, 219–220
  at Cassino, 373
  on Cassino, 376–377
  character, 24–25
  childhood, 17, 18

C-in-C, MAAF (1944), 2, 5,
239–240
CO at Hamilton Field, 270
command of 20th Pursuit Group,
117
command of all Army Air Forces,
in 1945, 431
command of all US Army Air
Forces in Britain, 320
command of Eighth Air Force,
202
command of fighter defenses on
West Coast, 126
commissioned in army, 27
condemnation of Washington's
treatment of the Eighth,
245–246
in Corsica, in 1944, 418
dawn-to-dusk flight, failure, 78–79
departure from MAAF, 435
desire to go on mission to
Schweinfurt, 300
desk nameplate, 13
doubts about daylight bombing,
190–191
early ambitions, 22
early education, 20–22
early leadership ability, 25–26
on Eighth's losses in combat,
274–275
Eisenhower on, 435
enlistment, 1917, 26
exchange with Arnold, in
controversy over bomber
command leadership, 271–273
first parachute drop, 62–63
first six weeks in Mediterranean,
368–369
flies to Ukraine, in 1944, 398–399
flying instruction, 30
forced landings and crashes, 31
in 1929, 79
at Bolling Field, 1925, 50
due to pilot error, 62
first crash, at Rockwell field, 31
in P-12 test flight, 79–80
in Philippines (1919), 36
in rice paddy (1918), 30–31
in Tolu, Kentucky, 80–82
fourth star, 492–493
in France, in 1944, 417
on German response to day
bombing, 315–316
at High Wycombe, 104
instrument-only flight across US,
99–100
journalism, 473–474

in journalism school, 86–87
lectures on Army Air Forces,
446–447
loses temper, 321–322
loyalty, 56, 469
marriage to Ruth, 84
meeting with Churchill at
Marrakesh, 345, 351
mentors, choice of, 22, 24, 32
mission to England, in 1941, 121
in Mitchell trial, 46, 47
to North Africa for conference, in
1942, 205–212
in North Carolina maneuvers, in
1941, 125
opinion of Soviets, 11–12, 404,
476–477
parents, 17–18
as Patrick's assistant in
Washington, 43
personality, 139–140, 175
plays volleyball at Poltava,
401–402
poker playing, 209–210
policy for dealing with Russians,
411
postwar activities, 12
postwar plans, 430
praised by Portal, 333
predicts war, 117
presentation for daylight
bombardment, in Washington
in 1942, 181
presentation to Joint Chiefs, in
1943, 253
presidency of Strategic Institute,
479, 482
press conferences, 295
proposed as assistant for Tedder,
239–240
publications. See specific title
reaction to bombing of Poltava,
407
recent health, 491
relations with Tito and Yugoslavs,
426–427
reports to Arnold on Eighth's
performance, 198–199
resignation from Hughes Aircraft,
470
retirement, 446
returns to 20th Pursuit Group in
1941, 126
role in creation of independent air
force, 119, 443
role in Question Mark flight,
70–75

role in saving Hughes Aircraft, 469
on Russian bomb-lines, 428–429
on Russian workers, 402–403
secondary education, 23–24
sent overseas in 1942, 128
Slessor on, 189
speeches, in postwar years, 463
spokesman for national security, 474–475
start in aviation, 27–30
statement on growth of Eighth, 295–297
stay at Southdown, in 1942, 134
target systems selection team, 252
tests P-47, 126
tests P-51, 126
third star, 308
on TORCH, 182–183, 208–209
tour of Eastern Command bases, 403–404
transfer to head of Mediterranean Air Command, 336–346
trips to Moscow, in 1944, 5–11, 394–395, 399–400, 404
trip to England, in 1944, 377–379
trip to Germany after war, 443
trip to North Africa, in 1943, 300–302
trip to Washington, in 1944, 429–430
visits to combat units, 238
visit to Pacific bases, 435–439
weekly column, 473–475
work for Douglas Aircraft, 471–473
work for Hughes, 455–463
writing, 12–13. See also specific pieces
writing style, 43
Eaker, Leah (first wife), 42
Eaker, Ruth Apperson, xi-xii, 85, 96, 102, 113, 132, 180, 181, 184, 247, 279, 335, 336, 430, 435, 447, 453, 454, 459, 471, 486–487, 491–493
first meeting with Eaker, 83
marriage to Eaker, 84
personality, 84–85
Eaker, Young Yancy (father), 17–18, 20–21, 79, 463–464
Eaker family, 18
Eaker Horses, 489
Eaker Plan, 262–263, 290, 312
Earle, Edward M., 250
Early, Stephen, 102

Eastern Command, 392, 401
bases, 332–333, 367. See also Poltava
antiaircraft defenses, 403, 405, 407
Eaker's tour of, 403–404
Russians take back, 410
in Ukraine, 393
Eastern Front, in 1943, 285
Eden, Texas, 18–20
welcomes Eaker after war, 442
Edison, Charles, 108
Edwards, Idwal H., 262, 276, 297, 338, 354, 355
Eighth Air Force, 5, 141, 223, 333
15th Bombardment Squadron, 166
in 1943, 189
advance echelon, 154
aircraft diversions from, 158, 305
to North Africa, 212–213, 263–264
to Pacific, 147–148, 160, 180
to Twelfth, 194
airfields, 154–155
anniversary book, 298
build-up
in 1943, 247
Andrews on, 232
final plan for, 254
lag in, 323
logistics of, 155, 237–238
coordinated attacks with Fifteenth, 364–366
Eaker takes command of, 202
establishment in Britain, 129, 155–157
Eaker on, 157
first 1,000 sorties in one day, 307
first aircraft received, 168
first air divisions, 287
first combat mission, 166–167
first heavy bomber mission into Germany, 230–231
first POW, 167
growth in 1943, 289
lack of balance between combat and service units, 290–291
losses, average for 1943, 328
public relations, 293–295
shortages, 204–205, 241–242, 271–272, 305
size, 155
strength in 1943, 284
training procedures, 156
training Twelfth, 183
Eighth Air Force Historical Society, 489

VIII Bomber Command, 158
44th BG, 213
91st BG, 231
92nd BG, 196–197
93rd BG, 178
97th BG, 168–170, 174, 183–185,
  207, 211
97th BG(H), 395
301st BG, 178, 183–185, 196–197,
  207, 208, 211
303rd BG, 231
305th BG, 205, 206, 236
306th BG, 178, 196–198, 213, 230
385th BG, 315
B-17s, first combat mission,
  174–175
Bomber Nights, 161–163
bomber operations, 177
Churchill urges build-up of, 190
first 1,100 sorties, 217
losses per mission, 185
organization, 168
participation in night attacks, 191
wingdings, 161–163
Eisenhower, Dwight D., 159, 164,
  167, 169, 175, 179–180, 186,
  205, 210, 218–219, 228, 239,
  289, 305, 332, 334–335, 338-
  341, 346, 354, 377, 378, 396,
  415, 417, 420, 421, 434, 438,
  444, 446, 464, 509n
CG of NATOUSA, 223
commander of OVERLORD, 334
Eaker's relationship with, 164–166
gifts to Eaker on his retirement,
  448
letter to Eaker on his retirement,
  524n
on Mediterranean Air Command,
  341–342
personality, 164–166
reaction to TORCH, 182–183
and unified air command, 201
visits to PINETREE, 195
Eisenhower jacket, 195, 510n
Ellis, John, Cassino, The Hollow
  Victory, 360
Embassy Operations Unit,
  aiming-point studies, 248–249
Emden, bombing of, 306, 315
Emmons, D.C., 127
Erickson, John, 481
Ervin, Robert G., 419
Essen, bombing of, 160, 284
ETO
command changes, in 1943,
  287–289

total US combat aircraft in, in
  1943, 289–290
ETOUSA, 223

F
Fairchild, Muir S., 52, 54, 57–58,
  68–69, 249–250
Farley, James A., 89, 91
Faulkner, Eugene, 38–39
Fear, Eaker on, 326–327
Fechet, James E., 50–51, 67, 78,
  84–85, 197, 321, 465
abilities as commander, 51
in Bremen rescue attempt, 68, 69
Eaker's relationship with, 51,
  55–56, 96
Eaker's service with, in twenties
  and thirties, 62–64
in planning Pan American
  Goodwill flight, 51–52
and Question Mark flight, 71
relationship with Davison, 65
school policy, 64–65
Fechet, Mary, 78
Fechet, Mrs. James E., 78
Fifteenth Air Force, 5, 289, 292,
  322, 334, 344, 353–354, 356,
  365, 373, 384–385, 394, 395,
  427
Task Force, Eaker on, 396
Fifth Army, 359
Fighter pilot, Eaker on, 118
Fighters. See also Aircraft
as bomber escorts, 5, 97, 98, 124,
  173, 241, 265
Eaker on, 118–119, 123
Century series, 460
command, controversy over,
  273–274
concepts and tactics for, views at
  Air Tactical School, 97, 99
development, 124
in England, Eaker's 1940 study of,
  121–124
gas tanks for, 264–265, 273, 274,
  279
German factories, bombing of, 292
German tactics for, 265–266
long-range, 279
Churchill on, 190
Eaker on, 280–281
as pursuit of hostile fighters, 266
Soviet. See Aircraft, YAKs
transoceanic hops, 154–155
Fire control devices, Hughes'
  development of, 459, 461
First Air Force, 288

Flack, Rudy, 174
Flak, LeMay's calculations for
    avoiding, 236–237
Flying Tigers, 120
Focsani airport, Rumania, 404
Forrestal, James V., 445
Fort Bliss (TX), 27
Fort Leavenworth, 100
Fort Logan H. Roots, 27
Foulois, Benjamin D., 89–93
Four-star generals, Eisenhower on,
    434–435
France, invasion of. See ANVIL;
    BOLERO; DRAGOON;
    Normandy;
    SLEDGEHAMMER;
    STARKEY
Frank, Walter H., 194
Frankland, Noble. See Webster, Sir
    Charles, and Frankland,
    Noble
FRANTIC, 392, 406–410
    historical importance of, 412
FRANTIC JOE, 394–398
Freeman, Roger, *Mighty Eighth War
    Diary,* 315
French Air Force, 420
    training and equipping, 419
French Riviera, German defense of,
    415
Freyberg, Bernard, 360–361, 372,
    374, 377

G

Gable, Clark, 295
Gabriel, Charles A., 492, 493
GAF. See German Air Force;
    Luftwaffe
Galatz, Rumania, 396–397, 400
Gallagher, Wes, 239
Garrick, David, 150
Gates, Artemus L., 368
Gates, Byron E., 249–250,
    252
Gay, Frank William, 473
Gaylord, Bradford, 209–210
Gdynia, 313, 409
Gee device, 145–146, 324
Gellhorn, Martha, 367
General Headquarters Air Force,
    108, 116
    formation, 92–94
    maneuvers, in 1938, 110–111
General Headquarters Air Service
    Reserve, 93
General Staff, 45–49, 62, 76, 92–95,
    107–110, 116, 504–506

George, Harold L., 102, 179, 435,
    458–459, 466, 469
George, Violet (Mrs. Harold L.), 102
George VI, 320, 390
    inspection of American bomber
    stations, 195–196
German Air Force. *See also*
    Luftwaffe
    in 1944, 330–331
    defense of Germany from day
    bombing, 305
    in Russia, 407
Germans, inroads in South America,
    in twenties, 51
Germany, US estimate of situation
    in, in 1944, 330–331
GHQAF. *See* General Headquarters
    Air Force
Gibraltar, 211
    Allied Force headquarters at, 195
Giles, Barney M., 267, 271, 279–280,
    430, 433, 435, 436, 439
Giraud, Henri Honoré, 209, 220
Gliders, 416–417
Goebbels, Joseph, 284
Goering, Hermann, 285–286
    on air defense, 284–285
Goldwater, Barry, 476, 493
Goodman, Ruth, 18, 25, 39
Gordon, Arthur, 298
Gotha, bombing of, 365
Govier, Alfred, 151, 204, 435
Grafton Underwood, 154, 168,
    174
Graham, John H., 18, 21
Gray, Edward, 163, 213–214, 408,
    487, 493
Greig, Sir Louis, 215
Grendal, Dimitri D., 399
Gruenther, Alfred M., 102, 520
Guadalcanal, 185
Gustav line, 359, 371, 381, 383
GYMNAST, 164, 170. *See also*
    TORCH

H

H2S, 291–292, 306, 515n
H2X, 9, 156, 322, 324
Hahn, Walter F., 481
Haig, Alexander, 483
Hailey, Travis, 187
Hall, William E., 434
Halverson, Harry, 71, 74, 102
Hamburg, bombing of, 284, 309
Hansell, Haywood S., Jr., 179–181,
    185–187, 200, 201, 204–206,
    212, 214, 238, 252, 253, 263,

266, 272, 287–288, 325, 430,
436
on Arnold, 320
on Eaker's accomplishment with
Churchill, 222
Harlan, John M., 252, 293
Harmon, M.F., 247
Harriman, Kathleen, 7, 399
Harriman, W. Averell, 148, 239, 241,
253, 263, 270, 273, 278, 320,
332, 367, 392, 394, 396, 404,
406–408, 410, 411, 430, 434,
487, 489, 514n
on American-Soviet cooperation at
Poltava, 10
in Moscow, June 1944, 6–7, 9
relationship with Eaker, 10–11
on Russians, 413
Harris, Arthur T. "Bert" (later Sir
Arthur), 104, 129–130, 134, 135,
139, 148, 159–161, 192, 216,
218–219, 223, 224, 228,
242–243, 245, 252, 253, 258,
263, 275, 278, 284, 292, 307,
309, 311–313, 327, 343–345,
378–379, 435, 443, 483–484
belief in strategic air power, 147
on bomber commanders going on
missions, 144
bombing of German cities, 152
on bombing tactics, 129–130
on first American raid, 175
letter to Arnold on bombing
strategy, 158
on panacea targets, 264
personality, 139–140
physique, 139
at Southdown in 1942, 134–135
support of American bombing
policy, 193
support of area bombing, 140–141
Harris, Jacqueline "Jackie," 135,
137
Harris, Jill (Mrs. Arthur T.) (later
Lady), 129, 435
Harte, Houston, 474
Hearst, William Randolph, 79
Hellman, Lillian, 390
'Hell's Angels," 456
Henley, Nadine, 473
Hewes, James E., Jr., *From Root to
McNamara*, 504n-506n
Hicks, Sam, 489
High Wycombe
ceremonies at, commemorating
Eighth Air Force and RAF
teamwork, 483

Eaker in, 153
Eaker's speech in, 153–154
Hitler, Adolf, 284, 312
air defense policy, 284–285
Hobby, Oveta Culp, 159, 307
Hodges, Jimmy, 238, 300
Hoffman, Callen J., 400
Holisso (yearbook), 25–26
Hollinghurst, L. G., 203
Holloway, Bruce K., 480–481
Hooe, Roy, 71, 74, 80
Hopkins, Harry, 116, 147, 148, 170,
187, 190, 192, 220, 329, 335,
413
Hopper, Bruce, 518n
Howard, Leslie, 133
Howard, Roy, 239
Howard Hughes Medical Institute,
IRS refuses tax-exempt status
to, 467–468
world's biggest philanthropy, 493
Hoyte, Ross G., 71, 73
Hughes, Big Howard, 456
Hughes, Howard, 455–463, 466, 473
business methods, 457
Eaker's first meeting with, 113, 114
latter years, 469–470
range of talents, 456–457
Hughes, Richard D'Oyly, 248, 252,
300
Hughes Aircraft Company, 12, 457,
458, 461
in 1954, 460
Eaker's work for, in sixties, 473
sale to General Motors, 492
sales, 469
transfer to HHMI, 467
Hughes Tool Company, 456, 458
Hull, Cordell, 332, 410–411
Hull, Harris B., 111, 120, 131–132, 135,
161, 166, 167, 181, 186, 187, 217,
238, 355, 396, 398, 424, 487,
493
Hunter, Monk, 127, 194, 262,
264–265, 273, 274, 288, 465
HUSKY, 223
Hyland, Lawrence A. "Pat," 469,
473–475, 493
HZX, 292

I

IFF, 156
ILS, 156
Incendiaries, in American bomb
loads, 311
Indian theater, Eaker's visit to, 437
Infield, Glenn B., 407

Instrument flying
Eaker's early experiments with,
36–37
Eaker's work on, in P-26, 95
first flight across US using, 99
Instrument landing system. See ILS
International Flight Research
Corporation, 489
Irving, David, The Destruction of
Dresden, 526
Italian campaign, 330, 371, 372, 380,
384, 434. See also
STRANGLE
Northern, discussed in
QUADRANT, 303–304
target selection in, 380–381
Italy, 355
German air power in, 356
Russian air base in, 393
shuttle missions from, Eaker on,
322

J

Jackson, Glenn, 121, 389, 453–454,
466
Jackson, Henry M., 482
Japan
B-29 bombardment of, 11, 179, 436
Doolittle's raid on, with B-25s,
166
Eaker's trips to, in 1920, 39–40
Japanese, Eaker on, 39–40
Jeschonneck, Hans, 311
Johnson, Davenport, 288
Johnson, Leon, 206, 210, 213, 238,
412, 493
Johnson, Louis, 109, 110
Johnson, Lyndon B., 463
Johnson, Samuel, 150
Joint Air Commission, 419
Joint Strategic Survey Committee,
249
Jones, David, 486
Jones, Gwyneth, 203, 322, 344
Jones, R. V., 248
Juin, Alphonse, 360
Julian, Thomas A., 407, 412
JUNIOR, 183, 184

K

Kammhuber, Joseph, 284
Kane, Francis X., 481
Kassel, bombing of, 284, 291
Kaye, Milton W., 515n
Kegelman, Charles C., 166, 167
Kenefic, Oklahoma, 23
Kennedy, John F., 269

Kenney, George, 246, 254, 266, 318,
433, 436, 438
Kepner, William E., 99, 102, 125,
273–275, 288, 417
Kesselring, Albert, 357, 359, 380
Kiel, 297
Kilner, W.G., 109
Kindelberger, James H. "Dutch,"
125, 280, 454
King, Ernest J., 170
Kirk, Charles, 186, 187
Knerr, Hugh, 108–110, 124, 254, 271,
305, 306, 343, 354, 411, 435
Knox, William F., 270
Kraigher, George, 422, 424
Kuter, Laurence S., 200, 201, 205,
211, 212, 214, 288, 289, 319,
320, 435, 439

L

Lamont, Thomas W., 250
Law
Eaker's early ambition to study,
23, 25, 38
Eaker's study of, 41–43
Lawrence, C. W., 396
Lay, Beirne, Jr., 131, 163, 187, 198,
202, 300, 422, 454
Leach, W. Barton, 249–250
Leavenworth, Henry, 100
LeClerc, Jacques Philippe, 421
Leese, Sir Oliver, 375
Leigh-Mallory, Sir Trafford, 287,
378–379
Leipzig, bombing of, 365
LeMay, Curtis, 98, 112, 205, 206,
234–236, 238, 272, 277, 288,
292, 299–300, 302, 370, 408,
433, 436, 438, 441, 472, 487,
517n
Le Muy, 416–417
Lend-Lease, 11, 404, 406, 411
Lessig, Cecil P. "Brick," 120–121,
172, 173, 186, 187, 202, 419,
435, 465, 466
Lessig, Ethelyn, 435
Lewis, Roger, 467
Lexington, 96
Lezard, Selwyn, 203
Libby, Ruthven E., 481
Lille, bombing of, 178
Lindbergh, Charles A., 13, 66, 90,
450, 461–462
Lindeman, E.A., 248
Linscheid, A., 24, 26, 443
Lippmann, Walter, 475–476
Lisbon, Portugal, 133

Litton Industries, 466, 488
Loening, Grover, 52
Longfellow, Laura, 83
Longfellow, Newton, 33, 36, 37, 40,
    79, 83, 168, 169, 196, 201, 202,
    205, 217, 238, 240, 244, 264,
    271, 272, 274, 287, 288
as bomber commander, 213–214
Lorient, bombing of, 183
Lovett, Adele (Mrs. Robert), 270
Lovett, Robert, 114, 116, 181, 214, 226,
    253, 268–271, 278–279, 281,
    295, 297–298, 307, 313, 352,
    355, 356, 402, 404, 430, 432,
    436, 439, 445, 486, 514n
on Eaker's transfer to
    Mediterranean, 343–344
on Schweinfurt-Regensburg losses,
    306
Lübeck, bombardment of, 145–146
Lucas, John P., 357
Luce, Clare Booth, 12, 476, 481,
    483
Luftwaffe. See also German Air
    Force
day fighters, 285
decline of, 307, 318–319, 366,
    377–378, 415, 417–418
defeat of, Speer on, 484–485
Eaker on, 148
fighter losses, AAF claims for,
    240–241
in Italy, 384
losses, in 1943, 241
night fighters, 284–285
at Normandy, 6
offensive tactics, 237
opposition to VIII Bomber
    Command, 178
as priority target system, 223
response to Combined Bomber
    Offensive, 284
Lyon, Ben, 294, 298, 435, 454

M

MAAF, 2, 5, 239–240, 351, 381–382,
    414, 421
administrative staff, 353–354
air crew rescued, 522n
fighting units, 354
headquarters, 355, 386–391
help to Russian advance through
    Eastern Europe, 12
operational staff, 353–354
sorties in DRAGOON, 417
sorties in STRANGLE, 382
structure, 353

MacArthur, Douglas, 66–67, 86, 436,
    438, 441, 442
in airmail episode, 90–91
and Mitchell court-martial, 66
Maclean, Fitzroy, 426
Macmillan, Harold, 220, 414–415,
    426
March Field, Eaker's service at, 88,
    95
Marcus, H. B., 489
Mariana Islands, invasion, 11
Marienburg, bombing of, 313–314
Marrakesh, 228–229
Marshall, George C., 116, 125–126,
    147, 148, 158, 164, 170, 180–182,
    184, 187, 218, 224–226, 228,
    232, 256, 263, 296, 297, 303,
    318, 320, 329, 331–334,
    339–342, 346, 390, 414–415,
    429, 430, 433–435, 439, 440,
    444, 505n, 523n
as likely supreme commander, 517n
support of build-up of Eighth, 243
Masefield, Peter, 170, 174, 179
Mason, Clarence O., 244–245, 345,
    389, 435
Mason-MacFarlane, Frank, 211
McAuliffe, Anthony C., 102
McCain, John S., Jr., 481, 482
McCrary, Reagan "Tex," 200, 355,
    367, 381, 398, 418, 419
McDonnell-Douglas Corp., 473
McFadden, Bernarr, 113
McGinnis, Harold, 266, 267
McNarney, Joseph T., 262, 417, 446
McPherson, John B., xi
Medford, Oregon, 453, 465
Medford Mail Tribune, 453–454
Mediterranean, operation of air
    forces in, 201
Mediterranean Allied Air Forces.
    See MAAF
Melcheor, Frederick, 68, 69
Memphis Belle, 295, 296, 515n
Meredith, Burgess, 295
Metcalf, Arthur G. B., 478–480, 489,
    493
personality, 483
Middleton, Drew, 482
Midway, 160–161, 185
Mielec, Poland, aircraft factory,
    bombing of, 400
Miller, Henry S. F., 306
Minefields, Russian system for
    clearing, 406
Mirgorod, 393, 409
Mitchel Field, Eaker's service at, 41

Mitchell, William "Billy," 13, 45–46,
    93, 110, 450, 485
  clashes with Patrick, 45–46
  court-martial, 46–47, 66
  Eaker on, 48
Molesworth, 154
Molotov, Vyacheslav M., 7, 9, 332,
    400, 401, 404, 405, 410
Monte Cassino Abbey, 359–364,
    367–368
Montgomery, Bernard, 289, 346,
    379
Morale
  of Eighth Air Force combat
    crews, 234–235, 516n
  German, 312
  effect of bombing on, 152–153,
    223
  military
    Eaker's understanding of, 143
    Fechet's precept for judging, 51,
    197
Moscow, German offensive on, 147
Moss, Malcolm, 250
Mountbatten, Louis, 227, 464
Münster, bombing of, 314
Murphy, Robert E., 220
Murray, Williamson, *Strategy for
    Defeat: The Luftwaffe
    1933–1945*, 241
Murrow, Edward R., 200

N

National Security Act, 445
NATO Armed Forces, Eaker on,
    472
NATOUSA, 223
Navy
  aviation, 96–97
  objections to independent air
    force, 445
  reaction to *Rex* flight, 112
  in suppression of army air, 107–108
Nelson, Otto, *National Security and
    the General Staff*, 504n-506n
Nevins, Allen, 485
New York, 58, 60
New York Herald Tribune, 475–476
New York Times, on Eaker's transfer
    to Mediterranean, 344
New Zealand Corps, 360–361, 371,
    374, 376
Nikitin, A. V., 7–9, 400, 405, 408,
    412
Nimitz, Chester, 438, 441
Ninth Air Force, 289, 307
Nolan, Pat, 398

Norcross, Carl, 135, 142, 152, 282,
    487
Normandy, 5–6, 328, 357, 375, 414,
    439–440. *See also*
    OVERLORD
  air statistics, 6
Norstad, Lauris, 302, 354, 355, 379,
    381, 384, 445
North Africa
  air operations in, 208
  invasion of, 160, 182, 195. *See also*
    GYMNAST; TORCH
  shuttle missions to, 302
  tactics of interdiction used in,
    379–380
North African Theater of
    Operations, 223
Novikov, A. A., 7–9, 400,
    412

O

Oboe, 156, 292, 322, 324
O'Donnell, Emmett R. "Rosie," Jr.,
    273, 335, 436
Office of Air Force History, xi
Oil, German sources of, as targets,
    385–386, 405, 421–422
Oliver, T. K., 424
Operational Research, 247
Operational training units, 204
Operations analysis, 249–253
Oschersleben, bombing of, 284, 291,
    326
Overacker, Charles B. "Chip,"
    197–198, 205
OVERLORD, 164, 228, 263, 268,
    287, 302–303, 330, 332–334,
    341, 377, 378, 381, 382, 385,
    392, 394, 397, 414. *See also*
    Normandy
Oxford, Mr. and Mrs. Russell, 82–83

P

Pacific theater, Eaker's visit to,
    435–439
Page, Edward, 6–7
Pan American, 78
Pan American Airways, 60
Pan American Goodwill Flight,
    51–60, 67
Paris, retaking of, 421
Parton, James, xi-xii, 6, 164, 196, 197,
    202, 206, 209–210, 298, 345,
    367, 368, 373, 396, 398, 418,
    435, 437, 443, 454
Partridge, Earle E., 380
Patch, Alexander M., 416

Patrick, Mason M., 41, 43, 62
abilities as commander, 51
as chief of Air Service, 45–46
and development of Air Service,
47–50
Eaker's relationship with, 55–56
idea for Pan American Goodwill
flight, 52
and Mitchell trial, 46–47
Patton, George, 98, 219, 376
Peace, military's role in preserving,
Eaker on, 476
Pearl Harbor, 107, 126
Peenmünde, 311
Pendleton, George C., 39
Pendleton, George C., Jr., 39
Pendleton, Mrs. George C., 39, 442.
See also Goodman, Ruth
Perera, Guido R., 250
Perminov, A. R., 7, 10, 399, 402,
403, 405, 408
Eaker's friendship with, 9
Pershing, John J. 41, 45
Peters, Jean, 462
Philippines, Eaker's service in,
1919–21, 33, 35–41
Phillips, Charles T., 33, 89–90, 168,
204, 205
Photo-reconnaissance planes,
Russian resistance to flights
of, 404
Photo Reconnaissance Unit, 244
Pilot error, 62
PINETREE, 149–150, 168, 169, 184,
201, 202, 238, 244, 293, 354
accommodations at, 150–151
attitude toward air raids at, 153
Bomber Nights, 275
operations room, 187
visitors to, 194–195
war room, 186
Piryatin, 393, 409
Ploesti, Rumania, bombing of,
263–264, 277, 323, 385–387,
421, 427
Pogue, Forrest, 224, 433
POINTBLANK, 263, 287, 290–292,
302, 303, 305, 307, 309, 312,
313, 319, 323–327, 336, 342,
365, 377, 384, 394
diversions from, 291
Poker, 506n
marathon session at Caserta,
367–369
Polebrook, 168
Polish Home Army, MAAF aid to,
12, 409–410

Poltava
base at, 5, 7, 9–10, 393, 409, 411
bombed by Germans, 405,
407–408
pictures of, fall into Nazi hands,
404–406
life at, 401
Portal, Sir Charles "Peter," 121, 123,
129, 139, 148, 159, 184, 188–190,
192, 216, 217, 224–225, 227,
228, 242, 247, 252, 253, 271,
275, 292, 303, 307, 311–312,
318, 328, 331, 332, 336, 338,
343, 345, 352, 369, 377, 378,
390, 435, 443, 516n
on Arnold, 224
Arnold's needling of, 319
on Harris, 312–313
on H2S, 291
opposition to central control of
strategic air, 332–334
support of Eaker Plan, 262–263
support of US Army Air Forces
at QUADRANT, 304–305
on Vegesack bombing, 244
views on bombing strategy, 136,
193–194, 225, 226
Post, Robert B., 292
Pound, Sir Dudley, 148, 159
Preservation of force, Eaker on,
233–234
Puckett, Allen E., 469
Pue, Ed, 70
Putnam, Claude, 198
Pyle, Ernie, 367, 377

Q

QUADRANT, 302, 303, 305, 329
Quesada, Elwood R. "Pete," 69, 70,
71, 74, 102, 417
Question Mark flight, 70–75
lessons and implications, 75–76

R

Radar, 508n
for air force, 460–461
Radio, air-ground, 95
RAF
205 Group, 385
acceptance of American bombing
strategy, 178–179
American collaboration with, 129,
135, 141–142, 203
American relations with, 294, 344
bombing of Germany in 1941,
effectiveness, 137–138
bombing strategy, 138–139, 186–187

Eagle Squadrons, 265
escort fighters for, 124
first thousand-bomber attack, 160
Group, definition, 188
losses, in 1941, 139
pleas for build-up of Eighth, in
    1943, 242–243
in Singapore, Eaker's early
    experience with, 40
squadron, definition, 188
Squadron 226, 166
strength, in 1943, 351
support of American bombing
    strategy, 216
RAF Bomber Command, 134–135.
    See also Southdown
size, in 1942, 135
sorties in 1943, 284
RAF Coastal Command, 352
Railways, bombing of, 8–9, 173,
    380–381
Ramo, Simon, 459, 466, 469
Rapido River, 359
Raymond, Gene, 163
Red Air Force
Americans to train, 411–412
bomb-line liaison with, 393,
    428–429
Redline, 357
Refueling, midair
Eaker on, 75–76
Eaker's work on, 70. See also
    Question Mark flight
Regensburg, bombing of, 285, 292,
    298, 299, 302, 306, 310, 357,
    365, 366
Reverse Lend-Lease, 141
Rex, interception by B-17s, 111–112
Richards, Denis, 136, 193, 228,
    312
Richardson, John, 462
Richardson, Ralph, 245
Rickenbacker, Eddie, 90
Robinson, J. Roland, 294, 298
Rockwell Field
Eaker at, in 1918, 30–32
hospital, construction, 32–33
Rogers, Will, 90
Rogue River (Oregon), 453
Eaker's cabin on, 465–466
Eaker's introduction to, 120–121
Rome, assault on, 371, 382–383, 414.
    See also DIADEM
Rommel, Erwin, 160
Roosevelt, Eleanor, visit to
    PINETREE, 194–195
Roosevelt, Elliot, 301–302, 367, 368

Roosevelt, Franklin D., 89, 90, 102,
    109–110, 116, 129, 164, 180, 190,
    304, 329, 332, 333, 335, 356,
    410, 436
Root, Elihu, Jr., 250–251
Rostock, bombing of, 152, 158
Rostow, Walt, 249
Rotterdam, bombing of, 178
Rouen, railway yard, bombing of,
    173–174, 395
Round-the-world flight
Air Corps (1924), 52, 54, 67
Howard Hughes', 113
ROUND-UP, 182, 223
Royal Air Force. See RAF
Ruhl, Robert, 454, 455
Ruhland oil refinery, 405
Rumania. See also Ploesti
rescue of airmen from, 422
shuttle-bombing missions to, 11
Russia. See also Moscow; Poltava;
    Shuttle-bombing missions, in
    Russia
American heavy bombers for, 8,
    406, 411
medical practices in, 401
Russian-American relations, 6, 7, 12,
    412–413, 427–428
Russians. See also Red Air Force
Eaker on, 11–12, 404, 476–477
Russian soldiers, hygiene, 401–402
Russian workers, 402–403

S

Saint-Exupéry, Antoine de, 419–420
St. Louis, 60
St. Nazaire, bombing of, 236
Salvo bombing, 235–236
Samford, John A. "Sammy," 274
San Antonio, 58, 60
Sandefeur, Bill, 77
San Francisco, 52, 54, 58, 60
Saundby, Robert, 135, 345
Saville, Gordon, 208
Saward, Dudley, 146, 192
Schacht, Hjalmar Horace Greeley,
    434, 523n
School of the Line, 101
Schweinfurt, bombing of, 252, 285,
    287, 292, 298–302, 306, 309,
    312–318, 325, 327, 365
conclusions on, 327–328
Searle, Richard, 151, 196, 204, 435,
    523n
2nd Aero Squadron, in Philippines,
    33, 36–37
SEXTANT, 329–330, 332, 335, 342

SHAEF, 425
Sharp, A. C. H. "Bobby," 298
Sharp, Robert S., 181
Shenandoah, 46
Sherman, William Tecumseh, 100–101
Sherrod, Robert, 442
Sherwood, Robert, 244
Short, Walter C., 126
Short-snorter, 227, 245
Shuttle-bombing missions, to and
    from Russia, 5–7, 11, 367, 392,
    405. *See also* FRANTIC;
    FRANTIC JOE
  first victory in, 400–401
  target selection for, 8–9
Sicilian campaign, 223, 380
Sinclair, Sir Archibald, 187, 188, 189,
    191, 216, 343
Sixth Army, 383
Slavin, N. V., 7, 399, 400, 408
SLEDGEHAMMER, 159, 160, 164,
    170, 184
Slessor, John C., 187–189, 216, 225,
    227, 275, 352, 355, 357, 360,
    379, 381–383, 410, 414, 434,
    443, 464
  on air power in land campaigns,
    384
  The Central Blue, 425
Smith, Beadle, 335
Smith, C. R., 322
Smith, Mrs. Robert J., 489
Smith, Robert, 150
Smith, Walter Bedell, 6, 340, 342,
    355, 438, 454
Smith, William R. "Smitty," 300,
    302, 345, 377, 435
Snow, C. P., 247–248
Southdown, 134, 142–143
Southeastern Normal School
    (Durant, OK), 23
Southeastern Oklahoma State
    University, 24
Spaatz, Carl A. "Tooey," 32, 33, 64,
    66, 87, 109, 119, 126, 131, 134,
    145, 154, 155, 157, 161, 166,
    169–172, 174–175, 179, 181, 184,
    186–188, 190, 191, 195–198, 202,
    205–210, 220, 221, 231, 234,
    242, 244, 262, 265, 275, 289,
    292, 301, 302, 307, 313, 318,
    335, 338–340, 351, 353, 354,
    356, 357, 367–369, 375,
    377–379, 381, 392–397, 404,
    407, 408, 411, 433–435, 437,
    439, 444, 464–466, 485,
    487–488, 512n
  in airmail episode, 89
  as air officer for ETO, 200–201
  on bomber commanders going on
    missions, 144
  build-up of AAF in Britain, 194
  chief of staff of USAF, 445
  commander of North African Air
    Force, 223
  command of Eighth Air Force,
    129
  command of USSTAF, 331–332,
    341, 342
  conference with Eaker at Caserta,
    364–365
  diary, 518n
  Eaker's relationship with, 96,
    114–115
  first arrives in England, 163–164
  head of US Strategic Force, 336
  and independent air force, 443
  meeting with Eisenhower at Tunis,
    340–341
  in Mitchell trial, 46–47
  orders to drop atomic bomb, 442
  personality, 115–116
  postwar plans, 430–431
  retirement, 446
  role in *Question Mark* flight, 71–75
  sent to Europe, in 1940, 116–117
  sent to Pacific theater, 438,
    440–441
Slessor on, 189
  speech on Eaker's retirement,
    447–448
  on strategic bombing, 444
Spaatz, Ruth (Mrs. Carl A.), 42, 71,
    115, 466, 487, 489, 493
Spaatz, Tattie, 71
Space, weapons in, Eaker on,
    472–473
Spareball, 300–301
Spasso House, 7, 9
Speer, Albert, Eaker's interview of,
    309–310, 484
Stalin, Joseph, 9, 10, 216, 329, 332,
    392–393, 406, 408–410, 413
  on Churchill, 333
  reaction to Normandy, 7
Stalingrad, German offensive on, 185
Stameshkin, Sol, 355, 462
Starduster, 377, 420, 435
STARKEY, 307
Steinbeck, John, 239
Steinhoff, Johannes, 286–287
Stewart, Jimmy, 454
Steyr, bombing of, 365
Stilwell, Joseph W., 232

Stimson, Henry L., 270, 181, 303, 430
Stirling, Yates, 108
Stovall, W. H., 465
STRANGLE, 381–384, 392, 520n
Strategic Review, 13, 479–481
  press coverage, 482
  reprints, 481–482
  testimonials, 482
Strategic superiority, Eaker on, 478
Stratemeyer, George E., 212, 232,
    242, 267, 279, 437
Streett, St. Clair, 41
Strickland [Lt.], 71, 73
Stroud, Leslie, 151, 204, 307, 355,
    435, 523n
Sudakov, [Lt. Gen.], 425
Sulzberger, Cyrus L., 239, 367–368
Sutterlin, F. J., 407, 408
Swanton Morely, 166
Switzerland, downed airmen in, 424
Symington, Stuart, 445–446

T

Talbott, Harold, 466–467
Tarawa, 327
Target Germany, 298–299
Target systems
  choice of, 223–224. See also
      Operations analysis
  for American shuttle missions
      from Russia, 8–9
  British approach to, 248
  EOU in, 248–249
  for Russian shuttle missions,
      397–398
  in COA report, 252
  in Italy, choice of, 380–381
  Speer's evaluation of Allies'
      effectiveness against, 309–310
Tedder, Arthur, 223, 227, 239, 292,
    307, 335, 336, 340–344, 351,
    355, 378–379, 512n
Teheran conference, 332, 335
3rd Aero Squadron, in Philippines,
    33, 36
This Flying Game (with Arnold),
    87–88, 94, 113, 247, 369
Thompson, Bernard S., 79
Thomson, C.R., 258
Thornton, Charles B. "Tex," 459,
    466, 469, 488
Thruelson, Richard, 298
Thyssen, Fritz, 434
Tibbets, Paul W., 174
Tierman, Cordes, 187
Tighe, Dixie, 292–293
Timberlake, Ted, 238, 277

Tinker, Clarence L., 89–90, 127, 162
Tito, Marshal, 390, 423, 425–426,
    428
  cooperation with Allies, 427
Tolbuhkin [Marshal], 406
Toolco. See Hughes Tool Company
TORCH, 170, 177–179, 182, 184, 190,
    194, 201, 204–206, 208–209,
    228
  air force requirements for, 183
Transcontinental flight, Eaker's
    attempt at, in 1930, 79
Trenchard, Lord, 343, 435, 464, 485
TRIDENT, 253, 262–263
Truman, Harry S., 441, 444
Truscott, Lucian K., 358, 383
TRW, Inc., 466
Tuck, Stanford, 121–122, 125
Tuker, Francis, 361
Turner, Stansfield, 482
Twelfth Air Force, 5, 155, 183, 184,
    194, 212, 289, 373
XII Bomber Command, 380
Twelve O'Clock High, 198
'Twelve O'Clock High," 454
20th Pursuit Group
  Eaker's command of, 117
  maneuver on Rogue River, 120–121
  sent to China, 120
Twining, Nathan F., 102, 336, 354,
    355, 375, 385–387, 395–397,
    409, 422, 427, 435, 438, 455,
    472

U

U.S. Strategic Air Forces in Europe.
    See USSTAF
U-boats
  attacks on convoys, interdiction,
      183
  crisis, of 1943, 282–283
  in pens, bombing of, 183, 233, 236
  as priority target systems, 223
Ukraine, American bases in. See
    Eastern Command, bases
ULTRA, 145, 285, 311, 313
United States Strategic Institute, 13,
    479–483
USAAF, in UK, in 1943, 188
USAF, independent. See Air force,
    independent
USSI. See United States Strategic
    Institute
USSI Report, 481–482
USSTAF, 342, 353, 354, 356, 367,
    392, 397, 407–409, 438
  British opposition to, 332

communication with Eastern
Command, 394
establishment of, 331–332, 335
Spaatz as commander, 339
value of, 366–367

V

V-1 and V-2 launching sites,
bombing of, 291
Vandenberg, Arthur, 433
Vandenberg, Hoyt S., 417, 433, 435,
438, 446
Vegesack, bombing of, 230, 243–244,
283
VHF sets, 156
Vietnam, Eaker on, 477
Villa Vismara, 395
Vinnitsa, 408–409
Vishinsky, Andrei, 9
Vladivostok, Americans' proposed
air bases at, 10–11, 410–412
von Braun, Werner, 462
von Rundstedt, Gerd, on air power,
439
von Senger und Etterlin, Fridolin,
371, 383

W

WAAF, at PINETREE, 151–152
WACs
Chaney's refusal to use, 159
sent to Eighth, 307
Walsh, Robert L., 396, 399, 407,
408, 411
War
men in, Eaker on, 476–477
principles of, as applied to air, 99
tactical decisions in, Eaker on, 477
talking about, Eaker on, 476
War correspondents
on bombing missions, 292
women, 292–293
War Department, general staff,
opposition to autonomous air
force, 504n-506n
Weaver, Elizabeth (Mrs. Walter), 129
Weaver, Walter R., 41, 109, 127, 129
Webster, Sir Charles, and Frankland,
Noble, 136
Weiler, Mary, 307–308, 355
Weiner-Neustadt, bombing of, 292
Wesley, John, 150
SS Westcadoa, 40–41

Westover, Oscar, 98, 99, 109, 113, 114
West Point, Eaker on, 43–44
Whitehead, E.C., 60
Whitney, John Hay "Jock," 294,
298, 355, 367, 368, 418–419,
423, 438, 465, 476, 484, 486
Wickstead Heath, 154
WIDEWING, 163–164, 202, 204,
293–294, 342–343, 354
Wigglesworth, Philip, 512n
Wilcox, Mark, 110
Wilcox bill, 110
Wilder, Thornton, 426–427
Wilhelmshaven, bombing of, 230
Williams, Robert B., 299–300
Wilson, Anna W., 516n
Wilson, Sir Henry Maitland, 335,
351–353, 356, 364, 367, 376,
381
Winant, John G., 159, 239, 248, 271,
435, 438
Winged Warfare (with Arnold), 31,
113, 117–120, 147, 291
Wolfe, K. B., 460
Women. *See also* WAAF; WACs;
War correspondents
in war tasks, Eaker on, 122–123
Wood, Leonard, 38
Wood, Sir Kingsley, 136
Woodring, Harry, 71, 73, 109
Wooldridge, Dean E., 459, 466,
469
Woolsey, [Capt], 60
Worner, Manfred, 482
Wray, Stanley, 238
Wright, Orville, 66
Wright Trophy, 13, 489
Wuppertal-Barman, bombing of, 284
Wycombe Abbey, 142, 149, 152. *See
also* PINETREE
Wyler, William "Willie," 295, 454,
462

Y

Yankee Doodle, 174, 175, 395
Yankee Doodle II, 395, 399
Yardbird, 377
Yeager, Charles "Chuck," 13, 450
Yugoslavia, 423–425

Z

Zero-level attacks, 266–268
Zuckerman, Solly, 248, 378, 380, 382

ABOUT THE MAKING OF THIS BOOK

The text of *"Air Force Spoken Here"*
was set in Times Roman by
ComCom, a division of The Haddon
Craftsmen, of Allentown,
Pennsylvania. The book was printed
and bound by Fairfield Graphics of
Fairfield, Pennsylvania. The
typography and binding were
designed by Tom Suzuki of Falls
Church, Virginia.